# RECORDS OF DISPOSSESSION

## The Institute for Palestine Studies Series

| | |
|---|---|
| Muhammad Y. Muslih. *The Origins of Palestinian Nationalism.* | 1988 |
| Justin McCarthy. *The Population of Palestine.* | 1990 |
| Camille Mansour. *Beyond Alliance: Israel in U.S. Foreign Policy* | 1994 |
| Michael Dumper. *The Politics of Jerusalem since 1967* | 1997 |

THE INSTITUTE FOR PALESTINE STUDIES SERIES

# RECORDS OF DISPOSSESSION

*Palestinian Refugee Property and the Arab-Israeli Conflict*

MICHAEL R. FISCHBACH

COLUMBIA UNIVERSITY PRESS   NEW YORK

Columbia University Press
Publishers Since 1893
New York Chichester, West Sussex



Library of Congress Cataloging-in-Publication Data

Fischbach, Michael R.
Records of dispossession : Palestinian refugee property and the Arab-Israeli conflict / Michael R. Fischbach.
p. cm.
Includes bibliographical references and index.
ISBN 978-0-231-12978-7
1. Arab-Israeli conflict—Claims. 2. Refugee property—Israel. 3. Palestinian Arabs—Claims. 4. United Nations. Conciliation Commission for Palestine. 5. Diplomatic negotiations in international disputes. I. Title

DS119.7.F565 2003
956.04—dc21 2003051514

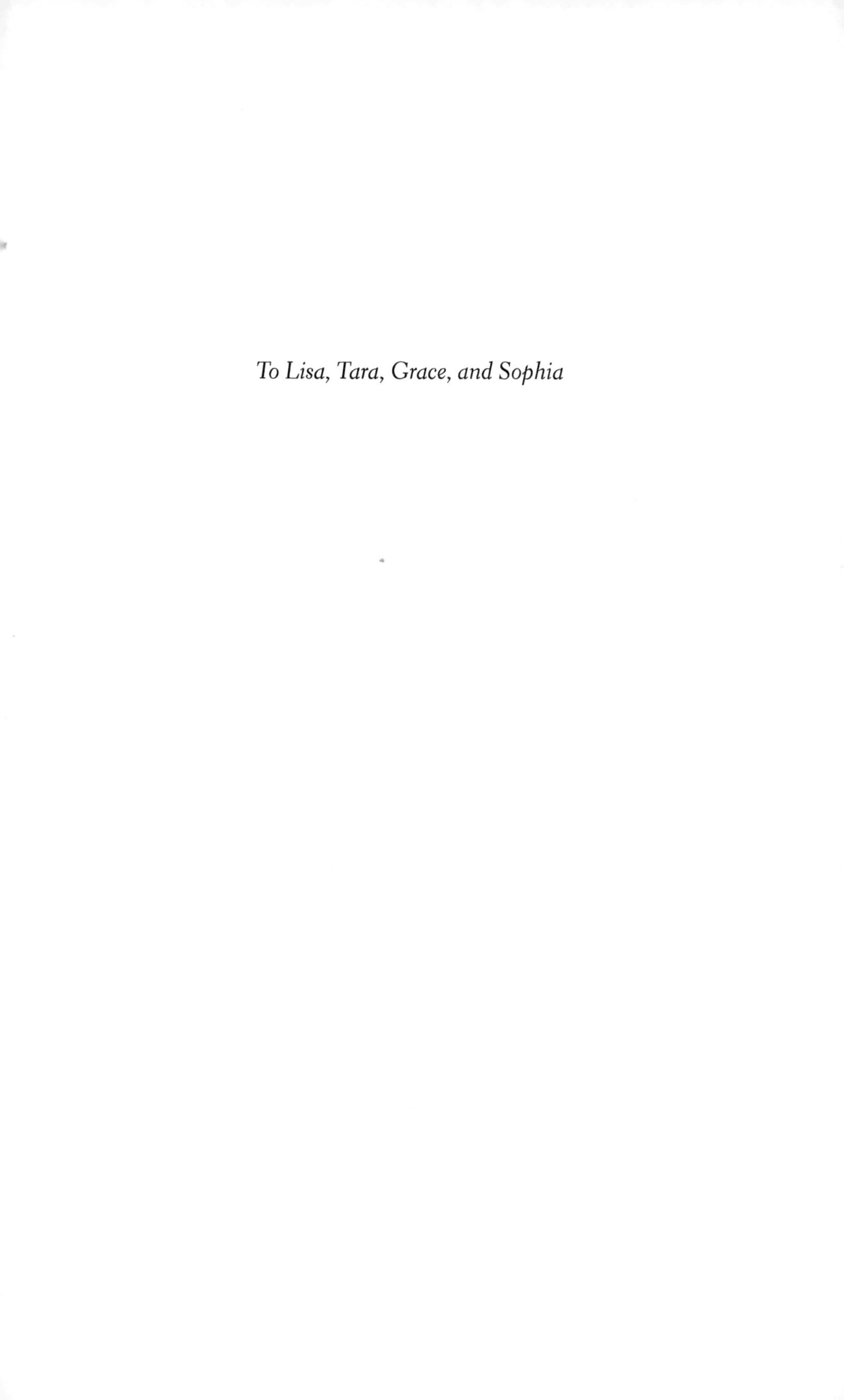

*To Lisa, Tara, Grace, and Sophia*

# CONTENTS

# LIST OF TABLES

# ABBREVIATIONS

| | |
|---|---|
| ASF | American Sephardi Federation |
| CZA | Central Zionist Archives |
| ILA | Israel Lands Administration |
| ISA | Israel State Archives |
| JA | Jewish Agency |
| JNF | Jewish National Fund |
| NARA | United States National Archives and Records Administration |
| PICA | Palestine Jewish Colonization Association |
| PLO | Palestine Liberation Organization |
| PRO | Public Records Office |
| UNCCP | United Nations Conciliation Commission for Palestine |
| UNSA | United Nations Secretariat Archives |
| UNRWA | United Nations Relief and Works Agency for Palestine Refugees in the Near East |
| UNTSO | United Nations Truce Supervisory Organization |
| WJC | World Jewish Congress |
| WOJAC | World Organization of Jews from Arab Countries |

# ACKNOWLEDGMENTS

I could not have completed this study without the support of a number of individuals and institutions. I gratefully acknowledge the financial support of a Research and Writing Grant from The John D. and Catherine T. MacArthur Foundation, given through the Friends of the Institute for Palestine Studies, as well as a Rashkind Endowment grant and a Walter Williams Craigie Teaching Endowment grant, both from Randolph-Macon College. Financial assistance was also forthcoming from the Institute for Palestine Studies, the Friends of the Institute for Palestine Studies, and James Abdo. I am particularly grateful to the Institute for Palestine Studies for permission to view its copy of the United Nations' collection of data on Palestinian property, just as I extend special thanks to the United Nations Conciliation Commission for Palestine for permission to examine the virtually untouched material in its archives. Thanks also go to Rex Brynen's FOFOGNET Internet network for keeping me current on refugee issues.

Thanks go to a number of individuals who helped along the way through their hard work, assistance, guidance, and hospitality. These include Walid Khalidi, Philip Mattar, Linda Butler, Eric Hooglund, Paul Perry, Marilla Guptil, Eric Scott Kincaid, Yoram Mayorek, Kamil Nasrawi, Adnan Abdelrazek, Issam Nashashibi, Carreen Lawrence, Nicholas Benne, Timothy Nolan, and Donna Geisler. A special thanks to Geremy Forman for his research and translation assistance, his careful reading of parts of the text, his comments and valuable suggestions, and his friendship. As always, my grateful thanks go to my wife Lisa and my ever-patient family, who have suffered through the years of worry and inconvenience I have put them through.

Michael R. Fischbach
February 2003

# A NOTE ON TRANSLITERATION

I have utilized the system for transliteration of Arabic into Latin characters established by the *International Journal of Middle East Studies*, and the Library of Congress system for transliterating Hebrew, with the exception of omitting most diacritical marks. Inevitably, however, inconsistencies emerged. This is especially true of certain words and proper names that have become widely recognized in English under a different spelling, or where individuals use a particular spelling of their names in English. In these cases, I have used the more popular spelling or the spelling used by those persons in their public lives. Thus, the reader will find "kibbutz" instead of "kibbuts"; "Yosef Weitz" instead of "Yosef Vaits"; "Izzat Tannous" instead of "'Izzat Tannus"; "Chaim Weizmann" instead of "Hayyim Vaitsman"; "Adnan Abdelrazek" instead of "'Adnan 'Abd al-Raziq"; and so forth.

Arabic place names are almost always properly transliterated from their written form and not how they are pronounced locally. For example, residents in the village of 'Arraba, in the northern region of Galilee, would pronounced their village name as "'Arrabi." A village by the same name in central Palestine is pronounced "'Arrabeh" by its inhabitants. Villagers in Nayn would pronounce the name of their community as "Nein." Once again, certain widely used alternative spellings in both Arabic and Hebrew place names have been kept, such as "Acre" instead of the Arabic "'Akka" and the Hebrew "'Akko," and "Jerusalem" instead of the Arabic "al-Quds" and the Hebrew "Yerushalayim."

# INTRODUCTION

In the late fall of 2000, the plane taking me home from conducting research at the United Nations Secretariat archives in New York made a direct pass over the city just after takeoff from LaGuardia airport. As the aircraft banked over midtown Manhattan, I looked down and could see the exact part of town where I had just completed several days examining documents from the United Nations Conciliation Commission for Palestine (UNCCP) relating to the land left behind in Israel by Palestinian refugees in 1948. Among these documents were detailed records of almost every parcel of Arab-owned land in Israel that the UNCCP carefully compiled in the 1950s and 1960s in the hopes that they could prove useful should Israel ever compensate the refugees for their losses. How poignant, I thought, that a detailed and fairly accurate reckoning of the refugees' losses, including the property lost by individual persons, has lain behind locked doors at the UN archives in New York for nearly four decades and thousands of miles from the Middle Eastern refugee camps that still house descendants of the original 1948 refugees. These unutilized records stand as mute testament to the fact that despite the considerable effort and diplomatic activity that has been expended over the years on how to deal with the Palestinian refugee exodus in general and the refugees' property claims in particular, wide-scale restitution or compensation never have been forthcoming, and these claims remain unsettled to this day.

In focusing on the history of abandoned Palestinian refugee property and how this question has fit into the wider Arab-Israeli conflict, this study examines one dimension of what surely ranks as one of the core unresolved issues of that conflict: the Palestinian refugee problem. The refugees' plight long ago emerged both as one of the most central challenges facing the world community in the aftermath of the first Arab-Israeli war of 1948 as well as one of the Arab-Israeli conflict's most intractable problems. The flight of the refugees was the direct result of the partition of Palestine and the subsequent war that broke out between Jews and Arabs in 1948, and constituted a socioeconomic and political tragedy of the first order of magnitude for the Arab population of Palestine. More than 726,000 Palestinians—about one-half of the entire population—left their homes in Palestine from late 1947 through

1948. Some fled, while others were driven out by Zionist forces. Some of the refugees left during the Jewish-Palestinian "civil war" that broke out after the November 29, 1947 United Nations General Assembly's decision to partition Palestine into Jewish and Arab states and that lasted through May 14, 1948. This was particularly true of wealthier Palestinians in the towns and cities, the so-called "middle class refugees." Many of the rest of the refugees, mostly poorer villagers, departed during the subsequent international phase of the fighting that occurred following the entrance into the fray of forces sent by neighboring Arab states on May 15. In the course of their flight, these refugees left behind huge tracts of farmland, tools and animals, shops, factories, houses of worship, homes, financial assets, and personal belongings.

The refugees' property losses only served to compound the tremendous political, social, and demographic catastrophe that had befallen them. Not only were they refugees, but by and large destitute refugees as well. The loss of rural farmland was particularly devastating to a village society that had largely been made up of small-scale cultivators. Their abandoned land did not represent only the loss of their homeland, but also of landed capital and, indeed, the loss of a way of life. Unlike some of their middle-class compatriots who managed to take some of their liquid capital with them, these rural refugees were thus lacking the material basis for reconstructing their former livelihoods in exile.

The opposite was true for the new state of Israel that emerged out of the 1948 fighting. Israel quickly extended control over the Palestinian refugees' land, the exact scope and value of which has been and continues to be debated by scholars and governments alike. Within a few short years of the refugee exodus, the refugees' property formally was taken over by the Israeli government. After the war Israel had been established on a full 77 percent of the surface area of Palestine even though Jews had owned only some 6.59 percent of that surface area prior to 1948.[1] While much of the resultant difference that accrued to Israel had not been owned by individual Palestinian refugees, the huge amount of land that the refugees did abandon in their flight proved to be an immensely valuable windfall for the struggling Israeli state. The war helped Zionist authorities deal with the nagging demographic "problem" that had faced them before the war: more Palestinian Arabs lived in Palestine than Jews. How could they create a Jewish state amidst large number of non-Jews? After 1948, four out of five of the Palestinians who had lived in what became the Jewish state were gone. But beyond helping to relieve Israel's demographic "problem," the vast tracts of abandoned property proved immensely helpful to Israeli authorities on a financial level. The Israeli government profited from the property by leasing some areas and selling much of it to the Jewish National Fund, the premier Zionist land purchasing agency whose charter forbade it ever from alienating its land or from leasing it to non-Jews. Produce from abandoned fields, orchards, and citrus groves was exported for hard currency. Moveable property was sold. The government even leased abandoned stone quarries and sold cactus fruit from abandoned areas. Beyond this monetary gain, control of the refugees' property allowed Israel and the Jewish Agency to settle as cheaply as possible the hundreds of thousands of new Jewish immigrants who began pouring into Israel after 1948. Some of these newcomers were Jews from Arab countries who themselves had left behind homes and property under duress. While declaring that this land had been alienated permanently out of the refugees' hands and would not be returned, Israeli authorities pledged to compensate the refugees for their losses. In this lies the kernel of the refugee property question.

This last point is one of the few aspects of the refugee property dilemma on which many parties have agreed over the decades since 1948: The refugees should be compensated for their abandoned property. Israel, the Arab states, some Palestinians, the United States, and the United Nations have all agreed on this issue. Yet to date, compensation has not taken place. Why? The answer to that question forms one of the major subjects handled by the present study. In short, the humanitarian dimension of the Palestinian refugee property issue has not been resolved because the question became enmeshed in the political dimensions of the Arab-Israeli conflict, and its importance—even its parameters—have ebbed and flowed over the decades since the onset of the first Arab-Israeli war of 1948. Much serious talk and research on refugee property compensation initially took place in the first fifteen years after 1948, especially on the part of the United Nations Conciliation Commission for Palestine (UNCCP). The UNCCP held conferences, tried to effect compensation plans, developed a general "global estimate" of the refugees' property losses, and eventually carried out a massive program to identify and valuate virtually every parcel of Arab-owned land in Israel as part of its efforts on behalf of the refugee property issue. During these early years the compensation issue became embroiled with and complicated by a number of factors, among which were Israel's linkage of compensation with compensating Jewish emigrants from Arab countries for their own property losses; Israel's insistence that compensation be dealt with as part of a wider peace process; U.S. attempts to link compensation with the controversial subject of refugee resettlement; and the Americans' reluctance to stray beyond certain "red lines" they had drawn for the refugee issue (red lines that usually corresponded with Israeli stances); the Arabs' converse insistence that compensation could not be equated with the abandonment of the refugees' "right of return" (right to repatriation); and the different directions taken by the Arab-Israeli conflict after the 1956 Suez War and, especially, the 1967 Arab-Israeli war, directions that sidelined the property issue. The UNCCP's efforts eventually foundered, the commission ceased to function actively, and after the 1967 war the property compensation question generally faded from active public consideration for more than two decades. Talk of property compensation again returned to the level of active discussion as a result of Arab-Israeli peace process that started in Madrid in 1991. This was particularly true of the Israeli-Palestinian peace process that followed the September 1993 Oslo Accord. But little progress had been made at all on the compensation issue by early 2003, at which point the Israeli-Palestinian talks were stalled amidst the onset of renewed Israeli-Palestinian violence and the virtual collapse of the peace process.

This study examines this issue with an eye toward answering certain questions. How much land did the Palestinian refugees actually leave behind in the areas of Palestine that became Israel, and how much was it worth? Why have the refugees' claims to this vast amount of land and moveable property remained unsettled over the past fifty years, despite widespread recognition of the refugees' right to compensation for their losses? How has the property issue affected—and been affected by—the overall, changing nature of the Arab-Israeli conflict? Why did the UN prove unable to effect compensation for the refugees' property and ultimately end up as at best a marginal player in resolving the Arab-Israeli conflict? How did U.S. policies toward the conflict and the refugees in particular contribute to the marginalization of the UN in this regard? How have the various parties to the conflict dealt with the property question, and why did it fade from active discussion twenty years after the refugee exodus? How and why did Israel raise counter claims for Jewish property in Arab countries? Who produced studies of the scope and value of Palestinian refugee property, and why even today is there no consensus on this issue? Why has the Arab-Israeli peace process, a process that has led to two full-scale peace treaties (Israel and Egypt, and Israel and Jordan) along with the ongoing peace talks between Israel and the Palestinians, not led to a breakthrough on the property issue?

The Palestinian refugee property issue is examined here in roughly chronological fashion beginning with its inception in late 1947. The study focuses broadly on the interconnectedness of this issue with the wider, ever-changing diplomatic context of the Arab-Israeli conflict, and more narrowly on the specific question of property compensation (as distinct from the right of return). Among the specific aspects of this issue covered here are the legal mechanisms by which Israel seized and utilized the land; the UN's efforts on behalf of property compensation in the 1950s; the Arabs' insistence that compensation not be equated with the forfeiture of the refugees' right of repatriation to their homes; American thinking to the contrary; Israel's linkage of compensation to compensating Jewish emigrants from the Arab world; the various (and contradictory) Israel, Arab, and UN estimates of the scope and value of the abandoned property; the UNCCP's massive study of the property question, a study that never publicly released its figures on the land's value (but that are presented here for the first time); the eventual failure of the UNCCP in its compensation efforts and its relegation (as well as that of the UN generally) to mere tertiary status in Arab-Israeli diplomacy; the fading public prominence of the refugee property issue after 1967; and its return to open discussion but not resolution after 1991.

In the final analysis, this study tackles the question of why the world community has not proved able to effect compensation or restitution for the 1948 Palestinian refugees and thus why the refugee property question remains unresolved. The central thesis it argues is that the property issue immediately became intertwined intimately with the diplomatic vicissitudes of the wider Arab-Israeli conflict after 1948 despite considerable global concern over the refugees and their plight and despite repeated regional and international efforts to isolate and solve this human tragedy separately from the wider political context of the conflict. The losers in this process were of course the refugees and their descendants. Efforts toward compensation, restitution, or the lack of such efforts, thus were politicized and subject to the changing nature of the Arab-Israeli conflict from the beginning.

Despite the rhetoric, the refugees and their property were never isolated from the overarching context of the conflict and dealt with on a strictly humanitarian level. This was played out on two different levels. First, it meant that the refugees' needs for resolving their property claims waxed and waned in the minds of Arabs, Israelis, Americans, and the global community in direct correlation to the various political and military crises that punctuated the Arab-Israeli conflict over the decades. The early 1950s witnessed a high level of activity on this question, given that the refugee exodus was still fresh in the minds of all concerned and given the absence of major military flareups among Arabs and Israelis. The outbreak of the Arab-Israeli wars of October 1956 and particularly of June 1967, however, eventually shifted the focus of the conflict away from the refugees and other lingering problems from 1948 and toward securing peace among states on the battlefield. Israel's growing military strength over the decades hardened its resolve, ironically just as their continuing defeats did for the Arabs, just as the cold war rivalry between the United States and the USSR (Soviet Union) also changed and hardened the conflict.

The second level on which the property question also has been fundamentally affected by the vicissitudes of the wider Arab-Israeli conflict over the years is seen in the ways in which it was subject to the shifting conceptual approaches to the conflict that have emerged over time. These conceptual approaches were related to political and military events on the ground, but still constituted an entirely different dimension of the conflict. In the first years after 1948, diplomatic efforts at resolving the Arab-Israeli conflict were understood conceptually to involve managing the effects of 1948. In addition to armistice agreements, borders, and cease-fire lines, the fate of the refugees displaced by the fighting was another micro-level problem that loomed large on the global stage given that the refugees constituted one of the most visible legacies of 1948.

With flareup of armed conflict between Israel and the Arab states starting in 1956 and most significantly in 1967, however, the world began viewing the Arab-Israeli conflict as an ongoing interstate matter that transcended 1948. The Arab states now saw that their involvement in fighting Israel was not limited to that first war. Diplomats viewed solving the conflict on the macro level by arranging cease fire agreements among nations, of bringing about conciliation on the basis of "land for peace," while the fate of the stateless refugees retreated from active consideration. Another conceptual shift concerned how the parties viewed the UN's role in the conflict and the refugee problem in particular. The failure of the UN to effect a resolution to either problem was in no small way the result of American muzzling of its efforts via certain political "red lines," and led to the world body's marginalization as a significant player. Finally, the refugees were affected by their own changing conceptualizations of themselves. The growth of a Palestinian national movement in the 1960s and the strength of the Palestine Liberation Organization (PLO) hardened the refugees' earlier resolve to continue the armed struggle for their homeland and not to accept anything that symbolized the abandonment of their right to return to their homes, including accepting compensation for the lost property. And just as war did not resolve the refugee property question, neither has the Palestinian-Israeli peace process as these lines are being drafted (early 2003). Ironically then, if the shifting nature of the conflict has continually confounded resolution of the refugees' property claims as it ebbed and flowed over the decades, the supposed "end" of conflict between Israel and some of her Arab neighbors has likewise confounded such efforts at resolution.

Chapter 1 examines the Palestinian refugee exodus of 1947–1948 and what the State of Israel did with the property the refugees left behind. It details the legal mechanisms by which the new Jewish state confiscated this land and then utilized it for economic production, leased or sold it to a variety of groups, associations, settlements, and the Jewish National Fund, and settled it with Jewish immigrants. It also discusses initial Israel attempts to determine the scope of this land.

Chapter 2 examines early global diplomatic activity on behalf of the refugee property question during the first several years after the refugee exodus. Particularly important in this regard was the establishment of the UNCCP, which would be the agency that expended the greatest amount of energy on the refugee property question over the years. The UNCCP soon produced the Global Estimate, the first of two official reckonings of the scope and value of refugee land that the commission would produce. The chapter also studies the reasons why its failure to realize progress on the issue prompted the UNCCP to adopt a new, less ambitious role for itself within a few short years of functioning.

The third chapter examines early Israeli policies toward the refugee property issue in the 1950s and 1960s, including Israel's decision to link Palestinian refugee compensation with counter claims for compensation for Jewish property abandoned in Arab countries. The question of German reparations to Israel also became wrapped up in the politics of the refugee issue. During this time the UNCCP was able to make some progress on the property issue by arranging for Israel to release frozen refugee bank accounts. Chapter 4 deals with early international activity on behalf of the question, including Arab and UN estimates of the property's value and the international political activity on behalf of compensation. It also notes how the 1956 Suez War shifted the Arab-Israeli conflict in a direction that further sidelined attempts to compensate the refugees.

Chapter 5 is devoted entirely to the second and most thorough of the UNCCP's attempts to calculate the scope and value of refugee property losses, the Technical Program. Completed from 1952 to 1964, the results of this study still remain the most thorough and accurate reckoning of the question despite criticism directed at it both by Arabs and Israelis. Although the UNCCP publicly released figures on the scope of the property, it kept the value of the property secret, literally locked up in the UN Secretariat archives in New York. This chapter reveals these figures for the first time. Chapter six examines the follow up to the Technical Program, including the UNCCP's Johnson Mission and other activities that explored whether or not compensation for the refugees could be arranged. It also discusses the effective demise of the UNCCP in 1966. Finally, the last chapter looks at how the refugee property question was affected by the vicissitudes of the Arab-Israeli conflict as the struggle meandered from war to cold peace, to war again, and eventually to a halting peace process. The chapter examines how the June 1967 Arab-Israeli war further minimized the property question and also sheds light on how the Arab-Israeli peace process has revived the issue since 1991, particularly as a variety of Jewish, Israeli, Arab, and Palestinian parties have sought statistics and data to support their eventual claims for compensation or, in the case of some Palestinians, restitution.

This study reflects research carried out on a number of levels and in a number of places in six countries on three continents. The main basis for this study are primary source documents. In the course of my research I conducted and commissioned research into primary archival sources at the Central Zionist Archives in Jerusalem; the Israel State Archives in Jerusalem; the British Public Records Office in London; the United Nations Secretariat archives in New York; the United States National Archives and Records Administration in College Park, Maryland; and the Jordanian National Library/Center for Documents and Documentation in Amman. I also carried out research into non-archival primary sources at several offices of the Jordanian government in Amman and at the Institute for Palestine Studies (IPS) in Washington and Beirut. At IPS I was able to access the records produced by the UNCCP's Technical Program from 1952 to 1964. A full listing of these sources, as well as other primary and secondary sources, is found in the bibliography.

# RECORDS OF DISPOSSESSION

# CHAPTER ONE
# REFUGEE FLIGHT AND ISRAELI POLICIES TOWARD ABANDONED PROPERTY

In 1948, during the first Arab-Israeli war, 726,000 Palestinian Arabs—one-half of the entire Arab population of Palestine—fled or were driven out of their homes in Palestine by Zionist forces. In the process they left behind farmland, tools and animals, homes, factories, bank accounts, and personal property. Israel did not allow the mass repatriation of the refugees and quickly confiscated their property. In this lies the genesis of the refugee property issue.

In recent years much has been written about the massive exodus of Palestinians from their homes but it is beyond the scope of this study to revisit this issue to any detailed extent. The entire issue remains to some extent shrouded in controversy, particularly concerning the causes of the refugees' flight. Did they voluntarily leave their homes out of fear of the fighting? Were they motivated by fear of Zionist atrocities, such as that at the village of Dayr Yasin outside Jerusalem in April 1948? Or were they expelled by Zionist forces in a campaign of ethnic cleansing? And if this was the case, was this part of a some wider Zionist plot to use the war as an opportunity to rid Palestine of as many of its Palestinian Arab inhabitants as possible, or was it done by local military commanders who wanted to remove potential enemy combatants from behind their lines? It appears that it was a combination of fear of battle, fear of atrocities, and deliberate expulsion that explains why some 726,000 members of an overwhelmingly settled, rural population attached to its homes and fields would abandon them.

## Flight of the Refugees

There were distinct waves of Palestinians fleeing their homes, and the refugees can be divided into socioeconomic categories. The so-called "middle class refugees" from the towns and cities constituted the first wave of the refugee exodus, and fled as the fighting between Zionist military organizations and local Palestinians began to escalate shortly after the United Nations partition decision of November 29, 1947. More well-to-do Palestinians in towns either harboring mixed Jewish-Arab populations or that were immediately adjacent to Jewish communities began leaving their homes and property for the safety of surrounding Arab cities like Cairo and Beirut as early as December 1947. That month saw the first movement of urban dwellers from Haifa and Jaffa, followed by an exodus from the Qatamon district in western Jerusalem in January 1948. The sharp escalation of urban fighting in mixed towns by the spring of 1948 prompted further departures, especially following the capture of Haifa by Zionist forces on April 21–22, 1948.

Many of these Palestinian urban dwellers were quite wealthy. They left behind not only luxurious homes replete with expensive furniture and other consumer goods but also shops, warehouses, factories, machinery, and other commercial property. This was in addition to financial assets like bank accounts and valuables such as securities held in safe deposit boxes in banks. Others left behind large citrus groves. Not only were the trees and land temporarily abandoned but so too were irrigation pipes, water pumps, and other capital goods present on the land. None felt that their departure was anything more than a temporary move away from a war zone.

The other sector of the refugee population were the villagers from the countryside. The Hagana, the official militia of the Zionist movement in Palestine, and other Zionist forces began assaulting strategically located Arab locales that they felt constituted a threat to Jewish settlements and supply lines, just as Arab forces attacked Jewish settlements. But in many ways the greatest impetus for the refugee flight came when Zionist forces began to initiate a full-scale offensive in the spring of 1948 against Palestinian villages that lay outside of the area assigned to the so-called Arab state by the UN partition plan. As the fighting spread, Palestinian villagers began to leave an environment replete with mutual violence, atrocities against civilian populations, and fear. Like their urban counterparts, they left behind—temporarily they believed—their homes, farms, farm animals and equipment, and personal property. Generally not possessing bank accounts like their urban counterparts, some buried money in the ground for safekeeping.

By May 1, 1948, 100,000 persons had fled the civil war between Zionist and Palestinian fighters, the latter assisted by a force of foreign Arab volunteers called the Arab Liberation Army. They abandoned ninety villages in the process.[1] The large-scale fighting between Israeli and Arab armies that began in mid-May 1948 and eventually lasted until armistice agreements were signed in 1949 created a total of 726,000 Palestinian refugees who fled into Lebanon, Syria, Jordan, the West Bank, and Gaza, as well as Egypt, Iraq, and beyond. Middle- and upper-class Palestinian urbanites moved in with relatives or rented new accommodations. The poor were relegated to refugee camps. The war also triggered the exodus of 30,000 Syrian, Lebanese, Egyptian, Jordanian, and Iraqi Arabs living in Palestine as well.[2] In total, these persons left behind a massive amount of moveable and immoveable property, the scope and value of much of which could not be proven either with deeds or by other documents.

By the end of 1948, vast stretches of Palestinian farmland, towns, and villages lay vacant. By the spring of 1949, the untilled fields were covered with wildflowers.[3] An American who traveled through Israel in 1951 described the sight of the abandoned towns and villages in this way:

> As we went through Israel, the former Arab villages were a broken, distorted mass of mud bricks and falling walls. They were slowly going back into the earth where they came. In the cities, the Arab quarters were being demolished for new streets and modern shops . . . . These old buildings, already partially demolished by the war, were unsanitary and unsafe for habitation. They had to be torn down so that the incoming Jewish refugees would not live in them and so that modern sanitation, water mains, sewers and wide streets could replace them.[4]

Not all Palestinian refugees were content merely to mourn their lost homes and fields from their new refugee camps. Some began infiltrating through Israeli lines to retrieve property or till their overripe fields, risking being shot in the process, as hundreds were. In at least one case, they chose certain death over the mere risk of death: one distraught Haifa businessman who had left behind his home and business only to end up in a refugee camp in the Jordan Valley near Jericho took his two sons behind their tent quarters one day in November 1948, shot them, and then turned the gun on himself.[5]

Israeli authorities found themselves in possession of a major economic and demographic windfall in the form of the massive amount of refugee land at their disposal. Exactly how much land the refugees left behind has been the subject of numerous and contradictory studies over the years since 1948. One reason for the difficulties in determining the scope of the property is that British mandatory authorities never completed a thorough cadastral accounting of land in Palestine. Various individuals and official bodies that study the question of refugee property ran against this problem of inadequate sources for documentation. Compounding the difficulty, what records had been created by the British were scattered as a result of the fighting. This entire subject is discussed in great detail later in this study.

Even determining the number of abandoned villages is problematic, in part because the definition of a "village" has varied from source to source. Not all locales from which the refugees came were recognized officially as settlements in the eyes of mandatory authorities, who therefore kept no information on them nor included them on survey maps. Because others were so small or only populated during part of the year they similarly never were considered "true" villages. Defining the term "abandoned" also has proven difficult. Some villages were abandoned totally, while only part of the population fled in others. Such imprecision also has bedeviled attempts to determine how many abandoned villages were razed later by the Israelis.

Over the decades several studies have attempted to quantify the number of villages abandoned by Palestinians in 1948. In some cases, researchers also have tried to determine how many of these villages later were destroyed. Most estimates mention between 360 and 429 destroyed villages. The Israeli government cited a figure of 360 abandoned villages to the U.S. State Department in 1949.[6] A study from the 1960s by the Palestinian lawyer Sabri Jiryis claimed that 374 abandoned Palestinian communities were destroyed by the Israelis.[7] Anti-Zionist Jewish activist Israel Shahak cited a figure of 385 destroyed villages in 1973.[8] Recent studies by Israeli and Palestinian scholars also vary, with Israeli estimates once again somewhat lower. Israeli scholar Benny Morris's detailed study of the question produced a figure of 369 abandoned localities.[9] Palestinian geographer Ghazi Falah cited a figure of 418 "depopulated" villages,[10] the same number as Palestinian scholar Walid Khalidi's thorough study of the issue (Falah and Khalidi used some of the same sources, which helps account for the fact that they arrived at the same figure).[11] Basheer Nijim and Bishara Muammar claim the highest number of "destroyed" villages: 427 and possibly 429.[12]

Nijim and Muammar's work indicates the geographical spread of the destroyed villages they uncovered, and also notes which districts ended up as part of Israel, the West Bank, and/or Gaza (see table 1.1). A more detailed discussion of the various estimates for the scope of the refugees' land appears later in this study.

The question of to what degree Jewish authorities deliberately expelled Palestinians is a hotly contested one.[13] For many historians of the Arab-Israeli conflict, the issue comes down to whether Zionist authorities ordered the deliberate expulsion of the Palestinians according to a master plan of ethnic cleansing. It is beyond dispute that some expulsions occurred as it is that, even before the fighting began, various figures in the Zionist movement were actively investigating the idea of what they euphemistically called "transferring" the Palestinians out of the country. One such person was Yosef Weitz of the Jewish National Fund [Heb.: Keren Kayemet le-Yisra'el]. Weitz was born in

TABLE 1.1 Palestinian Villages Destroyed in 1948, by Mandatory District

| *District* | *Sub-District* | *No. of Villages in 1948* | *Demolished* |
|---|---|---|---|
| Galilee | Safad | 83 | 78 |
| | Acre | 64 | 29 |
| | Tiberias | 29 | 24 |
| | Nazareth | 31 | 4 |
| | Baysan | 33 | 31 |
| Haifa | Haifa | 72 | 45 |
| Samaria | Jenin * | 19 | 6 |
| | Tulkarm * | 34 | 4 (maybe 6) |
| | Nablus ** | n/a | n/a |
| Lydda | Ramla * | 56 | 56 |
| | Jaffa | 26 | 26 |
| Jerusalem | Ramallah ** | n/a | n/a |
| | Jerusalem * | 41 | 37 |
| | Hebron * | 19 | 15 |
| Gaza | Gaza * | 46 | 46 |
| | Beersheba | 26 | 26 |
| TOTAL DESTROYED | | | 427 (maybe 429) |

* = subdistricts that ended up both in Israel and the West Bank and/or Gaza
** = subdistricts that ended up in the West Bank only
Source: Basheer K. Nijim, ed., with Bishara Muammar, *Toward the De-Arabization of Palestine/Israel 1945–1977*. Published under the Auspices of The Jerusalem Fund for Education and Community Development (Dubuque, Iowa: Kendall/Hunt Publishing Company, 1984).

Russia in 1890 and immigrated to Ottoman Palestine in 1908. He began working for the Jewish National Fund (JNF) in 1918. The JNF was established by the World Zionist Organization [Heb.: ha-Histadrut ha-Tsiyonit; later, ha-Histadrut ha-Tsiyonit ha-'Olamit] in December 1901 to acquire land in Ottoman Syria for the establishment of a Jewish state. It acquired its first land in Palestine in 1904. In 1907, the JNF was incorporated in London as the Jewish National Fund, Ltd., although its offices were located on the continent and moved several times over the decades. Starting in 1932, Weitz had risen to serve as the director of the JNF's Land Development Division. He was also involved in the establishment of the Histadrut, the all-encompassing Zionist labor federation.

By 1948, Weitz was one of the most knowledgeable Zionist land officials in the country. While he was not a leading political figure in the Zionist movement but rather a JNF bureaucrat, he had considerable access to such top officials and made his views known. He was indefatigable in his zeal for pursuing the twin Zionist goals of acquiring land in Palestine and settling it with Jewish immigrants to build the Jewish national home. Indeed, his determination to pour his life into the Zionist project was deepened by personal tragedy. His son Yehi'am was killed by Palestinians in northwestern Galilee in 1946 while participating in a raid carried out by the full-time Zionist strike force, the Palmah. A kibbutz in his name was erected nearby that same year. Weitz's determination to continue his work furthering the Zionist goal of building the Jewish state "dunum by dunum" (one dunum = 1,000 sq.m.) only intensified during the critical years of 1946–48. Weitz's dream of a Jewish state included little room in it for the indigenous Palestinian population, who still outnumbered Jews two to one by the time that the United Nations voted to partition Palestine into neighboring Jewish and Arab states in November 1947. Many Zionist leaders had run up against this over the decades. Some simply seemed to ignore the demographic reality that the state they were building would consist of an Arab majority. Others actively pondered ways to solve what was called the "Arab problem." This became particularly true after the UN partition vote, when it became clear that 45 percent of the population within the proposed Jewish state would be Palestinian.

Weitz was one of the latter types of Zionists, and the idea of "transferring" Palestinians out of the Jewish state occupied his thoughts for several years before the momentous events of 1948. Weitz met with the surveying engineer and JNF land valuer Zalman Lifshits in Jerusalem in December 1946 to discuss the future of the Zionist endeavor. Lifshits stated that they needed to collect detailed information on Palestinian villages in the country. Weitz countered with a hard-line vision of transferring the Palestinians completely out of the country. He detailed his ideas in his diary:

> It should be clear to us that there is no room in Palestine for these two peoples. No "development" will bring us to our goal of independent nationhood in this small country. Without the Arabs, the land will become wide and spacious for us; with the Arabs, the land will remain sparse and cramped .... The only solution is Palestine, at least Western Palestine [i.e., Palestine without Transjordan], without Arabs. There is no room here for compromises![14]

Weitz and Lifshits agreed to try to work toward this goal. In fact, in 1948 they served together on a committee that investigated transfer (see below).

When the fighting broke out in 1948, Weitz believed that it provided a golden opportunity to effect such a transfer. By the spring of that year, thousands of Palestinians were already in flight and leaving behind large stretches of land. For Weitz, the proper course of action was simple: prevent their return and take over their land. On May 20, 1948, Weitz noted in his diary that the refugee flight would create "a complete territorial revolution ....The State is destined to expropriate...their land." [15] Once the fighting was underway, he would move to realize this.

## Initial Israeli Attitudes Toward Utilizing Refugee Land

The flight of the refugees and their massive property losses presented both challenges and opportunities for the Jewish population of war-torn Palestine and its leadership, already consumed with the war. During the fighting, the Jewish Agency for Palestine [Heb.: ha-Sokhnut ha-Yehudit le-Erets Yisra'el] and, after May 1948, the Provisional Government of Israel, quickly recognized the major challenge presented by the refugee flight: preventing a return of the refugees to their lands behind Jewish lines where they could pose a demographic and potential military threat. The Jewish conquests of Palestinian towns and villages had left large areas vacant of their populations and, like Weitz, other Zionists also were determined to capitalize on this situation by preventing the refugees from returning. Indeed, some spoke of the refugee flight in emotion-charged terms. As early as June 1948, Israeli Provisional Foreign Minister Moshe Shertok (later Sharett) noted the possibilities presented by the huge demographic vacuum created by the still-developing refugee flight as follows:

> The opportunities which the present position [the refugee flight] open up for a lasting and radical solution of the most vexing problem of the Jewish State are so far-reaching as to take one's breath away. Even if a certain backwash is unavoidable, we must make the most of the momentous change with which history has presented us so swiftly and so unexpectedly. [16]

Weitz expressed similar sentiments shortly after the war:

> To begin with we must admit in retrospect that the flight of the Arabs was a positive development. It was a miracle almost as great as the [ancient Hebrew] exodus from Egypt. I cannot imagine how we would have shaped and stabilized the state had the Arabs remained ....The flight of the Arabs came like a gift from heaven, and we should not belittle it.[17]

The Zionist leader and first president of Israel, Chaim Weizmann, spoke frankly to the first American ambassador to Israel of the refugee exodus as a "miraculous simplification of our tasks" and evoked the Holocaust when dismissing international concern about the refugees. Weizmann groused:

> What did the world do to prevent this genocide [the Holocaust]? Why now should there be such an excitement in the UN and the Western capitals about the plight of the Arab refugees? [18]

Interestingly, the Palestinians' leadership in the Arab Higher Committee (AHC) also initially opposed the repatriation of the refugees as the war was winding down and the full scope of the refugee tragedy was becoming apparent. An August 1948 AHC note to the Arab League that was published in Syria rejected the notion of repatriation at that point in time because it would constitute recognition of the new state of Israel and would place the returnees in the position of being Israeli hostages.[19]

For Israeli authorities, preventing a return of the refugees was one thing. But deciding to take hold of their lands and exploit them for agricultural purposes or even for settling Jews was quite another. Here they were overtaken by events in the confusion of wartime and the preoccupation of the fledgling provisional government with the military situation. Some Jews began spontaneously to move into abandoned Palestinian homes in the towns and cities in the spring of 1948 while the battles still were being waged. The population of the Jewish Quarter of Jerusalem's Old City, for example, surrendered to the Jordanian Arab Legion on May 28, 1948 and was expelled across the front lines into Jewish West Jerusalem. The next day, the UN official Pablo de Azcárate witnessed some of them moving into the abandoned Palestinian houses in the upscale Qatamon district. He noted that some were living in "the magnificent houses which had been abandoned by their Arab owners in the early days of the struggle."[20] Some 1,200 Jewish refugees from the Old City eventually moved into Qatamon in addition to 4,800 others, mostly women, children, and the elderly.[21] Israeli soldiers with tanks seized abandoned areas in Jaffa.[22]

Jews began settling in Ramla in November 1948. Some new Jewish immigrants who were Holocaust survivors had initially been housed in rural kibbutzim. Having found their barracks-like accommodations in the kibbutzim too similar to those they faced in the Nazi concentration camps, they broke into Palestinian homes in Haifa. They took over well-appointed homes in such Palestinian quarters of the city as Wadi Nisnas and along 'Abbas Street. While the homes taken over in Qatamon had been abandoned, some of these homes were in fact still occupied by Palestinians who had remained. Some Jews simply evicted the owners by force. One Palestinian, Sa'id 'Atma, reported that Jews broke into his home, assaulted him, threw out his furniture, and began living in his house.[23]

Along with squatters taking up residence in empty Palestinian homes came a wave of looting of Arab homes by Jewish soldiers and civilians. The entire contents of expensive homes were carted away. Electric fixtures, plumbing pipes, and other such items were also removed. Although a Custodian of Absentee Property was created to protect the refugees' property (see below), this office reported to the new Israeli parliament, the Knesset, in April of 1949 that only £I4 million in moveable refugee property ever reached its storerooms. Millions more had been looted.[24] The UN estimated that the moveable property looted from the Arab College alone, located on Jabal al-Mukkabir (the Mt. of Evil Counsel), in Jerusalem, and occupied by Israeli troops during the second truce in September 1948, was worth £P18,000.[25] Despite "stiff jail sentences" meted out by the provisional government in an attempt to prevent looters, Israeli authorities were unable to contain the wholesale theft of Palestinian property.[26] Some Jews exploited the chaos of wartime to ransack the homes of fellow Jews as well. A group of Jewish residents of the Talpiyot and Sanhedriya sections of Jerusalem later submitted a bill to the Israeli government for the contents of "scores" of their homes looted by Israeli troops.[27]

Soon more organized attempts to place Jewish immigrants into Palestinian homes were underway. Jewish Agency (JA) head and future prime minister David Ben Gurion issued orders to the Hagana to begin settling Jews in captured Palestinian homes early in the war. In fact, he instructed the Hagana's commander in Jerusalem, David Shaltiel, to settle Jews in captured Palestinian areas of Jerusalem in early February 1948.[28] Nor did he intend that this be done on a temporary basis pending a final resolution of the Palestinian refugee problem; Ben Gurion was one of the Zionist leaders who early on had decided upon the permanent alienation of urban Palestinian property into Jewish hands. When speaking of using refugee homes in Jaffa for Jewish immigrants, Ben Gurion stated in May 1948 that "[t]he property belongs to the government" and "Jaffa will be a Jewish city. War is war."[29] In 1949, Yitshak Ben Tsvi, a MAPAI politician and member of the pre-state national council called the Va'ad Leumi (in 1952 he would become the second president of Israel), justified the seizure of abandoned housing by citing the need to placate Jewish donors abroad:

> If we go to the leaders of the Jewish communities abroad they too will ask how the vacant Arab residences were occupied. With more than 400,000 people evacuated and only 70,000 settled, it could be interpreted as negligence on our part. The proper utilization of abandoned residences is imperative.[30]

Officials of a variety of both Israeli government offices and Zionist institutions such as the Jewish Agency's Absorption Department [Heb.: Mahleket ha-Kelita] began formally to allow Jews to take up residence in abandoned refugee housing by the fall of 1948. As the former British barriers to Jewish immigration disappeared beginning in May 1948, Israel threw its doors open to new Jewish settlers and began placing many of them in Palestinian refugee dwellings. In September of that year, a four-member ministerial committee was established to divide up Palestinian apartments in Jaffa.[31] The first new Jewish immigrants to receive housing in urban refugee homes were those whom the British had turned away from Palestine in the mid and late-1940s and interned in detention camps in Cyprus, as well as former residents of Displaced Persons Camps in Europe and new Bulgarian immigrants. As the first new arrivals, they received the best choices of Arab homes and apartments in Jaffa, Lydda, and Ramla. Jews from North Africa were next in line, and moved into accommodations in Jaffa and Haifa.[32] By 1952, the Jerusalem Town Planning Commission had drawn up a planning scheme for the city that included all of West Jerusalem, not just the formerly Jewish neighborhoods. They clearly had accepted as a *fait accompli* the Jewish takeover of Palestinian homes in districts like Qatamon, Greek Colony, Baq'a, and other areas and made plans on the assumption that this situation would never change.

As a result of both the spontaneous and planned occupation of Palestinian homes by Jews, the numbers of Jews living in abandoned Arab urban districts began to swell. By April 1949, leaders of the main Zionist political party, MAPAI, noted that a total of 75,000 new immigrants were living in the Palestinian quarters of the formerly mixed cities of Haifa, Safad, Jaffa, and Jerusalem; 16,000 in the formerly Palestinian towns of Ramla, Lydda, and Acre; and 18,800 others in abandoned Palestinian villages.[33] By 1950, the number of new immigrants occupying refugee homes reached 7,000 in Jerusalem, 1,500 in Baysan, and 2,000 in al-Majdal.[34] Between May 1948 and May 1952, 123,669 of a total of 393,197 new immigrants were settled in refugee homes.[35] The total number of Jews settled in urban Palestinian residences eventually were as shown in table 1.2

Some of the new Jewish immigrants were not settled in the towns but in Palestinian homes in abandoned villages. This was particularly true for Jews from Middle Eastern and North African countries whom Zionist officials deemed socioeconomically suitable for rural agricultural life. By February 1950, some 15,000 were given housing in abandoned Palestinian villages.[36] In this context the Absorption Department of the Jewish Agency allowed Jews to move into the abandoned village of Dayr Yasin just west of Jerusalem, the scene of the most notorious Zionist massacre of Palestinians of the 1948 war, although such Jews as the scholar Martin Buber had publicly opposed the move. After its initial inspection by health authorities in August 1948, just four months after the massacre, the JA allowed immigrants from Poland, Slovakia, and Romania to settle there. The new villagers plowed under 20 dunums of olive trees and began growing plums and grapes instead in the village that was renamed Giv'at Sha'ul Bet.[37] In total, one-third of all immigrants entering Israel during the years of peak immigration in the late 1940s and early 1950s found accommodations in Palestinian refugee homes (more on the settlement of rural refugee land is found below).

TABLE 1.2 Number of Jews Settled in Abandoned Urban Properties

| *Town* | *Number of Jewish Settlers* |
|---|---|
| Acre | 5,000 |
| Haifa | 40,000 |
| Jaffa | 45,000 |
| Jerusalem | (400 apartments in the Greek Colony, German Colony, Baq'a districts for government officials who moved from Tel Aviv) |
| Haifa | 40,000 |
| Lydda | 8,000 |
| Ramla | 8,000 |
| TOTAL | 146,000 (plus government officials in Jerusalem) |

Source: Tom Segev *1949: The First Israelis*. Arlen Neal Weinstein, English language editor. An Owl Book (New York: Henry Holt and Co., 1998), pp. 76, 78

While Zionist officials in the cities were exploiting the flight of urban Palestinians, Yosef Weitz looked to the countryside in the spring of 1948. In late May of that year, he proposed to the new Israeli government that he be allowed to establish what he called a "Transfer Committee" to investigate proactive ways in which Israel could take advantage of the course of events and prevent a return of Palestinian refugees to their villages. Although he did not receive official cabinet approval to operate, Weitz simply formed the committee and went about his business. Working with him were two other seasoned officials with experience dealing with Arabs and/or land: Eliyahu Sasson and 'Ezra Danin. Sasson was a Syrian Jew born in Damascus in 1902 as Ilyas Sasson. A native speaker of Arabic, he was involved in Arab nationalist politics in Damascus before immigrating to Palestine in 1927. He directed the Jewish Agency's Arab Division from 1933–48 and later worked as director of the Middle Eastern Affairs Department of the Israeli Ministry of Foreign Affairs. Danin's father, Yehezkel Suchowolsky, immigrated from Europe to Palestine in 1886. 'Ezra was born in Jaffa in 1903, and became an orange grove owner. From 1940 to 1948 he served under Sasson in the Jewish Agency's Arab Division and later became a long-time special advisor on Arab and Middle Eastern affairs in the Israeli Ministry of Foreign Affairs.

Together the three men wrote a memorandum entitled "Retroactive Transfer. A Scheme for the Solution of the Arab Question in the State of Israel." Weitz presented it to Ben Gurion on June 5, 1948. The memorandum contained an ambitious proposal to consolidate Israeli territorial gains during the fighting. Weitz proposed that Israeli authorities prevent the return of Palestinian refugees; prevent Palestinian farmers from cultivating their abandoned fields; settle Jewish immigrants in 90 abandoned villages (20 of which lay within the boundaries of the UN-designated Arab state); and destroy the remainder of the abandoned villages. Ben Gurion reportedly agreed with the findings, but opposed destruction of large numbers of villages and wanted to create more a formal committee.[38]

Weitz was not to be deterred, however. Although Ben Gurion refused to authorize Weitz's sweeping suggestions formally, he did favor shorter term uses of the refugees' land. Jews quickly began taking over abandoned Palestinian farmland as well once the military situation stabilized by mid-June 1948 and the Israeli army essentially had neutralized any Arab threats. Initially, this movement was not for settlement purposes as Weitz wanted but for immediate economic reasons. Agricultural settlements were anxious to harvest the ripening grain left by the Palestinians to help compensate the wartime Jewish economy for losses suffered during the fighting. As early as the spring of 1948,

Jewish farmers began harvesting the grain left by their former Palestinian neighbors. Some of these actions were carried out spontaneously; in other instances, the military supervised these operations. The Hagana's Department of Arab Affairs sold the rights to harvest grain from abandoned fields to Jewish agents. In order to coordinate the usage of abandoned fields in a more centralized fashion, Zionist agencies stepped in to formalize more orderly procedures.

The most important Jewish agricultural planning organization during the mandate had been the Histadrut's Agricultural Center (Heb.: ha-Merkaz ha-Hakla'i). The center was the link between the Histadrut—and from there, the kibbutz movement—and the World Zionist Organization. It was the Agricultural Center that discussed matters of land allocation, etc., with the WZO and generally coordinated the agricultural activities of Jewish settlements by grouping individual settlements into block committees and regional councils. Given its central role in the creation of centralized Zionist plans for settlement and agriculture, it was the Agricultural Center and its regional councils that began entertaining applications for permission to cultivate abandoned farms from individual settlements and signing lease agreements with them. For example, the kibbutz Bet ha-Shittah sought the Center's permission in July 1948 to use some 5,400 dunums of refugee land in the villages of Yubla and al-Murassas. The Gilboa Regional Council later approved the request.[39] In October 1948, Weitz and Avraham Hartsfeld of the Agricultural Center divided an additional 23,500 dunums of refugee land in Yubla, al-Murassas, Kafra, Qumiya, and Zir'in to Gush Nuris [Nuris Bloc] settlements.[40]

In June 1948, the provisional government of Israel itself decided to get involved with assigning usage of refugee farmland rather than leave the matter totally to Zionist agencies and committees. By December 1948, the Israeli government had extended £I400,000 to kibbutzim to cultivate some 115,000 dunums of refugee land.[41] A nationwide survey was carried out to classify land and soil qualities. Yitshak Gvirts, formerly head of the Hagana's Department of Arab Affairs, began working with the Ministry of Agriculture to lease refugee farmland to Jewish settlements and individual Jewish farmers. Gvirts also had recently been a member of the Committee for Abandoned Arab Property that was established in March 1948 and was now head of the Department for the Property of Absentee Owners within the Ministry of Minority Affairs. Most abandoned areas in the northern and central parts of Palestine were leased to nearby Jewish settlements. In the central and southern areas of the Sharon Plain, however, private sector Jewish farmers from Hadera, Nes Tsiyona, and Petah Tikva also were involved.[42] However, because it was a new institution with little institutional history, the Ministry of Agriculture turned back to the

Histradrut's Agricultural Center to oversee the leases given as it had been doing so since the spring of 1948 anyway. The Agricultural Center in turn worked with its regional committees and with the Farmers' Organization [Heb.: Irgun 'Ovedei ha-Falha]. To devise an orderly plan for distributing refugee land, the Agricultural Center established a committee in July 1948 to meet with the various regional councils. Gvirts also served on this committee, along with Z. Stein, Y. Shutsberg, and Y. Levi.[43]

Jewish agricultural settlements from across the political spectrum began petitioning to lease abandoned refugee land during the summer of 1948. These included socialist kibbutzim (communal farms) as well as less communal moshavim and religious settlements. The following settlement movements, each representing a different ideological current, leased refugee land: ha-Kibbutz ha-Artsi—ha-Shomer ha-Tsa'ir, a kibbutz movement oriented toward the semi-Marxist MAPAM party; ha-Kibbutz ha-Me'uhad, another kibbutz movement oriented toward MAPAM, with some of its members associated with the left-wing of the main labor party, MAPAI; Hever ha-Kevutsot, the kibbutz movement that leaned toward MAPAI; Po'alei Agudat Yisra'el, the labor wing of the religious Agudat Yisra'el party; and various moshavim. Unlike communal kibbutzim, the extent of cooperation found on moshavim consisted of group marketing of crops. Individual farmers lived on their own and farmed their own separate land.

The question lingered, however, of going beyond simply using the abandoned villages' land to expropriating the land and settling it with Jews. The issue arose again during the summer of 1948 when the Israeli army destroyed villages during its operations. Weitz's Transfer Committee had proposed such destruction to Ben Gurion in May 1948. Believing that no one specifically had told him *not* to go ahead and that Shertok was reporting on his activities to Ben Gurion, Weitz pressed ahead with the Transfer Committee's plans to destroy abandoned villages in June and July 1948. Table 1.3 lists some of those he had destroyed.Although Weitz's program provoked intense criticism within some quarters in the Israeli government who disagreed with destroying abandoned villages, he carried out the demolitions anyway.

## The Legal Basis for Israeli Expropriation: The Custodian of Absentee Property

The Zionist takeover of refugee homes and farmland occurred for the most part in an *ad hoc*, uncoordinated fashion during the spring of 1948. In some

TABLE 1.3 Villages Destroyed by the First Transfer Committee, 1948

| *Village* | *District* |
|---|---|
| al-Mughar | Gaza |
| Fajja | Jaffa |
| Biyar 'Adas | Jaffa |
| Bayt Dajan | Jaffa |
| Miska | Tulkarm |
| al-Sumayriyya | Acre |
| Sabbarin | Haifa |
| al-Butaymat | Haifa |

Source: Benny Morris, *Birth of the Palestinian Refugee Problem, 1947–1949*. Cambridge Middle East Library (Cambridge: Cambridge University Press, 1987) p. 137

instances decisions to farm land and squat in refugee homes were taken by officials of the Jewish Agency, the Agricultural Center, the army, and individual Jews. However the huge amount of Palestinian property captured by Jewish forces soon prompted pre-state Zionist officials to establish a series of bodies to take formal control of refugee land, initially referred to as "abandoned lands" (Heb.: adamot netushot), and coordinate its usage. The first of these committees lay within the Hagana. This was not surprising given that it was the Zionist military that actually was occupying the land. In late March 1948, the Hagana created the Commission for Arab Property in Villages. This soon became the Hagana's Department of Arab Affairs.

Two other military committees quickly were created to deal with captured urban property as well. The first of these was established in April 1948 by Ben Gurion following the fall of Haifa, Tiberias, and Safad: the Supervisor of Arab Property in the Northern District. In May, the Ministry of Defense of the provisional government created the Supervisor of Abandoned Property in Jaffa. In addition, by April 1948 a civilian body, the Committee for Abandoned Arab Property, also was established. It was headed by Gad Makhnes, a Tel Aviv citrus grove owner who formerly had been involved in Jewish attempts to buy Palestinian property during the Mandate. Makhnes later served in the Israeli Ministry of Minority Affairs and became director general of the Ministry of the Interior. The committee's members included Makhnes' brother, Moshe, another orange grower and director of the ha-Note'ah Company; Yoav Tsukerman, a land purchasing official of the Jewish National Fund; 'Ezra Danin; and Yitshak Gvirts.

We can learn details of how Palestinian property was managed in the early days after the refugee exodus through a U.S. diplomatic document highlighting a June 1948 meeting between an official from the American consulate in Haifa and the Supervisor of Arab Property in the Northern District (Heb.: ha-Mefakeah ‘al ha-Rekhush ha-‘Aravi be-Mahoz ha-Tsafon), Naftali Lifshits. American Consul Aubrey E. Lippincott had received a letter from a refugee holding American citizenship, Evelyn Gebara, who had taken refuge in Beirut. She was inquiring about her family home and furnishings in Haifa. On June 21, 1948, someone from the consulate interviewed Lifshits, a prominent lawyer in Haifa. Lifshits offered a number of details about the operations of the office that he opened in late April of that year. The American interviewer came away with the opinion that the Supervisor's office was very well-organized. Lifshits had divided Arab property in Haifa into three categories: Palestinian refugee property, property of Palestinians still living in the city, and property of non-Palestinian Arabs. Lifshits' office was concerned with the first and second categories only. Property in the third category was taken over by the state as "enemy" property.

Lifshits divided Palestinian property, both refugee and resident, into three types. The first was arms and ammunition, which the state confiscated from all persons (refugees, resident Palestinians, as well as Jews). Lifshits reported that he had not uncovered sizeable quantities of such war materiel. The second type of property was that which could serve the Israeli war effort, such as cloth, large amounts of foodstuffs, and petroleum products. These also were confiscated and inventoried. If this property were sold, the amounts realized were duly recorded. The Supervisor deducted three percent of the value of the sale as commission for the sale. Resident Palestinians could receive some of this money generated by the Supervisor from the sale immediately, but not all of it. Israeli authorities were worried that they might smuggle the money out of Israel whereupon it could be used to finance the Arab war effort.

Finally, the third type of property was personal and household goods. Refugee household goods were sold, destroyed if in poor shape, or used to furnish abandoned residences for new Jewish tenants. Lifshits' office recorded all information in order to be able to credit the refugee. Resident Palestinians could get their household goods back immediately, unless they too had been sold. Since military authorities had herded those Palestinians who remained into certain areas of the city following its surrender, some were cut off from their homes and property. In cases where the Supervisor had sold residents' property, they eventually were given a receipt that noted how much money the state owed them, which they could collect "later."

Lifshits admitted to the American official that most of the credits for refugees and residents alike would not be paid right away. "Eventual compensation will be worked out by act of the Israeli parliament," he said. Still, the U.S. diplomat felt that Lifshits' office was trying to be as fair to those Palestinians still living in the city as possible to ease ethnic tensions. But the official noted that "considerable looting and burgling has gone on," and the Supervisor was trying to maintain order through the police and civilian guards. He also noted that with goods in such short supply at a time when the new state was at war, Arab goods were still being requisitioned despite the political sensitivities.[44]

The declaration of Israeli statehood in May 1948 prompted the reorganization of the several bodies that had been established to deal with the refugees' property. The provisional government moved to consolidate the various military and civilian committees dealing with abandoned refugee property into one. The Hagana committees and the Committee for Abandoned Arab Property became known as the Arab Properties Department (Heb.: ha-Mahlaka le-Nekhasim 'Aravim) within the new Ministry of Minority Affairs, and was headed by Gvirts. This arrangement quickly was superseded by the establishment of the Ministerial Committee for Abandoned Property in July 1948. This committee, sometimes known as the "committee of six," brought together six officials from different parts of the new government to establish joint policy regarding the refugee property. Its members were high-powered Zionist officials.

The foremost member was Provisional Prime Minister David Ben Gurion, born David Gruen in Poland in 1886. He had immigrated to Palestine in 1906 and became active in the socialist Po'alei Tsiyon labor movement. He helped found the Histadrut labor federation and later rose to lead both the MAPAI party and the Jewish Agency. Another MAPAI member, Provisional Foreign Minister Moshe Shertok, was born in the Ukraine in 1894. After immigrating to Palestine in 1906, Shertok (later Sharett) headed the Jewish Agency's Political Department from 1933–1948 and later became Israel's second prime minister. Provisional Finance Minister Eli'ezer Kaplan was born in Russia in 1891 and immigrated to Palestine in 1923. A member of MAPAI, he rose to become the Jewish Agency's treasurer from 1933–1948 and thereafter became Israel's first Minister of Finance. Provisional Justice Minister Felix Rosenblueth, who later changed his name to Pinhas Rozen, was born in Germany in 1887 and was a leader of the centrist Progressive Party. Provisional Minorities Affairs Minister Bekhor Shalom Shitrit was a Mizrahi Jew (Jew of Middle Eastern or North African origin, in this case of Moroccan descent) born in Tiberias in 1895 who served in the Palestine police and later rose to became Minister of Police in the Israeli government. A speaker of Arabic, Shitrit spoke Hebrew with an Arabic accent characteristic of some Mizrahi Jews. The final member was Provisional Agricultural Minister Aharon Tsizling, who was born in Russia in 1901 and immigrated to Palestine as a young boy in 1904. He rose to become a leading official in the ha-Kibbutz ha-Me'uhad movement and the Ahdut ha-'Avoda party.

The new ministerial committee decided on a plan to expropriate refugee land on August 20, 1948. This marked a departure from leases, and represented a major new direction in the Israeli government's attitude toward the land and thus for the refugee property question in general. From now on, Israel was set to separate the refugees from legal title to their land and use it instead for permanent settlement of Jewish immigrants. The committee approved a plan to settle Jews on 120,000 dunums of which 58,000 dunums were refugee land, a plan based on the JNF's earlier recommendations to use "surplus" refugee land. The committee hoped that, by seizing "surplus" land only, the government might avoid excessive criticism for taking refugee land.[45] The committee assigned authority over the refugee land to two ministries. It transferred legal authority over the land itself to the Finance Ministry, but gave the Agriculture Ministry the power to manage it. Finally, a new office was established to take possession of the refugee land: the Custodian of Abandoned Property (Heb.: ha-Apotropos 'al ha-Rekhush ha-Natush).

On July 15, 1948, Minister of Finance Kaplan appointed Dov Shafrir as the first Custodian of Abandoned Property. Shafrir, who assumed his duties two days after the Israeli capture of the Palestinian towns of Ramla and Lydda, was an immigrant from the Ukraine. Before assuming his duties as custodian he had been the head of the Neve 'Oved Company, the construction company of the Histadrut's Agricultural Center. In a pattern that would create controversy and charges of partisan political disposals of refugee land, Shafrir was also a member of the ruling MAPAI party. By the fall of that year the former Arab Property Department of the Minorities Affairs Ministry had been transferred to the Custodian's office where, known as the Villages Department, it was tasked with overseeing rural refugee property. The Custodian's office was responsible both to the Ministry of Finance and a semiannual review by a subcommittee of the legislature. The Custodian's policy was determined by the Custodian of Abandoned Property Council consisting of representatives of the Prime Ministry, as well as the ministries of Finance, Agriculture, Justice, and Interior. The council determined the rents charged by the Custodian, and approved any releases of abandoned property to its owners. Shafrir and the Custodian's office technically controlled refugee land although it continued the policy of empowering the Ministry of Agriculture to lease the land to cultivators for up to 35 months. Profits were turned over to the Ministry of Finance. (The Custodian's office and responsibilities would quickly change yet again toward the end of 1948, which is discussed further below).

The provisional state government also moved toward providing some sort of legal framework for the seizure of abandoned lands by these various bodies. In early June 1948, the provisional cabinet examined a draft proposal prepared by the Ministry of Minority Affairs for a Law of Occupied Territory, although nothing came of it. Thereafter the provisional legislature, and later the regular legislature (the Knesset), passed a series of laws and regulations that laid the legal basis for the expropriation of refugee land and its eventual disposal. The first of these laws was the Abandoned Property [Heb.: nekhesim netushim] Ordinance No. 12 of 5708/1948, enacted on June 21, 1948. The law was made retroactively valid as of May 16, 1948, two days after Israel declared its independence. Its purpose was to stop the impromptu seizures of refugee land described above and create a modicum of state control over the situation. Minister of Agriculture Aharon Tsizling, who was responsible for leasing refugee property, described the ordinance's purpose to the provisional cabinet as such:

> ...to regularize the legal situation in the abandoned areas. So far there is no single central authority and no legal system by virtue of which action can be taken as regards Arab property in the towns and the dozens of villages which have been abandoned by the majority of their inhabitants. I permit myself to say that there is a degree of chaos in this field which can only do harm to and prejudice the general interests of the state and the interests of the Arab inhabitants, which must not be prejudiced.[46]

A second law was passed three days later, on June 24, to provide a legal basis for extending Israeli jurisdiction, including over abandoned property, to "abandoned areas" of Palestine: the Abandoned Areas Ordinance. This second law defined an "abandoned area" [Heb.: shetah netush] as follows: "'Abandoned area' means any area or place conquered by or surrendered to armed forces or deserted by all or part of its inhabitants, and which has been declared by order to be an abandoned area."[47]

Such a definition meant that almost all Arab land that came under Israeli control—whether through capture or surrender—could be labeled "abandoned." The law also stated clearly that not all of the land's inhabitants need to have fled for it to be labeled abandoned. The law further allowed the state to take over buildings, crops, and just about anything else located on the land. Indeed, the definition of "property" included: "...animals, crops, fruits, vegetables and any other agricultural produce, factories, workshops, machinery, goods and commodities of all kinds, and also a right to moveable or immoveable property and any other right."[48]

Declaration of an abandoned area was a declaratory act by the government, which delegated its authority to the Ministry of Finance. The minister was then empowered to pass regulations regarding the confiscation of abandoned property within that area as he saw fit.

A third law was enacted that empowered the Minister of Agriculture to "assume control" of any land that he deemed was not being cultivated: the Emergency Regulations for the Cultivation of Fallow Land and the Use of Unexploited Water Sources of 5709/1948, passed on October 11, 1948. Drafted by the Ministry of Agriculture, these regulations allowed the minister to declare land he deemed "uncultivated" to be "waste lands" [Heb.: adamot mubarot] and order their use, including retroactive authorization for any planting of refugee property prior to the law's passage. The law included the following explanatory note:

> War conditions have resulted in lands being abandoned by their owners and cultivators and left untilled plantations being neglected and water resources remaining unexploited. On the other hand, the interest of the State demands that, without prejudice to the right of ownership of land or other property, agricultural production be maintained and expanded as much as possible and the deterioration of plantations and farm installations prevented. For the attainment of these objects it is necessary that the Minister of Agriculture should have certain emergency powers, which are conferred upon him by these Regulations.[49]

It was up to the Minister of Agriculture to determine what constituted "waste land." The regulations did not authorize the actual confiscation of uncultivated land but merely its use for a period of up to two years and eleven months. Any profits from the land were to be kept for the owners. The law was later extended on January 6, 1949 by the Emergency Regulations (Cultivation of Waste Lands) (Extension of Validity) Ordinance No. 36 of 5709/1949, by which time some 500,000 dunums of "waste land" were under cultivation by Jews.[50] Significantly, the second law extended the time the Minister of Agriculture could keep uncultivated lands under his control from two years, eleven months to five years.

The most sweeping of the initial Israeli laws affecting abandoned refugee land was the Emergency Regulations (Absentees' Property) of 5709/1948, drafted by the Ministry of Justice and enacted on December 2, 1948. These regulations shifted the legal definition of what constituted abandoned land from the land itself to its owner: instead of declaring land to be "abandoned," people were now declared "absentees" whose property could be seized by the state. The law created a new legal category—"absentee" [Heb.: nifkad]—into which refugees were fit but which in fact incorporated more types of people than the conventional understanding of a refugee. A person could be declared an "absentee" if s/he was a person who, on or after November 29, 1947 (the date of the UN partition resolution) was a citizen or subject of an Arab state; was in any of these states for any length of time; was in any part of Palestine not under Jewish control; or was "in any place other than his habitual residence, even if such place as well as his habitual abode were within Israeli-occupied territory."

Thus the law declared persons who were citizens of Arab states at any point after November 29, 1947 to be absentees, whether or not they were actually absent from any land they owned in Palestine. It declared Palestinians absentees if they ever traveled to an Arab country for any length of time after November 29, 1947, including those who fled temporarily to an Arab state and then returned, or even those who briefly traveled to an Arab country for business. It declared Palestinians absentees if they were ever in any part of Palestine not under the control of Jewish forces after November 29, 1947 for any length of time—which under those definitions included most of the country. Lastly, it declared as an absentee anyone who was temporarily away from his/her normal place of residence, for any reason, even if both that place and the normal place of residence lay *within* areas under Jewish control.

The law therefore potentially targeted almost all Arabs and not merely those who actually abandoned the land, fled across the borders as refugees, and remained there. Indeed, many who remained refugees inside Israel, including those who actually remained in their homes inside Israel, could be and were declared absentees. This was no accidental technicality. Shertok had objected to the initial wording of the draft legislation that would have categorized "absentees" as those persons who fled over the borders into Arab territory. He noted in a meeting of the Ministerial Committee for Abandoned Property that under this definition, the thousands of Palestinian refugees who remain huddled in camps near Nazareth, within Israeli territory, would be allowed to regain their property. He also noted the hypothetical case of Israel capturing the northern West Bank sometime soon and incorporating it into Israel. Under such a scenario, refugees in the newly captured areas then no longer would be "absentees" living across the borders but Israeli citizens who would be entitled to get back the land they had abandoned in Israel.[51]

Shertok's logic won the day, and the regulations were carefully worded so as to guarantee that Israel retained as many of the fruits of its 1948 conquest as possible. The Absentee Property Regulations further stipulated that the state could seize the property of any absentee and turn it over to a new office that replaced the Custodian of *Abandoned* Property: the Custodian of *Absentee* Property (Heb.: ha-Apotropos le-Nikhsei Nifkadim). The Custodian was granted control over all rights associated with land, business, and other property where at least one-half of the persons or companies owning rights to such property were declared to be absentees. The new Custodian's office could not permanently transfer refugee land under his control, but rather merely lease it for periods up to five years. Finally, the law stipulated that the burden of proof lay with the individual to prove that s/he was not an absentee.

The law reflected a sweeping change in legal thinking. In an effort to lay hold of as much Arab property as possible, the Israeli government shifted the focus from the land to its owner. The law created a broad definition of who constituted an absentee so that huge areas of Arab land could be seized. Instead of viewing the refugees' land as temporarily "abandoned property" or "fallow" land, the new law understood it as left behind under legal Israeli control indefinitely. The alienation of the refugees' property out of their hands thus allowed for the long-term uses of the land they left behind in Israel. This thinking is reflected in the fact that Kaplan later told the Knesset in 1949 that the regulations had been based on laws in the Indian subcontinent that dealt with the land permanently left behind by Hindu and Muslim refugees from Pakistan and India, respectively, in 1947.[52] Those drafting the law also clearly had in mind British mandatory legislation passed during the Second World War that had created a Custodian for Enemy Property. The Trading with the Enemy Law of 1939 allowed this Custodian to sequester land in Palestine belonging to citizens of Germany, German allies and satellites, and German-occupied territories.

The Absentee Property Regulations were greeted with dismay and hostility by a variety of circles. Within Israel, liberals and some centrists decried the law for confiscating the land of Arabs who until quite recently had been fellow citizens of Palestine, not enemy aliens. Knesset member J. Klebanoff of the

General Zionists urged his fellow legislators to consider the impact of legislation that essentially relegated the refugees to the status of enemy whose land could be seized:

> We are not dealing with enemy property, but with the property of a substantial part of the population of our country, who have and must have very important rights—people who can come to us with very serious claims, financial and moral. We cannot treat their property as enemy property.[53]

Internationally, the U.S. government also opposed the new law because it prejudiced the refugees' rights. The Americans urged the Israelis not to take unilateral action regarding the land, as the United States was committed to "safeguarding Arab absentee property interests in Israel against application of the Israeli ordinance of December 12, 1948 authorizing sale of such property."[54]

The initial legislation of 1948 provided the legal basis for the indefinite seizure and administration of refugee land, as well as the land of other Palestinians who remained in Israel. These laws further gave the government the legal authority to lease cultivable land to Jewish farmers, including retroactive permission for land already in use as described above. But what these laws did not do was allow the government to lay claim to the land's title and dispose of it permanently (i.e., sell it). Still, the new Custodian's office quickly moved to lease the refugees' land to a variety of quarters. By early 1949, Israeli authorities began moving to expropriate permanently the abandoned refugee property and to do so on some type of legal basis. Ben Gurion was anxious to sell a significant amount of the newly conquered land to the JNF as a fundraising effort. The JNF, however, was demanding that any such sale involve the legal transfer of the lands' title. This was one of a number of factors that led the state to obtain such title.

The result was the drafting of what came to be the single most important piece of Israeli legislation dealing with refugee land, the Absentees' Property Law of 5710/1950, passed by the Knesset on March 14, 1950. An expanded version of the Emergency Regulations (Absentees' Property), this law would govern the fate of the refugee property for decades to come. The Absentees' Property Law defined "absentees" in similar terms to the earlier Emergency Regulations but narrowed the definition somewhat to someone who left such residence for a part of Palestine under hostile control or, prior to September 1948, to a place outside Palestine:

(1) a person who, at any time during the period between the 16th Kislev, 5708 (29th November 1947) and the day on which a declaration is published, under section 9(d) of the Law and Administration Ordinance, 5708–1948), that the state of emergency declared by the Provisional Council of State on the 10th Iyar, 5708 (19th May 1948) has ceased to exist [Israel has never published such a declaration to this day], was a legal owner of any property situated in the area of Israel or enjoyed or held it, whether by himself or through another, and who, at any time during the said period -

(ii) was a national or citizen of the Lebanon, Egypt, Syria, Saudi-Arabia, Trans-Jordan, Iraq or the Yemen, or

(iii) was in one of these countries or in any part of Palestine outside of the area of Israel, or

(iv) was a Palestinian citizen and left his ordinary place of residence in Palestine

(e) for a place outside Palestine before the 27th Av, 5708 (1st September 1948); or

(f) for a place in Palestine held at the time by forces which sought to prevent the establishment of the State of Israel or which fought against it after its establishment.[55]

Absentees also could be groups of persons, such as co-owners of businesses, cooperative societies, and so forth. The law further defined "absentee property" as property owned by a person who, at any time after November 29, 1947, met the qualifications of an absentee. The law also specified that the Custodian of Absentee Property could seize what he felt constituted absentee land without the necessity of determining who was the legal owner of the land and that any debts owed to an absentee were henceforth due to the Custodian.

The wording of the law meant that others besides Palestinian Arabs were declared absentees. Certainly non-Palestinian Arabs who owned land in Palestine were declared absentees. However, non-Arabs also were declared absentees. For example, Israel seized land belonging to members of the Baha'i community of northern Palestine, most of whom had U.S. or Iranian citizenship. When Israel allowed the return of some 150 Baha'is who had fled, Sharett requested funds from Kaplan to help move fifteen Jewish families out of Baha'i homes they had occupied in Haifa.[56] Property belonging to Britons, Canadians, and other foreigners who absented themselves to an Arab country similarly was declared absentee property, although Israel generally looked favorably upon requests for compensation from such persons unless they were Arabs with dual citizenship.[57]

Finally, even Jewish citizens of Arab countries who owned land in Israel were technically absentees subject to having their property sequestered. Jewish absentees owning property in Israel were treated differently from Arabs. The Custodian generally released to them any property they owned in Israel upon their immigration to Israel. On other occasions, such land was released to their representatives (although the latter could not sell the land for the Jews in question).[58] Beyond this, Jews from Poland and other German-occupied territories who had purchased land in prewar Palestine also had their land sequestered by the government but under a different law. The mandate-era Trading with the Enemy Ordinance of 1939 had established a Custodian of Enemy Property that was carried over by the new government of Israel. When Jews who survived the Second World War immigrated to Israel, the Custodian of Enemy Property released their sequestered land to them or to their heirs.[59]

Another intent of the law was to tighten the Custodian's control over refugee land and prevent any attempts by the refugees to liquidate their property in exile. The land required all persons in possession of absentee property to notify the Custodian and also forbade anyone from acquiring absentee property. The law also outlawed any attempt by refugees to liquidate their property from over the borders. It specifically aimed to prohibit refugees selling their land to someone remaining inside Israel and then arranging for the money to be sent outside the country. Likewise, it sought to stop refugees from giving their land to a relative who remained behind in order to keep it out of the hands of the Custodian:

> (1) A transfer or handing-over of property to an absentee or to another for the benefit of an absentee during the period between the 21st Adar bet, 5708 (1st April, 1948) and the day of publication of the appointment of the Custodian, effected with intent to smuggle the whole or a part of the property or the whole or the part of the consideration received for it to a part of Palestine which at the time of the transfer or handing-over was outside the area of Israel, or to the Lebanon, Egypt, Syria, Saudi-Arabia, Trans-Jordan, Iraq or the Yemen, is null and void.
>
> (2) A transfer or handing-over of property from the hands of an absentee to another person during the period referred to in paragraph (1), effected for a fictitious or insufficient consideration or without consideration, or under unfair pressure, is null and void.

However, the law conversely validated the actions of anyone whom the authorities deemed to have dealt with absentee property "in good faith"—which allowed collaborators to hand over refugee land to the Custodian. Lastly, it validated any acts done before the law had been enacted, if such acts would have been valid under the law at that time.

The law allowed the Custodian to release absentee property to persons he deemed were no longer absentees or who had been improperly declared absentees. Such persons were required to pay the government a sum equal to four percent of the land's value to cover the Custodian's expenses in administering the property during the period of its sequestration; a sum representing any maintenance, improvements, etc. that the Custodian performed; plus interest of six percent per annum on the amount of such improvements. This provision worked to the advantage of some Palestinians who remained in Israel but was generally of little value to the vast bulk who were in exile. Still, some 2,000 properties were returned to legally repatriated refugees by January 1953 although not necessarily their own land. It appears that this land was rented to them, not necessarily sold.[60] The law also technically allowed the government to seize any property owned by an absentee, including land legally acquired *after* 1948 by "present absentees" [Heb.: nifkadim nokhahim]—refugees who had settled and were living within Israel. This proved too onerous even for the Israeli government, and the Knesset passed the Absentees' Property (Amendment) Law on March 15, 1951 that allowed "present absentees" who were lawfully resident in Israel legally to own property that they acquired after the war. Another Absentees' Property (Amendment) Law passed later in 1956 further clarified this issue by restricting the definition of absentee property to property acquired before 1947.

Perhaps the signal point of significance of this new law was that it allowed the Custodian of Absentee Property to sell land under his disposal to a "Development Authority" should such a body come into existence. This was the only exception to the rule that the Custodian could not sell the land under his jurisdiction. Similarly, he could lease refugee land for periods up to six years with the only exception to this requirement being any future Development Authority, which would be allowed to sign longer leases. The law specified that the Custodian must sell land under his care to a Development Authority only at the land's "official value," which the law specified.

Despite the clear prohibition against selling abandoned land to anyone other than the soon-to-be-created Development Authority, the Custodian of Absentee Property in fact agreed to sell a large amount of refugee land to other parties. The biggest deal involved the sale of some 1.1 million dunums to the Jewish National Fund in January 1949. This is described in detail below. Other, lower-profile deals occurred as well, and at a time when the Israeli government was scrambling to secure as much coveted hard currency as possible. In June 1952, a staff member of the UN's Conciliation Commission for Palestine was told that a building in Jerusalem left by a member of the Makhluf family of Bayt Jala was being offered for sale—for foreign currency only. The building had been purchased ca. 1941 for £P17,500. The UN staff member noted to the source of the information, a member of the Jerusalem Town Planning Commission, that the Absentees' Property Law of 1950 specified that the Custodian could sell property only to the Development Authority, not to the highest bidder on the open market. He was told that "the Development Authority itself was inviting offers from anyone who could pay in foreign currency."[61]

One final Israeli law of note was the Land Acquisition (Validation of Acts and Compensation) Law of 5713/1953, passed by the Knesset on March 10, 1953. This law retroactively validated the seizure of any land that Israeli authorities had deemed necessary "for purposes of essential development, settlement or security" that occurred between May 14, 1948 and April 1, 1952 if on the latter date that property was still in the government's hands. The law also stated that owners were entitled to compensation. However, this law was designed to deal with the situation faced by Palestinians *within* Israel who had lost land. It did not override the Absentees' Property Law in terms of refugees outside Israel.

## Policies of the Custodian of Absentee Property, 1948–1953

Together, these laws created the legal framework by which the Custodian of Absentee Property had consolidated his control over millions of dunums of refugee land as well as moveable property by 1950. The Custodian quickly moved to consolidate moveable property into his warehouses, but found that much of it had disappeared in the early wave of looting that spread through the towns in the spring of 1948. Most of the goods that he managed to collect were sold or leased in 1948 and 1949 to merchants, government and public bodies, the army, and private individuals. For example, a tender issued by the Custodian in 1951 requested bids for the following abandoned commercial property in Haifa: one 100-liter boiler; one glass polishing machine; one 15-horsepower engine; tables; tools; tubes; and a cupboard.[62] Between June 24, 1948 and March 31, 1950, the Custodian sold £I3,806,035 worth of abandoned moveable property.[63]

The Custodian was also granted control over financial assets and instruments held by persons deemed absentees. The questions of refugee bank accounts, safe deposit boxes, and Palestine Government bearer bonds quickly rose to become the most immediate and pressing issues surrounding such moveable refugee property, and are discussed below in detail. Less well known is the fate of other moveable property such as shares in companies that the Custodian took over. The Custodian of Absentee Property was empowered to take control of all shares of stock that were owned by persons who had been declared absentees as well as companies in which at least 50 percent of the owners were absentees. The earliest accounting of data relating to this that I could locate dates from January 1957. In that month, the Custodian's office issued a report indicating that it controlled absentee shares in forty-one different companies. According to a report compiled nearly three decades later in February 1984, the Custodian still controlled absentee shares in thirty companies although of these, only thirteen were companies that appeared on the 1957 list (the rest being new additions). The Israeli State Controller estimated in 1990 that the shares in five companies alone in which the Custodian still controlled shares by that time were worth tens of millions of New Israeli Shekels (NIS), there being approximately two NIS per U.S. dollar at that time.[64]

The Custodian's major concern after 1948 was not administering moveable property but abandoned immoveable property (land). Prior to the creation of the Development Authority in 1950, the Custodian could not sell absentee land but merely lease it. The Custodian's policy toward urban land was to try to assert his legal control over the thousands of Palestinian homes that had been requisitioned for new Jewish immigrants in the confusing legal and social atmosphere of the years 1948–50. As noted above, a variety of agencies and individual squatters had seized hold of abandoned refugee homes immediately following the refugee flight. As early as July 1948, Dov Shafrir, the first Custodian, had tried to allocate abandoned urban properties rationally in the face of opposition from local officials of the Jewish Agency, military officers, and individual Jews who all sought to control these buildings. The Custodian later managed to work in cooperation with the JA and other institutions to settle immigrants in abandoned urban housing. One was the Histadrut's powerful construction subsidiary Solel Boneh, which helped build housing for immigrants.

The Custodian found himself the largest legal urban landlord in Israel after 1948. One of the first things that his office undertook, beginning in the second half of 1948, was a survey to identify abandoned urban property throughout the country. The results were drawn up in special registers. Given that the surface area involved was much smaller than the rural areas and that taxation documents more precise, it was much easier to determine the scope of refugee property in the towns. The task was largely completed by 1950. Table 1.4 indicates the Custodian's official estimate of the scope of urban refugee property.

By March 31, 1950, the Custodian estimated that the value of the abandoned buildings alone (not including the value of the land) that he controlled totaled £I11,770,169.[65]

Table 1.5 provides figures on the number and location of abandoned dwellings controlled by the Custodian as of December 1951 according to figures available to the Jewish National Fund, as shown in table 1.5.

By 1952, the Custodian had a total of 39,627 dwellings under his control, containing 65,429 rooms and 7,880 businesses.[66]

By the early 1950s, the Custodian's office had finished surveying and recording abandoned urban property and established a Dwellings Division. It also studied mandatory tax records left behind by the British. Table 1.6 shows the scope and assessed tax value of urban refugee buildings according to mandatory *wirku* (land value) records, as shown in table 1.6.

Table 1.7 indicates the scope and value of the land alone, not including buildings, according to the *wirku* records.

Beyond determining the scope and value of the urban property under his control, the Custodian quickly surveyed the buildings for damage and made arrangements to lease the land and buildings. A thorough inspection survey began in early 1951, and was completed in Jaffa by that May. It revealed that

TABLE 1.4 Custodian of Absentee Property's Report on the Scope of Urban Refugee Property, 1949–1950

| *Date* | *Rooms* | *Businesses* | *Enterprises* | *Parcels* | *Misc. Bldgs.* |
|---|---|---|---|---|---|
| 1) Controlled by Custodian of Absentee Property | | | | | |
| 31/3/49 | 54,976 | 6,050 | 36 | 980 | 1,254 |
| 31/3/50 | 81,152 | 7,819 | no info. | no info. | 47,786 [apartments] |
| 2) Controlled by Israeli army | | | | | |
| 31/3/49 | 6,069 | 886 | no info. | no info. | no info. |

Source: Israel State Archives [ISA] (43)5440/1582, report of Custodian of Absentee Property (March 31, 1949) and (March 31, 1950)

of the 6,162 abandoned buildings inspected in the city only 658 were in good condition. The Custodian determined that 114 buildings must be demolished and the rest repaired.[67] By 1950, the Custodian's Dwellings Division had spent £I800,000 on repairing abandoned urban buildings, in addition to £I1,026,000 that the Jewish Agency paid for repairs to buildings in abandoned villages that were located near existing Jewish settlements.[68] Allocating the buildings was carried out in conjunction with Israeli governmental and Zionist settlement agencies. Once Ben Gurion ordered that government offices be moved to West Jerusalem, the government undertook a concerted effort to promote development in the city even though it was isolated from the rest of the country and that Tel Aviv was the center of Jewish life. The Custodian's registers revealed that by 1951 he controlled 5,736.048 dunums of abandoned land in West Jerusalem. Note the figures in Table 1.8: In addition to 400 apartments allocated to government officials, the Custodian leased 20 dunums of abandoned buildings in Jerusalem to some 200 commercial enterprises established by new immigrants, including a shoe factory, cigarette factory, and a clothing factory.[69]

TABLE 1.5 Number and Location of Urban and Rural Refugee Dwellings, 1951

| *Location* | *Dwellings* |
|---|---:|
| Jaffa | 16,327 |
| Haifa | 14,000 |
| Jerusalem | 7,033 |
| Ramla | 3,257 |
| Lydda | 2,588 |
| Petah Tikva area | 1,316 |
| al-Majdal | 1,208 |
| Nes Tsiyona area | 1,059 |
| Safad | 923 |
| Tiberias | 439 |
| Baysan | 406 |
| Nazareth | 282 |
| Beersheba | 227 |
| in villages | 5,000 |
| TOTAL | 54,065 |

Source: A. Granott, *Agrarian Reform and the Record of Israel,* trans. E.M. Epstein (London: Eyre & Spottiswood, 1956), p. 72

TABLE 1.6 Scope and Assessed Tax Value of Urban Refugee Buildings According to Mandatory Tax Records, early 1950s

| *Location* | *Shops* | *Residential Rooms* | *Tax Value of All Buildings (£I)* |
|---|---|---|---|
| Jaffa | 4,108 | 29,825 | 3,649.499 |
| Tel Aviv | 178 | 2,152 | 17.206 |
| Lydda | 478 | 4,912 | 329.638 |
| Ramla | 507 | 4,349 | 131.049 |
| Jerusalem | 1,076 | 16,541 | 2,977.006 |
| Haifa | 2,056 | 24,437 | 3,249.217 |
| Tiberias | 278 | 1,665 | 196.484 |
| Safad | 352 | 3,316 | 296.238 |
| Acre | 639 | 5,528 | 923.832 |
| Balad al-Shaykh [village] | 52 | 1,005 | N/A |
| TOTAL | | | |

Source: ISA (130) 2401/21II [undated, but early 1950s]

TABLE 1.7 Scope and Assessed Value of Urban Refugee Land According to Mandatory Tax Records, Early 1950s

| *Location* | *Total Area (Dunums)* | *Built-Up Area (Dunums)* | *Registration Blocs* | *Parcels* | *Tax Value (£I)* |
|---|---|---|---|---|---|
| Jaffa | 9,408.980 | 1,104.072 | 107 | 8,936 | 3,851.489 |
| Tel Aviv | 14,258.248 | 9.161 | 65 | 2,264 | 463.841 |
| Lydda | 3,037.497 | 163.744 | 36 | 3,565 | 284.390 |
| Ramla | 1,334.100 | 66.817 | 28 | 2,619 | 52.355 |
| Jerusalem | 4,967.676 | 625.910 | 99 | 3,216 | 3,871.716 |
| Haifa | 5,059.966 | 822.453 | 129 | 4,614 | 3,792.812 |
| Tiberias | 530.332 | 76.855 | 31 | 589 | 186.354 |
| Safad | 694.285 | 155.116 | 22 | 1,792 | 87.157 |
| Acre | 962.826 | 224.461 | 16 | 1,596 | 514.245 |
| Balad al-Shaykh [village] | 5,313.487 | 30.333 | 25 | 891 | N/A |

Source: ISA (130) 2401/21II (undated, but early 1950s)

TABLE 1.8 Scope and Value of Abandoned Land in Jerusalem, According to Custodian of Absentee Property

| *Amount (Dunums)* | *No. of Parcels* | *Net Annual Value (£P)* | *Value/Dunum* |
|---|---|---|---|
| 5,736.048 | ca. 3,660 | 444,076 | 77 |

Source: United Nations Secretariat Archives [UNSA], Record Group DAG 13–3, UNCCP. Subgroup: Refugee Office, 1951–1952. Series: Records of the Land Specialist, 1951–1952/Box 35/Jerusalem Urban Assessment; Document: "UNCCP—Jerusalem Urban Area: List of Absentee Property Register (Custodian of Absentee Property Register) 1951"

Leasing the abandoned buildings was the next step. By July 1949, the Custodian had leased 66,724 rooms in Jaffa, Acre, Haifa, Safad, and other towns to soldiers and immigrants. By July 1950, 170,000 such persons plus 40,000 other Jews and Palestinians who were tenants of absentee owners were living in buildings controlled by the Custodian. The Custodian leased an additional 7,800 shops to immigrants.[70] In the 1949–50 fiscal year, the Custodian collected £I1,740,173 from leases. In 1950–51, this had risen to some £I2,600,000 in lease fees collected from some 65,000 persons ranging from £I1,500–6,750/room.[71] In April 1951, the Knesset's finance committee approved lowering the rents for 80 percent of the Custodian's apartments. The new rental rate was established at £I1.5–3.0/room. Rent for the other 20 percent of apartments remained the same.[72] Table 1.9 illustrates rents collected from urban leases by the Custodian.

According to Israeli legislation, the Custodian was to set aside all net profits he received from the refugee property under his sequestration and keep them for the benefit of the absentees. These accounts actually were held by the Ministry of Finance, and by mid-1949 reportedly totaled £I3–4 million.[73] Most of this came from the sale of moveable goods inasmuch as most of the lease fees collected by the Custodian went toward expenses, repairs, taxes, and the like. Although the accounts of refugees were credited for the funds generated from the rent and/or sale of their property, the Israeli government did not actually hold onto the money. It quickly spent it. In 1953, Custodian Mordekhai Schattner noted that "All money accruing from these sales would go to the development authorities. This means, in fact, that it would be used for the settlement of new immigrants."[74] In addition, the Custodian was required by law to contribute to the Arnona Defense Insurance tax along with other Israeli landowners. This was a national tax created in February 1951 by

TABLE 1.9 Urban Lease Fees Collected by the Custodian of Absentee Property, 1948–1953

| *Year* | *No. of Lease Contracts* | *Lease Fees (£I)* |
|---|---|---|
| 1948–49 | 21,487 | 501,000 |
| 1949–50 | 45,706 | 1,745,000 |
| 1950–51 | 56,367 | 2,601,000 |
| 1951–52 | 60,500 | 3,023,000 |
| 1952–53 | 60,504 | 3,583,543 |
| TOTAL | 244,564 | 11,453,543 |

Source: *Israel Government Yearbook Vol. 5713/1952*, p. 118 and *Vol. 5714/1953–54*, p. 142

the War Risks Insurance Levy Law of 5711/1951. The purpose of this was to create an insurance fund against which Israeli citizens could apply for reimbursement for any property damage caused by Arab infiltrators. The distribution of the lease fees collected by the Custodian is indicated in Table 1.10 detailing 1951 and reveal that only seven percent represented net profit.

At least some people involved in the question of abandoned refugee land truly felt that they were safeguarding the refugees' interests as the law suggested. One of the first Custodians, Dr. Arno Blum, was one such person. He later claimed to have been shocked to find that, in his opinion, the refugees in fact would not be getting "a square deal." He resigned as Custodian in protest after discovering that the office was doing something other than merely guarding the refugees' property.[75]

Some 250,000 immigrants eventually were settled into 49,065 dwellings controlled by the Custodian in the cities. The only exception was about five

TABLE 1.10 Distribution of Lease Fees Collected by Custodian, 1951

| *Item* | *% of Fees* |
|---|---|
| National and city taxes | 25 |
| Repairs and inspections | 40 |
| Local development | 12 |
| Administration, incl. guarding empty buildings | 23 |
| Arnona Defense Insurance tax | 3 |
| Net profit | 7 |

Source: *Jerusalem Post*, April 19, 1951

percent of abandoned housing in Jerusalem, Haifa, and Jaffa, which was granted to others (including government offices).[76] By 1957–58, a total of £I2,114,700 had been received in lease fees for abandoned buildings. By then, the fees were paid to local municipal councils and not the Custodian.[77] This was because the Custodian gave up administering urban property. In early 1953, the Custodian yielded the administration of abandoned housing in big cities to the ‘Amidar company. ‘Amidar [the Israeli National Housing Company for Immigrants, Ltd.] was established in 1949 as a national company to house new immigrants. Starting March 1, 1953, the government handed over government housing for immigrants to ‘Amidar. Later that same year, the Custodian of Absentee Property likewise handed over responsibility to ‘Amidar for administering abandoned residential properties in small towns like Ramla and Lydda as well. The company acted as the Custodian's agent thereafter "on the grounds of efficiency and economy."[78] He later sold most abandoned property to the Development Authority in 1953.

The Custodian faced a more massive task when trying to allocate the millions of dunums of rural abandoned property. As noted above, the Israeli government was initially most concerned about utilizing this huge amount of land to produce crops. During its first months of operation in 1948, the Custodian's office tried to manage abandoned agricultural property itself through its Villages Section, established in the fall of 1948. In so doing, the Custodian's Villages Section essentially became a commercial agricultural firm that managed refugee land. This was particularly true for abandoned olive plantations and citrus groves, given that agricultural settlements by and large had taken over cereals land. In 1949, the Custodian adopted a new policy by which he leased land to a variety of groups, most of which consisted of veteran farmers and not new immigrants. Indeed, the Vegetable Growers' Association was worried that abandoned land planted with figs, grapes, and olives would be lost if the Custodian allocated such land to new immigrants who had no tools.[79] These leases were for short periods, generally one year, and were signed with Jewish settlements, agricultural groups, companies, and individual Jewish entrepreneurs. Groups like the Yemenites Association, the Farmers Organization, and the Soldiers' Settlement and Rehabilitation Board leased land from the Custodian, as did companies and cooperatives like the Pardes Syndicate and Hakal-Yakhin. So too did the government agricultural corporation Mata‘ei ha-Umma ["National Plantations Co."], which farmed fruit and olive land. The Custodian soon began extending longer, five-year leases.

The Custodian faced numerous problems with certain types of abandoned land, particularly olive plantations and citrus groves. By the end of the summer of 1948, he controlled 100,000 dunums of abandoned olive plantations. By 1951, the Custodian owned more than two-thirds of all the citrus groves and olive plantations in Israel.[80] In the case of olives, however, he discovered that Jews were not particularly anxious to lease abandoned Palestinian olive plantations. In the first place, olive cultivation traditionally had been an Arab industry. In 1946, Palestinian Arabs owned 650,000 dunums of olives; Jews owned only 7,000.[81] Secondly, Jewish agriculture was conducted differently from Arab: it utilized more machinery and thus spaced individual trees farther apart from one another. Some Jewish farmers thus considered it less than cost-effective to farm abandoned Palestinian olive groves barring the introduction of expensive investments to raise productivity. So the Custodian's office initially undertook to reap the abandoned olive crop itself. Israel's first olive harvest season in the fall of 1948 saw the Villages Section of the Custodian of Absentee Property's office hire 3,000 workers, mostly Palestinians who had remained in Israel, to harvest some 6,000 tons of olives. These were then sold for £I250,000.[82] In 1949, the Villages Section cultivated 30,000 dunums of olives itself and harvested 5,000 tons. It also transferred an additional 80,000 dunums to new Jewish immigrants.[83] Olive exports in 1949 comprised the country's third largest export item.[84] But in that same year, the Villages Section estimated that it cost more to farm abandoned olive plantations than the crop was worth: the income derived from one dunum of abandoned olive trees was £I62.200 while expenditures for harvesting one dunum stood at £80.[85] The cold and drought in 1950–51 hurt the plantations as well, and lessees began refusing to renew leases to avoid losses. Jewish settlements found it more profitable to plant their own olive trees from scratch.

By the end of 1952, only 95,344 out of 262,181 dunums of abandoned plantation land was under cultivation.[86] Table 1.11 gives the breakdown of who had leased plantation land lying in completely abandoned Palestinian villages.

Similarly, the 120,000 dunums of abandoned citrus groves controlled by the Custodian presented him with problems. Before the Second World War, citrus exports had been a highly lucrative business for both Jews and Palestinians and a driving force in the Palestinian economy. The Shammuti orange (also called the Jaffa orange) was world famous. Indeed, Palestine was the world's third largest exporter of oranges in 1936–37. But the war years witnessed the deterioration of orange groves due to the cutoff of traditional markets caused by Axis submarine activity in the Mediterranean, the lack of domestic demand, and the wartime lack of spare parts for installations such as irrigations pumps. The 1948 fighting and the resulting chaos led to the

TABLE 1.11 Utilization of Abandoned Plantation Land, December 1952

| *Lessee* | *Area Leased (Dunums)* |
|---|---|
| Jewish settlements | 40,157 |
| Mata'ei ha-Umma | 36,903 |
| Private leases | 18,284 |
| TOTAL | 95,344 |

Source: Central Zionist Archives [CZA] A202/97, Custodian of Absentee Property report of February 22, 1953

destruction of water pumps and the theft of pipes. A 1949 study by the Villages Section and the Ministry of Agriculture revealed that only 40,000 of the 120,000 dunums of abandoned Palestinian citrus groves were worth cultivating. The reasons cited for the poor quality of the rest of the land were the inadequate quality of the soil and trees; the proximity to urban areas, which made the land a prime target for urban sprawl; the lack of water; the proximity to disturbed border areas; the isolation of some groves; and disease (10,000 dunums in Galilee were diseased).[87] A shortage of Jewish labor also complicated the task of cultivating the abandoned groves.

Once again, the Custodian undertook the task as best he could. Under the direction of its head, S. Givon, the Villages Section itself farmed 11,000 dunums of citrus groves during the 1949–50 season. After March 1950, it began farming an additional 7,000 dunums.[88] While some in Israel argued that it would be cheaper and more efficient simply to replace the deteriorating refugee groves with new trees, the Villages Section countered that new trees would not be able to produce fruit until 1960 at the earliest.[89] Others besides the Villages Section stepped in and leased orange groves. These included Hakal-Yakhin, a Histadrut company for agricultural contracting, which leased 10,500 dunums; Pardes Syndicate, which leased 1,200 dunums; Polani & Co. leased 1,500 dunums; others (including the Polish Association), 5,000 dunums.[90] The Polish Association leased 1,700 dunums in 1950. Moshe Porat, the second man to occupy the Custodian's office, estimated that these groves earned some £I500,000 in foreign currency exports in 1950, allowing the government to recoup the entire amount of hard currency it had poured into the citrus industry.[91]

The Villages Section estimated that it could harvest 80 cases of oranges per dunum if it could receive all the equipment it deemed necessary for the task. It invested some £I2.5 million in citrus groves from the spring of 1949 to the spring of 1951 out of the state's Rehabilitation Budget. Some of this was spent on water for irrigation. The Custodian was also able to obtain funds to improve the citrus industry from the United States. The U.S. Export-Import Bank extended a $100 million loan to Israel in 1948, $8 million of which was used for the citrus industry.[92] Given the fact that citrus fruits constituted two-thirds of all Israeli exports, the Ministry of Finance allotted £I700,000 for restoring groves and an additional £I250,000 for irrigation schemes. Shmu'el Zagorski, director of the Custodian's Agricultural Department, estimated that 31,000 of the 120,000 dunums of abandoned groves had been rehabilitated by 1950.[93] In 1951–52, 400,000 boxes of oranges were exported, providing Israel with 64.7 percent of its foreign currency in 1951.[94] In addition to 17,000 dunums of abandoned citrus groves that the Villages Section cultivated directly, the Custodian leased out 13,000 dunums to contractors and 4,000 dunums to settlements and individual Jews.[95] Table 1.12. illustrates production figures.

Despite this, only a fraction of the abandoned citrus groves were under cultivation by the early 1950s. In 1951, the figure stood at 26,261 dunums.[96] By the end of 1952, only 30,708 out of 117,343 dunums of citrus groves in completely abandoned Palestinian villages were under cultivation. Most of this area was cultivated by the Villages Section given the overall reluctance to invest in citrus.[97] Table 1.13 details this.

The Custodian dealt with other types of rural land as well. He harvested and packed 225 tons of tobacco on abandoned land in 1948. He controlled stone quarries in Safad, along the Haifa road, and other locations. Fifty-two such quarries had been leased to 'Even Vasid by 1950.[98] By 1952, he determined that 65 stone quarries constituted abandoned property. Together they produced 545,000 cubic meters of rock in 1951–52. The Custodian leased all of them for the lease fees shown in table 1.14.

TABLE 1.12 Production in Abandoned Citrus Groves, 1949–1952 by Cultivator (in Boxes)

| *Season* | *Villages Section* | *Hakal-Yakhin* | *Pardes Syndicate* | *Polani & Co.* | *Total* |
|---|---|---|---|---|---|
| 1949–50 | 40,000 | 43,000 | 3,000 | 5,000 | 91,000 |
| 1950–51 | 250,000 | 250,000 | 50,000 | 40,000 | 590,000 |

Source: *Ha'aretz*, June 21, 1951

TABLE 1.13 Utilization of Abandoned Citrus Groves, December 1952

| *Lessee* | *Area Leased (Dunums)* |
|---|---|
| Hakal-Yakhin | 8,172 |
| Other contractors | 1,641 |
| Individuals | 5,424 |
| Worked directly by Villages Section | 15,471 |
| TOTAL | 30,708 |

Source: CZA A202/97, Custodian of Absentee Property report of February 22, 1953

The Custodian also controlled plantations of figs, apricots, grapes, apples, and almonds. By 1950, such land included 20,000 dunums of grape vines and 5,000 dunums of other fruits. Most were leased to institutions like Mata'ei ha-Umma, although the Villages Section cultivated some itself.[99] By 1953–54, the Custodian controlled 126,000 dunums of fruit (and olive) plantations that it leased as follows: 55,000 dunums to settlements; 55,000 to Mata'ei ha-Umma, and 16,000 to others.[100] Once again, however, much of this land remained unused. It was reported that only some 16,000 out of 40,000 dunums of abandoned vineyards were under cultivation by mid-1951.[101] The Custodian even found ways to make money from marginal lands, lands for which the Israelis later would state that they owed no compensation because they were uncultivable. In 1952, the Custodian "took care of all incidental abandoned properties" and collected 1,100 tons of fruit from cactus plants growing on such land. The Custodian then sold the fruit for the production of alcohol.[102]

TABLE 1.14 Lease Fees Generated from Abandoned Stone Quarries, 1948–1954

| *Year* | *Lease Fees (£I)* |
|---|---|
| 1948–51 | 32,885 |
| 1951–52 | 34,733 |
| 1953–54 | 35,000 |

Source: *Israel Government Yearbook Vol. 5713/1952*, p. 119 and *Vol. 5714/1952–53*, p. 142.

The Custodian also leased some abandoned land to Palestinians who had remained in Israel. By the fall of 1950, some 150,000 dunums had been so leased.[103] Some of this land was leased to its original owners, who despite having remained in Israel had been declared "present absentees" and whose land was seized. But the "present absentees" were not always interested in long-term solutions to their plight that involved leasing other Palestinians' land. In a bid to settle Palestinian refugees who remained within Israeli territory, the government even moved to build housing on abandoned land for the resettlement of the "present absentees." Even though the government built stone houses on such land, the refugees refused to move into them out of principle because they were constructed on fellow Palestinians' property.[104]

By August 1950, the Custodian along with the Ministry of Agriculture had leased a total of some 980,000 dunums out of 3,500,000 dunums of agricultural land. This figure included 800,000 leased to workers' cooperatives; 150,000 to Palestinians in Israel; and 30,000 to new immigrants, the army, and so forth. The Custodian's own Villages Division was still farming 100,000 dunums.[105]

A particularly sensitive issue was the Custodian's takeover of religious endowment land, called waqf— land that had been set aside for a charitable purpose, after which it became permanently indivisible and inalienable. This classic type of waqf was called charitable waqf [Ar.: waqf khayri]. During the long years of Ottoman rule in Palestine, another type of waqf emerged whereby the beneficiary of the land's income was not a charity but a family. This was called family waqf [Ar.: waqf dhurri]. Estimates vary about the size of waqf holdings in Palestine in 1948, but they were substantial. The Custodian confiscated most waqf property just as other abandoned property, particularly endowment land controlled by the Supreme Muslim Council. Since most of its leaders were in exile, the government declared the council to be an absentee and confiscated its property.[106]

Although Israeli authorities decided to retain the absentee status of all abandoned family waqf land, they arrived at various solutions to the problem of what to do with charitable waqf dedicated for religious purposes. Most Christian waqf land ended up being returned to the respective churches by 1950 given the sensitivities generated by the presence of foreign churches in the country. Israeli authorities even made some concessions to Muslims. Given that the tens of thousands of Muslim Palestinians were still resident in the country, the state decided that some type of arrangement should be made whereby they could benefit from the religious charitable waqf properties in their communities. In 1951, the Custodian came to an agreement with the

Ministry of Religious Affairs whereby he released the power to administer religious waqf land to the ministry's Division of Muslim and Druze Affairs. In 1954, the Custodian upgraded this relationship when he declared the division to be his "agent."

Another problem faced by the Custodian was the criticism levied at his office by various circles within Israel. Some of this criticism was directed at what some called the Custodian's "incompetent" and "irresponsible" management of the abandoned land. The state controller's report to the Finance Committee of the Knesset in 1951 scored the Custodian for the high percentage of abandoned land that remained uncultivated. The newspaper *Ha'aretz* ran a series of articles in the summer of 1951 describing the Custodian's shifting policies for utilizing the land and allowing olive plantations and citrus groves to deteriorate at a time of great economic adversity in the new state. Equally serious were the charges that the Custodian (and later, the Development Authority) was granting preferential leasing treatment to political cronies from the MAPAI party. Not only was MAPAI the leading party in the government and within the labor Zionist movement as a whole in Israel, but also Dov Shafrir, the first Custodian of Absentee Property, was a MAPAI stalwart. Prior to assuming the post of Custodian, he had headed the Neve 'Oved Company, the construction company of the powerful Agricultural Center. During one Knesset session in 1949, for instance, Ya'akov Gil of the General Zionists complained that the Custodian was giving away 90 percent of the abandoned land to MAPAI organizations on a partisan basis:

> Other parties, and ordinary Jews who belong to no party, are left out and receive no benefit from this property. The Custodian handles the property as he pleases, to suit himself and the party to which he belongs, his friends and associates.[107]

Regardless of what Israeli parties benefited from the refugees' property, there is no denying the tremendous overall benefit that this property represented to the struggling new state.

## Early Israeli Estimates of the Scope and Value of Refugee Property: The Weitz-Danin-Lifshits Committee

Exactly how much Palestinian refugee land Israeli authorities took over has long remained an extremely contentious point. As central a question as that is to the entire saga of Palestinian refugee property, there is no single answer to it. Arabs, Israelis, and others have argued over this point for years. Much of the problem depends upon what kind of land is classified as abandoned refugee property. A variety of estimates and commissions would later surface to investigate this very point: Israeli estimates, Arab estimates, and UN estimates.

One of the first Israeli attempts to quantify the extent of the refugee property was a commission appointed by Ben Gurion in August 1948 to look at the abandoned property question in the context of refugee resettlement. Almost from the beginning, the Israeli government argued that the only solution to the Palestinian refugee exodus was resettlement in the surrounding Arab countries. Massive repatriation was out of the question. The new committee was essentially a reconstitution of Yosef Weitz's unofficial Transfer Committee of earlier that year, and proceeded from this fundamental principle. The three-man committee consisted of two leftovers from the first Transfer Committee, the JNF's Weitz and 'Ezra Danin, now at the Ministry of Foreign Affairs. They were joined by Zalman Lifshits (b. 1900)—who would later change his name to Lif—a cartographic engineer who worked as a chief land valuer for the JNF. He was also an advisor on land affairs for the Ministry of Foreign Affairs and for Ben Gurion. It was Lifshits to whom Weitz had detailed his vision of transferring Palestinians out of the country during their meeting in Jerusalem in two years earlier in December 1946. Their vision of a formal committee to investigate the subject had come true.

The Weitz-Danin-Lifshits Committee was tasked to study several things. Its major focus was resettlement possibilities for the refugees in surrounding Arab countries. Weitz himself had traveled to Syria and Transjordan in the 1940s investigating this very topic. Danin was given the task of writing the section on the recent international history of population transfers. He looked at several twentieth-century examples, including the cases of Czechoslovakia and the Sudeten Germans; Romania, Hungary, and Yugoslavia; Iraq and the Assyrians; and the Turks and Armenians. Danin found one particular book on the subject "invaluable": Joseph B. Schechtman's *European Population Transfers 1939–45*. [108] Schechtman was no stranger to that topic. A Russian Jew born in 1891, he later moved to the United States where in 1944–45 he served as a consultant on population movements to the Office of Strategic Services, the precursor to the Central Intelligence Agency. Schechtman had reason to be interested in population transfers: he was a hardliner on Arab-Israeli matters and a co-founder of the Zionist Revisionist movement along with Vladimir Jabotinsky. Lifshits was given the task of examining the scope and value of the refugees' property based in part on sales information recorded in British mandatory land registries along with JNF land department records. Weitz devoted his attention to resettlement possibilities.

The committee members worked quickly through the fall of 1948, and signed their report entitled "Report on a Settlement of the Arab Refugee [Issue]" on November 25, 1948. It is their study of the scope and value of refugee land that concerns us here. The committee presented a bleak picture of the destruction of Palestinian moveable property, homes and buildings, indeed the Arab economy as a whole, designed as it was to illustrate the three men's position that the return of the refugees was out of the question:

> They [refugees] are, however, either unaware of, or wish not to know, the state of their abandoned property. A distinction must be made between property that is real estate and property that is not real estate. The latter has been completely destroyed, in both villages and cities. The Arab farmer's household economy has been completely destroyed. Nothing is left of its herds, and it is safe to say that, whatever herds were brought by the fleeing Arabs across the borders have decreased in number. This is both because they serve as a means of subsistence for their owners, who now sell them in exchange for other goods, and because of the thievery from both them and their brothers within the refugee camps. Work animals have disappeared, as has equipment. They did not harvest their fields, and they have no seeds. Their orchards were not tended to and not irrigated, and the financial value of most of them has decreased to an extremely low level. Many plantations also suffered from a lack of cultivation, and we can assume that some of the trees have died, and that the value of most of them has declined. Furniture in homes has been destroyed, and many of the houses themselves have collapsed due to damage caused by war. Moreover, in some cases entire villages were completely destroyed by the effects of the war.
>
> The entire urban, industrial, labor, and commercial economies have also completely collapsed. Along with the disappearance of equipment, machinery, tools and goods, many structures have suffered damage, some destroyed and others collapsed on their foundations. The value of this type of real estate property—structures—has decreased a great deal, and the dwellings that have survived cannot be used as shelter for the Arab refugees, as refugees of Israel are now living in them.[109]

The committee may have presented the grim outlook to serve its wider goal of proposing resettlement, not return, of the refugees as the only possible solution to their plight. Given the role Weitz played in arranging for the destruction of refugee villages earlier in the year, the stark description of destroyed villages "by the effects of the war" was disingenuous.

The only type of property that survived and that the refugees "might possibly" consider was the land itself. But here too the committee suggested that the government use the land as a way to engineer the refugees' resettlement within the Arab world:

> The only type of property that the Arab refugees might possibly be able to consider is land. We emphasize the words *might possibly*, as the Government of Israel can make an argument for its expropriation as property of enemies that fought against us. Czechoslovakia acted in this manner when it expropriated all the property of Germans from the Sudetenland and expelled them from within its borders with its victory after World War II. The governments of Romania, Hungary and Yugoslavia also acted in this manner, and the Government of Iraq expropriated property of the Assyrians when it expelled them in 1933, even though they had not fought against Iraq. The Turkish government expropriated all the property of Armenians due to acts of violence perpetrated against it in the context of nationalism-based hostility. However, we can also assume, as do the authors of this report, that the Government of Israel will not want to act in a similar manner, especially due to the fact that the present political situation demands a settlement of the Arab refugee issue that will be acceptable to Israel, the Arab states, and other nations. For this reason, we intend this asset to be used as a means and a factor of encouragement for achieving such a settlement.[110]

The 1948 committee's estimates of the scope of abandoned property that ended up in Israeli hands are listed in table 1.15. Specifics on the towns are found in table 1.16.

The rather modest amount of land they identified as abandoned points to the narrow definition of "abandoned" land the committee members used. In a pattern that would characterize future Israeli reckonings of the amount of refugee land seized, they did not count a huge amount of land that Palestinians would later claim, including communal pasture lands categorized as *matruk* land during the mandate. They also did not consider arid, "dead" lands categorized as *mawat* in their calculations. Like the British, the authors of the report considered these to be "state lands" that were not the personal or even communal property of Palestinian villagers. They stated, "Villagers have no property rights for this type of land located within their village boundaries,

TABLE 1.15 Scope of Abandoned Land According to Weitz-Danin-Lifshits Committee, 1948

| *Type* | *Amount (Dunums)* |
|---|---|
| 1) Rural | |
| Orchards | 92,615 |
| Bananas | 513 |
| Irrigated land, olives, fruit, grapes | 164,832 |
| Cereal | 1,645,183 |
| Built-up area in villages | 10,844 |
| TOTAL | 1,913,987 |
| 2) Urban (all types; see details in Table 16) | |
| Acre | 1,430 |
| Safad | 3,699 |
| Tiberias | 3,861 |
| Jaffa | 10,639 |
| Lydda | 21,570 |
| Ramla | 37,961 |
| Jerusalem | 8,698 |
| Haifa | 6,269 |
| TOTAL | 94,127 |
| GRAND TOTAL: | 2,008,114 |

Source: ISA (130) 2445/3, "Report on a Settlement of the Arab Refugee [Issue"" (November 25, 1948), appendix 9; CZA A246/57, "Comments on Value Assessments of Absentee Landed Property" (November 12, 1962)

and they therefore are not eligible to receive payment for them."[111] On the contrary, they believed in fact that the British had allowed Palestinians to trespass and settle illegally on such lands:

> There was also an absence of decisive agrarian policy to ensure state ownership over vast areas of land throughout Palestine that belonged to the state according to the law, but that had been seized by Arabs with no such rights of possession, by force and by trespassing.[112]

This issue would later rise to become one of the most basic points of differences between the Arab world and both Israel and the UN when it came to the question of the fate of abandoned refugee property.

TABLE 1.16 Scope of Abandoned Land in Cities by Type, According to Weitz-Danin-Lifshits Committee, 1948

| *City* | *Orchard* | *Built-up* | *Irrigated; Unirr Plantation* | *Cereal* | *Grazing* | *Uncult* | *Banana* |
|---|---|---|---|---|---|---|---|
| Acre | — | 1,137 | 293 | — | — | — | — |
| Safad | — | 879 | 163 | 1,103 | 736 | 818 | — |
| Tiberias | — | 478 | 7 | 1,041 | 1,746 | 589 | — |
| Jaffa | — | 8,206 | — | 1,095 | — | 1,338 | — |
| Lydda | 3,186 | 3,090 | 7,942 | 7,278 | — | 71 | 3 |
| Ramla | 1,455 | 3,645 | 15,808 | 16,866 | — | 187 | — |
| Jerusalem | — | 7,738 | 179 | 721 | — | 60 | — |
| Haifa | — | 6,269 | — | — | — | — | — |
| TOT. | 6,831 | 29,252 | 24,392 | 28,104 | 2,482 | 3,063 | 3 |

Source: ISA (130) 2445/3, "Report on a Settlement of the Arab Refugee [Issue]" (November 25, 1948), appendix 9

Weitz, Danin, and Lifshits exerted considerable efforts trying to place a value on the abandoned land. The men adopted a complicated formula to arrive at the figures. For rural lands, they started by using land values from 1938 as a base. They chose that year as a baseline for several reasons. First of all, it represented the last full year prior to the coming of the Second World War, which witnessed the decreasing value of currency in Palestine. Secondly, the authors of the report blamed what they called the artificially high land prices in Palestine thereafter on Zionist land thirst and Arab greed. Thirdly, they claimed that the threats directed by the Palestinian nationalist movement against Arabs who sold land to Jews helped drive up prices. Finally, they blamed the skyrocketing land prices after 1939 on the land transfer laws enacted by the British in 1940 that limited Jewish land purchases to certain areas of the country only. To cite again from the report:

> Jewish immigration and Jewish settlement constituted the sole source of the excessive land prices that were standard practice in Palestine until the end of the mandate. They far exceeded prices in the neighboring Arab countries, and they were not at all proportionate to the land's economic value... [I]t was necessary to acquire land for Jewish settlement, both private and national, principally by means of purchase on the open market from genuine and false Arab land brokers. They exploited the

> Jewish people's impatience and thirst for land, and gradually raised prices.
>
> Another cause of the fierce price increases since 1939 were the laws that limited [the purchase of land]....In these conditions, standard prices in Palestine were based on emotion and political considerations, not on economic value, based on income capacity ....And thus, due to the various conditions described above, and their interaction with one another, land prices in the country at the end of the mandate period exceeded the normal economic value of the land by two or three times.[113]

Starting with rural land values from 1938, the committee then added the estimated value of buildings erected on the land as if all structures were intact. Figures were derived from sales information recorded in extant mandatory land registers, plus material from the records of the JNF's Land Department. How these mandatory land records came into Israeli hands is discussed in chapter 4. They then multiplied the combined values by roughly three to account for inflationary effects and the fall in the value of the Palestinian pound from 1938–48. In the case of land with irrigation installations present on it, the committee members considered the "actual values, and their worth in terms of the land's current usage and future development."[114] Plantation land was valuated separately than the trees planted on it, the values of which varied according to type of tree, age, quality, and so forth. A notable exception was land planted with citrus groves. Despite the immense value of the citrus export industry prior to the Second World War, the committee decided to valuate not the citrus trees but merely valuate the land they stood on. They reasoned that the trees were in poor condition because of the previous two bad seasons and because the collapse of Arab marketing and shipping had ruined the citrus sector. Besides, the committee reasoned that they already had added the value of irrigation works, if any. Rocky land, grazing land other than matruk, and so forth was assigned a lower value than cultivable land. As noted above, they denied that the refugees had a right to any compensation for matruk and mawat lands.

In valuating urban property with buildings, they started with national and municipal tax figures. The value was based on capitalizing the land's annual income as stated in the tax records. Consideration was given to future development and the percentage of the land allowed for building according to municipal zoning plans. If no zoning plan existed, they deducted 25 percent from the valuation to account for future roads and open areas that may have been constructed. They also considered the quality and age of buildings and the potential development for the various urban areas. In cases where the poor quality of buildings meant that the land was worth more than the buildings, consideration was given only to the value of salvageable goods after their destruction. Where buildings were in good shape, they valuated them on the basis of their age, structural quality, and income from rent for the next ten years. Land within municipal limits but that lay outside urban construction plan zones was valuated as if it were rural agricultural land. Total urban valuation figures also reflected the combined value of land and buildings. The prices that the committee used are listed in table 1.17. For purposes of comparison, Weitz had estimated on his own that unirrigated land in two villages in Galilee "according to present conditions" was worth £I14.53/dunum.[115]

The total value for urban and rural land was then computed. However, the committee decided to subtract a considerable amount from the totals in the following cases. First, the committee members decided it was impossible to determine information about damaged or destroyed buildings. Secondly, they decided to reduce the amount to account for "the quick liquidation of a large amount of property during a very short period of time. This process in itself considerably reduced the value of such property."[116] Accordingly, they deducted a full 25 percent of urban property and 15 percent of rural property for these two situations.

Table 1.18 shows the total values of refugee land as determined by the committee, both the gross value and the net value reflecting the deductions described above.

The committee considered its estimates fair. Indeed, they felt that they had given the refugees the benefit of the doubt:

> These prices also possess a considerable emotional aspect, and at the same time exceed their economic value. Still, we believe that it is impossible to disregard the fortune of the Arabs of the country and their property, [which was] not in the Arab deserts, but in Palestine itself ....The benefit deriving from geographic location and from the high value of land in Palestine did not disappear altogether, even with the outbreak of violence and the war between Israel and the Arabs ....We have decided to retain the advantage deriving from geographic location, reflected in favor of the property owner, in determining the value of land.[117]

Israel did not release the Weitz-Danin-Lifshits report publicly. However, authorities did acknowledge the committee's existence and made sure that certain of its conclusions, especially regarding resettlement, were publicized.

TABLE 1.17 Prices per Dunum Used to Valuate Abandoned Land and Buildings by Weitz-Danin-Lifshits Committee, 1948

| *Type* | *Class A (£I)* | *Class B (£I)* | *Class C (£I)* |
|---|---|---|---|
| 1. Cereal land in valleys; non-cereals on coastal plain | 30 | 20 | 12 |
| 2. Cereal land in valleys and central part of coastal plain along transportation routes | 40<br>30<br>20 | | |
| 3. Cereal land in lower Galilee hills and near Baysan | 18 | 14 | 10 |
| 4. Cereal land in hills of Judea and Samaria | 18 | 12 | 3 |
| 5. Privately-owned grazing land | 6 | 4 | 3 |
| 6. Medium-age olive groves on flat land, in addition to land value | 20 | 15 | 10 |
| 7. Olive groves in hilly areas | 15 | 10 | 7 |
| 8. Medium-age vineyards | 15 | 12 | 10 |
| 9. Deciduous fruit tree plantations | 17 | 15 | 12 |
| 10. Land in close proximity to cities and housing areas (according to statutory use) | 300 | 200 | 100 |
| 11. Citrus orchards uncultivated in recent years, based on land value only | 50 | 40 | 35 |
| 12. Irrigated, based on region, in addition to value of irrigation installations | 50 | 40 | 35 |
| 13. Urban land without buildings | 200 times net annual income, based on tax figures; adjusted for actual land value, considering expected development | | |
| 14. Modern buildings | capitalization of net annual income based on tax figures for a period of 20–25 years | | |
| 15. Old buildings | either value of rent for next ten years or value of the land | | |

Source: ISA (130) 2445/3, "Report on a Settlement of the Arab Refugee [Issue]" (November 25, 1948), appendix 8

TABLE 1.18 Value of Abandoned Land According to Weitz-Danin-Lifshits Committee, 1948

| *Type* | *Gross Value (£I)* | *Net Value (£I)* |
|---|---|---|
| 1) Rural | | |
| Rural land | 46,498,000 | — |
| Rural buildings | 2,829,000 | — |
| TOTAL RURAL | 49,877,000 | 42,000,000 |
| 2) Urban (land and buildings) | | |
| Acre | 1,430,000 | — |
| Safad | 950,000 | — |
| Tiberias | 1,125,000 | — |
| Jaffa | 15,900,000 | — |
| Lydda | 2,200,000 | — |
| Ramla | 4,300,000 | — |
| Jerusalem | 14,600,000 | — |
| Haifa | 12,000,000 | — |
| TOTAL URBAN | 52,505,000 | 39,500,000 |
| | (excluding Beersheba, Baysan, al-Majdal) | |
| GRAND TOTAL | 102,382,000 | 81,500,000 |

Source: ISA (130) 2445/3, "Report on a Settlement of the Refugee [Issue]" (November 25, 1948), appendix 9

Danin even met with U.S. Ambassador to Israel James McDonald on February 25, 1949 at the ambassador's residence and briefed him with a sanitized version of the committee's report. Danin told the American that the committee had been formed to study the resettlement of refugees, of which they estimated there were between 581,000 and 600,000. He reported that all the refugees could be resettled for £UK100/person or £700/family, especially if they were resettled in Iraq. The total figure would be some £60 million. Danin assumed that Christian refugees might want to live in Lebanon; the rest could be resettled in Iraq, Syria, and Jordan. Significantly, he told McDonald that Israel could help pay for resettlement by paying compensation for the land, after subtracting the costs of war damages Israel sustained in 1948. He thought that a UN loan to the governments hosting the refugees, or the refugees themselves, could cover the rest. When discussing the scope and value of the abandoned land, Danin was much more circumspect. He said that the committee came up with global figures for the scope of the land, but not figures for individual persons' ownership. However, he apparently did not offer what that global figure was. Danin then apparently misled McDonald about the land's value, claiming that the committee could not determine its value because the three men could not decide upon a basis for valuation. Danin said that such a figure could be determined during any eventual peace talks between Israel and the Arab states.[118] Nor was McDonald the only one to be told that the committee could not establish figures on land values. Joseph Schechtman, the Revisionist Zionist expert on population transfer whose work proved helpful to the committee, followed the entire refugee issue carefully and also put out the story in his various writings that the committee could not determine land prices.[119]

Other Israeli estimates of the scope and value of refugee land began surfacing in the months and years after 1948. Weitz was quick to publish his own estimates in 1948 and 1950, although they did not include land in the Beersheba district. Weitz stated that 372 villages had been abandoned by Palestinians (see table 1.19).

Weitz also offered the following figures for values, but only for land suitable for settlement (see table 1.20).

The Custodian of Absentee Property also issued reports detailing how much land he estimated had come under his control, which varied over the first several years as his office had more time to ascertain the scope of the refugee land. In all cases, his figures were higher than Weitz's (see table 1.21). Minister of Agriculture Aharon Tsizling provided an even higher figure for 1949 (see table 1.22).

Various figures on the value of the land also began appearing in the Israeli press. In July 1948, the independent daily *Ha'aretz* ran an article entitled "A Plan for Arab Refugees" written by an economist, A. Ater. According to American diplomats, the attitudes found in Ater's piece were not official Israeli government views but had generated a good deal of public discourse about the topic. Ater estimated the scope of refugee land at approximately 5 million dunums. Basing himself on land values used by the 1946 Anglo-American Commission, Ater estimated that this land was worth £P30 million. If one included buildings and land together, he raised the figure to £P50 million.[120] The figure of £50 million seemed to carry a good deal of credence with the Israeli public. *Herut*, the paper of the Revisionist Herut party, stated in November 1950 that this figure was the maximum that Israel would consider paying as compensation to the refugees.[121] The Haifa publication *Business Digest* ran an article in May 1951 by a Dr. Duesterwald claiming that the value of

TABLE 1.19 Scope of Abandoned Land Outside the Beersheba District According to Yosef Weitz, 1948 and 1950

| *Type, Location* | *Amount (Dunums)* |
|---|---|
| 1. Good land | |
| Coastal plains | 959,701 |
| Jezre'el Valley | 128,714 |
| Hula Valley | 51,847 |
| Baysan | 81,274 |
| Galilee hills | 348,458 |
| Samarian hills | 82,476 |
| Judean hills | 85,910 |
| Judean lowlands | 331,890 |
| 2. Poor land | 136,530 |
| 3. Matruk | 751,730 |
| 4. "Government" land | 486,750 |
| 5. Land held by Custodian of German Property (included because this land had Arab tenants who later became refugees) | 39,320 |
| 6. Urban | 100,000 |
| TOTAL | 3,584,600 |

* included: land lying outside Israel belonging to villages lying within Israel
* not included: Beersheba district, land in partially-abandoned villages
Source: Yosef Weitz, "le-Hanhil Adama Hadasha" [Bequest of New Land], *Molad* 2, 12 (March 1949), p. 325; Yosef Weitz, *The Struggle for the Land* (Tel Aviv: Lion the Printer, 1950) p. 113–14

TABLE 1.20 Value of Abandoned Land Appropriate for Settlement, Including Beersheba, According to Yosef Weitz, 1948

| *Type* | *Amount (Dunums)* | *Value (£I)* |
|---|---|---|
| Rural | 2,070,270 | |
| Urban | 99,730 | |
| Good land in Beersheba district | 1,230,000 | |
| TOTAL | 3,400,000 | £I65,000,000 |

Source: Weitz, "le-Hanhil Adama Hadasha"

TABLE 1.21 Scope and Value of Refugee Land According to Custodian of Absentee Property, 1949–1954

| *Date* | *Amount (Dunums)* | *Value (£I)* |
|---|---|---|
| March 24, 1949 | 3,986,493 | N/A |
| March 31, 1950 | 3,299,447 | 13,100,691 |
| March 29, 1951 | 4,500,000 | N/A |
| February 22, 1953 | 4,063,669 | N/A |
| September 5, 1954 | 4,450,000 | N/A |

Source: ISA (43) 5440/1578, "Interim Report on Real Estate Held by Custodian" (24 March 1949); ISA (43) 5440/1582, "Report of Custodian of Absentees' Office" (March 31, 1950); ISA (130) 2402/4, "State Controller Report on the Custodian of Absentee Property" (March 29, 1951); CZA A202/97, "Custodian of Absentee Property Report" (February 22, 1953); CZA KKL5/22273, "Report on the Land Administration System of the State" (September 5, 1954)

TABLE 1.22 Scope of Abandoned Land According to Ministry of Agriculture, 1949

| *Type* | *Amount (Dunums)* |
|---|---|
| 1. Total | |
| Cultivable | 1,373,000 |
| Waste and barren | 2,720,000 |
| Northern Beersheba | 1,700,000 |
| Southern Beersheba | 10,800,000 |
| TOTAL | 16,593,000 |
| (only 400,000 dunums were deemed available for leasing) | |

Source: Aharon Tsizling, "Ways of Settlement Development in the State of Israel," *Kama* (1951), p. 111, in Granott, *Agrarian Reform*, p. 89; Labor Party Archives, IV-235–1, file 2251A, in Arnon Golan "The Transfer to Jewish Control Control of Abandoned Arab Lands during the War of Independence," S. Ilan Troen and Lucas, Noah, eds., *Israel. The First Decade of Independence*. SUNY Series in Israeli Studies. Russell Stone, editor (Albany, N.Y.: State University of New York Press, 1995), p. 423

abandoned property that had been used by Israel up to that point stood at some £130 million.[122]

## The Custodian Sells Refugee Land to the Development Authority

The next step in the Israeli government's legal strategy for transferring refugee land was for the Custodian of Absentee Property to sell the land to a "Development Authority." Following up on the Absentees' Property Law and the legal framework for the Custodian to sell the land to a "Development Authority," the Development Authority (Transfer of Property) Law of 5710/1950 subsequently was enacted on July 31, 1950. This legislation created a body called the Development Authority [Heb.: Reshut ha-Pituah]. The first members of the Development Authority council were Yosef Gurion, Levi Shkolnik, Hayyim Halperin, Yosef Weitz, Yitshak Finkelshtain, Binyamin Fishman, and Asher Rozenblum. Later the Development Authority was chaired by the veteran Zionist financial official, David Horowitz.

The Development Authority started functioning as of January 1, 1951. It was empowered it to "buy, rent, take on lease, take in exchange or otherwise acquire property" from the Custodian of Absentee Property and from there to "sell or otherwise dispose of, let, grant leases of, and mortgage property" to others. However, the law ensured that the vast majority of any land sold by the Development Authority was sold to governmental and Zionist organizations, not private individuals. It stipulated that the Development Authority only could sell land to the state, to the JNF, to a local authority, or to a government-approved institution for settling landless Arabs. The only exception to this rule was urban land under its jurisdiction as long as such land had not been set aside by the government for settling Jewish immigrants, building low-cost housing, or for other developmental purposes. Even then, the Development Authority was required to offer such land to the JNF first and the total amount of such land sold could not exceed 100,000 dunums per transaction, not including any land sold to the above-mentioned types of institutions. Such state institutions could not resell the land thereafter but rather merely lease it.

The Development Authority could buy land from the Custodian at only the official value for it specified in the Absentees' Property Law of 1950. The law used British mandatory land tax classifications as the basis for establishing the value of absentee property. These classifications differed depending on whether the land in question was urban or rural land. The Absentees' Property

Law stated that land in the towns that the British had taxed under the classification of urban property during 1947–48 would be valued at 16.67 times the amount of the net annual tax value for that property as determined by the last British tax assessment. The value of land in the countryside varied according to what British rural tax category the land belonged to and whether or not there were buildings on the land. Land with industrial buildings on it was valued at 16.67 times the amount of the net annual tax value; prime agricultural land belonging to British land tax categories 1, 2, 3, 4, and 17 was valued at 300 times the amount of the tax assessment for category 1 regardless of whether or not the land actually was category 1 land; rural land in all other tax categories was valued at 75 times the amount of the assessment. The law empowered the Minister of Finance to reduce any of these rates if he determined that the land in question was damaged or left neglected. Table 1.23 illustrates the value of absentee land by tax category according to the law.

Together, the Absentees' Property and Development Authority Laws of 1950 allowed the Custodian of Absentee Property to sell refugee land permanently. But the actual sale of the land did not occur until three years later.

TABLE 1.23 Official Value of Rural Absentee Land for the Purposes of Selling to the Development Authority According to the Absentees' Property Law of 1950

| *Land Type* | *Tax Category* | *1947–48 Tax/ Dunum (£P)* | *Israeli Value/ Dunum (£P)* |
|---|---|---|---|
| Citrus (excluding Acre district) | 1 | 0.100 | 30.000 |
| Citrus (Acre district) | 2 | 0.100 | 30.000 |
| Bananas | 3 | 2.240 | 672.000 |
| Built-up | 4 | 0.640 | 192.000 |
| Irrigated and fruit (first class) | 5 | 0.160 | 12.000 |
| Irrigated and fruit (second class) | 6 | 0.140 | 10.500 |
| Irrigated and fruit (third class) | 7 | 0.140 | 10.500 |
| Cereals (first class) | 8 | 0.100 | 7.500 |
| Cereals (second class) | 9 | 0.080 | 6.500 |
| Cereals (third class) | 10 | 0.072 | 5.400 |
| Cereals (fourth class) | 11 | 0.060 | 4.500 |
| Cereals (fifth class) | 12 | 0.048 | 3.600 |
| Cereals (sixth class) | 13 | 0.032 | 2.400 |
| Cereals (seventh class) | 14 | 0.016 | 1.200 |
| Cereals (eighth class) | 15 | 0.008 | 0.600 |
| Uncultivated | 16 | 0 | 0 |

This was apparently a source of some concern to the government, which issued a decision on November 2, 1952 to speed up the process.[123] But it was not until February 24, 1953 that the Custodian and the Development Authority signed an agreement by which the Custodian would sell some of the land under his authority to the authority for £I7 million. "The main object of the transfer," noted the official Israeli state yearbook, "was to step up the rate of development of the properties, especially by way of sale."[124] But a second agreement later was signed by the two agencies in Tel Aviv on September 29, 1953 by which the Custodian agreed to sell the Development Authority even more land. This was done in order to speed up the process by which the Development Authority could sell land to the Jewish National Fund. Under this second agreement, the Development Authority agreed to purchase 3,465,334 dunums of land from the Custodian, including some 600,000 dunums in the Beersheba district.[125] The land was described as follows:

> (a) I. Cultivable agricultural land, including the wells located on such lands and all their equipment.
>
> II. Plantations, including all trees and plants, structures, apparatuses, irrigation installations, wells, water rights, and all other rights pertaining to the plantations.
>
> III. Built-up areas within villages.
>
> IV. Land in the Beersheba sub-district within the borders of the State of Israel that is marked as fallow on maps from the mandate period, located within an area bordered in the east by longitude 40, in the south by Wadi Shinik, and in the north and west by the borders of the Beersheba sub-district from the mandate period. Details regarding the properties referred to in paragraphs I through IV are found in the lists and/or maps attached, or those that shall be attached, which constitute an inseparable part of this agreement and are indicated by the letter "A."
>
> (b) Land in urban areas, including structures standing on such land, according to the attached itemized lists [which were not attached to the original document]
>
> (c) other immoveable property not included in sections (a) and (b), according to the itemized lists and/or maps attached, or those that shall be attached, which constitute an inseparable part of this agreement and are indicated by the letter "C." [which were not attached to the original document][126]

The September 1953 agreement amended the official price of the land that had been established by the Absentees' Property Law of 1950. In addition to the price listed in that law, the agreement specified that the Development Authority add to that the following sums:

1. £I100 for each dunum of plantations and groves that were outlined in an attachment to the agreement.
2. The cost of pumps and other equipment attached to wells. The cost was to be determined by the chief government assessor.
3. The cost of any debt, including tax liabilities, accumulated by a specific parcel of land if that amount exceeded the land's official value.

The agreement also set forth a payment plan. The Development Authority was to pay the Custodian £I46 million for the land, but over a ten-year period. Of this, the Development Authority would pay £I9 million upon signing the agreement, in addition to the £I7 million from the earlier agreement of February 1953. Thereafter, the Development Authority would make an annual payment of £3 million to the Custodian on the first of October for ten years, and would also be liable for interest of 2.5 percent per annum of the unpaid amount. The interest would be paid in monthly installments of £I20,000. The legal transfer of title took place effective October 1, 1953, after which the Development Authority was entitled to all proceeds from the land.

Did the Development Authority actually transmit funds to the Custodian, which amounted to one Israeli government agency paying another? The Development Authority's budget for 1954–55 did reflect the fact that it had to pay £I3 million to the Custodian that year for the absentee land it acquired in addition to £I240,000 in interest payments at £I20,000/month.[127] While I could not locate records to indicate whether the Development Authority finished all of its annual payments to the Custodian, it was still paying the amount as of October 1959.[128] In any event, the "sale" simply represented one branch of the Israeli government selling land to another, possibly involving little more than the transfer of funds on paper within the Israeli government's budget.

Despite the agreement to sell the Custodian's land to the Development Authority, it took quite some time for the actual transfer of title to take place in the Israeli land registries. Deeds were drawn up for some 840,000 dunums of agricultural land and 50,000 dunums of urban property by the end of 1953.[129] But this was possible only because the Jewish National Fund lent some of its employees in Jerusalem and Haifa to assist in the task.[130] However, while one-third of the land—1,027,340 out of 3,465,334 dunums—had been legally transferred by March 1954, legal transfer of title from the Custodian to the Development Authority in the land registries continued in some cases for at least another two decades.[131]

The sale of the Custodian's land to the Development Authority radically transformed the Custodian's office, then under the direction of Moshe Levin. Because refugee land was now in the hands of the Development Authority, Levin's office had little need for its large staff. On October 1, 1953, 180 persons were transferred from the office of Custodian and began working for the Development Authority, including former Custodian Mordekhai Schattner. Schattner was born in 1904 in Hungary to a family that originated in Kuty, Ukraine. He was an early Zionist pioneer involved in the kibbutz movement in the 1920s who returned to Europe in the 1930s as a Zionist emissary and immigration recruiter. He also became an industrialist and served on the pre-state Va'ad Leumi. A close associate of Ben Gurion, Schattner was among those who signed the Israeli Declaration of Independence in 1948. He later became Custodian of Absentee Property before assuming the post of head of the Development Authority council. The Custodian's office now had to deal with only three essential tasks: the ongoing process of transferring title to the Development Authority; the question of blocked refugee bank accounts and other forms of moveable property and assets; and handling various claims (over abandoned land, claims against refugees, and claims to release refugee land). In the words of the U.S. State Department, "The Custodian's office therefore has now changed its character from that of a large landowner to that of an accountant."[132]

Lastly, the Israeli government enacted several laws in the three years after 1948 that dealt with refugee property, although less directly. One such law vested so-called "state land" into the care of the new state. Israeli authorities were eager to lay hold of all land that had been the property of the mandatory government of Palestine. Palestinians later would assert rights to this property, and the original UN partition resolution had called for this type of property to convey to each of the two sides. In January 1949, the government established the State Properties Division within the Ministry of Finance. The office initially was located in Haifa, but was moved to Jerusalem in November of that year. The State Properties Division collected mandatory documentation on "state property." In September 1950, the prime minister's office for land affairs was transferred to the State Properties Division. The following month, the State Property Law of 5710/1950 was passed to lay the legal framework for the seizure of all state lands. It vested all land in the state that was without a clear owner as of May 15, 1948 or as of the date it became ownerless. Importantly, this included all land that had been the property of the mandatory government of Palestine. A second such law, the State Property Law of 5711/1951, was enacted on February 6, 1951 and dictated that the government could not transfer ownership of state land except to the JNF, the Development Authority, or a local authority. Regulations for state land also were established by the State Property (Lands) Regulations of 5712/1952. In February 1952, the State Properties Division changed its name to the State Lands Department.[133]

## The Jewish National Fund Acquires Refugee Land

The Jewish National Fund (JNF) had long considered itself the premier national (i.e., Jewish) body dealing with land within the Zionist movement. It felt it possessed the experience and the staff power to manage the question of Jewish acquisition of land in Palestine. Yet in the early, confused atmosphere surrounding abandoned land, with a variety of institutions and individuals taking over land in ad hoc fashion, it ended up that the Histadrut's Agricultural Center and the MAPAM-dominated Ministry of Agriculture in the new provisional Israeli government were the agencies designated to allocate abandoned land to the kibbutzim. Some in the JNF, including the veteran Yosef Weitz, began pushing for the JNF to be given control over some of the land abandoned by the refugees. In July 1948, some JNF officials floated a proposal by which the JNF would buy "surplus land" in the abandoned villages. JNF officials believed that any Palestinian refugee families allowed to return could survive on smaller estates than they previously had tilled through the use of "modern," intensive Jewish farming techniques. "Excess land" was that portion of village farmland deemed to be in excess of what this new, intensive agriculture would require. In the JNF proposal, the state would take over such excess land, which would be located far from the village centers, and sell it to the JNF. But not all senior JNF officials liked the idea of buying the land of small-scale Palestinian landowners. JNF head Avraham Granovsky demurred, and favored Zionist authorities taking over the land of big land owners and nonresident absentee landowners only. The idea never materialized.[134]

Some of the first JNF acquisitions of refugee land were leases it obtained. On August 16, 1948, the JNF established a Subcommittee for the Cultivation and Maintenance of Abandoned Lands to manage such properties. Thirteen days later, the JNF formally requested to lease 193,500 dunums of abandoned land from the Ministry of Agriculture.[135] In November 1948, it leased

154,000 dunums for one year from the Ministry of Agriculture. The JNF then sublet the land to settlements.[136] It continued to lease land into 1949, "ordering" land on one-year leases from the Custodian of Absentee Property's Villages Section according to a settlement map prepared by the Jewish Agency's Settlement Department. Weitz continued to press for expanded JNF control over refugee property. He wanted legal JNF ownership of the land, not merely leases. He was anxious to open up the lands for Jewish immigrants, and expressed his impatience shortly after the JNF acquired its first refugee land from the state in 1949:

> Of the entire area of the State of Israel only about 300,000–400,000 dunums . . . are state domain which the Israeli government took over from the mandatory regime. The JNF and private Jewish owners possess under two million dunums. Almost all the rest belongs at law to Arab owners, many of whom have left the country. The fate of these Arabs will be settled when the terms of the peace treaties between Israel and her Arab neighbors are finally drawn up. The JNF, however, cannot wait until then to obtain the land it requires for its pressing needs. It is, therefore, acquiring part of the land abandoned by the Arab owners, through the government of Israel, the sovereign authority in Israel.[137]

Weitz was not alone in the JNF in pushing for its legal ownership of the abandoned land, not continued state control. This was not only because of impatience brought on by the flood of incoming Jewish immigrants but also because of ideological reasons. The JNF felt that only it could guarantee that land become and remain Jewish land, or "national land" [Heb.: karka' hale'om] in Zionist terminology, and thus be subject to exclusive Jewish usage. The new State of Israel, while self-consciously a Jewish state, was also a democracy containing non-Jews. The JNF feared that if captured refugee land remained in the hands of the state, the state might be forced to allocate land for development on an equitable basis between its Jewish and Palestinian citizens instead of reserving it exclusively for Jewish usage.

The JNF faced no such obstacles and was free to discriminate against Arabs in favor of Jews. Its charter mandated that all land that it purchased thereafter would be inalienable, to be held by the JNF on behalf of the Jewish people in perpetuity. Because the JNF could not sell land it acquired, it leased land to Jewish settlements and individual Jews on the condition that it not be re-let to non-Jews and that only Jewish labor be used on the land—the policy of "Hebrew labor" [Heb.: 'avoda 'ivrit]. Thus as a nongovernmental organization free to manage its own land on an exclusivist basis within the new state, the JNF argued for its control of refugee land on this ideological base: if the JNF obtains the land, it will be the best way to guarantee that it is used for Jewish settlement only. This attitude was expressed by a JNF official at the 23rd congress of the World Zionist Organization held in 1951, the fiftieth anniversary of the JNF's establishment, who stated that the JNF "will redeem the lands and will turn them over to the Jewish people—to the *people* and not the *state*, which in the current composition of population cannot be an adequate guarantor of Jewish ownership" [emphases in the original].[138]

The JNF felt strongly that refugee land should not merely be expropriated but duly purchased. This was not only in keeping with the Zionist movement's historical mission to secure a Jewish homeland legally but also in order to sever the refugees' legal title to the land forever. The JNF believed that a purchase was a sounder basis for such a desire than outright expropriation. Weitz argued that the JNF should raise funds from Jews around the world and pay compensation to individual refugee land owners for their abandoned property.[139] He discussed the situation regarding the refugees, their rights, and the JNF's needs and desires in succinct fashion in 1948:

> As for the property they have left behind, we are prepared to pay for it, after deducting proper compensation for the damage caused by the Arabs. This money will help the Arab refugees to re-establish themselves wherever they may be, whether in Transjordan, Iraq, Syria or Nablus .... Israel has no legal way of appropriating these lands, unless it wishes to follow totalitarian methods, and I do not believe that is possible. The land in question is legally owned by people who will not give it up even if they have to remain in exile for many years. Sooner or later we shall have to make compensation, and later it may be financially more disadvantageous than it would be now .... The future stability of the state, its population and its development demand a rapid settlement of the Arab refugees' claims and a complete severance of their link with their past property. Otherwise these claims will remain as a permanent source of friction and give rise to threats and recriminations. The attachment between past owners and their lands can only be eliminated by the payment of the full purchase price for these lands. Those who are reluctant to make financial sacrifices for this purpose should remember that expropriation will lead in the future to greater and more prolonged sacrifices on the part of the Yishuv [Jewish community in Palestine], perhaps even to loss of life.[140]

Others in the JNF shared this view. A November 1948 article in *Karnenu* ("Our Fund"), the organ of the JNF head office in Jerusalem, noted that: "the [JNF] will compensate owners of land which will be required for this public development, and any land passing from private Arab ownership to the Jewish National Fund will be paid for."[141] The article stated that since the JNF could not actually pay the refugees, the compensation funds would be deposited with the Israeli government, which "will act as trustee holding such funds against legitimate claims of Arab owners whether they remain abroad or return." The JNF repeated the vow to compensate the refugees at the 23rd congress of the World Zionist Organization in 1951: "...considerations of ethics and of state constrain us to pay compensation for the abandoned properties, after the requisite reductions have been made for damages incurred by us through the Arab invasion."[142]

As it waited for the state to decide what to do, the JNF moved to purchase abandoned land directly from individual refugees. Weitz noted in 1948 that:

> We have heard echoes from the Arab world that some Arab refugees wish to sell their property in Israel in order to settle down permanently in their country of refuge. What has been proposed in the case of a few individuals, could be extended to embrace most if not all of the Arab refugees.[143]

Weitz, supported by Shertok, proposed cutting deals with wealthy refugees residing in Cairo, Beirut, and Europe. Eventually, the JNF dispatched two men who had served on the Committee for Abandoned Arab Property earlier in the year, Yoav Tsukerman and Gad Makhnes, to Paris to seek out refugees interested in selling their land in Israel. Both men had experience buying land from Palestinians. But the Israeli cabinet ordered the JNF to stop all efforts at buying land from Palestinians directly, and the men returned to Israel.[144] Ben Gurion told Weitz and Danin in December 1948 that "The JNF would buy land only from the State. There was no need to buy land from Arabs."[145]

The veteran land purchaser and Hagana officer Moshe ("Musa") Goldenberg was another JNF official involved in the purchase of land directly from refugees. Born in Rishon le-Tsiyon in 1897, Goldenberg had started working for the JNF in 1934. In response to requests from Palestinian refugee landowners in exile who managed to contact him, he and others from the JNF's Haifa office would travel to the Israeli-Jordanian border near Tirat Tsvi, Kfar Ruppin, and other settlements to meet with refugees along the porous border. For what he called a "fair price," Goldenberg stated that at each such meeting he purchased "hundreds and thousands" of dunums of land that the refugees had left behind. The JNF would determine the prices it was willing to pay in advance, in hard currency, so the refugees had little bargaining room. According to Goldenberg, "The Arabs swarmed to these meetings, and it was hard to accept all the proposals."[146] Even Jewish settlers living near the borders arranged for refugees to meet with Goldenberg. His name and willingness to buy up land soon spread among refugees living in Jordanian-controlled territory, so much so that some refugees would sneak across the border just to meet with him. The Israeli police would notify Goldenberg in Haifa that they had apprehended yet another Palestinian infiltrator who was asking to speak with him. Goldenberg used to travel to the police station in question but was no longer able to offer the refugee any money for the land after the JNF later decided to stop buying land in this manner.[147] Goldenberg deeply regretted that the JNF no longer could carry out such sales, believing that such purchases offered a chance for Palestinian-Israeli reconciliation. He noted:

> In this way all work stopped of buying land with foreign currency, in which I saw great benefit to the state and a chance to soften the outcry of the refugees over the plunder and theft of their land and property. If we had expanded and deepened this work in the early days, many Arabs would have rehabilitated themselves in the neighboring states. In consequence there would not have been created such large concentrations of destitute refugees, who cause trouble in trying to return and to recover their property, and who serve as a sharp weapon in the hands of our ill-wishers.[148]

Despite the orders to stop purchases directly from refugees, in 1949 reports still spread that refugees were continuing to sell their abandoned land to Israeli purchasing agents. The radio station in Ramallah, in the West Bank, broadcast a report in May 1949 stating that some refugees were liquidating their land to Israeli agents in Cyprus (such rumors about Cyprus resurfaced in the early 1960s; see chapter 3).[149] That same month U.S. diplomats confirmed that some refugees had managed to sell their abandoned land from exile, although the venue was not indicated: "The category of [refugee] property owners in general desire to return principally to liquidate their holdings; some have already done so in absentia."[150]

One month after Ben Gurion told Weitz that the JNF should buy land only from the state, the two sides finally concluded a major deal by which the

JNF would purchase a huge amount of refugee land in January 1949. Despite his mistrust of sharing power with the JNF, Ben Gurion had long wanted to sell captured Palestinian land to the JNF. In fact as early as May 13, 1948, the day before he publicly read Israel's declaration of independence, Ben Gurion offered to sell a massive 2 million dunums of land to the JNF for £P0.5/dunum. He was trying to sell land he did not yet control to raise money for arms. It was clear that he was in no position at that time to hand over legal title to such land to the JNF, which refused the offer.[151]

The situation had changed by January 1949. In the months after Israel's victory in 1948, Ben Gurion initially deferred making any final decisions on the permanent fate of refugee land. During his December 18, 1948 meeting with Weitz and Danin, Ben Gurion decided to raise the subject of a large state-JNF land sale once again. This time he offered the JNF 1 million dunums. Three days later, the two held another meeting along with three other leading Zionist land and financial officials: Finance Minister Eli'ezer Kaplan, Avraham Granovsky, and Levi Shkolnik. Born in 1890, Granovsky (later Granott) was a JNF official and co-founder of the Progressive Party who rose to head the JNF in 1945. Levi Shkolnik (later Eshkol) was a leading figure in Zionist land and financial circles and head of the Jewish Agency's Settlement Department since September 1948, and is discussed in greater detail below. The men finalized the deal by which the JNF would purchase 1 million dunums for a theoretical price of £I10 million. Weitz and Granovsky insisted upon a legal transfer of title. Ben Gurion was annoyed; he cared little for such technicalities and besides, Israeli legislation at that point did not allow for sale of refugee property.

On January 27, 1949, the state and the JNF closed the deal. Ben Gurion himself joined with Kaplan in signing on behalf of the state. The state raised the price to £I11 million, although the actual price, payable in installments, would be determined by a joint state-JNF committee and would vary according to location and type of land. In addition, the JNF agreed to pay an additional £I7,250,000 to the state and the Jewish Agency to assist in settling immigrants on the land.[152] The eventual price paid was much higher, although this may reflect the devaluation of Israeli currency: approximately £I23,421,685.[153] The JNF insisted that the land be legally transferred to it within one year of signing the contract in order to assure that the JNF right of ownership.[154]

Varying figures have surfaced as to the exact amount of land transferred in the January 1949 sale, the so-called "first million" (because the JNF later bought another million dunums; see below). The JNF's report to the 23rd

TABLE 1.24 Partial List of Refugee Land Sold to the Jewish National Fund in January 1949

| *Region* | *Amount (Approximate, in Dunums)* |
|---|---|
| Jerusalem corridor | 2,000 |
| Northern Negev desert | 250,000 |
| Coastal Plain | 150,000 |
| Sharon Plain | 150,000 |
| TOTAL | 552,000 |

Source: Granott *Agrarian Reform*, pp. 107–111

congress of the World Zionist Organization in 1951 stated the amount at 1,109,769 dunums: 1,085,607 dunums of rural land and 24,162 urban.[155] Granovsky reported several years later a slightly lower amount: 1,101,942 dunums of which 1,085,607 were rural and 16,335 urban.[156] A partial list showing the location of some of the lands is shown in table 1.24 The rest of the land lay in the Hula Basin and near Baysan.[157]

Where did the cash-strapped JNF obtain the funds to pay for this land? Certainly the JNF's traditional fundraising activities continued among diaspora Jewry. The first JNF head, Johann Kremenezki, had established a vigorous tradition of fundraising, encouraging Jews outside Palestine to contribute money through buying JNF stamps, dropping coins into small blue-and-white collection cans, and inscribing the names of larger donors in the JNF's Golden Book. These fundraising activities continued in the wake of the Holocaust, the establishment of the State of Israel, the first Arab-Israeli war, and the massive immigration of Jews from Europe and the Middle East starting in 1948. American Jews were crucial in providing funds with which the JNF could purchase land. During the October 1946–October 1947 fiscal year, the American branch of the JNF—The Jewish National Fund, Inc. of New York—donated $9,106,388 to the JNF head office in Jerusalem. Between October 1, 1947 to June 15, 1948, a nearly nine month period that witnessed the birth of the State of Israel and the darkest days of the first Arab-Israeli war, the U.S. branch of the JNF more than trebled its previous contribution, making available $31,037,145 to the head office. Most of these funds were donated through the United Jewish Appeal drive. Between 1910 and mid-1948, the American JNF had donated a total of $85,760,732 to the JNF. Other Jews contributed funds to the JNF as well during 1948: Canadian Jews donated $132,410; South African Jews £154,072; and British Jews £2,047,000.[158]

Another source of vital funding for the JNF was a $15 million loan extended by the Bank of America National Trust and Savings Association of San Francisco, founded by A.P. Giannini. The JNF dispatched Yosef Weiss (not to be confused with Yosef Weitz) to explain the JNF's need for the loan to Giannini. Weiss was born in Germany in 1902, and was the director of the Financial Office at the JNF's head office in Jerusalem. He was also an advisor to the Minister of Finance on Israeli claims for compensation abroad. Negotiations between the bank and the JNF began in May 1949. Weiss managed to convince Giannini of the necessity of the loan, along with the fact that the Jewish National Fund, Inc. in New York agreed to guarantee one-third of its amount. The Bank of America extended the loan one month later on June 9, 1949.[159] The loan was significant for several reasons. First of all, it provided the JNF with badly needed cash. The Fund needed money not only to pay the state for the land but also to build Jewish settlements on the land. The loan enabled it to complete its "Series A" settlement plan as well as construct eighty new "Series B" settlements. Beyond that, the loan was important because it represented the first major nongovernmental, noncharitable loan extended to a corporation in Israel, although the JNF was legally registered as a British entity.[160]

Execution of the deal with the state and the JNF's usage of the land took some time. Between signing the deal on January 27, 1949 until March 31, 1954, the state had legally transferred only 35.9 percent of the land, or 396,149 dunums.[161] The land first had to be transferred from the Custodian of Absentee Property to the Development Authority and then to the JNF, which complicated this process. For its part, the JNF had put only 770,271 dunums of the land it bought in completely abandoned villages to use by the end of 1952.[162]

In September 1950, the JNF and the state decided on a second sale before the JNF even had paid for the first million dunums it bought the previous year. The deal involving the so-called "second million" dunums was finalized on October 4, 1950, and involved the transfer of an additional 1,271,734 dunums by the Custodian of Absentee Property on behalf of the Development Authority to the JNF, 99.8 percent of which (1,271,480 dunums) was rural land. Granott later placed the amount at 1,278,200 dunums. The amount of £I66 million was to be paid to the government over a ten year period. Some sources indicate that the JNF was actually to turn the money over to the Jewish Agency on the government's behalf; the amount then would be considered a loan by the government to the JA. Others claim that the JNF never actually paid the amounts it owed under the two deals.[163]

TABLE 1.25 JNF Usage of the "Second Million" Dunums of Refugee Land Purchased in 1950

| *Usage* | *Amount (Dunums)* |
|---|---|
| Completing construction of new settlements | 500,000 |
| Expanding existing settlements | 500,000 |
| Afforestation | 160,000 |
| Various agricultural purposes | 100,000 |
| Settlement housing | 16,200 |
| Urban housing | 2,000 |
| TOTAL | 1,278,200 |

Source: Granott, *Agrarian Reform*, pp. 108, 111

The JNF quickly put the land to use for development purposes, including agricultural development, settlement building, industrial and commercial development, and construction of public housing. Since its charter forbade it from ever selling its land, it continued its policy of signing long-term leases with Jewish organizations and institutions. Its standard lease term was for 49 years. It frowned upon leasing large tracts of its land to private companies, refusing, for example, requests from citrus companies like Hakal-Yakhin to lease land to them as the state did. Table 1.25 indicates what uses the JNF put to the "second million."According to Weitz, the JNF's purchasing policy was to buy entire tracts of land from the government rather than parcels here and there. Examples of such tracts include one north of the Hula Basin consisting of 30,000 dunums; one in the Baysan Valley of 60,000 dunums; one between al-Tantura and al-Tira of 60,000 dunums; and a 400,000 dunum stretch in the Jerusalem corridor and the Shefelah.[164] Table 1.26 illustrates the location and price paid for the land in both JNF purchases.

The two sales saw the JNF's holdings grow and future plans expand. Granovksy chose the JNF's Jubilee Convention in Washington in January 1951, convened to celebrate the fiftieth anniversary of the founding of the JNF, to announce its ambitious new five-year plan. The plan revealed the new circumstances in which the JNF found itself and sought to raise the kind of funds necessary to achieve its ambitious goals. The plan envisioned a massive outlay of $250 million for a variety of projects in Israel. These included $70 million to pay for the more than 2 million dunums that the JNF had bought from the Israeli government; construction of some 500 new Jewish settle-

TABLE 1.26 Location and Prices of Land in 1949 and 1950 Purchases of Refugee Property by the Jewish National Fund

| *Location* | *Amount (Dunums)* | *Price (£I)* | *£I/Dunum* |
|---|---|---|---|
| 1. Rural land | | | |
| Northern Negev | 352,850 | 4,001,934 | 11.3 |
| Judea | 608,280 | 32,002,849 | 52.6 |
| Coastal Plain | 204,667 | 3,557,687 | 17.4 |
| Sharon Plain | 205,342 | 14,628,380 | 71.2 |
| Haifa region | 250,967 | 9,706,274 | 38.7 |
| Acre region | 150,657 | 6,933,266 | 46.0 |
| Nazareth region | 21,370 | 837,047 | 39.2 |
| Jenin region | 47,553 | 1,822,112 | 38.3 |
| Baysan region | 82,328 | 1,972,179 | 24.0 |
| Tiberias region | 57,414 | 1,584,457 | 27.6 |
| Safad region | 162,813 | 4,179,650 | 25.7 |
| Jerusalem corridor | 210,847 | 2,188,142 | 10.4 |
| 2. Urban land | | | |
| Various | 18,589 | 6,007,708 | 323.2 |
| TOTAL | 2,373,677 | 89,421,685 | 37.7 |

Source: Granott, *Agrarian Reform*, p. 111

ments; and purchasing some 500,000 dunums of land for forests and other projects.[165]

The two sales trebled the amount of land the JNF owned—by 1956, 68 percent of all JNF land consisted of the land bought in the two sales.[166] The JNF owned 17 percent of the surface area of the state, including 39 percent of cultivable land and 23.1 percent of Jewish-owned land in the cities.[167] By the mid-1950s, 577 of 698 Jewish agricultural settlements in Israel (82.7 percent) had been built on JNF land, while 80 percent of all agricultural produce was grown on its land.[168]

A final indication of the new circumstances in which the JNF was operating was the incorporation of the JNF as an Israeli company and the transfer to it of the assets formerly held by the British-registered Jewish National Fund, Ltd. In November 1953, the Knesset passed the Keren Kayemet le-Yisra'el Law of 5714/1953 that created an Israeli company by that name, the Hebrew name for Jewish National Fund. The company came into existence on May 20, 1954, after which the British JNF transferred all the land that it owned within the boundaries of the State of Israel. However, the British JNF retained ownership of JNF land that lay outside Israeli jurisdiction in surrounding Arab countries. This undoubtedly was because the state of war existing between Israel and the Arab world made it untenable for an Israeli company to own land beyond the borders in hostile territory, land the JNF had acquired in Jordan, Syria, and Lebanon prior to 1948.

For its part, the state was content to have sold the land to the JNF. By 1958, almost all of the land had been transferred to the JNF. The government's official yearbook stated the effect of the two sales on the office of the Custodian of Absentee Property:

> The transfer of land to the Jewish National Fund marks the beginning of a process, the main object of which is to convert the activities of the Custodian from temporary activities—as they appeared a first to be—to a systematic restoration of property at his disposal in order to make it an instrument for the development of the country.[169]

## Settling the Refugees' Land with Jewish Immigrants

Zionist and Israel policy toward refugee land in the spring and summer of 1948 was initially focused on housing new Jewish immigrants in captured Palestinian homes in the towns and cities and on temporarily utilizing agricultural land. By fall 1948, the situation also allowed the entertainment of longer-term policies toward the land. Several factors account for this. In the first place, the Ten Days Fighting of July 9–18, 1948 saw the Israeli army conquer even more parts of Arab Palestine. These victories helped to prompt the government toward the new strategy because such lands, lying deep in Arab territory far from any Jewish settlements, could not be leased to Jewish farm communities as before. Secondly, the legal consolidation of the land first into the hands of the Custodian of Absentee Property and later the Development Authority and the JNF laid the basis for the permanent alienation of refugee land. The extensive legal and administrative maneuverings regarding refugee land in Israel between 1948–53 laid the groundwork for the fundamental transformation of the cadastral landscape within Israel. The Custodian of Absentee Property's sale of the land to the Development Authority and their joint transfer of much of the land to the Jewish National Fund at the government's directive represented a huge windfall for the Zionist movement.

With the land securely in the hands of the government and the JNF, both parties undertook the decision to begin constructing Jewish settlements on the land. The shift from leasing land to seizing it permanently and building settlements on it stemmed from a third factor as well. Zionist officials argued that the best way to block either mass refugee repatriation or slow repatriation through infiltration of individual refugees was to settle the land with Jews. The success of the Zionist enterprise until that point in history lay partly with Zionism's ability to create facts on the ground through the acquisition of land and settling it with Jews. Consolidation of Israel's gains in the war were another reason for this success. This fact seemed to demand nothing less than the prevention of refugee repatriation by the speedy erection of Jewish settlements on their land.

The cry to prevent the refugees from returning to their lands began arising from a number of sources by the summer of 1948. One looming factor in this regard was the army's keen desire to prevent the infiltration of refugees across the porous borders and cease-fire lines. In fact, refugee infiltration had become a major concern for the defense and political establishments by the early summer of 1948. Armed incursions by certain refugees were prompting the flight of some Jews living in existing communities near the borders. The military was also concerned that once they returned the refugees could constitute a fifth column behind Israeli lines. The Israeli army urged a speedy decision to shift from leasing refugee land to settling it to prevent "a serious danger that these villagers would re-establish themselves in their villages deep behind our lines. . . . There is no time to be lost in taking a decision."[170] Zionist settlement officials like Weitz echoed such concerns:

> Slowly but surely, abandoned villages are vanishing as they are resettled, partially or completely . . . . Many thousands of dunams formerly considered abandoned lands—are now being [cultivated] or claimed by their owners.[171]

The Foreign Ministry noted:

> The infiltration of individual Arabs, ostensibly for reaping and threshing, alone, could in time bring with it the re-establishment [of the refugees] in the villages, something which could seriously endanger many of our achievements during the six months of the war.[172]

Even ordinary Jews urged the government to prevent the refugees' return. In June 1948, a delegation from Safad asked the government not to allow

Palestinian refugees back into the town, noting that most of their property had been looted anyway. Instead, delegation members requested, the empty Palestinian quarters of the town be settled with Jews.[173] Such logic prevailed: the provisional cabinet decided on June 16, 1948 not to allow refugee repatriation, and ordered the Israeli military to prevent infiltration. An advisory meeting called by Ben Gurion in August 1948 discussed settling the land to forestall refugee return. The committee, consisting of Shertok, Kaplan, Weitz, Danin, Shitrit, and Gen. 'Elimelekh Avner (head of the military government imposed on the Palestinians who remained in Israel), among others, even examined the possibility of selling the abandoned refugee land to American Jews and paying the refugees compensation with the proceeds.[174]

While agreeing to prevent the return of refugees, the provisional government was still reluctant in the fall of 1948 to go one step further and authorize the erection of new settlements on the land. Ben Gurion's government chose not to accept a November 1948 settlement plan drawn up by the army in conjunction with the Jewish Agency's Settlement Department and the JNF that proposed building 96 new settlements on refugee land. Kaplan and Tsizling were leading voices opposing such a move. But others in the Zionist establishment continued to push for settling the refugees' land and permanently guaranteeing Israeli military successes during the war. Weitz argued tenaciously for this. For him, settling refugee land was not simply of strategic value but actually essential for the future of the Zionist venture. He noted his deeply held ideological vision in this way in January 1950:

> The struggle for the redemption of the land [Heb.: ge'ulat ha-adama] means simply this—the liberation of the land from the hand of the stranger, from the chains of wilderness; the struggle for its conquest by settlement; and last but not least, the redemption of the settler, both as a human being and as a Jew, through his deep attachment to the soil he tills.[175]

Beyond the strategic need to settle the borders and prevent refugee repatriation, the demographic pressures presented by mass Jewish immigration immediately after the declaration of Israeli statehood and the end of the fighting also pushed the government toward erecting new settlements on the refugee land and not merely leasing it to existing settlements. The wave of new immigrants placed enormous demands for housing on the new state, which aimed to provide land for the "ingathering of the exiles" [Heb.: kibbuts ha-galuyot]. Note the immigration statistics shown in table 1.27.

TABLE 1.27 Jewish Immigrants into Israel, 1948–1958

| *Year* | *No. of Immigrants* |
|---|---|
| 1948 (May 15–December 31) | 101,819 |
| 1949 | 239,076 |
| 1950 | 169,405 |
| 1951 | 173,901 |
| 1952 | 23,375 |
| 1953 | 10,347 |
| 1954 | 17,471 |
| 1955 | 36,303 |
| 1956 | 54,925 |
| 1957 | 71,100 |
| 1958 | 26,093 |
| TOTAL | 923,815 |

Source: Ernest Stock, *Chosen Instrument. The Jewish Agency in the First Decade of the State of Israel* (New York: Herzl Press and Jerusalem: Hassifriya Haziyonit, 1988), p. 261

In May 1948, a meeting was held between two officials of the new provisional government and Israel and the JA to discuss a division of labor with regard to settling new immigrants. Tsizling and Kaplan met with the JA's Settlement Department [Heb.: Mahlakat ha-Hityashvut] to devise a strategy for the large-scale settlement of the thousands of new immigrants coming into the country. They decided that the new state would manage existing Jewish settlements and that the JA and other Zionist organizations would deal with creating new ones.[176] This arrangement was formalized when a joint state/JA committee, the Committee for Agriculture and Settlement Planning, decided in the summer of 1949 that the government's Ministry of Agriculture would be responsible for existing settlements while the JA's Settlement Department would deal with new ones.[177]

By that time, the JA's Settlement Department had a new head: Levi Shkolnik, who later changed his family name to Eshkol. Born in the Ukraine in 1895, Eshkol immigrated to Palestine in 1914. A leading Zionist figure in the realm of land, water, and finance, Eshkol was one of the central figures in the drama of Israel's transformation of the abandoned refugee land. Eshkol's resumé was impressive. A member of MAPAI, he had worked with the Histadrut's Agricultural Center during the mandate. From 1935 to 1951 he served as the founding director of the Mekorot Water Company. Starting in

1934 Eshkol also headed ha-'Avara, Ltd., a corporation that had worked to transfer the assets of Jewish immigrants who left Germany for Palestine. During the 1940s, he became head of the Hagana's Finance Department. In September 1948, Eshkol rose to head the JA's Settlement Department, a position he held until 1963. Capping off a busy career, Eshkol later became Treasurer of the JA in 1949, Israel's second Minister of Finance during 1952–63, and its prime minister from 1963 until his death in 1969.

One day in late 1948, Eshkol was driving to Jerusalem when he passed an abandoned village overlooking the road to Latrun. With him was his driver and his aide, Ra'anan Weitz (born in Rehovot in 1913), the son of Yosef Weitz and future head of the JA's Settlement Department. Together with the younger Weitz, Eshkol walked through the village and later recalled, "I didn't know the details, yet, but I believed that the desolate and abandoned place might help solve the problem of settling the nation." Continuing on the way to Jerusalem, Eshkol and Weitz began devising a plan for settling new Jewish immigrants in more than 45 abandoned Palestinian villages.[178] Eshkol's energy eventually helped found 371 new settlements and the expansion of 60 existing ones during his tenure as head of the JA Settlement Department. Most of the new settlements developed in Israel from 1948–52 according to the JA's settlement plans were built on abandoned refugee land in the Sharon Plain along the Mediterranean coast, in Galilee, and near Jerusalem, land that the JNF had acquired in its purchases from the state in 1949 and 1950. Thereafter, settlement activity focused on building in the Lakhish and Adullam areas in southern Judea, the Ta'anakh area of the eastern Jezre'el Valley, and Wadi 'Arava and other parts of the Negev desert. Most of these new settlements were moshavim, as JA settlement officials determined that the communal life of the kibbutz did not suit the new arrivals. These were by and large Holocaust survivors, Jews from North Africa and the Middle East, and other refugees whose immigration was spurred by reasons other than the Zionist zeal to take up agriculture in socialist communities.

The number of new settlements began to burgeon. Between May 1948 and June 1949, a total of 89 new Jewish communities were established on refugee land. Of these, 63 were built as new settlements and 26 consisted of former Palestinian villages that were merely repopulated with Jews.[179] By 1952, Eshkol's Settlement Department had established new settlements on a total of 854,900 dunums, of which 734,900 were rainfed.[180] By the end of 1953, Eshkol had overseen the erection of 345 new Jewish settlements—251 moshavim and 96 kibbutzim—which together cultivated a full 1,048,000 dunums of land.[181] Other sources put the figure at 370 new settlements, of

TABLE 1.28 Settlement Building in Israel by Type of Settlement, 1948–1958

| *Type of Settlement* | *Number* |
|---|---|
| Workers' [Heb.: 'ovedim] moshavim | 257 |
| Communal [Heb.: shitufi] moshavim | 17 |
| Kibbutzim | 100 |
| Educational institutes, training farms, etc. | 27 |
| Middle class settlements | 22 |
| Expansion of older settlements | 44 |
| TOTAL | 467 |

Source: *Israel Government Yearbook Vol. 5719/1958*, p. 459

which a full 350 had been built on refugee land.[182] By 1958, the JA Settlement Department had built and supervised a total of 467 settlements in Israel. Table 1.28 indicates the type of settlements.

The massive construction boom carried out by Eshkol and the JA during the 1950s was made possible by the use of refugee land, a significant amount of which ended up in the hands of the JNF. By 1954, one-third of Israel's entire Jewish population lived on refugee property, including 250,000 new immigrants housed in urban refugee housing.[183] One advantage to utilizing abandoned refugee housing was that it was much cheaper than constructing new homes. Settling immigrants in new housing amounted to between $7,000 and $9,000 per family in 1950, compared to $750 per family for repairs to existing Palestinian homes in the villages plus another $750 for animals and farm equipment.[184] The massive settlement building on refugee land did more than just alienate the land permanently from its Palestinian owners and allow for the absorption [Heb.: kelita] of hundreds of thousands of new immigrants. It also transformed the spatial and cultural landscape of Palestine. New Jewish communities dotted the landscape where formerly hundreds of Palestinian villages had stood. Sometimes the new settlements appropriated the former villages' names. Thus in 1949 the settlement of Nurit was erected on the abandoned lands of Nuris. The village of 'Ayn Hawd was replaced in 1953 by an Israeli artists' community called 'En Hod.[185] Other abandoned areas were not settled but planted with groves of trees under Weitz, who was busy with forestation and other projects as head of the JNF's Land Development Division until 1959.

Settling new Jewish immigrants on refugee land and sometimes in their very homes was not greeted with universal acclaim by Jews in Israel. The

Yiddish-language journalist David Pinsky related an account in October 1949 of one Holocaust survivor who felt great misgivings living in an abandoned Palestinian house in the village of Yazur, near Jaffa. The entire Palestinian population had left, and their homes and personal property were in fairly good order. Jews from Poland, Czechoslovakia, and other European countries occupied the village, which was renamed Mishmar ha-Shev'a:

> Mr. Pinsky tells of one woman he met in Yazir [sic], who had become openly obsessed by the problem. She was a young woman, a mother of two children who occupied a home of a former well-to-do Arab family. The house was spacious; the garden well-kept; they had plenty of everything and could live comfortably. One day the children discovered a closet full of toys which belonged to the children of the exiled Arab family. The children were overjoyed with their find and began to play noisily with the toys. But the mother was suddenly struck by the thought that her children were playing with the toys of Arab children who were now exiled and homeless. She began to brood: where were those children whose toys were being played with by her own children? have they a roof over their heads? a bed to sleep in, or a toy to play with? What right have her children to be happy at the expense of the unhappiness of others? She ordered the children to put the toys back into the closet and forbade them to play with them. But this did not restore her peace of mind: what right had she and her family to occupy a house which does not belong to her? use a garden and field which were taken by force from other people who ran away in a panic of war and are not permitted to return? Is she and her family not living on goods robbed from others? Is she not doing to the Arabs what the Nazis did to her and her family?[186]

Like the earlier leasing of refugee land, settlement building on abandoned land spanned the ideological spectrum of Zionist politics. The Rural and Suburban Settlement Company, or RASSCO, was a subsidiary of the JA established in 1934 to encourage middle-class Jewish immigration. It leased refugee land from the Development Authority to help fulfill its mission. On the other side of the ideological spectrum, the leftist MAPAM built socialist communities on refugee land. In June 1948, MAPAM had issued a liberal-minded policy statement toward the question of refugee repatriation. The document, entitled "Our Policy Toward the Arabs During the War," opposed the ongoing expulsions of Palestinians from territory under Israeli control and called for refugee repatriation. However, this did not stop MAPAM members from erecting kibbutzim on refugee land anyway. The MAPAM kibbutz of Sassa was built on land belonging to the abandoned village of Sa'sa' in northern Galilee, close to the Lebanese border. The village had been the scene of two massacres during the 1948 fighting, after which its inhabitants fled or were expelled by Israeli troops. The new collective settlement of Sassa was then established by some 100 American Jews in 1949. Sassa's leader, a graduate of the University of Minnesota, justified the conflict between his leftist beliefs and the reality of living on refugee land in this manner: "It was a hard decision for us to make. It was against our principles to take over the homes of Arab laborers. But the government insisted that Sassa be occupied for security reasons. We had little choice."[187]

Nor were all the settlers who lived in the new settlements recent immigrants. Veteran Israelis settled there too. Some 76,000 dunums of land were given to the survivors of Jewish settlements destroyed during the 1948 fighting, including those whose land lay across the cease-fire lines in the West Bank and Gaza after the war. Survivors from four destroyed settlements of Gush 'Etsiyon [the 'Etsiyon Bloc] founded the settlement of Nir 'Etsiyon on land formerly belonging to the village of 'Ayn Hawd near Haifa. Beyond that, survivors from the Gush 'Etsiyon settlement of Massu'ot Yitshak received several hundred dunums of abandoned vineyards with which to start a new community within Israel. Of the 76,000 dunums granted to such communities, 29,000 was JNF land. But the remainder consisted of refugee land, "enemy property" (German property seized by the British during the Second World War; discussed below), and so forth.[188]

Even as settlement of the abandoned land continued apace into the early 1950s, the cry to hasten erection of settlements near the borders continued. A major Israeli concern remained preventing the return of refugees, hundreds of whom continued to cross the borders in an effort to return to their homes. According to the army, there were 16,000 instances of what was termed "infiltration" during 1952, most (11,000) across the cease-fire lines from Jordan and the Jordanian-controlled West Bank.[189] Ben Gurion noted to the Knesset in that year that:

> The settlement of the borders and the empty spaces—is also a security task of the first order .... The War of Independence revealed the military value—not only the tactical, but also the strategic value—of the settlements around Jerusalem, in the South, in the Galilee and in the Jordan Valley .... Security ... commands us swiftly to populate the border areas and the empty spaces.[190]

Most "infiltrators" were not terrorists who threatened Israel's security but merely refugees seeking to return to their lost homes and villages. Some merely sought to glimpse their former homes. Lt.-Gen. John B. Glubb, commander of the Jordanian Arab Legion who tried to halt as much cross-border infiltration as possible in order to reduce Jordanian-Israeli friction, tried to explain the motivating behavior that gave rise to this phenomenon as:

> Some deep psychological urge which impels a peasant to cling to and die on his land. A great many of these wretched people are killed now [by the Israeli army], picking their own oranges and olives just beyond the [frontier] line. The value of the fruit is often negligible. If the Jewish patrols see him he is shot dead on the spot, without any questions. But they will persist in returning to their farms and gardens.[191]

The economic and strategic value of this huge windfall cannot be overstated, a fact that dampened any talk of allowing the refugees back to claim their land. Indeed, forestalling such a move became a bedrock principle of Israeli and Zionist officials from that time forward. In 1956, Granott noted that the ultimate success of settling Jewish immigrants on refugee land depended upon Zionist retention of the abandoned land:

> Settlement operations in the years 1950–52 strengthened the conviction that there could be no return to the old status: the lands vacated by the Arabs during the War of Independence were by this time settled, for the most part cultivated, and governed by a progressive agrarian regime, in harmony with the aspirations of Zionism and the rules of the Jewish National Fund .... Thus, as a result of a combination of unanticipated factors it has been possible to implement the great principle of land nationalisation proclaimed at the inception of the Zionist Movement, which in the State of Israel is now a reality with every day bringing nearer its complete fulfillment.[192]

## Disposal of the Balance of the Refugee Land

The sales of abandoned land to the JNF had left a significant percentage of refugee land out of the state's hands by the mid-1950s. But the Development Authority still retained some land both in the towns and in the countryside and continued to dispose of it. Nearly a million dunums—920,000—were still administered by the Development Authority or the Ministry of Agriculture by 1953.[193] By 1954, incomplete figures showed the Authority still possessing 101,000 dunums. As of May 12, 1954, the Development Authority owned 50,171 residential and commercial buildings in towns as follows: 47.4 percent in Tel Aviv-Jaffa; 30.4 percent in Haifa; 19.6 percent in Jerusalem; and 2.6 percent in Nazareth and Beersheba.[194] The Development Authority's Urban Property Department leased some 59,000 residential dwellings and 11,000 businesses in 1956 and a total of 57,497 residential dwellings and 10,727 businesses in 1958.[195] From 1952 to 1956, it leased plantations to the governmental corporation Mata'ei ha-Umma. The following year, all of the 48,000 dunums of plantation land it still controlled were leased to Mata'ei ha-Umma and the rehabilitation of this land was completed.[196] By 1956, the Development Authority still owned 85,000 dunums of citrus groves as well that it granted to agricultural bodies, companies, and individual farmers on 49-year leases. This included 10,000 dunums that were included in the "Grove by Saving" investment project, in which the Development Authority and Hadarei Yisra'el Co. were partners along with the Hakal-Yakhin company and the Pardes Syndicate.[197] In 1957, the Development Authority leased 10,000 dunums to Hadarei Yisra'el Co.; 22,000 dunums to Mehadrin Co.; 11,000 dunums to Hakal-Yakhin; and 3,000 dunums to RASSCO.[198] Besides leases, the Development Authority continued disposing of abandoned land under its jurisdiction as well. During the first half of 1953, it transferred 17,884 residential and commercial units in abandoned buildings in the cities to the 'Amidar company.[199]

As a postscript, the Israeli government consolidated several agencies that controlled land into one in 1953 and called it the Property Department. The new department consisted of the Development Authority, the Custodian of Absentee Property, the Custodian of Enemy Property, the State Lands Department, and the Custodian of German Property. The latter resembled the Custodian of Enemy Property but dealt only with property of German nationals that had been sequestered by mandatory authorities during the Second World War. Israel retained control of this land after 1948 by virtue of the German Property Law of 5711/1950 that created the office of Custodian of German Property on October 1, 1950 to manage this property. The Custodian of German Property eventually sold property belonging to the Roman Catholic and Lutheran churches to the Development Authority while negotiations began between Israel and the West German government in 1954 for release of secular German property. Table 1.29 shows which state agencies held land in 1954.

TABLE 1.29 Amount of Land Administered by Israeli Government Agencies, 1954

| *Agency* | *Amount (Dunums)* |
|---|---|
| Ministry of Agriculture | 819,000 |
| Development Authority | 101,000 |
| State Lands Division | 745,000 |
| Others | 6,425 |
| TOTAL | 1,671,425 |

Source: CZA KKL5/22273, "Report on the Land Administration System of the State" (September 5, 1954)

Despite Israel's desire to utilize the refugees' land, much abandoned land still remained vacant by the 1950s, especially in the rural areas. This was a source of major concern to Weitz and others. In February 1953, the Custodian of Absentee Property's office prepared a report on the utilization of land in totally abandoned Palestinian refugee villages that showed that only 2,474,958 out of 4,063,669 dunums had been put to use by Jews since the war (see tables 1.30 and 1.31). Ever critical of state land agencies, Weitz estimated

TABLE 1.30 Utilization of Refugee Land by Type of Land, 1952

| *Use of Land* | *No. of Dunums* |
|---|---|
| Citrus orchards | 30,708 |
| Olive plantations | 95,344 |
| Leased to settlements | 909,879 |
| Held by settlements without lease | 371,735 |
| Jewish National Fund land leased to settlements | 770,271 |
| Lased to individuals | 108,349 |
| Housing (including that in the planning stage) | 112,097 |
| Ma'abarot [transit camps for new immigrants] | 13,445 |
| Industrial and commercial installations | 18,928 |
| Israeli army bases, etc. | 44,232 |
| TOTAL | 2,474,988 |

Source: Source: CZA A202/97, Custodian of Absentee Property report of 22 February 1953

TABLE 1.31 Location of Refugee Land by Mandatory Sub-District, 1952

| *District* | *Amount (Dunums)* |
|---|---|
| Acre | 148,580 |
| Baysan | 147,477 |
| Nazareth | 86,395 |
| Safad | 435,660 |
| Tiberias | 160,731 |
| Haifa | 258,488 |
| Jaffa | 145,254 |
| Jenin | 125,825 |
| Nablus | 8,814 |
| Tulkarm | 234,209 |
| Hebron | 1,006,547 |
| Jerusalem | 209,352 |
| Gaza | 640,503 |
| Ramla | 455,834 |

Source: CZA A202/97, Custodian of Absentee Property report of 22 February 1953

that the amount of unused refugee land actually was much higher, closer to 2 million dunums. Following a 1954 study he carried out of land under state control, Weitz determined that 680,000 dunums of cultivable land and 1,400,000 dunums of uncultivable land still were not being used (see table 1.32).

The result of all of this activity was that within a few short years of their flight, the refugees would scarcely have recognized their abandoned lands even if they had been allowed to return. It had been incorporated *mutatis mutandis* into the Jewish character of the State of Israel. Israel refused to give the land back, but agreed to compensate the refugees for it. The call for compensating soon became a major international issue for diplomats seeking conciliation among the parties to the Arab-Israeli conflict.

TABLE 1.32 Scope of Abandoned Land According to Yosef Weitz, 1954

| *Type* | *Amount (Dunums)* |
|---|---|
| Transferred to Development Authority | 3,465,334 |
| Uncultivable | 1,400,000 |
| TOTAL | 4,865,334 |
| Not being used: | |
| Cultivable | 680,000 |
| Uncultivable | 1,400,000 |
| TOTAL | 2,080,000 |

Source: CZA KKL5/22273, "Report on the Land Administration System of the State" (5 September 1954), section 3

CHAPTER TWO

# UNCCP'S EARLY ACTIVITY ON THE REFUGEE PROPERTY QUESTION

The plight of the Palestinian refugees was one of the most visible manifestations of the havoc wrought by the first Arab-Israeli war. Almost immediately the international community began expressing a considerable degree of concern over their fate, including the property they left behind. Certainly the United Nations concerned itself with this issue given that it was its decision to partition Palestine. Indeed, the first major international discussion of land and property matters in the context of solving the Arab-Israeli dispute came from the UN. Even before the fighting and the refugee exodus, the UN General Assembly had been thinking about the question of the fate of property in the wake of the creation of the neighboring Jewish and Arab states that were called for in its partition resolution of 1947. General Assembly Resolution 181 (II) of November 29, 1947 addressed the issue of what might happen to Palestinian property in the new Jewish state, and vice versa. As far as land was concerned, the resolution stated that the new Jewish authorities only could expropriate Arab-owned property for "public purposes" and that they must compensate the owners for the land. The same would be true for Jewish property in the Arab state. According to Section I.C.2.8.: "No expropriation of land owned by an Arab in the Jewish state shall be allowed except for public purposes. In all cases of expropriation full compensation as fixed by the Supreme Court [of the Jewish State] shall be paid previous to dispossession."

The General Assembly also anticipated that the land and other property belonging to the mandatory government would be split between the two communities. Each community was to inherit moveable property on an "equitable" basis as determined by the United Nations. State land would be taken over by the state in whose territory such land lay:

> The moveable assets of the Administration of Palestine shall be allocated to the Arab and Jewish States and the City of Jerusalem on an equitable basis. Allocations should be made by the United Nations Commission referred to in section B, paragraph 1, above. Immoveable assets shall become the property of the Government of the territory in which they are situated. (Section I.E.1.)

Thus even before the 1948 war broke out, the UN already considered that the Palestinians should receive their share of land and moveable assets held by the British mandatory government, a belief flatly rejected by Israel as noted in chapter 1.

The 1948 fighting and the massive dislocation suffered by the refugees prompted immediate concern in the halls of the UN. On May 14, 1948, the last day of the British mandate and the day on which Israel declared its independence, the General Assembly enacted Resolution 186 (S-II) that created the office of a UN mediator for Palestine. The mediator was to try to do nothing less than "promote a peaceful adjustment of the future situation of Palestine." The person selected for this daunting task was the Swedish Count Folke Bernadotte. Born in Stockholm in 1895, Bernadotte was a member of the Swedish royal family and had served as president of the Swedish Red Cross. Bernadotte worked tirelessly during the summer of 1948, effecting two truces in the fighting among other accomplishments.

Bernadotte submitted a report on the situation and his activities to the General Assembly on September 16, 1948.[1] Bernadotte addressed the refugee problem in his report, and indeed was the first highly-placed person to focus international attention on this crucial dimension of the conflict. He stated that "the right of the Arab refugees to return to their homes in Jewish-controlled territories at the earliest possible date should be affirmed by the United Nations." Beyond this, he discussed the fate of the refugees' property, which he felt should be secured pending a solution to the refugee exodus. Bernadotte was particularly shocked at reports of the widespread looting of Palestinian property that was taking place and was the first international figure to charge Israel publicly with responsibility for private Palestinian property left behind under its jurisdiction. He also had received reports of the willful destruction of villages that Yosef Weitz and others were undertaking. Bernadotte's report noted:

> There have been numerous reports from reliable sources of large-scale looting, pillaging and plundering, and of instances of destruction of villages without military necessity. The liability of the Provisional Government of Israel to restore private property to its Arab owners and to indemnify those owners for property wantonly destroyed is clear irrespective of any indemnities which the Provisional Government may claim from the Arab States.

His report also called for the "payment of adequate compensation to those choosing not to return to their former homes." Lastly, he called on the UN to create a "conciliation commission" to carry on the work of Arab-Israeli mediation.

On September 17, 1948, the day after he signed his report, Bernadotte was shot and killed in Jerusalem by militants associated with the "Fatherland Front," which was connected with the Revisionist group Lohamei Herut Yisra'el ("Fighters for the Freedom of Israel," or LEHI). The LEHI was bitterly opposed to his peace proposals, and one week later issued a statement warning others not to repeat Bernadotte's mistake of trying to give away part of the historical Jewish patrimony to "foreigners:"

> The Fighters for the Freedom of Israel will fight by any means at their disposal against foreign regime [sic], be it Arab, Anglo-Arab, or a combined imperialist regime under the mask of U.N. They will fight against any such regime exactly like they fought against direct British regime. A special warning is hereby issued by the Fighters for the Freedom of Israel against any attempt to establish a non-Hebrew regime in Jerusalem . ... The Fighters for the Freedom of Israel do not wish to do harm to representatives of other nations and countries which are not enemies of the Hebrew People and his freedom in his country .... Any such [foreign] supervision or any such ruling will be considered by us as service to imperialism and foreign occupation and we will treat them as we treated the British regime and its representatives.[2]

## Establishment of the UNCCP

The UN replaced Bernadotte with the American Ralph Bunche and subsequently put into action Bernadotte's proposal to create a "conciliation commission." This latter step was accomplished when the General Assembly passed the landmark Resolution 194 (III) on December 11, 1948. Among other provisions, the resolution created a new UN agency, the United Nations Conciliation Commission for Palestine (UNCCP). The UNCCP was to assume the duties of the mediator. The commission would exert a profound role in the drama of Palestinian refugee property over the next two decades.

The UNCCP was structured as a body made up of three members that was responsible to the General Assembly. The members were not persons but member states of the UN: France, Turkey, and the United States of America. The position of chair was rotated among the three nations, initially on a monthly basis. As an agency within the UN Secretariat's bureaucracy, the three-member body employed the services of UN employees, the highest ranking of which was the UNCCP's Principal Secretary. The first Principal Secretary was Pablo de Azcárate of Spain. Bunche later observed that both he and Bernadotte naively had assumed that the representatives on the conciliation commission he proposed would act independently from their respective governments. According to a member of the U.S. delegation to the UN, Bunche had said as much to him during a meeting in 1949: "In closing, Dr. Bunche observed that when Count Bernadotte and he had recommended a conciliation commission, it never occurred to them that the members of the commission would act on the basis of instructions from their respective governments."[3]

However, that is precisely how the UNCCP would act over the coming decades of its existence. The American seat on the UNCCP in particular served to guarantee that the body never strayed too far from overall U.S. policies toward the Arab-Israeli conflict in general and, importantly, toward the refugee property in particular. This fact would prove to be fundamentally important in understanding the limits of the UNCCP's abilities on behalf of the property question.

General Assembly Resolution 194 (III) also discussed the Palestinian refugees and specifically called on Israel to compensate them for abandoned and damaged property. This resolution would be the major catalyst in the efforts exerted by a number of parties over the coming decades when dealing with the matter of the refugee property. Specifically, Resolution 194 (III) called for:

> the refugees wishing to return to their homes and live at peace with their neighbors should be permitted to do so at the earliest practicable date, and that compensation should be paid for the property of those choosing not to return and for the loss of or damage to property which, under principles of international law or in equity, should be made good by the Governments or authorities responsible.

Partisans of the Arab-Israeli conflict have long argued over just what the resolution calls for. Does it affirm *both* the refugees' right to repatriation *and* their right to be compensated? Exactly what is meant by "compensation"? Are only nonreturning refugees entitled to it? The UNCCP offered its own interpretation early on when it drew up a background paper on the question of compensation in early 1950. This document states the commission's interpretation of just what Resolution 194 (III) called for. The UNCCP background paper stated that the resolution's text covered compensation for *both* returning and nonreturning refugees. That is, compensation should be paid both for the property left behind by refugees who do not return to live in their homes *and* to repatriated refugees whose property had been looted or otherwise destroyed without military necessity. However, the commission opined that repatriated refugees returning to homes and property damaged or destroyed during normal military operations would not be eligible for compensation.[4] Despite the UNCCP's own opinion on the question, just which refugees were eligible for compensation would later become a major controversy among the parties to the conflict.

The UNCCP commenced functioning on January 24, 1949 from its field offices in Government House in Jerusalem. The fate of the refugees was one of the leading stumbling blocks to its early efforts on behalf of conciliation. Its first major endeavor was a series of meetings with Arab representatives in Beirut from March 21, through April 5, 1949. This would become a pattern for the UNCCP over the next several years during the time when it exerted most of its conciliatory efforts: separate meetings with Israel and the Arab states. The atmosphere between Israel and the Arab states was frosty after the armistice agreements signed between January and June 1949, and the Arab states initially demanded that the refugees' right of return was the *sine qua non* of any discussions with Israel. During the Beirut meetings, however, the representatives of the so-called front-line Arab states—Egypt, Syria, Jordan, and Lebanon—indicated that they had dropped their insistence upon the right of return prior to any talks with Israel. At Beirut, the UNCCP's three delegates, Claude de Boisanger, Mark Etheridge, and Hüseyin Cahid Yalçin, met with representatives of the four front-line states plus Iraq and Saudi Arabia. The issue of who would represent the Palestinians themselves proved contentious. The commission refused to invite representatives from the Palestinian nationalist group, the Arab Higher Committee (AHC), to the meetings to sit as official participants, but rather invited the AHC to attend only as one of a number of nongovernmental organizations that met with the UNCCP. The AHC refused. However, the UNCCP conducted hearings with a number of other delegations representing Palestinian refugees in late March. Among these was a delegation from the Association of Arab Landlords of Haifa, including Gabriel Abyad, Faris Sa'd, Raja Rayyis, Hamad Abu Zayd, and the group's secretary, Sulayman Qutran.[5] When discussing both moveable and immoveable refugee property, the delegations from the Arab states complained bitterly about Israel's actions. They stated that Israel was creating facts on the ground by blocking refugees' access to their accounts in banks in Israel and by liquidating other refugee property. For their part, the nongovernmental Palestinian organizations issued pleas for the return of their property. Afterwards, the three UNCCP members met with Ben Gurion in Tel Aviv on April 7, 1949 to discuss what had occurred in Beirut.

Realizing the importance of the refugee property issue to the Arabs, the UNCCP decided to act quickly by bringing up the matter formally with the Israelis. Four days after the commission met with Ben Gurion, the UNCCP delivered a memorandum on the subject to Michael S. Comay of the Israeli Ministry of Foreign Affairs. Comay was a South African born in 1908 who had served in the Jewish Agency's Political Department from 1946–48 before joining the Israeli foreign ministry. He later became Israel's ambassador to the UN, and would come to play an important role in the refugee property question. The UNCCP's memorandum requested that the Israeli government suspend the Emergency Regulations (Absentees' Property) of December 12, 1948 until such time as a final peace settlement could be reached. It further requested "placing of refugee property in the category of 'enemy property' under a custodian."[6] On May 6, 1949, Israeli diplomat Walter Eytan wrote a reply to UNCCP Chair Mark Etheridge. Eytan, born Walter Ettinghausen in Munich in 1910 and schooled in Britain, had only recently immigrated in 1946 after a stint of lecturing at Oxford. He had, however, risen quickly to direct the Civil Service and Diplomatic College of the Jewish Agency in Jerusalem from 1946–48 before becoming Director General of the Israeli Ministry of Foreign Affairs in 1948. In 1949, Eytan headed the Israeli delegation to the armistice talks at Rhodes. Eytan responded to the request to place refugee property under some type of custodian by pointing out that Israel had done precisely that when it authorized the Custodian of Absentee Property to sequester the abandoned land and property. He noted in his letter, "we *did* place property under a custodian, as you requested on April 11, 1949 [emphasis in the original]." Eytan also pointed out that the Israeli government recognized that the refugees were entitled to compensation for the land. But he went on to state what would become a bedrock Israeli principle for decades to come: While Israel owed the refugees compensation, it was keeping their land and would not consider restitution. The Israeli government, he noted, reserved the right to use the abandoned property as it saw fit and may "enact legislation for the more rational use of absentee property."[7] Eytan reaffirmed the Israeli conviction that the refugees' land had been alienated permanently from them when he spoke to the French representative to the UNCCP, Claude de Boisanger, that same month. "If an Arab refugee counts on living again in the house he abandoned... or tilling the fields in the vicinity of the village he once knew, he is living under an illusion."[8]

Indeed, the Israeli government had stated that it would compensate the refugees for their land. Israeli politicians like Moshe Sharett had indicated as much on several occasions. On February 7 and again on February 24, Sharett told the UNCCP prior to its departure for the Beirut meetings that Israel was willing to pay compensation for the abandoned land. His statement also was published in the international press.[9] However, he made clear another cardinal Israeli condition: Compensation would be paid globally and not to individual refugees. Israel from the beginning was making it clear, as Eytan had already done, that it considered individual refugees' legal connection to their lands to have been severed. Israel was responsible to them for compensation as a corporate lot, not individually, but their title to the land was now gone. Sharett noted: "We are definitely ready to accept in principle, that property has to be compensated. What we do not accept is the question of the individual [and] juridical rights."[10]

Internally, Ben Gurion also let it be known to his government that he favored compensating the refugees but only "in principle."[11] Ben Gurion soon clarified this by restricting the land for which Israel was willing to pay compensation to land that actually had been under cultivation—reserving for itself free of compensation the huge stretches of pasture land, arid lands, and so forth that had fallen into Israeli hands. The prime minister was ready to compensate refugees "who had actually cultivated their land."[12] Thus the Israeli attitude toward refugee property quickly was becoming clear: Israel would not return the land (restitution); the refugees' legal title to it was now null and void; and Israel would pay compensation, but only for land actually cultivated and only on a collective basis.

The issue of compensation continued to occupy the international stage in 1949. In May, it was discussed when the UN General Assembly voted to admit Israel into UN membership. Israeli diplomat Abba Eban reaffirmed Israel's readiness to pay compensation during the General Assembly debates on May 5, 1949. One week after General Assembly Resolution 273 (III) of May 11 admitted Israel to the UN, the Arab delegations demanded of the UNCCP the "abrogation of the Absentee Act and annulment of all measures taken in conformity with this act." The Syrian representative summed up some of the Arab objections in a subsequent letter on May 27, 1949. While admitting that countries may supervise the property of enemy aliens during war, he pointed out that the Palestinian refugees were neither enemies nor foreigners. He also noted that such a law could not be valid because it was being applied retroactively to events that had occurred months before the law at a time when the State of Israel did not even exist.[13]

## Early American Approaches to the Question

The United States also was starting to take a look at the issue of refugee property. As a member of the UNCCP, as a major international supporter of Israel, and as a superpower, the United States was keenly aware of the implications of the refugee issue. Although many Americans were concerned about the refugees' fate on humanitarian grounds, U.S. policymakers first and foremost were concerned that without a resolution of the refugee problem in all its aspects, the region might destabilize. U.S. policy toward the refugees was derived from this central point. Early on, the United States established certain policy positions that became "red zones" beyond which it—and through its influence in the commission, the UNCCP too—would not cross. Three early U.S. documents reveal this thinking concerning how to resolve the problem. The first is a memorandum that the Department of State delivered to President Harry S Truman on May 9, 1949 entitled "Palestine Refugee Problem: Financing Repatriation and Resettlement of Palestine Refugees."[14] From the outset, the State Department made two fundamental assumptions. First, the purpose of compensation payments would be to finance the massive resettlement of most Palestinians into the surrounding Arab countries. Second, the United States and the world community would end up paying most of the costs of compensation, not Israel itself. Although the document spoke of the American expectation that Israel would pay compensation for Palestinian land, it also noted that compensation would constitute only a small part of the total cost of repatriating some refugees in Israel and resettling *most* of the refugees in the Arab world. The document estimated that Israel should pay between $US30–50 million in compensation to help defray a total cost of $267.5 million for repatriation and resettlement. The United States, the Export-Import Bank, international banks, and other states and organizations would pay the rest. Table 2.1 details the compensation figures outlined in the document.

Three weeks later on May 31, 1949, the newly formed Central Intelligence Agency drafted a second memorandum on the refugees that is instructive for the light it sheds on American thinking on three particular points. First, it stated that the Palestinian refugee problem threatened U.S. interests by heightening instability in a region already vulnerable to such instability. Second, nowhere did the document mention compensation. This was clearly not a major issue for the CIA as it was for the State Department. Third, the memorandum stated that resettling the refugees in the surrounding Arab countries was the most likely solution to the problem, not repatriation to Israel. Thus, this solution was the one that merited the most American attention.

TABLE 2.1 US State Department Estimate of Israeli Compensation and Costs to Repatriate and Resettle Palestinian Refugees, 1949

| *Item* | *Cost ($US)* | |
|---|---|---|
| 1. Expenses | | |
| Repatriation of 200,000 refugees | 30,000,000 | |
| Resettlement of 500,000 refugees | 160,000,000 | |
| Direct and indirect work relief for refugees | 27,500,000 | |
| Development projects in Arab world | 50,000,000 | |
| TOTAL | 267,500,000 | |
| 2. Revenues | | |
| *To be Received From* | *Minimum ($US)* | *Maximum ($US)* |
| Israeli compensation | 30,000,000 | 50,000,000 |
| International banks; Export-Import Bank | 15,000,000 | 50,000,000 |
| Other states, organizations | 25,000,000 | 50,000,000 |
| US [by reducing capital outlays] | 150,000,000 | 117,500,000 |
| TOTAL | 220,000,000 | 267,500,000 |

Source: United States National Archives and Records Administration [NARA], RG 59, Lot File 53D468/Records of the Bureau of Near Eastern, South Asian, and African Affairs/McGhee Files 1945–53/Box 18. Document: "Palestine Refugee Problem: Financing Repatriation and Resettlement of Palestine Refugees" ( May 4, 1949)

To cite from the report:

> The 725,000 Arab refugees produced by the Palestine war contribute directly to instability in an area of great strategic importance to the US. If this instability is permitted to develop unchecked, it may well lead to the breakdown of the present weak political, economic, and social structures of the Arab states. Even now the Arab states represent a liability in US global strategy. Because of their weakness they could contribute only insignificantly to their own defense or to the defense of US interests in the event of war between the U.S. and the USSR. Before they can become strong and cooperative allies, a long process of political stabilization and economic development must take place. Neither can take place unless the corrosive effect of the refugees on the Arab society is eliminated.[15]

The document went on to state that practically speaking, most refugees would have to be resettled outside Israel. This mammoth task would require international capital outlays to pour into irrigation and land reclamation in the Arab world. Although it stated the cost would be high, the memorandum noted that this would be a small price for the U.S. to pay to shore up so strategically important a region. This was the justification for the proposed massive cost to the American taxpayer of paying for resettling the Palestinian refugees in the Arab host countries.

The third document was a massive briefing book assembled by the Department of State entitled "The Palestine Refugee Problem" and dated August 2, 1949. Throughout this huge set of documents, resettlement of the refugees loomed once again as the only real solution to the refugees' plight. The diplomats who assembled the document devoted no significant discussion either to repatriation or to compensation despite their earlier detailed comments discussed above in the memorandum to President Truman.[16]

The CIA and Department of State documents underscored initial American concern with the refugees, but from the point of view of moving quickly to resettle most of them in the surrounding Arab countries in order to reduce regional instability. The questions of refugee property and compensation payments were subordinate to that goal. This was in line with Israeli thinking. This is not to say that American diplomats were avoiding studying the compensation question; some certainly did. George McGhee of the Department of State asked an official of the American Friends Service Committee whether records existed in Israel that might be helpful in determining the amount of compensation that ought to be paid to refugees.[17] Ultimately, however, the United States remained focused on refugee resettlement first and foremost. Compensation fit into this vision to the extent that it might help facilitate such a goal. It was also clear to the United States from the beginning that Israel would be asked to contribute only a small proportion of the total cost of repatriating some and resettling most of the refugees.

These positions became red lines that American policymakers drew on the theoretical road map of a proposed solution to the Arab-Israeli conflict and the refugee dilemma, lines beyond which they were not prepared to go. Given the Americans' important role on the UNCCP, they were largely able to enforce these red lines within UNCCP policy decisions as well. The United States was clearly the dominant force in the commission. It was one of two global superpowers. It largely financed the UN's operations. The other two members of the UNCCP were American allies in the North Atlantic Treaty Organization (NATO)—France as of NATO's inception in 1949, and Turkey starting in 1952. American insistence on resettling most of the refugees and financing this project with compensation payments would end up playing a crucial role in ebbs and flows of the refugee property question in coming decades.

## Lausanne Conference

Following up on its initial foray into Arab-Israeli conciliation in the Middle East in the early spring of 1949, the UNCCP spent several months later that spring and summer trying to bridge the gaps between Israel and the Arab states at an international diplomatic conference in Lausanne, Switzerland. From April 27 through September 12, 1949, the UNCCP met separately with the Israelis and the Arabs carrying out what the UNCCP called an "exchange of views." In addition to the presence of diplomats representing Israel and the Arab states, three delegations arrived purporting to represent the refugees, including an organization called the General Refugee Congress that had been formed in Ramallah on March 17, 1949. Represented by Aziz Shehadeh and Muhammad Nimr al-Hawwari, the General Refugee Congress was one of a number of Palestinian groups that had sprung up after 1948, each trying to represent a variety of Palestinian interests. The General Refugee Congress was particularly interested in thwarting the efforts of the Arab states and the Arab Higher Committee, the leading pre-1948 Palestinian nationalist body, which was also present to speak on behalf of the refugees. Indeed, the congress later changed its name to the Palestine Arab Refugee Congress and claimed to speak on behalf of many of the refugees. Relations between the refugees groups and the delegations from the Arab states were reportedly hostile, according to chief Israeli negotiator Walter Eytan, who later wrote that Egyptian delegates forcibly ejected a group of refugees who had tried to secure a meeting with them. Eytan also claimed that at a secret meeting he held with one of his Egyptian counterparts the latter revealed his disdain of the refugee question in general by noting, "Last year thousands of people died of cholera in my country, and none of us cared. Why should we care about the refugees?"[18]

The different parties discussed a number of issues with the UNCCP's members, but once again the fate of the refugees loomed large over the proceedings. It was at this important meeting that Arabs, Israelis, and the UNCCP for the first time discussed in detail some of the issues relating to the refugee property question. Along with repatriation, the property question lay at the heart of the discussions. The Israelis explained the activities of the Custodian of Absentee Property. The UNCCP in return hinted to the Israeli delegation that portions of the Absentees' Property Regulations could "aggravate the problem of refugee property and make its eventual solution more complex."[19] Beyond presentation of such mechanical matters, several important issues relating to the refugee property issue were discussed: whether the issue could be addressed separately from overall resolution of the Arab-Israeli conflict; Israeli counter claims for war damages; the fate of refugee orange groves; and the fate of refugee bank accounts blocked in Israel. Already the specific humanitarian question of the refugee property was becoming embroiled in and affected by the wider course of Arab-Israeli relations.

On the broad level, the Israelis insisted on discussing the refugee problem generally and the property question specifically only within the context of resolving the overall Arab-Israeli conflict and not as a separate issue as the Arabs had been demanding. They offered to repatriate 100,000 refugees but insisted that the remainder be resettled in the Arab world as part of a final settlement. Israeli negotiators also set forth their basic demands concerning compensation. They explained that they only were willing to discuss property compensation, not restitution. They explained that Israel was willing to pay compensation into a "common fund" although they made it clear that such compensation would not cover all the abandoned property. Eytan stated on May 5 that Israel would not pay compensation for moveable property. The Israelis also insisted that Israel only would pay compensation for lands that had been cultivated prior to being abandoned. They also noted that the question of compensation could be settled through direct negotiations with the Arabs and the creation of a board to examine the questions. Compensation payments would not be paid to individual refugees or even to the Arab states, but to a "common fund." Beyond all this, Israeli negotiators also stated that any compensation for Palestinian refugee property must be reduced by an amount equal to the cost of war damages suffered by Israel in the 1948 fighting. The Israeli government had begun publicly to demand that any settlement involving compensating Palestinian refugees also must take in account the costs of war damages suffered by Israel during the fighting. Israel insisted that the Arab "invasion" was unprovoked, was the Arabs' fault, and it was thus they who should pay for the damage they had inflicted. Far from just throwing out this issue as a negotiating ploy, the Israeli government hoped to subtract such amounts from any compensation it would have to pay Palestinian refugees. The issue thus became a useful tool when discussing the matter with the UNCCP. The war damages question also was the first example of what would come to be a basic Israeli negotiating position on the property compensation issue that has continued to be asserted until today: Deduct certain costs from any compensation payments to Arabs.

How much had Israel sustained in war damages? As with that of Palestinian refugees, different types of property were damaged. The most pertinent property to this discussion was land and buildings. During the 1948 fighting, 22 Jewish settlements were destroyed. Ten of these were overrun by Arab forces while twelve were destroyed but held by Israeli forces. Besides the loss of buildings, the land on which seven settlements had stood ended up behind Arab lines in the Jordanian-occupied West Bank after the armistice agreements along with one in Egyptian-occupied Gaza. An additional 32 Jewish localities suffered property damage.[20] Yosef Weitz stated that the number of destroyed villages was 23, not 22. Details on these eight settlements left behind Arab lines are discussed later in this study, as is the fate of other Jewish land in the West Bank, Gaza, and the Arab states. The number of Jews made refugees during the fighting varies. U.S. diplomats cited a figure of 7,000 in 1949.[21] The UNCCP's Clapp Mission put the figure much higher at 17,000, although this may have been a typographical error in the document.

Various figures for the amount of war damages suffered in Israel began surfacing publicly in 1948–49. Weitz arrived at a total figure of £I1.5 million, based on rebuilding costs.[22] Press accounts cited a figure of over £P8 million, which was very close to the official amount that the Israeli government had arrived at. Israel began asking its citizens to register any property damages with the Department of Property Damage within the Ministry of War Victims. As of December 12, 1949, the department had recorded 8,598 claims for damaged property totaling £I8,624,100. In addition to this, the Ministry estimated that £I4 million had been suffered in damages to agriculture in addition to the loss of public Jewish institutions in the West Bank and Gaza.[23] By December 31, 1950, a total of 9,510 urban claims had been recorded totaling £I9,197,717.[24] Jerusalem was one of the most heavily damaged areas. By 1950, the Israelis claimed losses of £I2.6 million in that city alone, including agricultural losses.[25]

Israeli attitudes toward the question of war damages are revealed in a 1952 document from the Ministry of Foreign Affairs. The document, entitled "Claims for Jewish Property Frozen in Arab States," discussed Israeli claims for war damages as well. The document is significant first in outlining an overall diplomatic approach for arguing for war damages from the Arabs as it had emerged by 1952. It outlined four types of damages for which Israel should seek compensation from the Arab states. The first was the cost of the Israeli army's expenditures incurred in the "repulsion of the Arab invasion." The second was direct and indirect war damages suffered by individual Jews, private companies, the state, and public institutions. Third, Israel should demand payment for physical and psychological damages sustained as a result of hostile action and the subsequent burden this put on the state. Finally—and significantly—the document outlined yet another dimension of Israel's counter claims that had emerged by 1952: a demand for compensation for the damages to private individuals, companies, the state, and public institutions caused by the Arab states' boycott of Israel and companies doing business with Israel. Besides outlining the overall diplomatic approach, the document also makes it clear that while the Israelis had been publicly using their claim for war damages as a bargaining chip to seek a reduction in the total amount of compensation due to Palestinian refugees, on an internal level they were only just beginning to formulate this policy clearly and establish definite amounts due to them by 1952. The document's author, Shim'on Shapir, noted this point clearly: "It is important to note that work on the wording of these claims and their translation into monetary totals is still in the beginning stages, or even earlier."[26]

Israel's raising of the war damages issue in connection with Palestinian property compensation sidetracked the UNCCP's efforts to deal with the property question separately. In the first place the UNCCP did not go along with the idea that either Israel or the Arabs should demand reparations or war damages from each other. It adopted this line for two reasons. The first was that the commission's overall approach was to seek some kind of limited movement among the parties on tangible issues such as refugee compensation as it was working toward an overall peace settlement. In this regard, it rejected linking Palestinian compensation with other outstanding issues between Israel and the Arab states, although Israel refused UNCCP requests to disconnect refugee property compensation from the framework of an overall Arab-Israeli settlement and deal with it on a piecemeal basis. When the UNCCP wrote to Sharett on June 8, 1950 asking how Israel proposed dealing with compensation, Sharett replied that it would serve no useful purposes to de-link the compensation question from the other dimensions of a settlement, including Israel counter claims. Secondly, the UNCCP had decided as early as October 1949 that war damages lay outside of the specific framework of compensation as delineated in General Assembly Resolution 194 (III) of 1948. The commission understood its mandate to deal with property compensation in the terms of the resolution, which in its opinion dealt only with refugee property, not compensation claims generally. In this context, the UNCCP felt that the section of the resolution dealing with compensation for property destruction only covered the refugees and only covered "illegal" war damages caused by acts such as looting. The UNCCP specifically noted the fact that: "ordinary war damages do fall outside the scope of the resolution of the General Assembly would seem to be clearly illustrated by the legislative history of paragraph 11 of the resolution."[27]

The UNCCP also had to struggle with the Arabs' demands on the refugee issue. Despite Eytan's claim that they did not care about the refugees except as a bargaining ploy, the Arab states did present specific demands in a joint memorandum to the UNCCP on May 18, 1949: a halt to the seizure of Palestinian homes and property; freeing of sequestered waqf property; release of Arab bank accounts frozen by Israel; and repatriation of refugee orange grove owners, plus their workers and technicians. A number of Palestinian nongovernmental organizations also delivered letters to the UNCCP. The Arab Higher Committee demanded, for example, that Israel return both moveable and immoveable property to the refugees in addition to an indemnity. The Jaffa and District Inhabitants Committee dispatched a letter demanding compensation for those refugees who freely chose not to be repatriated.[28] However, the Arabs spoke not just of compensation but also of repatriation and Israeli territorial compromises to allow for this as well, issues that bound up their immediate demands for the refugees with wider diplomatic issues. Thus it was clear as early as the Lausanne Conference that both Israel and the Arabs had extracted the refugee property question from any humanitarian setting or UNCCP attempt to isolate it and had intertwined it instead with the overall international political dimensions of the Arab-Israeli conflict complete with ripostes and counter ripostes.

The question of abandoned orange groves, blocked bank accounts, and abandoned safe deposit boxes also emerged at Lausanne. There was a particular reason for this. The presence of the Palestinian nongovernmental organizations at Lausanne and those that dispatched letters to the UNCCP at the conference underscored another significant point that would affect early diplomatic activity on the property question: the concerns of wealthy refugee land and property owners, such as those who had owned valuable orange groves and maintained bank accounts and safe deposit boxes, received the lion's share of the diplomatic attention. It was clearly these notables who formed the various nongovernmental organizations that besieged the UNCCP with letters about their property, not poor refugees. Representatives of big landowners were present at Lausanne, including Sa'id Baydas of the Jaffa-Lydda Large Property and Orange Grove Owners and Shukri al-Taji al-Faruqi of the Land Owners and Real Interests in Palestine group.[29] Despite Eytan's claims about the poor relations between them, the lobbying of such propertied refugees might explain why the Arab states demanded of the

UNCCP that Israel readmit the owners of abandoned orange groves—generally wealthy Palestinian landowners—as well as their workers in order that they be able to harvest their fruit and reap the financial benefits. It also explains the surfacing of another Arab demand: that Israel release Arab bank accounts and safe deposit boxes that it had frozen in banks now under its jurisdiction. Again, it was generally only the urban wealthy and middle class refugee who possessed such things, not the average poor rural refugee. The focus of Arab efforts at Lausanne to deal with the refugee property question thus dealt with ameliorating the situation of precisely those Palestinian refugees who most easily could weather the financial exigencies of exile in comparison to their poorer compatriots. As is detailed below, this fact was not lost on the Israelis, who in fact would try to dangle the prospect of compensation or access to bank accounts as a way of buying influence among wealthy refugee opinion makers.

In an effort to do something tangible for the refugees besides just talk to the various parties, the UNCCP decided at Lausanne to establish the first of what would come to be several subcommittees and sub-agencies focusing on the rights and interests of the refugees. This marked a new development in the committee's history, one which saw its growth from a three-nation conciliation committee to a more institutionalized body that would carry out its own projects, initiatives, and research independent of the wider twists and turns of conciliation efforts among Arabs and Israelis. The aim of this first body, created on June 14, 1949 and called the Technical Committee, was to assist overall UNCCP conciliation efforts at Lausanne by developing some practical steps on tangible issues relating to the refugees and reporting back to UNCCP mediators. The Technical Committee's terms of reference included eight items, the sixth of which dealt directly with compensation:

> ...study the question and practicable methods for the payment of compensation to refugees not choosing to return to their homes and for loss of or damage to property which under principles of international law or in equity should be made good by the Governments or authorities responsible.

The Technical Committee started its work in Jerusalem on June 22, 1949 and continued to function until September 7, 1949, at which time it issued its report to the American, French, and Turkish diplomats who made up the parent body of the UNCCP. The report reflected the twin desires of seeking specific solutions to the compensation problem and arranging for direct

Arab-Israeli cooperation in the matter. Not only would this approach create movement on the refugee issue but also it would facilitate the UNCCP's wider conciliatory mission by encouraging bilateral Arab-Israeli cooperation in the process. The Technical Committee's report recommended that the UNCCP create a mixed Arab-Israeli working group on refugee compensation that would be headed by a neutral expert or a UN staff member. This mixed committee would supervise the preservation of refugee property in Israel, including the orange groves; determine ownership of the land and evaluate the extent of damage suffered by the property; and gather documents to assist in these tasks, including films of land registers that the British had made prior to their withdrawal from Palestine and that they had stored in London. Israel, however, believed that such a proposal encroached on its sovereignty because the land that the proposed mixed committee would supervise lay within its borders; it thus rejected the idea.

However, the UNCCP nevertheless took up the issue of the orange groves. The commission in fact had begun to look into the matter even before receiving the Technical Committee's final report. The Arab states had delivered a memorandum to the UNCCP on May 18, 1949 calling on it to arrange for repatriation of the grove owners and their workers. "The orange groves constitute the principal wealth of the Arabs in the territory at present occupied by the Israelis," they noted. "According to representatives of the refugees, the value of these groves is approximately £150 million sterling."[30] Shortly after its creation, the Technical Committee tried to form a mixed Arab-Israeli team to visit the groves, but Israel refused to allow this. The Israelis also noted that there was no need for them to repatriate agricultural workers given the presence of labor in Israel. The committee then dispatched a French consultant named Delbes to carry out an inspection tour of the abandoned orange groves. Delbes spent four days (July 7–11) examining about one-third of the groves. He reported back that 50 percent of the groves had deteriorated beyond any hope of revival; one quarter of the remainder was under the care of Israeli authorities. Only the final 25 percent could be saved and used by the refugees if proper care were given to the groves, and with the use of machinery. He also noted that a complete examination of the groves would require eight experts a full two months to carry out. As a result of the study, the UNCCP proposed creating a Mixed Working Group on Oranges that could estimate damage to the groves and recommend measures for their conservation. Terms of reference were drawn up for the Mixed Working Group on September 2, 1949. Once again the idea never got off the ground although the archival record is silent on the reason.

The other issue relating to refugee property that kept surfacing at Lausanne was the matter of frozen refugee bank accounts and items left behind in bank safe deposit boxes. The banks now were located in Israel, which had frozen the accounts of absentees after May 15, 1948. Earlier, on February 22, 1948, Britain excluded Palestine from the sterling area and blocked access to accumulated accounts belonging to the Palestine government to prevent any of the parties involved in fighting in Palestine from accessing them. These accounts consisted of the assets of the Palestine Currency Board and the unspent balance of three different bond issues. Basing itself on the British mandatory Defense (Finance) Regulations of 1941 that dealt with Axis assets, the Israeli government later blocked access to refugee funds in banks in its territory on June 20, 1948. Estimates of the amount of money in the refugees' accounts varied. American diplomats reported in 1951 that the UNCCP estimated that Israel controlled some £P6 million in accounts in Barclays Bank, the Ottoman Bank, the Arab Bank, and the Arab Nation's Bank, along with another £P500,000 in Jewish-owned banks. The commission estimated that these accounts belonged to some 10,000 refugees.[31] For their part, the Americans felt that there was slightly less money involved, some £P5 million. They also felt that a "large proportion" of this money was owned by "not more than 12 ex-Palestinians."[32] One such large account holder was Sidqi al-'Alami. He told a UNCCP official in 1952 that his accounts in Barclays Bank totaled £UK21,000 as of February 1948.[33] Various Israeli sources cited even lower figures, both for the total amount of money involved and the number of accounts. As of December 1948, Israeli press accounts mentioned that the government had blocked 5,833 accounts (see table 2.2 ). The Custodian of Absentee Property later estimated in 1952 that the total amount of blocked accounts was £I4 million, or some $US12 million. By contrast, Israeli authorities that same year reported that only $US1,252,944 in Israeli accounts were frozen in Arab countries.[34]

Israeli negotiators were well aware that the question of bank accounts, like that of the orange groves, was a reflection of vocal propertied refugees' concerns. Some Israeli delegates even declared that the representatives of the Palestinian refugee landowners present at Lausanne cared little for wider national issues but were concerned only with their own personal property. Gershon Avner of the Ministry of Foreign Affairs noted:

> When we met them at Lausanne, they talked only about property and the reunion of families. The talks revolved around bank accounts. They had left the jewelry of their wives in a safe deposit box in Barclays Bank

TABLE 2.2 Refugee Bank Accounts Blocked by Israel as of December 1948

| *Size of Account (£P)* | *Number of Accounts* |
|---|---|
| less than 49 | 2,800 |
| 50–99 | 523 |
| 100–149 | 435 |
| 150–199 | 275 |
| 200–249 | 300 |
| 250–499 | 300 |
| 500–999 | 520 |
| more than 1,000 | 680 |
| TOTAL | 5,833 |

Source: *Ha'aretz* ( July 17, 1951), in Rony E. Gabbay, *A Political Study of the Arab-Jewish Conflict. The Arab Refugee Problem (A Case Study)* (Geneva: Librairie E. Droz and Paris: Librairie Minard, 1959) pp. 366–67

in Jerusalem, for example, and they wanted it back. They had abandoned their orange groves and the fruit picking season had arrived and they wanted to be allowed to go back to pick their fruit or to be compensated for their lost property. They did not ask anything of [Israeli negotiator] Gideon Rafael except the safe deposit boxes and the orange groves. They did not talk at all about the future of the country or about its borders and the talks were devoid of any political meaning. They themselves did not advance any proposal for a political settlement. They sat like sheep in front of Gideon Rafael. They were subservient. They said, "We are pulverized refugees, we are finished as a nation, we lost everything, the Arab states betrayed us, give us back our property." We agreed but there were technical difficulties in carrying out this agreement. In their flight they frequently forgot to take with them their papers and the keys to their safe deposit boxes.[35]

The UNCCP did take up the question of the blocked bank accounts for the first time at Lausanne. Seeking the release of the accounts would not just represent progress in its conciliation mission; the UNCCP knew that proposals for repatriating or resettling the refugees would cost vast sums of money and sought ways to free up capital that could stimulate job creation among the poorer refugees. As early as April 1948, an internal UNCCP memorandum proposed asking the British government what it intended to do with the former Palestine government accounts it had blocked since February 1948.[36] Several days later on April 11 the UNCCP also proposed to the parties at Lausanne that they unblock their respective accounts. The UNCCP discussed the matter with both the Israeli and Arab delegations and received memos from representatives of the refugees. Israel finally agreed on June 27 to discuss reciprocal agreements by which it would release blocked funds but only if the Arab states would release accounts belonging to Israelis that they had blocked. Accordingly, the UNCCP formed another subsidiary body comprised this time of Arab and Israeli representatives, the Mixed Committee of Experts on Blocked Accounts. This body represented the first example of direct Arab-Israeli discussions engineered by the UNCCP and the only mixed committee that the commission ever managed to set up. The mixed committee consisted of one Egyptian, one Israeli, and a chair, who was the UNCCP's highest ranking UN civil servant, Principal Secretary Pablo de Azcárate. These three men met after the Lausanne Conference from October to November 1949 in an attempt to work out an arrangement. The problem that they encountered was that while Israel controlled between £P4–5 million in Arab bank accounts, only Egypt had blocked accounts belonging to Israelis and this amount was significantly smaller than the Arab accounts frozen in Israel. Since the amounts were not at all comparable, Israel refused to release large sums of money for deposit to Arab banks for so little in return.

The committee continued to meet, however, and finally decided on a procedure at the subsequent Geneva Conference on February 15, 1950 that involved a partial, indirect payment of such accounts. Pending a final peace settlement, each refugee who possessed a blocked account in Israel could obtain an advance payment of £P100 in local currency from a financial institution or government in the Arab state where s/he lived. For its part, Israel would deposit £P100 into a fund outside Israel that would be credited to the account of the Arab state involved. A trustee would administer this fund pending a final peace settlement.[37] Israel signed the agreement with Egypt, which acted on behalf of the other Arab states. However, the agreement never was actualized for reasons the archival record does not detail, and the question of the blocked accounts would linger for two more years before another agreement could be reached.

As the Lausanne Conference was winding down, the UNCCP decided to try yet another new approach to the question of the refugees, including compensation. Shifting away from the idea of mixed committees and back toward unilateral commission action, as well as shifting away from micro-level issues like bank accounts and back to macro-level issues of compensation and resettlement, the UNCCP decided to dispatch a study mission to the Middle East. This decision was a follow up to one of the earlier recommendations of the UNCCP Technical Committee to develop a comprehensive regional economic development plan to assist in the resettlement of the refugees in the Arab states. This decision also represented the three-nation UNCCP's essential concurrence with American and Israeli thinking that massive refugee resettlement, not repatriation, represented the most realistic solution to the problem. Basing itself on the charge it received from Resolution 194 (III) of December 1948, the UNCCP officially established the United Nations Economic Survey Mission for the Middle East on August 23, 1949. Part of this plan would include payment of compensation for the refugees' lost property. But the overall "flavor" of the mission's charge was to develop a regional economic development plan that would ease the bitter political feelings about refugee resettlement within the Arab world. This study mission is discussed further below.

In the end, all parties were disappointed with the Lausanne process. The UNCCP had very few tangible gains to which it could point and went on to change its entire approach to the refugee issue and to Arab-Israeli conciliation in general. The United States was frustrated with Israel's refusal to do more about the refugees although by and large it agreed with Israeli priorities. During the conference on May 29, President Truman sent a note to Ben Gurion expressing his "deep disappointment" about Israel's attitude toward the refugees and threatening to re-examine U.S.-Israeli relations as a result. Truman's favorable position regarding Israel in part had been based on his deeply felt humanitarian concern about Jewish Holocaust refugees. He was angry at what he viewed as Israeli hard heartedness toward the Palestinian refugees. Israel did not budge, however, and Truman did not fundamentally alter his stance toward Israel.[38] In fact, the United States adopted a much friendlier tone with Israel thereafter. But its retreat came at a cost: "Far from achieving its intended objective, this abruptly applied and hastily withdrawn attempt at exerting influence had antagonized Israel, impaired future U.S. power, and had had the indirect effect of weakening the CCP since it discredited the Commission's most powerful member."[39]

For its part, Israel emerged from Lausanne frustrated with the role played by the UNCCP. Israel formally notified the UNCCP in the fall of 1949 that it felt that its role should not be one of initiating proposals but rather mediating between the Arabs and Israel, who would respond directly to one another's initiatives. The UNCCP countered on December 10, 1949 that its mandate indeed empowered it to initiate proposals inasmuch as Resolution 194 (III) had transferred the role of the former UN mediator to it. This was not to be the last time that Israel complained about the UNCCP. For the Arabs, movement on the refugee issue remained the *sine qua non* of any wider discussions with the Israelis and so they too came away disappointed from Lausanne.

The Lausanne Conference failed to achieve tangible results on the refugee property question for several reasons. In the first place, Israel insisted on discussing compensation arrangements only as part of a wider set of peace talks between it and the Arabs, even though the UN had called for refugee compensation independent of other factors and issues. (Israel did, however, agree to talks on the specific issue of the bank accounts.) The Arabs refused to enter into wider peace talks until Israel acted on the refugees, immediately embedding the property question within wider diplomatic scuffles between Israel and the Arabs and harnessing the Palestinians' own parochial issue to that of others. Another major reason why compensation was not forthcoming was that the Arabs were suspicious of compensation talks. They categorically refused resettlement of the refugees in the Arab world as an alternative to repatriation, and correctly understood that Israel, the United States, and the UNCCP viewed compensation as the main vehicle by which such resettlement could be financed. This problem further was complicated by the fact that the Arab ranks were split at Lausanne. This was true not only of the Arab states versus the Palestinians, but also among Palestinians as well. Lausanne saw several Palestinians and Palestinian groups vying to represent the refugees. While the General Refugee Congress officially participated, the Arab Higher Committee and other groups were there as well offering testimony and lobbying delegates. The differing priorities between wealthy, propertied refugees and their poorer compatriots was yet another factor that worked against progress on an overall compensation scheme. Since Israel and the United States hoped to use a *collective* compensation payment to finance refugee resettlement, rich refugees knew this meant they would not be compensated for their *individual* property and thus lobbied against the idea. The result was gridlock.

## Clapp Mission

The UNCCP quickly followed up on the idea of dispatching a study mission to the Middle East. It selected an American, Gordon Clapp, to head the United Nations Economic Survey Mission for the Middle East, thereby giving rise to the name the Clapp Mission. Gordon Rufus Clapp was born in 1905 in Wisconsin. After receiving a M.A. from the University of Chicago, Clapp began working for the Tennessee Valley Authority (TVA) in 1933. The TVA was a huge Depression-era governmental project to provide electricity in the southern United States. Clapp rose to chair the TVA starting in 1946, and took time off three years later to serve the UNCCP. The three nations of the UNCCP contributed members to the Clapp Mission: France appointed the diplomat Eirik Labonne while Turkey's delegate was that country's Minister of Public Works, M. Cemil Gökçen. A fourth member was a British diplomat, Sir Desmond Morton, appointed to deal with the financial aspects of the mission's recommendations.

The Clapp Mission reflected the UNCCP's embrace of the American belief that resettling the refugees in the Arab world was the best solution to their dilemma without prejudice to their compensation rights. This belief is reflected in the mission's terms of reference, which included the following charge: "[study] the problem of compensation to refugees for claims for property of those who do not return to their homes, and for the loss of or damage to property with special reference to the relationship of such to the proposed settlement projects."

The UNCCP, then, was officially adopting the U.S. linkage between compensation and resettlement, a policy wholeheartedly embraced by Israel as well. But after touring Lebanon, Jordan, Syria, Israel, and Gaza starting on September 12, 1949, Clapp had his eyes opened to realities in the Middle East. He quickly became eager to caution his own government against undue emphasis on the politically explosive concept of resettlement, however logical such a policy may have been to him. Clapp was made aware of the deep emotional attachment the Arab world had to the Palestinian refugees and the great hostility to any solution to their plight that appeared to compromise their rights to repatriation and/or compensation. He quickly realized that any progress he and the mission could make among the Arabs would be jeopardized by public discussion of the mission's goal of resettlement through regional economic growth. While in Lebanon, Clapp drafted a remarkable letter to Assistant Secretary of State George C. McGhee reporting on his new deference to Arab opinion and laying out his concerns about American policy. He reserved his clearest frustration with American officials who were "berating" the Arabs for their alleged "lack of realism" and for not accepting the concept of refugee resettlement:

> The formal papers which are under preparation setting forth the US position on problems of resettlement and repatriation of the refugees

> cannot, or at best, do not reflect all the circumstances underlying this issue. The purpose of these lines is to enable you, if you wish to advise those concerned in the Department and the UN Delegation, of what the thinking is here and why "resettlement" or even "settlement" are explosive terms.
>
> On the one hand there is the strong moral case of the refugees, recognized by the UN in the December 11 resolution, to repossess properties which were abandoned or from which they were ejected during the war. Unless the US is prepared to argue for a revision of the judgment embodied in the UN resolution, it seems only right that the US should avoid pressing concepts which are regarded as attempts to abrogate the rights recognized in the resolution. To these rights, it is only natural for all refugees to cling. Action by any of the Arab States waiving or prejudicing these rights would be political suicide. Any offer from the outside to finance resettlement, however lavish it might be, would be doomed to failure. Any success the idea of "resettlement" might have promised at one time has been blasted by the fact that "resettlement" has been adopted and promoted by the Israelis as the answer to the problem. It is regarded as their method of disregarding the UN resolution. The Arabs might consider resettlement if Israel were against it. They do not take kindly to a formula originating with the ones who now possess their lands and homes. For all these and other reasons, E.S.M.'s [Economic Survey Mission] success to date in local contacts has been achieved by studious avoidance of reference to resettlement and emphasizing only the advantages of temporary employment for refugees in areas adjacent to their present whereabouts. There is little or no support here, then, for a policy of berating governments and refugees alike for their lack of realism in not accepting a fait accompli in Palestine and proceeding to make the best of a new world with the assistance of friendly Western powers.[40]

Clapp clearly was annoyed at the direction of U.S. policy toward the refugees and, through U.S. domination of it, the UNCCP itself. This is not to suggest that Clapp abandoned the concept of resettlement. To the contrary, he still believed it was "obvious" that massive repatriation by Israel would not take place soon and that resettlement therefore would prove to be the only workable solution. The mission in fact carried out a quick survey of resettlement possibilities in the regions of Aleppo, Hums, and Ladhdhaqiya in Syria, a survey which was "taken very kindly" by Syrian authorities. But Clapp remained committed to what he considered the justice inherent in the refugees' claims, and thus understood Arab opposition to public discussion of resettlement as more than mere bellicosity for the sake of Arab public opinion. He noted as much in his letter to McGhee:

> It appears to those here in the field that considerations which are obviously good local politics in the short run have a substantial basis in terms of justice, whatever may have been the cause of the Palestine war; and a full appreciation of the Arab point of view and patience in reconciling our own plans with Arab susceptibilities, will pay off in all our negotiations with the Arab leaders . . .
>
> This approach accords with the moral judgment expressed in the General Assembly's resolution; it waits for refugees to change *their* minds in circumstances of time and enlarged alternatives; it avoids using the refugees as a club against the Arab States or against Israel. It is a course which has a chance of winning the confidence of people in the Near East, including the people who are refugees.[41]

In addition to gaining an appreciation for what Clapp termed the "justice" inherent in the Palestinian refugees' plight and the extreme sensitivity of discussing their resettlement in the Arab world, the Clapp Mission also came away with a taste for Israel's tough bargaining stance on the matter. On October 10, 1949, the mission met with Dr. David Horowitz, Director General of the Israeli treasury and one of Israel's senior governmental economists. Horowitz was a veteran Israeli financial expert with diplomatic experience. Born in Poland in 1899, he immigrated to Palestine in 1920 and assumed a position on the Histadrut's executive committee. He later served as director of the Jewish Agency's Economic Department from 1935–48, helping to finance Israel's victory in 1948 in the process, before running the new country's treasury from 1948–52. Horowitz later became Israel's second Minister of Finance and, starting in 1954, the governor of the Bank of Israel. His diplomatic experience included organizing Jewish witnesses before the 1946 Anglo-American Commission of Inquiry, serving as a Jewish liaison officer for the UN Special Committee on Palestine in 1947, and serving as a member of the Jewish Agency's delegation at the General Assembly that year. Horowitz offered a frank and acerbic commentary on Israeli policy to Clapp and his committee. He said that his government regretted having publicly committed itself at Lausanne to readmitting 100,000 Palestinian refugees and would try to get out of that promise by claiming Israel already had fulfilled this. He also stated that Israel was highly receptive to the concept of resettling refugees through economic development in the Middle East and felt that Israel would contribute experts for this purpose—something that Clapp clearly felt lessened the idea's appeal to the Arabs. In a comment clearly aimed at compensation, Horowitz stated that Israel could not contribute any money toward resettlement. Just the opposite: He expected that the UN would extend a large international loan to Israel as the industrial and financial center of the Middle East. Horowitz also told the Clapp Mission members that Israel could beat it at the game of international public relations. According to a British account of the meeting:

> Horowitz said openly that he would never admit in public what he had admitted to us in private conversation. He claimed that the Jews were masters of propaganda and distortion and gave many instances. For example, although he knew quite well how we defined the word "refugee" he would make a play in public when the time came that by this word the Jews meant refugees from European persecution. He said that even if the enthusiasm of world Jewry for Israel was waning financially he could always whip it up politically by various devices.[42]

Horowitz also confirmed to the mission that Israel considered buildings as part of abandoned urban land. And a representative of the Israeli government whom Clapp did not name also informed the mission that the amount Israel intended to claim as war damages was expected to be less than the amount payable by Israel as compensation to the refugees.[43]

Chastened by its frank discussions with Arab and Israeli leaders, the members of the Clapp Mission returned to New York and drafted their first report to the UNCCP in November 1949. The "First Interim Report of the United Nations Economic Survey Mission for the Middle East" was quickly showed to UN General Secretary Trygve Lie. The mission's final report, "An Approach to Economic Development in the Middle East," was released to the UNCCP on December 18, 1949. Remarkably, neither of these public documents nor the later "Technical Supplement of Mission" made any detailed reference to compensating the refugees. In a separate November 22, 1949 memorandum to the UNCCP that was not released publicly at the time, however, Clapp discussed the entire topic of refugee property at some length. First of all, Clapp noted that Israel reaffirmed its belief that, while it owed compensation, this should be part of a final peace settlement with the Arabs that would include appropriate deductions for Israeli war damages. It was for this reason that Clapp felt it was premature for the mission to recommend detailed mechanisms for paying compensation to the refugees. Based on legal analysis by the mission's legal advisor, Paolo Contini, Clapp offered the following suggestions to the UNCCP. First, the commission should try to convince Israel to separate the issue of compensation from a general peace settlement and, significantly, to pay compensation both for land *and* moveable property that had been abandoned. He also affirmed the UNCCP's position that the compensation question was not connected to Israeli claims for war damages because the Palestinian refugees were not citizens of the Arab states, and the question of war damages must be carried out among states. To avoid a lengthy process, any compensation should be paid as a lump sum rather than to individual refugee landowners.

One of Clapp's most ambitious private recommendations was that the UNCCP establish a "Refugee Property Trustee." The idea of a property custodian would resurface several times in the ensuing decades, and would be opposed fiercely by Israel and Clapp's own government. Anticipating Israeli objections, Clapp suggested some interesting amended ideas. This body could serve a number of purposes. It could create and manage a trust fund into which Israeli compensation would be paid. The trustee could also appraise the value of the abandoned property based on sampling methods with available records. It could also encourage Israel to accept the principle of compensation without linking it to a peace settlement inasmuch as the General Assembly has established the refugees' rights in this regard. Thereafter, the trustee could negotiate with Israel an amount that the latter would pay as compensation. Beyond this, the trustee could recommend to the UNCCP, its successor, or the General Assembly whether to divide up compensation sums among the refugees on a pro-rata basis or to pay it to a rehabilitation fund that would be administered by a different UN body. Early payment of compensation to the refugees would give them monetary incentives to resettle. If Israel refused his plan, Clapp recommended asking Israel to pay 10–15 percent of the compensation sum right away and pay the rest after a peace settlement. In this case, the UNCCP would *not* exclude war damages from the equation. Additionally, the UNCCP would ask Israel to add an additional amount as compensation for property losses and damages sustained by repatriated refugees.[44]

Clapp's suggestions and his willingness to shift principles underscored what was already becoming clear by late 1949: The compensation issue had become a political football being kicked around by the parties as a bargaining tool. Beyond this, the United States clearly was interested in seeing that the refugee problem be solved via resettlement not repatriation. This soon became the most challenging aspect of the refugee property issue because it hardened the attitudes of the parties and made it more and more difficult for the UNCCP to seek tangible remedies for the refugees. It is worth noting that at the same time the Clapp Mission also considered a subject that some in the UNCCP hoped would lead to at least some modicum of progress on the refugee property issue regardless of whether wider issues of compensation could be resolved: the status of the refugees' blocked bank accounts in Israel. During their tour of the Middle East in the fall of 1949, the commission members made informal inquiries about the possibility of using these funds as part of its overall recommendations for economic development. Clapp and Sir Desmond Morton had been told that the refugees who owned some of the larger accounts apparently were willing to invest the total amount blocked in their accounts toward economic development projects in Jordan. During the same time, officials at the British embassy in Washington met with representatives of the International Bank for Reconstruction and Development (the World Bank) and discussed a related idea: a World Bank loan to Jordan secured by the frozen accounts. British government officials later discussed the idea with Horowitz, who refused any general release of blocked accounts.[45]

The UNCCP accepted some of the Clapp Mission's ideas but rejected others. On the specific question of compensation, it considered Clapp's private recommendations for creating a property trustee "too ambitious" in light of the refusal of the parties to budge from their respective positions, and his proposed property trustee was never created.[46] The UNCCP noted that it did not wish to "prejudice the question at issue," which essentially meant that it did not want to be seen as adopting a position that Israel would reject. The UNCCP did welcome, however, Clapp's suggestion that it make its own "appraisal" of the value of the abandoned property. This independent venture on the part of the UNCCP soon would be carried out as part of a major shift in the conceptualization of its role.

## New Directions for the UNCCP

In 1950, the UNCCP began shifting its attitude toward the appropriate course of action it should take regarding the refugees' property. This attitude reflected its failure to make any meaningful progress on the issue to that point because the parties refused to separate the question of refugee property from their wider diplomatic entanglements. The UNCCP ultimately decided that it should forgo active attempts at mediation and focus instead on tangible, "technical" efforts it could do on its own on behalf of the refugee property. These studies then could be utilized should conditions among the parties reach a stage where they could be implemented.

Before this, however, the UNCCP tried once again to break the diplomatic logjam between Arabs and Israelis when it met separately with the parties in

Geneva from January 30 through July 15, 1950. Like Lausanne, the Geneva Conference tried to deal with a host of issues relating to the Arab-Israeli conflict including the refugee question. Once again, it attempted to establish mixed committees. In January and February, it suggested one mixed committee; this idea failed. In March, it suggested creation of several. This too failed. Overall, the meeting produced no breakthroughs because the UNCCP was unable to overcome the entrenched differences among Arabs and Israelis over basic procedural matters such as whether they should negotiate face-to-face or merely respond separately to UNCCP initiatives.

In light of this, the UNCCP began rethinking its entire approach to "conciliation" in general and problems relating to the refugees—including property compensation—in particular. Such thought actually pre-dated the Geneva talks. Several weeks before the conference on January 3, 1950, the two American delegates to the UNCCP at that time, John W. Halderman and James W. Barco, sent a memorandum to the UNCCP suggesting that it shift course and begin to work on secondary issues where it actually could make some progress on its own without trying to get the parties to work together. In the wake of the Geneva deadlock, the UNCCP still was interested in making some kind of tangible progress on the compensation issue that it could point to and use as a stepping stone to its wider conciliation efforts. It held a series of meetings in August on this subject and decided to create a new subcommittee without joint Arab-Israeli membership, rather like the Technical Committee had been, to carry out a legal and technical study into the compensation question. The UNCCP decided preliminarily that the tasks this subcommittee should perform should mirror those proposed by the Clapp Mission. These included determining what documentation was available for estimating the scope and value of refugee property and then actually estimating this value. The subcommittee also would collect information on the land from the British government and the three governments of the UNCCP, as well as secure information about the Israeli Custodian of Absentee Property from public documents and press reports. The subcommittee would also be tasked to collect information on Israeli laws regarding absentee foreigners, data from Knesset debates, and other Israeli data. After obtaining a preliminary assessment of the land and its value, the subcommittee then would approach the Israeli authorities about the matter. The subcommittee was also preliminarily to find information about sequestered German property in Israel as well as about Israeli claims for compensation and/or reparations from West Germany that first had been raised publicly in 1945 prior to Israel's establishment.[47] The UNCCP knew that it would be very hard to establish a value for every parcel of refugee land because "an appreciable proportion of rural property and agricultural land seems to have been distributed to Jewish immigrants" and so chose to come up with an overall figure.[48]

It is important to note that the UNCCP's shift in approach did not stem just from its failure to realize progress on the refugee question to date. As early as its decision not to forge ahead with Clapp's recommended property trustee for fear it would alienate Israel and thus complicate its mission, the UNCCP had taken a clear decision not to adopt an activist agenda vis-à-vis the parties and particularly not Israel. As the leading force in the UNCCP, the Americans soon had other reasons not to antagonize Israel unduly. These reasons dealt with the geopolitics of the Cold War. In June 1950, the Korean War had broken out. Essentially a proxy war between the United States on the one hand and the USSR (Soviet Union) and China on the other, Korea prompted the United States to shift its foreign policy priorities and alignments. Israel was quick to take advantage of this American desire to court new friends and allies. Despite the presence of pro-Soviet forces in Israel such as MAPAM, Ben Gurion began moving more closely toward the United States and the West as the Korean War became a major international crisis. The United States reciprocated, and began adopting a much more conciliatory attitude toward Israel at a time when it needed allies in the Middle East. The Israelis certainly noticed this new American stance after the beginning of the war. The seasoned Israeli diplomat and Arabist Re'uven Shiloah (born in Jerusalem in 1909 as Re'uven Zaslani) wrote to Walter Eytan in October 1950 noting how the U.S.-Israeli atmospherics had changed for the better "in the last few months." "This shift," he wrote, "can be attributed to Israel's position on the international issues." But Shiloah warned that Israel had been told that it must nonetheless issue a public statement about its "political and moral obligation" to pay compensation for the refugees' property.[49]

In October 1950, the UNCCP followed up on its ideas and established the Committee of Experts on Compensation without seeking to include both the Arab and Israeli membership on a joint committee. Several men eventually were appointed to staff the UNCCP's new compensation committee. Tevfiq Erim was a Turk already in the employ of the UN secretariat in New York. He had experience in the Greco-Turkish population exchange in the 1920s, and was to be the committee's legal expert. Dr. René Servoise of France was the economic advisor. However, this new body soon was sidelined by more serious issues faced by the Americans and the UNCCP and does not appear to have carried out much work at all.

After the failure of Geneva, the Arab states moved their struggle into the halls of the UN itself in an effort to break out of a UNCCP diplomatic process that was not going to pressure Israel unduly. By the fall of 1950, the Arabs clearly were frustrated by the lack of progress on the question of compensation. This frustration was based on Israel's continued insistence on discussing compensation only in the context of peace talks and refugee resettlement outside of Israel. Even though throughout 1950 Israel had restated its intention to pay what Sharett called in May of that year a "vast sum" as compensation, it continued to link compensation with a general peace settlement with the Arabs, and refused to discuss compensation separately.[50] Sharett stated this succinctly in a July 9, 1950 letter to the UNCCP: "no useful purpose would be served by the subject of compensation... being torn out of the general context and treated in isolation from the rest."[51] In fact, Sharett ordered Israel's ambassador to the UN and the United States, Abba Eban, to tell the UNCCP that it should convey to the Arabs an Israeli threat: the Arabs' refusal to come to the negotiating table was liable to prompt Israel to withdraw its compensation offer.[52] Israel also continued to offer compensation only collectively.

In the fall of 1950, the Americans began prompting the Israelis to make some kind of movement on the compensation issue in order to blunt Arab criticism and diffuse Arab attempts at using the General Assembly to pressure the UNCCP. American diplomats urged Israel to consider paying a large sum of money to a "Reintegration Fund," an idea that had germinated within a sister UN organization, the United Nations Relief and Works Agency for Palestine Refugees in the Near East (UNRWA). Following up on the Clapp Mission's recommendations, the UN General Assembly had created the agency through Resolution 302 (IV) of December 8, 1949. The resolution was the initiative of the Americans, British, and French, who wanted to replace the temporary body called the United Nations Relief for Palestine Refugees with something more permanent. UNRWA almost immediately had faced serious funding difficulties. In response, UNRWA's Howard Kennedy proposed creation of a reintegration fund that could receive UN contributions, other contributions, and compensation payments from Israel. Funds would not be paid to individual refugees but would assist UNRWA's overall mandate to aid the refugees. The United States embraced the idea, and asked Israel to declare its willingness to pay an initial sum into a fund in order to be seen as taking steps toward complying with its obligations to pay compensation under paragraph 11 of Resolution 194 (III) of 1948. The United States agreed with Israel that compensation should be viewed as "logically linked with non-return" and so hoped Israel would accede to such a public statement.[53] Beyond that, however, the Americans do not appear to have thought much about how such a fund would deal with the question of compensation. British diplomats seemed to confirm the overall political nature of the fund idea when they reported to London that the Americans actually had not given much thought to the modalities of compensation.[54]

Several months after Israel's announcement, the General Assembly voted to create such a $US30 million fund through Resolution 393 (V) of December 2, 1950. The move did not placate the Arab states, however, which had objected to the idea of a reintegration fund. Speaking for Jordan, Ahmad Tuqan told the UN General Assembly's Ad Hoc Political Committee that it "would be prejudicial at [this] stage to suggest a reintegration fund designed to absorb the private wealth of the compensated refugee."[55] Israel, however, quickly accepted the idea. Eban announced at a New York press conference on December 21 that Israel was willing to pay £I1 million into the Reintegration Fund but only if it were released from paying individual compensation. Sharett also announced to the Knesset that Israel would pay into such a fund if it absolved the Jewish state of having to pay individual compensation. He also had ideas about where to get the money: he directed Israeli diplomats to include a certain amount for compensation in Israel's application for American grants-in-aid. Israel then could sell donated American aid for hard currency which would be paid into a counterpart fund, which is what India was doing.[56] Interestingly, the United States later had similar thoughts about Israel using American aid to finance compensation. In November 1952, the Department of State felt that perhaps Israel could set aside some of the aid money it received from the United States for compensation, or at least service a loan with compensation with it.[57] Frustrated with the lack of progress on compensation and their perception that the UNCCP was unable to stop Israeli seizures of refugee land, the Arabs simultaneously were working on a different strategy in the General Assembly in the fall of 1950. In the assembly's Ad Hoc Political Committee, Egypt called on the UNCCP to create an office to protect refugee property and deal with compensation. The campaign succeeded. On December 14, 1950, two weeks after agreeing to creation of the Reintegration Fund, the General Assembly passed Resolution 394 (V) calling on the UNCCP to establish an office that would oversee implementation of paragraph 11 of Resolution 194 (III) of 1948 calling for compensation.

Having just decided to create the Committee of Experts on Compensation that October, the UNCCP responded to the resolution by establishing the Refugee Office on January 25, 1951 and transferred its compensation staff to it. The Refugee Office marked a real departure for the UNCCP. It heralded the fact the UNCCP had all but given up hope of realizing a comprehensive diplomatic solution to the Arab-Israeli conflict. Instead, it had chosen to focus on narrower issues where its efforts might make progress, helping to create good will among the parties on which to base future efforts and assisting the refugees in concrete ways in the process. It also represented the UNCCP's admission that compensation had become so politically loaded that the commission would have to develop ideas about it on its own and not rely on direct Arab-Israeli discussions. The Refugee Office's real work commenced in May 1951 with the appointment of Holger Andersen as director of the office. Andersen was a Dane who, like Erim, had been involved in the Greco-Turkish population transfers in the 1920s. The UNCCP notified the concerned governments of Andersen's appointment on May 15; one week later he arrived at its offices in Jerusalem. The Refugee Office's terms of reference regarding the compensation issue were to determine a method for compensating refugees who chose not to return to their homes in consultation with the Arab states and with UNRWA. Furthermore, the office was charged with investigating compensation for individual refugees as well as studying how Israel would be able to pay. Finally, it was tasked with studying how Israel would pay for damages to the property of repatriated refugees.

If the UNCCP hoped its shift toward focusing its efforts on technical aspects of the refugee problem would clear the way for it to make meaningful progress on the question of refugee property, it was mistaken. The UNCCP placed great hope in the formation of its new Refugee Office under Holger Andersen and earnestly looked for it to create, as de Azcárate expressed, a "miracle" that could erase the stigma of the UNCCP's failures.[58] The commission still faced Israeli opposition to its very existence and efforts. Publicly, Eban pledged on November 7, 1950 that Israel would cooperate with the UNCCP's efforts to evaluate how much property the refugees had left behind. Privately, however, Israel placed conditions upon its cooperation with the efforts of the new Refugee Office and its attempts to deal with compensation. In a January 30, 1951 internal memo, Israeli officials laid out five overall conditions for such cooperation. Israel clearly was willing to pay compensation only for cultivated land, only on a collective basis, only if it were used for resettling the refugees in Arab countries, only if it released Israel from any further payments to the refugees, and only if it were part of a general peace settlement with the Arabs. Beyond this they discussed four specific conditions. First, Israeli payment of compensation was dependent upon signing a peace treaty with the Arabs. Second, payment only would go toward the Reintegration Fund, an act that subsequently would release Israel from any claims to or responsibility for payment to individual refugees. Third, Israel only would pay compensation for cultivated land as recorded in mandatory tax records. Finally, Israel only would pay compensation if UNRWA were then obligated to resettle the refugees in the Arab world. Israel thereafter would have no more financial obligations to them.[59]

Israel continued to attack the UNCCP throughout 1951. At a meeting in Paris on December19, Sharett told Britain's representative to the UN that the UNCCP actually had hindered rapprochement between Israel and the Arabs. He went on to say that Israel was in favor of dissolving the UNCCP and creating a new body called the "Good Offices Committee" that would not be stationed in the Middle East, as the UNCCP had been, but in New York. Revisiting Israel's earlier complaints about the UNCCP's mediation role, Sharett proposed that this new body would not devise peace initiatives on its own nor even issue annual reports to the UN as the UNCCP did.[60] Israel suggested that this new committee be made up of the same three members as the UNCCP, although the Israelis indicated they preferred dropping Turkey in favor of the UK.

## UNCCP's Global Estimate

The UNCCP's new Refugee Office was given a major task soon after it began functioning in May 1951: to undertake a study to determine the scope and value of the property abandoned by Palestinian refugees in Israel. This would be the first of two major studies of the question undertaken by the UNCCP. The UNCCP wanted the Refugee Office to conduct a survey of the value of refugee property as well as to study specific procedures for compensating the exiled owners. While this occurred, the parent body would discuss with the parties whether the compensation question should be settled prior to a general peace settlement and whether compensation should be paid for noncultivated lands. The UNCCP's specific ideas about what the Refugee Office should accomplish were developed in the spring of 1951 and laid out in a March 16, 1951 meeting between the Deputy U.S. Representative to the UNCCP, James W. Barco, and British Foreign Office official Geoffrey Furlonge in London. The plan called for tasking the Refugee Office to survey mandatory land records for Palestine that the British government had preserved in order to arrive at a general estimate of the value of abandoned refugee land. Israel then would be told the amount, without prejudice to the questions of Israeli counter claims or the methods of paying compensation. UN member states would then contribute to a loan fund in order to lend money to Israel to cover the costs of compensation. Israel would then begin repaying its debts to a separate fund controlled by the UNCCP (presumably, the Reintegration Fund called for by the General Assembly).[61]

While they were formulating the procedures that the UNCCP Refugee Office should adopt, American diplomats also were assuring the Israelis that they would not be responsible for paying the entire amount developed by the office. Barco and fellow American UNCCP official Ely E. D. Palmer met with Sharett to discuss how the UNCCP envisioned compensation would work. They assured Sharett that while the Refugee Office would base compensation figures on the abandoned property's *value*, the method of payment would be based on Israel's *ability to pay*. Israel would pay into a fund as it had agreed to, and not to Arab governments or individual refugees. The fund in turn would issue compensation payments to specific refugees, not to the governments of the states in which they resided. The UNCCP in general would restrict usage of the payments for resettlement purposes as the Americans wanted. In order to do this, the commission would try to "scale down" compensation claims from big landowners and "scale up" those from smaller owners given that the poorer refugees stood in great need of money for resettlement. The two men also told Sharett that Israel would need to settle the compensation first before dealing with any counter claims.[62] The UNCCP's insistence on de-linking compensation with Israeli counter claims also was discussed at Andersen's June 23, 1951 with Jordan's King 'Abdullah and Prime Minister Samir al-Rifa'i. Andersen assured them that Israeli counter claims were "unconnected" with compensation. He outlined that figures for compensation would be global, which was the best method, and would include Jerusalem.[63]

The UNCCP was in a hurry for the Refugee Office to arrive at compensation figures. Part of the reason was because the UNCCP needed to report its progress on the matter to the General Assembly session that would begin in November 1951, and it wanted to be able to report progress. However, the compensation question also had seemed to take on a new urgency for a different reason by the spring of 1951: UNRWA indicated to the UNCCP that it thought the Arab states were preparing to resettle the refugees. Because compensation had long been linked with resettlement in the minds of many, including the UNCCP, it ordered its Refugee Office to carry out its study of refugee land quickly. The UNCCP also sought UNRWA's cooperation in the matter by distributing a questionnaire asking refugees about compensation. The UNCCP assured UNRWA that compensation would be paid to individuals because this is what the United States wanted.

Creation of the Refugee Office also coincided with the emergence of a second American red line around the property compensation issue: the UNCCP should not produce compensation figures that were too high for Israel to pay. This thinking was spelled out in a working paper drawn up by the UNCCP in February 1951. Referring to any compensation figure that Israel cannot pay, the document noted "[i]t would be useless... it is clear that compensation—being part of the general Palestine problem—is a *political* and not a *book-keeping* question [emphases in the original]." Reflecting the American red line, the UNCCP felt that producing a figure that was too high for Israel realistically to pay would be ill-timed and unnecessary. It believed that compensation was a political matter, and that the real issues were not paying individual refugees the value of their abandoned property but Israel's willingness and ability to pay, the procedures for payment, and the international aid required for payment. Thus, the working paper noted that the Refugee Office should develop an informed *estimate* of the overall value of the abandoned land that could help the political work of the commission.[64] Such work included resettling the refugees, so the UNCCP sought to base compensation in part upon the cost of resettlement. The UNCCP also decided that its mission was only to compensate *Palestinian* Arabs who had abandoned property in Israel. Non-Palestinians could seek redress from their respective governments.[65]

Since the refugee land was situated in Israel, the UNCCP also knew that Israeli cooperation with the study of the property was crucial. Israel had said it would cooperate with the UNCCP's efforts to determine figures on the refugees' land, but as noted above, privately it conditioned its cooperation upon certain outcomes. The private conditions soon became public reality when the Refugee Office began asking the Israelis pointed questions about the policies adopted by the Custodian of Absentee Property. Even earlier, in November 1950, the UNCCP had tried to get the Israelis to discuss what the Custodian had been doing with the land. As part of the Refugee Office's efforts to study the question, Holger Andersen also asked the Israelis about the Custodian. He met with Sharett in Jerusalem on June 7, 1951 and with staff members of the Ministry of Foreign Affairs in Tel Aviv the next day. Andersen discussed with them the idea of the Refugee Office carrying out a study of compensation, although he admitted that the office did not yet have a clear idea about how to go about it. He also gave a questionnaire to the Israelis that inquired about the Custodian and other Israeli agencies dealing with refugee land. The Israelis stated that they were ready to hand over the Custodian's property lists but would not reveal what they actually had been doing with the land since its sequestration, calling this "irrelevant" to compensation. Interestingly, the Israelis hinted to Andersen that they might not provide the Refugee Office any information on abandoned urban property. To them, these Palestinian buildings were not assets: the fighting had damaged many of them, and Israel was not liable for such war damages. The buildings may have to be demolished. Bringing up the war damages claim, they noted that damage to Jewish buildings must also be considered in the equation.[66]

The man assigned to carry out the global estimate of refugee property losses was the Refugee Office's British land expert, John Measham Berncastle, who would end up becoming one of the most knowledgeable and influential persons ever to become involved in the long story of the refugee property. He would go on to become the architect of the UNCCP's later lengthy endeavor to quantify the refugees' individual property losses in the 1950s and 1960s. Born in 1906, Berncastle had worked as a land valuer for the Government of Northern Ireland from 1932–35, before transferring to the Palestine government in 1935. After working as Assistant Agent and later Acting Agent for the Haifa Harbour (Reclaimed Area) Estate from 1935–38, he became a land officer and eventually rose to serve as Chief Land Valuer for the mandatory government's Department of Land Settlement. After termination of the mandate, Berncastle returned to Britain and continued his government service in the Ministry of Local Government. He thus possessed an expert background for the responsibility he had to shoulder. The British government agreed to second him to the UNCCP in February 1951, and he arrived in Palestine on April 23, 1951 to begin work at the Refugee Office in Jerusalem in May.

The Global Estimate of overall refugee losses that Berncastle worked on was to do two things: determine estimates of how much land the refugees had left behind and how much it was worth. Berncastle also studied the value of moveable property left behind. The first step in this huge task was to search for available records upon which to base this task. Berncastle initially was nonplussed that Israel did not eventually follow through with information from the Custodian of Absentee Property. Such information would be coming from an "interested party" in the matter, he reasoned, and would also make the Arabs suspicious. The UNCCP never went so far as even to ask to inspect abandoned land.[67]

Berncastle wanted more neutral records. As a former employee of the mandate government, Berncastle was well aware of the rich land registration and land taxation records maintained by the British in Palestine from 1920–48. He traveled to London and visited the Palestine section of the Colonial Office in March 1951 to discuss access to these documents. He was given a copy of the mandatory publication, *Village Statistics, 1945*, an exhaustive study of land throughout Palestine. He also took an index to 2,160 films that the British had made of mandatory land records shortly before the end of British rule in 1948 (see chapter 4). If he decided that he needed a particular roll of film, Berncastle made arrangements with Kodak, Ltd. of London to copy that roll. He also borrowed some Colonial Office maps showing the location of state land, Jewish-owned land, and the progress of the mandatory "land settlement" process in Palestine. Back in Jerusalem, the Israelis gave him a 1/150,000 map of villages in Palestine entitled the "Index to Villages and Settlements." Armed with these basic documents, Berncastle set to work.

Determining what land to count and how to count it as refugee land was a major challenge. Berncastle later noted that four possible methods of estimating the scope of abandoned land presented themselves. The first was to submit a questionnaire to all refugees asking them for details about their lost land, including submitting any deeds or other documents they still might have in their possession. The Refugee Office staff then could check the results against the British films as well as from mandatory land tax records. This method, Berncastle noted, was fraught with problems. Not the least of these challenges was the fact that it first would necessitate copying and purchasing all the films from British authorities in London. It would also require considerable expertise both from the refugees, in terms of accurately listing the exact details of their land, and from the Refugee Office's staff in interpreting the British records. Berncastle also noted that much refugee land was collectively owned and that describing any individual's particular share of ownership in such land "would probably be quite beyond the powers of the average Arab fellah unless he had expert assistance to complete the questionnaire for him."[68]

The second method that could be used to determine the amount of abandoned land would be to use the films only. Berncastle noted that the nature of the records on film varied, making the task of identifying specific parcels of Arab-owned land difficult in a short period of time. The Refugee Office also would need either to print the films' images onto paper or project them in order to read them. The third method would be to base the study on the records of the Custodian of Absentee Property, an idea Berncastle dismissed for reasons noted above. The final method, which Berncastle adopted, was to use the information on land and land values contained in the copy of *Village Statistics, 1945* that Colonial Office authorities had given him in London. Berncastle was aware that certain Arabs already had criticized the accuracy of the information contained therein. Yet he upheld *Village Statistics* as sound and unbiased. As a former employee of the British Department of Land Settlement in Palestine, his belief in the impeccability of "neutral" British record keeping was undoubtedly a personal assessment of his own years of colonial service. He wrote of the figures in *Village Statistics* as representing:

> years of conscientious work by officials of the mandatory government, and may at least be regarded as unbiased since they were prepared at a

> time when their use for the present purpose was unthought of. Although it may be easy to point to inaccuracies of particular figures from which the statistics were compiled, e.g. of assessments of particular properties; nevertheless when taken as a whole, they are at least as likely to be accurate as the opinions of individuals, especially of interested parties.[69]

Berncastle decided that the quickest and most accurate way of measuring the scope of refugee losses would be to use the fourth approach, i.e., to base his study on the data contained in *Village Statistics*. He consequently did not purchase copies of the British films at that time. Although using *Village Statistics* was the quickest approach, Berncastle was anxious to allay suspicions that he resorted to this method for reasons of expediency alone. He took great pains to explain that this was also the soundest method, and pointed out the figures in *Village Statistics* had been "prepared by an authority [the former mandatory government] which has no direct interest in the outcome of any dispute as to the amount of compensation payable by Israel for lands of Arab refugees."[70]

How much land should be counted as "abandoned" refugee land? The UNCCP already had decided on May 31, 1951 to exclude from the assessment land in the Israeli-Syrian and Israeli-Egyptian Demilitarized Zones (DMZs) and from the so-called No Man's Land along the Israeli-Jordanian front lines in Jerusalem.[71] Given these exceptions from the Refugee Office's parent body, Berncastle adopted a very important definition of what constituted Palestinian refugee land: all lands "which were formerly held by Arabs and which have now passed into the hands of the Israel Government or its agencies."[72] To arrive at this, Berncastle resorted to maps. He took the 1/150,000 scale map showing village boundaries that he had obtained from the Israeli government and superimposed on it the armistice lines he took from a map supplied to him by the United Nations Truce Supervisory Organization (UNTSO). The result showed him which Palestinian villages were now under Israeli jurisdiction. Since the UNTSO map did not show the DMZs, Berncastle's staff had to draw those lines on the map themselves. He then referred to *Village Statistics* to determine how much land was contained in each of those villages. In cases where the armistice lines cut through a village, Berncastle resorted to maps showing state land and Jewish-owned land and to simple estimation of what percentage of a village's lands remained in Israel. While admitting that this produced "approximate" figures, Berncastle felt that overall any resulting errors would balance themselves out in the end.

Berncastle faced a different problem concerning those Palestinians who had not fled as refugees but remained in what became Israel. Clearly, their land could not be counted as "refugee" land in his opinion and must be deleted from the totals. Israeli census data from December 31, 1949 showed 95 Palestinian villages in Israel. Eleven of these were not included in the mandatory statistics; Berncastle felt these were probably parts of other villages counted by the British. The result, he believed, was that 84 villages remained under Israeli control and that most of their population had stayed. He then concluded that this population had remained in control of their land. However, although these people were not "refugees" in the sense that they had not fled outside the borders of Palestine in 1948, thousands of them in fact had been declared "present absentees" by the Israeli government and had their land confiscated. In other cases, land within a village may have been owned by a refugee who had fled, in which case the Custodian of Absentee Property could confiscate it. So while Berncastle's assumptions served the purpose of his approximate study, they did not reflect the actual status of all Palestinian land left in Israel. The UNCCP considered that its mandate covered only Palestinian refugees in exile who had lost their lands, not those remaining within the sovereign territory of Israel.

Berncastle worked separately on land in Jerusalem because of its special status. The Israeli-Jordanian armistice agreement had left the city in three parts: Israel-controlled West Jerusalem, Jordanian-controlled East Jerusalem, and the so-called "No Man's Land" straddling the cease-fire line between them. Israel was more accommodating in supplying information to Berncastle on Jerusalem, and actually provided access to the Custodian of Absentee Property's register of abandoned land in Jerusalem. He also consulted mandatory "field valuation sheets" used for assessing urban taxes.

Berncastle worked on his study throughout the summer of 1951. His final report of August 14, 1951 was entitled "Valuation of Abandoned Arab Land in Israel." He concluded that a total of 16,323,971 dunums of Palestinian land had passed into Israeli hands, excluding Jerusalem, which was assessed separately. In Jerusalem, the figure was 5,736 dunums. This is detailed in table 2.3.

Berncastle's estimate of the scope of abandoned refugee land was *eight times* larger than the one arrived at by the Israel's Weitz-Danin-Lifshits Committee, although Israeli authorities had denied his request to see that committee's report. In particular, Berncastle had included *all* land that he considered Arab-held that had ended up in Israeli hands, not just privately owned, regularly cultivated farmland as the Israelis had been insisting. Besides collectively

TABLE 2.3 Scope of Refugee Land According to UNCCP's (Berncastle's) Global Estimate, 1951

| *Type of Land* | *Mandatory Tax Categories* | *Amount (Dunums)* |
|---|---|---|
| 1. Northern and Central Palestine | | |
| Citrus | 1–2 | 120,564 |
| Bananas | 3 | 620 |
| Village built-up areas | 4 | 14,602 |
| Irrigated, plantations, etc. | 5–8 | 303,750 |
| Cereal land | 9–13 | 2,113,183 |
| Cereal land | 14–15 | 201,495 |
| Uncultivable | — | 1,431,798 |
| TOTAL | | 4,186,012 |
| 2. Beersheba District | | |
| Cultivable | — | 1,834,849 |
| Uncultivable | — | 10,303,110 |
| TOTAL | | 12,137,959 |
| 3. Jerusalem | | 5,736 |
| TOTAL | | 5,736 |
| GRAND TOTAL | | 16,329,707 |

Source: "Valuation of Abandoned Arab Land in Israel" (see note 67)

owned land, he also included millions of dunums of non-Jewish, uncultivable land in the southern Beersheba district as Arab-held. But what proved most controversial when his figures became public were not Berncastle's estimates of the scope of the land but its value. Since ultimately the question of compensation came down to a monetary figure reflecting the land's value, not its scope, it was valuation that the Arabs and Israel paid the most attention to. Much of the controversy would boil down to the basis upon which Berncastle valued the land and the prices he used. Berncastle systematically explored how to do this. His report outlined three methods that he could have used. The first was to study the prices paid for land in Palestine as recorded in the filmed copies of mandatory land records. There were several problems with this approach. First, the land registers did not include a detailed description of each parcel of property. This meant that someone would need to inspect each parcel of land. Nor did they record the sale price and officially estimated value of each parcel for the same date: this was only recorded on a piecemeal basis when an individual parcel was sold. The second method was to look at the assessed value of land contained in mandatory tax records that were available in condensed form in *Village Statistics*. The final method was for Berncastle to use his own experience as a land valuer in Palestine together with consensus opinions of land prices—if these were possible—from among Palestinian and Israel land experts. Berncastle decided to adopt a combination of the second and third approaches, using the *Village Statistics* as his base.

Berncastle once again defended his choice of relying upon the *Village Statistics*. He argued that it was not only simply quicker to do so but also more reliable. He once again asserted that the figures for land values contained in the book were collected by a neutral authority several years before the entire question of refugee land was even an issue. Berncastle also noted that *Village Statistics* offered figures for all Palestinian land and not just what had been registered. He also felt that the land values reflected true land values and not the speculative high prices caused by high demand and laws that restricted where Jews could buy land. Berncastle stated that the basis for mandatory land valuation had been the estimated agricultural productivity (for rural land) and estimated rent (for urban land).

Even after arguing that the *Village Statistics* constituted the best basis for determining land values, Berncastle still wanted his bosses sitting on the UNCCP itself to make the political decision of how to determine the method of establishing actual prices. He therefore prepared a working paper for the UNCCP that offered five methods for arriving at values from the tax assessments and asked the Americans, French, and Turks to choose from among them.[73] The five methods were: to capitalize the assessment value in *Village Statistics*; capitalize and then "weight" the figures to account for actual prevailing prices both by the end of the mandate and as of mid-1951; use actual market values as the basis instead of *Village Statistics*; estimate the replacement value of land ("what it would cost Israel to create the abandoned Arab assets if she [sic] had to start from scratch"); and estimate the value on the basis of reinstatement. By "reinstatement" Berncastle meant: "what it would cost to reinstate each refugee in one of the Arab countries in a position as nearly as possible equivalent to the position which he has lost."[74]

In other words, what would it cost to buy similar land in a neighboring Arab country? The three member states of the UNCCP met on May 14, 1951 and decided to combine the second and fifth methods. Berncastle later came to the conclusion, however, that the fifth method was impractical. It was simply too difficult to obtain land prices in surrounding countries and to try to determine what types and qualities of land in Jordan, Lebanon, Syria, etc. were comparable to the lands abandoned in Palestine.

Ultimately, Berncastle ended up using the following formula for valuating refugee land:

> Under the prevailing circumstances the [Refugee] Office concluded that the fairest basis was the value of the abandoned land in its existing use with regard to its capacity to produce income in the form of crops or rent, but ignoring any speculative elements of value which might be due to the possibility of its being converted to some different and more valuable use, in so far as such speculative elements exceeded the normal. It must be appreciated that in Palestine much of the land had what might be called a fictitious market value which was in no way justified by the income derived from its existing use or by a normal expectation of development. This fictitious value, in so far as it exceeded the normal developmental value which attaches to undeveloped land on the outskirts of towns everywhere in the world, was due almost entirely to the pressure of Jewish immigration and land hunger and to the flow of Zionist capital from all over the world into Palestine for the purpose of land purchase.[75]

That is, he decided to put a value on refugee land based on a formula of "existing use value plus normal development value" and to disregard the land's potential value in the future to Jewish land purchasers. In this he agreed with the prevailing Israeli view. He would assign values to land used for agriculture, for example, on the basis of the income it could produce from crops—not on the basis of higher prices that such land *might have* fetched at some future date. Berncastle dismissed outright the high prices for land in Palestine in the late 1940s as "fictitious," something that later would outrage Arab critics of his study. Berncastle not only just credited Jewish demand for land for causing prices to rise to such fictitious levels, but also pointed out that mandatory restrictions on where Jews could buy land and Palestinian nationalist efforts to halt sales of Arab land to Jews had conspired to drive up the price.

Berncastle was indifferent to Arab complaints that his values were too low and did not reflect the reality of land prices in Palestine. He dismissed the Arab argument that even land sold between two Palestinians without regard to Jews or land transfer regulations was expensive:

> it appears that in the past, Arabs who sold their land benefited personally as a result of the Arab national policy, by obtaining greatly enhanced prices. The argument, which is sometimes put forward, that

> similar prices were paid in sales between Arabs, is a superficial one because, obviously no Arab would sell land to another at £P x per dunum knowing that the buyer could promptly resell to Jews at twice the amount.[76]

Berncastle also pointed out that had the Palestinian national movement succeeded in its aim of halting Jewish land purchases, these artificially high land prices would have come to an end. Now that the Palestinians had lost the struggle and become refugees, he deemed it "unreasonable" that they should receive high levels of compensation reflecting high prices for land that they had tried to keep out of Jewish hands by force:

> Had the Arabs succeeded during the mandatory regime in bringing about their avowed object of completely prohibiting further Jewish immigration or land purchase; or had they succeeded in liquidating the State of Israel when they resorted to arms in 1948; these fictitious values would have disappeared. It seems unreasonable that, having been unsuccessful in their resort to arms, the Arabs should get more by way of compensation for their land than they would have been able to get by way of sale had they been successful.[77]

He was also sure that the Israelis never would agree to pay compensation based on the high, fictitious land prices anyway and agreed that this would be an unreasonable expectation. Berncastle did have a soft spot in his heart for the "peace loving refugee who took no part in politics and only left his property in the hope of avoiding trouble." Cases where a Palestinian had bought land at high prices for her/his own use deserved "sympathy and special consideration" in any future plan for payment of individual compensation, although he did not specify on what basis a refugee would prove his or her innocent, nonpolitical nature. Berncastle also rejected the proposal submitted by representatives of the refugees that in determining the value of urban land he should use the "contractor's method" of adding the value of the land together with the value of any buildings on it. Berncastle argued that most of the time the total value of urban property did not equal the sum of the land and the buildings and in some cases, like rent-controlled buildings, actually might be less than if the site were vacant and then developed.

After deciding that he would base refugee land values on the formula of "existing use value plus normal development value," Berncastle then had to decide the date on which the existing use value would be based. After consultations with the UNCCP's legal advisor, he decided to establish land values as of November 29, 1947, the date that the UN General Assembly passed the partition resolution. Berncastle knew this date would infuriate the Israelis, who continued to argue that they were responsible for refugee property only after it had come under the authority of the Custodian of Absentee Property several months later. They believed that any compensation figures therefore should be based on the value of the land once the Custodian took hold of it. Since the war had damaged some of the property, it naturally would be worth less. Berncastle noted, however, that although the Israelis did not want to assume the costs of depreciation to Arab property associated with the war, they continued to insist that the Arabs indemnify *them* for war damages to their *own* property:

> In short, the Government of Israel repudiates any liability in respect of damage which occurred to the abandoned property between 29 November 1947 and 2 December 1948, no matter how or by whom such damage was occasioned. On the other hand, the Government has stated that it intends to counter-claim against the compensation due to refugees for damage which occurred to Jewish property during the same period.[78]

He also defended use of the November 29, 1947 date on the grounds that the Israelis in any event had refused to allow him to investigate any changes to the property made by the Custodian, claiming that such an investigation would be irrelevant.

Having established the bases of his valuation work, Berncastle set about the business of actually determining the amounts. As noted in table 2.4 below, he listed how much land had been abandoned in each mandatory tax category. His next step was to capitalize this figure, i.e., establish the land's actual value as of November 29, 1947 based on the tax figure assessed by the British on each category of land. The last year of tax data Berncastle had at his disposal was from 1947. Berncastle then multiplied the 1947 tax rate by ten to achieve the "net annual value." He then obtained the capital value from the net annual value by multiplying the latter by 30. In the case of land in tax categories 5–8 (irrigated land, fruit plantations, and first grade crop land), he first "weighted" the net annual value before multiplying it by 30. He did this to account for the fact that while the value of all land rose during the Second World War, largely due to the drop in purchasing power of the currency, the value of irrigated land rose comparatively more than cereal land.

The cases of land planted with citrus and banana trees presented special problems. Berncastle agreed with those Israeli negotiators who had argued that Palestinian citrus groves had deteriorated considerably as a result of the Second World War. He decided that the figures for the mandatory tax categories 1 and 2 were consequently of no value to him. Instead, Berncastle consulted with Palestinian and Israeli experts as to the value of citrus land in 1947. The former cited values of £P120/dunum, while the latter cited £P75/dunum. Berncastle believed that other evidence pointed to the Israeli assessment as closer to the mark, and he settled on a figure of £P80/dunum. He also felt that the tax value of banana land in tax category 3 was also useless, and adopted a figure of £P80/dunum based on the similarity of the "lot viable" for each kind of fruit (the amount a cultivator would need to have to be economically viable). Berncastle felt that putting a value on the built-up, residential parts of villages (category 4) was even more complicated. Using tax figures, he compromised with a figure of £P150/dunum. When it came to uncultivable land, Berncastle assigned this land no value at all. Finally, Berncastle tackled the problem of rural land in the Beersheba District. Mandatory authorities did not tax cultivated land in this southern region of Palestine according to one of the 16 tax categories. Certainly one reason for this was that most of these lands were never registered. Instead, they assigned a lump sum tax on the entire area that was subdivided. Using a variety of sources, Berncastle arrived at a figure of £P3.600/dunum for cultivated land in the Beersheba District (see table 2.4).

Turning to urban land, Berncastle noted that the following Palestinian towns that had been legally classified as municipalities by the British were now within Israeli territory: Acre, Baysan, Beersheba, Haifa, Jaffa, Lydda, al-Majdal, Nazareth, Ramla, Safad, Shafa' 'Amr, and Tiberias. In these cases, he multiplied the rate of urban tax that had been assigned to land in these towns by ten to arrive at the total net value of land. However, Berncastle admitted that arriving at a value of urban Palestinian land by capitalizing the tax assessment usually resulted in an undervaluation. To account for this, he added 25 percent to the net annual value that he derived from the tax figures. He then added an additional 25 percent to account for the steep rise in values between the last urban tax assessment and the year 1947. Finally, he multiplied this by 16.67 to capitalize this figure.

As he had when estimating the scope of land, Berncastle addressed the question of the value of land in Jerusalem separately, given the unique situation of the city. Berncastle finally succeeded in securing statistics on abandoned Palestinian land in Jerusalem from the Israeli Custodian of Absentee

TABLE 2.4 1947 Palestinian Rural Land Values Used by UNCCP's (Berncastle's) Global Estimate, 1951

| *Tax Category* | *Description* | *1947 Net Annual Value (including Weighted Figures)* | *Value/ Dunum (£P)* |
|---|---|---|---|
| 1 | Citrus (outside) Acre sub-district) | | 80.000 |
| 2 | Citrus (Acre s.d.) | | 80.000 |
| 3 | Bananas | | |
| 4 | Village Built-up | | 150.000 |
| 5 | 1st grade irrigated<br>1st grade fruit | 2.000 | 60.000 |
| 6 | 2nd grade irrigated<br>2nd grade fruit | 1.750 | 52.500 |
| 7 | 3rd grade irrigated<br>3rd grade fruit | 1.500 | 45.000 |
| 8 | 1st grade cereal<br>4th grade irrigated<br>4th grade fruit | 1.250 | 37.500 |
| 9 | 2nd grade cereal<br>5th grade irrigated<br>5th grade fruit | 0.800 | 24.000 |
| 10 | 3rd grade cereal<br>6th grade irrigated<br>6th grade fruit | 0.720 | 21.600 |
| 11 | 4th grade cereal<br>7th grade irrigated<br>7th grade fruit | 0.600 | 18.000 |
| 12 | 5th grade cereal<br>8th grade irrigated<br>8th grade fruit | 0.480 | 14.000 |
| 13 | 6th grade cereal<br>9th grade irrigated<br>9th grade fruit | 0.320 | 9.600 |
| 14 | 7th grade cereal<br>10th grade | 0.160 | 4.800 |
| 15 | 8th grade cereal | 0.080 | 2.400 |
| 16 | Forest and uncultivated | 0 | 0 |
| — | Cultivable land Beersheba District | | 3.600 |

Source: "Valuation of Abandoned Arab Land in Israel," p. 17, and Appendix II

Property. He hired an Israeli assistant to translate and transcribe the register. Using all these procedures and figures, Berncastle determined that the value of abandoned rural Palestinian refugee property as of November 29, 1947 was £P69,525,144. The value of abandoned urban property was £P21,608,640. Urban refugee property in Jerusalem was worth £P9,250,000. The totals are shown in table 2.5.

It is worth noting that the UNCCP also instructed the Refugee Office to estimate the value of *moveable* property that had been abandoned by the refugees. Here Berncastle had to concede that developing such a figure was impossible. Instead, he made three different calculations following three different methods to arrive at rough overall figures for abandoned household articles, industrial equipment, vehicles, agricultural equipment, commercial stocks, and livestock. The first of these methods was to develop a figure based on a percentage of the value of refugee land. He did this based on a percentage used in the 1920s during the Greco-Turkish population exchanges. Using this for the Palestinian case, Berncastle's figure came to £P21,570,000. His second method was to take 40 percent of the national income of the Palestinian sector of the economy during the last years of the mandate. This meant that moveable refugee property amounted to £P18.6 million. Finally, he tallied up the "aggregate value of the various categories of moveable property owned by Arabs under the Mandate." This last figure came to £P19.1 million. The UNCCP decided that the three different methods provided very similar results, and it rounded the figure to £P20 million for abandoned moveable property.[79]

Berncastle also studied the distribution of compensation by families, producing statistics on the number of refugee families that would benefit from various levels of compensation (see table 2.6).

TABLE 2.5 Value of Refugee Land According to UNCCP's (Berncastle's)"Global Estimate," 1951

| *Type of Land* | *Value (£P)* |
|---|---|
| Rural land | 69,525,144 |
| Urban land | 21,608,640 |
| Jerusalem land | 9,250,000 |
| TOTAL | 100,383,784 |

Source: "Valuation of Abandoned Arab Land in Israel," p. = 20

TABLE 2.6 UNCCP Estimate of the Number of Landowning Refugee Families by Value of Holdings

| *Value of Property (£P)* | *Number of Families* |
|---|---|
| 1–99 | 63,950 |
| 100–1,000 | 75,760 |
| 1,000–10,000 | 18,478 |
| more than 10,000 | 1,672 |
| TOTAL | 159,860 |

Source: United Kingdom, Public Records Office [PRO], FO371/98519, "A Study of the Distribution of Arab Land in Palestine According to the Value"

Just days before concluding his study in early August 1951, Berncastle met with a man whose estimates of refugee property he felt were quite sound and whose expertise in general impressed him: Yosef Weitz. Before agreeing to see Berncastle, Weitz sought and secured permission from the Israeli Ministry of Foreign Affairs. Berncastle told Weitz, "as if discovering a secret," that he had found Weitz's published figures on the value of the abandoned property the most accurate. Weitz also claimed that Berncastle expressed his intention to "bring his estimate closer to my figures, although in the end his estimate would be slightly higher than mine."

The two men sparred on Berncastle's use of 1947 land values as the basis for his forthcoming estimate. Weitz argued that prices that year were too high, in part because of the development being carried out in Palestine by the Jews with their capital. Berncastle agreed with him and, while sticking to his guns, said he would note Weitz's point of view in his report "which appears to him to be justified." Berncastle then asked Weitz why his figures on abandoned land in the Beersheba district were lower than his. Weitz stated that that he did not include land in tax category 16—uncultivable land. While *Village Statistics* included this land as Palestinian simply because it was not registered to Jews or the government, Weitz claimed this was uncultivable waste land that belonged to the state. It was for this reason that Weitz did not include this vast area in his estimates of abandoned property. When Berncastle asked why their two figures also differed in the scope of cultivable land, Weitz countered that he had not included land in tax categories 14 and 15 in his own estimates of abandoned land. Weitz stated that mandatory authorities had listed these as cultivable when they in fact were not. As proof he pointed out that the government had not levied taxes on this land because it was so marginal (this was true but only until April 1944, when the mandatory government *did* levy a low rate of taxation on land in tax categories 14 and 15). Weitz, also skilled in public relations, told Berncastle that in any event, the actual scope of refugee land was not yet determined because the government was releasing some to its owners in Israel who had proven that they were not absentees.[80]

Interestingly, another Israeli whom Berncastle respected quite highly, Moshe Ellman, would later determine that Berncastle's figures were actually too *low* compared to market values. Ellman, the Ministry of Justice's Chief Valuer in its Land Assessment Division, and a personal friend of Berncastle's, compared the various Israeli and UN figures on the refugee land in a November 1962 report to the Israeli government (see chapter 6). In that report, Ellman contrasted Berncastle's assessment system with his own, and found that Berncastle's led to valuations that were too low, at times drastically so:

> It is interesting to note at this juncture that, when I conducted my assessment of the property of the [German] Templars in Jerusalem, Haifa, and Jaffa, there were many visible differences between the assessment based on the system adopted by Berncastle and assessment of market value. We assessed lots and vacant Templar land in Haifa at £P895,000, while Berncastle's method yielded a figure of £P615,000. Our assessment of built-up lots was 87 percent higher than the figure rendered using Berncastle's method. The situation in Jaffa was similar to that in Haifa, and our assessment in Jerusalem resulted in a figure 45 percent higher than that of Berncastle's method for vacant lots, and 88 percent higher for built-up lots.[81]

Overall, Ellman later thought that the refugee land was worth more than Berncastle's estimate, somewhere over £P140 million.

In the end, then, both Arabs and Israelis would agree that the UNCCP's first major attempt to quantify the refugees' property losses was too low. At the time, however, the UNCCP was eager for Berncastle and the Refugee Office to present it with figures that could be used as the basis for compensation talks. The reason: It had convened yet another conference at which it intended to present the findings.

## Paris Conference

From September to November 1951, the UNCCP convened one final conference at which it hoped to bridge some of the gaps between Arab and Israeli stances on the refugees and other questions. Rather than use its earlier strategy of trying to develop consensus on initiatives, the commission instead presented the parties with its own proposals and ideas. Among these were the compensation figures that Berncastle had developed. Berncastle presented his overall estimates of refugee land—16,329,707 dunums, worth £P100,383,784—to the Refugee Office's Holger Andersen on August 14, 1951. Andersen then drafted a "Preliminary Report" on September 7 for the UNCCP to use in Paris. These figures represented the first—and to that date, the only—official UN figures on the scope *and* value of the refugee's property losses. Andersen's report never was given an official number to circulate as a UNCCP document, although the estimates were presented to the parties at Paris. Beyond just numbers, the Refugee Office's report also dealt with compensation and other questions. It noted that the UNCCP had decided upon payments to individuals and recommended that it take steps to determine how much land individual refugees had lost through a questionnaire circulated among the refugee camps. The report also recommended creation of an "authority" to which the Israeli Custodian of Absentee Property must show details of his accounts and from which the Custodian must obtain permission prior to selling any refugee land.[82]

Among the five proposals that the UNCCP offered the parties at Paris were three that dealt with the refugee property issue: cancellation of mutual war damages claims; the mutual release of all blocked bank accounts; and an Israeli pledge to pay compensation to nonrepatriated refugees. The last was worded as follows: "That the Government of Israel accept the obligation to pay, as compensation for property abandoned by those refugees not repatriated, a global sum based upon the evaluation arrived at by the Commission's Refugee Office."

The UNCCP was careful to note that the compensation sum would not be Berncastle's figures but instead would be *based* on those figures. Ultimately, the actual amount that it expected Israel to pay would be subject to its ability to pay. The UNCCP stated that a committee of economic and financial experts established by a UN trustee would determine a payment plan. This trustee in turn would pay individual claims. Regarding compensation, the UNCCP explained what it had been saying for some time (and what was stated in Andersen's report): that despite the global nature of the Refugee Office's figures, it expected that compensation would be paid to individual refugees.

The Israelis agreed that Berncastle's figures would not be the amount they would pay. Indeed, they already had indicated even before he had finished his report that any figures he produced would not be "the measure of the burden to be laid on Israel."[83] It came as no surprise when the Israelis scoffed at his estimates in public once they were made public. Foreign Minister Sharett dismissed the £P100 million figure as merely "academic," noting that Israel had not acquired the land as the result of an ordinary business transaction, but through war.[84] He told the Knesset on November 4, 1951 that compensation figures could not be based solely on the value of abandoned property. His speech also stated that Israel would require international aid to help it pay compensation, and that it would pay compensation only to a UN organ and not to Arab states or individual refugees.[85]

In private, however, the Israeli government liked Berncastle's figure of £P100 million ($280 million in 1951 dollars) because it approximated their own estimates. As discussed in chapter 1, the Weitz-Lifshits-Danin Committee of 1948 had estimated the value of the abandoned land at £I81.5 million ($228.2 million in 1951 dollars). Custodian of Absentee Property Mordekhai Schattner and other Israelis privately told Berncastle that his study was an "excellent and well reasoned document."[86] In discussions with the British Secretary of State on December 3, 1951, Israeli officials indicated their pleasure with Berncastle's figures by stating that Israel now was willing to negotiate with the UN about the entire compensation issue under certain conditions. Israel must have a role in determining the amount; it would not just have a figure dictated to it. Secondly, Israel was not prepared to pay compensation that was based on the market value of the land (which Berncastle already had ruled out as well). Thirdly, Israel's contributions to compensation must be based on its ability to pay, given its tremendous outlays for settling Jewish immigrants. Lastly, compensation would need to be linked with the issue of Jewish property left behind in Arab countries.

British diplomats felt that the Israelis were talking out of both sides of their mouths: they spoke of the financial burdens they labored under but yet the bulk of the money for compensation would end up coming from the U.S. anyway. Besides, they noted, the UK had just agreed to release £UK5 million in sterling securities that Britain had frozen since February 22, 1948.[87] Two years later, in 1953, a senior Israeli government economic expert told U.S. diplomats in Tel Aviv that the Israelis still were insisting on negotiating the sum of compensation. Even though they liked Berncastle's figure of $280 million inasmuch as they too believed the property was worth somewhere under $300 million, this was only a starting point for negotiations.[88]

Israel's publicly harder line toward compensation manifested itself at Paris in other ways as well. It continued to refuse even to consider compensation for the value of former mandatory government property such as railroads,

Haifa Harbor, etc., and still wanted to secure an international loan to help pay for compensation. Israeli guidelines for talks at Paris also included a warning to its diplomats not to allow any compensation agreement to suggest any Israeli blame for the refugee flight. Compensation also should be linked to a "nullification" of calls for refugee repatriation; such payments should be directed toward resettling the refugees in the Arab world and would signal the end of Israeli obligation to them in the future. Lastly, Israel would not waive its rights to seek reparations for war damages or compensation for Jewish property in Arab countries like Iraq. Indeed, the waiver of war reparations was "absolutely out of the question."[89] Secretly, the Israeli delegation also felt that despite its calls for direct talks with the Arabs, the real battle over compensation would be waged between them and the Americans.[90] On the other hand, the Israeli government decided in October 1951 to move in the new direction suggested by Abba Eban: approve the idea of a reintegration fund that the General Assembly had called for the previous December and agree to pay compensation into it.

Israeli delegate to Paris Maurice Fischer spelled out Israel's position in his statement to the UNCCP on November 14, 1951. He reaffirmed Israel's willingness to pay compensation. Interestingly, he reaffirmed Israel's refusal to drop its claims for war damages as well despite the strict instructions he had been given. In discussing compensation, Fischer laid out seven points. First, Israel was ready to discuss compensation with the UNCCP or any other UN body. Second, the value of the property must be determined first. Third, all concerned must consider the fact that the Arabs started the war; this in turn led to property damage and is the very reason why Israel ended up controlling the abandoned land in the first place. Fourth, Israel's capacity to pay compensation was being hindered by the Arab boycott, the Arab blockade of the Suez Canal, and the influx of Jews into Israel fleeing oppression in Arab lands. Fifth, compensation talks must consider Jewish land left behind in the West Bank and Gaza, as well as property left behind by immigrants from Arab countries. Sixth, compensation must end all Israeli responsibility for the refugee property. Finally, individual refugees' claims must be taken up with the UN body that receives the compensation. Israel itself would entertain no claims for individual compensation. Throughout the conference, Fischer had been instructed by Eban to do the "minimal": "Our objective should now be to assess the minimal Israel concession which would have the result of diverting the pressure of American mediation away from us and towards the Arab states."[91]

After weeks of effort at Paris discussing Berncastle's numbers and other topics relating to compensation, the UNCCP informed the parties on November

19, 1951 that the conference had failed and that it could not carry out its mandate. The UNCCP's failure to translate Berncastle's global estimate into the starting point for serious talks on compensation further chastened it. The new directions it had embarked upon starting in 1950 had not produced the anticipated results. The UNCCP then decided to take up Berncastle's ideas on compensation directly with the Israelis, who after all were the party from which the UNCCP most needed cooperation.

## UNCCP's Compensation Efforts

After the failure at Paris, the General Assembly expressed its own frustration with the inability of the parties to make progress on the refugee problem. It passed resolution 512 (VI) on January 26, 1952 calling upon the UNCCP to continue its efforts to secure implementation of Resolution 194 (III) and to make itself available to the parties. The resolution recognized that it would need to be the parties themselves who made peace: "the governments concerned have the primary responsibility for reaching a settlement of their outstanding differences in conformity with the resolutions of the General Assembly on Palestine." The UNCCP with its plans, ideas, and statistics could assist, but these ultimately would be mere aids to efforts that the Arabs and Israelis themselves would need to expend. This resolution was the final nail in the coffin of the UNCCP as an active mediator in the Arab-Israeli conflict. From early 1952 onward, the new direction of the UNCCP would be refined further, until it would essentially confine itself to, as it later described, "efforts to the solution of concrete problems which might be of direct benefit to a great number of refugees and on which progress could be made independently of the readiness of the parties to reach over-all agreement." Since Israel controlled the property and it would be Israel that paid compensation, this meant that henceforth the commission *de facto* would deal only with Israel on the specifics of how compensation would be paid. The move away from active involvement in mediation also prompted the UNCCP to stop meeting in Jerusalem. It decided in Paris on January 28, 1952 to meet next in New York. At that meeting on April 21, the UNCCP decided to continue meeting in New York, where it could be close to the parties' delegations to the UN and could meet on short notice.

Although staying in New York themselves, the American, French, and Turkish delegates to the UNCCP ordered Berncastle on April 28, 1952 to proceed to Jerusalem and commence discussions on a "technical level" about the modalities of a compensation regime with Israel and the Arabs. He was to travel there as a technician—the "Land Specialist" of the Refugee Office—and as not a representative of the UNCCP as a whole authorized to negotiate. Although the UNCCP knew that it primarily would need to talk to the Israelis about compensation, it still envisioned an Arab presence in certain aspects of the compensation question. This was particularly the case when dealing with the issue of exactly how much would be paid, given that the Arabs considered Berncastle's figures far too low. By the spring of 1952, the Refugee Office had established the broad parameters of how it would go about the business of estimating compensation. As Berncastle had done, it felt that valuation should reflect the condition of the land on November 29, 1947. It also felt that the UNCCP should return to the idea of setting up a mixed Arab-Israeli committee of technical experts—not politicians or diplomats as before, but people with experience in land affairs. For the Israeli representative to such a committee, Berncastle recommended Moshe Ellman. From the Arab side, Berncastle thought the Palestinian land expert Sami Hadawi would be the best. In a nod to politics, Berncastle noted that if the UNCCP deemed it politically necessary to appoint a nontechnical but more high-profile Palestinian like the refugee spokesman Izzat Tannous to the committee then the UNCCP should balance the mixed committee with a second Israeli, Yosef Weitz, whom Berncastle had quoted in his 1951 report.[92] The mixed committee idea never materialized.

Berncastle's mission to the Middle East would be fraught with challenges from the outset. The Israelis already had served notice to the UN that their willingness to pay compensation would not stand forever and was dependent upon their ability to pay. In the fall of 1951, they began serving notice that the Arab boycott of Israel and Egypt's closure of the Suez Canal to Israeli shipping was hurting their economy and ultimately their ability to pay compensation. Sharett told UNRWA's John Blandford in December 1951 that if "unlimited demands for repatriation" are made of Israel, "its commitment on this matter [compensation] would not remain valid indefinitely."[93]

On the other hand, Israel had made an important change to its policy by the time Berncastle arrived in the region. A committee from the Israeli Ministry of Foreign Affairs agreed that the valuation of abandoned land should be based on land conditions as they existed on November 29, 1947 and not when the Custodian of Absentee Property gained control of the land months later.[94] For their part, the Arabs had their own thoughts on compensation. The Arab League announced on September 1, 1951 that Israel should pay compensation to international bodies like UNRWA, essentially agreeing with the Israelis that they would not take the money directly from Israel themselves. The League continued to insist that Israel pay for damages to property as well, and that it pay in pounds sterling based on November 1947 values. Besides discussing compensation with the parties, the UNCCP wanted Berncastle to begin moving beyond his global estimate of property losses and investigate how the UNCCP might determine individual refugees' losses.

Berncastle arrived in Palestine on May 14, 1952. He spent five months in the Middle East meeting with people in several countries working out a plan for compensation, devising a plan for individual assessment of refugee losses, and trying to nail down the Israelis on specifics. His first official meeting took place in Jerusalem on May 22 with Michael S. Comay, then Assistant Director General of the Ministry of Foreign Affairs. Comay already had accumulated three years experience dealing with the UNCCP on the abandoned property issue. The two men's discussion reflected Israel's increasingly confident and tough position on compensation, particularly the basis for determining the total amount. According to Berncastle's diary entry for that day, Comay "suggested that the amount which Israel would pay would bear very little relation to the value of the property."[95] Berncastle quickly told him that the UNCCP had decided that Israel "should not be asked to commit herself to accepting the findings of any group of experts which might be set up." As he noted in his diary, "this seemed to reassure Mr. Comay considerably."[96]

Trying to woo the Israelis further into concrete discussions, Berncastle tried to assure them about other aspects of compensation. When he met with Dr. A. Biran, an Israeli District Commissioner, on June 19 in Jerusalem, Biran asked Berncastle how compensation would be linked with resettlement.[97] Would not most of the money go to a few wealthy landowners? Biran inquired. Berncastle replied that he believed compensation payments should be related directly to refugee resettlement. In fact, the money should be paid only for expenses associated with this, like education, new land, steamship fares, and so forth. Berncastle later confided to his diary, "My general impression from the conversation was that Dr. Biran was not very optimistic about the possibility of the Israel Government paying any substantial amount of compensation."[98]

Berncastle also met with a number of Palestinians in the West Bank as part of his mission. Berncastle held a meeting in Ramallah on May 24 with Sami Hadawi and Izzat Tannous, the two Palestinians who had emerged as the Arab world's most knowledgeable figures on the refugee property issue. The two urged Berncastle not to involve the Arab governments in any future attempt to carry out an assessment of individual refugee losses. Instead, they suggested inviting the participation of committees representing the refugees' interests. Only with such direct refugee participation in the assessment would Palestinians accept the results. Three days later Berncastle and Hadawi traveled again to Ramallah and met with Yahya Hammuda, a lawyer from the General Refugee Congress that had met with the UNCCP at Lausanne. Hammuda later would become the second chairman of the Palestine Liberation Organization in December 1967. He told Berncastle that the refugees had no faith in the UN. He claimed that the poor among the refugees would not waive their right to repatriation for a few pounds in compensation whereas the rich only cared about their money and did not care where they lived. Hammuda also complained that Berncastle's global estimate figures were too low. Berncastle countered that the Refugee Office had done its best in the absence of any help from the refugees or the Arabs at large, despite its pleas. Hammuda also asked how communal property left behind by the refugees fit into the UNCCP's thinking. Berncastle said that dealing with that matter only would delay progress and that for now, his efforts at exploring individual assessment of losses would focus only on land that was registered in a specific person's name. By this he included companies and religious organizations.[99]

Berncastle met again with Hadawi in Ramallah two weeks later. Having also worked in land affairs in the mandatory government, Berncastle was well aware of Hadawi's expertise on land issues both during and after the mandate. One question he was anxious to find out was the question posed to him by Biran earlier: What percentage of compensation payments would likely end up in the hands of big landowners? This was a concern shared by many, inasmuch as it would militate against using compensation to resettle the bulk of the poorer refugees. Together, Berncastle and Hadawi guessed that between 40–50 percent of the total value of refugee land would be divided among some 40,000 members of the "effendi class" who were not living in refugee camps or receiving UNRWA rations. The remainder would be divided up among the large number of "fellahin," most of whom were living in the camps. The two men also met again with Hammuda and several other representatives of the General Refugee Congress: Aziz Shehadeh, the congress's secretary general; Anton 'Atallah, a former Palestine supreme court justice; Hanna 'Atallah; and Jabr Akram. The congress representatives urged that Berncastle conduct an individual assessment on the basis of a questionnaire handed out to refugees, and that he publicize it as widely as possible. To minimize refugee fear of the political consequences of filling out the form, they also suggested that he call it a "census of property" without mentioning compensation. The men also rejected Berncastle's 1951 global estimate of £100 million not so much because of the amount of the final figure but because it was a global figure, not the sum of individual assessments.[100]

Berncastle also met with Palestinians outside of Palestine to discuss, among other things, this vexing issue of global versus individual compensation. In late June, he traveled to Beirut. While there he met with members of various refugee committees. The Arabs had been hostile to the concept of a Reintegration Fund since the idea first developed if for no other reason than the wealthy refugees whose spokespersons were the loudest would be shortchanged. He told them that the UNCCP's plans for compensation did *not* envision payments to a Reintegration Fund but rather to individuals. "It [UNCCP] will have nothing to do with payments to governments or to a reintegration fund."[101] The refugees also complained that the tax values on which Berncastle had based his 1951 estimate of £100 million was lower than the actual value of the land. He countered that using the 1947 values was the only thing on which the Arabs and Israelis he had talked to could agree. Berncastle also had some of Hammuda's earlier assessments about wealthy refugees confirmed when he met with Munir Haddad in July. Haddad fled Palestine for Lebanon in 1948 with £600. Within four years he headed INTRA Bank & Trading Company, which Haddad claimed possessed more capital than any other bank in Lebanon. He ventured that he had no interest in being repatriated to Palestine but would accept compensation if it were offered, which he doubted ever would be.[102]

Between his meetings with Israelis and Palestinians Berncastle had been doing some other thinking about his charge to investigate how individual payments could be made. By August, he had determined enough to predict that the aggregate value of individual refugees' properties would exceed his global figure of approximately £P100 million. The difference in values was because the global figure represents the value of the land to the state that acquired it, whereas the individual figure represents the value of the lands to their former owners who, unlike Israel, would factor in the value of future development rights. In any case, he did not estimate that the aggregate figure for individual properties would exceed his figure by more than fifty percent.[103]

Berncastle's summer-long campaign in the Middle East was taxing on him in many ways. While in Jerusalem, he and his wife enjoyed comfortable accommodations at the YMCA in Israeli-controlled West Jerusalem. Crossing back and forth across the cease-fire line into East Jerusalem, however, could present problems. Berncastle experienced a particularly disagreeable incident on June 12, 1952 that greatly infuriated him. As he was attempting to cross over the cease fire line at St. Clare's Gate to go to the UN offices in Government

House, an Israeli border policeman asked if he were carrying any Israeli currency. When he pulled out £I95.5, the policeman grabbed the funds and cited new customs regulations forbidding the export of Israeli money. Berncastle snatched the bills back out of his hand and protested that he was a UN employee exempt from such procedures, whereupon the policeman in turn grabbed the money back out of Berncastle's hands. During the ensuing argument over diplomatic immunity, the policeman also confiscated Berncastle's "white card" that had enabled him to pass across the cease-fire line. Berncastle then stormed off to Government House to lodge a protest and try to get his money and white card returned, and was stranded and unable to return to the Israeli side until the matter was resolved.[104] Beyond this particular incident Berncastle was also clearly frustrated with the parties' behavior during his talks with them. He grew weary of what he called the Israelis' "stalling tactics." As for the Palestinians with whom he spoke, Berncastle derided what he felt was their hyperemotional behavior. "Arabs are always inclined to over-emotionalise such situations and tears come to their eyes very easily."[105]

By late summer Berncastle finally had devised an ambitious plan for compensation. His September 10, 1952 report to the UNCCP was entitled "A Plan for the Payment of Compensation for Abandoned Arab Immoveable Property."[106] The genesis of his plan extended back to a suggestion sent to him by Fayiz al-Hajj, a representative of a Palestinian refugee committee in Lebanon. Al-Hajj had proposed a novel idea for dealing with the refugees' property and paying compensation. Al-Hajj suggested establishing a special bank with international capital. This bank would pay compensation to refugee landowners. To recoup its outlays, Israel would release the property of the refugees to the bank. These were in some sense fictitious transfers, for the bank then would sell the land to interested Jewish buyers around the world. The funds it raised from the sales would be used to pay back the original lenders, less the costs for overhead. Berncastle's own plan for compensation was a derivative of this idea. The plan adopted al-Hajj's idea about a bank. Berncastle suggested that the UN establish a financial group that in turn would create a fund with some $US50 million or so. The fund would pay compensation to refugee landowners and receive the legal title for their land from the Israeli Custodian of Absentee Property. The fund would then sell the land to Jews throughout the world in order to pay itself back. The Jewish National Fund and the Israeli government would have the right of first refusal on this land. Israel would make up any losses in these transactions.

Berncastle was frank about both the advantages and disadvantages of his plan. He noted several of the former. First, it would remove the compensation issue from the tortuous realm of diplomatic politics and bring it down to the level of business. Second, it would separate compensation from Israel's continued insistence on deductions for war damages. Third, it would avoid the appearance of compulsion; refugees would be free to participate or not. Beyond that, Berncastle noted that Israel would not be obligated to pay a specific amount in advance, nor would it be forced to acquire a large sum of hard currency. Such a compensation plan also would help the process of resettlement but would not be connected to that loaded issue in the minds of Arabs. Finally, the process would be gradual in order to lessen the inflationary impact on regional economies that the sudden influx of millions of dollars would cause. A gradual process also would be easier to administer. On the down side, Berncastle noted that the devaluation of the Israeli pound and Israeli rent control laws might make Jewish investors abroad less likely to buy the land from the fund. Most problematic of all, he noted that "it is very unlikely that it would be acceptable to the Government of Israel" and also stated that the Arabs already had rejected his £P100 million figure. Still, he felt that his plan could work and that the £100 million figure "would represent just and reasonable compensation for the loss of their [refugees] immoveable property."[107]

Berncastle also devised a plan for how to go beyond his global estimate and carry out a much more thorough individual assessment of refugee losses. His August 7, 1952 plan entitled "The Individual Assessment of Abandoned Arab Immoveable Property in Israeli Held Territory" laid out the basis.[108] In this plan, Berncastle noted that a massive campaign to ascertain the value of each parcel of refugee land would produce an aggregate total that would be greater than his 1951 global estimate. This was because the new amount would reflect the value of each parcel of land to each individual refugee, and thus would include the potential development value of the land. The global estimate tallied the value of all the land that Israel received at once, the value of which (to Israel) was less. To this point, Berncastle noted that what counted in the individual assessment was that each refugee eventually would be compensated, not that the aggregate figure ever be published.

In this Berncastle disagreed with the Americans. U.S. delegate to the UNCCP James Barco feared that if the new figure were much higher or even lower than Berncastle's 1951 figure that it would undermine confidence in the UNCCP.[109] Berncastle, however, believed that the work of the individual assessment could be arranged so that this new value might be kept secret. Berncastle estimated that the Refugee Office would need a staff of some fifty persons working for two years to complete the task. He specifically recommended hiring ex-employees of the mandatory land department because they had the necessary experience dealing with land in Palestine and also because hiring refugees would help solve refugee unemployment in a small but meaningful way.

As summer turned to fall, Berncastle had completed two plans: one for how to compensate the refugees, the other for how to carry out a second, more detailed assessment of individual refugee losses. He was now anxious to achieve some modicum of progress in practical talks on compensation and the new assessment with the Israelis before leaving the region. Berncastle had decided that the best records upon which to base an individual assessment were the mandatory land and tax records that the British had produced. This would be a better method than circulating a questionnaire among refugees as he previously had thought. On June 10 Berncastle had already asked the Second Secretary of the UK legation in Amman, Peter Wakefield, whether he felt the Jordanians would provide the UNCCP with access to mandatory records in the Jordanians' possession. Wakefield replied that the Jordanian cabinet ministers would "do anything they were advised by Mr. Walpole," referring to the long-serving and influential British Director of Lands and Survey in Jordan, George Frederick Walpole.[110] He also ran the idea of using mandatory records past Sami Hadawi, who agreed that it was practical but that the land registers were insufficient and the UNCCP would need to secure tax records that were now in Israeli hands. When Berncastle told Comay of his ideas on carrying out an individual assessment, he responded that while it could not commit to it *en toto*, Israel had liked his 1951 global estimate of £100 million. Why do an individual assessment, Comay asked? The numbers would be different, and it would be just as easy to divide the amount in the 1951 estimate among the number of claimants seeking compensation. Berncastle noted the contradiction in Comay's thinking in his diary:

> On thinking over my interview with Comay it seems to me that he wants to have the best of both worlds. Without committing himself to acceptance of 100 million sterling, he is anxious that we should not carry out an investigation which might lead to the establishment of a higher figure.[111]

Still committed to the individual assessment and in need of documents in Israel's possession, Berncastle wrote to Comay on September 4, 1952 requesting access to three types of records. These were Tax Distribution Sheets, which the British had prepared in order to assess taxes on rural property under the Rural Property Tax Ordinance of 1935; Field Valuation Sheets, which did the same for urban property under the Urban Property Tax Ordinance of 1928; and the land registers for Tel Aviv and Netanya.[112] The UNCCP told him five days later the Americans were willing to back up his request with their own if necessary. After receiving a noncommittal letter from Comay on September 17, Berncastle lost his patience and asked the UNCCP to bring in the promised American help to pressure Israel. He wrote the following to the Principal Secretary of the UNCCP, Feng Yang Chai, on September 25:

> It [the letter from Comay] is in line with the usual stalling tactics with which I have become all too familiar in my dealings with the Israeli authorities. I think it would be a very good thing if the U.S. Government brings its influence to bear [in pressuring Israel to allow use of its documents].[113]

In addition to getting hold of Israeli documents Berncastle was still pressing Comay for a meeting to discuss the modalities of compensation now that he had a specific plan. As his departure date drew near, Berncastle finally met with Comay on September 26. Comay said his immediate response to Berncastle's plan was that Israel would not want to allow a foreign agency like Berncastle's proposed international bank to be given title to the abandoned land because Israel had a planned economy and wanted to control the land. Berncastle spoke frankly of his discouragement with the Israeli authorities' lack of overall cooperation. Afterwards he noted in his diary, "I said that I would be bitterly disappointed to have to return to New York and report that no progress at all had been made in this matter."[114]

Comay thereafter had to leave the country himself, and Berncastle offered to delay his own return to New York for a week to give the Israelis more time. Comay indicated that Berncastle would be contacted in his absence by Mordekhai Kidron, head of UN affairs at the Ministry of Foreign Affairs. With his departure from the Middle East now only 48 hours away, Berncastle finally received a telephone call from Kidron on October 5. Kidron promised to read the documents relating to compensation, and Berncastle once again offered to postpone his flight in order to give the Israelis more time. The next day, Berncastle received a telephone call at 4:15 P.M. from one of Kidron's subordinates at the Ministry of Foreign Affairs. The employee apologized for Kidron, stating that he had tried to call Berncastle himself but could not get through. In any event, the subordinate reported that Israel rejected Berncastle's plan because it only would discuss compensation with a UN body (not an international financial group). Furthermore, the employee relayed that Kidron felt there was no need for Berncastle to postpone his trip again for another week but had wanted to assure him that Israel was ready to enter into negotiations with the UNCCP on global compensation at any time. A frustrated Berncastle later would record his response to the Israeli in his diary:

> In reply I said that I had been in Palestine four months as the representative of the Commission to undertake the very negotiations which the Israel Government expressed their readiness to take part in at any time. I wondered therefore exactly what the Israel Government expected of the Commission.[115]

Kidron's subordinate replied that he was not in a position to respond but was merely relaying a message from Kidron. With that, Berncastle left Jerusalem the next day and traveled to New York to report on his lack of success in creating movement on the compensation issue. It marked the end of an era for the UNCCP.

## CHAPTER THREE

# EARLY ISRAELI POLICIES TOWARD THE PROPERTY QUESTION

One reason why Israel disliked the UNCCP was that it had long favored direct negotiations with the Arabs, rather than indirect talks with them through the good offices of the commission such as at Lausanne and Paris. Israel had good reason for this desire: it had managed to achieve a great deal of progress in direct, secret negotiations with Jordan that actually predated 1948 and felt that this offered the best prospects for forging peace with the Arabs. In the course of such talks Israel believed that it could best address the compensation issue. For in addition to borders and other matters, the various public and secret contacts between Israel and Jordan that continued into the early 1950s also dealt with refugee property and compensation. Israeli Jews had lost property that ended up both in Jordan and the West Bank after 1948, and wanted it back. Jordan was now home to tens of thousands of Palestinian refugees seeking the return of their property in Israel.

## Secret Israeli-Jordanian Talks on Compensation

Drawing on a history of generally amicable relations between the Zionist movement and Jordan's King 'Abdullah, both sides sought to address their respective property claims almost immediately. Article eight of the Israeli-Jordanian armistice agreement of April 3, 1949 called for the creation of a special committee to examine compensation for Jewish property in Jordanian-controlled East Jerusalem and Palestinian property in Israeli-controlled West Jerusalem. Compensation thereafter loomed large in the secret bilateral talks that aimed at producing a follow-up Israeli-Jordanian peace treaty. 'Abdullah himself participated in these secret negotiations. Israel dangled the prospect of compensating Palestinian refugees in Jordan for their valuable property in Jerusalem as an incentive for peace. A draft peace treaty—actually, a five-year nonaggression pact—was formalized in March 1950 although the treaty was never actualized for a variety of reasons including Arab opposition. In its article six, the treaty proposed creation of a mixed commission to examine the compensation question, again only for property in Jerusalem. It went further to propose compensation "for [all] persons permanently resident in the territory of either" party. This included permission for property owners to return to Israel temporarily or to send lawyers to sell or rent their property for them.[1] Israeli diplomats were keen on letting the Americans and British know of their plans, undoubtedly in hopes that they would try to pressure Jordan to follow through with implementing the treaty.[2]

Concern for property compensation also loomed large among those Palestinians who opposed King ʿAbdullah's secret talks with Israel. The Israelis knew this and proposed using the issue as a way of buying off their opposition to talks with the Jewish state. Israeli diplomat Shmu'el Bendor felt that wealthy refugee property owners in the West Bank who were looking out for their own interests had been able to "tie the hands" of ʿAbdullah and Prime Minister Samir al-Rifaʿi in their efforts to negotiate. He suggested that Israel consider a compensation compromise to assist ʿAbdullah and al-Rifaʿi: Israel would pay compensation for refugee homes in the Jerusalem Demilitarized Zone that straddled the Israeli-Jordanian cease-fire line in the city.[3] This could help ʿAbdullah bring opponents of his peace moves on board through the hope of receiving money for their abandoned property that lay in this area.

The king's opponents hoped to realize compensation in other ways too. Some large landowning Palestinian Christians who allegedly opposed ʿAbdullah's position supported instead the UN's official policy of pushing for the internationalization of Jerusalem. They felt that such a political arrangement would provide a better guarantee of getting their property back than Jordanian-Israeli cooperation.[4] Israel continued to try to co-opt those Palestinians who publicly opposed peace talks between the Arabs and Israel into supporting such talks by dangling in front of them the prospects of getting their property back as an incentive. A key architect of this policy was the Israeli diplomat Abba Eban. Born Aubrey Eban in 1915 in Capetown, South Africa, the young, eloquent speaker became a rising star in Zionist and Israeli diplomatic circles. In 1949, he became Israel's first ambassador to the UN and, in 1950, concomitantly assumed the post of Israel's ambassador to the United States. In January 1951, Eban proposed co-opting Palestinians in the Jordanian government and parliament by offering them compensation for their property. However, fellow diplomat Moshe Sasson, the son of Eliyahu Sasson, investigated and found out that most of the afore-mentioned Palestinians in the ranks of the Jordanian establishment in fact did not own land in Israel.[5]

Israel was also aware that some wealthy refugee landowners feared that any compensation arrangement would involve Israel paying into a general compensation fund rather than to specific individuals. Obviously, such persons wanted to receive personal compensation for their expensive homes and property rather than see it go into a fund that would benefit poor refugees. British diplomats shared this concern. [6] Those refugees in Jordan who had supported Israeli-Jordanian talks had done so because they believed that individual compensation for their property would be about the best possible outcome for them that a settlement could yield. The concept of personal payments thus would help generate support for a peace treaty in the face of generalized opposition to such an idea in Jordan and elsewhere in the Arab world. Among those who hoped to link a peace settlement with individual compensation was a delegation of influential refugees who traveled to Iraq and met with Iraqi Prime Minister Nuri al-Sa'id. Delegates included Ahmad al-Khalil, a Haifa lawyer who was Jordan's representative on the United Nations Truce Supervisory Organization's (UNTSO) Jordanian-Israeli Mixed Armistice Committee; Hikmat al-Taji al-Faruqi, a lawyer from Ramla; 'Ali al-Mustaqim, former vice mayor of Jaffa; Muhammad Najjar; and 'Ali Abu Ziyad. [7]

Israel's continued insistence upon global and not individual compensation thus engendered a negative reaction among the only Arabs actively pushing for peace with Israel, pro-Hashemite Palestinians in Jordan. Even some Israeli diplomats urged the government to adopt a different stance, at least in the case of influential refugees in Jordan. In January 1951, the Middle East Division of the Israeli Ministry of Foreign Affairs suggested that the government could split the ranks of rich refugees by paying personal compensation to certain of them in Jordan to show that it benefits a person who "acts in accordance with Israel's interests [i.e., signing a treaty with Jordan]." It was also recommended that the government stress to any Arabs who would listen that time was running out. [8] Certainly King 'Abdullah wanted Israel to allow wealthy refugees the chance to return to Israel briefly to sell their property. He told an American official of the UNCCP on June 27, 1951, just weeks short of his assassination, that he did not expect that total repatriation or total compensation was going to happen. However, Israel could help alleviate some of the refugees' bitterness by allowing the propertied ones to return to Israel to deal with their property. If they could not get it back maybe Israel at the least would allow them access to its income. If Israel would do this and release the blocked bank accounts, it would go far in helping the refugees resettle and eliminating their bitterness. [9]

The Israelis actually followed through with this strategy by using the subject of the refugee bank accounts it had frozen to woo Palestinian decision-makers in Jordan. The issue of these accounts had loomed large in 1949–50 at

Lausanne and beyond, but nothing had occurred despite a February 15, 1950 Egyptian-Israeli agreement on the matter. During secret Israeli-Jordanian talks in the spring of 1951 the issue was discussed again. The Israeli government agreed behind the scenes to release frozen accounts for those refugees living in Jordan. An internal Israeli memorandum from May 15, 1951 records that the government decided to "release an appreciable part of the accounts frozen in Israeli banks in favor of account holders in Jordan" for this purpose.[10] King 'Abdullah also confirmed as much to Eliyahu Sasson on April 28, 1951.[11] It is unclear, however, if any funds actually changed hands. Certainly 'Abdullah's above-cited comments to a UNCCP official about the accounts in late June 1951 suggest that in fact such a release had not occurred.

Secret Israeli attempts to connect compensation with making peace with Jordan continued even after 1951 but for different reasons. Whereas the emphasis on compensating the wealthy had focused on pushing the refugees toward accepting peace with Israel, it changed to getting the wealthy refugees to work for resettlement. John B. Blandford, Commissioner of UNRWA, told Berncastle in May 1952 that rich refugees were leading the charge against resettlement schemes because Israel was insisting that compensation payments only be made to a "Reintegration Fund." In such cases, the rich would not receive any money. According to Blandford, Israel was becoming more willing to separate the issues of compensation and resettlement. The reason was because Israel believed that if it paid personal compensation to the wealthy, they would be satisfied, cease their pressure on the bulk of refugees, who then would accept resettlement.[12] In August 1952, Berncastle met with Comay in Jerusalem. Comay confirmed Blandford's assessment, opining that paying compensation to wealthy refugees would lead them in turn to push for resettlement of the bulk of the refugees. Comay also claimed that Israeli government Arabists had provided him with a long list of names of wealthy refugees to consider.[13]

Ultimately, the assassination of King 'Abdullah at the hands of a Palestinian in July 1951 ended the prospects for Israel to conclude a separate peace treaty with Jordan. With 'Abdullah's death came a temporary halt in the prospects for compensation for refugees living in Jordan.

## Lif Committee

The Israeli government appeared concerned about the growing international interest in refugee compensation by late 1949. The most clear example of this interest was the UNCCP's various attempts to seek progress on the issue, including the dispatching of the Clapp Mission to the Middle East. On October 20, 1949, a mere ten days after the Clapp Mission met with Israeli treasury director David Horowitz, the Israeli government decided to establish a commission to examine the entire question of compensation. It turned to Zalman Lif to head the commission, called the Committee to Examine the Issue of Compensation for Absentee Property. Lif was the former Zalman Lifshits, the JNF colleague of Yosef Weitz who had served with Weitz and 'Ezra Danin on the first Israeli commission to look at refugee land in 1948. He was assisted in his new task by Yehoshu'a Palmon, the prime minister's advisor on Arab affairs, and Dr. G. Meron, director of the Ministry of Foreign Affairs' Finance Department.

Unlike the earlier 1948 wide-ranging study of the refugee issue, including abandoned property, the Lif Commission's sole purpose was to study compensation. The committee's point of departure was the assumption that refugee repatriation was out of the question except for small numbers "in exceptional cases." The question of refugee land was thus one of expropriation and compensation. The committee also started its study on the assumption that full legal ownership of the land would be transferred to the state to be used for development purposes. Specifically, the committee agreed to study the following questions:

1. Do generally accepted standards exist, from the perspective of international law, that obligate the State of Israel to pay compensation?
2. Does the UN General Assembly Resolution of 11 December 1948 [calling for compensation] possess any authority, and if so, how much?
3. What should be the political circumstances upon which negotiations regarding refugee property compensation payment should be conditioned?
4. In the event that the State of Israel will be obligated to pay compensation—should compensation be individual or collective? And in the event that compensation will be collective, what body should be authorized to receive the compensation, and what should it be used for?
5. For what types of property will it be necessary to pay compensation?
6. In the event that it will be necessary to pay compensation for specific types of property, what will the basis of property valuation and the determination of the amount to be paid as compensation?
7. How is this property being safeguarded against decay and depreciation, and how has the Israeli government taken responsibility for the integrity of this property since its transfer to the Custodian of Absentee Property?

8. How is it possible to link the payment of absentee property compensation with Israel's counter claims against the Arab states for war reparations and indemnities?[14]

These questions reveal fascinating insights into the Israeli government's thinking about the refugee property at the time. Various government officials had issued statements throughout 1949 to the effect that compensation only would be paid for cultivated land, that only a collective payment would be made, and that Israel would take into account its claims for war damage when considering compensating the refugees. The questions used by the committee as the basis of its deliberations clearly indicate that at least some within the Israeli government were not yet willing to accept these as foregone conclusions prior to a serious legal study. During its first meeting, the three-man committee invited various experts to assist in the general discussion and help formulate recommendations. These were S. Rozen, Legal Advisor to the Foreign Ministry; Z. A. Beker, deputy legal advisor to the government; Prof. Y. Shaki, assistant to the government's legal advisor; Moshe Kohen Elhasid, Department of the Advisor for Land Affairs; Dr. Y. Gera, Financial Department of the Foreign Ministry; M. Kortemar, Legal Advisor to the State Controller; and Yosef Teko'a, assistant to the Foreign Ministry's Legal Advisor.

After four months of study, the Lif Committee issued its report on March 17, 1950. Entitled "The Report of the Committee to Examine the Issue of Compensation for Absentee Property," the 17-page document examined a wide range of issues relating to the eight questions that had informed the committee's deliberations. Despite the degree of doubt that might have been indicated by the committee's starting questions, the Lif Committee report overall offered a carefully researched and firm affirmation of the tough public line adopted theretofore by the Israeli government. First, the report set the historical context for the refugee flight and the abandonment of property. It first noted that Jews too had fled their homes during the fighting. It ascribed the Palestinians' flight as part of the political and strategic military strategy of the Arab states. It furthermore noted that the state essentially had neglected the abandoned land up to that point [this was prior to enactment of the Absentees' Property Law and the subsequent sale to the Development Authority]. It also studied two specific legal questions: Do the refugees still possess the right of title to their sequestered land, and is the UN resolution calling for compensation legally binding for Israel? Lif and his associates decided that the Emergency Regulations (Absentees' Property) of 5709/1948 did *not* pass legal title to the refugees' land to the state:

> The legal situation resulting from the above-mentioned regulations is that the property rights of absentee owners, or their rights to the value of their property in the case of their sale, is harmed neither by the original version of the Emergency Regulations regarding Absentee Property nor by the version currently under debate in the Knesset [which was debating a temporary extension of the law; this was prior to passage of the Absentees' Property Law of 1950]. This right is also not harmed by any other Israeli law .... From a legal and theoretical perspective and in the absence of a peace treaty with the neighboring Arab countries, this right will remain intact and valid until either a final settlement regarding the issue of refugee property is achieved, or a law specifically annulling the property rights of refugees is legislated. [15]

This "liberal" interpretation of the ongoing nature of the refugees' right to the land's title was premature: the Knesset enacted the Absentees' Property Law three days before the Lif Committee's report was signed and delivered. That law, discussed in chapter 1, allowed the Israeli government to claim legal title to the abandoned land. As for the UN General Assembly's Resolution 194 (III) that called for compensation, the Lif Commission investigated whether a resolution of the General Assembly was legally binding for member states of the UN and determined that it was not. However, it cautioned the government that the resolution still carried "political weight" that Israel should consider in its eventual decisions regarding compensation.

The Lif Committee report then set out 27 conclusions about compensation that overall endorsed the hard line previously adopted by the Israeli government and set forth further tough policy recommendations. A number of these conclusions are worth examining. The Lif Committee went to significant pains to discuss the legal status of the refugees insofar as the question of whether they constituted "enemies" of the state was concerned. The three committee members noted the similarity between the 1948 Israeli legislation governing the abandoned law and the laws of "enemy property" that a number of countries had adopted in the twentieth century to deal with the property of enemy aliens residing in those states during times of war. In such cases, the report noted that any negotiations regarding compensation for damaged or expropriated "enemy land" was conducted by the two belligerent states themselves after the end of hostilities, not between one state and the property owners of the other state. Thus, under these situations, the one state pays compensation to the other state, which then resolves the claims submitted to it by its own citizens (or does not resolve them, as the case may be; this is an internal domestic matter of no concern to the government that paid compensation). However, the committee noted that several aspects of the Palestinian refugee case made it difficult to address in this way. In the first place, the writers stated that certain parties within the international community did not view the Arab-Israeli war of 1948 as a true "war" from the perspective of international law, both during the stages of the Jewish-Palestinian civil war between November 29, 1947 and May 14, 1948 and the period after declaration of Israeli statehood and the entrance of regular Arab armies into the fray thereafter. It was thus not a simple matter to apply the usual international precedents for two former belligerent states that deal with confiscated property after a war.

On a similar issue, the Lif Committee stated that Palestinian refugees outside the borders of Israel could not in fact be considered "enemy citizens." This further complicated the matter of applying the usual international laws governing the use or expropriation of the land of enemy aliens by a belligerent nation. Nor was it the case that the refugees could be classified as "rebels" by the State of Israel. The report noted that:

> The Arabs of Palestine that today live outside of Israeli territory should not be regarded as "enemy citizens"; rather, with the end of the Mandate, they became devoid of any citizenship. There is no agreement as to whether or not it is possible to classify those that undertook hostile actions against the State of Israel as "traitors" or "rebels."[16]

The committee also informed the Israeli government that its policy of linking counter claims for war damages with refugee property compensation was illegal. The report noted that Israel could not simply blame the Palestinians for a war that Israel believed was forced on it by the neighboring Arab states. In this regard, Israel could not legally pass along its demands for war damages from the Arab states to the refugees and their claim for compensation. The situations and the parties involved were different. On the other hand, the Lif Committee believed that such international legal ambiguity presented Israel with certain opportunities to demand war damages anyway, as did the Arab states' refusal to negotiate directly with the Jewish state.

> Actually, the lack of a clear set of rules in international law and the absence of a uniform procedure in the case of compensation and the payment of damages enables Israel to make its arguments and to condition the Arab states' representation of the refugees on the payment of war

> indemnities to Israel ....As long as the Arab states refuse to enter into peace negotiations with Israel, there is no reason for Israel not to adopt a firm stance on the issue of compensation for refugee property. This would be in order to make it necessary for them to begin negotiating, and to adopt a more conciliatory stance on the issue of war indemnities.[17]

Another possibility for Israeli negotiators, according to the committee members, was to make an issue of the fact that certain Palestinian refugees "identified" with the Arab armies' struggle against Israel. While there was no legal basis to consider these persons "traitors," Israel could push to seize these refugees' property in exchange for war damages. "We must insist that the value of the property of refugees that identified themselves [with the Arab states] be deducted from the total sum that Israel agrees to pay for refugee property."[18] It stated that Israel must differentiate between refugees who were "hostile" to Israel versus those who actually participated in "hostile acts" against the Jewish state. Since later portions of the committee report stated that it was impossible to evaluate the property of each individual refugee, it is unclear how the committee proposed quantifying either the number of refugees who had been involved in "hostile acts" or the value of those persons' property. It was also noted that it might prove impossible to maintain such a stance but that nonetheless it could serve Israel's interests in the UN. The report also declared that Israel could hold the refugees' property hostage to pressure the Arab states into paying war damages. The Arabs could not be forced to pay war damages or to negotiate directly with Israel, but Israel could use the fact that it controlled refugee property to try to force Arab compliance on these issues. The authors hoped that the refugees would realize that they would not receive any compensation outside of peace talks.

Like the Weitz-Lifshits-Danin Committee the year before, the Lif Committee pushed for resettlement of the refugees in the neighboring Arab countries as the only solution to their exile. Lif and his colleagues noted, however, that Israel could drop its demand that compensation be discussed only with the Arabs as part of comprehensive peace talks if it received "persuasive and guaranteed" evidence that resettlement of the refugees in the Arab world in fact was taking place prior to such a peace process. In that case, the committee recommended that Israel contribute money to that resettlement process, subject to its ability to pay, subject to the conditions that the Arabs states and the UN "pledge to be responsible toward Israel for the funds contributed, and that the amount of the installment be deducted from total compensation to be paid in the future." [19] Israel would decide on the amount of this installment on the basis of how extensive the resettlement efforts were and how much the Arab states and the international community were contributing. In similar fashion, the report recommended that if no negotiations with the Arabs took place and the UN created a fund for the permanent resettlement of the Palestinian refugees, then Israel should make a contribution to that fund, a contribution that would be deducted from future compensation.

Turning to the question of how to identify and place a value on refugee property, the committee flatly ruled out the possibility that Israeli authorities could determine such information for each and every parcel of abandoned property. This was:

> due to the situation that resulted from the course of events, the use of refugee property by residents of Israel who were forced to take possession for reasons caused by the war, and the process of development that has been taking place during the past few years. [20]

For this reason, Israel must insist upon collective, not individual compensation:

> It is therefore important that the Israeli government insist on the principle of collective compensation for refugee property and agree neither to individual valuation of each specific item nor to the payment of compensation to property owners themselves. [21]

Not only was it technically impossible to valuate individual refugees' land, it was politically undesirable as well. The report hinted that individual payments would not help the overall refugee problem—an allusion to the fact that Israel feared that a good percentage of the total amounts paid would go to a certain few wealthy landowners with insufficient amounts left to finance resettlement of the bulk of poorer refugees. Individual payments also might lead to demands that refugees be repatriated to help in the process of valuating their land, which could create security nightmares. It also might foster the false belief that they could remain permanently in Israel. Israel must refuse to take any steps that might lead to this. As the report noted:

> Only complete, unmistakable refusal on the part of Israel to allow the entrance of refugees will convince them they have no other option aside from permanently settling elsewhere, and that the sooner they do this, the better they will fare. [22]

The report was clearly fearful that the Arabs would demand such a temporary repatriation for the purposes of disposing of land, as in fact the Arabs had called for at Lausanne. The report affirmed that Israel's statements that it had an obligation to compensate the refugees in no way implied that it must settle accounts with individual refugees or allow them a direct hand in the process of resolving the issue. The most Israel should go toward including the Arabs in this process would be to participate in a mixed committee that had one Arab member.[23]

The Lif Committee's report also reaffirmed Israel's narrow interpretation of just what types of property merited compensation. Only privately owned land that was regularly cultivated would be considered. No compensation would be paid for other lands, including land belonging to the former mandatory government:

> In the event that compensation is paid, it will only be applicable to property that can be proven to have been held as private property, in contrast to property of local authorities, state property, and other public property. Private family endowments will be considered private property for the sake of compensation. Listing of a specific property in the registry in an individual's name will not be sufficient evidence that this property was privately-owned, unless registration was accompanied by possession and regular use of the property before its abandonment, and unless taxes were paid on it for an extended period of time. Compensation will only be paid for cultivable land that was regularly cultivated.[24]

The committee also made it clear that Israel should pay compensation only for property that the Custodian of Absentee Property actually received in good condition. It made clear that the government of Israel was not responsible for property damage inflicted during the war, nor "for the degeneration or decrease in value of property located inside of Israel that took place before it was actually transferred to Custodian supervision." This was a major point, because Arab spokesmen—and later, the UNCCP—estimated compensation on the basis of what the land was worth prior to the war. The Lif Committee argued that Israel only should be accountable for the property's value months later, when the Custodian of Absentee Property took hold of it. The Israeli claim that it was not liable to pay for damages to refugee property caused during the war came despite Israel's own insistence that the Arabs were liable for war damages sustained by the Jewish state.

The report particularly repudiated the Arabs' claims for the value of the orange groves that they had made at Lausanne, and stated that the UNCCP had been "affected by the propaganda of the refugees on this issue."[25] The report detailed how the orange groves had deteriorated during the Second World War but remained registered as active groves because their owners wanted to take advantage of favorable British tax policies toward citrus groves. The report pointed to a 1949 study carried out by the Israeli Ministry of Agriculture that showed the true extent of Arab orange groves, and stated that this study should be used to calculate any compensation. They also noted that the records of the Custodian would be helpful in this regard. Finally, it did not rule out compensation for moveable property that actually was received by the Custodian in useable condition.

Regarding valuation of the property, the report repeatedly stressed that this should be a collective figure and not a figure for each refugee's individual property. It stressed that the government should be in negotiations with other parties regarding the amount of compensation to be paid and proposed the following formulas for arriving at values:

1. In the case of moveable property that was actually transferred to the Custodian—values will be based on the property's value at the time of its transfer, if such a valuation was made. If the property was leased by the Custodian, valuation will take into account the amount actually received, after deduction of all expenditures of the Custodian, including management costs, taxes and all other such expenditures, according to a report approved by the Minister of Finance.
2. In the case of land—values will be based on the Government of Palestine's last assessment of the property for the purposes of urban or rural property tax, according to the circumstances. Another method of overall valuation of refugee property is calculating the national income of the Arab sector, to which the refugees belong, based on the estimation carried out by the Mandate government in 1946, and then multiplying this income by an agreed-upon factor. In the United States, the standard factor is four. Some propose taking this approach toward the national income of the Arab population of Palestine, but applying a factor of three.[26]

Overall, the report urged the government to continue negotiating over the final amount of compensation to be paid. This final amount should reflect Israel's ability to pay and must take into account war damages. The report did not offer its own estimate of the scope or value of refugee land. The Lif Committee ultimately upheld the stance that the Israeli government publicly had adopted by late 1949, and provided a reasoned, legal analysis to support this position. With some exceptions, these fundamental attitudes would continue to govern Israeli policy for years to come. Israel did not make the report public, much as the UNCCP wanted once it found out about its existence. Nor did Zalman Lif live to discuss it: he died within nine months of the report's submission.

## Counter Claims for Prewar Jewish Property Abandoned in 1948

Israel devised a number of counter claims to reduce or even cancel out what it expected to pay in compensation to Palestinian refugees. Certainly the first of these was the war damages claim that it first raised at the Lausanne Conference. Related to this was the question of land owned by Israeli Jews that was lost behind Arab lines after 1948, both in the parts of Palestine controlled by Egypt and Jordan as well as in surrounding Arab states. From the beginning of the Zionist movement in the late nineteenth century, Zionists committed to Jewish settlement throughout Greater Syria began buying land in a number of Middle Eastern areas. Most of this, of course, lay in what the British called Palestine after the First World War. Some lay in Lebanon, Syria, and Transjordan, however. The 1948 fighting saw the owners of this land separated from their property, much as Palestinian refugees found themselves on the other side of hostile borders and ceasefire lines from their own property in Israel. Among this lost Zionist land in Palestine was the land on which several settlements had been constructed. All but one of these settlements lay in the West Bank, which was occupied and later annexed by Jordan. The other one was in Gaza, which was administered by but never annexed by Egypt. The settlements were evacuated in May 1948 (see table 3.1).

Besides these lost lands belonging to Zionist land purchasing institutions, individual Jewish landowners, companies, and civil and religious institutions left behind real estate in the West Bank (including East Jerusalem) and Gaza after 1948. Individual Jews owned land in localities like Bayt Jala, East Jerusalem, Silwan, Bayt Iksa, Bayt Safafa, Hebron, and the Triangle area bounded by Nablus, Tulkarm, and Janin. Corporate entities owning land in the West Bank included the Mizrahi Land Improvement Co., Ltd.; the Palestine Jewish Colonization Association (PICA); the Jewish National Fund; the Anglo-Palestine Bank; the Hebrew University of Jerusalem; the Vilna, Hayy 'Olam, and Ashkenaz waqfs in Jerusalem; the Jewish cemeteries in Hebron and Nablus; and others. All total, 16,684 dunums of Jewish-owned land lay in the West Bank after 1948, a full 6,676 of which was located in the four former settlements of the 'Etsiyon Bloc. This land is detailed in table 3.2.

TABLE 3.1 Jewish Settlements Abandoned in the West Bank and Gaza in 1948

| *Locality* | *Type* | *Date Est.* |
|---|---|---|
| 1. West Bank | | |
| Bet ha-'Arava | kibbutz | 1939 |
| Gush 'Etsiyon ['Etsiyon Bloc] | | |
| a. Kfar 'Etsiyon | religious kibbutz | 1943 |
| b. 'En Tsurim | religious kibbutz | 1946 |
| c. Massu'ot Yitshak | religious moshav | 1945 |
| d. Revadim | kibbutz | 1947 |
| 'Atarot | moshav | 1922 |
| Neve Ya'akov | moshav | 1924 |
| Rabbat Ashlag | * | 1930 |
| Kaliya | ** | 1930s |
| 2. Gaza | | |
| Kfar Darom | religious kibbutz | 1946 |

** Palestine Potash Company works
** hotel complex
Source: *Encyclopaedia Judaica* (Jerusalem: Keter Publishing House, Ltd., 1971); *Geography*. The Israel Pocket Library (Jerusalem: Keter Publishing House, Ltd., 1973)

Besides Jewish land in the West Bank, Jordan also controlled more than 6,000 dunums of Zionist-owned land on the East Bank, in Jordan proper. In 1921, the mandatory government granted an electric concession to a Jewish industrialist in Palestine, Pinhas Rutenberg. Born in the Ukraine in 1879, Rutenberg moved to Palestine after a brief involvement in the 1917 Russian revolution. His concession extended across both sides of the Jordan River, including both Palestine and Transjordan. In February 1927, mandatory authorities prompted the Transjordanian government to sell 6,000 dunums of state land in the Sukhur al-Ghawr region of the northern Jordan Valley to Rutenberg's Palestine Electric Corporation (PEC) for £12,965. [27] This land lay near the confluence of the Yarmuk and Jordan Rivers. The inhabitants were resettled and in June 1928 the area was renamed Jisr al-Majami' by the Transjordanian government after the bridge spanning the Jordan located nearby. Zionists referred to the area as Naharayim. Rutenberg built an electric generation plant on the lands, which were so vast compared to his needs that he petitioned the British to allow him to sell some of the excess to Jewish settlers. They refused, although later he allowed some Jews to live and farm on his land without selling it to them. [28] Rutenberg's plant was overrun by

TABLE 3.2 Jewish Land in the West Bank Controlled by Jordan After 1948

| *District* | *Amount (Dunums)* |
|---|---|
| Nablus | 5.850 |
| Tulkarm | 688.118 |
| Ramallah | 145.976 |
| Jerusalem | |
| 1. Urban | |
| E. Jerusalem | 77.108 |
| No Man's Land | 25.458 |
| Government House | 47.494 |
| Hebrew University/ Hadassah Hospital enclave | 880.195 |
| 2. Rural | |
| Government House | 119.675 |
| Villages | 8,708.693 |
| Bethlehem | 2,928.095 |
| Hebron | 3,031.759 |
| TOTAL | 16,684.421* |

* The author could not locate comparable figures for the amount of Jewish land in Gaza.

Source: UNSA DAG 13–3, UNCCP. Subgroup: Land Identification and Valuation Office. Series: Records of the Land Specialist, 1937–1967/Box 38/1964–66/Israel; Document: Jarvis to Comay (March 17, 1966)

Jordanian forces on May 14, 1948 and later looted by local villagers. Its ruins still stand to this day. According to one source, the PEC eventually transferred title to its lost land in Jordan to the JNF.[29]

Besides actual ownership of property, at least one Zionist company also leased land in Jordan. The war saw these leases broken by the Jordanian government. The Palestine Potash Company (PPC) was directed by a Russian Jewish immigrant to Palestine, A. Moshe Novomeysky (b. 1873). The PPC built a potash and bromine plant at Rabbat Ashlag at the northern end of the Dead Sea—on the Palestinian side of the lake—in 1930. The kibbutz of Bet ha-'Arava also was located on this PPC land and settled by German and Central European Jews associated with the ha-Kibbutz ha-Me'uhad movement in 1939. The PPC also leased 2,149 dunums of state land on the Jordanian side of the Jordan River just north of the Dead Sea, in the Zawr Kattar area of Ghawr al-Rama. The Jordanian treasury leased the land to the company for

72 years. Beyond this, the treasury also leased the PPC both land and water rights in Ghawr al-Safi on the southern end of the Dead Sea. These water rights consisted of one-third of the river water flowing through Wadi Hasa into Ghawr al-Safi. [30] The land and leases of the PEC and PPC represent the only examples of Jews or Jewish-owned companies that owned land in Jordan by 1948. Despite rumors and numerous attempts by Zionists to acquire land, including through subterfuge, no concrete evidence has surfaced showing other Jewish ownership of land in Jordan besides the examples noted here. [31]

In the wake of 1948, Jordan and Egypt sequestered Jewish-owned property in the West Bank and Gaza, respectively, much as Israel had done to Palestinian property. Unlike the Palestinian refugees, Jews in Israel who owned land under Jordanian and Egyptian military administration were now legally "enemy aliens" given that Egypt and Jordan were technically at war with Israel. Jordan simply used the same mandatory era "enemy property" law that had been enacted in 1939 upon the outbreak of the Second World War. In 1948, Jordan established a Guardian of Enemy Property (Ar.: Haris Amlak al-'Aduww) in accordance with article nine of its Trading with the Enemy Act. The Guardian officially was granted legal control—but not legal title—to land in the West Bank that was owned by residents of Israel, whether Jews or Palestinians. When Jordan ended military rule in the West Bank, the Guardian was placed under the rubric of the Ministry of the Interior. The guardian also assumed control over Jewish-owned land in the East Bank, in Jordan proper. Thus the Jordanian government served public notice in October 1953 that it had cancelled the Palestine Electric Corporation's concession. [32] The PEC's land in Jordan was placed under the Guardian of Enemy Property in April 1954. [33] The Palestine Potash Company's concession was cancelled in December 1952 although no land was placed under the Guardian since it merely leased land in Jordan. [34]

The fate of Jewish land under Jordanian control came up immediately in talks between Israel and Jordan and between the UNCCP and Jordan. The PEC's land in particular quickly loomed large in Israeli-Jordanian relations after 1948. Israeli negotiators brought up the future of the electric works during the armistice talks on Rhodes in 1949. The Israelis insisted on placing a clause in the draft Israeli-Jordanian non-aggression pact of March 1950 stating that Jordan would allow resumption of the plant's operation. Several months later, acting upon Israel's interpretation of the extent of its territory under the 1949 armistice agreement, Israeli forces occupied a small part of the PEC lands along the Jordan River in August 1950. When Holger Andersen of the UNCCP's Refugee Office discussed Israel's claim for Jewish property in the

West Bank with Jordanian Prime Minister Samir al-Rifa'i in mid-1951, al-Rifa'i "agreed to this property being taken into account in the final compensation settlement." [35] In addition to diplomatic moves, the PEC—which later changed its name to the Israel Electric Company in 1961—also engaged lawyers in the United States to investigate what the Americans could do about its property. In July 1953, the New York law firm of Cahill, Gordon, Zachry & Reindel (Cotton & Franklin) met with the U.S. Department of State to discuss Jordan's cancellation of the PEC concession and UNRWA's plan to finance a dam on the Yarmuk River. [36] As noted above, one source claims that the PEC eventually transferred title to its lost land to the Jewish National Fund. Regardless of any such move, however, the land has remained sequestered by the Jordanians to this day.

Throughout the 1950s and 1960s, Jordanian authorities published orders in the official government newspaper listing villages and regions in the West Bank where Jewish land was being placed under the Guardian of Enemy Property. At times, the publication listed the land of individual persons as well. In April 1954, land belonging to the following "enemy citizens" was placed under the Guardian, among others: Yona Born; Yona Friedman; the Palestine Electric Corporation; Shlomo ben Avraham Abu Jadid on behalf of the Hayy 'Olam waqf in Jerusalem; the Jewish cemetery in Hebron; the Jewish cemetery in Nablus; and the Jewish National Fund, Pinhas Liebkin, and partners. [37] Land owned by enemy citizens in Jerusalem was sequestered by the Guardian in October 1966. [38] Land of the Anglo-Palestine Bank, which became Bank Le'umi le-Yisra'el in 1951, was placed under the Guardian in 1963. [39] Even Palestinian Arabs in Israel had their land sequestered by the Guardian, such as Muhammad Mustafa al-Sha'bani of Jaffa. In his case, he was not referred to as an "enemy citizen" but simply "the absentee." [40]

The policy of the Jordanian government concerning the 16,684 dunums of Jewish land in the West Bank was to preserve the original owners' legal title to the land. Unlike Israeli legislation toward the Palestinian refugees' land, Jordanian law preserved the legal rights of the "enemy" landowners and did not allow its sale. This does not suggest, however, that the government did nothing with the land. In fact, it rented it out. For example, the state rented two dunums of enemy land in Hebron to Jawda Salim al-Bakri for JD[Jordanian dinars]5/year for some seven years. [41] The Custodian allowed UNRWA to use 68 dunums in 'Atarot for the Qalandiya Vocational Training Center. American diplomats noted that while the land had been worth JD200/dunum in 1948, it was worth JD1,000/dunum by 1961. [42] Palestinian refugees were allowed to settle in the ruined Jewish Quarter of Jerusalem's Old City, although not all of the land in the quarter was Jewish-owned. In Gaza, Egyptian military authorities sequestered Jewish-owned property as well. Just one month after entering the Gaza region, they issued Order No. 25 of 1948, entitled Order for Administering the Property of Jews in the Areas Subject to Egyptian Forces in Palestine.[43] The land was placed under the authority of a Director General, and was used after 1948 for construction of refugee camps and leased for private use, among other purposes.

Besides Jewish land that ended up in Jordan, the West Bank, and Gaza, Zionist organizations also owned land in Syria and Lebanon. This land similarly was cut off from its owners after 1948. Most of this land lay in the southern regions of Syria in Hawran and the Golan. During the late nineteenth century, Jews from Palestine, Europe, and the United States tried unsuccessfully to settle in these regions.[44] In 1886, Jews from Safad established the settlement of Bnei Yehuda on the Golan Heights near the eastern shore of Lake Tiberias. A moving force behind Bnei Yehuda was reportedly an Algerian Jew living in Safad who had been a colleague of the anti-French Algerian resistance leader ʻAbd al-Qadir al-Jaza'iri. The amount of land that was purchased is unclear; the author has seen estimates ranging from 3,500 to 6,000 dunums. The land reportedly had belonged to a village called Bir Shaqum prior to that.[45] The Bnei Yehuda settlement survived only until the 1920s but the land remained legally controlled by Jews and eventually was owned by the JNF. The same was true of a larger area of land to the east in Hawran. Several foreign Jewish organizations were involved in that endeavor during the late Ottoman period. The Russian Agudat Akhim organization acquired land in the village of Jillin and several others in the districts of Fiq and Darʻa. The American group Shavei Tsiyon and a Romanian group tried to establish a Jewish settlement near the village of Sahm al-Jawlan.[46] In 1892, the Paris-based Jewish philanthropist Baron Edmond James de Rothschild bought the holdings of these three groups. He ended up owning a large amount of land in several villages in Golan by special order from Istanbul. The total amount of land varied according to the definition of "ownership": the amount of land for which Rothschild actually possessed a title deed versus the amount of land as it appeared on maps; the amount was at least 54,000 dunums.

Two organizations tried to settle Rothschild's land with Jews, although they too failed: the Paris-based Committee for Erets Yisra'el and, after it was established in 1924, the Palestine Jewish Colonization Association (PICA). The settlers planted extensive eucalyptus groves near Jillin and built a road stretching from Lake Hula in Palestine to Muzayrib in Hawran. Despite the failure of the Jewish colonies in Syria, the land on which they sat remained in Jewish ownership. Rothschild handed over his lands in the Middle East to PICA after it was formed. Title to the land in Hawran was legally transferred to PICA in 1929 and 1930.

PICA was cut off from this large expanse of land in Syria after the 1948 war. In fact, it had experienced major difficulties retaining legal control of its land even before 1948. The presence of Zionist-owned land in Syria was a touchy one with Syrian authorities, especially after Syrian independence from France. In 1942, the Syrian "land settlement" campaign to register title to land spread to the PICA lands. Part of the process was to register land in the name of the true legal owner. Despite its claims, the Syrians ruled against PICA and refused to register the land in its name. PICA appealed to the Court of Appeals in Aleppo in January 1946, but the dispute lingered until 1947. By that time, Syria was independent of France and PICA realized that the country's Arab nationalist government never would rule in favor of a Zionist organization. In fact, British diplomats in Damascus reported that Syrian Prime Minister Jamil Mardam had decided "in principle" that the Syrian government should buy the land "on the grounds that it was contrary to Syrian policy to allow Jews to own land in Syria." Apparently, Mardam wanted to wait until after the elections of that year before making a move.[47]

The 1948 war definitely cut off PICA from its land and the situation seemed even more hopeless. In April 1949, PICA wrote to the Israeli Ministry of Foreign Affairs about the matter.[48] PICA arranged for its tax liabilities for the land to be sent to Syrian authorities every year thereafter until 1957, when the payment was returned by the Syrian government along with a note stating that the land was now registered to "its legal owners."[49] This was probably due to a 1952 Syrian law that forbade foreigners from owning rural land. Syrian Legislative Decree No. 189 of April 1, 1952, later amended by Decree No. 155 of November 15, 1952, stated that no foreigner could own such land. In the event foreigners did own rural land, it could not be inherited by heirs but eventually would be taken over by the state. According to the decree, compensation would be paid by the Administration of State Lands.[50] Eventually, PICA decided to give its land in Syria to the Israeli government. James Rothschild, son of Edmond James de Rothschild and his successor in the drive to settle Jews in Israel, died in 1957. His will instructed PICA to transfer most of its land in Israel to the JNF. By that time, however, the JNF had become an Israeli company and was focused on developing its land in Israel. PICA then agreed to give its land in Syria to the Israeli government instead in the hopes that it could press a claim for compensation someday. A formal agreement was signed on December 31, 1958 by which PICA:

TABLE 3.3 PICA Land in Syria After 1948

| *Village* | *Area Owned by Deed (Dunums)* | *Area Owned by Map (Dunums)* |
|---|---|---|
| Jillin | 4,433 | 4,884 |
| Kawkab Qibliyya | 3,250 | 3,987 |
| Kawkab Shamaliyya | 1,000 | — |
| Muzayra'a | 3,555 | 3,600 |
| Sahm al-Jawlan | 27,952 | 27,739 |
| Bustas | 12,051 | 12,051 |
| Nafa'a and Bayt Akar | 2,000 | — |
| TOTAL | 54,241 | 73,974 |

Source: ISA (80) 5721/gimel/23

> has agreed to vest in the STATE OF ISRAEL its rights in the Properties and in relation thereto to execute an Irrevocable Power of Attorney for the transfer of all PICA's rights in the Properties to the State of Israel, or as the State of Israel may direct. [51]

Table 3.3 details PICA's holdings in Syria by that time. As already mentioned, the total amount of land varied according to the definition of "ownership."

In addition to PICA, the JNF also owned land in Syria. It claimed that it owned 76,000 dunums in Golan, Hawran, and Transjordan by 1923. [52] It continued to claim legal ownership of these lands after 1948 as well. Evidence also suggests that the government of Israel later transferred the former PICA land in Syria to the JNF, just as the Palestine Electric Company reportedly transferred title to its sequestered land in Jordan to the JNF. [53]

TABLE 3.4 PICA Land in Lebanon After 1948

| *Village* | *Amount (Dunums)* |
|---|---|
| Mawtil | 1,389.958 |
| Khiyam and Khiyam Marj 'Ayun | 394.400 |
| Kufr Kala | 784.578 |
| Ibil al-Kama | 1,782.698 |
| TOTAL | 4,351.634 |

Source: ISA (80) 5721/gimel/23, agreement of December 31, 1958

Finally, 1948 saw Lebanon in control of Zionist-owned land. PICA had acquired 4,351.634 dunums in several villages in the Marj 'Ayun district in far southern Lebanon. These formally were registered in PICA's name in Lebanon on April 26, 1938. These are detailed in table 3.4. As with its land in Syria, PICA continued to pay taxes on its land through 1958, at which time it transferred its rights in the land to the Israeli government. I could not find data to indicate whether Lebanon ever expropriated this land formally.

## Counter Claims for Property Abandoned by Jews in Arab Countries After 1948

The counter claim that Israel began trumpeting the loudest, especially starting in 1951, was the fate of Jewish land abandoned in Arab countries after 1948 by immigrants to Israel. This was worth much more than the above-mentioned property lost in 1948. Israel began demanding that this second type of Jewish property be taken into consideration in any talks about Israel's debt of compensation to Palestinian refugees. According to Israel's logic, it and the Arab world had carried out a population transfer: most of Palestine's Arabs for most of the Arab world's Jews. The Arab world absorbed the Palestinians; Israel absorbed the Arab Jews. The Arabs claimed compensation for abandoned property; so too did Jews from Arab countries. Thus Israel argued that the two compensation issues were linked, and raised the fate of Jewish property in Arab countries as a way to offset any claims it might owe the Palestinians.

The Arab world was home to several hundred thousand Jews prior to 1948. The presence of some, like in Yemen, Iraq, and Syria, dated back thousands of years. While sometimes speaking Arabic with a particular Jewish dialect, these people lived for all intents and purposes like the Christian, Muslim, and Druze Arabs in whose midst they resided. Other Jewish populations in Arab countries were more recent descendants of the Jews expelled from Spain in 1492. These were called the Sephardim. While living in an Arab environment and speaking Arabic, they also clung to their own Judaeo-Spanish language called Ladino. Thirdly, some Arab areas saw the immigration of small numbers of European Jews, called Ashkenazim. Many of these spoke a Judaeo-German language called Yiddish. Most of these moved to Palestine, although some were found in countries like Egypt as well. Finally, there were a number of foreign Jews in certain Arab countries. These were Jews from both Sephardic and Ashkenazic backgrounds from countries like Italy and France who lived in Egypt, Libya, Algeria, and other Arab states but who retained their European nationality. Whatever their background, Jews in the Arab world owned property and businesses. Some grew quite prosperous, especially in Iraq and Egypt.

The rise of Zionism and its clear impact upon the Arabs of Palestine evoked widespread hostility toward Zionism among Arabs in the Middle East in the years prior to 1948. At times this hostility was directed against the Jews in their midst, even though the vast majority of them were not involved in Zionist politics and intended to remain living in the Arab world, where their ancestors had lived for generations. The most notorious example of such persecution was the attack on Jews in Baghdad in June 1941, known to Iraqi Jews as the Farhud. However unfairly, the Jews of the Arab world were caught up in the rising Zionist-Arab conflict in Palestine. With the coming of the 1948 war, the implications of this connection were to have far-reaching consequences. Almost immediately after the war, both Israelis and Arabs began quietly to ponder the possibilities of a population and property transfer. Why not have the Arab world absorb the 726,000 Palestinians refugees while Israel absorbs Jews from Arab countries? Such thinking was in line with Zionist concepts of population transfers. Some Arab politicians, notably Prime Minister Nuri al-Sa'id of Iraq, also proposed such an idea. Al-Sa'id told the Clapp Mission in Baghdad in October 1949 that Iraq would exchange 100,000 Iraqi Jews for 100,000 Palestinian refugees if Iraq were permitted to keep the Jews' property.[54] Although none of these plans came to real fruition, the details of some are discussed below.

Much more than transfer, the real issue that motivated Israel to link Palestinian refugee issues with Jewish property in the Arab world was the enactment of restrictive legislation in several Arab countries in 1948 and thereafter, legislation that at times permitted confiscation of Jewish property. Israel was anxious not only to absorb Jewish immigrants from the Middle East but also to secure their wealth as well. Sequestration of Jewish property in several Arab states made this impossible, and Israel began assuming for itself the role of protector of the frozen assets of its new citizens. The eruption of open hostilities between the new Israeli state and troops from several Arab countries (Egypt, Jordan, Syria, Lebanon, Iraq, and Saudi Arabia) prompted some of these states to enact sequestration laws that affected the property of the Jewish citizens living in their midst. The reasons for such laws included retaliation for the Israelis' seizure of Palestinian land and fear that Jewish property in their countries somehow would be used to benefit Israel.

Certainly the country where the issue of Jewish property affected the question of Palestinian refugee property and indeed the entire Arab-Israeli conflict the most was Iraq, home to a thriving and ancient Jewish community of some135,000 persons. As a result of the events of 1948, Zionism was declared illegal and Jews were persecuted even though many displayed no sympathies with Zionism or Israel. A prominent Jewish businessman, Shafiq ‘Adas, was executed in September 1948 for allegedly having business contacts with Israel. Restrictions on the buying and selling of Jewish property were put in place. The country was placed under martial law until December 1949. Especially given the Palestinian refugee flight, there was much discussion in Iraq about the fate of its Jewish community. Like Israel's concern that Palestinian absentees would be able to smuggle assets out of the country, the Iraqi government was concerned about illegal Jewish emigration and the smuggling of assets out of the country. In Iraq this was seen as a major problem, given that a good percentage of the business assets in Iraq was in Jewish hands and the effect on the Iraqi economy could be severe.

By 1950, the governor of the southern Basra district estimated that between 30–40 Jews a day were crossing illegally into Iran by resorting to bribery. Making their way to Tehran, they then flew to Israel. Jews who had not yet left devised a way to smuggle out their assets. Each year Iranian Muslim pilgrims would visit the Shi‘i holy cities of Karbala' and Najaf in Iraq. Using their connections with Jewish business persons in Iran, Iraqi Jews would persuade the pilgrims to use a system of credit slips in order to buy things while in Iraq. The funds were credited to their partners in Iran for eventual pick-up by the Iraqi Jews upon their arrival in Iran. [55] Subsequently, Israeli intelligence officers involved in the immigration complained that upon arrival in Israel the Iraqi Jews discovered that the Israeli treasury charged the newcomers a 20 percent commission for exchanging their assets, compared with only 5 percent charged in Britain. One native Iraqi-born Israeli officer involved in the underground immigration project, Mordekhai Ben Porat, complained about this to Israeli officials in December 1949 and February 1950 but received no response. [56]

On March 5, 1950, the Iraqi parliament legalized Jewish emigration but denationalized those wishing to emigrate. Law No. 1 of March 5, 1950 was enacted as an annex to Law No. 62 of 1933, the Ordinance for the Cancellation of Iraq Nationality. One of the supporting arguments circulated with the draft law stated the following:

> It has been noticed that some Iraqi Jews are attempting by every illegal means to leave Iraq for good and that others have already left Iraq illegally. As the presence of subjects of this description forced to stay in the

> country and obliged to keep their Iraqi nationality would inevitably lead to results affecting public security and give rise to social and economic problems, it has been found advisable not to prevent those wishing to do so from leaving Iraq for good, forfeiting their Iraqi nationality. This law has been promulgated to this end.

The law gave Jewish Iraqis who wished to leave the country one year to sign a form from the Ministry of the Interior, at which time they would forfeit their Iraqi citizenship. Prime Minister Nuri al-Sa'id had estimated that between 6,000 and 7,000 Jews would leave, although this was a mere fraction of the number that eventually would emigrate. [57] Interestingly, British diplomat Sir Henry B. Mack had intended to meet with al-Sa'id to discuss the proposed legislation several days before it actually was enacted. He reported that he was going to tell the prime minister to examine Israel's legislation affecting Palestinian refugee property when drafting the Iraqi law. [58] Thousands decided to take advantage of this opportunity, signed forms, and awaited planes that the Israel government was organizing to fly them out of the country. Adult emigrants were allowed to take out only 50 Iraqi dinars when they left but could retain ownership of any property that they left in Iraq. According to Yusuf al-Kabir, a respected member of the Jewish community in Iraq, Jews in the country possessed assets of some £UK90 million. [59] According to S.P. Sasson of the Sephardic Association of Tel Aviv, Jews owned £I76,150,000 in land, homes, and communal property. [60] A total of 129,292 Iraqi Jews ended up immigrating to Israel between 1948–72, mostly between May 1950 and August 1951 during the Operation 'Ezra and Nehemya airlift. [61]

One year and five days after passing the denationalization law but at a time when many of the denationalized Jews were still awaiting emigration, the Iraqi parliament passed a second law freezing the assets of ex-Iraqi Jews. Law for the Control and Administration of Property of Jews Who Have Forfeited Iraqi Nationality No. 5 of March 10, 1951 sequestered the property of ex-Iraqi Jews who were still waiting to leave the country. According to one source, this law affected 104,670 Jews. [62] American diplomats felt that the law was designed not only to stop the smuggling of Jewish assets out of Iraq but also to force the Israelis to speed up the airlifts. One wrote that "it appears likely that the freezing legislation was designed not merely to prevent the illegal removal of Jewish assets from Iraq but also as a means of pressure upon the Israeli Government to speed emigration." [63] Law No. 12 of March 22, 1951 later froze the assets of those Jews who already had left the country after January 1, 1948 as well.

The Iraqi government then set about the complicated task of sequestering the property of ex-Iraqi Jews. A new office was established called the Custodian General (Ar.: Amin 'Amm) for the Control and Administration of the Assets of Jews Who Have Renounced Iraqi Nationality. The first Custodian General was 'Abd al-Hamid Rif'at, the former Director General the Ministry of the Interior and former Controller of Foreigners' Property, who was appointed by a special committee composed of Jamil al-Midfa'i and Muhammad Sharif Husayn.[64] Israeli officials monitoring the situation felt that Rif'at was honest and reliable, unlike many of those his office employed. An immediate problem the Custodian General faced was how to determine what property belonged to denationalized Jews and what belonged to those Jews who had not renounced their citizenship. On March 12, 1951, two days after passage of the law, *all* Jewish businesses were ordered closed for inspection to determine this. Banks and government offices were instructed to submit statements detailing Jewish assets. The period of time for this later was extended to June 1951. Given the strong position of Jews in Iraqi business circles, especially banking and money changing, Iraq's economy was severely affected by the closure of Jewish businesses. The Custodian General then decided to issue identity cards to those Jews who intended to remain in Iraq so they could reopen their businesses. Sometimes even denationalized Jews could obtain cards through bribery.

The Custodian General also established a procedure for inventorying the sequestered property in the closed businesses. Some forty committees were created to record the assets of each closed shop and other businesses. Each committee consisted of a police official, a custodian (who was a lawyer), and a clerk. Each committee examined businesses in a certain area and made a report to the Custodian General's office. The committees would inquire about the owner of a certain shop and agree to meet him on a certain date to open the shop and inventory the contents. Both committee members and the owner would sign the resultant inventory statement, the shop would be closed again, and the keys turned over to the committee. The contents of shops were to be moved to the Custodian General's warehouse in the Khan al-Daftardar area of Baghdad. Many times the Jews would bribe the committee members to allow them to remove cash, documents, and other items prior to inventorying. Gold, jewelry, and other such items were removed from the shops and stored in the Rafidain Bank. By mid-April 1951, such work had been completed in nearly 720 businesses.[65]

The government was now faced with the serious problem of what to do with the sequestered property. Business life throughout the country already had been badly disrupted by the closure of Jewish enterprises. Were the Custodian General to auction the sequestered goods immediately as was contemplated, it would worsen the situation of the non-Jewish business sector by creating havoc with prices. The Chamber of Commerce in Baghdad met several times with the Custodian about this situation. The Custodian was not planning on selling land and other immoveable property. As a result of the passage of Law No. 12 of March 22, 1951, which froze the assets of those Jews who already had left the country after January 1, 1948, special custodians were also established to reopen businesses of such emigrants and run them under their supervision. According to a report sent to the Israeli government, this affected about fifteen companies, including firms like Lawee, Stanley Shashoua, Heskel Abed, and Mashal. The companies were to remain open pending the return of their owners to Iraq. If that did not occur, some other course of action presumably would need to be undertaken. [66]

How much Jewish property was sequestered? Given the wide coverage of the issue in the West and in Israel, a variety of figures emerged. Some Israeli officials guessed that the total value of the Jewish community's assets in February 1950, prior to the various sequestration laws, was ID[Iraqi dinars]600 million (£UK600 million). [67] 'Ezra Danin felt that the community's wealth prior to freezing was $US60 million in land and $5 million in gold and jewels. [68] The Ministry of Foreign Affairs, citing an "internal" Iraqi estimate, offered a figure of ID8–9 million. [69] The Beirut newspaper *Bayrut* cited figures on January 31, 1951 contained in the Baghdad paper *al-Sha'b*: £UK2 million in bank accounts and £2 million in land. [70] British officials obtained estimates from three British banks in Iraq and from American government information that was in turn received from Iraqi Jews. These estimates were ID600,000–1 million in bank accounts. The figures for land and moveable property varied. The banks estimated land at ID4–5 million (1951 values) while the Iraqi Jews felt this land was worth ID12–15 million. The banks estimated the value of moveables at ID1–2 million while the Jewish figure was ID3–6 million. [71]

A knowledgeable Israeli informant actually on the scene in Iraq in April 1951, however, offered much lower figures in the following "rough estimate" of Jewish assets that were actually sequestered (as opposed to the total value of Jewish property prior to passage of the legislation). Bank accounts probably did not exceed ID750,000, including those belonging to Jews who remained in the country. The informant felt that since some denationalized Jews were obtaining residency cards through bribery and would be able to withdraw their funds, the eventual amount in blocked accounts actually would probably not exceed ID500,000. An additional ID100,000 was probably contained in safe deposit boxes in banks. The informant estimated that ID1.5 million was sequestered in shops and ID150,000 in port, customs, and railroad warehouses. The value of bullion and jewelry was thought to be ID150,000, although this figure included the value of such items that were owned by non-Jews but were in Jewish shops at the time of sequestration. The informant believed that some 4,000 homes were frozen of which perhaps one-half actually were owned by Jews and the other half leased. Assuming a value of ID600 for a leasehold unit and ID1,200 for a home that actually was owned the informant estimated the value of sequestered homes at ID3.6 million. As for household goods, no estimate was provided because the informant stated that it was fairly easy for Jews intending to emigrate to arrange for a remaining Jew to sell their furniture, etc., for them. In total, the informant estimated the value of sequestered Jewish property at ID5.9 million. [72] These figures were later cited in other internal Israeli memoranda. [73]

A decade later the Iraqi government renewed its steps to freeze the property of Jews who had immigrated. Law No. 12 of 1951 was amended on December 7, 1963 to require that all Iraqi Jews, whether in Iraq or abroad, must register themselves and receive new identity papers. Those failing to do so within 90 days would forfeit their nationality. In addition, Jews living abroad had to submit proof that they had not acquired new citizenship elsewhere. Those who forfeited their Iraqi nationality would have their property frozen and placed under the Custodian General. Why did Iraqi authorities carry out what appear to be duplicate efforts to those made in 1951? The U.S. State Department felt the reason was that the Iraqi government sought to update its records on the more than 120,000 Jews who had left the country since 1948. The Americans also felt that the government was trying to stem the continued smuggling of Jewish assets to Israel. [74] Starting in September 1964, the Iraqi press carried the names of hundreds of Jews who forfeited their Iraqi citizenship as a result. By November 1965, more than 400 names had appeared. [75]

The 1948 war had a detrimental impact upon the property rights of Syrian Jews as well. Approximately 30,000 Jews lived in Syria in 1948, mostly in Damascus, Aleppo, and Qamishli near the Turkish border. As early as December 22, 1947, the government halted Jews in Syria from buying or selling land in order to prevent Jews from emigrating to Israel with funds. Like the Israeli and Iraqi governments, the Syrians were worried about the expatriation of assets into the hands of its enemies. [76] Bank accounts reportedly were frozen in 1949. Most Jews succeeded in liquidating their assets anyway and emigrating. American officials noted that "the majority of Syrian Jews have managed to dispose of their property and to emigrate to Lebanon, Italy, and Israel." [77]

Some 10,402 Jews from both Syria and Lebanon emigrated to Israel between May 15, 1948 and May 22, 1972.[78] Palestinian refugees were housed in certain of their empty homes in Damascus's Jewish Quarter in the early 1950s. The Director General of Public Security, Ibrahim Husayni, evicted Arab tenants who had been living in empty homes belonging to Jews who emigrated to Israel in order to make room for incoming Palestinian refugees. The rent for these properties had been paid by the tenants to agents of the departed Jewish owners, but the police formed a committee and began collecting the rent themselves to use for "public interest" projects.[79] It also has been reported that the Syrian government eventually established a committee for managing the property of Jewish emigrants.[80]

The U.S. government took an interest in the matter of Syrian Jews and studied their treatment and the question of their property after 1948. In 1952, the American embassy in Damascus reported that the president of the remaining Jewish community in Damascus claimed that the value of all Jewish property in Syria that faced restrictions since 1947, was some £S15–25 million ($US1 = £S3.75).[81] American diplomats reported to Washington on a February 1, 1949 meeting they had with Ibrahim Ustuwani, the Acting Director General of the Syrian Ministry of Foreign Affairs. Ustuwani decried Israel's Absentees' Property Regulations directed at Palestinian property and hinted that "reciprocal treatment of Jewish property in Arab countries" was under consideration. He stated that Syria had a right to sequester the property of "collaborating families" of Jews whose children had emigrated to Israel to fight with the Israeli army. Ustuwani claimed that 80 percent of remaining Syrian Jewish families were such "collaborators" with Israel.[82]

Later that year, an American Jew originally from Aleppo contacted the U.S. Department of State in Washington in an attempt to get around the ban on Syrian Jews selling land. Her brother in Syria, 'Ayyash bin Musa Jerro, wanted to sell his land and move to Israel but was forbidden to do so by the sequestration orders. However, since the land actually had been inherited by the sister in the United States, Latife Sutton, Jerro and his family wanted her to sell the land because she was now a foreign citizen. Sutton wrote to the State Department to get a copy of her certificate of naturalization proving that she was an American citizen in order to send it on to Jerro, who would sell the land for her.[83] Still, the Americans believed that the Jews of Syria generally were not being mistreated. The embassy in Damascus wrote that the Syrian government's treatment of Jews was similar to that of the Israeli government toward the Palestinians who remained under military rule within Israel: "The Syrian government's policy toward the small Jewish minority here appears disinterested and certainly compares favorably with that of the Israeli authorities toward the Arab minority in Israel." [84] Press reports stated that in October 1952 the Syrian cabinet discussed going beyond sequestration and actually confiscating Jewish property to benefit Palestinian refugees in the country.

Lebanon and Jordan did not replicate the actions of their Iraqi and Syrian neighbors. Although some in Lebanon like Emile Bustani of the Socialist and Nationalist Front argued for confiscating the property of the country's 5,000-member Jewish community, it does not appear that the Lebanese government ever took such action. [85] Jordan had no indigenous Jewish population. Only a very small number of foreign Jews had lived in Jordan in the late nineteenth century and it is unclear whether or not they owned any land. German writers noted the presence of Jewish traders in three locales in the northern 'Ajlun district: Irbid, Dayr al-Sa'na, and Malka. Those in Malka, and perhaps the others as well, were Jews from Palestine who established small stores in the village in partnership with local Arabs. [86] By mandate times, the number of Jews in Jordan appears to have numbered just a few individuals from Palestine, including a carpenter who did work at the palace of Amir 'Abdullah. [87]

Further west in the Arab world, authorities did enact legislation dealing with Jewish property. About 75,000 Jews lived in Egypt in the late 1940s. In the general atmosphere of anti-Zionist feeling, Egyptian authorities moved against Jews suspected of Zionist connections. On May 30, 1948, two weeks after intervening in the fighting in Palestine, the government issued Proclamation No. 26. This law allowed the government to sequester the property of persons who were interned on security charges, as a number of Jews were. A Director General was created to manage their property while they were in detention. In 1949, some of these persons were released, as was some of their property. The connection between the Jews of Egypt and their property and the property of the Palestinian refugees also arose at this time. Egyptian Prime Minister Ibrahim 'Abd al-Hadi had "given an intimation" of exchanging Egyptian Jews and their property for the Palestinian refugees to the UNCCP's Mark Etheridge in February 1949. However, he acknowledged that Egyptian laws made the export of valuables difficult. The prime minister also told Etheridge that Egypt had already sequestered some Jewish property, and opined that this property in particular would be very difficult to export to Israel if the Israelis went ahead and began taking over the Palestinian refugee land according to their new Absentees' Property regulations.[88] Egypt also blocked access to bank accounts owned by persons residing in Israel.

During the first half of 1951, Israeli officials became worried over reports that Egypt and other Arab states were intending to follow Iraq's example and take over the property of their own Jewish citizens. On April 11, 1951, the Research Department of the Israeli Ministry of Foreign Affairs published a report on Arab states' "plotting" against Jewish property in the Arab world. The ministry then sent the report to its embassies and consulates worldwide. According to Israeli documents, the Syrian Foreign Ministry sent a report to the Arab League on January 16, 1951 proposing that the Arab League "discuss taking steps of reprisal against Israel (which seized the abandoned Arab property located in its territory) and to find a practical and effective solution to the problem." The Arab League's Legal Department apparently thereafter reported that Arab reprisals against Jewish property in their own countries might constitute recognition of Israel. The Legal Department suggested instead that Arab states follow the example of Iraq by denationalizing Jews. They could be declared enemy aliens and have their property taken over. [89]

Israeli diplomats also nervously gleaned information from open and secret sources about Egyptian intentions. An opinion piece in the November 27, 1950 issue of the influential *al-Ahram* newspaper reportedly questioned the government's tolerance in allowing Egyptian Jews to emigrate to Israel with their property, which only served to help Israel overcome its budget deficit. An informant reported to the Israelis on April 7, 1951 that certain senior government officials supported the expropriation of Jewish property but that important politicians like Mustafa Nahhas and Fu'ad Sarraj al-Din opposed this and even warned the Chief Rabbi, Hayyim Nahum, of such plots on April 5. Finally, the Israelis received a report from a second, "unverified" source on April 9 that the Egyptian government had established a special commission to study the possibility of seizing Jewish property. The informant cited the following members of the commission: Wahid Rif'at, an advisor in the Foreign Ministry; Ahmad al-Shuqayri, the Palestinian serving as Deputy Secretary of the Arab League; 'Abdullah al-Shu'ayb, director of the Ministry of the Interior's Department of Supervision; and Kamal Salih from the Ministry of Finance. According to the report, the commission petitioned Iraq for information on how it handled the matter of its own Jewish property. [90]

A second and much more massive wave of Egyptian seizure of Jewish property occurred later in 1956 after Israel, Britain, and France attacked Egypt in October of that year. Egypt passed Military Proclamation No. 4 Relative to Commerce with British and French Subjects and to Measures Affecting their Properties in November 1956, which allowed authorities to sequester the property of British and French nationals that was located in Egypt. Once again, a Director General was assigned to manage this property. He deducted 10 percent of the value of assets plus 10 percent of any income for administrative costs. According to American accounts of published lists, some 486 persons and firms were subject to this sequestration—most of them Jewish. Other U.S. documents speak of 539 Jewish individuals and 105 Jewish firms excluding British and French Jews. Still other accounts claim that the assets and bank accounts of 500 Jewish-owned firms were sequestered between November 1956 and March 1957, along with the assets alone of 800 more. [91]

While some Jews residing in Egypt in fact maintained British and French citizenship, the land of certain Egyptian Jews was frozen as well. Beyond this, Egypt began expelling Jews possessing British and French citizenship and "stateless" Jews starting in mid-November 1956. These persons were allowed to take only a small amount of money with them: £E200 for each head of a family plus £E100 per dependent. Single persons were limited to £E20 per capita. But authorities deducted from this the value of wedding rings, watches, the cost of boat tickets, etc. [92] The Finance Minister later cancelled Military Proclamation No. 4 on April 21, 1957.

A large number of Jews left Egypt during the years 1956–58. Out of a community of 60,000, an estimated 23,000–25,000 emigrated after being issued travel documents stating that they gave up all claims against Egypt. [93] Estimates have varied as the value of property seized from British, French, Egyptian, and stateless Jews in 1956–57. One estimate stated that 101,255 feddans of land (1 feddan = 4,200 sq. m.) and 2,807 buildings were confiscated worth £E24,200,000. [94] The B'nai B'rith organization claimed that £E14 million in moveables and £E27 million in immoveable property was seized. It also claimed that the Egyptian authorities were auctioning off Jewish households goods and realizing between £E500–3,000 per week. [95] A third wave of property seizures occurred in Egypt after the June 1967 Arab-Israeli war. Between June 1967 and September 1968, an estimated 1,500 Jews left or were expelled without their assets. In all, the Israeli government claimed that a total of 29,325 Egyptian Jews arrived in Israel between 1948 and 1972. [96]

The property of Jews in Libya also was affected by the Arab-Israeli conflict. Some 40,000 Jews lived in Libya by the late 1940s, of whom some 2,650 emigrated to Israel in 1948. Some 30,000 more moved there from 1949–51, leaving behind property. British military authorities, who ruled the former Italian colony after the Second World War, allowed some Palestinian refugees from Gaza to move there and settle in empty Jewish homes in the fall of 1950, but most of them returned to Gaza in September 1951. [97] A more serious threat to Jewish property in Libya occurred in 1961, by which time the country had become an independent monarchy. Law No. 6 of March 1961 Concerning the Sequestration of the Properties of Some Israelis was enacted. It did not affect all Jewish property, but targeted only the property of owners who had an alleged tie to Israel. The law allowed the state to freeze the property and bank accounts of persons or institutions who were in Israel, who were citizens of Israel, or who allegedly were working on Israel's behalf. In the wake of Colonel Mu'ammar al-Qadhdhafi's coup of 1969, two other laws were passed in 1970 that affected Jewish property. The second of these, Law No. 57 of July 21, 1970, created a "Custodian's Administration" to take control of the land of persons who left Libya to live abroad. The government published a list of 643 names, of which 628 were those of Jews. The property was not confiscated, but was to be paid for with Libyan government bonds. An organization of Libyan Jews living in Italy estimated that the total amount of sequestered Libyan Jewish property was probably between £UK110–120 million. [98]

Finally, the Arab-Jewish struggle in Palestine affected the 55,000 Jews living in Yemen, plus 8,000 more in British-controlled Aden. Most ended up leaving for Israel shortly after 1948, a dramatic and sudden continuation of an older historical tradition of Yemeni emigration to Palestine that began in the late nineteenth century. Israel's Operation Magic Carpet airlift flew more than 48,800 Yemeni Jews to Israel from 1949–50. While many Jewish activists over the years have noted that the emigrants were forced to leave behind their homes and property upon their departure, the author could not locate any figures detailing the amount of such property losses.

Israeli negotiators began discussing property left behind in Arab countries by Jews immigrating to Israel almost immediately after the cessation of hostilities in 1948. In the beginning they included compensation for this land within the rubric of "war damages" in talks with the UNCCP. The government launched a campaign in 1949 to get Israelis to declare all their assets around the world so that it could negotiate agreements to secure these assets for the cash-strapped Israeli treasury. The Foreign Claims Registration Office within the Ministry of Finance collected 29,357 claims in 1949. [99] The government also made a specific effort to quantify the scale of property left in Arab-controlled areas. The Israeli government soon asked its citizens to report voluntarily any property that lay behind enemy lines in Arab territory. Citizens were called upon to register claims with the Foreign Claims Registration Office in Jerusalem in a public announcement issued by S. Hirsh, the Registrar of Foreign Claims in the Ministry of Finance on November 3, 1949. Israeli citizens were asked to complete forms detailing assets in Egypt, Saudi Arabia, Iraq, Yemen, Syria, Lebanon, and Jordan by December 31,

TABLE 3.5 Value of Jewish Property Left in Arab Countries Recorded by Israeli Registrar of Foreign Claims, 1949–1950

| *Country* | *Claimants (N)* | *Claims (N)* | *Amount (in currency)* | *Total Amount ($U.S.)* |
|---|---|---|---|---|
| Libya | 203 | 203 | £L629,636,340 | |
| | | | £Egypt. 19,135 | |
| | | | FF1,248,620 | 1,065,927 |
| Egypt | 153 | 153 | £Pal.17,901 | |
| | | | £UK45,287 | |
| | | | £E619,473 | |
| | | | 74,357 Rupees | |
| | | | $US3,025 | |
| | | | FF107,500 | 1,977,856 |
| Iraq | 1,619 | 50 | £UK3,525 | |
| | | | 709,955 Iraqi Dinars | 1,997,184 |
| Yemen | 15 | 15 | £Pal.15,000 | |
| | | | 167,024 Riyals | |
| | | | 116,217 Rupees | 83,512 |
| Syria | 121 | 121 | £Pal.100,902 | |
| | | | £S2,453,090 | |
| | | | 4,608 Gold Pounds | |
| | | | 34 Ottoman Pounds | 1,410,467 |
| Lebanon | 74 | 74 | £Pal.90,417 | |
| | | | £L289,946 | |
| | | | £Syr.2,459 | |
| | | | $US253 | |
| | | | £UK1,667 | 390,981 |
| Jordan | 38 | 38 | £Pal.3,509,180 | |
| | | | £Syr.1,950 | 9,826,590 |
| West Bank | 1,414 | 1,284 | £Pal.13,094,294 | 36,664,023 |
| Palestinian Absentees | 111 | 111 | £Pal.219,015 | |
| | | | £UK998 | 616,036 |
| TOTAL | 3,748 | 2,049 | | $54,032,576 |

Source: ISA (130) 1848/hts/9, "Overall Summary of the Work of the Foreign Claims Registration Office as of December 31, 1950"

1949, although the office continued registering claims through the last day of June 1950. Applicants were to list all abandoned land, factories, bank accounts, stocks and bonds, and other claims. This included debts, etc. owed to them by Palestinian refugees in the Arab world. They were also asked to assess the value of the property in local currency. In that short time, Israelis registered $US54,032,576 in assets in Arab countries. By far the largest amount of this—$36,664,023—represented land and other assets in the Jordanian-occupied West Bank. Table 3.5 details the results of this registration.These figures included $131,600 in bank accounts left behind in Arab countries ($31,920 in Iraq alone).[100] By August 1, 1952, Israel had recorded a total figure of $86,870,456, of which $1,252,944 were bank accounts.[101]

The Israelis were disappointed that the figures were not higher. Some Israeli diplomats now were concerned that raising the counter claims issue might backfire given that the amount was so low—a foreshadow of what actually was to come in the late 1990s. The Israeli Ministry of Foreign Affairs' UN Department reported to the Israeli embassy in Washington in 1952 that $US86,869,000 of property in Arab countries had been registered. One diplomat cautioned, "Considering this I would like to draw attention to the danger of emphasizing our claims to the frozen Jewish property in Arab countries."[102] Israel decided to carry out a second campaign to register assets left behind in Arab countries by Jewish emigrants in 1952, especially because Iraq recently had frozen the property of Jews who emigrated to Israel. The decision was made on September 30, 1952, and the Foreign Claims Registration Office announced the second registration on October 8. Once again, Israelis were asked to register assets in Egypt, Saudi Arabia, Iraq, Yemen, Syria, Lebanon, Jordan, and Arab-controlled areas of Palestine.[103] By early 1956, a grand total of $103,373,000 had been registered.[104]

Unlike the Israeli government, some Jews did not want to use their lost property merely as a bargaining tool with the Arabs. They wanted monetary compensation as soon as possible and they wanted it directly from the Israeli government. After the publicity surrounding the loss of Jewish property in Egypt following the Suez War of 1956, the vice president of the Association of Egyptian Immigrants in Israel, Shlomo Cohen-Sidon, asked the Israeli Minister of Finance, Levi Eshkol, to keep records of Jewish property in Egypt. Eshkol agreed, and in March 1957, a special body headed by Cohen-Sidon was created to register the property claims of Egyptian Jewish immigrants to Israel. Between July and September 1957, this commission registered 640 claims totaling £E5,531,755.370.[105] (A similar special commission on Iraqi property is discussed below.) Eshkol apparently thought that registering the property would end the immigrants' clamoring. It did not. Cohen-Sidon pressed the Israeli government itself to begin paying compensation to Egyptian immigrants from the value of enemy Egyptian property in Israel taken over by the government in 1948. He was referring to the railroad station in Lydda, which technically had been registered in the name of the Egyptian government and seized by Israel during the 1948 war. Cohen-Sidon actually filed suit against the Israeli government in early 1960 to receive a share of the value of the seized Egyptian property. He later dropped the suit following a promise from the government that the Egyptian Jews' rights would not be forgotten. [106]

It was the Jewish property in Iraq that concerned the Israelis the most. The reasons for this were because the amount of frozen property was the highest anywhere in the Arab world and because the sequestration occurred in March 1951, at a time when the issue of Israeli compensation for Palestinian refugee property was occupying center stage in the mind of the UNCCP and others concerned with resolving the Arab-Israeli conflict. Even before Iraqi Prime Minister Nuri al-Sa'id proposed exchanging Iraqi Jews for Palestinian refugees, some in Israel were developing similar thoughts. Minister of Police Bekhor Shalom Shitrit suggested as early as a March 1949 cabinet meeting that Israel compensate Iraqi immigrants with abandoned Palestinian refugee land. That same month, another Mizrahi proposed a similar idea in the Knesset. Eliyahu Elyashar of the Sephardic List linked the Palestinian refugee exodus with the growing influx of Iraqi Jews as well. Shitrit brought up the idea again in the cabinet in September, but Sharett dismissed it. [107]

One reason why Sharett dismissed the idea is that he and other Israelis thought this kind of linkage could set a "dangerous precedent" by encouraging the Arabs to take over their Jewish citizens' property. In fact, Sharett later told the Israeli cabinet in March 1951 that he believed that the Iraqi decision to sequester Jewish property had done precisely this: Iraq looked to Israel's own actions regarding Palestinian refugee property as an example of what to do with the property of its own Jews who had registered to leave for Israel. [108] Indeed, these ideas of linking the Palestinian refugees' land with that of Iraqi and other Arab Jews were taking place in 1949, *before* the widespread sequestrations in Iraq and Egypt. Sharett also objected to the idea on other grounds. When the cabinet discussed Nuri al-Sa'id's offer to swap 100,000 Iraqi Jews for 100,000 Palestinian refugees, Sharett felt that such an exchange only would lead to resettlement of a fraction of the Palestinian refugees. Israel might be asked to repatriate the rest. Sharett also felt that since Iraq would keep the Jews' property, the immigrants might press Israel to compensate them for this land—leaving Israel with the double burden of compensation for the Palestinian refugees and the Iraqi Jews. Israel would prefer if Iraq took in closer to 300–400,000 refugees.[109] Other Israelis also warned against provoking the Arab states. Teddy Kollek, later the long-serving mayor of Jerusalem, told Sharett in June 1949 that he had a meeting with Emile Najjar, a self-appointed spokesperson for Jews in Arab countries (probably the same Emile Najjar who was the last president of the Egyptian Zionist Federation). Najjar had warned him against linking Palestinian refugee property with the property of Jews in the Arab world. Were Israel to compensate the refugees only on a global and not a personal basis, it "will be a dangerous precedent with regard to Jewish property in Arab countries."[110]

Others in Israel still were interested in probing for a connection between Palestinian Arab and Iraqi Jewish property. Finance Minister Eli'ezer Kaplan authorized £I1,000 for 'Ezra Danin in July 1950 to explore the possibility of exchanging Iraqi Jewish property and the property of those 120,000 or so Palestinians who remained in Israel after 1948.[111] The Palestinians would leave Israel and settle in Iraq, and be replaced by incoming Iraqi Jews.[112] Danin's idea apparently was put into motion. The British consulate in Haifa reported several months later in October 1950 that certain Palestinian citizens in Israel, led by one Sulayman Qutran, were involved in negotiations with Iraqi Jewish landowners. Qutran may have been the same Palestinian who met with the UNCCP in Beirut in the spring of 1949 as secretary of the Association of Arab Landlords of Haifa. The talks focused on exchanging Palestinian land in Israel, worth some £1 million, for Jewish land in Iraq. As the British diplomatically stated it, "it is understood" that the Israeli government was not opposed to this initiative.[113]

But other Israelis were still reticent about pressing the connection too much.[114] Not enough Palestinians would be involved, while Iraqi immigrants might come to expect compensation from Israel. On March 5, 1950, the day after Iraq allowed Jews who wished to emigrate to forfeit their nationality, Israeli Mossad intelligence officer Mordekhai Ben Porat proposed exchanging the Jews for Palestinians in one of his secret communications to Israel. Ben Porat was born in Baghdad in 1923 and emigrated to Palestine in 1945. He became a key player in Operation 'Ezra and Nehemya, and later sat in the Knesset. Ben Porat was rebuffed and warned not to raise the hopes of Iraqi emigrants that they would get either land or compensation from Israel upon their arrival. The Israeli treasury told the Mossad,

> You have to warn Dror [Ben Porat's code name], firmly, not to promise any compensation to Jews who are leaving their homes in Berman

> [Baghdad] and no exchanges are to be made with the refugees. An incautious arrangement from our side will invite claims and difficulties in Israel.[115]

Ben Porat continued his activities. He had Na'im Yitshak Shammash, manager of the Ottoman Bank, work as a liaison between himself and a group of Iraqi Jews. Among other things, Ben Porat asked Shammash, Salim Qahtan, and Naji Efra'im to produce a report on public and private Jewish assets in Iraq that Ben Porat passed on to the Mossad and the Israeli treasury on March 7, 1951, just days before Iraq froze Jewish property. He also told Israeli authorities, "It is better that you start questioning all the immigrants and listing their frozen assets."[116] The Israelis agreed that immigrants should be instructed about what kinds of documents testifying to property ownership they should bring with them when they left Iraq, but were starting to think that they should form a "public" agency to deal with the question of Iraqi property as opposed to a governmental one. This would give Israel some deniability with the Iraqi immigrants, who should not be encouraged to think that Israel would compensate them. Shamai Kahana of the Ministry of Foreign Affairs noted succinctly:

> It must be taken into consideration that such a process of registration is likely to create illusions among the immigrants and the agency that gathers the claims will be burdened with a great responsibility towards them unless it objects to this from the outset.[117]

Some also began contemplating creating some type of Iraqi-American-Turkish holding company, another international company, or a Bank of America subsidiary that could transfer the assets to Israel.[118]

For these reasons, the Israeli government took special if indirect pains to ascertain how much land Iraqi Jewish immigrants had left behind in Iraq. The earlier registration campaign of 1949–50 clearly did not include the property of the recent immigrants. In fact, only 50 claims had been filed by Iraqi Jews prior to June 1950. After the influx of tens of thousands of Iraqi immigrants in 1950–51, 2,150 more claims were registered. Still, the vast majority of new immigrants did not register their assets with the Israeli government. By August 1, 1952, a mere 2,220 declarations on assets in Iraq had been filed. The amount claimed was valued at approximately $US35,850,000. Table 3.6 shows those assets that had been claimed as of August 1.

Overall, Israeli authorities were disappointed with the low numbers. Most immigrants had not filled out registration forms: the 2,150 applications from

TABLE 3.6 Value of Jewish Property Left in Iraq Recorded by Israeli Registrar of Foreign Claims, 1949–1952

| *Item* | *Value (Iraqi Dinars)* |
|---|---|
| Land | |
| Houses | 4,417,470 |
| Urban land | 1,454,355 |
| Agricultural land | 714,110 |
| Moveable goods | 688,135 |
| Factories | |
| Commercial | 2,810,945 |
| Industrial | 381,570 |
| Goods confiscated at customs posts, in route, etc. | 124,260 |
| Bank accounts | 411,880 |
| Stocks and bonds | 93,860 |
| Mortgages | 168,075 |
| Business agreements | 1,203,235 |
| Insurance policies | 21,960 |
| Confiscated cash, fines for "Zionist" activities | 187,740 |
| Salaries | |
| Private | 3,720 |
| Government | 300 |
| Iraqi railroad | 270 |
| Pensions and trust funds | |
| Private | 31,968 |
| Government | 17,985 |
| Iraqi railroad | 5,450 |
| Running pensions | 9,375 |
| Other claims | 53,635 |
| TOTAL | 12,800,295 |

Source: ISA (130) 1791/1, document of Department of Transfer and Registration of Foreign Claims (7 August 1952). See also ISA (130) 2401/22, "Claims for Jewish Property Frozen in Arab States" (October 6, 1952)

Jews who left Iraq for Israel during Operation 'Ezra and Nehemya constituted less than six percent of the 37,124 families who arrived. [119] Besides immigrants who had not registered, other Jews who left Iraq decided to take their assets to other, choicer destinations than the austere, postwar socialist economy of Israel.

The Israeli government moved ahead with plans to have a nongovernmental, "public" body led by Iraqi immigrants carry out a second registration specifically of Iraqi property. Although apparently established in June 1955, the existence of the Commission for the Registration of the Claims of Iraqi Immigrants was not announced by Sharett until January 25, 1956. It was chaired by a banker, Shlomo Noah. Other commission members included 'Ezra Korin, Ya'akov Lev, Shlomo Darvish, Binyamin Sasson, and Shlomo Hillel. The commission worked all year and issued an unpublished, interim report to the Ministry of Foreign Affairs on December 17, 1956. This commission was not much more successful than the 1949–52 registration campaign. Of the more than 37,000 Iraqi Jewish families, only between 3,000 and 4,000 bothered to register assets. The commission decided to focus only on Jewish land in Iraq, not moveable property. The reason for this once again lay with Israeli diplomacy: Israel wanted to link Iraqi Jewish with Palestinian refugee property. Since it had already announced that it would only consider compensating the Palestinians for abandoned land and not moveable property, the commission thus felt that it should look only at land. [120]

Besides trading the property of Iraqi Jews for Palestinian property, the Israeli government devised schemes involving other Jewish property in the Arab world as well. One dealt with Libya, which the Ministry of Foreign Affairs developed in March 1950. The plan was to replace the 17,000–18,000 Jews who had left Libya for Israel with Palestinian refugees. By March 1952, another idea had emerged, this time focusing not on the refugees but once again on Palestinians still living in Israel. Foreign ministry official Moshe Sasson wrote a memorandum proposing to exchange Jewish property in Libya for that of Palestinians in Israel. The Jewish National Fund would be involved in the exchange. The Libyan idea was still alive in May 1954, when the JNF's Weitz proposed to Sharett, Eshkol, and others that he and fellow JNF official Yoav Tsukerman travel to North Africa to investigate the possibilities of the exchange. [121] Libyan scheme continued to be examined in 1956, when Israel raised money to buy the land of Italians who had left Libya after it achieved independence. They purchased or were close to purchasing some 100,000 dunums near Tripoli. The idea was to settle Palestinian refugees living under Jordanian rule on this land in return for their agreeing to drop any claims for monetary compensation. [122]

Another scheme dated from 1954, when the Israeli Ministry of Finance began playing with an interesting idea for compensating Israeli citizens for property left in parts of Palestine then under Arab control. The vast majority of this lay in the West Bank. In May 1954, the government placed advertisements in the Israeli media asking citizens to register claims for such lost land in Arab-occupied territory. As a result, some 500 people responded. Most of these claims related to buildings in East Jerusalem and land in the "Triangle" region between Nablus, Janin, and Tulkarm. According to a plan developed in 1955, Israel would compensate the claimants by providing them with land under the control of the Development Authority. In return, they would sign agreements transferring their rights to the abandoned land to the state, much as PICA had done in 1958. One of the major claims was made by an attorney named Oster. The proposal was shown to the legal division of the Ministry of Foreign Affairs. R. Migdal of the division commented that Jewish citizens from Arab countries might feel discriminated against because they were not being offered compensation as well. He was also concerned that the fact that compensation was being provided only to citizens holding land in Arab-controlled Palestine might be construed as prelude to an Israeli plot to invade the West Bank and Gaza to get the land back. [123] It is unclear whether or not this scheme ever was carried out; indications are that it was not.

Jewish organizations outside the Israeli government also were quite concerned about Jewish property in the Arab world. Meeting in Tel Aviv on March 21, 1949, the International League for Saving Arabian Jewry appealed to the government to condition its cooperation with the UNCCP upon the latter's attempts to safeguard Jews and Jewish property in all Arab countries.[124] The loss of property in Egypt after the 1956 Suez War prompted considerable activity. In 1957, several international Jewish organizations started a campaign to register the property lost by stateless Jews in Egypt. These groups—the World Jewish Congress, the American Joint Distribution Committee, the Alliance Israélite Universelle, and the American Jewish Committee—founded a body called the "Joint Committee (Central Registry of Jewish Losses in Egypt)." They estimated that the value of this property was $US28 million. [125] In 1958, an Egyptian Jewish immigrant in Israel, Sami 'Attiya, formed an association called the Organization of the Victims of Anti-Jewish Persecution in Egypt that also collected statistics on property. [126]

While Israel was initially hesitant to make the connection between Palestinian refugee land and Jewish property internally with its own immigrants, it had showed no hesitation in linking the issues externally for foreign diplomatic consumption. At the time of the Iraqi sequestration in March 1951, the Israeli cabinet decided that the best way for the Israeli government to respond was to deduct the value of sequestered Jewish property of Jewish immigrants from Iraq and elsewhere in the Arab world from any future amount paid to Palestinian refugees. [127] Indeed, this would come to be the most consistent, longest-lasting Israeli diplomatic riposte to the entire Palestinian compensation issue. The issue would remain a staple of Israeli thinking about compensation for decades to come. Israeli officials began making public statements linking Palestinian and Jewish property compensation almost immediately, in June 1948, and discussions were held in the cabinet. When UN Mediator Count Folke Bernadotte met with Sharett in Tel Aviv on July 26, 1948, Sharett linked the future of the Palestinian refugees with that of a final peace settlement and with Jewish property in Arab-controlled Palestine. [128] On March 19, 1951, nine days after the freezing of the property in Iraq, Foreign Minister Sharett addressed the Knesset and announced the government's new policy of linking Palestinian refugee property with Jewish property in Iraq: "The government of Israel . . . views this incident of robbery in the guise of law as a continuation of the oppressive and malicious governance traditionally practiced by Iraq towards its defenseless and helpless minorities." [129]

Sharett went on to link Iraq's seizure of the property with compensation for the Palestinians. The official basis for this linkage was that Israel now would have to shoulder the costs of absorbing penniless immigrants from Iraq. The Israelis also notified the United States and the UNCCP of their intentions to link the issues. Walter Eytan wrote to the UNCCP on March 29, 1951 that Israel could not fully assume its obligation to pay compensation into the Reintegration Fund if it now was obliged to cover the expenses of propertyless Iraqi refugees. [130]

As they prepared for the Paris conference in the fall of 1951, the Israelis demanded that blocked Jewish funds in Iraqi banks be included in any agreement to release blocked Palestinian accounts in Israel. In Washington, Abba Eban later pleaded with Sharett in May 1952 to provide him with statistics on sequestered Jewish bank accounts in Iraq in particular so he could use the information as *quid pro quo* when dealing with the UNCCP on the release of blocked Palestinian bank accounts. [131] The Israeli Ministry of Foreign Affairs wanted to use the frozen Iraqi accounts and other assets as a counterbalance to the Palestinian refugees' claims. [132] Israel did not press this connection later when it released the blocked accounts because it was never able to document that Jews in Iraq possessed more than a fraction of what Palestinians had frozen in Israeli banks. As Table 3.6 above shows, Israel had registered only 411,880 Iraqi dinars in frozen Jewish bank accounts in Iraq compared to more than £UK3.2 million in blocked Arab accounts in banks in Israel.

While generally supportive of the Israeli situation regarding compensation for Palestinian refugees, the United States did not agree with Israel on all points regarding the Iraqi property question and demurred from pressuring the Iraqi government concerning its Jews. In the first place, U.S. officials did not believe that Iraq's Jews were suffering from intense persecution. Secondly, they believed that Iraq's actions definitely were linked with Israel's prior sequestration of Palestinian refugee property more than two years earlier and were thus a response to a course of action begun by Israel. American diplomats actually told the Israelis that the United States would not pressure the Iraqis without positive Israeli action on the Palestinian compensation issue. In that case, the United States might reconsider approaching the Iraqi government:

> there is no reliable evidence available to the United States Government to indicate that, aside from the inevitable hardships involved in mass population transfers, the treatment of Jewish residents of Iraq has not been generally correct... [but] constructive action by the Government of Israel to regulate and expedite liquidation and transfer of frozen property and assets of former Arab residents of territory now under Israeli control would permit consideration of an approach to the Government of Iraq for comparable disposition of Jewish assets in that country.[133]

Internally, American diplomats stated to one another that it would be difficult to pressure the Iraqis on the frozen Jewish property when Israel had done essentially the same thing to the Palestinian refugees:

> There is very little choice between the policy being applied by the Government of Iraq in freezing assets of denationalized Jews and the policy previously instituted by the Government of Israel with respect to assets of Arab refugees and displaced persons. Anyone approaching Iraq on this score would be in a very weak position unless it could be shown that Israel had taken constructive action to return Arab properties or give adequate compensation in lieu thereof. [134]

The Department of State also took this line when pressured by American congressional representatives to do something about the Iraqi situation. One letter to a member of the House of Representatives stated:

> With respect to the freezing of assets of Jews who have voluntarily given up their Iraqi nationality in order to go to Israel, you will appreciate that the freezing of assets where mass transfers of populations occur is not

> unprecedented. As you are no doubt aware, the Government of Israel in 1948 considered itself obliged to immobilize the assets of former Arab residents of territory now under Israeli control.[135]

On the other hand, the Americans agreed that it was fair to link the two property questions in the context of an overall peace settlement:

> It certainly would be desirable to have property settlements accomplished for both the Arab and Jewish properties involved. However, it is hard to see how this can be done except within a framework of a general settlement of the Arab-Israeli conflict.[136]

Because it hoped to deduct the value of the Iraqi Jewish property from any compensation it eventually would pay to the Palestinians, the Israeli government did not want to create the illusion among Iraqi Jewish immigrants that they would receive compensation for their property from the Israeli government pending some final arrangement. The government therefore sought to register the value of Iraqi Jewish assets not to guarantee that individual Jews be compensated someday but "with the aim of deducting the value of the Jewish property frozen in Iraq from the payment of compensation for the abandoned Arab property." This attitude also was stated succinctly by Ministry of Foreign Affairs official Shim'on Shapir in an internal October 6, 1952 memorandum entitled "Claims for Jewish Property Frozen in Arab States." In the document, Shapir stated:

> Mutual material claims of Israel and the Arab states related to the failure of the Arab invasion of Israel constitute a problem, the future solution—and the possibility of solution—to which will not depend on the legal justification of these claims. A solution will depend, rather, on political issue and on the political nature of the relations between Israel and the Arab states.[137]

In the end, Israel pressed on with its linkage of the two questions in diplomatic discussions throughout the 1950s and into the present. Foreign Minister Golda Meir reiterated to the Americans in December 1959 that Israel would pay the Palestinian refugees compensation, but would deduct the value of property taken from its immigrants in Iraq, Egypt, and Yemen.[138] The Americans already had gone on record as telling the Israelis that their claim for property in some Arab countries was weakened by the fact that those countries were not fully independent from Britain or France in 1948. Specifically, the Americans noted that Morocco, Tunisia, and Libya were "not under Arab sovereignty" in 1948 and that Israel might have difficulties pressing its claims from the present Arab governments of those countries for actions taken prior to independence.[139]

Ben Gurion again linked the two issues in a speech to the Knesset in 1961. He later brought up the matter of the Mizrahi claims to American ambassador to Israel Walworth Barbour in April 1963 and opined that UN resolutions on "refugees" applied to them as well. Ten days later the State Department bluntly informed Barbour, "Re Jewish refugees, these have not repeat not been covered by UN resolutions."[140] The Ministry of Justice later created a special department in September 1969 to maintain records on the subject. Prof. Ya'akov Meron was appointed to head the department, which was closed in the 1990s. While Israel has maintained this linkage to this very day, its data on Jewish property in the Arab countries eventually was filed away in the Israel State Archives in Jerusalem although not all of it is available to the public.[141] The subject, and the archived data, would return to the spotlight with the onset of the Arab-Israeli peace process in the 1990s.

## Linking German Reparations with Palestinian Compensation

In the spring of 1952, an issue arose that once again became entangled with the compensation question. Negotiations were underway in Europe between the World Jewish Congress and the Federal Republic of Germany to discuss the question of German reparations for Nazi crimes against Jews before and during the Second World War. The Arabs and, privately, others (including the United States and certain members of the UNCCP staff) saw in this potentially huge outlay of German reparations the capital with which cash-strapped Israel could begin paying compensation to the refugees. The compensation question then spread and became a truly international issue.

The origins of the German reparations go back to the first days after the formal end of the Second World War. On September 20, 1945, the Jewish Agency, through the venerable Zionist leader Chaim Weizmann, demanded reparations (Heb.: shilumim), restitution, and indemnification from Germany for crimes related to the Holocaust. Weizmann addressed his letter to the victorious Four Powers that now controlled the defeated Germany—the United States, France, the United Kingdom, and the USSR. Israel later demanded reparations as well when Sharett wrote to the Four Powers on March

12, 1951 asking for $US1.5 billion from West Germany. Sharett explained that Israel was seeking the money to cover the costs it absorbed in settling 500,000 Holocaust survivors in Israel at $3,000/person. On September 27, 1951, West German Chancellor Konrad Adenauer agreed to negotiations. The World Jewish Congress's Nahum Goldmann was the senior negotiator inasmuch as the final settlement would involve not only payments to Israel but also to Jewish organizations around the world. Although born in Lithuania in 1895, Goldmann spent his formative years in Germany. He lived in Germany from when he was five years old until Hitler rose to power in 1933. Goldmann was instrumental in the formation of the World Jewish Congress three years later in 1936, and was the first chair of its executive board. He also headed the Conference on Jewish Material Claims Against Germany that had been called in October 1951. During negotiations, Israel reduced its demand to $1 billion with the reservation that it would obtain the rest from the German Democratic Republic (East Germany) someday.

A final agreement was signed on September 12, 1952 in Luxembourg. West Germany was obliged to provide Israel DM3,450 million ($845 million) in reparations, mostly in goods. This was in addition to a further DM450 million ($110 million) that it would provide to the Conference on Jewish Material Claims Against Germany for allocation to Jews living outside Israel. These amounts were to be paid in annual installments for fourteen years, from April 1, 1953 to March 31, 1966. The amount was not paid in cash but as credit to be used to purchase goods. Of the amount going to Israel, for instance, 30 percent went toward purchases of crude oil in the United Kingdom. The other 70 percent would be used for steel, industrial and agricultural products, and the like that would be exported by Germany to Israel. These goods ended up accounting for 12–14 percent of total Israeli imports during those years.[142]

The Arabs reacted to the reparations talks even before an agreement was signed. In March 1952, Syria, Lebanon, and Iraq approached the United States, the United Kingdom, and France, and stated that the Palestinian refugees should benefit from any future German reparations to Israel. Jordan wrote a similar note to the United Kingdom and France, while the Yemenis gave their verbal assent in April 1952 to the idea. In June, the Arab Higher Committee wrote directly to the West German government asking it to sequester the reparations for use by the refugees. The Germans simply ignored the letter, arguing that the Arabs were not a party to their talks with Israel. Some Arab governments approached the Germans as well. Privately, however, the German government conceded that the Arabs had a point, and stated that some of the money should in fact benefit the refugees. The Arabs then threatened to boycott West Germany, something the United States was desperate to avoid. The Americans told the Syrians that "they would be killing their own case for compensation" by such a course of action.[143]

The reality was that many, including in the United States, Israel, and international Jewish circles believed that some of the reparations *should* be shared with the refugees. They argued that it would be difficult for Israel to maintain the argument that it was too poor to pay compensation given this massive transfer of German products which amounted to direct financial aid by another means. American officials confided to one another that Israeli payment of compensation soon was "increasingly advisable" because of Israel's success in gaining the reparations.[144] But it was not just the Americans who agreed that talk of compensation in the wake of the reparations agreement would make sense. Nahum Goldmann, the senior Jewish negotiator with the Germans and a man who would frequently adopt what some Jews considered controversial stands on Arab-Israeli matters, himself wrote to Eshkol that it would be "good for Israel" and "essential" for the Germans if some of the reparations went toward compensating the refugees.[145] In fact, the Israeli government itself had been among the first to tout the idea. Sharett told U.S. Undersecretary of State George McGhee in March 1951 that the reparations were a possible source of funding for compensation, while about the same time Ben Gurion noted:

> Certainly we wish to give reparations to the Arabs, but we cannot until we have been paid for all we lost in Germany, Hungary, Poland or Austria. We have our demands now before the United Nations. When this is adjusted, we will be glad to make an adjustment with the Arabs. Besides, you must remember we Jews have claims against the Arabs for all we lost in the territory now in their hands.[146]

Similarly, Sharett and David Horowitz told American UNCCP delegates Ely Palmer and James W. Barco in mid-1951 that American grant-in-aid and eventual restitution from Germany would enable Israel to pay compensation.

Some UNCCP staff personnel also were attracted to the idea. The reparations agreement occurred at the same time that John Berncastle was about to undertake his four-month mission on compensation in 1952. He also felt that linking German reparations to Israel with Israel's obligations to the Palestinian refugees was a logical idea. He felt that whereas Israel's claim for reparations was based on its absorption of half a million Holocaust refugees, this absorption had been made possible precisely because Israel confiscated the refugees' land. Some of what the Germans gave to the Israelis for this same purpose (absorbing refugees) logically should go to pay back the refugees. However, he realized that nothing would come without the strong support of the three member states in the UNCCP, particularly the United States. Berncastle began confiding his thoughts to his diary, discussing the "direct relationship between the two matters":

> It seems to me that the PCC should now consider whether, and in what way, it will link up the Israel-German and the Arab-Israel claims. If the PCC decides in favour of representing to Israel that a proportion of what she receives from Germany should go towards satisfying the refugees' claims, it would be necessary to have the strong backing of the Member Governments. As it may take time for these latter to formulate their views, the matter is one of some urgency.[147]

In July 1952, he wrote this to a fellow UNCCP staff member, Alexis Ladas:

> The Arab [refugee] property has, therefore, made a direct contribution to the very operation [resettlement of Holocaust refugees in Israel] of which the expense is about to be recovered from Germany. I think that it is legitimate for me to suggest to the Commission that it should take cognizance of the matter and consider what would be the consequence of taking my action or of not taking any action. In the past, one of the main arguments against proceeding actively with the work on compensation was that Israel had no money to pay. Now, it seems that she will get a windfall of money, or money's worth, the value of which will be several times the amount of our estimate of compensation due to the refugees . . . . Any proposal to them [the Israelis] that part of what they receive from Germany should go to the refugees would need to be backed up by pressure from the governments [on the UNCCP], particularly the U.S. Government, and by plans for implementation.[148]

On June 30, 1952, Ladas wrote back to Berncastle that he, or the Arabs, should formally suggest such a course of action to the UNCCP. The commission is not likely to take action based on your diary alone, Ladas told him. In fact, Berncastle had written to UNCCP Principal Secretary Dr. Feng Yang Chai in New York on June 11 discussing linkage between the reparations and refugee compensation. Berncastle laid out both the practical and "moral" reasons for linkage:

> there is a possibility of linking the questions of Israeli claims against Germany with the Arab refugees' claim against Israel, in the sense that if Israel succeeds in her claim she should have the means to satisfy the refugees' claim against her and is under a moral obligation to do so.[149]

He later told Chai, "Now that this agreement has been concluded it is surely time for Israel to do something about compensation for the Arab property."[150] Berncastle also surmised that the reason why Israel signed a deal whereby Germany would pay in kind instead of cash was precisely to forestall Arab demands that cash reparations be set aside for compensating the refugees.[151]

The United States continued to examine linkage between the two issues. The State Department drafted a memorandum in January 1953 entitled "Arab Refugee Compensation and the Israeli-German Reparations Agreement." Among the ideas contained in the document was the postulation that *theoretically* the two issues were separate but that *politically* it would be helpful to connect the two issues so as to forestall an Arab boycott of West Germany. The document suggested that the Americans use Israel's great anxiety about securing German parliamentary approval of the deal as a "sanction" to get it to move forward on the compensation issue. The United States could reasonably ask Israel to link the two issues, however, only if it increased its aid to Israel. The maximum amount necessary for this was $20 million/year. This would require the United States to give up its hope of ending Israeli grants-in-aid sometime around fiscal year 1957.[152] Later on March 4, 1953, American ambassador to Israel Monnett B. Davis suggested to Sharett that Israel issue a public statement renewing its willingness to pay compensation in order to forestall the threatened Arab boycott of West Germany. Sharett told Davis that he already had passed on an indirect message to Egypt through the good offices of Ralph Bunche that Israel's offer still stood "for the time being." He added, however, that Israel's domestic political scene made it difficult for him to issue such a statement at that time. Indeed, the opposition Herut party's Menachem Begin had led the charge against accepting the reparations on principle: accept no blood money from Germany. Ben Gurion insisted on accepting the aid, arguing that Israel badly needed it. Sharett believed that adding the already hotly emotional issue of German reparations to another hot button issue for many Israelis would be courting political suicide.[153] Soon other Israelis in the newly formed Horowitz Committee also began exploring the question between reparations and compensation. In the end, however, no German reparations payments were diverted to the Palestinian refugees.

## Horowitz Committee

So much diplomatic activity had taken place on the property compensation question in the four years since the Israeli government studied the matter via the Lif Committee in 1949 that it decided to undertake a major new study of the issue in mid-1953. Beyond the passage of time several other issues arose in early 1953 prompting this course of action. In February 1953, the Custodian of Absentee Property formally sold the bulk of the abandoned land to the Development Authority. The Arab states lodged a complaint to the UN one month later about this sale. The Israeli Ministry of Foreign Affairs also wanted to have a more recent study in order to prepare for the upcoming UN General Assembly meeting in the fall. To study the issue once again, the government turned to David Horowitz, the veteran Israeli economist and diplomat. Horowitz had met with the Clapp Mission in 1949, had been Director General of the Israeli treasury until 1952, and would become the first governor of the Bank of Israel in 1954. The Israeli cabinet took a secret decision on June 21, 1953 to establish a commission under Horowitz "to investigate the issue of the Arab refugees and to propose solutions." The committee was appointed officially eight days later and included members from the JNF, the Ministry of Foreign Affairs, and the Ministry of the Interior. Horowitz was chair; the other members included Yosef Weitz, Yehoshu'a Palmon, Z. Sozayev, A. Livni, and a certain Dr. Kramer. The committee was not expected to submit a massive report like the Weitz-Lifshits-Danin Committee's report but rather a shorter one that would offer policy suggestions to help Israeli diplomats as the Lif Committee report had done.

The Horowitz Committee was significant in that it marked a shift in Israeli thinking about the compensation issue. Horowitz proposed that the committee examine the refugee problem from a "humanitarian" perspective, noting that "we have no political obligation to help." This point of departure was that the best solution for the refugees would be resettlement in the Arab world. In this light, compensation should be global, not individual, and should be part of a wider campaign by the UN, the superpowers, and the Arab world to resettle the Palestinians. During the discussions that followed, several interesting new developments were revealed. Gideon Rafael of the Foreign Ministry indicated a shift in Israeli thinking. Instead of Israel trying to avoid the public spotlight about compensation, Sharett now wanted to court such attention. This would then shift the global focus away the present Arab clamor for refugee repatriation toward Israeli payment of compensation. Finding a workable plan for this was thus crucial in bringing this about. Rafael also stated that the government wanted to find ways to decrease the amount Israel would need to pay. His colleague Kramer also noted a second shift in official Israeli thinking: the Foreign Ministry had given up the demand that compensation be settled as part of a comprehensive peace deal with the Arabs. Rafael conceded that Israel had pledged to pay compensation, but wondered if it could shift its position to one of paying for rehabilitation instead of compensation. Rafael also brought up the question of war damages and damages to Israel's economy as a result of Egypt's closure of the Suez Canal. He claimed that all of these damages totaled £UK250–280 million. Rafael also mentioned other ideas for reducing the Israeli payment, like offering to pay for "reparations" instead of "compensation," or paying compensation via bonds instead of cash. Finally, he opined that the wealthy, propertied refugees were holding their poorer refugee countrymen hostage by insisting upon individual compensation, and that the Arab states were concerned that compensation would leave the refugees better off than the indigenous population. Weitz cautioned against linking compensation with Jewish property in Arab countries or even Israeli property in the West Bank and Gaza. Echoing the concern of some in the Israeli government, the JNF official felt that doing the former only would encourage Iraqi immigrants to press the state to pay them for their lost land, while the latter issue involved war reparations and should not be linked with the refugees.

Weitz also took issue with one of Horowitz's ideas: using the shilumim (German reparations) to help pay. Horowitz, Rafael, and others also discussed this point. In the end, the committee members agreed that Israel could not expect the money for compensation to come from the United States but would need to acquire it itself. Rather, Israel should borrow the money from the World Bank, using the German reparations as collateral on the loan since the Israelis were sure to receive this annual payment from the West Germans. As Horowitz noted, "It [the reparations payments] is excellent security. There is no better debtor today than Germany." All the men agreed that the two—reparations from Germany and compensation to the Palestinians—must be kept formally separate, however. As Horowitz noted, "We must mention this to the Government. We will, however, perform it in the form of two separate transactions. The Bank will lend [the money] to us, and we will put up the shilumim as collateral."[154]

In December 1953, the Horowitz Committee issued its report to the cabinet labeled "Top Secret." One of its first points was that Israel's traditional twin arguments (that the refugees fled of their own accord and that the Arab states were ultimately responsible for their flight because of their attack on

Israel) did not obviate the problem: the refugees still needed to be resettled. The report's authors ruled out repatriation. Israel was already too densely populated and returning refugees would constitute a fifth column. By contrast, the Arab countries constituted a familiar ethnic environment and stood in need of labor. It would be most beneficial for the refugees to be resettled there, especially in Syria, Jordan, and Iraq.

Turning to compensation, the Horowitz Committee report stated clearly that Israel alone could not "take upon itself the burden of individual compensation." Not only would this amount be greater than a collective compensation, it would not facilitate refugee resettlement. The committee members felt that a "large portion" of the refugees owned little or no property, so individual compensation would not alleviate their plight. Israel's payment of compensation should facilitate the resettlement of the refugees in the Arab countries with a standard of living that approximated what they had experienced in Palestine. But the committee did not rule out individual compensation to wealthy landowners at the same time. While calling such payments "acts of grace," the report made clear that they were based on political calculations:

> It is of course possible to compensate specific people as "acts of grace" based solely upon political and utilitarian considerations in order to acquire their support for the resettlement program, if they possess significant influence over large groups of Arab refugees. All such payments, however, can only be made as acts of grace, without damaging the principle of global payment.[155]

What basis should be used to determine the amount that Israel would pay? The report first noted the difficulties in trying to determine assessments because of currency fluctuation, the high price of land in pre-1948 Palestine that was the result of Jewish development, and so forth. The report also noted that the number of refugees had been inflated. The committee members concluded that resettlement in Arab countries would cost between $US300–350 per person. Since there were between 700,000–900,000 refugees, multiplying the higher figure of $350 by the higher estimate of refugees would be $315 million. Israel would be able to pay only some $100 million of this toward a resettlement program; the rest would need to come from the UN and the Arab states. The report noted that UN "wasted" a great deal of money each year caring for the refugees. "It would be worth its while for the UN to make a one-time investment of a larger sum of money in order to solve the problem once and for all." While not specifically calling for American assistance, the report noted that the superpowers also had an interest in a stable Middle East. Barring this, the only alternative would be to accept the UNCCP's global estimate, which was approximately the same amount. Israel, which would garner considerable international approval, would benefit from this latter approach.

The report then dropped its bombshell. It stated flatly that "Israel can acquire such a sum [$100 million] in one way only: by using the last installment of the shilumim. We must assume that use for such a goal is possible." Since it was in Germany's interest to negate continued Arab hostility over its reparations deal with Israel, Germany surely would agree to use the reparations as collateral for a loan secured in the United States. Horowitz and his colleagues were aware that this could set off a fire storm of criticism in Israel, and went to great lengths to qualify what they meant:

> It is clear that there should be no official linkage between this investment in the Arab refugees and the issue of the shilumim. Any such connection would be met with moral, political, and public opposition. The equation must be a loan to the State of Israel secured by the stable income of the shilumim. In other words, there can be no formal connection between the shilumim and investment in refugee rehabilitation, rather only a technical-financial one. But there is no chance of funding this project in any other way or from any other source.[156]

The government noted the committee's report, but undertook no major initiatives on the refugee property question as a result. The West German government continued to pay reparations to Israel until 1966 but the Israeli government did not use the payments as collateral on a major loan to pay the refugees compensation.

## Release of Blocked Refugee Bank Accounts

Israel agreed to one major initiative regarding refugee property the year before. This proved to be the most significant Israeli action on the property question and the UNCCP's most tangible success in the matter. As noted above, the question of refugee bank accounts blocked by Israel had come up early in the UNCCP's mediation efforts. Despite a February 15, 1950 agreement between Israel and Egypt, nothing happened. On May 5, 1952, American representative to the UNCCP Ely Palmer met with Eban to discuss the blocked accounts. The UNCCP felt that between 20,000 and 30,000 refugees possessed such blocked accounts. Palmer had been empowered by the UNCCP to approach the Israeli government formally and request that it consider releasing these funds "as a manifestation of good-will on the part of Israel." When Eban inquired whether Palmer was speaking for himself, for the UNCCP, and/or for the U.S. Department of State, Palmer replied that the UNCCP had deputized him to make the request, which also reflected the views of the State Department. He mentioned that a February 1951 meeting in Istanbul of U.S. ambassadors to Middle Eastern countries urged that the blocked accounts be released as an expression of Israel's good will and in order to help alleviate the plight of the Palestinian refugees. Eban promised to bring it up with the Israeli government.

Eban wrote home to the Ministry of Foreign Affairs' United States Division urging cooperation. He frankly admitted that Israel had been amazingly successful in stonewalling the Americans up to that point in time, far beyond what even he had imagined possible. "[I]t is fantastic what we get away with here without our eve[n] meeting USA requests but there is [a] limit which we may well have reached." Eban then proposed that Israel tell the United States that it was ready in principle to discuss releasing the accounts. As for linkage with Jewish bank accounts held in Arab countries, he suggested discussions with the UN. In the case of Iraq, Eban said that Israel should approach the United States for help. To underscore his plea for cooperation, Eban wrote Sharett on May 8, 1952 imploring action on Israel's part. He again stressed that Israeli cooperation need not come at the expense of Israeli demands: the Jewish state should continue to demand the *quid pro quo* release of frozen Jewish accounts in Iraq. But continued generalized stonewalling, he warned, would worsen U.S.-Israeli relations. "[W]e have taken our exploitation [of] their [U.S. Congress] sympathy to [the] saturation point," he warned.[157] Eban succeeded. In June, he told the United States that the Israeli government had agreed to revisit the issue of the blocked accounts. He indicated that Israel would discuss a gradual release "subject to the overall foreign exchange position of the country." A meeting between Israeli and UNCCP representatives was set for July 21, 1952 at the UN Secretariat building in New York.[158]

The UNCCP came prepared with a briefing paper containing questions that its representatives wanted to ask of the Israelis. The first thing that the UNCCP sought to determine was exactly what Israel meant by "blocked accounts." What the UNCCP was trying to find out was whether Israel was willing to release merely bank account balances or the contents kept by refugees in safe deposit boxes and items placed on "safe custody" with the banks as well. The former were boxes rented by refugees, who then placed in them articles they wished to store in the bank for safekeeping: jewelry, gold, other valuables, and so forth. The banks had no idea what the contents were. "Safe custody" items were different. They were usually paper securities such as bearer bonds that were left in the bank's vault for safekeeping. These were not anonymous transactions because the bank registered the items and thus had a record of them. Occasionally, however, banks also accepted sealed envelopes containing documents and kept them in safe custody as well. Most of the other questions that the UNCCP delegates wanted to pose to the Israelis at the meeting dealt with the modalities of the release. They were particularly anxious to know if Israel would agree to the operation being a bank-to-bank exchange with the UNCCP only acting in a "supervisory role."[159]

At the July 21 meeting, UNCCP staff personnel Feng Yang Chai, John Reedman, and Alexis Ladas explained to the Israelis how they envisioned the release taking place. First, Israel would make a public declaration of its intent to release the accounts and develop a release procedure that would be reviewed by the UNCCP. Then the refugee depositors would complete applications forms seeking the release of funds. Third, banks in the Arab countries where the refugees lived would "represent the interested banks in Israel to carry out the complicated task of clearing the applications and submitting them to their correspondent banks for Israel for clearance and liquidation." The UNCCP's representatives stressed that the UNCCP itself was not competent to execute the actual transfer; it would be a bank-to-bank operation. The Israelis noted that on their end the procedure would involve the Custodian of Absentee Property first releasing the funds to banks in Israel. Both sides agreed that complicated claims, such as those involving joint claims or law suits, should be handled separately and that the entire operation not be needlessly delayed by these. The Israeli diplomat Gideon Rafael insisted that the funds of the Palestinian-owned Arab Bank that were being held by Barclays Bank and other banks in Israel represented a special case that must be dealt with separately from foreign banks.[160]

After several months of working on the issue, Israel and the UNCCP came to an agreement on October 9 regarding the procedure of releasing the accounts. On December 4, 1952, Israel publicly announced its intention to carry out a limited release. It would release a total of £I1 million from the accounts at the rate of £I1 = $US2.80—that is, it would release about 20 percent of the total amount of blocked funds. Israel also agreed to release funds only from those accounts belonging to persons who had lived in Palestine up to November 29, 1947 and who fled prior to September 1, 1948. The accounts of expatriate Palestinians who lived abroad prior to November 29, 1947 as well as accounts belonging to refugees who fled after September 1, 1948 would not be affected by the release. Israel also would only release funds blocked in two foreign banks: Barclays Bank and the Ottoman Bank. Refugees with blocked accounts in these two banks could start filling out applications in quadruplicate requesting the release of funds. They would have until May 31, to do this. Payments would commence in March, and would total £UK50 per month per account only. The payments only applied to accounts owned by individuals, not companies, partnerships, or other impersonal bodies. The payment scheme would start on March 1, 1953 and would last for ten months only, meaning that persons holding blocked accounts of more than £500 would have to wait for the future to receive the balance of their funds inasmuch as the Custodian of Absentee Property had taken all balances over £500 from the banks as a type of loan. Additionally, the £50/month payments would be subject to having the same 10 percent compulsory loan to the Israeli government deducted from them just like any other bank account in Israel, but this amount would be refunded to the refugees when the final payment was made on each account. It was also agreed to begin procedures for future releases of safe deposit boxes and safe custody items.

To facilitate the work, the UNCCP established a Liaison Office in Jerusalem in mid-August 1953 to maintain contact both with local officials and with the UNCCP home office in New York. The first Liaison Officer was John P. Gaillard, who later was succeeded by Alexis Ladas in January 1954. Ladas would end up serving the commission in the position for several years. On a side note Ladas felt compelled to inform the UNCCP about a personal matter that he hoped would not compromise his official position. He told the commission in 1955 that he was engaged to be married to Theamaria Ackermann Husayni, the widow of Musa Husayni, whom the Jordanian government had tried and executed for alleged complicity in the assassination of King ʻAbdullah. The commission had no problem with this, however, and Ladas continued in his position.[161]

There were 6,246 blocked Arab accounts by 1949, according to the figures supplied to the UNCCP by the Custodian of Absentee Property's office. Of these, 45.1 percent (2,820) were small accounts of less than £50. Thus the total amount of funds in these small accounts would be paid out during the scheme. Table 3.7 shows the number and value of blocked accounts at the time that release was about to begin.

Refugees with accounts in the two banks began applying for their funds in March 1953. However, the program almost immediately ran into political

TABLE 3.7 Number and Amount of Blocked Arab Accounts, 1953

| *Amount of Account (£UK)* | *Number of Accounts* |
|---|---|
| less than 50 | 2,820 |
| 50–99 | 532 |
| 100–149 | 435 |
| 150–199 | 279 |
| 200–249 | 302 |
| 250–499 | 681 |
| 500–999 | 523 |
| over 1,000 | 683 |
| TOTAL £3,218,775* | 6,246** |

*Approximate: excluding £582,931 claimed by Arab Bank, Ltd., against Barclays Bank
** includes corporations, etc., not eligible for participation in release scheme; also excludes deceased account holders

Source: NARA RG84, United Nations/USUN Central Files—UN Letters/2450, "Blocked Arab Accounts;" Document: "Interim Memorandum on Results of First Instalment [sic] of "Blocked Accounts' Release Agreement" (September 18, 1953)

troubles that suspended its operations in April and May. Some of the refugees objected to the wording of the application form, fearing that signing it implied recognition of Israel. Following negotiations that concluded with the Jordanian government on June 3, a new form was devised and the process resumed in mid-June. The Jordanian government was anxious for the release to continue because it desired the influx of hard currency into the country. By May 21, at which time the process was still on hold, 907 applications already had come in from refugees in Jordan, Egypt, and Iraq. The Israeli Custodian of Absentee Property had approved 549 of these, rejected four, leaving 358 still in process. The total amount approved for release by the Custodian up to that date was £148,783.[162]

The two banks began making their first payments in June and dispersed approximately £50,000 by the end of the month. The refugees obtained the money from a branch of their bank in the country where they lived. The Joint Control Office established by the two banks in Jerusalem began receiving the first applications from Lebanon on July 3 and from Syria on August 19. Payments to the former began in August. The Banque de Syrie et du Liban handled the transfers in Lebanon and Syria on behalf of Barclays and Ottoman. By September 15, 1953, 2,880 applications for release of blocked accounts were received by the Joint Control Office. Of these, 2,173 were passed on to the Custodian; 400 were still being processed; and 300 were rejected by the two banks. Of those passed on to the Custodian, 1,536 were approved; 44 were rejected; 1 was approved but later withdrawn by the applicant; 6 were returned to the Joint Control Office for further examination; and 626 were still being processed by the Custodian.

The Custodian had to deal with a number of what were called "hard cases." Most of these were applicants for whom the Custodian could not easily determine their absentee status. Under terms of the release scheme, only absentees could apply for their bank accounts. But in a region strapped for hard currency, other people with accounts in the two banks sought to gain access to their frozen hard currency accounts as well. Among these were Palestinians who, while considered "refugees" by certain quarters in the UNCCP, were not technically "absentees" under the Israeli Absentees' Property Law of 1950. One of the main criteria used to determine this status was whether the applicant was a resident of Palestine on November 29, 1947. Palestinians who had taken up residence in surrounding Arab countries before that date and were subsequently unable to return because of the war were thus ineligible. The UNCCP, however, considered these persons as "refugees," as it did those Palestinians who had been out of the country only temporarily on November 27, 1947 and could not get back, and therefore tried to assist them. Palestinians who were still resident in Israel also were not included as their accounts were not frozen (they could simply go and withdraw funds from their accounts, although in Israeli currency, not sterling). Other hard cases included applicants who did not themselves own a blocked account but possessed drafts (checks) drawn on a blocked account. On the other hand, the Custodian *did* agree to release blocked accounts of some Palestinians whom he considered were not absentees: certain Palestinians from the Old City of Jerusalem who had not fled from territory now under Israeli control (the Old City was under Jordanian control) but who had accounts in the western part of the city. Overall, the UNCCP believed that both the Custodian and the Joint Control Office had been liberal in their interpretations in an effort to guarantee the success of the release.[163]

UNCCP officials were puzzled by the low number of applicants in several categories. The first was among persons owning small accounts—precisely the needy people officials thought would jump at the chance to receive their blocked funds. Only nine percent of eligible applicants owning accounts of less than £50 (260 of 2,820 accounts) had applied and had their requests approved by September 15, 1953. Similarly, only 36 percent of those owning accounts of between £50–499 had applied and been approved, along with 37 percent of those owning large accounts over £500 (who would receive only the first £500 of their accounts during the release). Also, the number of applicants living in Lebanon and Syria was strikingly low.

Several explanations for the low turnout were advanced. Perhaps negative publicity in the Arab press and among refugee leaders may have deterred refugees from applying—especially inasmuch as Israel had announced that it had deducted the ten percent loan from all blocked accounts. This allowed Arab commentators to allege that Israel and the banks were conspiring to rob the refugees. In addition to such negative comments, the overall level of publicity was low and may have contributed to the small response. Some refugees may also have feared that submitting a form was tantamount to recognizing Israel, especially since the first application form that was used contained language that implied this in some refugees' minds. The fact that the scheme was halted after Jordanian complaints and a new form used only served to increase the mistrust. Certainly the announcement that Israel was deducting a percentage as part of the mandatory loan discouraged others and contributed to the feeling that applying somehow was legitimizing Israel's seizure of their money. Beyond the loan, some applicants who did apply found that the Custodian had deducted amounts to cover his "expenses": one £800 account showed that £200 had been deducted to cover such expenses from 1949–52. Finally, political reasons also were cited for noncooperation: some refugee leaders were opposed to a piecemeal, "economic" solution to the refugees' plight which they feared might somehow negate their political rights. Izzat Tannous, for example, encouraged refugees not to apply.[164]

Another major reason for the low number of applications was a series of lawsuits that refugees had brought against Barclays Bank and the Ottoman Bank. These suits were seeking to force the banks to pay the depositors their account balances outside of any general release scheme with Israel. Some refugees undoubtedly felt that such suits constituted a more politically palatable way to get hold of their money without having to participate in a process that was connected with Israel, with loan deductions, and so forth. This process had started two years before the release scheme was announced. In October 1950, the Arab Bank in Amman sued Barclays Bank in a British court for £P1 million. The Arab Bank had been the leading Palestinian Arab bank during the mandate, having a total of some £P6 million in Barclays and the Ottoman Bank in addition to £P500,000 in Jewish banks like the Anglo-Palestine Bank. The Arab Bank had deposited funds with Barclays' Allenby Square branch in western Jerusalem prior to 1948 and ended up moving to the Old City of Jerusalem during the initial fighting and then to Jordan in June 1948. After the war the

Israeli Custodian of Absentee Property considered the Arab Bank's accounts with Barclays to be absentee property because they were owned by an absentee company. Accordingly, the Custodian requested in January 1951 that Barclays Bank in West Jerusalem turn over to him the Arab Banks' accounts. The following month Barclays Bank handed over £582,931. Because the Arab Bank reportedly had paid refugees the amounts they had left in the blocked accounts without receiving the actual money from its blocked account with Barclays Bank in Jerusalem, it sued Barclays in London to obtain the amount.[165] The Arab Bank's venerable chief executive, Abd al-Hamid Shoman, flew to London for the court proceedings.[166] After eventually hearing the case of Arab Bank, Ltd. v. Barclays Bank (Dominion, Colonial and Overseas) in the spring of 1954, however, the House of Lords dismissed the claim. Another high-profile case filed against Barclays Bank in Jordanian-controlled East Jerusalem by a Mrs. Barakat, however, saw the Jordanian district court in Jerusalem rule in her favor on June 25, 1953.

The release continued, but remained plagued by difficulties. One such problem was the long period of time between the times refugees applied for a release of their bank accounts and when the funds were actually received. By August 31, 1953, only £100,000 had been paid out. Payments first were made to refugees in Jordan and Egypt, because they had been the first to send in completed applications. Releases were made to Iraq and Lebanon starting in August. While the UNCCP believed that the delays were not out of the ordinary given the complexities of the entire scheme, it still feared that the delays would discourage other refugees from applying for release of their money.

The UNCCP felt by the fall of 1953 that the first phase of the release scheme had been a partial success at best. The UNCCP recognized that there was a general lack of good will among the parties, to no small degree because while Israel may have sought a degree of appreciation from the Arab world for its willingness to release the funds, the refugees considered that getting back their money was their right and not something they should view favorably as an Israeli compromise. Alexis Ladas noted:

> No spectacular reaction can be expected from the Arab States. Expressions of appreciation are not likely to come from refugees who consider payment of long-blocked balances merely the liquidation of a definite obligation. This aspect of the problem well might be impressed on Israel representatives who consider their gesture a heavy sacrifice calling for acknowledgment in the form of a reciprocal gesture. A longer term view could be suggested.[167]

The UNCCP then began discussions with Israel for a second phase of the release program in order to allow more refugees to apply for their blocked accounts and to keep momentum going on Arab-Israeli contacts. The UNCCP was told in May 1954 that Barclays Bank had agreed to lend the government of Israel £UK5 million, of which £3 million was to help cover a second phase of releasing blocked accounts. The loan was approved on September 26, 1954, and Israel announced the following day that it would agree to a second phase of the release. Israel stated that in this phase all account holders could apply, including corporate entities. It also announced that safe deposit boxes and safe custody items would be included in the second phase of the release. Israel further reserved the right once again to refuse to pay but limited the total amount it could refuse to release to £I290,000 (approximately £UK50,000). Lastly, it would cancel all further deductions for the compulsory loan. However, Israeli diplomats informed the UNCCP on August 11, 1954 that this time Israel insisted on negotiating the terms of the release directly with duly elected representatives of the refugee account holders. These representatives then would be required to sign a legal agreement with Israel. One of the two Israelis at the August 11 meeting, Gideon Rafael, claimed that Israel had placed this requirement purely in order to remove the obstacles to payment that had arisen during the first phase. In the event that no delegation was willing to step forward and negotiate with them, the Israelis stated, Israel would consider any further responsibility toward the account holders to be over.

The insistence on direct negotiations with the refugee account holders was clearly a calculated move designed to bring Israel into face-to-face talks with Arabs outside of UNCCP-sponsored talks. The Israelis were angry at the UNCCP for failing to conciliate, in their opinion, and would take whatever steps they needed to start direct negotiations. This was a direct turn around from earlier Israeli policy, when the Israelis tried to minimize the UNCCP's diplomatic role. Rafael berated UNCCP staff member Alexis Ladas at the August 11, 1954 meeting with the UNCCP, saying that the UNCCP had no right not to conciliate. The UNCCP should remember, Rafael snapped, that it was a servant of Israel and the Arab states, not vice-versa.[168] The UNCCP saw through the ploy right away. Ladas knew that Israel's insistence upon meeting directly with the refugees was not in order to work out any problems but simply a way to force Arabs into direct talks with Israel. The UNCCP always had encouraged the entire release scheme to be a simple business transaction, bank-to-bank. How could such a new arrangement be any more advantageous than the previous one? Ladas believed that Israel had pulled a "fast one" and shared his feelings with UNCCP Principal Secretary Chai:

> What makes the Israeli proposal so unnecessary in any real sense is that since the money will be made available by Barclays to the banks the method of payment could be left up to the banks themselves acting upon applications from their clients. It is very hard to see what the "beneficiaries" [account holders] would contribute to the negotiations other than the propaganda value of their presence.[169]

Israel eventually dropped its demand for negotiations with the refugees and agreed to a second transfer on September 26, 1954, although it delayed a formal announcement of such until November 16, 1954. The second phase of the release began with the announcement that applications could be submitted in January 1955. By May 1, 1955, the Custodian of Absentee Property had received 1,628 new applications of which 1,053 were approved for £1,745,298.[170] By August 31, 1955, the Custodian had released a total of £UK2,292,339 to date. Barclays Bank still had £UK442,845 in outstanding refugee funds eligible for release, while the Ottoman Bank still had £298,459.[171] Table 3.8 shows how much had been released by December 31, 1955. By June 1956, the Custodian had approved 2,025 applications for release of the equivalent of £2,618,683. By September, 87 percent of the funds in Barclays Bank and the Ottoman Bank had been released.[172]

As mentioned, the second phase of the release in 1955 also allowed refugees to petition for the release of safe deposit boxes and items left on safe custody. In February 1955, Jordan was the first Arab country to agree to a procedure for transferring these items. The boxes and other items would be opened in the banks in Israel in the presence of the following officials: Israeli customs and censorship personnel; UNCCP Liaison Officer Ladas; a representative from

TABLE 3.8 Blocked Accounts Released by 1955

| *Country of Refugee's Residence* | *Amount Released (£UK)* |
|---|---|
| Jordan | 1,528,400 |
| Lebanon | 602,900 |
| Syria | 144,000 |
| Egypt | 74,900 |
| Gaza | 26,000 |
| Others | 162,442 |
| TOTAL | 2,538,642 |

Source: UN Document A/3199, 15th Progress Report of UNCCP (October 4, 1956)

TABLE 3.9 Refugee Safe Deposit Box and Safe Custody Items Released by 30 September 1955

| | *Number Originally Held by Custodian of Absentee Property* | *Number Released* |
|---|---|---|
| 1. Safe Deposit Boxes | 153 | 10 |
| 2. Safe Custody Items | | |
| Boxes and parcels | 51 | 10 |
| Open dossiers | 658 | 121 |
| Dossiers of Palestine Bearer Bonds | 416 | 199 |
| Items held abroad | 9 | 2 |

Source: NAR/RG 84, United Nations, USUN Central Filest—UN Letters/2450, "Blocked Arab Accounts;" Document: Ladas to Bang-Jensen (November 3, 1955)

the Joint Control Board; and two representatives from the bank. All items would be inventoried before being transported across the cease-fire crossing point at the Mandelbaum Gate in Jerusalem into Jordanian-controlled territory. Jordan agreed to waive customs duty on such incoming items and agreed to provide armed police escort for the UN vehicles that physically would carry the goods from East Jerusalem to Amman. The first convoy crossed over on April 15, 1955 without incident. Lebanon later agreed to the same procedure, with the first convoy driving north into south Lebanon from Ra's Naqqura (called Rosh ha-Nikra by the Israelis) in August. However, the Lebanese government began charging customs duties as high as 26 percent on the value of most of the goods.[173] Syria later agreed to a procedure, although it never came to fruition. By September 30, 1955, a number of safe deposit boxes and safe custody items had been released, as indicated in table 3.9. By April 1, 1957, 108 safe deposit boxes had been released.[174]

Releasing Palestine bearer bonds owned by refugees represented yet another challenge. A number of Palestinians had left dossiers containing these bonds on safe custody in the banks before 1948. Since these represented an obligation of the British government, Israel ordered all banks to register such bonds with the government in early 1950 to prepare for negotiations with the British government over lingering financial matters between Israel and the United Kingdom. Israel dispatched David Horowitz to London for the talks, which ended on March 30, 1950. In the resulting Agreement Between the United Kingdom and Israel for the Settlement of Financial Matters Outstanding as a Result of the

Termination of the Mandate for Palestine, the United Kingdom released to Israel £UK5 million in assets of the former Palestine government that it had blocked since February 1948. Israel also acquired all British crown property and mandatory government assets in its territory except for some property in Jerusalem. The United Kingdom was to have £UK3 million returned over the next fifteen years.[175]

Prior to the release of the refugees' safe deposit boxes and safe custody items, the banks discussed what to do with these bonds. Those held on safe custody had been registered. Upon their release, Israel would have to pay the amounts they represented in sterling to the British government as part of the 1950 financial agreement. Those bonds that had been kept anonymously in safe deposit boxes, however, would be treated differently. Since the banks had no knowledge of them and did not register them with the Israeli government, any refugee who sought to redeem such bonds obtained through the release would need to approach the British government directly.[176] By April 1, 1957, 480 of 520 applications for the release of Palestine Bearer Bonds had been approved for a total of £UK92,100.[177]

By 1955, the UNCCP was quite happy about the progress it had made in returning the blocked refugees' funds and property after the second release. Unlike compensation for land, here the commission felt it had realized tangible and demonstrable progress. It felt that this success had created an air of optimism that it hoped could be built upon:

> There is no doubt that a great number of people have benefited significantly from the implementation of the release scheme and the beneficial effects on their state of mind can be easily felt. This is one of the few times when international action has produced tangible advantages to individuals and the effect is a somewhat exaggerated expectation that other more serious problems can be speedily resolved in a similar way. In particular the return of the [safe deposit box] valuables to their owners, which incidentally were of considerably greater value than was supposed, has led to a feeling of optimism which constitutes quite a solid achievement for the Commission.[178]

Applications and releases of blocked accounts continued into 1957 and 1958. By April 1, 1957, the Custodian had approved 2,153 of 2,415 applications received to that date for a total of £UK2,644,003. This figure rose to some £2,750,000 by March 31, 1958 and by 1959, a total of £2,781,164 had been released. There were still some outstanding accounts in Barclays Bank by that point. Lists of outstanding account owners were provided to UNRWA offices in

Jordan, Lebanon, Syria, Egypt, and Gaza in order to publicize the fact that these accounts were still outstanding and could be claimed. The UNCCP also issued press releases. By July 31, 1966, £2,802,110 had been released.[179]

While the vast majority of the accounts in Barclays Bank and the Ottoman Bank had been released by 1959, the issue of accounts in other banks in Israel remained. The UNCCP estimated in early 1956 that these consisted of some £UK300,000.[180] Such banks included the Holland Bank Union in Haifa and what had been called the Anglo-Palestine Bank. This latter had been the leading bank for the Jewish community in Palestine prior to 1948. With Israeli independence in May 1948, the Anglo-Palestine Bank became the government's banker and changed its name to Bank Le'umi le-Yisra'el in 1951. It continued to provide this function until the establishment of the Bank of Israel in December 1954. Bank Le'umi therefore had no branches in Arab countries, and could not transfer accounts with the ease that Barclays Bank and the Ottoman Bank could. The amount of blocked funds in Bank Le'umi was also considerably less. The UNCCP discussed the question of accounts in other banks with Israeli authorities on several occasions. The UNCCP noted that Israel's November 16, 1954 announcement regarding the second phase of the first release scheme had referred to accounts in "banks in Israel," not just those held by Barclays and the Ottoman banks: "there is no valid reason why the depositors of other banks should be discriminated against particularly since no such distinction was made under the first instalment [sic]."[181] The Israelis had, in fact, released some safe deposit boxes from other banks after 1955, which tended to support this argument.

Ladas approached Gideon Rafael and other officials of the Israeli Ministry of Foreign Affairs about releasing funds from other banks in February 1956. Relations between the ministry and the UNCCP were still somewhat strained from 1954 when the Israelis had presented—and then dropped—their demand to negotiate directly with the refugee account owners. The Israelis wanted to know why the UNCCP was involving itself in a matter that it earlier had striven to have carried out on a bank-to-bank level without its intervention. Ladas responded that the UNCCP was only trying to facilitate the further release of accounts and always reserved the right to express concern over the refugees' property. Later he confided to UNCCP Principal Secretary Povl Bang-Jensen:

> [t]hey are still pretty annoyed with us for having refused to fall in with their scheme to negotiate with the refugees. Personally I don't think it matters very much as long as we get results and I don't see that there is much point in including these things in the Commission's report.[182]

The Arab-Israeli conflict heated up considerably in 1955 and 1956 to the detriment of the UNCCP's attempts to broker a second release scheme for blocked bank accounts and for the wider goal of compensation for land. This worsening situation was particularly true of relations between Israel and Egypt. A Middle Eastern arms race started in 1955, with Israel obtaining modern weaponry from France and Egypt from the USSR via Czechoslovakia. In October 1956, Israel joined with France and Britain in attacking Egypt following Jamal 'Abd al-Nasir's nationalization of the Suez Canal Company. The UNCCP wrote to Israel about the remaining blocked accounts on May 10, 1957, but was told that the Israeli treasury was not providing the foreign currency necessary for a release.[183] It was therefore not until November 11, 1959 that Israel agreed to a third major release involving accounts in banks "other than Barclays Bank and the Ottoman Bank." By that time, however, the entire question of refugee accounts had faded into relative obscurity. In fact Israeli officials apparently forgot to follow up on their promise to arrange for a third release. On June 8, 1960, officials from the American embassy approached Gershon Avner, Director of the U.S. Division of the Israeli Ministry of Foreign Affairs, to inquire why no progress on the third release had been made to date. Avner was completely unaware of where the matter stood. When told that the UNCCP's representative in Jerusalem had approached Foreign Ministry official Michael S. Comay about the issue, Avner expressed surprise and replied that he was not even aware that the UNCCP had a representative in the region. He was also uncertain if the UNCCP's request ever was received. The Americans wrote to Washington that it "was the latter's [Avner's] hope, he remarked smilingly, that such a situation would continue."[184] Indeed, it would not be until May 1962 that Israel announced that it was prepared to release the accounts blocked in the other banks. By July 31, 1966, £UK52,642 had been released as a result of this third release scheme.

As the number of applications relating to the release schemes trickled into oblivion by the eve of the June 1967 Arab-Israeli war, the following statistics reveal the overall progress of the three releases. By 1966, a total of £UK3,595,160 in blocked bank accounts had been released to refugees.[185] By July 1966, about 2,000 unclaimed or unapproved blocked accounts worth some £UK250,000 remained (most were unclaimed). Of these, 1,440 were in Barclays Bank totaling £UK150,000. Some £UK10,000 remained in the Ottoman Bank. By that same month there were still 30 unclaimed safe deposit boxes and 205 unclaimed items on safe custody hold.[186] At least one of these boxes later was claimed: Fuad W.F. Boustany requested the release of a safe deposit box that had been held for decades at the Barclays Bank branch in Haifa. The box was opened at the bank on December 13, 1967, in the presence of representatives of the Joint Control Office, the Custodian of Absentee Property, Israeli customs, the Israeli censor's office, and the UNCCP liaison officer. Thus released, the contents of safe deposit box number 246B left Haifa nearly twenty years after their owner had fled the city.[187]

## Reorganization of Israeli Land Agencies

Almost as a postscript to its confiscation of refugee land, Israel reorganized the structure in which landed property was managed in the country. In the years after the state transferred several million dunums of land to the JNF, the variety of different agencies responsible for land management in Israel continued to cause confusion. This confusion came in the context of the overall problem faced by the Zionist movement after 1948: who was now responsible for policy in Israel, the World Zionist Organization or the Israeli government, or both? While the overall relationship between the WZO and the Israeli government was formalized in 1952, it was not until 1960 that a new land regime was created that brought together under one rubric land under state control and land belonging to the Jewish National Fund. Following negotiations between the two sides, the Knesset passed the Israel Lands Law of 5720/1960 on July 19, 1960, after which the JNF and the state signed an agreement. Shortly thereafter on July 25 the Knesset enacted the Israel Lands Administration Law of 5720/1960. These laws along with a state-JNF agreement created a new public body that would control the land of both the state and the JNF: the Israel Lands Administration (Heb.: Minhal Mekarke'ei Yisra'el). Under this arrangement, both the state and the JNF played a role in policy making and administration of what thereafter were called "Israel Lands" (Heb.: Mekarke'ei Yisra'el). Two policymaking councils were created that were made up of representatives of both the state and the JNF. The first was the Israel Lands Council, in which the state held the majority of the thirteen seats. The second was the Land Reclamation and Development Council, in which the JNF held the majority. The agreements also created two administrative councils: the Israel Lands Administration, with a state majority, and the Land Development Administration, with a JNF majority. By the 1990s, 93 percent of all land in Israel was under ILA control, of which 80 percent was state land, 10 percent was Development Authority land (also a type of state land), and 10 percent JNF land.[188]

This reorganization did not lead to any movement on compensation nor significantly alter the international equation regarding the refugees' land. As a result of the agreement, the Custodian of Absentee Property's office moved in 1962 from the Ministry of Finance to within the rubric of the ILA, even though the 1950 Absentee Property Law—still the controlling legal mechanism governing the Custodian's activities—stipulated that the Ministry of Finance alone would be responsible for carrying out the law's statutes. This apparently did not present any major problems because by that time the Custodian's office no longer controlled any land but only managed refugee accounts and some moveable assets.

## Secret Israeli Moves to Compensate Individual Refugees in the 1960s

Where Israel did expend some energy on the compensation question about this time was a surreptitious campaign to pay compensation to certain refugees. Rumors began circulating in the Middle East in the early and mid-1960s of refugees secretly conducting land transactions with Israeli agents in third countries. Such reports had been in circulation almost from the beginning of the refugee exodus. The radio station in Jordanian-occupied Ramallah had broadcast a report on May 2, 1949 that refugees were selling land to Israelis in Cyprus.[189] Starting in 1963, rumors of secret deals on Cyprus resurfaced. This time, there seemed to be more to the stories than mere idle speculation. The Middle East was set abuzz by an April 1963 issue of *Newsweek* magazine reporting that "[Israel] has started reimbursing former Palestinian Arabs (most of them are now in Jordan) for lands and properties lost during the 1948–49 Arab-Jewish war. Budget for the plan: $4 million."[190] (189) Several Arab UN delegates approached UNCCP Principal Secretary John Gaillard and asked whether he could confirm the reports. Gaillard asked the UNCCP's liaison officer in Jerusalem for information, but came up with nothing concrete. Gaillard later told American diplomats at the UN in July 1963 that in recent months he had received "indications" that such rumors were true: that special Israeli officials were negotiating in Cyprus with lawyers representing refugees, and that Israel was paying compensation to individual refugees through Bank Le'umi and other Israeli banks.

The U.S. Department of State immediately instructed its embassy in Tel Aviv to ask Israeli officials about this story. American diplomats then approached Gideon Rafael and another diplomat from the Israeli Ministry of Foreign Affairs. These two informed the Americans that the story was partially true. They claimed that a Palestinian citizen of Israel living abroad mentioned to an Israeli official that a number of refugees wanted to settle compensation claims directly with Israel. Was Israel interested? The Israeli government informed the man through an intermediary that it was indeed interested. The government then established a £I3 million–4 million contingency fund in the state budget for this. However, the two Israelis insisted to the Americans that Israel heard nothing more from the Palestinian after that. The Americans kept digging. The State Department asked the American embassy in Nicosia what it knew of the story. U.S. diplomats there replied that they had no knowledge of such dealings, but "discreetly" asked an Israeli embassy official in Nicosia whether Israel was using Cyprus as the venue for contacts with Arabs on a variety of issues. The Israeli contact denied any talks were underway on Cyprus or anywhere, and denied that any progress was being made on the refugee property issue in particular.[191]

Other information began to surface pointing to the possible veracity of the reports of secret compensation deals between Israel and refugees on Cyprus. In August 1963, Israeli Prime Minister Levi Eshkol granted an interview with the London-based *Jewish Chronicle* in which he stated that he was ready to present the Knesset with a request for a special budget for compensating the refugees. Israel then would use intermediaries to "establish direct contact with refugees." He also added the usual Israeli provisos that compensation only could come through a general solution to the refugee problem and must take into consideration Jewish property in Arab countries. The Israeli opposition newspaper *Herut* reported a dramatic story in November 1963 that Egyptian agents had tried to assassinate a wealthy Palestinian citizen of Israel living in Cyprus, Sa'id Hajjaj, in early 1963. According to the report, Hajjaj had sold land in Israel and then moved to Cyprus and had been told, "presumably by pertinent Israeli authorities," to encourage Palestinian refugees to sell their land to Israel.[192] It is unclear to the author whether Hajjaj was the Palestinian citizen of Israel whose case Israeli officials had discussed with American diplomats (see above). Later that month, the State Department received reports from Tel Aviv that the "Israelis [are] quietly working on compensation payment schemes." The rumors continued to circulate for several years. In February 1965, the American embassy in Amman reported on rumors of refugees negotiating the sale of land "in Cyprus and elsewhere." That July Mordekhai Gazit of the Israeli mission to the UN told an American UN official about a "small, token [compensation] plan which would have to be carried out surreptitiously." Even if it worked, Gazit said, it could not be part of a larger plan.[193]

The Arab states were quick to respond to the rumors by trying to stop such sales. The Arab League issued a resolution asking member states not to provide any information to individual refugees that might facilitate land deals with the Israelis. This was particularly aimed at Jordan because the Jordanian Department of Lands and Survey had been providing refugees with certificates noting how much land they had owned in pre-1948 Palestine and where. Jordanian land authorities derived this information from captured mandatory land registers in their possession since 1948. Some of those who requested the information simply may have wanted a record that they had owned land in Palestine, or sought proof of their origins in order to secure Jordanian passports. Others in fact may have wanted to use the certificates as a type of deed in order to sell their land. In either event, the Jordanian government responded to the Arab League request by stopping the issuance of certificates that showed the amount of land that refugees had owned, although it continued to provide documents stating that so-and-so owned land in such-and-such village, but without listing how much. Overall, hard facts about the rumors of land sales on Cyprus and elsewhere have yet to surface. It is thus difficult to determine how widespread this activity was. However, it did not alter the refugee property equation significantly and has remained largely a curious historical footnote.

## CHAPTER FOUR

# EARLY ARAB AND INTERNATIONAL POLICIES TOWARD THE PROPERTY QUESTION

The Arab world continued to be outraged at Israel's confiscation of refugee property and its subsequent stance on the compensation issue, while also expressing little faith in the UNCCP. The Arabs scoffed at its 1951 Global Estimate of refugee property losses as being far too low. Like the Israelis, various Arab individuals and groups had publicly floated a variety of figures for the value of the abandoned refugee property since 1948, all of which were much higher than Berncastle's numbers. The premier Arab expert on land in Palestine undoubtedly was Sami Hadawi. He had impressive credentials to back up this claim. He was born in Jerusalem in 1904 to a Palestinian mother and an Iraqi father. Although he never completed school after the age of eleven, Hadawi learned English and German while attending Christian schools as a youth in Jerusalem. During the First World War his mother took the family to Transjordan for safety. After serving as a translator for German troops in Amman he later translated for the British commonwealth troops that captured the city. Back in Palestine after the war, Hadawi began working for the mandatory government in 1919, and in 1927 took a position in the Department of Land Settlement. From 1938 until the end of the mandate, Hadawi assessed land values for urban and rural taxation. He played a major role in the production of the mandatory publication on land tenure, *Village Statistics, 1945*, upon which Berncastle had relied when carrying out the Global Estimate. Hadawi eventually was awarded the M.B.E. (Member of the British Empire medal) and granted British citizenship.

Besides knowledge about land, Hadawi also possessed documents. As the fighting escalated in 1948 and both sides prepared for the future, Hadawi's friend Yusif Sayigh convinced him to hand over Palestinian land records under his control to the Arab Higher Committee. When Hadawi received orders from the British to transfer all documents in his office to the French Building next to the King David Hotel in western Jerusalem, he packed them off to the Christ Church Hostel in East Jerusalem instead. The armistice found him a refugee in Jordanian-controlled East Jerusalem with his documents but with his home and the aviary containing his beloved canaries now in Israeli-controlled West

Jerusalem. From 1949–50, Hadawi's experience proved beneficial to the Jordanian government, for which he worked as director of tax assessments for the West Bank. In 1949, Hadawi moved the records he had secured to the police building in Ramallah, and separated the ones that he would need for the West Bank from the rest. He sent eleven bags of documents not dealing with the West Bank to Sayigh, who by then was working in the economic section of UNRWA. Sayigh later delivered the records to Hadawi's wife in Beirut. After the Syrian government came across his name in an article he had published on Palestinian land, he met with Syrian leader Adib Shishakli and took up the latter's offer to head an official body established by the Syrian government to deal with Palestinian refugees. He handed over the eleven bags of records he had been keeping in Beirut to Shishakli in order that some use might be put to them, and they were housed with the organization that Hadawi headed. As he later noted ruefully, he never saw the majority of the records again after he left his post in Syria.[1]

Hadawi also became the leading land expert for the Palestinian refugee cause thereafter. As a former expert on the scope and value of Palestinian land, he was in a good position to assist representatives of the refugees in their communications with UN officials. He provided figures to some of the refugees who made representations to the UNCCP in Beirut in March 1949. Berncastle studied some of his other recommendations. In early 1951 Hadawi had proposed determining the scope of refugee property by issuing a questionnaire to refugees that could be checked against mandatory land records. His detailed proposal suggested that it would take five years to carry out 250,000 such interviews with refugees. At the time of the Global Estimate in 1951, Hadawi also urged Berncastle to establish land values based on the average market value of land in 1947 rather than rely on the British tax assessment data, which Hadawi and other Palestinians said were too low. Having been a tax assessment office himself during the mandate, Hadawi noted that tax assessment committees in Palestine had consisted of four persons: two government employees and two civilians. Only one of these had any training in the field, and he claimed that the committees rarely actually carried out inspections of property. Hadawi maintained that the "official" tax assessments Berncastle used were inaccurate and almost always low. Hadawi also said that the assessed net annual value of land had no meaningful connection to the real capital value of property. As for buildings, he suggested using the 1947 replacement cost because the tax assessment figures were based on pre-Second World War costs. Lastly, Hadawi noted that most of the urban tax assessments dated from 1939, before rent restrictions came into force in 1940, and were thus far below what the actual rents that landowners managed to charge illegally.[2] Berncastle was generally not persuaded by Hadawi's arguments, but it would not be the last time that Sami Hadawi's expertise proved important both to the Arabs and to the UNCCP.

## Early Arab Estimates of Refugee Property

When the Arab League met in Alexandria in August 1950, press reports indicated that estimates of the value of the refugees' property up to $US5 billion were being floated at the conference.[3] Some refugee leaders from Jaffa told a journalist in Beirut that the 122,000 dunums of abandoned orange groves in Israeli hands were worth $1–2 million and that the value of land and moveable property in Jaffa alone totaled $120 million.[4] On November 30, 1950, two of Jordan's representatives to the UN, Ahmad Tuqan and Yusuf Haykal, told the General Assembly's Ad Hoc Political Committee that the refugees' property was worth $3 billion.[5] In mid-1951, the Egyptian Ministry of Foreign Affairs asked Palestinian refugees living in its territory to send a statement of their abandoned property in Israel to the ministry in order to tally the results.[6]

Surely one of the most thorough, if questionable, of these early Arab attempts to quantify the Palestinians' losses came from the Arab Refugee Property Owners in Palestine and its indefatigable spokesman, Dr. Izzat Tannous. No stranger to the Palestinian national cause, Tannous was born in Nablus in 1896, and obtained his M.D. from the Syrian Protestant College (now called the American University of Beirut). He became involved in politics after returning to Palestine to pursue medicine. Associated with the Arab Party established by the "Councilists"—followers of al-Hajj Amin al-Husayni, president of the Supreme Muslim Council and Mufti of Jerusalem—Tannous became a major spokesman for Palestinian issues. He headed the Arab Information Office in London in the late 1930s, the London office of the Arab League starting in 1945, and the Arab Palestine Office in Beirut in 1949.

Himself an exile who left behind land in Palestine, Tannous also worked with an organization of refugee landowners called the Arab Refugee Property Owners in Palestine in Beirut. He took it upon himself to estimate the value of the refugees' losses in order to present it to the UNCCP. On May 7, 1951, the organization dispatched an official letter to the UNCCP suggesting the compensation figures detailed in figure 4.1.

Berncastle found Tannous' figures "quite impossibly high."[7] Confidentially, so too did Sami Hadawi. The following year Hadawi approached his

TABLE 4.1 Value of Refugee Property According to Izzat Tannous and the Arab Refugee Property Owners in Palestine, 1951

| *Type* | *Value (£UK)* |
|---|---|
| 1. Cities (Jerusalem, Jaffa, Haifa) | |
| Land | 100–500/sq.m. |
| Buildings | 10–25/sq.m./floor plus value of land |
| 2. Towns | |
| Land | 3–30/sq.m. |
| Buildings | 10–25/sq.m. plus value of land |
| 3. Villages | |
| Built-up land | 250–500/sq.m. |
| Buildings | 3–10/sq.m./floor plus value of land |
| 4. Agricultural land in the plains | |
| Fruit trees | 300–500/sq.m. |
| Other | 75–150/sq.m. |
| 5. Agricultural land in the hills | |
| Fruit trees | 50–100/sq.m. |
| Other | 25–50/sq.m. |

Source: UNSA DAG 13–3, UNCCP. Subgroup: Reference Library. Series: United Nations/Box 10/ORG; Document: ORG/37, "Letter Addressed to the Conciliation Commission by the Committee of Arab Refugee Property Owners in Palestine" (May 7, 1951)

friend Tannous and told him that the memo on land values was "absurd." Tannous reportedly admitted his ignorance on technical land matters, but told Hadawi that he had done his best given that no one else in the Arab world seemed to be working on the issue.[8]

The month before dispatching his own estimates, Tannous sent the UNCCP statistics on refugee property generated by another Palestinian, Sa'id Baydas, who had a long history with land and agriculture in Palestine. During the mandate, he had been a member of the Committee for Agricultural Economics and Marketing, the Citrus Control Board, the Citrus Marketing Board, and the Union of Arab Villages Society. He also met with the UNCCP at the Lausanne Conference. Table 4.2 details Baydas' figures.

Berncastle noted Baydas' figures in his final report on the Global Estimate in 1951, and generally was impressed with them—much more so than with those of Tannous. Berncastle noted, however, that Baydas' numbers seemed to include the land of Palestinians who remained in Israel. Nevertheless, the

TABLE 4.2 Scope and Value of Refugee Land According to Sa'id Baydas, 1951

| *Type* | *Scope (Dunums)* | *Annual Production (£UK)* |
|---|---|---|
| Citrus trees | 130,000 | 5,845,000 |
| Olive trees | 240,000 | 1,800,000 |
| Fruit trees | 150,000 | 750,000 |
| Cereal land in the plains 4,500,000 | 13,500,000 | |
| Cereal land in the hills 2,100,000 | 4,200,000 | |
| Uncultivable | 2,180,000 | — |
| Buildings, warehouses in towns and villages | | 6,000,000 [annual rent] |
| TOTAL | 9,300,000 | 32,095,000 |

Source: UNSA DAG 13–3, UNCCP. Subgroup: Reference Library. Series: United Nations/Box 10/ORG; Document: ORG.38, "Statement by Said M. Beidas" (May 7, 1951)

Arab world continued to reject the UNCCP's figures and would continue to determine its own estimates in the years to come. So, in fact, would other parties, including the UNCCP itself.

## UNRWA Estimates of Refugee Property

It was not only Israel, the Arabs, and the UNCCP that were generating estimates of the Palestinian refugees' property losses in the early 1950s. Even within the UN other agencies were interested in this question. By 1950, the UNCCP found itself embroiled in a bitter rivalry with UNRWA over responsibility for the refugees. The existence of a second body dealing with refugee matters had set the stage for a collision between UNRWA and the UNCCP over who had jurisdiction over the refugees' future. UNRWA took care of the refugees' basic needs in exile, such as food rations and education for children. The UNCCP was working on matters of compensation and resettlement. However, since these impinged directly upon UNRWA's work and future, a rivalry quickly developed between the two agencies. UNRWA wanted sole authority to discuss matters of permanent refugee resettlement, leaving repatriation and compensation to the UNCCP. When the director of UNRWA, American diplomat John B. Blandford, met with Sharett in Paris on

December 3, 1951, he told the Israeli outright that UNRWA cannot handle compensation and that money for compensation and money for resettlement should be separate. Blandford said this even though his own government viewed compensation as the very means for resettlement. UNCCP Principal Secretary Pablo de Azcárate complained of the rivalries among the various UN agencies especially between the UNCCP and UNRWA. "But the fact is that no collaboration of any sort ever existed between the Conciliation Commission and UNRWA, much less cordial collaboration."[9] The rivalry stemmed in part because some felt that the UNCCP considered itself higher up on the chain of UN command than UNRWA. "In the exchange between personnel of the two organs, which became heated at times, Frenchman argued against Frenchman, and the US representative in one organ against his counterpart on the other organ."[10]

The two agencies did work together at times, however, particularly on the matter of quantifying the extent of the refugees' property losses. In 1950, UNRWA's advisory commission asked the UNCCP if it had any data on abandoned refugee property.[11] At that point the UNCCP did not have very specific information. Therefore, UNRWA decided to conduct its own brief survey of refugee landholdings that year by distributing registration cards to heads of refugee households in Jordan. Subsequently, on March 6, 1951, the UNCCP proposed such an operation to UNRWA, but it seems clear that UNRWA was already in the process of doing this because it reported the results of the survey within a few short weeks. Some Arab quarters also had privately called for such forms. A few days after the UNCCP proposal to UNRWA, de Azcárate had a meeting in Jerusalem on March 19, 1951 with Anton 'Atallah, a former supreme court judge in the mandatory government. 'Atallah had recommended that the UNCCP consider distributing a "conditional form" for compensation for those Palestinians who were refugees from the UN-envisioned "Arab state."[12]

UNRWA distributed questionnaires to 84,000 heads of refugee families in Jordan (including the West Bank), apparently in 1950. This represented some 340,000 persons. The UNCCP then tallied the results for 8,400 questionnaires that were randomly selected and extrapolated cumulative results from this statistical sample. The results were instructive. Some 66 percent of refugee families in Jordan (55,400) claimed they had abandoned 3,508,540 dunums of land. Fifty-nine percent (49,500 families) claimed they lost a total of 47,500 homes with 158,00 rooms (see table 4.3).

The UNRWA sampling survey is also instructive for the figures it produced on how many of the refugees had abandoned small, medium, and

TABLE 4.3 Refugee Property Losses According to UNRWA Sampling of Refugees in Jordan (including the West Bank), 1950

| *Type* | *Number* | *% of Families With Losses* | *Number of Families With Losses* |
|---|---|---|---|
| 1. Structures | | | |
| Houses | 47,500 | 34 | 49,500 |
| Independent structures | 331 | N/A | N/A |
| Shops | 4,150 | N/A | N/A |

| *Type* | *Amount (Dunums)* | *% of Families With Losses* | *No. of Families With Losses* | *Amount/Family With Losses (Dunums)* |
|---|---|---|---|---|
| 2. Land | | | | |
| Cultivated | 2,000,000 | N/A | N/A | 36.2 |
| Citrus | 138,000 | N/A | N/A | 2.7 |
| Other Trees | 315,000 | N/A | N/A | 5.1 |
| Built-up | 5,540 | N/A | N/A | 0.1 |
| Other | 1,050,000 | N/A | N/A | 18.9 |
| TOTAL | 3,508,540 | 66.0 | 55,400 | 63.0 |

Source: UNSA DAG 13–3, UNCCP; Subgroup: Office of the Principal Secretary. Series: Records Relating to Compensation/Box 18/1949–51/Working Papers; Document: W/60, "Sampling Survey of Abandoned Property Claimed by Arab Refugees" (April 12, 1951)

TABLE 4.4 Size of Refugee Landholdings According to UNRWA Sampling of Refugees in Jordan (including the West Bank), 1950

| *Size of Abandoned Holdings (Dunums)* | *Number of Families with Losses* |
|---|---|
| Less than 63 | 42,600 |
| 63–200 | 8,400 |
| 200–2,000 | 4,290 |
| More than 2,000 | 110 |
| TOTAL | 55,400 |

Source: UNSA DAG 13–3, UNCCP; Subgroup: Office of the Principal Secretary. Series: Records Relating to Compensation/Box 18/1949–51/Working Papers; Document: W/60, "Sampling Survey of Abandoned Property Claimed by Arab Refugees" (April 12, 1951)

large landholdings. The vast majority of the refugee families surveyed had abandoned small holdings of 63 dunums or less (see table 4.4.).

## Arab and International Efforts on Behalf of Refugee Property

The United States continued to look into the question of compensation in the early 1950s in part because it believed that "a reasonable solution of the compensation question could play an important part in stabilizing the area" and because the UNCCP had been unable to prompt Israel toward taking any concrete steps.[13] American efforts began in early 1953. Berncastle had failed to make any progress in his compensation talks with the Israelis the previous summer and fall. In addition, the transfer of refugee land from the Israeli Custodian of Absentee Property to the Development Authority in February 1953 had outraged the Arabs who lodged an official complaint with the UN the following month. With such renewed focus on refugee property and compensation, the United States devoted considerable thought to these questions and tried to create movement on the issue.

The Americans first approached the Israeli government on several occasions in early 1953 inquiring about refugee property. The Ministry of Foreign Affairs provided American diplomats with the figures (shown in table 4.5) for abandoned land—a vastly lower number that Berncastle's 1951 Global Estimate.

The American embassy in Tel Aviv also tried to meet with the Custodian of Absentee Property, Moshe Levin, to obtain information. When U.S. diplomats finally succeeded in meeting Levin, he provided them with opinions but no documents. Levin reaffirmed Israel's refusal to entertain individual refugee claims, noting that since the passage of Israel's Absentees' Property Law, "no individual absentee has a claim against the State of Israel." In a nod toward the UNCCP's attempts to determine individual ownership, he stated that this would be hard to do which is why a final figure for compensation should be a negotiated one.[14]

In its study of compensation, the U.S. government also was concerned that most of the payments would go to a few rich landowners and leave the bulk of the poor refugees without funds with which to resettle in the Arab world. In a May 1953 document entitled "Palestine Refugees: Alternative Methods of Compensation of the Arab Refugees," State Department officials estimated that "fewer than one-fifth" of the refugees would receive "substantial benefits" from a compensation regime.[15]

TABLE 4.5 Scope of Abandoned Palestinian Land According to the Israeli Ministry of Foreign Affairs, 1953

| *Type* | *Amount (Dunums)* |
|---|---|
| Cultivable | 2,600,000 |
| Non-cultivable | 900,000 |
| Underdeveloped urban land | 100,000 |
| GRAND TOTAL | 3,600,000 |

Source: NARA RG 59, 884A.16/5–453, Tel Aviv to Department of State (4 May 1953)

That same document outlined five alternatives for compensation, and these sum up American thinking on the subject as it had crystallized by 1953. The first alternative would be direct compensation by Israel. However, this was dismissed as too expensive and the Americans felt Israel could not pay this. The lowest estimate of what was due was $300 million. A second alternative would be for the UN to pay. However, it would be difficult for the UN to raise that much money, and the Arabs would complain that such an arrangement was letting Israel off the hook. Thirdly, UNRWA could resettle the refugees with the money, although propertied refugees would still have claims. A fourth alternative would be to have Israel pay compensation through a grant or a loan. It was felt that it would be difficult for the Israelis to find the money, and that the Arabs likely would object that this entailed "no sacrifice" from Israel.

Lastly, the State Department laid out what it considered the best idea. This was a variation of Berncastle's 1952 plan for an international financial corporation. Under the American scenario, an international corporation for compensation and resettlement would be formed. Israel would pledge to pay the corporation in annual installments. The United States and other parties would also extend interest-free loans to the corporation. Property-owning refugees then would have two options. The first would be to receive credit from the corporation to buy land that the corporation had reclaimed in the Arab world, along with houses built by it. Alternatively, the refugees could receive cash which would be invested in a business that would make them self-sufficient. Those refugees who did not own property in pre-1948 Palestine would be extended similar credits, but would need to pay them back to the corporation. The State Department conceded that it was difficult to say whether the corporation would end up receiving all the money owed to it by

Israel and the landless refugees, and thus whether or not it could pay back the interest-free loans from the United States and other interested parties. The diplomats submitted that such losses to the United States would nonetheless be acceptable because the overall solution would lead to a solution of the refugee problem.[16]

The U.S. embassy in Tel Aviv directed a number of memoranda and opinions to Washington in the spring and summer of 1953 concerning this subject. American diplomats reiterated how important the issue was, even though the "present moment is not opportune for raising the compensation problem with the Israel Government."[17] The embassy also agreed with the Israelis that "serious problems" exist in determining individual compensation. Part of this problem was that the Israelis had so radically transformed the refugee land:"[the] tide of events has swept beyond the point of restitution of abandoned Arab property and possibly beyond the point where an Israeli accounting of its administration of this property would serve a useful purpose."[18] The embassy also noted that the U.S. government intended to follow up on one of its suggestions. This was to reduce American aid to Israel and hand over the amount saved as an American contribution to compensation if this could be part of a settlement that would "contribute significantly" to a lessening of Arab-Israeli tension.[19] Once again, nothing came of the Americans' ideas.

It was not only the Americans who exhibited interest in the refugees' property and compensation during 1953. On March 23, 1953, one month after the Israeli Custodian of Absentee Property agreed to the first sale of refugee land to the Development Authority, the delegations of most of the Arab states to the UN—Egypt, Iraq, Lebanon, Saudi Arabia, and Yemen—raised their first official complaint about this by writing to the Secretary General of the UN. They claimed that Israel was financing Jewish immigration and settlement with the sale of refugee land. In addition, the Ministers of Foreign Affairs of Jordan and Lebanon sent separate letters. The Arabs repeated their charge on July 10 of the same year after receiving no response. The UNCCP agreed to investigate the matter, and made inquiries of the Israeli government that triggered a series of back-and-forth letters. On July 7, 1953, Eban sent a letter to the UNCCP noting that his government already had stated its policy on compensation for the refugee property and was prepared to discuss it. Nonetheless, Eban essentially confirmed what the Arabs had charged—i.e., that Israel was selling land—by noting, "The [Israeli] Government's declared policy on this question is not affected by any internal arrangements which might be made for dealing with the property according to the laws of Israel." The UNCCP wrote back on July 29 stating that its concern was the "manner in which Arab property [is] being dealt with in Israel, and not on the questions of compensation." It asked point blank if the Israeli government had authorized the disposal of refugee land, and if so, how this was done and was it completed. The UNCCP also asked if the consideration received for the land was being held in the name of the previous Palestinian owner for compensation should s/he choose not to return. As for those choosing repatriation, what measures had been taken to ensure restitution of their property?

After several months of nagging by the UNCCP for a response, Eban responded on October 9, 1953. He noted that the Custodian of Absentee Property indeed had sold abandoned land to the Development Authority according to the Absentees' Property Law. He stated that the funds realized were kept for the refugees' benefit according to the law. Eban went on to note that if any refugees are authorized to reenter Israel, then the government would ensure their reintegration. Lastly, he stated that Israel was starting preparatory work on a compensation proposal. The study would end soon and then the Israeli government would be in a position to present concrete ideas about compensating the refugees.[20]

The 1953 sale of refugee property prompted the Arabs to demand that the UN create a property custodian to safeguard the refugees' property interests in Israel. This concept would end up becoming a staple Arab demand over the coming decades. The genesis of the idea extended back to 1949 and a private recommendation by Gordon Clapp. In 1950 the Palestinian land expert Sami Hadawi also proposed such an idea. On November 8 of that year, Hadawi sent a written suggestion to the UNCCP that a "trustee" be appointed to take over the refugees' land from the Israeli Custodian of Absentee Property. The UNCCP's Refugee Office later proposed just such an idea in its final report. It noted that the UN should establish an "authority" to which the Custodian of Absentee Property must provide access to his accounts and to which the Custodian would need to secure permission prior to transferring any refugee land. The Refugee Office felt that idea was "eminently reasonable, and it is difficult to see what valid grounds the Government of Israel could have for refusal."[21]

Thus the concept of some type of property custodian was not a new one when Izzat Tannous proposed it publicly during a speech to the Ad Hoc Political Committee of the General Assembly on November 25, 1954. However, Tannous introduced a new concept that would come to be another key Arab demand for decades to come: this neutral custodian, he maintained, should work to secure the income being made from the refugees' property until the final status of the land were resolved. Tannous carried out a study of the sale of refugee property through the aegis of the Palestine Arab Refugee Office, an information office he established in New York in 1954. He later complained to the UNCCP in a memorandum of November 3, 1955 that the UNCCP had done nothing to protect refugee land or even investigate the sale of abandoned property, as he had done, since the Arab states' original complaint of March 23, 1953. His letter of complaint received wide comment in the Arab press. During discussions held by the UN General Assembly's Ad Hoc Political Committee from November 14–30, 1955, the Arab states reintroduced the idea of a property custodian to whom Israel should hand over any income generated from refugee land. They deftly asserted that such funds could go to supplement the UNRWA budget and assist in its relief work among the refugees. The argument was a shrewd one: Why should the UN continue to solicit contributions from the global community when the refugees had property sequestered in Israel with which they could support themselves? In fact, the UNRWA Advisory Commission had discussed just such an idea, and said it would refer the matter to the UNCCP.[22] The introduction of the property custodian proposal also represented a significant conceptual shift in some Arab parties' thinking about the property question, a shift away from demanding compensation and, however implicitly, toward the notion of restitution. Acceptance of Israeli compensation for their abandoned land implied the Arabs' acceptance of an Israeli fait accompli—the transfer of legal title to the land from the refugees to Israeli authorities. Acceptance of compensation therefore involved the cessation of further claims. Calling for the creation of a property custodian, however, implied that the Arabs considered that title to the abandoned land remained vested with the refugees themselves, not Israel, despite the passage of the years since 1948. Under such a proposal Israel would therefore be required to forward the income it was generating from the refugees' land to the custodian, rather like a tenant would pay a landowner's agent. Such an arrangement would allow the refugees in exile to benefit financially from their land without conceding their ultimate rights to title, rights that they hoped they could once again claim in the future. The Arabs were thus laying the basis in the mid-1950s for what would come to be a bedrock principle for some Palestinians by the time the Palestinian-Israeli peace process started in the 1990s: property restitution, not property compensation. Despite the Arabs' efforts, no resolution was forthcoming. The issue would resurface, however.

Two Arab organizations also released new studies of the value of the refugee losses at this time. In 1955, the Arab Higher Committee published its estimate: P£1,626,100,000. This is detailed in table 4.6. The following year, the Arab League issued its own report containing statistics on the refugees'

TABLE 4.6 Value of Refugee Property According to the Arab Higher Committee, 1955

| *Type* | *Value (P£)* |
|---|---|
| Citrus | 100,000 |
| Banana | 1,000,000 |
| Orchards | 275,000,000 |
| Cultivable and Pasture Land | 250,000,000 |
| Urban and Rural Built-up | 1,100,000,000 |
| TOTAL | 1,626,100,000 |

Source: Arab Higher Committee, "al-Laji'un al-Filastiniyyun: Dahaya al-Isti'mar wa'l-Sahyuniyya" [The Palestinian Refugees: Victims of Imperialism and Zionism] (Cairo: 1955), pp. 81–93, and Arab Higher Committee, "Statement" (Beirut: 1961), pp. 19–24, both in Yusif Sayigh, *al-Iqtisad al-Isra'ili* [The Israeli Economy] (Cairo: League of Arab States, Institute for Higher Arab Studies, 1966), pp. 112–113

losses that were determined by unnamed "neutral experts." They are listed in table 4.7.

One of the most wide-ranging plans for compensation at this time emerged from the United States and the United Kingdom in 1955. These two powers were in the process of reevaluating their overall foreign policies toward the Middle East. The end of the Korean War in 1953 offered the United States in particular some breathing room to begin dealing with the full implications of

TABLE 4.7 Value of Refugee Property According to the Arab League, 1956

| *Item* | *Value (£UK)* |
|---|---|
| Citrus plantations, including buildings, machinery, etc. | 100,000,000 |
| Banana plantations | 1,000,000 |
| Olive groves, fruit plantations, other trees | 275,000,000 |
| Cereal lands, good quality | 30,000,000 |
| Cereal lands, medium quality; grazing lands | 220,000,000 |
| Urban lands, buildings; factories, machinery; livestock | 1,100,000,000 |
| Moveables of all types | 200,000,000 |
| Blocked securities and deposits in banks | 6,000,000 |
| Blocked insurance companies' funds | 1,000,000 |
| TOTAL | 1,933,000,000 |

Source: J. Khoury, *Arab Property and Blocked Accounts in Occupied Palestine* (Cairo: League of Arab States, General Secretary, Palestine Section), 1956), p. 20

its growing role as a Cold War-era superpower in the Middle East. The CIA had played a role both in the downfall of the Egyptian monarchy in 1952 and the stabilizing of the Iranian monarchy the following year. The United States invited Turkey and Greece to join NATO and began extending military aid to Iraq. The growing neutralism of the regime of Jamal 'Abd al-Nasir in Egypt also concerned the Americans, for he steadfastly refused to thrust Egypt into the West's anti-Soviet security plans. For the United Kingdom, Nasir conjured up a different ghost: the end of empire in Egypt and the Middle East. Not only had he negotiated an agreement for the final withdrawal of British troops from the area around the Suez Canal but also he had become a champion of anti-imperialist republicanism that threatened the United Kingdom's monarchical Iraqi and Jordanian allies. All of these developments were taking place in a region awash in much-needed oil reserves.

With these concerns in mind, the Americans and the British started in 1954 to work earnestly on a new approach for healing the rift between Arabs and Israelis in order to deflate the continuing destabilizing effect of the Arab-Israeli conflict on the region. In November 1954, the United States and the United Kingdom devised a confidential plan code-named "Project Alpha." While the plan had wider goals, it also contained a scheme for dealing with the Palestinian refugees. The Israelis were sending signals at that time that they were giving "fresh consideration" to the idea of compensation, including in a November 26, 1954 statement. At the time, this statement was viewed by some as a "hint" that Israel was seeking a foreign loan to help it pay compensation.[23] Israel in fact had been conducting secret talks with refugee leaders about compensation. On June 30, 1954, Moshe Sharett met Aziz Shehadeh and another official of the Palestine Arab Refugee Congress.[24] Once their idea was formulated, the United States and United Kingdom secretly sent the Project Alpha plan to the governments of Israel, Egypt, Syria, and Jordan in 1955. Among other points, Project Alpha called for Israel to repatriate between 75,000 and 100,000 refugees and pay £100 million—Berncastle's global figure—in compensation for property. Israel would renounce its counter claims, while the Palestinian refugees would give up demands for communally owned land and moveable goods. Funds for compensation would come from a variety of sources. Israel and Jews around the world would raise 30 percent of the £100 million. Banks and Western governments, mostly the United States and United Kingdom, would lend the remainder to Israel. Compensation payments would be made to individual refugees through the UN.

In July 1955, Assistant Undersecretary Charles A.E. Shuckburgh of the British Foreign Office told American officials that his government was ready to provide £10–15 million to Israel for its compensation fund. The United States publicly committed itself to the idea as well. On August 26, 1955, U.S. Secretary of State John Foster Dulles delivered a speech to the Council on Foreign Relations in New York in which he stated that "compensation is due from Israel to the refugees." He went on to outline the Alpha Project's idea about an international loan and noted that President Dwight D. Eisenhower would recommend a "substantial participation" by the United States in such a loan.[25] Israel responded positively to Dulles' speech at the Special Political Committee of the UN General Assembly in November 1955. But it continued to link compensation with other issues, in this case such matters as the Arab boycott. Meanwhile, the years 1955 and 1956 witnessed tremendous turmoil in the Middle East and the worsening of Western relations with the Arab world. Project Alpha fell victim to these events, and yet another plan for compensation failed to reach fruition.

The sweeping Anglo-American plans came when the UNCCP was giving thought to a new idea about compensation: "phased compensation," whose origins stemmed from Berncastle's earlier failure to make progress with the Israelis on his September 10, 1952 plan for compensation. The UNCCP thereafter had asked the Israelis on several occasions about their own ideas about compensation. On October 9, 1953, Eban told the UNCCP that Israel was studying the matter—a reference to the Horowitz Committee—and that it would hear from Israel soon. On August 1, 1954, Israel told Alexis Ladas that it would reveal its findings on compensation as soon as they were ready, although the secret Horowitz Committee report in fact had been completed eight months earlier. The mood of the UNCCP grew dispirited. Just three days before Eban's discussions with it, the UNCCP wrote a remarkable progress report that reflected its frustration and its conviction that compensation was urgently needed in frank terms. Among other things, the report stated:

> Ever since 1949, the Government of Israel has formally accepted the obligation to pay compensation for lands abandoned in Israel by the Arab refugees. The fact that compensation has not been paid constitutes one of the most serious obstacles, whether real or artificial, to every effort made to bring about an improvement of Arab Israel relations and even positively contributes to the deterioration of those relations .... the Commission is the only body competent to attempt a settlement of the compensation issue and as long as it does not it acts, by the mere fact of its existence, as an obstacle to the efforts which other interested parties might make in this direction .... In conclusion it must be said again that

> though compensation by itself cannot bring about a solution of the refugee problem, progress in this field would facilitate the settlement of other aspects of the question whereas the lack of progress on the compensation question obstructs their solution. It also follows that the compensation question can probably not be settled without reference to other related problems, such as resettlement and the return of a certain number of refugees to Israel. The refugee problem is still perhaps the greatest irritant in the relations between Israel and the Arab States. Its solution lies, no doubt, in increasing the wealth and absorptive capacity of the whole area, but it also requires the preservation of certain basic political and property rights of the refugees, for otherwise every effort will simply be interpreted by the Arabs as an attempt to bribe them into silence.[26]

By early 1955, the UNCCP was busy with its Technical Program to identify individual refugee property losses (see chapter 5) and was not in a position to press for immediate compensation. It also feared that if detailed discussions about compensation failed, its work in identifying refugee property might seem pointless thereafter. Thus, while deciding to focus on its technical work, it nonetheless drew up a document entitled "The Compensation Question" on March 8, 1955.[27] This UNCCP document noted that "no compensation can be paid until the current [identification] work has been completed." Thus "it was best to put off the day of decision while preserving the impression that all necessary preparations were being made for the eventual payment of compensation."

Certainly the length of the project would justify such a delay. But the document did discuss certain wider issues about compensation that indicate the UNCCP's thinking on compensation by 1955. First, it reiterated its stance that compensation should be paid to individuals, not governments. Second, compensation payments must be made to the refugees by the UNCCP or some other international body and not paid to them directly by Israel. Third, compensation must be paid for the value of refugee land as it was at the time it was abandoned. Fourth, refugees were free to accept or reject compensation, but if they accepted they must relinquish their right to be repatriated—the fear that had prevented many refugees from showing interest in a compensation plan. The document went on to suggest a theoretical compensation plan. Israel might be asked to pay part—one half, for instance—of Berncastle's £100 million compensation figure. The other £50 million would be covered by UNRWA and other bodies or governments. The individual identification project then underway would lead to a individual valuation project. If the sum total of each refugee's property exceeded the £100 million figure, then Israel would agree to pay up to an additional £50 million of this balance. Anything over that amount would by paid by others. Thus, Israel's total liability would lie somewhere between £50 and 100 million. Payments would be made to individual refugees upon application, but not all at once. They would be spread out over time or paid by subdistrict of origin in Palestine.

This last point—a phased compensation plan—intrigued the UNCCP and others in the UN by early 1955 as a possible way to start movement on compensation. The UNCCP's land identification project had started and was nearly completed for abandoned villages in the mandatory subdistrict of Gaza. The idea surfaced that compensation could begin right away if it began with the refugees in Gaza, given that the UNCCP now possessed detailed information on Arab property in that area. The idea was of interest to other UN agencies as well. On April 20, 1955, a three-man meeting was held in Beirut among UNCCP Liaison Officer Alexis Ladas; Henry R. Labouisse, the American commissioner of UNRWA; and Maj.-Gen. E.L.M. Burns, the Canadian chief-of-staff of the UNTSO.

After Ladas explained the UNCCP's thinking, Burns indicated he was strongly in favor of the idea. He felt that the technical work necessary for it was nearly complete and that it stood a better chance of success than other schemes because of its limited, piecemeal approach. Burns also stated that it would benefit the neediest of all refugees, namely, those in Gaza whom he, as head of the UN organization patrolling the front lines between Israel and Egypt, saw on a regular basis. Labouisse was more cautious. The American was worried that if this limited scheme failed, it could damage the only issue (compensation) on which the Arabs and Israelis could agree to meet about. He wanted to keep alive the idea of a partial repatriation, as the refugees were entitled to. He also wanted to maintain the connection between compensation and resettlement. Labouisse suggested that compensated refugees could leave Gaza for resettlement in Syria, Iraq, or in Sinai, where UNRWA was contemplating such a scheme. The UNRWA commissioner also was concerned that the UNCCP should publicize the fact that its identification project was working only on compensating refugees for abandoned land. He later urged the UNCCP to avoid generating expectations among the majority of refugees, who owned no land, if word of the phased compensation plan leaked out.

Labouisse still believed that the UN should undertake a wholesale resettlement of propertied and property-less refugees as a form of "restitution." He thought a good way to begin this would be to pay compensation to the vocal, property-owning refugees who were opposed to resettlement because they were holding out for compensation. General Burns agreed with Labouisse that such a phased compensation would provide little more than a psychological boost to refugees unless it were linked to some form of resettlement. They also agreed that the first step should be to prompt Israel to issue a clear statement on the amount and modalities of its compensation plan now that the Horowitz Committee had met. This would help the UN agencies to determine whether Israel really was willing to pay and whether most refugees would receive anything. The two men also told Ladas that the UNCCP needed to speed up its program of identifying refugee land and should adopt a new global figure for the value of the land, one based on actual land prices in 1948 as opposed to the method of capitalizing tax values that Berncastle had used in his 1951 global estimate. In fact, Labouisse felt that speeding up the identification program was so important that, if the UNCCP could not find enough funds to do this, then UNRWA would try to find them itself.

For his part, Ladas suggested several days after the meeting that the phased "Gaza first" compensation scheme would work only if the compensated refugees could leave Gaza and use their compensation payments to begin new lives in a more hospitable environment. Since getting other Arab countries to agree to resettle Gazan refugees might be difficult, Ladas wondered if such a phased approach might be started more profitably among refugees already in Syria. Most of these came from the subdistricts of Tiberias and Safad. As with the Gaza idea, the UNCCP's land identification program could exert its initial efforts toward these two subdistricts. Compensated refugees then could leave the camps in Syria and move to the country's Jazira region.[28]

The UNCCP decided to talk with Israel once again about compensation in light of these ideas. On February 2, 1956, the UNCCP instructed Ladas to approach the Israelis. He was to remind them that the UNCCP had inquired about compensation in 1953 and was told to wait until Israel completed studying the issue at which time it would announce its views. Now that the UNCCP was accelerating its identification program, it was particularly anxious to hear about Israel's thoughts on the matter. Significantly, Ladas also was instructed to ask not just about compensation but also about restitution and to mention that the Arab states had asked about whether the refugees at least could gain access to the rent that the Custodian of Absentee Property was realizing from their property. Was Israel studying either of these two ideas?[29]

After sending the letter on February 14, Ladas received the Israeli response on March 11. Although Israel had several years earlier given up on linking compensation with peace treaties, the letter indicated that it was still insisting on connecting compensation with "the general context of Arab-Israeli relations." At that moment in time, the letter went on, Israel saw no purpose in its coming forward with a compensation plan if the overall conditions in the Middle East were not conducive. But if the Arab states reversed their stepped-up economic blockade of Israel and assumed an attitude toward Israel more "in conformity with the Charter of the United Nations," Israel would let its detailed plan for compensation be known. The letter made no reference to the potentially explosive concepts of restitution and a property custodian. The UNCCP found this response "unfortunately negative and inconsistent with Israel's previous statements concerning compensation."[30] UNCCP Chair Pierre Ordonneau later wrote back to the Israelis on September 28, 1956. He noted:

> It appears from this letter [March 11, 1956] that the Government of Israel has now altered its previous position with regard to the question of compensation for Arab refugee property holdings in Israel, as set forth in Amb. Eban's letter to the Commission of 9 October 1953.[31]

Ordonneau also noted that Israel's letter did not address some of the questions the UNCCP had raised, for example, about how Israel was administering the refugee property. The UNCCP also had asked about information on the land. He reminded the Israelis that the UNCCP was responsible for more than just compensation. The UN General Assembly Resolutions of December 11 and 14, 1950 gave the UNCCP responsibility for protecting the refugees' property rights as well, and the UNCCP was seeking to do that. Restating the requests, Ordonneau asked once again that Israel provide the UNCCP with information about its administration, protection, and safeguarding of the identity of refugee property as well as what Israel thought about turning over the funds it received from renting these properties so that the refugees could benefit from them. The archival record did not indicate whether the Israelis answered Ordonneau's letter or what, if anything, transpired as a result.[32]

Privately, American diplomats complained that Berncastle and Ladas were connected so resolutely and intimately with the details of their compensation mission that they were woefully out of touch with political reality in the Middle East. Despite the U.S. oversight on the commission, UNCCP staff members had urged that concrete steps be taken toward compensation without waiting for the parties to agree on overall solutions to the Arab-Israeli conflict.

They believed that such positive, practical steps in fact might work toward creating the proper atmosphere for wider talks. The Americans, including their Consul General in Jerusalem, felt just the opposite. The consul wrote to the Department of State on September 11, 1956 warning that Berncastle:"is suffering from too close a concern with the potentially explosive effect of proposing to compensate the refugees before a political settlement or positive atmosphere of willingness to accept compensation by the refugees is reached." He added that Berncastle and Ladas underestimated the "fanatical attachment of the refugees to the idea of returning to their homes," and that both the refugees and the Israeli press would interpret payment of compensation as a scheme to deny the right of repatriation.[33]

None of the various moves, plans, and initiatives for compensation reached fruition in the 1950s. Certainly a major factor that explains this is the Suez War that erupted in October 1956. That war would permanently alter the character of the Arab-Israeli conflict and with it, the refugee property question. With interest in the fate of the abandoned property still high, however, various parties began inquiring about what the United Kingdom had done with its mandatory land records.

## Britain Disposes of Filmed Copies of Mandatory Land Records

The growing importance of the compensation question prompted a search by several parties for records that could assist them in determining the scope and value of the refugee property. By far the richest source of data on the refugee land losses were the land registers and land tax data compiled by the British during the Palestine mandate. It was not long after the fighting subsided in 1948 that appeals were being made to the British to secure this data.

British authorities had maintained several types of land documents. The most significant of these were Ottoman land registers and mandatory registers of deed and registers of title. Britain's withdrawal from Palestine caused these documents to end up in a variety of places after 1948. One place was Britain itself, where British authorities stored 2,160 films they had made of land records prior to quitting Palestine. The idea to film the records first had been raised in 1944 after a bomb destroyed the Jerusalem land registry. No action was taken at the time, and approval to photograph the documents was not finally granted until October 1947 as Britain was preparing to vacate the mandate. That December, three Watson recording cameras were purchased in England and flown to Palestine. Supplemented with two cine cameras,

British officials began photographing their land registers in January 1948 at the former Park Hotel in Jerusalem. As of November 17, 1947, the mandatory government possessed 844 Ottoman land registers, 2,192 of its own registers of deeds along with 1,424 registers of title produced by the land settlement process. Registers of writs and orders and the deeds book for Jerusalem also were to be photographed. The contractor hired to carry out the photography was Jewish, although most of the employees actually doing the work were Palestinians. To maintain impartiality, the British invited Jewish and Palestinian representatives from the land department to be present during the entire period of the photography process, although usually only the Jews attended. Units from the British army and the mandatory police brought the documents from the various land registries scattered throughout Palestine to Jerusalem. Those relating to the Gaza, Nablus, Tulkarm, and Beersheba districts later were returned but the rest were kept in Jerusalem after the process was completed.

At times the photography process was arduous because Jewish-Palestinian fighting had broken out in late November 1947. Sami Hadawi was able to observe the process from his office. The workers sometimes had to stop work and take shelter because of the shooting around them. There were also some serious errors in the filming. The registers of deeds consisted of ledgers containing two side-by-side pages relating to the same land transaction. Yet the photographer filmed all of the left hand pages and then all of the right hand ones. It was later virtually impossible to coordinate the films in order to see both halves of the same transaction. Not all of the registers of deeds were photographed in any case. The films later were developed and stored in London for the Crown Agents for Palestine by J. F. Spry, formerly assistant director of land registration. The cost of the entire process was a little over £P8,000.[34]

Mandatory officials decided to take the films with them and leave the originals with representatives of the Jewish and Palestinian communities. Registers dealing with Jewish land would be given to the Jewish Agency for Palestine, while those from Palestinian areas would be given to the Supreme Muslim Council. The ultimate plan for dividing up the records was as follows. To the Supreme Muslim Council the British gave some of the Baysan district's registers, as well as those relating to Hebron, Jaffa, Janin, Nazareth (excluding the Plain of Esdraelon), and one-half of Safad. The Jewish Agency received most of the rest, plus parts of other registries that related to Jewish holdings. Thus, the JA was given the other one-half of the records relating to Safad, and was also granted certain registers transferred from Jaffa to Tel Aviv. The Haifa registers, including the Plain of Esdraelon, were handed over to the Haifa Municipal Corporation. Lastly, since the UN had voted to create an international zone in Jerusalem, the British decided to leave the Jerusalem records at the Jerusalem YMCA. The YMCA was under the flag of the International Red Cross of Geneva at that time. All remaining land records other than the actual registers were left in the land department's headquarters at the Russian Compound in Jerusalem. These included departmental records, statistics, ledgers from the Ottoman Agricultural Bank, and the Ghawr Mudawwara Agreement.[35]

During the fighting, the documents suffered various fates. The Jerusalem records were stored in the library gallery of the Jerusalem YMCA. Sami Hadawi took some of the miscellaneous records left behind in the Russian Compound to the Old City. The Israelis later reported that the registers for the Beersheba district had been lost. A particularly colorful episode involved the bulk of the land registers that were accepted by the Supreme Muslim Council. These were hidden in the women's section of the Marwani mosque in Jerusalem's Haram al-Sharif complex, which was controlled by the Jordanian Arab Legion during the fighting. Afterwards, they were kept by Ya'qub Ibrahim 'Atallah, a former employee of the mandatory land department. 'Atallah (b. 1895) had first begun working for the British as an interpreter for British forces during the First World War and continued his service after that. In December 1948, the Jordanians made him their first land registrar in the West Bank where he was able to use the registers. 'Atallah later transferred the registers under his control to the central office of the Jordanian Department of Lands and Survey in Amman where several hundred registers (including 403 Ottoman registers) eventually were stored.[36] Eventually, the Jordanians placed those registers relating to areas in the West Bank in the land registries that they later opened in certain West Bank towns, and retained those relating to Arab land in Israel at the central office.

The presence of the films in London soon acted like a magnet, attracting the attention of a variety of parties seeking to acquire them or at least gain access to them. The first mention of the possible uses of these films came from the UNCCP's Technical Committee, whose September 7, 1949 report recommended that a proposed mixed Arab-Israeli committee on compensation could study these films as part of its work. When Berncastle was working on the Global Estimate, he visited with officials from Britain's Colonial Office in March 1951 and took an index to the films. He also secured permission to obtain copies and made arrangements to purchase copies of any of the films that he might need. Shortly thereafter, in May 1951, the Israeli government approached the British and formally asked them to hand the films over to Israel as the successor government to the mandate. Israel already had the original land registers relating to Jewish-owned property in Palestine. What it wanted was information to help it identify the vast amount of Arab-owned refugee land that it now possessed. In fact, the Israelis openly told the British that they needed the films to assist the Custodian of Absentee Property in his work.[37] It was not only the Israeli government that was interested in the films: so was the JNF. About the same time as the Israeli government's request, the JNF's London office asked the British government for the films relating to land in the Tulkarm, Jaffa, and Gaza regions.[38]

News of Israel's request for films soon jolted others to action. During a meeting at the British consulate in Jerusalem in July 1951, Berncastle was told of Israel's recent request. He immediately asked that the British give the films to the UNCCP instead, citing the fact that the Israelis were not the only interested party that could benefit from the material. He later argued that the UNCCP, as an international agency responsible for the individual assessment of Arab property, at least should be granted access to a copy of the films first. Britain eventually decided that it was duty bound to hand 95 percent of the films over to Israel and the rest, relating to areas under Jordanian control, to Jordan. It also offered to provide both Israel and Jordan with copies of the films that related to border villages where the armistice line divided the villages' lands. Each side was to pay one half of the reproduction costs (£700 each). The Israelis later sent £700 to London on November 12, 1951. The Jordanians declined the offer, citing the fact that they possessed the original registers. But they objected vociferously to Britain's decision to give to Israel those films relating to Arab property now in Israeli hands, even writing directly to Sir Anthony Eden. The British were unsympathetic, and asked why Jordan had not objected earlier.[39]

The British yielded in part to Berncastle's pleading that the UNCCP should get the films and not the Israelis. Britain decided that it would still give the original films to Israel but agreed to allow the UNCCP to copy the films for itself at its own expense first.[40] The British also had filmed copies of loans made by the Anglo-Palestine Bank and the Ottoman Bank to citrus grove owners. The UNCCP agreed to pay for copying the films, and informed Berncastle on January 31, 1952. The UNCCP thereafter made copies and the original films were given to Israel. The British later refunded the £700 that the Israelis had sent for the films of the border areas. The Kodak Company in London made the copies, and sent the films to the UNCCP at the UN headquarters in New York. Eventually, the UNCCP ended up with 1,642 rolls of 35 mm acetate film. All but one of them contained Ottoman registers, mandatory registers of deeds, and mandatory registers of title. One roll contained mandatory state domain records. For some reason the Netanya and Tel Aviv registers were not copied. Then, on September 4, 1952, Berncastle wrote to Comay and asked if he could make copies of the original films for these areas that the Israelis now had, in addition to filming mandatory tax records. Archival record does not indicate whether Comay responded.

Once the UNCCP was finished copying the films, the British sent them to Israel in batches, apparently as the copying process was completed. Israel quickly put them to use in reconstructing registers for the abandoned areas. Israel's Director of Land Registration was Binyamin Fishman (b. 1897), who had worked as a land officer for the British beginning in 1920 and thus was intimately acquainted with the mandatory land records. He later served on the first Development Authority council in Israel in 1950. In order to make use of the films in helping to reconstruct land registers right away, Fishman bought a film projector for $100. He then projected the image onto the wall of a room and had a female secretary who could read English copy the information into new, blank Israeli land registers. The Jewish National Fund, which was anxious to transfer the large amount of refugee land it bought from the Israeli government and obtain deeds, later donated some of its staff to help in the process. By September 1954, JNF staff members had reconstructed registers for 174 abandoned villages covering about 1.5 million dunums.[41]

Following up on the Jordanian complaint to the British about providing the films to Israel, the Arab League wrote to the UNCCP on April 26, 1953 and formally requested that paper copies be made from the films and given to the league. This marked the beginning of a twenty-year Arab effort to secure copies of such records.The commission politely refused, noting that:

> only one copy of the records exists in the archives of the United Nations and it forms the essential basis for the Commission's experts in examining, identifying and valuing the properties of individual Arab refugees, in accordance with the directives of the General Assembly of the United Nations. The Commission attaches great importance to this work in the interests of the refugees, and therefore regrets that it is unable to make these unique records available.[42]

The rebuff was not the end of the matter. In August 1961, the Arab League and individual Arab states once again began petitioning for copies of the films. (see chapter 6).

## The Property Question After the 1956 Suez War

The mounting tensions in the Middle East in the mid-1950s erupted into open war on October 29, 1956 when Israel attacked Egypt. France and the United Kingdom soon joined in the war on Egypt. Israel occupied Gaza and the Sinai Peninsula for five months and only withdrew after pressure from both Washington and Moscow. Egypt was left to rebuild its Soviet-equipped military with new shipments of Eastern bloc armaments. The war marked a clear shift in the direction of the Arab-Israeli Conflict. Whereas the cold war of 1948–56 had seen Israel and the Arab world essentially dealing with the fallout of 1948, the Suez War demonstrated to both sides that their fighting would continue. Egypt and the Arabs also now clearly believed that Israel constituted a threat not only to the rights of the Palestinian refugees but to their own territory and armed forces as well. The Arab-Israeli conflict increasingly was becoming a political and military battle among states. The fate of the stateless Palestinians and their property began fading from view as all parties began changing strategies and priorities. Israel clearly had emerged as the military giant of the Middle East, more confident and assertive. The Arabs began building up the size of their armies. The 1956 war had seen Western powers (France and the United Kingdom) directly enter into the Arab-Israeli conflict. Both the United States and the USSR now approached the Arab-Israeli conflict differently. Finally, the UN increasingly became the venue for talks about peace that understood "peace" as the end of armed conflict among states, not just settling issues relating to the 1948 refugees.

This major conceptual shift worked to the detriment of the attention that had been focused on Palestinian refugee property. The property issue continued to attract attention although it sank lower and lower in terms of its relative importance compared to other issues in the conflict after 1956. Both Israel and the Arabs continued to talk about it, albeit in a more ritualistic fashion. As soon after the war as February 1957, Israel's delegate to the UN General Assembly's Special Political Committee noted that Israel still was willing to pay compensation for refugee property outside of a general peace agreement. However, he noted that the Arabs' economic blockade of Israel prevented Israel from moving on the compensation issue. Failure to pay thus lay at the doorstep of the Arabs. In the late spring of 1957, Israel told American diplomats that if Jordan and Iraq worked to encourage refugees to move from Jordan to Iraq, then Israel would pay compensation to those willing to emigrate.[43] Israel publicly repeated its willingness to pay compensation if the Arabs lifted the blockade that November as well. Indeed, Israel continued to state that it was willing to compensate the refugees throughout the last years of the 1950s and into the 1960s.

The Arabs in particular changed their strategies regarding repatriation and compensation after 1956. Some observers thought they were starting to give up hope that repatriation ever would occur and were beginning to concentrate more on compensation in lieu of repatriation. In the minds of some Americans, this was starting to take place even before the Suez War. American representative to the UNCCP James Barco came away with this feeling after holding a meeting with the Syrian and Yemeni ambassadors to the UN on March 1, 1956 in which the two Arabs discussed protection of refugee property in Israel.[44] The mantle of leading Palestinian spokesman at the UN on the refugee problem also was shifting, from Izzat Tannous to Ahmad Shuqayri. The latter had a long history of service to the Palestinian cause. A Palestinian born in Lebanon in 1908 during a period when the Ottomans had exiled his father, Shuqayri returned to the family's hometown of Acre in 1916. He worked with the Arab Information Office in Washington during the 1940s and later headed the Arab Information Office in Jerusalem. After fleeing Palestine for Lebanon in 1948, Shuqayri became a diplomat. He served with the Syrian delegation to the UN from 1949–50 and later became assistant general-secretary of the Arab League from 1950–57. From 1957–63, he served as Saudi Arabia's representative to the UN. He later would become the first chairman of the Palestine Liberation Organization in 1964. Shuqayri was an adamant upholder of Palestinian rights at the UN in the late 1950s and early 1960s who forcefully pushed the issue to the forefront. He was disliked by many, including his fellow Arabs. He refused to abandon the right of return and focus instead on compensation. In November 1959, he declared that the concept of refugee repatriation was still an option. Indeed, he felt that only those refugees who came from areas of Palestine that the UN had designated as the so-called Jewish state should have the choice between repatriation and compensation. Those refugees from the Arab state should be repatriated immediately to Israel.[45]

For its part, the United States still held out some ideas about compensation. Secretary of State Dulles requested a review of U.S. policy toward the refugees on May 13, 1957 inasmuch as the Department of State felt that 1957 represented more "favorable" conditions for dealing with the refugees now that the war was over and the Israelis had ended their occupation of Gaza and Sinai. The Americans also may have hoped that the Arabs would be more amenable to compromise solutions after the war. The result was a secret and quickly written memorandum entitled "Detailed Review of the Palestine

Refugee Problem." Only 28 copies of the document were made.[46] The Americans developed a plan that was based on two important assumptions. The first included a stark assessment of the UNCCP: its ongoing attempt quantify refugee losses was in "disrepute" among Arabs and so compensation therefore must be channeled through a different body. Secondly, the document noted that U.S. policy toward the refugees had wavered between seeing solution of the refugee problem as part of an overall resolution of the Arab-Israeli conflict and isolating it and trying to solve it separately through UNRWA, the economic plans of the 1949 Clapp Mission, and the August 1955 Johnston Plan developed by the American Eric Johnston for Arab-Israeli water sharing. The document noted that the Americans were leaning toward the comprehensive solution perspective once more, as seen in Johnston's memorandum of June 10, 1957 suggesting that the United States approach Iraq to accept resettled refugees and help Jordan develop the Jordan Valley.

There were several other operating assumptions in the American document. First, any future payment scheme must be "expeditious and equitable in the processing and payment of compensation claims." Second, the document openly reaffirmed traditional American thinking that compensation would come at the price of giving up the right of repatriation and "should, if possible, be [made] more attractive to the Arab refugees than repatriation." Even though the American Consul General in Jerusalem criticized the UNCCP for naively underestimating Palestinian resistance to compensation in lieu of repatriation, the State Department remained in favor of precisely that. Third, the funds must be distributed in such a way as to avoid the inflationary consequences of a large influx of capital into the region at one time. To do all this, the State Department proposed a plan by which the United States would announce its intention to provide a $100 million long-term loan to Israel for payment of compensation. The UN then should establish a "Compensation Board" to process refugees' claims given that the UNCCP was, in this viewpoint, in "disrepute" among Arabs. Each refugee would receive up to $100 in cash whether s/he owned property or not, but could petition for more by providing evidence of landholdings exceeding that amount. Once a refugee agreed to accept compensation, s/he gave up the right of repatriation and only could change his/her mind with Israeli permission. For their part, the Arab host governments were to regulate the spending of these amounts of money to avoid sudden inflation.[47]

American thinking on the compensation question was clarified when the State Department's Henry Villard later drafted a memorandum on November 21, 1957 entitled "The Palestine Refugee Problem." In it, Villard reaffirmed that the "compensation" the United States was talking about was not just paying for lost property but for resettlement. What the Americans were intending was to provide economic aid to Arab countries willing to resettle refugees. Such aid would be paid on a per capita basis according to the number of refugees accepted for resettlement. Villard agreed with many Israeli and UN officials in arguing that individual payments should be made to the wealthier refugee leaders who agitated against compensation in lieu of resettlement. He stated that "The political pressures in the refugees problem would tend to disappear if the principal agitators were silenced by compensation for their losses and if opportunities for permanent resettlement outside of Palestine were provided for the rank and file of the rest."[48] Villard and another American diplomat in fact had met earlier with UN Secretary-General Dag Hammarskjöld on September 19, 1957 and discussed this proposal. At that time, the Americans drew a distinction for Hammarskjöld between this notion of "compensation" for resettlement purposes and what they called "property reimbursement," insisting that these two were two different ideas.[49]

Increasingly the Arabs were sidetracking the UNCCP, criticizing UNRWA, and resorting to UN General Assembly sessions and committee meetings as venues for fighting for refugee property rights. Israel responded accordingly. Thus, the Arab states raised complaints about UNRWA in November 1957 and began discussing an alternative to it. Israel notified the General Assembly's Special Political Committee in November 1959 that it still was willing to pay compensation with the international assistance promised by Dulles in 1955 but only as long as compensation was linked to Jewish property in Arab countries and Israeli-owned property behind Arab lines in the West Bank and Gaza. The Arab campaign did produce some tepid results when the General Assembly expressed its frustration with the lack of progress on compensation in its Resolution 1456 (XIV) of December 9, 1959 that dealt with UNRWA. The resolution noted:

> *with deep regret* that repatriation or compensation of the refugees, as provided for in paragraph 11 of General Assembly resolution 194 (III), has not been effected, and that no substantial progress has been made in the programme endorsed in paragraph 2 of resolution 513 (VI) for the reintegration of refugees either by repatriation or resettlement and that, therefore, the situation of the refugees continues to be a matter of serious concern...[the General Assembly] *Requests* the United Nations Conciliation Commission for Palestine to make further efforts to secure the implementation of paragraph 11 of General Assembly resolution 194 (III).

At the 1959 session of the General Assembly, the Arab states also revived their campaign to have the UN appoint a "property custodian" to watch over refugee land in Israel. They reintroduced the idea before the General Assembly's Special Political Committee in November and asked that Israel turn over the revenue it was receiving from the property. No resolution was passed that year, but the Arabs brought up the idea the following spring and again during the next General Assembly session in November 1960. The Arab states called for the director of UNRWA to be made the administrator of the refugees' property. A motion to create a UN custodian for the Palestinian refugees' property actually was passed in the Special Political Committee and went to the General Assembly for a final vote despite strong opposition by the United States.

Israel was highly upset by the notion of a UN custodian for the abandoned property because it raised again a vital legal point: A custodian suggested that title to the land still belonged to the refugees, who logically were then entitled to the revenue derived from it. The Israelis were adamant that although the refugees were entitled to *compensation* for the land, their *legal title* to it had been severed long before when the Custodian of Absentee Property took custody of it. Israel was concerned that even if the Arabs failed to get the property custodian idea passed in the General Assembly that they might insist on inserting language in the UNRWA budget resolution implying that the refugees retained ongoing title to the land. Perhaps they feared this could lay the basis for calls for property restitution. Israeli diplomats at the UN complained to their American counterparts that Israel was cooperating with the UNCCP's Technical Program to identify and valuate refugee property on the basis of an understanding they reached with Berncastle in the early 1950s. According to them, this understanding was that the Technical Program was aimed solely at establishing title and values as of the late 1940s in order to prepare figures for future compensation. The UNCCP's work, they maintained, was not based on any notion of ongoing revenues from the land. They claimed the Americans had assured them that this was the U.S. understanding of the Technical Program as well. Israeli Ambassador to the United States Avraham Harman also told a State Department official in Washington on December 13, 1960 that Israel had reached an agreement with Berncastle years before that it would work with the UNCCP's identification program as long as it was understood that the refugees no longer possessed title to the land. The UNCCP contacted Berncastle in Britain about this issue. Berncastle denied that there was any sort of protocol between Israel and the UNCCP regarding the program.[50]

The Arabs continued with their diplomatic initiative in 1961 although the Lebanese Ambassador to the UN, Nadim Dimeshkie, confided to his American counterparts that the Arabs were raising the issue solely for "domestic consumption."[51] The Americans continued to oppose the property custodian idea as well on the basis that it constituted a gratuitous irritant to Arab-Israeli relations. This constituted another red line they were unwilling to cross. They agreed with the Israelis about the loss of the refugees' title rights and did not want to pressure them. In an internal study, American diplomats asserted that the refugees no longer possessed legal title to their land. The February 24, 1961 document, entitled "Title to Arab Property in Israel," based this assumption more on practical than legal grounds:

> [w]hile it is likely that the Arab states which protested to the Palestine Conciliation Commission against the transfer of title [from the Custodian of Absentee Property to the Development Authority] in 1953, may refuse to recognize the legality of these transfers, it is improbable in practical terms that the process could be reversed.[52]

Secretary of State Dean Rusk agreed. While noting that Israel still was obligated to compensate the refugees, he argued that it was free as a sovereign nation to do as it pleased with any property within its borders and compared the Israeli seizure of refugee land to Egypt's nationalization of the Suez Canal. Rusk stated that the

> [p]ertinent factor is that as [a] sovereign state Israel has [the] legal right to transfer title to absentee property... Therefore unless [a] recognized international court such as [the] ICJ were to rule to [the] contrary, [it] seems to us [that] measures which have been taken by GOI [Government of Israel] to transfer title to lands in question were in rightful exercise of its powers (cf. Egypt and Suez).[53]

The British Foreign Office was less certain and expressed doubt about the U.S. position. Still, it agreed to support the Americans and even offered to bring up a supportive 1954 British court case heard by the Queen's Bench Division that had upheld the legality of vesting refugee land with the Israeli Custodian of Absentee Property. In the case of F. & K. Jabbour vs. Custodian of Absentee Property for the State of Israel, Fouad Bishara Jabbour and Kamal Bishara Jabbour sued in an English court to obtain monies they claimed were owed to them by a British insurance company. In 1947 they had taken out a fire and theft policy against the contents of their automobile repair shop and garage in Haifa. The garage and its contents were destroyed in January 1948 and the two men left for Egypt two months later. They eventually settled in Lebanon and in November 1950 started legal action against the insurance company to obtain the money it owed them. The insurance company agreed that it was liable for the amount and paid the amount to the court. However, the Israeli Custodian of Absentee Property joined in the case and petitioned the court to grant the money to him instead inasmuch as the two refugees' assets had been vested in him by virtue of Israeli legislation. Ultimately, in 1954 the court upheld the Custodian's right to the money and awarded the sum to him, in effect upholding the legality of his control over the two refugees' assets.[54]

The British later came up with the idea to have the UNCCP think about asking Israel to hand over data on its usage of the refugee property as well as to allow on-the-spot inspections of the land. "[S]uch a request and Israel's granting thereof might at this junction serve as an effective tactic vis-à-vis the Arab drive for recognition of their 'ongoing title' property concept."[55] Jordan understood the U.S. position to a point, but still challenged it. Its Ambassador to the United States, Yusuf Haykal, admitted to State Department officials that Israel had a right to expropriate property within its borders, but only in a "normal situation." The flight of the Palestinian refugees, he maintained, was "abnormal." Haykal later told the Americans that the reason the Arab states were pushing the property custodian idea was that UNRWA's mandate was threatened by the lack of donations to it, raising the question of how the refugees could support themselves. The revenues from their seized property offered such a solution and could be considerable. Issa Nakhleh of the Palestine Arab Delegation office in New York claimed in 1963 that Israel would owe some $180 million/year in rent for the refugees' property.[56]

Other Arab representatives put on a tougher face with the Americans. The Jordanian Ambassador to the UN, 'Abd al-Mun'im al-Rifa'i, noted that the disagreement between the Arabs and both the United States and the United Kingdom was the first serious disagreement between them in ten years in dealing with the refugee issue. The Iraqi delegate to the UN asked American Ambassador to the UN Adlai Stevenson and other American diplomats: If a UN property custodian was not the best way to deal with the issue of the refugee property, then what was? He also noted that the Arab states were keenly aware that the Kennedy administration was evaluating the entire situation in the Middle East.[57]

Whatever the reason the Arabs pushed for the property custodian in the General Assembly in 1961, Israel was truly anxious about the prospect of its passage. The concept not only implied that the UN recognized that the refugees still possessed ongoing legal title to the land, which had been sold to the Development Authority and the Jewish National Fund, but it also laid the basis for UN interference in internal Israeli affairs and a potential Arab call for property restitution, not compensation. So important did this matter become that Foreign Minister Golda Meir threatened to withdraw Israel's longstanding offer to pay compensation to the refugees. Meir told the U.S. ambassador in Tel Aviv that Israel would "consider [the] advisability of withdrawing any compensation offers" rather than sit through a long and bitter General Assembly debate on UNRWA and the UNCCP. Meir also was worried when the Americans warned her about yet another Arab tactic in the UN. The Americans had information that the Arabs might accuse Israel of having violated General Assembly Resolution 181 (II), the partition resolution of November 29, 1947. That resolution stated that the proposed Jewish state could expropriate Arab property only if it was needed for "public use" (see chapter 1). U.S. diplomat Francis T.P. Plimpton told Meir that Israel should begin preparing to defend itself against the Arab charge that its expropriation of the refugees' property was not for such public use.[58]

The United States eventually used its influence in the UN to block the property custodian drive. It appeared keen to avoid seeing Israel suffer a diplomatic setback in the General Assembly even if its practical impact would be minimal. After working hard to secure dissenting votes, the idea for a custodian failed during debates in the General Assembly in April 1961 and again during the next session that December. Perhaps given the high level talks later undertaken by the UNCCP's Johnson Mission, the Arab states backed off from introducing the custodian idea again in 1962. The issue, however, would soon be resurrected.

Indeed, the idea of helping the refugees either through the revenues from the property itself or from the interest generated from the principle in a UN compensation fund lived on. The Palestine Arab Delegation, a body created by the Arab Higher Committee to present the Palestinian cause to the UN, sent two representatives to meet with members of the American delegation to the UN in June 1963. They suggested that the UNCCP should create a new office that would collect and distribute the rent monies generated from the refugees' property. The UNCCP's records could be used to determine if the rents charged by Israel were fair. The Palestine Arab Delegation's Issa Nakhleh told the Americans that the refugees did not seek compensation, which meant giving up their right to repatriation. Instead, they sought their legitimate rent.[59]

Such an idea had a following even within the UN. The following year UNRWA Commissioner-General Lawrence Michelmore mentioned in the first draft of UNRWA's 1964 report that means should be sought to allow the refugees to benefit from their property in Israel without prejudicing their claims to repatriation.[60] Even the UNCCP Land Specialist Frank Jarvis, hired in 1960 to complete the UNCCP's Technical Program to identify and valuate refugee property, was supportive to a degree. However he feared that the UNCCP's records would be dragged into the inevitable political morass that would accompany passage of the property custodian idea in the General Assembly. Indeed, in November 1964 he voiced such fears: the Arabs would point to the voluminous records the UNCCP had made (see chapter 5) as alleged proof both of the feasibility of such an idea and of UNCCP agreement with the idea when trying to garner votes. Jarvis thought that perhaps the UNCCP should preempt this by considering some method of providing the refugees with income from their property.[61]

The property custodian idea resurfaced in 1965 and 1966, but was defeated in the Special Political Committee each time when the Arabs could not collect enough votes to overcome American objections. In the wake of the 1967 Arab-Israeli war, it was debated during at the General Assembly in December 1967 but not actually voted on. The war knocked the idea, and the refugees' property in general, off the political radar screens of the Middle East for some time thereafter. The vicissitudes of the Arab-Israeli conflict propelled international interest in the Palestinian question in new directions. Nevertheless, the idea that the refugees should be able to benefit from the income generated by their property in Israel without conceding their title thereto would return over a decade later although by that point the issue had been relegated to the role of an Arab diplomatic stick with which to beat Israel at the UN.

## CHAPTER FIVE
# UNCCP TECHNICAL PROGRAM

As part of the new direction it took away from active mediation and toward more tertiary, "technical" aspects of the refugee problem, the UNCCP decided to expand on the 1951 Global Estimate of refugee property losses by conducting a more thorough study of such losses. This new study would go beyond the general statistics of the Global Estimate and study individual refugees' property losses. The resultant UNCCP Technical Program of 1952–64 went on to become the most detailed study ever made of the scope and value of Palestinian refugee property. The Technical Program produced a documentary record of almost every parcel of land that was owned by an Arab on May 14, 1948 in the areas of Palestine that later became Israel. The results of this study would be roundly criticized by both Arab and Israeli alike, but still remain the most thorough reckoning of the property question ever conducted by any party, as well as the most massive effort undertaken by the UNCCP itself.

## Origins of the Technical Program

The origins of the project date from 1952 and John Berncastle's mission in the Middle East. His August 7, 1952 plan entitled "The Individual Assessment of Abandoned Arab Immoveable Property in Israeli Held Territory" laid out guidelines for following up the Global Estimate of refugee property with a far more detailed study that identified and set a value for every refugee's holdings. Berncastle estimated that it would take a staff of fifty persons some two years to complete such a task. On September 5, 1952, the UNCCP took a formal, unanimous decision to implement Berncastle's plan. However, the UNCCP decided that a new Technical Office should carry out the work in New York because the UNCCP's diplomats were worried that if the project were conducted in Jerusalem it would become a "center of attraction such as would not be conducive to the settling process in Arab-Israel relations for which the Commission hopes."[1] This possibility could jeopardize the project's confidentiality and might even subject the UNCCP's locally hired employees to threats or enticements. As such, the UNCCP wanted the project done "by staff whose integrity is beyond doubt." The United States also voiced practical concerns about working in Jerusalem: The UN probably could not provide the UNCCP with a budget to establish a second office in Jerusalem. When news of the project emerged, one Arab politician worried about the implications of moving records to New York for use there. Jordanian Foreign Minister Musa Nasir feared that Jews might be able to destroy the records easily, much as Jews in Palestine had blown up the King David Hotel in Jerusalem in 1946.[2]

The entire program of identifying and valuing individual refugees' property holdings was assigned to a new office within the UNCCP called the Technical Office, and the project simply entitled the Technical Program. Once established, the next question was who would direct the Technical Office's work? John Berncastle was the UNCCP's land expert at the time the UNCCP initiated the Technical Program in 1952. But Berncastle was not a permanent UN civil servant. Rather, he had been seconded to the UNCCP by the British government in February 1951 and fully intended to return to Britain after his year and one-half service. Thus, one of the first major tasks faced by the UNCCP in starting the program was to decide who would head the Technical Office and oversee the Technical Program. The UNCCP decided to hire the knowledgeable Palestinian land expert, Sami Hadawi. Berncastle had worked with Hadawi during the mandate and had relied on his insights on the refugee property question during Berncastle's tenure with the UNCCP. He had consulted with Hadawi several times during his trips to the Middle East and felt that Hadawi's talents lay in his excellent administrative skills, his intimate knowledge of land in Palestine, and his familiarity with the mandatory records that would be used during the project. He was less confident of Hadawi's ability to assign values to the land, however. Berncastle was no doubt aware that Hadawi lacked formal training in land valuation, economics, and indeed any subject. Berncastle's thoughts on Hadawi were expressed earlier in a May 11, 1951 letter to UNCCP Principal Secretary Pablo de Azcárate: "I would describe him as a very able officer whose talents lie in the direction of organization rather than in that of profound thought. He has not much knowledge of valuation or economic theory but is essentially a practical man with considerable energy and ability to get things done."[3] The commission hired Hadawi, who left his job with the Jordanian government and began working in New York for the Technical Office with the title of Land Specialist on December 28, 1952.

The Technical Office started its work under several significant assumptions. The program aimed to determine a value for compensation based on the scope and value of Arab land and certain types of moveables. It was decided not to investigate the value of other moveable property such as household goods, nor for commercial and professional facilities or intangible items like rental contracts. It sought to determine what land in the area of Palestine that became Israel had been owned by Arabs as of May 15, 1948, the first full day of Israeli independence and the day that the Arab armies entered the 1948 fighting. The program also would determine the value of this land as of November 29, 1947, the date the UN General Assembly voted to partition Palestine. The UNCCP's logic for choosing this date for valuing the property was that the commission felt that the violence that broke out shortly after the partition decision led to an abnormal situation regarding land sales and prices. Interestingly, the UNCCP never established a definition of a "refugee." Accordingly, the Technical Office decided to identify *all* Arab-owned land in Israel as of May 15, 1948, knowing full well that some of this land was still in the possession of Palestinians who remained in Israel while a much smaller area had been owned by non-Palestinian Arabs.

## Identification of Arab Property

The Technical Office decided to start with the most time-consuming part of the project, identifying Arab-owned land. Valuation would come later. The staff based its identification work on the most detailed and credible records that it could find: mandatory land records, tax records, cadastral maps, and other documents. Earlier in 1952, the UNCCP had purchased copies of the films that the British had made of various land records prior to their departure from Palestine. These included Turkish-language Ottoman land registers, English-language mandatory registers of deeds, registers of title, and other land records. The UNCCP kept these on 1,642 rolls of 35 mm acetate film in New York. However, these records were deemed insufficient for the job. The Ottoman records were in Ottoman Turkish (written with Arabic characters, which had not been in use in Turkey since the mid-1920s) as opposed to modern Turkish. More important, the information contained in them was not linked to maps or to the cadastral system of block and parcel numbers that the British later used. This made it essentially impossible to link up the information contained in them with later records produced by the British. In addition, the Ottoman registers were very poorly photographed and the images were not clear.

The English-language mandatory registers of deeds suffered from similar problems. It was virtually impossible to determine to what specific parcel the registers were referring given the lack of precise cadastral information in the documents. Nor did they record *all* parcels: as registers of deeds, they only recorded instances where land was transferred. Furthermore, they suffered from a different kind of technical error. While each register contained two side-by-side pages relating to the same land transaction, the photographer in 1948 had filmed all of the left hand pages in each register and then all of the right hand pages. The Technical Office staff found it impossible to coordinate the films in order to see both halves of the same transaction.

The only films that were of value to Hadawi's staff were those containing the mandatory registers of title. These were a different kind of register created as part of the massive land settlement process initiated by the British according to the Land (Settlement of Title) Ordinance of 1928. Land settlement was a systematic attempt to survey and determine the legal rights associated with all land throughout Palestine. Settlement teams were sent to villages to perform this survey. In the process, they drew up new registers of title for each village that was settled, recording the size of each parcel, its owner(s) and noting what other rights existed regarding each parcel (e.g., mortgage liens). These then replaced the previous registers of deeds. The village was also divided into numbered registration blocks and each parcel assigned a specific number within one of the blocks. Maps were drawn of each village. The new registers of title showed exactly who had been determined to be the legal owner(s) of land rights to specific parcels of land that could be identified on maps. Both the British and, later, the UNCCP Technical Office considered these to be the only reliable, legal reckoning of land ownership rights in Palestine, not the registers of deeds or Ottoman registers. The problem for the UNCCP was that the British had not completed the land settlement process by 1948. The last public reckoning of the amount of land that had been settled was 5,243,042 dunums out of a total area of 26,320,000 dunums by April 30, 1947.[4] But given that the southern half of Palestine was largely desert, the area settled encompassed a much larger percentage of the cultivable land in Palestine than the figures suggested. Fortunately for its work, the Technical Office estimated that most of the 5 million dunums in the filmed registers of title lay in the areas that became Israel in 1948, covering about half of the land in Israel. Nonetheless, the records were incomplete.[5]

In order to complete the process of identifying Arab ownership in the other half of Israel not covered by the filmed registers of title, Hadawi and his staff utilized mandatory tax records. The British had not filmed these, so Hadawi and his colleagues had to resort to the originals that mandatory authorities had left behind in 1948. Berncastle previously had tried to secure permission from the Israelis to use these, inasmuch as most of them had ended up in Israeli hands after the fighting. There were two types of these tax records. The first were tax distribution sheets that the British had prepared in order to assess taxes on rural property under the Rural Property Tax Ordinance of 1935. The others were field valuation sheets that did the same for urban property under the Urban Property Tax Ordinance of 1928. Yet even these were of no help when it came to the southern subdistrict of Beersheba. This area had contained many semi-nomadic bedouin tribes prior to 1948, had not undergone land settlement, and was not subject to the normal rural tax procedures found in the rest of Palestine. It was subject instead to the Commutation of Tithes Ordinance that only applied to that region. A lump sum land tax was applied to the area and then divided up among the inhabitants by village tax distribution committees. While information on these taxes had been recorded, these documents disappeared in 1948. No registers of title or tax records were thus available for Beersheba land. The only documents from Beersheba available to Hadawi's staff were sixty registers of deeds for the area that were in the Israelis' possession.

Hadawi decided to start the process of identifying Arab land with the registers of title and then consult the tax records for those areas that were not covered by the registers or if any information in the registers was unclear. The Technical Office culled information from the various mandatory documents and recorded it on basic forms printed up by the office called "R/P" forms, for "refugee property." Hadawi's staff would prepare one R/P form for each parcel of land that was studied. There were different numbers assigned to these forms. Arab-owned land was recorded on R/P1 forms. "Excluded" land was recorded on R/P3 forms. This included non-Arab owned land such as Jewish land, state land, etc. R/P5 forms were drawn up for state land that had been leased to Arabs who were eligible to purchase it someday. Besides these, eighteen other R/P forms were used by the Technical Office for various purposes, including administrative. There was even variation within the color of the R/P1 forms that were used for Arab-owned property. The most common R/P1 forms were white, which designated individually owned Arab land. Green forms were used for Islamic waqf property. Red forms denoted Christian waqf land. Yellow forms were used to record parcels of Arab land that lay in the Demilitarized Zones along the Israeli-Syrian and Israeli-Egyptian armistice lines and in No Man's Land between the Israeli and Jordanian lines in Jerusalem. Finally, blue R/P1 forms were for those parcels that were cut by the armistice lines and lay partially in Israel and partially in Arab-controlled territory.

How did Hadawi's staff identify Arab property in the records, and what types of Arab property were included on the R/P1 forms? These issues later would constitute the grounds for both Israeli and Arab objections to the Technical Program. In determining what land was owned by Arabs, Hadawi's staff assistants simply were told to look for Arab names in the mandatory records and consider the land in question as "Arab." Hadawi and others realized that some Mizrahi Jews had Arabic-sounding names. However, it was decided that their full names usually contained some unmistakable Hebrew names as well, easily identifying them as Jews. Another problem concerned Palestinians of Arabized Slavic background who were considered "Arabs" but had Slavic family names that might be confused with Ashkenazic Jewish names. Once again the staff believed that these persons could usually could be distinguished from Jews with Slavic names by their clearly Muslim or Christian first names. The situation became further complicated when it came to Armenian and Greek names in the British records. It was decided to include Armenians in the R/P1 forms but not the Greeks. The Technical Office decided that Armenians generally had been considered local inhabitants of Palestine, whereas some Greeks maintained Greek citizenship and were in that sense considered foreigners. Greek names therefore were recorded on R/P3 forms (excluded properties forms).

As for the type of Arab land on which the Technical Office focused, the staff drew up R/P1 forms for individually owned land, land owned by companies and corporate bodies, waqf land, and *musha'* land (collectively owned by a large number of persons within a village). Land owned by municipal bodies or registered to *mukhtar*s (village headmen) on behalf of villagers was not recorded on R/P1 forms but rather on R/P3 forms. As R/P1 forms were completed, they were filed by subdistrict, village, registration block, and parcel number. All other R/P forms, except those used for administrative purposes, were simply filed by village or town.

Staff members took a variety of information from the mandatory records when completing an R/P1 form. The following procedure was used for rural land. If the land had undergone land settlement, Hadawi's staff extracted the following data from the filmed registers of title: the name of the village; the number of the registration block and the parcel number; the name(s) of the owner(s) and the share of the property owned by each; the surface area of the parcel in dunums; and information on mortgage liens or other encumbrances. To obtain a description of the land, they later turned to the tax distribution sheets once they had access to them. If the land had not undergone land settlement, the Technical Office used the tax distribution sheets to extract the village name; taxation block and parcel number (although these villages had no registration block and parcel numbers they did have taxation block and parcel numbers that had been assigned by mandatory tax authorities); name(s) of owner(s); shares owned by each; surface area; and description of area. Because information on mortgages and other encumbrances was not entered in the tax distribution sheets, staff members tried their best to find such information in the registers of deeds if they were available. The process for studying urban land went as follows. Since the British had not applied land settlement in urban areas, the field valuation sheets drawn up for taxation purposes were used in the first instance. From these staff members extracted the name of the town, taxation block and parcel number, the name(s) and shares owned by the owner(s), the surface area, and description of the land. They once again did their best to find information regarding encumbrances from the registers of deeds.[6]

Hadawi and his staff soon started work on a "pilot program" to determine how well the system they had developed would work. They began their identification work for villages in the mandatory Gaza subdistrict. The land belonging to 50 villages in the subdistrict ended up in Israel after 1948, along with some of the land belonging to seven other villages that straddled the cease-fire line. This amount totaled some 691,000 dunums. Hadawi had decided to begin with Gaza primarily because the British had completed land settlement operations in most of the Gaza subdistrict. Not only did this mean that the best possible records were available for most of the villages but also that the filmed copies of these records were in the New York office. Therefore, Hadawi's staff would not need to consult tax records in the Middle East. By the end of May 1953 after several months' work, the office completed identification work in two villages in the Gaza subdistrict: Isdud and 'Arab Suqrir. It is interesting to note the amount of land in the two villages that the Technical Office staff listed on R/P1 forms versus other types of R/P forms, and to compare the total results with figures established for the villages by the British in 1945 (see table 5.1).

It is not clear why there existed a discrepancy between the two figures as far as Arab-owned property was concerned. By March 1955, the Technical Program had been completed in fourteen villages in Gaza, and 173,039 dunums had been identified.[7] The fact that the identification work was well underway in Gaza by 1955 prompted some in the UNCCP, UNRWA, and UNTSO to consider a phased "Gaza first" compensation scheme although this never took place (see chapter 4).

## Work Issues

The work of the Technical Program could be demanding at times. Consulting the tax sheets in the Middle East was not as simple for the Technical Office

TABLE 5.1 Comparison of Mandatory and UNCCP Figures for Scope of Land in Isdud and 'Arab Suqrir Villages

| *Parcels of Individually-Owned Land on RP/1 Forms* | *Area** | *Jewish-Owned** | *State Land** | *Roads, Etc.** |
|---|---|---|---|---|
| 1. UNCCP Technical Office Figures, 1953 | | | | |
| 2,406 | 24,410 (plus 12 more that were "communally owned") | 656 | 44,121, | 1,162 |

| *Parcels of Individually-Owned Land* | *Arab-Owned** | *Jewish-Owned** | *"Public"Land* |
|---|---|---|---|
| 2. Mandatory Figures, 1945 | | | |
| N/A | 45,175 | 2,487 | 40,433 |

*Dunums

Source: NARA RG 84, United Nations/USUN Central Files—UN Letters./2450, "Blocked Arab Accounts;" Document: "Palestine Conciliation Commission. Individual Assessment of Arab Refugee immoveable Property in Israel. Progress Report for Month Ended May 1953"; *Village Statistics 1945. A Classification of Land and Area Ownership in Palestine*, with explanatory notes by Sami Hadawi (Beirut: Palestine Liberation Organization Research Center, 1970)

staff as using the filmed registers in New York. Most of the tax records were in Israel, which originally had refused to provide access to these. The Israelis later changed their mind in 1954, after Alexis Ladas had worked to convince them. Hadawi and his staff did as much work as they could from the filmed copies of the land registers in New York. In 1953, he suggested to the UNCCP that the Technical Office be allowed to establish a sub-office in Jerusalem where locally hired employees could consult local documents and provide any needed information requested from New York. The UNCCP discussed this with the Jordanian and Israeli governments, who agreed to the proposal. The sub-office was established at Government House in Jerusalem. The office began operations in April 1954 with two Palestinians with Jordanian citizensip, 'Adil Nammari and Gregory Issaevitch. An Israeli, N. Ben 'Uzziel, also was hired to work out of Tel Aviv.

Coordination among the Technical Office staff in three different countries was cumbersome. Whenever the New York office needed information that it lacked or that was illegible in the films, it wrote what it needed on a "query sheet." Hadawi then sent the query sheets village by village to the sub-office in Jerusalem so Nammari and Issaevitch could obtain the missing information from tax lists and return it to New York. This usually involved the sub-office in Jerusalem passing along the query sheets to Ben 'Uzziel in Tel Aviv, who was granted permission by the Israeli land department to travel to its registry offices around the country to consult the requisite records and answer the queries. The query sheets then were returned to New York. Complicating this cumbersome process even further, when Ben 'Uzziel needed to examine tax records (as opposed to land records), Israeli tax officials would only agree to allow him to see them at the Israeli government's tax offices in Jerusalem. Rather than visiting each local tax department, Ben 'Uzziel had to request the tax authorities to order the records shipped to Jerusalem where he could consult them.

Even though it had become much more forthcoming about UNCCP requests for documents by 1955, Israel still did not grant the UNCCP all of its requests. Despite the UNCCP's knowledge of them, Israel never gave it copies of the 1950 Lif Committee report or the 1953 Horowitz Committee report. Nor did the Israelis provide further access to the Custodian of Absentee Property's records after Berncastle had been granted copies of a few of these records in 1951. The Israelis refused to hand over more of the Custodian's records even though they insisted that these were the only valid records detailing the refugees' property. As Comay later told an UNTSO official, "Under Israel legislation, the records of the Custodian of Abandoned [sic] Property are the only authoritative source for determining the status or extent of such property."[8]

The Technical Office soon realized that other mandatory records that it needed (largely other tax records) were under the control of the Jordanian, Syrian, and Egyptian governments. The UNCCP formally requested access to the Jordanian records on March 15, 1955. The request went all the way to the Jordanian cabinet, which refused in early July. Among other reasons for the refusal was Jordan's objection to the UNCCP's 1951 Global Estimate of the value of the refugee property, which the Jordanians decried as too low. In February 1956, a notable refugee in Jordan who was a former Palestine supreme court judge offered to intervene on behalf of the UNCCP. Anton 'Atallah agreed with the UNCCP that Jordan's refusal to provide the records was ill advised, and promised to intercede with Minister of Finance Hashim Jayyusi, whose ministry controlled the records that were housed at the Department of Lands and Survey in Amman.[9] By that time, George Fredrick Walpole was no longer the director of the land department, having been replaced in 1954 by a Jordanian, Muhammad Isma'il, from the al-'Atiyyat family. Eventually the Jordanians acceded to the UNCCP's request and granted permission to access mandatory records under their control on June 19, 1956. In fact, the Jordanians eventually provided the Technical Office staff not only with the records but also with facilities for examining them. Syria lent the Technical Office tax sheets that it possessed, which were probably those it obtained from Sami Hadawi in 1950. Finally, Egyptian authorities allowed Technical Office staff access to its land registry offices in Gaza and starting in February 1955 provided part-time staff help as well.[10]

One reason why the UNCCP needed to consult records in Gaza was that the Egyptians allowed refugees to buy and sell abandoned land from the mandatory subdistrict of Gaza and record the transactions at the land registry office in Gaza City, even though the land was under Israeli control across the cease-fire lines. According to the UNCCP, this office did a "brisk business" in registering such transactions even though the UNCCP considered them of dubious legality. The Technical Office decided to record these changes to the information contained in its R/P1 forms for Gaza by drawing up supplemental forms to show such changes in data. By late 1955 it stopped doing this, at which time some 7,000 parcels had been affected by such sales. It was just as well: After Israel occupied Gaza in October 1956, its forces took all land registers and tax sheets with them upon their withdrawal the following March.[11]

The work of the Technical Office suffered a setback in April 1955 when a UN disciplinary body forced Hadawi to resign because of a purported conflict of interest. The circumstances behind Hadawi's removal underscore the extreme political sensitivities surrounding the UNCCP's identification work. In September 1954, Hadawi received a telephone call in New York from Meir Meyer of the Israeli delegation to the UN. Meyer told Hadawi that he had just come from Israel and had brought some family photographs given to him by one of Hadawi's former Jewish subordinates in the mandatory government. The subordinate wanted Meyer to pass the photos on to Hadawi. While the two men met over lunch, the subject of Hadawi's abandoned house in the Qatamon area of West Jerusalem came up. Meyer suggested that Hadawi should apply to the Custodian of Absentee Property for release of the house inasmuch as Hadawi was a British subject and might not be considered an absentee any longer. At minimum Hadawi could ask the Custodian to prevent sale of the home. Meyer suggested that Hadawi write the Custodian a letter that Meyer would pass along.

Hadawi did not immediately follow up, but eventually did so after Meyer brought up the matter again during a chance meeting the two had one month later. On October 20, 1954, Hadawi wrote a letter to the Custodian on UNCCP stationery requesting the return of his land in Jerusalem as well as that co-owned by his wife and aunt. He stated that he was a British subject and noted that he was working for the UN on the compensation question. The Custodian, Moshe Levin, responded to Hadawi on November 3, 1954. He declared that Hadawi was still considered an absentee under Israeli law, his British nationality notwithstanding, but that he would forward his request for release to the Special Committee that entertained such petitions under the Absentees' Property Law. Meyer passed this letter to Hadawi on December 24 and the matter appeared to be over.[12]

However, the Israelis apparently leaked the matter to the UNCCP. Clearly disturbed by Hadawi's actions, UNCCP Principal Secretary Dr. Feng Yang Chai confronted Hadawi the following February about the incident and asked for an explanation. Hadawi wrote a memorandum to Chai on February 8 that recounted what had happened and offered his opinion that he had not acted unwisely or in any way that would cause embarrassment to the UNCCP. He was simply inquiring about his own personal property, he noted, and claimed that he had in no way abused his official position with the UNCCP to obtain special favors for himself. Hadawi was a proud man who always was concerned about being able to provide for his family. He told Chai that while he regretted any problems his actions may have generated he saw no conflict of interest between his employment with the UNCCP and his desire as a refugee to secure his personal property for himself and his family. Chai notified the UNCCP members three days later of Hadawi's actions. Although Chai conceded that Hadawi "may have been induced" by Meyer to write the Custodian, he stated that Hadawi's action nonetheless raised questions about his "continued value to [the] Commission." The matter was sent before the UN Secretariat Joint Disciplinary Committee, which recommended Hadawi's removal from UN employment. Chai informed the UNCCP of the outcome on April 13, noting that UN Secretary General Dag Hammarskjöld himself had ordered that Hadawi be forced out by April 15, 1955. He would be allowed to resign and his personnel file would be kept among the Secretariat's confidential files. More seriously for the UNCCP, the possibility of terminating the entire land identification program had been discussed as well.[13]

The UNCCP thus suffered the loss of a man who had possessed intimate knowledge of land in Palestine. The Palestinian refugees saw their most highly placed colleague and expert on their land removed from a position of influence. Had he been set up by the Israelis in order to get him out of the UNCCP? The archival record consulted by the author is unclear. But what is clear is that word of Hadawi's letter to the Custodian—a letter that had been sent through an official of the Israeli mission to the UN—somehow found its way to the UNCCP under circumstances that suggest Israeli involvement. Even Chai had admitted that Hadawi "may have been induced" to write the letter by Meir Meyer. The Israelis clearly had had good relations with Berncastle, and no doubt disliked the fact that a Palestinian refugee had replaced him in such an important job.

Given this and given his background as a refugee landowner who had been involved with Arab governments and organizations in their attempts to defend refugee rights, why did the UNCCP hire Hadawi in the first place? The answer is unclear, except that Berncastle had felt that he was the most qualified person given his knowledge of Palestinian land and mandatory land records. Hadawi himself had boasted of this. Chai noted that "He himself [Hadawi] has told me that there was no one of sufficient training or expertise to fill his position. I have also consulted the Commission's former Land Specialist, Mr. John Berncastle, who confirms this."[14] The UNCCP was left to find a replacement for Hadawi, who found employment with the Palestine Arab Refugee Office in New York that was headed by Izzat Tannous. It would not be the last time that the UNCCP would have to face Sami Hadawi.

The UNCCP turned to John Berncastle and asked if he would return to work for the UNCCP. Four days after Hadawi's departure, Berncastle responded to Chai from England to express his willingness to return to UN service as Hadawi's replacement. After all, he had started the entire identification and valuation process himself and was committed to its success. However, he wanted the UNCCP to speed up its work. The UNCCP looked into the matter of accelerating its work as a precondition for rehiring Berncastle. A March 1955 UNCCP report on compensation underscored Berncastle's concern about the slow pace of the identification and valuation project. The report estimated that at the current rate of 100 parcels processed per staff member per day (85,000 parcels per year) that the program still needed six years to complete. However, two months later in June 1955, the UNCCP heard a different report on the progress of Hadawi's "pilot program" to date suggesting that it would take fifteen years to complete. The UNCCP decided to seek additional funding from the UN to accelerate the program, expand the Technical Office staff, and base them in Jerusalem rather than New York. On July 8, 1955, the UNCCP met with Hammarskjöld to discuss the proposal. Hammarskjöld agreed that the program should be hastened, and said he would get the UNCCP the additional $50,000 for its budget that this necessitated.[15]

Having secured permission to accelerate the project, the UNCCP offered Berncastle a two-year contract. He arrived in Jerusalem and commenced work as "Area Specialist" in late September 1955. Berncastle hired a number of new employees to help with the work. Berncastle found that his Arab staff enjoyed the work and got along with one another well. This was in marked contrast with his rather negative opinion of his Israeli employees. As he commented in early 1956: "Arab employees seem to like the work and are a happy team... the only flies in the ointment are the two Israeli employees who badger me with complaints and requests about salaries, hours of work, leave and the like."[16]

Politics continued to interfere with the Technical Office's work. In late 1955 and again in February 1956, the Israeli government complained to Berncastle that there were not enough Israelis working on his payroll. The government felt that at least two or three more should be hired and should work on the same premises as the Arab employees (i.e., at Government House in Jerusalem). The Israelis argued that the project was a UN mission of great concern to Israel, and that Government House was in Israeli territory anyway so there should be no problems with Israelis working there. Berncastle replied that he had not selected employees on ethnic lines; he mostly hired Arabs because they were the only ones who applied. He did not have the budget to hire new staff, and could not very well fire some of the Arabs to make room for new Israeli employees.[17]

About the same time, the UNCCP received a letter of complaint this time signed by representatives of eight Arab states. The letter was submitted on March 1, 1956, and complained about the Technical Office's work. Among other charges, the letter claimed that no representatives of the refugees were involved in the identification work—a clear reference to Hadawi's termination. In fact, Berncastle told UNCCP Principal Secretary Povl Bang-Jensen that the letter was "largely the work of the Arab Refugee Office which is headed by Dr. Izzat Tannous and in which Sami Hadawi is employed." Berncastle felt that the letter was largely Hadawi's work, inasmuch as Hadawi previously had shared such opinions with Berncastle.[18]

Not yet a year after his dismissal from the UNCCP, Hadawi had once again surfaced on the property question. He later met with the UNCCP in New York along with the Jordanian and Egyptian delegates to the UN on May 27, 1959 to complain about the Technical Office's work once again. Hadawi asked how the valuation process would take care of buildings in rural areas, communally owned land, state land, land in the Beersheba district, moveable property, and the former assets of the mandatory government.[19] Politics continued to affect the office's work in the fall of 1956 when work was stopped for three weeks during the Suez War of October and November 1956. The Jerusalem staff were given three weeks leave with pay.

At the height of the identification work in late 1956, Berncastle employed seventeen Arab and five Israeli staff members in the Middle East. Two of the latter were working at the Israeli land registry office in Safad and one at the Haifa registry. After a delay the sub-office in Jerusalem obtained ten microfilm viewers that the staff could use. In addition, three staff members continued to work in New York. By the time Berncastle's contract was due to expire in the fall of 1957, the Technical Office had almost completed the identification work. Table 5.2 indicates the progress made from the end of 1952 until August 31, 1957. By March 31, 1958, a total of 9,872 blocks had been finished as well as all of the Beersheba district.[20]

Identification work was completed in 1958. The Technical Office reported that it had created approximately 453,000 individual R/P1 forms, meaning that it had identified that number of parcels of individually owned Arab property in Israel, subject to certain reservations (this figure is actually incorrect, as chapter 7 will show). While the office had *identified* that many parcels, it freely conceded that there were more that it could *not* identify. Were the R/P1 forms a type of substitute land deed for the refugees' property that could be considered legally valid? Not all of them, according to Berncastle and his staff, who considered that the information on those R/P1 forms that had been taken from the registers of title was authoritative. The R/P1s drawn up from the information in other registers and tax documents were less solid because they were based either on presumptive title or recorded the name of whoever paid tax on the land, who may not have been the sole owner or even the "true" owner.

Another problem concerned uncultivable land located in those villages that had not undergone land settlement operations. Since the British did not tax this type of land, and the tax registers were drawn up in order to divide taxes among landowners, village authorities were not always careful to list every owner of land rights in such land in the village tax registers. The result was that this source of data was imprecise. The Technical Office therefore made the decision to exclude all of this land—some 460,000 dunums—that lay in unsettled villages because it could not definitively prove that it had been privately owned. R/P1 forms were not drawn up for this land.[21]

Another problem the Technical Office faced was how to identify Arab land in certain areas that were lacking documents altogether. This problem was most acute in the vast Beersheba subdistrict, which consisted of some 12.5

TABLE 5.2 Pace of UNCCP Technical Office's Work on Identifying Individual Refugee Losses, 1952–1957

| *Sub-District* | *Villages (N)* | *Blocks (N)* | *No. of Blocks Completed* |
|---|---|---|---|
| Ramla | 81 | 1,447 | 1,407 |
| Gaza | 55 | 1,586 | 1,586 |
| Jaffa | 30 | 827 | 818 |
| Tulkarm | 56 | 753 | 471 |
| Haifa | 60 | 1,759 | 1,648 |
| Safad | 83 | 913 | 666 |
| Tiberias | 32 | 535 | 459 |
| Acre | 52 | 645 | 274 |
| Baysan | 32 | 443 | 429 |
| Nazareth | 29 | 616 | 473 |
| Ramallah | 3 | 8 | 8 |
| Hebron | 26 | 269 | 252 |
| Janin | 23 | 156 | 156 |
| Nablus | 3 | 5 | 5 |
| Jerusalem | 53 | 503 | 299 |
| Beersheba | (not divided into villages and blocks; work finished for 30 of 60 land registers) | | |
| TOTAL | 618 | 10,461 | 8,951 |

Source: NARA RG 84, United Nations/USUN Central Files—UN Letters/2450, "Blocked Arab Accounts;" Document: "Report to P. Bang-Jensen, Acting Principal Secretary of the Commission, from J. Berncastle, Land Specialist" (November 1, 1957)

million dunums. As noted above, none of this land had undergone land settlement operations. Nor had regular tax registers been drawn up because it was subject to a special lump sum land tax under the Commutation of Tithes Ordinance. This lump sum was divided up among the inhabitants by village tax distribution committees. Data on these taxes had been recorded in different documents than the normal tax registers but these documents disappeared in 1948. To make up for the dearth of data, the office turned to the registers of deeds to try to locate information about Arab property. The staff ended up finding references to only 200,000 dunums out of the entire subdistrict, of which only 64,000 dunums were determined to have been registered to Arabs. R/P1 forms were drawn up only for these 64,000 dunums. The Technical Office assumed that the rest of the 1,935,000 dunums of cultivable land in the subdistrict was cultivated by Arab bedouin but did not record information for this land on R/P1 forms.

The vast lands in the Beersheba subdistrict were not the only examples of problems faced by the UNCCP's staff in trying to identify refugee land. Recent tax sheets were not located for urban land in Ramla, although 1940–41 sheets were found for some of the missing areas. These were used for constructing R/P1 forms where possible. Tax sheets were also completely missing for the villages of Burayj, Dayr Aban, Jarash, and Khirbat Ismallah. About one-half of the identification work was completed for Dayr Aban based on other documents (provisional land settlement records), but no work at all could be done for the others. Incomplete sets of sheets were located for Bayt Jimal, Dayr Rafat, Lifta, Suba, Dallata, Malikiyya, and al-Ras al-Ahmar, with the result that not all land from these villages could be included in R/P1 forms either.

## Valuation of Property

When Berncastle temporarily returned to the UNCCP in mid-1955, he originally had been thinking along the lines that the valuation work should produce a figure that conformed with his earlier 1951 global estimate of £100 million. He noted in an internal memorandum that was circulated to UNRWA against the UNCCP's wishes, "individual valuation should therefore be an analysis of the global figure already adopted rather than a synthesis of new valuations." UNRWA Commissioner Henry Labouisse was aghast when he learned of the memorandum. He felt that the new figure should be independent of the results of the earlier one, and let this be known to the UNCCP. Alexis Ladas agreed with him, and the UNCCP's Principal Secretary Povl Bang-Jensen quickly wrote to Labouisse assuring him that Berncastle's memorandum was not really an official memorandum but merely a written version of some of his initial thoughts. In any event, he said, it should never have been circulated. Berncastle's thinking had since evolved, and he too realized that it would be "unethical and politically unwise" to valuate the refugees' land in any way other than its true market value. Bang-Jensen went on to state categorically that the UNCCP's Technical Office was not bound by the earlier 1951 figure of £P100 million and would produce whatever the true figure was, come what may. In fact, he opposed the idea of limiting the amount of compensation artificially in order to conform to a certain amount: "It would be immoral for the United Nations to maintain that the refugees received full compensation if that were not so. Quite apart from the moral aspect, it is, of course, also entirely impossible to solve the problem in a politically satisfactory way by pretending, contrary to facts, that full compensation is paid."[22]

Berncastle's thinking on how to compensate the refugees also underwent modification since he had first devised a compensation plan in 1952. In his earlier plan of September 10, 1952 entitled "A Plan for the Payment of Compensation for Abandoned Arab Immoveable Property," Berncastle suggested that the UN establish a financial group to pay compensation to refugee landowners and receive the legal title for their land from the Israeli Custodian of Absentee Property. The fund would then sell the land to Jews throughout the world in order to pay itself back. The JNF and the Israeli government would have the right of first refusal on this land. Any losses in these transactions would be made up by Israel. The year after he proposed that idea, Berncastle discussed the idea for an "International Banking Organization for the Development of the Near East" with a French diplomat. He later discussed this new idea with an American diplomat in August 1956. It was a similar proposal, but instead of paying full compensation to the refugees the bank would pay most of them one-half of their compensation payment in cash and one-half in bonds, to limit the inflationary impact of a sudden influx of capital into the Middle East. The refugees then could invest the bonds as stock in new development projects in the region. Each year, the bank would compensate about 20 percent of the refugees and stretch out the entire operation to five or more years. Making the bulk of the refugees wait for their compensation payments would be a way of "promoting peace" because it would not be in their interests to push for a war that would upset the repayment schedule. Additionally, Berncastle argued that this method would facilitate resettlement because each refugee would receive enough money at one time, in cash and bonds, to help them resettle.[23]

Valuation work began in September 1956 and was carried out on a regional basis as the Technical Office staff studied data on rural and urban land prices by subdistricts. Since the data on prices was regional, the Technical Office initially did not establish values for individual parcels of land. By mid-1957, Berncastle had done enough of this work to increase his initial 1951 estimate of the value of the property by 50 percent. He now felt the value would end up being closer to $US460 million than his earlier 1951 estimate of $280 million (£P100 million). Ironically, he was discovering that his Arab critics were correct when they derided his earlier figures as being far too low.[24]

Berncastle also began exploratory work on establishing values for individual parcels of land. Once again focusing on the Gaza subdistrict because identification work was done there first, Berncastle chose one village at random to valuate and study in detail as a test. In particular, he wanted to investigate what percentage of the population had owned land on May 15, 1948 and thus stood to benefit from any future compensation regime. He chose the village of Julis. The Technical Office had determined that Julis comprised 13,584 dunums divided among 1,116 parcels as indicated in table 5.3.

He then valued the land in the village and studied the percentage of village land owned by small, medium, and large landowners. He determined that the total value of all privately owned Arab land in Julis as of November 29, 1947 was £P486,570. Berncastle also determined that 16 individuals among the 642 landowners in Julis—2.4 percent of the landowners and 1.6

TABLE 5.3 Technical Office's 1957 Study of Scope of Refugee Land in Julis, Gaza Sub-District

| *Type* | *Area (Dunums)* |
|---|---|
| 1. Land by category | |
| Built-up | 30 |
| Citrus | 1,355 |
| Banana | 5 |
| Other fruit | 931 |
| Cereal | 10,803 |
| Railroads, roads, other uncultivable | 460 |
| TOTAL | 13,584 |
| *Type* | *Area (Dunums)* |
| 2. Land by type of ownership | |
| Private Arab | 12,989 |
| In trust for the village | 15 |
| Jewish owned | 227 |
| State owned | 335 |
| TOTAL | 13,584 |
| *No. of Male Owners* | *No. of Female Owners* |
| 3. Land ownership by gender | |
| 526 | 116 |

Source: UNSA DAG 13–3, UNCCP. Subgroup: Principal Secretary. Series: Records Relating to the Technical Office/Box 16/1955–60/Mr. J.M. Berncastle; Document: "Property Ownership in an Arab Village" (March 11, 1957)

percent of the total population—controlled 40 percent of the land. The range of ownership by value is indicated in table 5.4.

Berncastle also examined the value of landholdings by extended family (Ar.: hamula). He found that most land (in terms of value) was owned by members of four such families. The al-Ghusayn family owned by far the most: £P232,095. They were followed by the al-'Assar (£P67,820), the Shaqliyya (£P21,455), and the Abu Sayf (£P21,380).[25]

Berncastle also compared global data on refugee compensation from his 1951 estimate with specific information from Julis to see how the percentage of families who would receive compensation compared with his earlier estimate. The comparison showed a great similarity: despite his random selection of Julis, the percentage of families in the village that would receive various levels of compensation was remarkably similar to his earlier, generalized estimates of 1951 (see table 5.5).

With Berncastle's contract set to expire on August 31, 1957 the UNCCP once again faced the task of selecting someone to carry on. Identification work was nearly complete, and the important job of assigning values to the refugee land lay ahead. Berncastle had two suggestions for his replacement. The first was Moshe Ellman, Chief Valuer at the Israeli Ministry of Justice and a personal friend of his. Berncastle had recommended him as a suitable valuer back in 1952 when the Refugee Office was contemplating a compen-

TABLE 5.4 Technical Office's 1957 Study of Value of Refugee Land in Julis, Gaza Sub-District, by Value of Landholding

| *Value of Holdings (£P)* | *No. of Individuals* | *Total Value (£P)* |
|---|---|---|
| less than 100 | 188 | 7,440 |
| 101–500 | 284 | 67,940 |
| 501–1000 | 79 | 56,565 |
| 1001–1500 | 29 | 36,660 |
| 1501–2000 | 12 | 20,370 |
| 2001–2500 | 11 | 24,025 |
| 2501–5000 | 23 | 75,520 |
| 5001–10,001 | 14 | 108,015 |
| more than 10,001 | 2 | 90,035 |
| TOTAL | 642 | 486,570 |

Source: UNSA DAG 13–3, UNCCP. Subgroup: Principal Secretary. Series: Records Relating to the Technical Office/Box 16/1955–60/Mr. J.M. Berncastle; Document: "Property Ownership in an Arab Village" (March 11, 1957)

TABLE 5.5 Refugee Families Benefiting from Compensation Comparison of UNCCP's 1951 Global Estimate with Data from Julis Village

| | *Families Receiving Compensation Julis more than* | *All Palestinians (1951 Figures)* |
|---|---|---|
| £100 | 60 % | 71 % |
| £500 | 36 % | 32 % |
| £1,000 | 12.5 % | 16.5 % |
| £P2,000 | 6.4 % | 6.9 % |
| £P10,000 | 1.04 % | 1.07 % |

Source: NARA RG 84, United Nations/USUN Central Files—UN Letters/2450, "Blocked Arab Accounts;" Document: Berncastle to Chai (June 28, 1957)

sation scheme. Were he selected, he would become the highest-ranking Israeli to work with the Technical Program. Berncastle's other recommendation was a fellow Briton, Roy Clifford Ward. During the mandate, Ward had replaced Berncastle as Assistant Agent at the Haifa Harbour (Reclaimed Area) Estate in 1938 when Berncastle vacated the position and moved to the land department. He later went into the private sector, and in 1957 was General Manager of the Iraq Petroleum Co. in Israel.

In the end, the UNCCP hired neither man and decided not to hire a permanent replacement for Berncastle. Instead, two local Palestinian employees in Jerusalem were tasked to oversee the project as it wound down its identification work. Most of the rest of the staff were dismissed. These two men were Gregory Issaevitch and Shukri Ibrahim Salih. Issaevitch was a Palestinian of Arabized Yugoslav background who had worked for Hadawi in the mandatory land department. A friend of the Issaevitch family, Hadawi had hired him as a favor to his mother. Berncastle liked him, although several years earlier he had described Issaevitch as a "very junior officer in the mandatory government—and was very much Hadawi's man."[26] Some in the UNCCP also worried that Arabs were suspicious of him because of his last name (presumably it sounded "Jewish"). Fifty-seven year old Shukri Salih was another Palestinian who was very much Issaevitch's senior in age and in terms of experience as well. He was another close friend of Hadawi and had been the best man in Hadawi's wedding. Salih had worked with the mandatory government since 1921 and later joined the Jordanian government after 1948, which seconded him to the UNCCP.

Since Issaevitch had worked for the UNCCP longer than Salih, technically he would become the senior person in the office. Berncastle worried, however, that Salih might resent this, given that he was older and had been a higher-ranking official in the mandatory government. He recommended that neither man be addressed as the office head. Valuation work began under their joint leadership in 1958. Part of the work was to obtain prices for land sales in the late 1940s from the various regions of Palestine. It was hoped to find these in mandatory records called Returns of Dispositions, books which gave such prices.

While Berncastle thought it might be a useful idea to publish the figures from the *identification* process (so that individual refugees could check them for accuracy and add pertinent details such as information on buildings located on the land), he argued for strict secrecy regarding the figures on land *values*. His main concern was that the Arabs would reject the entire identification and valuation project if they learned of the new figure, which although it would be larger than his 1951 figure would still undoubtedly be lower than what the Arabs publicly had been claiming the land was worth.[27]

The valuation work later was deemed too important to leave to subordinates so the UNCCP temporarily rehired Berncastle again as a "consultant" for one year from June 1959 until June 1960. During that time, the commission finally selected a permanent replacement to oversee the Technical Office's valuation work: Frank E. Jarvis. A Briton born in 1910, Jarvis was selected over 45 other candidates for the position. He was seconded by the British Board of Inland Revenue, left Britain, and began working as the new Land Specialist in New York starting in April 1960. Berncastle had this to say about Jarvis: "In Mr. Jarvis you have as director of the valuation program a man to whom no exceptions can be taken on political grounds, and who enjoys the highest professional reputation."[28]

Jarvis' arrival resulted in the acceleration of valuation work. He continued Berncastle's earlier strategy of determining general land prices for each subdistrict and even parts of subdistricts. Jarvis' staff in New York examined the mandatory records and obtained data on prices by looking at sale prices in 1946 and 1947. His staff of seven persons plus himself included trained valuators. Jarvis also had three consultants at his disposal: Berncastle in London and two others in Jerusalem. The data on sale prices were then entered into "valuation books" for rural property and "valuation files" for urban land. These contained values for each subdistrict and sometimes even portions of subdistricts. Jarvis told the UNCCP that his office would not assign a value to each specific parcel (although this in fact was done later starting in 1961). Instead, they would develop a "key number" and then create a formula for using this number in conjunction with the general data on land prices for each subdistrict found in the valuation books to arrive at values for parcels.

What did he mean by a "key number?" Jarvis felt that paragraph 111 of UN General Assembly Resolution 194 (III) of 1948 calling on Israel to compensate the refugees also discussed compensation as a way for nonrepatriated refugees to reestablish themselves. He felt that prices from 1947 would need to be multiplied to account for the passage of time and other, economic factors in order to make them relevant to the situation of the early 1960s. Given their high value, he did recommend that the Technical Office take the time to investigate and determine the specific value of each parcel of urban land, though. The UNCCP approved of his plan.[29]

On what basis did Berncastle and later Jarvis valuate the land? As noted, the basic criterion they aimed for was to determine value on the basis of what price a given parcel of land could have been sold for on the open market on November 29, 1947. To accomplish this, the men sought to make valuations consistent with the proviso that similar types of land would fetch different prices in different parts of Palestine. Urban tax sheets provided the basis for such nation-wide comparisons by listing the net annual value of all land. In rural areas, all taxable land (except in Beersheba) was listed in records by tax category. They also sought to base values on studies made of actual sale prices based on a consideration of all sales that took place in the two years proceeding November 29, 1947. A "declared price" was recorded in the registers of deeds for each parcel of land sold, based on the testimony of the parties to each transaction. Since they paid a transaction fee according to value, they had every reason to minimize the sale price. The Technical Office felt that since it would be hard to lie to an experienced registrar who anyway would be the final judge of what the "assessed price" of the land was, the prices listed in the registers of deeds probably reflected the actual price of the land in question. Where the "declared price" and the "assessed price" varied, the office adopted the higher figure.

Beyond these general guidelines, the office devised different strategies for valuing land. Urban lands constituted a particular challenge given the subtleties of price variation according to location in cities. The common criterion for all urban land was the "net annual value" (NAV) assigned by mandatory tax authorities. Under the Urban Property Tax Ordinance of 1928, the NAV for an urban building was the rent it could fetch less deductions for repairs. In valuating "buildings," what was meant was the value of the land and any buildings built on it. All NAVs were determined by assessment committees and reassessed every five years. However, the office determined that some NAVs were undervalued in 1947–48. A standard procedure for using an assessed tax value had been developed to arrive at the capital value for land. This was to multiply the NAV by a certain figure, called a multiplier, that was based on interest rates. The office modified this for the purposes of valuing buildings. It divided the sale prices of buildings it found listed in the registers of deeds and other documents by the NAV to arrive at a multiplier. It found that these figures tended to be very similar time after time. It then grouped property in brackets of £P25 and applied the same multiplier to all NAVs within the same bracket to arrive at capital values. Because some of the tax sheets for the town of Ramla were missing but the total tax was known, comparisons were made with nearby Lydda for valuation purposes. Since there were no tax records for Beersheba at all, nor were there any nearby towns for comparison, the office carried out two studies of urban land values for the town of Beersheba. It estimated the amount based on the capital value of smaller towns and dividing it by the tax payable. Secondly, the office created a mathematical formula based on the capital value of other towns and their populations, and applied the resulting figure to Beersheba town. For urban vacant lots without buildings, the NAV was six percent of the sale price were the land to be freely sold.

The procedure was different for valuating rural lands. The Rural Property Tax Ordinance established tax categories in April 1935 for all lands not subject to urban taxation except the Beersheba subdistrict. Land was classified into one of the sixteen tax categories by committees and reassessed periodically. The Technical Office valued rural land differently if it was cereal land, fruit land, or built-up land. In addition to using the mandatory tax categories, Technical Office staff also consulted a classification of soil qualities, rainfall, and topography that the mandatory government had prepared for the 1946 Anglo-American Commission of Enquiry. This study had classified rural land in Palestine into ten regional zones, which the office used in conjunction with the tax categories to determine parcels of similar value for each village. Once again the staff searched through mandatory records for evidence of land sales in each village, recording the amounts to create formulas that would help them determine general prices in the villages. Garden areas on the outskirts of towns used for planting gardens and whose value was higher because they potentially could be used for construction were valued separately based on sales records.

Village built-up areas presented a special problem. Since these buildings were not located in towns, they were not subject to the urban tax ordinance and thus no tax records were drawn up for them. Nor was land settlement applied in most village built-up areas. Nor were there very many sales of village houses, leaving a dearth of information about the value of rural houses and other buildings. The staff studied the mandatory village development survey maps of approximately fifty Palestinian villages. They measured the surface area of the built-up areas compared to that of the total village and found that this ratio was fairly uniform within each subdistrict. Beyond that, they devised a formula for estimating the value of houses based on the value of the land plus the cost of building materials. They decided upon a nation-wide figure of £P2 per square meter for rural buildings based on building costs, and multiplied this by an estimate of the number of estimated rooms in the village that was derived from mandatory population figures. To this was added a value for land equal to three times the corresponding value of garden areas in that village.

The Beersheba subdistrict presented problems for valuation just as it had for identification. Information on land sales was extracted from the registers of deeds which was plotted on maps of the region. This allowed the Technical Office to determine roughly what land prices were for the various parts of the large subdistrict. The staff faced an insurmountable problem dealing with grazing land in the area, though. Although it believed that there was indeed a value to this type of land, it could not find any sales data from which to make any estimates.

Table 5.6 indicates the values of rural land in each subdistrict, by tax category, that the Technical Office established and used in its valuation estimates. Since the office determined figures for individual villages, the chart shows the highest and lowest value that the office determined within each category. Table 2.5 lists Berncastle's 1951 valuation of land and for the explanation of what types of land were included within each tax category. It becomes clear that the land values that Jarvis developed were higher than those determined by Berncastle. Because the UNCCP tried to keep all valuation figures secret, the figures shown in table 5.6 are published here for the first time.

The final stage of the valuation process began in 1961, when the Technical Office began establishing a specific value for each individual R/P1 form. This involved taking the data on values in each subdistrict and village that had been painstakingly assembled as described above and applying it so that each individual parcel of Arab land was assigned a unique value. This was relatively simple for the urban areas given the presence of detailed tax figures for individual dwellings. For rural areas, the information described above was supplemented by resort to village cadastral maps in order for the office to get a sense of where in the village the various land sales for which it had data took place. This allowed them to be as detailed as possible in determining individual land values. Valuation figures were then written in red ink in the upper right hand corner of each R/P1 form, and appear as a whole number rounded to the

TABLE 5.6 Range of Values per Dunum (£P) for Rural Land in each Sub-District (by Tax Category) as Determined by UNCCP Technical Office

| | *Tax Categories* | | | | | |
|---|---|---|---|---|---|---|
| *Sub-District* | *1,2* | *3* | *5–8* | *9–13* | *14–15* | *16* |
| Acre | 50–127 | 40–75 | 28–110.8 | 12–35.1 | 12–18 | 11–22 |
| Baysan | 62–68 | 51–55 | 24.5–40 | 9.5–32 | 9–24 | 8.5–32 |
| Nazareth | 55–65 | — | 32–47 | 10–30 | 10–14 | 9–25 |
| Safad | 70–85 | — | 22–75 | 7.5–35 | 9–35 | 9–25 |
| Tiberias | 65–70 | 43–53 | 18.3–40 | 5–20.5 | 10–14.6 | 5–18 |
| Haifa | 70–74.3 | 52 | 21.4–60 | 10–41.7 | 10–25 | 9.5–23 |
| Janin | 60 | — | 30–45 | 10–25 | 10–16 | 9.5–24 |
| Nablus | — | — | 25 | 25 | 22 | 24 |
| Tulkarm | 55–151.4 | 48–108 | 16–82 | 10.3–82 | 22 | 10–43 |
| Hebron | 60 | — | 30–44 | 15–23 | 15–20 | 14–22 |
| Jerusalem | — | — | 33–110 | 18–65 | 17–65 | 17–65 |
| Ramallah | — | — | — | 20–24 | 24 | 19–23 |
| Jaffa | 102–165.3 | 70–125 | 58–140 | 41–127 | — | 59–100 |
| Ramla | 60–180 | 65–80 | 30–105 | 14.8–92 | 24–26 | 11–87 |
| Gaza | 50–123 | 49–72 | 22–60.9 | 15.7–51.5 | 15.7–30 | 15–33 |

Source: UNSA DAG 13–3, UNCCP. Subgroup: Principal Secretary. Series: Records Relating to the Technical Office/Box 16/1952–57/Land Identification Project/Jarvis Report; Document: A/AC.25/W.83, "Initial Report of the Commission's Land Expert on the Identification and Valuation of Arab Refugee Property Holdings in Israel" (September 15, 1961)

nearest Palestinian pound. The figure does not include a "£" sign nor is any other information listed to indicate what this figure means. This was no doubt done as a type of code to hide the meaning of what the figure means. Thus, a parcel of land that was determined to have a value of £P128 would simply have "128" written on the R/P1 form in red. This task was completed in 1962 after the office accelerated its work following a December 1961 General Assembly request that it hasten the project. The valuation figures later were added to an index of owners' names.

These UNCCP records are the most thorough reckoning of Palestinian Arab land ever produced by any quarter. They record the details of land ownership in hundreds of abandoned villages as well as in villages in Israel that remained inhabited. The following data on two refugee villages were taken from the relevant R/P1 forms to indicate the kind of macro-level information that can be derived from them (this stands apart from the obvious micro-level details the R/P1 forms show for individual parcels of land). The first village is 'Ayn Hawd, south of Haifa. This village was later renamed 'En Hod by the Israelis. The R/P1 forms contain information on 1,237 parcels of Arab-owned land there, totaling 5,825.744 dunums. The UNCCP Technical Program established a total value for this land at £P123,984, or £P21.280/dunum. Most of the land was cultivable cereal land: 3,974.274 dunums, or 71.7 percent of the total Arab land. However, this land was valued at £P65,514, and thus only constituted about one-half of the total value of land in the village. While comprising only one-fourth of the land (25.6 percent), the 1,439.780 dunums of land on which fruit trees had been planted was valued at £P45,745 (£P31.770/dunum) and thus constituted a much higher percentage of the total land value. The most valuable land of all lay in the 50 dunums of homes in the village's built-up area, where land was determined to be worth £P117.280/dunum. The value of 'Ayn Hawd's agricultural land in its various fiscal blocks ranged from £P11.950/dunum to £P32.000.[30]

The second village for which statistics have been collected here from the R/P1 forms is Khalisa, at the tip of the far northern panhandle of Palestine. It was renamed Kiryat Shmona by the Israelis. A careful study of the R/P1 forms reveals some problems with the data, which were gathered and collated in the pre-computerized era of the 1950s. Adding up total figures to arrive at a total number of parcels, for example, is difficult because of the presence of a number of uncategorized parcels of land in the records. These probably referred to land in the built-up portion of the village. The figure for the total surface area of Arab-owned parcels in Khalisa, including these uncategorized parcels, is 10,638.423 dunums spread throughout 658 parcels. It was thus a much larger village than 'Ayn Hawd although it contained only half as many parcels. The total value of this land was £P239,661 with the average value standing at £22.530/dunum. Most of the land—7,658.014 dunums or 71.98 percent—was cereal land, almost the exact percentage as in 'Ayn Hawd. But due to the relatively tiny amount of valuable fruit land that lay in Khalisa (240.184 dunums, or 2.26 percent of the total surface area, worth a total of £10,380 or £43.220/dunum), the value of this cereal land constituted a much higher percentage of the total land value in Khalisa. Cereal land was valued at £184,526 or £24.100/dunum, which constituted a full 76.99 percent of the total value of land in the village. The most valuable land in the village was land categorized as industrial land. The 151 parcels of this land totaled only 35.928 dunums but were valued at £3,607 or £100.400/dunum. The value of Khalisa's agricultural land in its various fiscal blocks was generally higher than for 'Ayn Hawd, and ranged from £P14.640/dunum to £P59.890.[31]

## Final Statistics on Scope and Value of Arab Property

By September 1960, Jarvis was in a position to report on the total scope and value of all refugee holdings in Israel based on the R/P1 forms. As mentioned, the Technical Office actually produced figures on the total scope and value of *all* Arab-owned property in Israel without reference to what was owned by Palestinian refugees, Palestinians who were still resident in Israel, and non-Palestinian Arabs. Not including Beersheba, this totaled 7,874,419 dunums, for which R/P1 forms were completed for 5,194,091 dunums. The figures for the Beersheba district were less precise, and the Technical Office published figures both on the scope of what it thought was Arab-owned land in Beersheba (12,445,000 dunums) and the (smaller) scope of land for which it prepared R/P1 forms detailing individually owned Arab property (64,000 dunums). This information, shown in table 5.7, later was released publicly.

Jarvis' office also estimated how much land was probably not refugee land but rather land still owned by Arabs living in Israel. The total of this rough estimate came to 1,012,059 dunums. The UNCCP never published this figure, which is presented here for the first time, as shown in tables 5.8 and 5.9. Therefore, the UNCCP Technical Office assumed that 4,246,032 dunums of the individually owned Arab land for which it created R/P1 forms probably belonged to refugees. It is difficult to determine what amount of the additional 1,811,000 dunums of land in Beersheba that the office assumed was also Arab owned should be excluded, since the office could not do this accurately.

By the fall of 1962, the Technical Office was able to determine the cumulative value of Arab-owned land in Israel. It tried to keep these figures secret and never published them for reasons discussed below. They are presented here for the first time, in tables 5.10–5.12.

Thus the total value of Arab land in Israel as of November 29, 1947 according to the individual assessment came to £P235,660,250. Jarvis estimated that the value of land still owned by Palestinians in Israel would approach £P31 million, which if subtracted would leave a grand total of £P204,660,190 in land belonging to refugees and other Arabs who fled. This figure was 1.75 percent higher than the initial estimate of £P197.1 million in refugee land that he had developed in 1961 before he had assigned a value to each R/P1 form.[32] It was also double what Berncastle's 1951 global estimate had been (£P100,383,784).

The Technical Office also developed estimates of the value of other types of property besides land. Jarvis studied several methods for estimating the

TABLE 5.7 Scope of All Rural and Urban Arab Land in Israel According to UNCCP Individual Assessment, 1952–1962

| *Sub-District* | *Total Area (Dunums)* | *Covered by R/P1 Forms (Dunums)* |
|---|---|---|
| 1. Excluding Beersheba | | |
| Acre | 795,357 | 507,707 |
| Baysan | 366,095 | 147,167 |
| Nazareth | 490,942 | 248,345 |
| Safad | 696,859 | 347,710 |
| Tiberias | 439,031 | 194,439 |
| Haifa | 972,312 | 405,580 |
| Janin | 257,212 | 228,407 |
| Nablus | 23,414 | 23,414 |
| Tulkarm | 503,676 | 332,571 |
| Hebron | 1,162,336 | 1,144,808 |
| Jerusalem | 296,943 | 221,482 |
| Ramallah | 6,240 | 6,240 |
| Jaffa | 285,084 | 140,425 |
| Ramla | 763,481 | 569,813 |
| Gaza | 815,437 | 675,983 |
| TOTAL | 7,874,419 | 5,194,091 |
| 2. Beersheba* | 12,445,000 | 64,000 |
| GRAND TOTAL | 20,319,419 | 5,258,091 |
| FINAL GRAND TOTAL** | | 7,069,091 |

* R/P1 forms were not drawn up for an additional 1,811,000 dunums of cultivable land in the Beersheba sub-district that were assumed to be cultivated by bedouin Arabs

** adding the 1,811,000 dunums of land in Beersheba assumed to be cultivated by bedouin Arabs but for which no R/P1 forms were drawn up

Source: UN Document A/AC.25/W.84, "Working Paper Prepared by the Commission's Land Expert on the Methods and Techniques of Identification and Valuation of Arab Refugee immoveable Property Holdings in Israel" (April 28, 1964)

value of moveable property as well. He ended up using the same three methods that Berncastle had used in 1951, but once again came up with three different figures. Unlike Berncastle's 1951 effort, though, Jarvis' figures never were made public and are presented here for the first time. His first method was to base the value of moveables on the value of the rural land. Using 4.7

TABLE 5.8 Estimated Scope of Land Owned by Arabs Still Living in Israel According to UNCCP Individual Assessment, 1952–1962

| *Sub-District* | *Amount (Dunums)* |
|---|---|
| Acre | 318,714 |
| Baysan | 9,390 |
| Nazareth | 190,182 |
| Safad | 30,222 |
| Tiberias | 50,323 |
| Haifa | 170,238 |
| Janin | 86,554 |
| Nablus | 0 |
| Tulkarm | 140,231 |
| Hebron | 7,649 |
| Jerusalem | 3,186 |
| Ramallah | 0 |
| Jaffa | 40 |
| Ramla | 5,320 |
| Gaza | 0 |
| TOTAL | 1,012,059 |

Source: UNSA DAG 13–3, UNCCP. Subgroup: Principal Secretary. Series: Records Relating to the Technical Office/Box 16/1952–57/Land Identification Project/Jarvis Report; Document: A/AC.25/W.83, "Initial Report of the Commission's Land Expert on the Identification and Valuation of Arab Refugee Property Holdings in Israel" (September 15, 1961)

percent as the basis of his calculations, Jarvis came up with a rough estimate of £P5,678,000 excluding the Beersheba subdistrict. He then added to this 60.9 percent of the value of urban land and arrived at approximately £P36,418,000. The total figure was then £P42,069,000 (excluding Beersheba). Jarvis' second method was to determine the value of immoveables as

TABLE 5.9 Scope of Rural and Urban Refugee Land in Israel According to UNCCP Individual Assessment, 1952–1962

| *All Arab Land in Israel (Dunums) (on R/P1 Forms)* | *Land Owned by Palestinians Still Living in Israel (Dunums)* | *Land Owned by Refugees (on R/P1 Forms)* |
|---|---|---|
| 5,258,091 | 1,012,059 | 4,246,032 |

TABLE 5.10 Value of All Rural Arab Land in Israel According to UNCCP Individual Assessment, 1952–1962

| *Sub-District* | *Value (£P)* |
|---|---|
| Acre | 15,051,225 |
| Baysan | 3,464,834 |
| Nazareth | 5,595,879 |
| Safad | 7,323,092 |
| Tiberias | 3,805,192 |
| Haifa | 11,757,629 |
| Janin | 4,357,696 |
| Nablus | 540,660 |
| Tulkarm | 11,987,299 |
| Hebron | 12,443,989 |
| Jerusalem | 10,598,408 |
| Ramallah | 135,150 |
| Jaffa | 23,560,057 |
| Ramla | 22,190,429 |
| Gaza | 19,579,534 |
| Beersheba | 15,000,000 |
| TOTAL | 167,395,073 |

Source: UNSA DAG 13–3, UNCCP. Subgroup: Principal Secretary. Series: Records Relating to the Technical Office/Box 16/1952–57/Land Identification Project/Jarvis Report; Document: A/AC.25/W.83 ADD 1, "Initial Report of the Commission's Land Expert on the Identification and Valuation of Arab Refugee Property Holdings in Israel" (September 10, 1962)

a percentage of the Arab share of the national income of Palestine. He came up with £70 million as "a reasoned guess" for the total Arab share of the national income using this method. Assuming that 700,000 out of 1,124,000 non-Jews became refugees, this left a total of £17.4 million in immoveables. The third method was to base the value of immoveables on the ownership of capital. Here Jarvis did have mandatory data on ownership of industrial equipment, etc. He came up with a total figure of £P30.6 million for the Arab sector of pre-1948 Palestine as follows: industrial equipment (£4 million); commercial stock (£5.5 million); vehicles (£2 million); agricultural livestock (£13.1 million); and household furniture (£6 million). Again deducting a percentage to represent the refugees only left him with a figure of £P19,125,000

TABLE 5.11 Value of All Urban Arab Land in Israel According to UNCCP Individual Assessment, 1952–1962

| *Area* | *Vacant Lots (£P)* | *Buildings (£)* | *Total (£P)* |
|---|---|---|---|
| Acre | 423,542 | 919,385 | 1,342,927 |
| ʻAfula | 984 | 0 | 984 |
| Bat Yam | 1,683 | 0 | 1,683 |
| Baysan | 53,691 | 457,186 | 510,877 |
| Haifa | 4,311,086 | 10,467,644 | 14,778,730 |
| Holon | 123,441 | 890 | 124,331 |
| Jaffa | 7,559, 740 | 14,094,203 | 21,653,943 |
| Jerusalem | 6,371,160 | 12,062,701 | 18,433,861 |
| Lydda | 438,690 | 1,403,399 | 1,842,089 |
| al-Majdal | 94,960 | 728,976 | 823,936 |
| Natanya | 0 | 36,497 | |
| Nazareth | 219,907 | 1,412,635 | 1,632,542 |
| Ramat Gan | 71,447 | 0 | 71,447 |
| Safad | 157,354 | 84 | 98,029 |
| Shafa' ʻAmr | 52,814 | 284,330 | 337,144 |
| Tel Aviv | 2,366,740 | 134,020 | 2,500,760 |
| Tiberias | 201,253 | 524,084 | 725,337 |
| * Beersheba (estimate) | | | 600,000 |
| * Ramla (estimate) | | | 1,850,000 |
| TOTAL | | | 68,265,177 |

Source: UNSA DAG 13–3, UNCCP. Subgroup: Principal Secretary. Series: Records Relating to the Technical Office/Box 16/1952–57/Land Identification Project/Jarvis Report; Document: A/AC.25/W.83 ADD 1, “Initial Report of the Commission's Land Expert on the Identification and Valuation of Arab Refugee Property Holdings in Israel” (September 10, 1962)

in refugee immoveables. The three different methods then produced figures of £42,069,000, £17,400,000, and £19,125,000.[33] Berncastle's corresponding figures from 1951 were £21,570,000; £18,600,000; and £19,100,000. The two men generally agreed on the last two figures; only in the first did they differ, because Jarvis' estimate of the refugee land's value was twice that of Berncastle's.

Jarvis conducted several other noteworthy studies which were never made public either. In one he estimated the value of *communally owned* Arab land

TABLE 5.12 Value of Rural and Urban Refugee Land in Israel According to UNCCP Individual Assessment, 1952–1962

| *All Arab Land in Israel (£P)* | *Land Owned by Palestinians Still Living in Israel (£P)* | *Land Owned by Refugees (£P)* |
|---|---|---|
| 235,660,250 | 31,000,000 | 204,660,190 |

Source: UNSA DAG 13–3, UNCCP. Subgroup: Principal Secretary. Series: Records Relating to the Technical Office/Box 16/1952–57/Land Identification Project/Jarvis Report; Document: A/AC.25/W.83 ADD 1, "Initial Report of the Commission's Land Expert on the Identification and Valuation of Arab Refugee Property Holdings in Israel" (September 10, 1962)

as well as an estimate of the proportion of refugees who were landowners. This first issue later would constitute a major Arab complaint against the UNCCP's various studies of refugee land: They did not publicly study the value of abandoned communal property. Jarvis in fact did study this, and compensation for it did feature into the UNCCP's unpublished plan for compensation. Jarvis estimated this land to be worth approximately $US56 million, although this rough figure was never published. As an internal 1962 UNCCP document noted, "For the purposes of an estimate a figure of 56 million dollars has been suggested but it is emphasized that this figure has no basis in valuation."[34] In September 1965, Jarvis issued to the UNCCP the results of a second study he had made detailing the ratio between landowners and non-landowning refugees. He based his research on 434 randomly selected rural villages not located near urban centers. Jarvis used 1945 mandatory population figures as a baseline figure and then added 6 percent to account for population growth since then. He thus determined that 133,495 out of 306,103 persons living in those 434 villages—43.6 percent—owned property. Basing himself on November 29, 1947 land values, he developed the following statistics (see table 5.13) showing the number of landowners according to the value of their total holdings. These figures likewise were never released. Jarvis also estimated that that 348,300 of 904,000—39.6 percent—of refugees registered with UNRWA had owned land in Palestine. He also felt that the percentage of the total refugee population that owned land but were not registered UNRWA refugees stood at 1.5 percent.[35]

As a final step, Jarvis' office compiled an index of Arab landowners starting in 1963. Because the R/P1 forms were organized by village and block, it was

TABLE 5.13 UNCCP Study of Arab Landowners in 434 Villages in Israel by Value of Holdings, 1965

| *Value of Holdings (£P)* | *Owners (N)* | *Owners %* | *% Total Value of Land* |
|---|---|---|---|
| 1–100 | 58,808 | 44.0 | 2.9 |
| 101–200 | 20,423 | 15.3 | 4.1 |
| 201–300 | 11,390 | 8.5 | 4.2 |
| 301–400 | 7,924 | 5.9 | 4.6 |
| 401–500 | 5,592 | 4.2 | 4.2 |
| 501–600 | 4,416 | 3.3 | 4.5 |
| 601–700 | 3,473 | 2.6 | 4.5 |
| 701–800 | 2,715 | 2.0 | 4.3 |
| 801–900 | 2,250 | 1.7 | 3.8 |
| 901–1000 | 1,932 | 1.4 | 4.0 |
| 1001–1300 | 3,935 | 2.9 | 8.9 |
| 1301–1600 | 2,648 | 2.0 | 6.0 |
| 1601–2000 | 2,335 | 1.7 | 6.3 |
| 2001–2500 | 1,764 | 1.3 | 5.9 |
| 2501–3000 | 1,108 | 0.8 | 4.4 |
| 3001– | 2,861 | 2.1 | 27.5 |

Source: UNSA DAG 13–3, UNCCP. Subgroup: Principal Secretary. Series: Records Relating to the Technical Office/Box 17/General Programme; Document: "An Analysis of Property Owners compared with Population and the Amount of Property in Various Categories of Value" (September 1, 1965)

extremely difficult to determine the landholdings of any particular individual when using them. The UNCCP therefore authorized Jarvis to develop an index of owners for ready identification of specific persons' land holdings. The Technical Office staff then prepared approximately 220,000 index cards listing the property holdings, with block and parcel number, of each individual landowner in each village. The cards also indicated the value of the holdings. The cards were arranged by village, with the owners appearing in alphabetical order. Since a person could own land in more than one village, the cumulative number of names appearing in the index cards was larger than the actual number of Arab landowners in Palestine. The office experienced considerable difficulties with the fact that land and tax documents transliterated Arabic names in a variety of different ways.

Jarvis wrote a detailed report of the Technical Office's efforts in 1963. In a marked departure from the policy that had been adopted for publishing

Berncastle's 1951 global estimates on value—and in fact, because of that experience—the UNCCP decided against publishing Jarvis' valuation figures. Only the Technical Office's estimate of the *scope* of Arab-owned land in Israel, and not its *value*, publicly was released in 1964 along with a detailed description of how the office went about the entire identification and valuation program. As noted above, the Technical Office always had been concerned about the program being ruined by leaked information about land values that would cause an uproar, particularly among the Arabs.

Even the decision to publish this sanitized report came after considerable debate. As the program neared completion, the UNCCP decided in early October 1961 to keep the valuation figures secret and not publish the abbreviated report of the program that Jarvis was writing. The reason for the second decision was that Jarvis had stated that publishing an abbreviated report without such figures would be meaningless. Thus the UNCCP opted for no public report at all. However, just weeks before, it did authorize Jarvis to show his report to Berncastle in Britain to get his opinions. In addition, the United States changed its mind and also called for keeping the figures secret. In so doing it was deferring to UNCCP Special Representative Joseph Johnson's recommendations that the figures remain secret (see chapter 6).[36]

Once Jarvis had prepared the text for a final report to be made public in early 1964, the United States apparently changed its mind again. It argued that publishing the values would help the UNCCP avoid charges of "concealment." The Americans also stated that representatives of interested parties should be allowed to examine the index cards of owners. Jarvis protested, noting among other things that consultation of the index cards without "explanatory information" would be meaningless. Impressed with Jarvis' points, the Americans changed their minds yet again and advocated keeping the land values secret. In any event, they noted, the total amount by itself would be too low without adding to it figures for moveables, accrued interest, etc.[37]

Although the UNCCP decided against publishing Jarvis' estimate of land values, it remained divided over when to release the public part of Jarvis' report. The commission's annual reports to the UN Secretary-General always had been carefully worded so as not to prompt an official rejection of the identification and valuation project from any of the parties to the conflict—particularly the Arabs. American representatives to the UNCCP also worked to delete certain passages from Jarvis' report itself that the United States feared would elicit objections from Israel. Even though Jarvis' report was basically ready in 1963, the UNCCP deferred issuing it to "avoid further exacerbating debate in [the] G[eneral] A[ssembly]."[38]

When Jarvis was completely finished with the last details of the report in February 1964 the UNCCP decided to issue the sanitized Technical Report on April 30, 1964. However, the Americans again urged a last-minute delay. The reason: Israel had asked them for the delay because Prime Minister Levi Eshkol was due to visit the United States in June—the first official visit to the United States ever by a sitting Israeli prime minister. On April 29, 1964, an Israeli official approached the Department of State and asked that the United States use its influence in the UNCCP to postpone publication of the Technical Report in order to forestall a negative Arab response that could mar Eshkol's visit. The State Department agreed to try. While the French representative on the UNCCP was sympathetic, he urged that the delay not be any longer than it needed to be. However, the Turkish chair of the commission, Vahap Asiroglu, was "very negative." He felt that the Americans already had ensured that the report "leaned too far towards respecting possible Israeli sensitivities" and worried that the Arabs would think that postponing issuing the report was because of Eshkol's visit—which of course, was true. Asiroglu commented that Turkey already was viewed negatively by the Arabs for failing to stand up to the pro-Israeli views of the United States and France. Still, he went along with the American request.[39] The UNCCP finally announced the end of the Technical Office's program on May 11, 1964 in its 22nd annual report. The Technical Report itself was published on May 13. Thus marked the close of the most far-reaching program under undertaken by the UNCCP, as well as its last.

## CHAPTER SIX

# FOLLOW UP TO THE TECHNICAL PROGRAM

As the Technical Program was winding down, the UNCCP undertook one final attempt at creating movement on the compensation question by dispatching the Johnson Mission to the Middle East in 1961. Although this appeared to mark a revived interest in compensation on the part of the UNCCP, the mission was in fact largely an *American* initiative. The mission's origins lay in the fact that UN General Assembly Resolution 1604 (XV) of April 21, 1961 again requested that the UNCCP do something practical to bring about compensation and report back to the General Assembly on its progress by October 15 of that year. The U.S. Department of State informed the new president, John F. Kennedy, that something now needed to be done for the refugees in light of this and the ongoing Arab diplomatic offensive in the General Assembly. It also notified Kennedy that the upcoming discussion of the UNCCP's annual report in the fall of 1961 was likely to be negative. Finally, the department told Kennedy that the U.S. Congress was unlikely to contribute more to UNRWA, so some other plan was needed to assist the refugees. As a result, Kennedy dispatched letters to the leaders of Egypt, Jordan, Syria, Lebanon, and Iraq in May notifying them of the continued U.S. commitment to solving the refugee problem as well of his intention to persuade all parties to work with any new UNCCP initiative on the refugees.[1]The Kennedy administration also pushed the UNCCP to send a "special representative" to the Middle East in the early fall of 1961 to see what progress could be made on the compensation question. The UNCCP initially selected the Swiss ambassador to the United States, August R. Lindt, but he delayed giving an answer because the Iraqi-Kuwaiti crisis of 1961 kept him preoccupied. Eventually the UNCCP selected an American, Joseph E. Johnson.

## Johnson Mission

Dr. Joseph Esrey Johnson was born in 1906 and possessed both an academic and diplomatic background. After completing his B.A., M.A., and Ph.D. studies at Harvard, Johnson taught at Williams College before joining the Department of State in 1942. During his service as a diplomat, he was a delegate to the Dumbarton Oaks Conference of 1944 and the first meeting of the UN in San Francisco in 1945. After briefly returning to teach at Williams in 1947, Johnson agreed to serve as president of The Carnegie Endowment for International Peace in 1950. He was appointed the UNCCP's "Special Representative" on August 21, 1961 and charged with exploring what practical steps could be taken to effect compensation for the Palestinian refugees. When U.S. Secretary of State Dean Rusk told him that his prospects for success were not good, Johnson quipped that he was not at that time applying for a Nobel peace prize. Two days later, Rusk summed up his low expectations of Johnson's mission when he told American diplomats in Cairo that "only a most modest low-key consultation with the Near East governments directly concerned with [the] refugee problem is envisaged at this point to let them set forth their views."[2]

Johnson traveled to the Middle East in September 1961 to conduct his mission, the first of two trips he would take. While in Israel he met with Prime Minister David Ben Gurion. The Israelis were not at all disposed to Johnson's mission nor talk of compensation at that moment and his meeting with Ben Gurion was tense. The Israeli became so "harsh" with him that Johnson actually contemplated storming out of the meeting. Ben Gurion later sent him an uncharacteristic letter of apology.[3] He later experienced trouble with the Arabs as well. A delegation representing Palestinian refugees called on him. The group consisted of Izzat Tannous, Emile Ghoury, Issa Nakhleh, and 'Umar 'Azzuni, and bore a letter from the Arab Higher Committee signed by the aging Palestinian leader al-Hajj Amin al-Husayni authorizing them to represent the Palestinians before the UN General Assembly's Special Political Committee. Johnson refused to see the delegation and dismissed their claim officially to have represented the Palestinians at the UN. He said that they had addressed the Special Political Committee as individuals and not in an official category. Since he was only visiting with officials, he would not agree to sit with them. In this he appeared to reflect official U.S. government policy.[4] After returning to the United States and submitting his report on November 24, 1961, Johnson was later reappointed on March 2, 1962 and made a second trip to the region in April and May of 1962. He wrote his second report on August 31, 1962.

Johnson's ambitious and controversial plan for compensating the Palestinian refugees that was rejected by Israel with such force that the Johnson mission was doomed to failure. Johnson based his plan on General Assembly Resolution 1604 (XV) of April 21, 1961 that had called on the UNCCP to take steps to implement paragraph 11 of Resolution 194 (III) regarding compensation. Johnson outlined his views on compensation to U.S. diplomats on September 29, 1961:

> Compensation of refugees, per se, constitutes no problem in the minds of people of the area, either Israeli or Arab, since they are convinced the U.S. will foot the bill. It is equally clear that compensation is not enough. It will help only a very small number of the refugees. Something will have to be done for the others to make them feel that they are being "compensated" and that they are receiving something with which to make a new start.[5]

He submitted his plan in its final form on July 27, 1962. In essence it provided for giving refugees a choice, via a questionnaire, whether they wished to be repatriated or to receive compensation. The Americans felt that perhaps ten percent of the refugees would request repatriation.[6] The UN would establish a fund to collect contributions, which would be paid to individual refugees as compensation and in the form of a "re-integration allowance." The total cost of compensation would be based on the value of abandoned land, immoveables, public property, plus a variety of allowances. Beyond that, Israel would need to allow some refugees to be repatriated and compensate them for their losses as well.

Johnson's plan revolved around his definition of compensation, its bases, and how it would be paid. He understood "compensation" as the amount of money required to place a refugee in a similar financial situation as if s/he had not lost property. Thus Johnson included the loss of livelihood in his definition of compensation, not merely property. Specifically, he wrote of six bases of compensation. The first was the value of land, in 1947–48 terms, "when he [the refugee] departed his home." This figure was set out in the UNCCP Technical Office's first secret estimate of 1961, some £P195.6 million (Jarvis later raised this value; see chapter 5). Second, Johnson included the value of abandoned moveable property as well. He once again took Jarvis' secret 1961 estimate, which at £P30 million was the average of the three different figures he arrived at. Whereas individual refugees would be compensated for the loss of their own land, the projected UN agency that would oversee compensation would distribute the compensation for moveable property as it would see fit. Third, Johnson's plan called for a monetary payment as an adjustment for the loss of interest on a refugee's property. He suggested that a full 50 percent be added to the value of the abandoned property to account for this, or £112.8 million. Fourth, he proposed adding a second adjustment to account for the depreciation in currency. Johnson estimated that this value had declined by

20 percent between 1948–62, so he added £P45,120,000. Fifth, he called for compensation for the loss of mandatory public property plus the adjustments for lost interest and currency depreciation. Here, Johnson did not have access to UNCCP values for the Palestinians' share of public property formerly belonging to the mandatory government—police stations, schools, transportation services, and the like—and so developed his own estimate of £P20 million. This amount would not be paid to the refugees, however, but to the host governments in the countries where they now lived. Finally, he added another component to his scheme that departed from the concept of compensation only representing lost property. Johnson recommended providing $250 as a "re-integration" allowance for all refugees whether or not they owned property in Palestine. The cumulative total would be £P87 million. *En toto*, Johnson estimated that compensation would require the equivalent of some $1,377,456,000.[7]

Johnson's ideas about the modalities of payment were as follows. Governments and private contributors would pay into a fund established by the UN General Assembly. He assumed that Israel would pay into this as well: "As the property for which compensation will be paid is now in Israel, it is assumed that Israel will make a substantial contribution."[8] The fund then would make payments to individual refugees, although the host governments in the countries where they were living could determine how this would be spent. The host governments themselves would receive the compensation for the public property in proportion to the number of refugees they harbored. These funds would be used to assist in resettling the refugees. He stated that the refugees should be allowed to choose repatriation or compensation but that Israel should compensate the repatriated refugees as well. Johnson expected that Israel itself, and not the UN fund, would pay compensation for seized property although "[i]t is hoped . . . that UN members [and] members of UN special agencies, will help." In order to establish themselves anew in Israel, Johnson also believed that the refugees should be allowed to buy other nonreturning refugees' property. Since he worried that Israel would not deal "fairly" with the returnees, Johnson recommended that the United States ask for an Israeli "modification" of its laws.[9] After his first trip to the Middle East, Johnson estimated that solving the refugee problem would take 10–15 years.

Johnson delivered his plan on September 10, 1962 at separate meetings in New York with the Israeli and Arab delegations to the UN. All parties were disturbed by elements of his plan. The Arabs were skeptical. Jordan earlier had sent a memorandum to the other Arab states in May 1962 following Johnson's second trip. This document, which was published in the Arab press, accused

Johnson of trying to get the refugees to "sell" their country.[10] President Kennedy then tried to help Johnson by writing a secret letter to King Hussein that was delivered on September 15, 1962. In the letter, Kennedy asked for Hussein's help in supporting the Johnson Mission's initiative. Four days later, the U.S. embassy in Amman reported to Washington that the Jordanian cabinet had decided not to oppose the Johnson plan after all and would even work to convince the other Arabs to give it a chance "for tactical reasons." However, the Jordanians noted that if the other Arabs rejected the plan, Jordan would be obliged to go along.[11]

For their part the Israelis were positively apoplectic about the Johnson plan. According to American diplomats, they reacted "violently" after Johnson's meeting with Israel's UN ambassador Michael Comay and thereafter launched a furious counterattack against him. What galled them the most among a variety of issues they opposed in Johnson's plan was his call for allowing the refugees the right to choose compensation or repatriation without allowing Israel to establish a limit on the total number of returnees.[12] While the Arabs always had continued to call for the Palestinians' right of return, no serious talk of repatriation had surfaced since the Suez War. The entire focus, and passive at that, had been on property. Now it was not the Arabs but an American in the service of the UNCCP who was reviving the call for Israel to repatriate some of the refugees, compensate them, and then help pay to compensate the rest who were not returning.

Israel's fierce diplomatic offensive against Johnson soon began. Details of Johnson's plan were leaked to the American press, presumably by the Israelis, and publicized. In September 1962, the American embassy in London passed along information that Golda Meir was about to inform Rusk that Johnson's plan was "totally unacceptable" to Israel. In particular, Israel objected to the fact that the number of refugees to be repatriated was open-ended. They also reacted negatively to two other of Johnson's ideas. The first was that any refugee refused repatriation by Israel for security reasons could appeal Israel's decision to an independent commission. Second, they opposed Johnson's proposal to allow refugees to change their minds; that is, those who elected for resettlement in the Arab countries later could decide that they wanted to be repatriated to Israel.[13] Although they pointedly refused to meet with Johnson, Israeli diplomats later met with officials of the Department of State in Washington on October 12, 1962 to lodge their protest over the plan. The meeting occurred only four days before the start of the Cuban missile crisis. On November 21, 1962, the day that Kennedy lifted the naval quarantine on Cuba, Meir told Rusk flatly that Israel rejected the Johnson plan and would not cooperate in any resettlement plans unless the Arabs agreed in advance to resettle at least 90 percent of the refugees. Additionally, Israel refused any talk of allowing the refugees to state their own preference about repatriation versus resettlement.[14]

Lastly, Johnson's plan thus presented his own government with some serious challenges. Even though they had initiated the idea for the Johnson Mission and had picked their fellow countryman to head it, the Americans were surprised to see Johnson cross several of their long-standing red lines on the compensation question. The fact that these suggestions had come from a highly respected American serving in the capacity as Special Representative of the UNCCP—a body whose policies toward Israel largely had been shaped by the Americans to avoid angering the Israelis as much as possible—came as an additional surprise. As they were made aware of the details of his forthcoming plan, American policymakers began noting the various ways that their fellow American was suggesting that the UNCCP cross U.S. red lines. In July 1962 the State Department noted that its "longstanding views" were that only those refugees who were resettled in Arab countries should receive compensation, not those who were repatriated as well. What happened to these persons was up to Israel. The Americans also had noted in April 1962 that the U.S. position "always" had been that compensation should not be paid for moveable property but only for land, along with the proper adjustments for the depreciation of currency since 1948.[15]

While disagreeing with these aspects of the Johnson plan U.S. officials did accept his overall estimates on the cost of compensation and urged that the administration accept this amount. An internal State Department document stated that Israel should pay the value of the refugees' land itself, some $560 million according to the document, as its basic contribution to the compensation scheme. The other $900 million needed for the total compensation package would come from a variety of sources. The United States might contribute half of the amount while other nations like the United Kingdom and West Germany would pick up the remainder. For budgetary purposes, the document estimated that the American contribution in calendar year 1963 would be $100 million. Beyond the value of the abandoned land, the document stated that Israel also should pay a certain percentage of the total compensation package above the value of the land. Any amount that Israel chose to pay as compensation to repatriated refugees could be deducted from the $560 million.[16]

In the end the Kennedy administration buckled under the ferocious Israeli campaign against the Johnson Mission. It certainly had other things to worry about given the fact that the United States and the USSR nearly came to nuclear blows over Cuba. When Meir met with Kennedy in November 1962, the president already had decided to cut his losses and back away from Johnson. Kennedy told Meir "that's gone" when referring to Johnson's plan.[17]

Stung by the hostile media campaign in the United States instigated by Israel and bereft of support from the Kennedy administration, Johnson decided to resign. He announced his resignation at a meeting of the UNCCP in New York on January 31, 1963 and diplomatically cited "compelling personal commitments" as the reason. His final comments to the UNCCP were delivered in a "friendly if emotional way" and revealed the depth of his frustration and bitterness toward both the Israelis and his own government for its refusal to support him. An American diplomat present at the meeting described Johnson's comments thus: in a "rambling discussion, Johnson revealed [the] intensity of his bitterness at American Jewish leaders ("many of whom [were] incorrectly informed by [the] Israelis about my proposals") who have continued successfully [to] frustrate attempts [to] reach [a] compromise solution."[18]

He also complained that the U.S. government had failed to support him when Israeli officials had pointedly refused to meet with him during their trip to the United States in the fall of 1962. Finally, Johnson told the UNCCP that he had marked his report "confidential" and hoped it would remain that way. The UNCCP agreed that his report and its controversial plan would not be published at that time, although the UNCCP noted that someday it hopefully could become "part of [the] public record." The American delegation eventually placed a copy of the report in the American archives, which is now publicly available following its declassification by the Department of State. One final order of business for Johnson was an invitation to call on Pres. Kennedy on February 6. The State Department prepared a brief for the president before the meeting that recommended both Johnson and the White House respond to media questions about Johnson's resignation by noting that Kennedy "greatly valued" Johnson's efforts. Responses to the media should also note that Johnson "had informed the Palestine Conciliation Commission many months ago that personal plans and other commitments...would oblige him to resign as Special Representative in February 1963." The brief concluded with the words, "We believe it would be an appropriate gesture were Dr. Johnson to be photographed in the President's company."[19] With that, Johnson departed and his ambitious proposals died, a testament to the power of American influence over the refugee property issue.[20]

## The UNCCP's New Plan for Compensation Fails

In one respect the Johnson Mission was not a failure. Based on Johnson's recommendations and the extensive figures on value that he had assembled, Frank Jarvis also developed a far-reaching plan for compensation that he presented to the UNCCP. Like Johnson's plan before him, Jarvis' far exceeded what U.S. officials in particular were willing to support. To his frustration, Jarvis' plan never led to the onset of compensation and the UNCCP never made Jarvis' plan public. Its details are presented here for the first time.

Starting in about 1961, Jarvis began formulating a number of ideas that he hoped would be implemented someday by some type of "UN Repatriation/Compensation Agency." He met with Johnson on March 12, 1962 along with UNCCP Principal Secretary John P. Gaillard and UNRWA official Sherwood G. Moe. The men discussed five types of payment that would be made as part of an overall compensation settlement. The first was compensation for the abandoned refugee land. In addition to the 1947 capital value of the land, Jarvis proposed adding an additional 70 percent of this value. Of this, 50 percent would account for a 4 percent per annum compound interest on the sum while the other 20 percent would account for changes in the value of currency. The second type of payment would be to cover the value of moveable property, plus an additional amount to cover interest and changes in currency as noted above. Third, they discussed paying a "disturbance allowance" that would represent the loss of a refugee's income until s/he could be reestablished. The fourth type of payment was an "ex-gratia" payment of between $500–1,000 that would constitute a general compensation for hardship. The same amount would be paid to all refugees, and was designed to help with resettlement.

Finally was the "reintegration cost," which would be $2,500 per family. The four men could not agree on this point. The reintegration cost would not actually be paid to each family but was instead more of a notional payment. It represented a cumulative amount for all types of compensation. The first four types of payments then would be deducted from the total amount of the reintegration cost (the total number of refugee families multiplied by $2,500). Any funds remaining either could be directed toward the refugees or the host governments. They also agreed that they had overlooked the question of compensation for public property. The four thought that perhaps this could form the basis of the $2,500/family reintegration cost.[21]

Jarvis later developed his ideas. He definitely felt that interest should be paid on the abandoned land and added to its value. Jarvis conceded that this amount would be subject to a political decision but that the principle remained nonetheless. He also insisted that the refugees be compensated for their share of mandatory police structures, schools, public transit, and other forms of public property. He noted that such things "are an essential requisite of any community and their loss has to be made good wherever the refugees are resettled other than in their country of origin." Jarvis thought that perhaps a lump sum could be paid to the host countries to cover this amount. Jarvis also remained committed to a "disturbance allowance" as a way of assisting the refugees in resettlement. Overall, he envisioned a grand compensation scheme working like this. Compensation would be paid for property, but only to nonrepatriated refugees. "Damages," on the other hand, were a different matter and could be sought by anyone, including non-Palestinians. Jarvis included moveables in his definition of "property." He admitted that compensation should be based on more than just the value of abandoned property in order to facilitate wide-scale resettlement. But compensation should "express the payment as a contribution designed to recompense the recipient, as far as is possible, for the loss which he has suffered."

Should the amount of compensation be subject to negotiation? Here Jarvis conceded that in the case of international contributors to a fund that the answer would be yes. However, he believed that it would not be difficult to convince them that the amount in question was "reasonable." When it came to negotiations with the refugees, he noted that "It is a natural characteristic of the Arab to try to drive a bargain." He also believed that not much would be gained from negotiations with individuals, unless an arbitration tribunal were created, because they inevitably would remember their property as being more valuable than the figures established by the UNCCP. Should payments be made in cash to individual refugees? On this question, Jarvis wanted to avoid having refugees invest money in advanced economies outside of the Middle East, just as he wanted to avoid the inflationary effects of a sudden, massive influx of capital into the area. His solution was that perhaps compensation payments could be made with some type of UN bond.

Finally, Jarvis also was willing to incorporate the Arabs' argument that a property custodian could secure the income from the refugees' property into his plan. He wrote a memorandum to the UNCCP on November 24, 1961 in which he discussed his idea for connecting a compensation fund with UNRWA's need for operating funds. Jarvis' idea was that the interest earned on the sums contributed to a compensation fund could be siphoned off and directed to UNRWA. This would help meet the Arab demand that the income from the refugees' property in Israel be used to their advantage.[22]

In total, Jarvis' secret plan to pay compensation based on the value of land, moveable property, interest, and so forth, totaled some £P400 million, or $1,125,000,000 compared to Johnson's $1,377,456,000.[23] Word of the various general figures being talked about began to leak out, and some people with UN connections began talking of $US1.5 billion in compensation while other figures were between two and seven times as large.[24] Several of Jarvis' suggestions crossed American red lines. One of these was American opposition to any property custodian idea. The State Department also was opposed to Jarvis' idea of adding figures representing interest and currency devaluation to the overall compensation package.[25]

As with Johnson, the UNCCP never decided to adopt Jarvis' plan. In early 1963, the United States proposed instead that the UNCCP carry out a series of scaled-down "informal talks" on the refugees with Israel and the four Arab host countries (Jordan, Syria, Egypt, and Lebanon) without preconditions. The UNCCP agreed, and a series of talks took place in the spring and summer of 1963. Despite the American desire for talks without preconditions, the Israelis would not offer any specific ideas on compensation and other aspects of the refugee problem at the April meeting in Washington unless the U.S. government secured several conditions from the Arabs. These were, first, a commitment to proceed with a comprehensive settlement. Second, the Arab states were to resettle the bulk of the refugees. The number of refugees that would be repatriated would be determined in advance and essentially be symbolic (the Israelis did not say what number of refugees it was willing to take). Third, this symbolic repatriation would be accomplished simultaneously with resettlement. Finally, the Arabs must agree to cease making the refugees an international issue.[26] Not surprisingly given long-standing Arab positions that flew directly in the face of these Israeli demands, the talks did not lead to anything concrete. Despite not achieving any real movement on the compensation problem, the United States eventually characterized the informal talks publicly as "useful." With that, the ambitious compensation plan developed by a second earnest UNCCP official came to nought.

## UNCCP Solicits Refugee Inquiries

Upon completion of the Technical Program the UNCCP decided to issue a press release inviting refugees to write to the UNCCP with details about their property. Frank Jarvis felt that he needed some type of input from the refugees to make his study more accurate. As it was, he said, the study was "unilateral."

Jarvis then could use the information contained in such inquiries to cross check the R/P1 forms and see if the Technical Program had produced accurate results.[27] The phenomenon of refugees writing to the UN in general and the UNCCP in particular inquiring about their property or seeking UN help in getting it back long predated this venture. Indeed, the UNCCP's archives contain dozens of letters from such refugees, some dating back to 1948. Many of the early letters were addressed to a variety of UN agencies or personnel, and directly or indirectly blamed the UN for the loss of their property. For example, Subhi T. Dajani, Chairman of the Board of the Arab Organization for the Welfare of the Blind in Palestine, wrote to UN Mediator Count Folke Bernadotte in August 1948 stating that all of the contents of the organization's headquarters on Jaffa Road in Jerusalem, worth £P10,000, were burnt on July 28–29, 1948 during the UN-imposed ceasefire that month.[28] Hanna Boutros Helou wrote to Trygvie Lie in July 1948 stating that all of the dyes and chemicals of the H. Helou & Fils company in Jaffa, worth £P156,180, were stolen by Jews, again during the same ceasefire. Helou stated flatly that he held Lie, as UN Secretary General, personally responsible for this loss since it occurred during a UN ceasefire.[29] Najib Ahmad Shabib and his sons sent a similar communication to the UN stating "we hold you responsible for the loss caused for us as a result of your declaration of Palestine partition on 29.11.47." They had left their home on Yarmuk Street in the Manshiyya Quarter of Jaffa on April 26, 1948, and £P5,750 in household goods subsequently were "stolen by terrorists."[30]

Typically the UN answered such letters by noting that it never exercised control in any part of Palestine and thus could not take responsibility for or action on such claims. At least one refugee was not satisfied with this response. As'ad Halaby had written to the Clapp Mission in September 1949 complaining that he had left the stores and depots for Lind & Halaby behind in Jaffa and Haifa when he departed Palestine for a safer locale. His goods, valued at £P153,200, were taken by Jewish authorities during one of the ceasefires. His home on al-Khadr Street in Jaffa was also looted, in early May 1948, with the loss of crystal, a piano, a radio, a refrigerator, and other items. He held the UN responsible. When he received the "usual response," he wrote back and had this to say about the UN's claim of no responsibility:

> The test is not whether the United Nations ever exercised control over Palestine but whether the United Nations is the cause, and this cannot be denied . . . . What Code of justice can decree a person in my predicament to be prevented from reaching his home and property; a person

> whose ancestors for hundreds of years have toiled and died on the land while newcomers and strangers are allowed with your approval to come in and appropriate what is most certainly not theirs?[31]

Other writers were not assigning blame, but rather seeking assistance or informing the UN about other matters. A British lawyer wrote to Secretary General Trygvie Lie in November 1948 informing him that his clients, Petroleum Development (Palestine), Ltd. and the Iraq Petroleum Co., Ltd., wished to continue to pay the royalties they had formerly been paying to the mandatory government. The companies had established accounts in the name of the "Successor to the Mandatory Government in Palestine" with Barclays Bank in London and were making payments into that account. The lawyer asked Lie to inform the relevant parties concerned.[32]

Shafiq G. Kawar, originally from Nazareth and then living in exile in Beirut, wrote several times to the UN asking that his claim for back rent owed to him be passed on to the Israeli government. According to Kawar, he for many years leased "large plots of land" in Jaffa and another location near Nazareth to the Jewish National Fund (JNF) for £P325/year. The last lease was renewed in 1947, and was carried out in the name of Avraham Druri of the Ginnesar settlement. Because of an assassination attempt on his life in October 1938 as part of the internecine Palestinian feuding during the Arab Revolt in Palestine, Kawar had fled Palestine for Lebanon under British escort. Kawar asked that the UNCCP pass along his request for the rent owed to him by the JNF for the years 1948–63 to the Israelis, and boasted of his formerly good relations with the JNF: "I am sure the said Company will support my statement and will vouch for the excellent relations which existed between us at the time."[33]

Finally, some who wrote in the early days after their flight sought not compensation but repatriation to their homes and businesses. Hasan 'Ali al-Hindi of Jaffa wrote to the Clapp Mission in October 1949 on behalf of his ten-member family living in exile in Lebanon. He noted that his family had owned six houses and two shops in Jaffa; a house in Ramla; goods in warehouses in Jaffa, Tel Aviv, and Haifa; and 82 dunums of orange groves. The family left Jaffa around the first of May 1948, and was living in Shuwit, Lebanon, on Red Cross rations and what was left of their cash. Al-Hindi was physically disabled, and pleaded for the UNCCP's help in being repatriated by Israel. He noted:

> if I am able to return to Jaffa, I can solicit the mercy of the Government of Israel to grant me permission to live as other Arabs are living under it

> . . . . I come with this petition requesting you to kindly mediate on my behalf to facilitate my return to my home in Jaffa by which you would save a family threatened with starvation and which nothing could save other than its repatriation with a guarantee of safety. May God bless you and give you long life to do good to suffering humanity.[34]

John M. Reedman, Principal Secretary of the Clapp Mission, responded that the mission could not help al-Hindi because his request dealt with matters outside of the mission's the terms of reference. He referred the refugee's letter to the UNCCP offices, although the author could find no indication whether the UNCCP ever responded.

The UNCCP also received letters over the years from persons seeking assistance in matters relating to Jewish property and Israel. An Iraqi Jew wrote the UN in 1955 and again in 1961 regarding frozen property in Iraq. The UNCCP responded to Elias Isaac Joseph Isaac in September 1961 that Israel had connected the question of Jewish property in Iraq with that of the Arab refugee property issue, and that the UNCCP could not help him at that time.[35] Others wrote seeking information about property in order to sell it to Israelis. The American lawyer representing the family of a deceased Lebanese who had owned land in Palestine wrote in 1963 seeking information that might help the family sell the land to a "Jewish-Israeli company." Robert Thabit of New York was the attorney for the widow and children of Fayyad Mas'ud Jabara, who had owned land in the village of al-Zuq al-Tahtani in northern Palestine. Thabit had some deeds to Jabara's abandoned land but was seeking information on its value for a possible sale to the company, to which he had been referred by an Israeli bank in New York City.[36] According to information contained in a 1946 Palestinian report, the Jabara family in Lebanon in fact had a history of selling land in al-Zuq al-Tahtani to Jews, dating from the mandate.[37] The lawyer was apparently unaware that Israel had long since confiscated abandoned Arab property.

Thus the UNCCP had a long history of receiving unsolicited letters when it decided in early 1964 to solicit letters inquiring about refugee property. The U.S. government thought that this would be of political benefit beyond Jarvis' more technical reasons for seeking such letters: it could refute the refugees' suspicions that the UNCCP was not doing anything actively on the property compensation question but in a way that would not lead them to believe that compensation was imminent. The State Department noted: "We think placing on file letters of inquiry and/or information submitted would have advantages without disadvantages, i.e., it would keep [the] process of fermentation going and allay suspicion without unduly [raising] refugee hopes of imminent compensation program or necessitating [a] large permanent PCC staff."[38]

As letters began trickling in, Jarvis checked the data contained in them against the owners index cards and R/P1 forms that the Technical Office had assembled. Jarvis wrote back with a response stating the particulars of the land in question as contained in the UNCCP records and also indicating that these records did not prove definitive title to land:

> I am able to confirm that the property described below is registered as being in the ownership of the above named gentleman on 14th. May 1948. This statement in no way constitutes proof of such ownership and is made solely for the purpose of indicating that the United Nations Conciliation Commission for Palestine recognizes a prima facie case for his ownership at that time, subject to the claims of a third party, if any, and to any dispute being resolved by normal process of law.[39]

The UNCCP later sent out a press release in November 1964 soliciting more responses. In response Jarvis received 49 inquiries between November 1964 and February 1965, all but two of which were written from Lebanon. None gave an UNRWA refugee camp as the return address, leading him to believe that these represented more well-to-do refugees for whom compensation for property might not be as pressing a need as poorer refugee landowners in the camps.

Inquiries continued to come in and Jarvis responded in detail to them. One example was a 1966 inquiry by Morad S. Nasif, son of the large landowner and mandate-era politician Sulayman Yusuf Nasif. Jarvis checked his records and responded to Nasif noting how many shares he owned in six parcels of land totaling 380.655 dunums in the village of al-Himma. Jarvis added that his brother, Nasri, owned a similar amount and that the rest of al-Himma was owned by the Bahhuth family. His father Sulayman owned 7.695 dunums in al-Himma as well, and the Mineral Springs, Ltd. company established in 1936 by their father had a long-term lease of 194.704 dunums of state land according to a June 5, 1946 lease.[40]

In September 1967, Sidney Reich, Morad Nasif's lawyer in White Plains, New York, wrote back to the UNCCP stating that he needed information on the land to help his client and his co-owners sell the land and the buildings on it or obtain an income from the land—presumably from Israel.[41] Georges W. Murr wrote from France in January 1967, and was told he owned 7.094 dunums in 11 parcels or buildings in Haifa.[42] Not only Palestinian refugees wrote: Hassan Hanna Jamal wrote to the UN Development Program in

March 1968 (which forwarded the letter to the UNCCP) asking if his Lebanese father, Hanna Dib Jamal of Dayr Mimas in southern Lebanon, was still registered as the owner of four parcels of land in Mettula.[43]

Overall, Jarvis was pleased with the degree to which his data matched that contained in the inquiries. He estimated that 90 percent of the information correlated exactly with that in his R/P1 forms. However, outside of providing him with a way to cross check his data and keeping the "process of fermentation [on the compensation question] going" as the Americans had noted, the solicitation of refugee inquiries did little else.[44]

## Response to the Technical Program

The U.S. Department of State was very satisfied with the Technical Report that had consumed so many of the UNCCP's efforts over the years 1952–64. The department believed that the Technical Office staff did a "thorough and resourceful job for which we [are] deeply indebted."[45] But while it was appreciative of the efforts of Hadawi, Berncastle, Jarvis and their staffs, the Americans were more equivocal when it came to predicting whether the voluminous information collected and assembled by the Technical Office ever actually would be used in a compensation regime: "We believe [that the] evaluation program definitely was worthwhile and hopefully will some day serve as [the] basis for [a] compensation program." The truth was that after a number of years following its new and more limited directions, the United States had all but given up on the UNCCP. the Americans were responsible for scuttling the compensation plans of both Johnson and Jarvis. Turkey and France also were apparently so uninterested in the refugee property issue by 1964 that their governments failed to notify their respective embassies in the Middle East that the UNCCP had issued Jarvis' report. Surprised French and Turkish diplomats in Amman and Beirut found out about it only when their American counterparts mentioned the fact to them.[46]

Others expressed greater interest in the results of the Technical Program. Interestingly, the West German government asked for a copy of the report in December 1964. More importantly, Israel awaited publication of the report with great interest. Israel initially had opposed releasing the report at all, but diplomat Shamai Kahana claimed to have convinced the government to drop its opposition.[47] Shortly after its publication, the UNCCP sent seven copies of Jarvis' report on the Technical Program to Theodor Meron, Israel's representative to the UN. The Israelis in fact already knew what was contained in the report. Their intelligence about UN activities was superb. In March 1961, for instance, Comay held a meeting with his American counterpart, Adlai Stevenson, to discuss matters relating to the General Assembly debates on UNRWA and the UNCCP. Comay's remarks revealed that he already knew how many of the Arab delegates were pushing for a showdown with the United States on these matters.[48]

Some eighteen months before public release of his data, the Israelis already knew specifics from Jarvis' report as well, such as amounts, methods of valuation, and so forth. This is revealed in a study of Jarvis' data dated November 12, 1962 that had been carried out by Moshe Ellman, the Chief Valuer at the Israeli Ministry of Justice's Land Assessment Division, a senior Israeli expert on land values, and a man twice recommended by Berncastle to head up UNCCP tasks. The Israelis clearly had obtained specific information about the Technical Program, probably from the Americans, and decided to have Ellman study it. In a report entitled "Comments on Value Assessments of Absentee Landed Property," Ellman compared the various statistics on the scope of refugee land collected by the Weitz-Lifshits-Danin Committee, the UNCCP Global Estimate, and Jarvis' more recent figures on the amount of refugee property. He also had access to Jarvis' supposedly-secret valuation figures. Overall, Ellman believed that Israel's own ongoing study of how much the refugee land was worth would be less than Jarvis's figure but would end up being somewhere over £P140 million.[49] Thus when Meron asked the Americans on March 31, 1964 about the U.S. position on the completion of the Technical Program, he already knew the contents of the report on the program because he made specific references to it.[50]

Comay then met with Jarvis on September 24, and October 8, 1964 to discuss the report with him and convey Israel's opinions. Comay came prepared with a detailed response to several specific sentences and paragraphs in the report, and shared these with Jarvis. Comay complained that Jarvis had included too much land in the Beersheba subdistrict as "Arab." He noted that Jarvis' use of the term "Arab-owned" to describe 12,445,000 dunums of land in the Beersheba subdistrict (mentioned in paragraph 15 of his report) was therefore incorrect. Jarvis later wrote Comay on November 13 and cited *Village Statistics, 1945*, the *Survey of Palestine*, as well as mandatory lists of state lands to support his claim. He told Comay:

> [the mandatory records] contain evidence of the ownership by the government of comparatively small areas of land in the Beersheba Sub District. The assumption was made that all other land in this sub-district

> was Arab owned, other than that for which documentary evidence indicated a non-Arab ownership . . . . I believe that the position was that the great bulk of the area was used and lived on by the Bedouin. There is however no documentary evidence in my possession of the type used for the rest of the country to establish ownership. The term "Arab-owned" in par. 15 of the working paper should, in consequence, not be construed as representing the formal position of the author of the paper on this point.[51]

Beyond Beersheba, Comay complained in subsequent correspondence with him that Jarvis had included too much of other types of land in his figures. For instance, he claimed that the R/P1 forms included the land of those Palestinian citizens of Israel who had not fled as refugees, of non-Palestinian Arabs and, potentially, even of Mizrahi Jews with Arabic-sounding names. Comay also felt that it was improper to complete R/P forms for state land, waqf, and so forth. Because of this Comay maintained that there were R/P forms covering a greater amount of territory than was actually refugee property. He also complained that no indication was made in the records of which land was disputed, nor did Jarvis' study deal with counter claims.[52] Reports in the Israeli press indicated that the Israelis also took exception to Jarvis including land that had been leased to Arabs on long-term leases on R/P1 forms, presumably because the Arabs in question had not actually owned the land. They also felt that all land that had not undergone the land settlement process should similarly be excluded because title had not been definitively determined. Israel also objected to individual compensation; compensation must be global and must take into consideration Israeli counter-claims.[53]

Comay's meeting was not the only time that Israelis met with Jarvis to discuss the Technical Report. In November 1964, the U.S. embassy in Tel Aviv granted a visa to Ellman, who officially secured the visa in order to travel to New York for talks with Israeli delegates to the UN. However, it was also clear that he was being sent to discuss the Technical Report with Jarvis given that he had already provided the Israeli government with his views on Jarvis' report in November 1962. Over the course of ten meetings in late 1964 and/or early 1965, Ellman met with Jarvis and went over the voluminous materials at Jarvis' disposal at UN headquarters.[54] On January 28, 1965, Comay and Meron paid another visit to Jarvis. The Israelis asked Jarvis for information in his files about Jewish-owned property under Jordanian control in the West Bank and, curiously, about *Jewish* property under Israel's control in West Jerusalem. Comay also asked him what the UNCCP intended to do with all of its records given completion of the Technical Program and Jarvis' impending departure from UN service. Jarvis responded that he was about to propose to the UNCCP that he immediately begin preparing the records for storage. Comay then asked whether the material would be available. Jarvis responded that he assumed it would be, but that in his absence it would be hard to use.[55]

The response of the Arabs to the Technical Program was completely negative. Unlike the Israelis, the Arabs were not initially interested in meeting with Jarvis and generally dismissed the report. None of the Arab delegations to the UN formally or informally informed the Americans that they had rejected the report, nor did it initially receive much press coverage in the Arab world. Part of this problem was that the UN itself did not expend many efforts at disseminating it in the Arab world. The UN information center in Beirut only received one copy of the report without any instructions about what to do with it. The office did not circulate it but instead treated the document and the UNCCP's annual progress report, in the words of an American diplomat, "virtually as classified documents."[56]

By August 1964 Jarvis was worried about the lack of response from the Arabs. He felt that information he was receiving from the Middle East indicated that the refugees did not know about completion of the UNCCP's Technical Report. He made three suggestions to the UNCCP for publicity efforts to make them aware of the project's completion. He first suggested that the UNCCP write to the host countries, re-inviting them to respond to the report. Second, it could start a public relations campaign to inform the refugees of the program's completion. Third, the UNCCP should move ahead to the next step on the road to compensation by creating a loan fund or a compensation fund. Jarvis was a firm believer in the righteousness of his efforts, and believed that the UNCCP now needed to "do something." He pointed out that the UNCCP no longer could justify its inactivity by claiming it was awaiting his report. He clearly underestimated the international consensus that the UNCCP's effectiveness had long since passed as well as American hostility to his ideas.[57]

At least one Arab government in fact did formally study Jarvis' report fairly shortly after it was issued. In June 1964, the Jordanian government created a three-person committee with representatives from the Ministry of Foreign Affairs and the Ministry of Finance. Among them were Taysir Tuqan, Director of Political Affairs for the Foreign Office, and Subhi al-Hasan, Director of the Department of Lands and Survey. The committee's work during the summer of 1964 was delayed because al-Hasan could not read English well and the report had to be translated into Arabic. The committee gave its findings to the prime minister in August 1964. The committee members stated that the report was based on "illegal grounds" because no UN decisions regarding Palestine could be made until all such UN decisions had been implemented. The committee also believed that the documents on which the UNCCP had based its findings were inaccurate and that the entire identification and valuation program was flawed because no estimate could be considered legal unless performed in the presence of refugees or their agents. The report also faulted the UNCCP Technical Report for technical reasons, among them failing to include all Arab land in the Beersheba subdistrict; for not including the land belonging to the Hijaz railroad; omitting property of the former mandatory government; and omission of moveable property.[58]

In November 1964, the UNCCP agreed to try to elicit response from the refugees by issuing a press release in the Arab world announcing the Technical Program's end and soliciting refugee inquiries about their property. As a result, Arab momentum against the UNCCP and the Technical Report grew. Two Beirut dailies that published the press release on November 14 criticized the report for failing to release the land's value and for ending a long period of inactivity with a flawed study. *Sawt al-'Arab* noted acerbically that "after a long silence the Commission which we thought dead has published a silly report."[59] Finally, the Arab Higher Committee condemned the Jarvis report in a press report issued in Beirut on November 17. The AHC called the UNCCP a group of "pro-Israeli states." It also scored the UNCCP's call for refugees to write it with details of their landholdings. The AHC considered this an effort by the UNCCP "to secure legal recognition by Palestinians of the legality of its action, and to bring them to recognize the unjust resolutions adopted by the United Nations on Palestine."[60] In an earlier March 14, 1963 communiqué, the AHC had condemned compensation in general, accusing Kennedy and Golda Meir of trying to "liquidate" the Palestinian problem through repatriation, resettlement and emigration, and compensation.[61]

The Arab states waited another full year before formally responding to Jarvis in 1966. On April 11, 1966, several Arab states sent the UNCCP an official response to Jarvis' report. The letter was based on numerous complaints about Jarvis' methodology. First, they contended that the mandatory records consulted by Jarvis did not cover all Arab holdings, particularly in areas that had not undergone land settlement. Second, they contended that buildings and trees were not fully covered by the UNCCP study. This was because neither a 1937 amendment to the Land Settlement law nor the 1935 rural property tax ordinance required that buildings be registered and thus they were not found in the mandatory records. Third, the study did not record communal-owned property such as grazing lands, uncultivable lands, or mandatory government property. The letter faulted the UNCCP for its reckoning of Arab land in the Beersheba subdistrict. In particular, it scored the Technical Office for omitting 10 million dunums of uncultivable land that the bedouin used for grazing their animals. Furthermore, the study did not include government moveable property nor did it mention destroyed Arab buildings in rural areas. Another complaint dealt with Jarvis' methodology. The Arabs objected to basing much of the study on mandatory tax lists because they contended that the land values they contained were too low. Finally, they objected to the use of mandatory data on land sales, contained in the registers of deeds, because they too listed land prices that were too low.[62]

The Arab letter prompted a series of back and forth correspondence. Jarvis digested the Arab states' complaint and responded to them later that year but only after considerable discussion within the UNCCP about the timing and the forum that would be appropriate. He defended the overall veracity of the Technical Report, including by citing examples of individual refugees who had corresponded with him about their property. Jarvis noted, " subsequent operations of the office of the Technical Report in responding to individual enquiries have demonstrated that the identification is substantially correct." Answering the charge that the study ignored state land, Jarvis admitted that this charge was correct. However, he noted that data on special Arab leases of state land was included.[63] The Arab states responded to Jarvis' response on February 3, 1967, noting that they still had reservations about the study. They also requested "all documents and materials" in the UNCCP's possession relating to property in Palestine. The Arab demand for the UNCCP's records was an ongoing issue between the Arab states and the UNCCP, and is discussed below. Israel in turn responded to the Arabs' observations on Jarvis' report, noting that the Arabs made some "unfounded" statements.[64]

Jarvis tried to meet with the Arab delegations face-to-face to discuss their observations. He first wrote to them in July 1964 shortly after publication of the report, suggesting that they hold an informal meeting. He received no response. Then Jarvis was made aware of an article that appeared in the August 6, 1965 issue of the Palestinian newspaper *Filastin* that seemed to shed light on why the Arabs had ignored him. The article claimed that the UNCCP sought a meeting with the Arab states but that they would refuse, because the real purpose of the meeting was the "liquidation of the Palestine returnees." Jarvis wrote again to the Arab delegates separately in September 1965, offering once again to meet with them and explaining that the press article indicated that his letter may have been misinterpreted. He tried to assure the host governments that completion of the identification and valuation project did not prejudge any possible solutions to the questions of repatriation and compensation. Jarvis wrote that the UNCCP had "not reached any conclusions concerning possible means of implementing the options and alternatives set forth in paragraph 11 of General Assembly resolution 194 (III)." Although they tentatively arranged a meeting with Jarvis for early February 1966, the Arab states sent identical letters to Jarvis in late January and early February of that year declining to follow through.

One probable reason why they demurred was because the Arab states simultaneously were involved in trying to formulate jointly a detailed technical response to the Jarvis report. They convened three conferences that brought together "land experts" from the various Arab states to study the report. Sami Hadawi apparently played a role in convening them. He was then head of the Institute for Palestine Studies in Beirut and later claimed that he had had to prod the Arab states into rejecting the Jarvis report and offering specific, technical reasons for their objections. Besides Hadawi's nagging, a conference of Arab foreign ministers that met prior to the third Arab summit in Casablanca in September 1965 adopted a resolution calling for a response to the UNCCP study, something the Arab League later did. The first conference of Arab land experts took place from March 23–27, 1966 in Amman. Attending the meeting were the departing Arab League Secretary General Dr. Sayyid Nawfal, Hadawi, the Jordanian Department of Lands and Survey's Assistant Director for the West Bank, as well as delegates from Lebanon, Jordan, Syria, and Egypt. The newly formed Palestine Liberation Organization refused to attend, citing the need for the total liberation of Palestine instead.

The conference produced a six-page document that apparently reflected Hadawi's view that the mandatory records on which the UNCCP Technical Program was based were inaccurate and incomplete, although it did not outright reject the Technical Report. Hadawi later confided to U.S. diplomats that he nonetheless was disappointed with the meeting. In his opinion none of the conferees knew anything about the subject and were just attending because they hoped to get a free trip to New York as part of any future Arab delegation that might meet with Jarvis. He also had urged the conference in vain to reject the Technical Program. Finally, the conference proposed reconvening in Amman on July 9. Egypt proposed instead that the Arab League council meet instead on July 16. This gathering decided that the land experts should meet again and be in contact with the Palestine Liberation Organization. The PLO, however, continued to refuse cooperation, citing that "[it] does not believe in an evaluation of property nor does it recognize anything called Israel." It also stated that it was not committed to any UNCCP procedures on Palestine.[65]

A second Arab land experts meeting did convene later from July 25 to August 13, 1966 in East Jerusalem. As the Arab world's leading expert on Palestinian land, Hadawi once again attended the conference. He clashed there with Sayyid Nawfal, urging that the Arabs needed to respond to the UNCCP's report with a detailed, well-documented response and not just rhetoric. The conferees agreed to a third such gathering, which began in Beirut on February 20, 1967. This time all Arab countries except Tunisia and Morocco were represented. Conspicuously, Hadawi was not invited. The main purpose of this third meeting was to continue the dialogue with the UNCCP on the report.[66] Jarvis' departure from UN service in 1966 plus the outbreak of 1967 Arab-Israeli war disrupted future Arab plans to carry on with their dialogue, however.

## Demise of the UNCCP

As a result of the completion of the Technical Program and the lack of U.S. enthusiasm for either Johnson's or Jarvis' plans for compensation, the year 1966 marked the effective demise of the UNCCP and its decades-long effort on behalf of the refugees. No one placed any faith in it. Israel always had kept its distance. The Arabs had all but given up on the UNCCP as it had been constituted as well. One of the signs of this came during the 16th session of the UN General Assembly in the fall of 1961, when the Arab states introduced an amendment to the draft of the annual resolution on UNRWA that would have expanded the UNCCP from three members to five. They had grown tired of the Americans' ability to influence the French and the Turks, both of whom were American allies. They sought to "reconstitute" the commission to allow it to "take measures for the protection of the rights, property and interests of the Palestine Arab refugees." The amendment passed in committee but failed to garner the requisite two-thirds majority at the General Assembly plenary session.[67]

The issue continued to float around for several years. U.S. State Department officials meeting in June 1964 decided that the United States might actually agree to a "controlled expansion" of the UNCCP to a maximum of five members. The following year the department prepared a position paper for U.S. diplomats at the UN to use during the UNRWA debate that fall. The document instructed the diplomats to recommend that the UNCCP remain constituted as it was, but if an expansion was deemed necessary to limit this to two new members. One of these was to be an African state and one a Latin American state.[68] But the UNCCP never was expanded, and Arab frustration with it as an active force in the Arab-Israeli conflict intensified. In fact, the Arab states had announced to the UN in November 1963 that they believed that the UNCCP's "general tenor" deviated from the mandate given in General Assembly Resolution 194 (III) of 1948, that the UNCCP's 21st progress report of 1963 contained factual errors about the "informal talks," and that their governments were not prepared to enter into talks with the UNCCP on the basis of that report.[69] The Technical Report did nothing to assuage Arab frustration.

The Americans, always the leading force in the UNCCP, also were questioning its effectiveness. The entire nature of the Arab-Israeli conflict and of conciliation had changed since 1956. As the macro level immensity of conflict resolution in the region had become clear, the Americans began running out of energy on the seemingly micro level property issue by the mid-1960s and began signaling their own belief that the UNCCP's effectiveness had reached its limit. American diplomats began exploring other options to deal with the refugees outside the context of the UNCCP Technical Office. In February 1965, the State Department discussed the idea of an "economic" solution to the refugee problem and wondered if it should ask the commission to study this possibility. The Clapp Mission had explored such an option in 1949 and the negative reaction from U.S. missions in the Middle East to a new such initiative killed the idea. The following month the department instructed American diplomats at the UN to let the Turks and French "carry the ball" in any further UNCCP initiatives. They could always remind their allies that it had been the United States that had done all of the work the last time the commission engaged in its "informal talks" in 1963.[70]

By late 1965 and early 1966, the United States essentially felt that no further UNCCP initiatives were likely to make any progress; the Americans, giving up on further hopes of a UNCCP-led breakthrough, were now content merely to let the Technical Office finish its valuation program and leave things at that. In fact, in January 1966 the State Department asked posts in the Middle East for their opinions about asking Israel to float unilaterally its own compensation plan without UNCCP involvement. American diplomats in Amman replied that "a number" of Jordanians said they would consider compensation if a choice was offered between repatriation or compensation. The department discussed the idea with Foreign Minister Abba Eban on February 7, 1966, asking that Israel consider some kind of initiative on the refugees.[71]

The clock was running down on Frank Jarvis' contract with the UNCCP, raising the question of just what the UNCCP's future, and the future of its massive collection of documents on refugee property, was to be.

Given the attitudes of the parties, the reality of the Arab-Israeli conflict since 1956, the lack of positive response to initiatives like the Johnson Mission and the "informal talks," the United States began calling into question the wisdom of keeping the Technical Office functioning. It was becoming clear to the Americans by the mid-1960s that there were no realistic possibilities for the commission to move the parties toward a solution of the refugee problem. If the Technical Office were kept open, what would Jarvis do? This engendered some opposition within the UNCCP, both from the French and the Turks and from paid UNCCP staff members. The French and the Turks argued for extending the Technical Office's mandate. For his own part, Jarvis—who with completion of the Technical Program changed his title starting on July 21, 1964 from UNCCP "Land Expert" to its "Technical Representative"—was quite anxious for the UNCCP to take steps toward implementing his ideas about compensation and particularly his idea on using the property's income. In October 1964, the UNCCP held informal discussions about this idea and talked about its similarity to the Johnson plan among other related topics. Turkish delegate Vahap Asiroglu argued strongly for doing something to follow up on the just-completed Technical Program. It was the UNCCP's "moral obligation," he insisted, to work toward any possible progress on the refugee question. The French delegate seemed to rise in cynical agreement when he replied, "Let's be moral from time to time."[72]

The question of whether to keep the Technical Office open and retain Jarvis on the UN payroll came up again in January 1965. UNCCP Principal Secretary David Hall informed the American mission to the UN that Jarvis's renewable contract was set to expire and that he would be leaving on March 31, 1965. Hall's question was, should Jarvis be asked to stay on again as he had in the past? Hall was opposed to the idea of the UNCCP being "strung along" on a monthly or quarterly basis. Some kind of longer term planning was needed. The American diplomats replied that they had not yet been informed of the State Department's position on the matter but that the U.S. government was unlikely to do anything significant regarding the refugees. Jarvis himself was quite anxious to stay. He told the UNCCP the next month that if it did not use the Technical Program's data for implementing his property income idea soon, the program probably would remain permanently dormant. Jarvis separately told the American UN delegation that he was reluctant to keep working with the UNCCP on a temporary basis if all he was going to do would be to answer the inquiry letters coming in from refugees and maintain his files. He complained that such an arrangement was costing him financially. He was, after all, being seconded to the UN from the British Board of Inland Revenue. He noted that by working in New York he was losing promotion opportunities and it also was affecting his British pension. Jarvis earlier had complained in 1963 about the salary he received as well. He told the Americans directly that if he was going to be retained, it must be for a good purpose and not just to "let the commission off the hook" by pointing to his continued employment as a sign of the UNCCP's good intentions toward the refugees.[73]

Jarvis' bluster failed to move the Americans. They had given up on the idea of an "economic solution" to the refugee problem in the spring of 1965 and in March of that year decided that there was really no hope for any future UNCCP initiatives on the refugee issue. The Technical Office should be closed and Jarvis let go. However, the Turks in particular continued to argue for continuing the office's mandate. Asiroglu described the UNCCP without Jarvis as a "car without wheels." It was "essential," he pleaded, for the UNCCP to request a continuation of his services.

The Americans had other reasons for closing the Technical Office besides the fact that they felt the UNCCP was becoming irrelevant. They disliked the way Jarvis continued to push ideas that went beyond their red lines. They felt that Jarvis thought of the refugees as "wards" of the international community and that the UN subsequently bore some "responsibility" for compensating them. They opposed the elements of Jarvis' compensation plan that called for adding sums representing currency devaluation and interest to the value of the abandoned land. They especially disliked the idea of having the UN use the income from the refugee property, because the U.S. position continued to be that the refugees no longer held legal title to the land. Jarvis' property custodian idea was virtually the same thing as the Arab states' property custodian idea that the United States and Israel had opposed so strongly.

In the end, the United States acceded to French and Turkish pleading and agreed to another extension of Jarvis' services. But American diplomats noted: "As [an] initial condition to our concurrence, we would wish [to] insist [that] Jarvis immediately get off [his] 'property custodian' kick. It would be senseless for [the] U.S. to allow [the] PCC tech rep to continue to push [the] very idea which USG [U.S. government] has exerted such labors year after year to halt."[74] U.S. diplomats in New York had a direct meeting with Jarvis on March 17, 1965 and explained that he thereafter should limit his services to conducting narrow technical studies, not anything approaching a diplomatic initiative that might obligate the UNCCP. They also conveyed the State Department's concern about any discussions he might carry out with the concerned parties.[75]

Jarvis was rehired and the Technical Office stayed open. Nevertheless, compensating the Palestinian refugees for their land remained as distant a reality as ever. By early 1966, even the Turks had despaired of realizing any progress by following up on the Technical Program. Their delegate to the UNCCP agreed in January 1966 with what their first delegate to the UNCCP had said back in 1950: that the UNCCP could accomplish little to nothing in and of itself. He added that Jarvis' desire to breathe life into the process by continuing with his technical efforts would accomplish nothing and might even make things worse. He argued that the UNCCP should just go through the formality of talking with the Arabs and Israel about "intensification" of the its efforts and issue yet another "bland" progress report to the 21st session of the UN General Assembly.[76]

With even Turkish support gone, the UNCCP agreed with the American logic and decided to close down the Technical Office. The UNCCP informed Israel and the Arab states in March 1966 that Jarvis would be leaving on the last day of that month. A farewell party for him was planned for March 22. But the day before the planned party, the Arab states wrote requesting that Jarvis's services be extended because their land experts still were considering his report. The Arabs wanted to send Sami Hadawi as their representative for technical discussions with Jarvis about the scope of the refugee land. In a follow-up meeting, the Egyptian delegate said that the Technical Office had taken a long time preparing the identification and valuation program, and that the Arabs themselves needed more time. Informally, the Arabs suggested a brief three to four months extension of Jarvis's tenure. The British Board of Inland Revenue agreed to one final extension of Jarvis's services. The UNCCP then gave in, rehiring him one more time through September 30, 1966. Part of the reason for the extension is that the Americans argued that in doing so the Arabs would not be able to say in the future that the UNCCP cut off their chance to discuss the Technical Program. "In any case," they noted, "Jarvis-Arab exchanges may fill out what may be [a] rather meagre PCC progress report next fall."[77]

Despite the Americans' desire for the Technical Office to fade away gently, Jarvis characteristically continued to promote ideas about compensation. He told the American delegate to the commission, John A. Baker, Jr., that he had wanted to present ideas at the April 13, 1966 meeting of the UNCCP but that the discussion of the Arab states' official letter of response to the Jarvis report had prevented him. Jarvis also recommended that the UNCCP establish a new "expert committee" to examine issues relating to completion of the Technical Program. The U.S. State Department did not like this idea. Jarvis also sought permission to write a letter-to-the-editor to the Beirut newspaper *al-Usbu' al-'Arabi*, which on May 9, 1966 had published an article entitled "A Trap Set by the Conciliation Commission." Jarvis took issue with the information in the article, especially since the figures it cited were not his but Berncastle's from 1951. He also suggested drafting a press release saying that the UNCCP had not made any announcements about values and that the figures cited in *al-Usbu' al-'Arabi* were not his work. His zeal came to naught: the Technical Office finally closed down for good on September 30, 1966 and Jarvis and his staff were released from UN service. All inquiries received thereafter received a stock reply noting that the UNCCP's Technical Representative no longer worked for the UNCCP and that it was not in a position to answer questions.[78]

The three-member UNCCP has continued to exist to this day on paper but with little tangible evidence of its existence beyond limited staff support and the drafting of annual reports. For all intents and purposes the UNCCP ceased to function in 1966. Its demise elicited no tears from any of the parties. The UNCCP's last remaining task was to decide what to do with the massive volume of material assembled by the Technical Office since 1952.

## The Arabs Obtain Copies of UNCCP Documents

Frustrated as they were with the UNCCP's various estimates of the value of refugee property, which were much lower than their own, the Arab states had begun requesting copies of some of the UNCCP's records as early as 1953. With completion of the UNCCP Technical Program in 1964 and the Arabs' desire to determine their own estimates of refugee property losses, the Arabs renewed their efforts to obtain the documents. The UNCCP had accumulated a huge amount of material relating to Arab property in Israel by the time the Technical Office was closed in 1966: 96 linear feet of paper, of which 90 feet were documents (two-thirds of which was the R/P1 forms). The other six feet consisted of several thousand maps, largely mandatory maps of Palestinian villages. The UNCCP had begun investigating how to store this material in the UN archives as early as 1963. One idea was to microfilm the paper documents, which would cost about $750 to produce some 150 rolls of 16mm film. After studying the situation, the UN Department of Records determined that it was best to microfilm the UNCCP's land records and then destroy the original paper copies to save money and space. Jarvis and UNCCP Principal Secretary David Hall countered that this would not be wise. Jarvis noted that it would be almost impossible to use the owners index cards if they were on microfilm only. The U.S. delegation to the UN agreed, and the records department later microfilmed the R/P1 forms and the index cards but saved the original paper copies as well. The UNCCP thus ended up with 226 additional rolls of 16mm film to add to its 1,642 rolls of 35mm films of the Ottoman and mandatory land registers. All of its voluminous records were stored at the UN Secretariat archives in New York away from public scrutiny under lock and key. To this day, special permission is required to gain access to them.[79]

The Arabs felt that they had a right to this material, however. The first Arab League request for paper copies of the mandatory films in the UNCCP's possession came on April 26, 1953 and was denied. Seven years later the issue of Arab usage of the material was revived when on April 26, 1960, Jordan's delegate to the UN asked the UNCCP to see its records for *Jewish* land in Shu'fat and Neve Ya'akov near Jerusalem. The UNCCP responded that it did not have such information. The Jordanian Ministry of Foreign Affairs had requested information on Jewish land in West Jerusalem as well from the British embassy in Amman two months earlier.[80] A second general Arab request for copies of the UNCCP's documents was made in August 1961. The U.S. delegation in particular opposed the move and tried to have the inquiry "deflected."[81] Eventually, the UNCCP denied the request again, telling the Arabs to wait until the Technical Program was finished using the films. However, this request prompted a great deal of political discussions among the UNCCP delegations and staff. Did the UNCCP had the authority to reproduce British government documents? Did it have the authority to allow the Arabs to copy the films if Israel objected? The UNCCP asked UN Legal Counsel C. A. Stavropoulos such questions, whereupon he produced a memorandum on the legal issues surrounding the films on September 11, 1961. Significantly, Stavropoulos' memorandum opined that Israel had no legal basis to object to the UNCCP providing copies of the films to the Arabs.[82]

In January 1962, the Arab League once again asked for copies of the mandatory films without having to wait for completion of the Technical Program. It was no doubt becoming clear to them that they would disagree with the UNCCP's final reckoning of the property and they wished to obtain the films so as to carry out their own studies of the property question if they wanted to. The United States again opposed the idea, with the State Department telling the American delegation in New York that the refugee property issue involves Israel and the four Arab host governments, not Israel and the

Arab League. The UNCCP once again denied the request but told the Arabs that it would review such requests at a later time when the Technical Program was finished.[83]

On June 17, 1963, Syria requested "complete photo copies of the properties of Arab refugees within Israel." Principal Secretary John Gaillard immediately sent a memorandum to the UNCCP delegates upon receiving the Syrian request. Gaillard noted that there was no technical reason why the UNCCP could not provide copies of the films, and the UN's legal counsel said that Israel had no basis for objecting. In fact, Gaillard noted that the Israelis had the original copies of the films made by the British and had made a study of refugee land that it had not made available to the UNCCP. The Arabs might feel that they should now have a chance to study the same data that had been available to the Israelis and the UNCCP. He concluded by opining that it was difficult to justify not making the films available. Gaillard noted:

> To do so would not, it seems to me, provide the Arabs with any more propaganda material than they already have. The films are of course only a small part of the data used by the Technical Office. It is hard to see what practical use could be made of them. Yet they might serve to delay any Arab demands for a full report on the Technical Office work which has cost so much money. Such a demand appears a possibility.[84]

The Americans were not so sanguine. They were anxious about Israel's reaction. They were concerned that Israel would object to such a release and that the information might be made available to Palestinians who might distort it to discredit the Technical Program. U.S. Ambassador to the UN Adlai Stevenson also feared that giving the Arabs the records might damage Israel's willingness to cooperate with the UNCCP. He thought that the UNCCP could tell the Arabs that the films were still in use and that when the project was done they could approach the British to obtain copies, getting the monkey off the UNCCP's back. Jarvis recommended telling the Syrians that the mandatory films were incomplete and that the UNCCP's other data (e.g., the R/P1 forms) were not available. The UNCCP held some informal meetings with the UN Secretary General's legal advisors on ways to turn down the request, and eventually told the Syrians "no."[85]

The Syrians made an additional request in the spring of 1964. The French delegate told an informal meeting of the UNCCP that his government had discussed the legality of providing copies of British documents with the British government. UNCCP Principal Secretary David Hall had replied that Britain had provided copies to Israel and Jordan, but should it have veto power over other countries receiving copies? The Turks and the Americans did not like using Britain's supposed veto power as the basis for rejecting the Arab request, although they were in favor of refusing the request for other reasons. Eventually, the UNCCP never officially responded to the Syrians.[86] For his part, Hall felt that the time was right in the wake of the 1964 public release of the Technical Report to release a copy of the films. He noted, that the "Commission has stated its desire to make the results of the work of the Technical Programme fully available to those concerned." He suggested that one copy of the films be made available.[87]

When the Technical Program was completed and Jarvis' summary report issued in the spring of 1964, the UNCCP's position regarding the films was forced to undergo a revision. In early 1966, Hall said that the UNCCP's continued refusal to release the films had become a symbol in Arab eyes of the its negative attitude in general toward them. That summer, the delegates of Jordan and Syria to the UN approached the chair of the UNCCP on behalf of the host countries and once again requested access to the documents used by Jarvis. The Turkish chair of the UNCCP thought they still were requesting copies of the mandatory films, but found out that the Arabs in fact sought a copy of *everything* that had been at Jarvis' disposal. That would include the R/P1 forms and their secret data on valuation. The Arabs wanted the material in order to reply to Jarvis' report during the General Assembly in a technical manner. However, the UNCCP thought that the Arabs in fact were seeking the documents for "political" and not technical reasons. The Arab states already had sent Jarvis their negative observations on his report and the UNCCP felt that perhaps the Arabs merely wanted the documents to form a plausible basis for rejecting the report at the General Assembly in the fall of 1966.

Even the United States had to agree that with the Technical Program completed, the UNCCP had no legal grounds to deny the Arab request. Besides, the Americans noted, the films of both the mandatory records and the UNCCP's own records offered only an incomplete record of Arab property and contained no data on the land's value (in this the Americans were mistaken; valuation figures were written both on the R/P1 forms and the owners index cards). The Americans told the Turks and French that they no longer objected to release of the films so long as the British agreed. At a September 22, 1966 meeting, the UNCCP finally agreed in principle to allow the Arabs to send a "formal written request" when the UNCCP was in a position to release the films. The UNCCP also decided to define the Arab requests for documents as meaning requests for the mandatory films, not other records like the R/P1 forms. The French still felt that the British and the Israelis would have to give permission. Israel objected to the UNCCP giving copies of land records to the Arabs on the very next day. Israeli diplomats held a meeting at the Department of State in Washington on September 23 to protest strongly any decision to hand over copies of the documents. The Israelis objected in principle, on the basis that they had provided Jarvis some of their own records and that the Arabs only wished to use the documents to cause trouble.[88]

Although the UNCCP decided to wait until the annual UNRWA debate was over in the General Assembly to reply to the Arabs, it eventually did so and invited an official written request. On February 3, 1967, representatives from Jordan, Lebanon, Egypt, and Syria sent a letter to the UNCCP responding to Jarvis' comments on their "observations" about his report. In that letter, they requested copies "of all documents and materials in the possession of the Palestine Conciliation Commission and its Technical Office relating to property in Palestine."[89] Israel twice dispatched diplomats to the State Department, on April 10 and May 27, 1967 during a time of increasing tension in the Middle East to seek U.S. help in defeating the request. The Israelis speculated that this time the Arabs were seeking to use the materials to strengthen their perennial calls for a UN property custodian, an idea they knew the Americans opposed as well. In between their two visits, Syrian Ambassador to the UN Rafiq Jouejati called Hall on April 21 to ask unofficially if Syria could obtain a list of Arab property owners in the Israeli-Syrian Demilitarized Zone. Besides seeking American help, the Israelis moved on a different front in such a way as to render the Arab request for the films irrelevant: a week and a half after meeting the Americans for the second time, Israel launched the June 1967 war, annihilating the armies of Egypt, Jordan, and Syria. One result of the war was to put a five-year halt to future Arab requests for copies of the UNCCP's material.[90]

On November 6, 1972, the Lebanese ambassador to the UN spoke with the U.S. Ambassador to the UN, George H.W. Bush, about whether the United States would support a renewed Arab request for copies of the UNCCP records. The UNCCP discussed the matter once again with the UN's legal counsel and decided to grant permission at long last. The UNCCP agreed to provide copies of the following documents: the films of the mandatory land registers; the R/P1 forms; and the owners index. It further asked that any party receiving such material keep the valuation figures confidential.[91]

The first Arab state formally to request and receive copies of the UNCCP material was Egypt, which asked to make copies of the material at its own expense in September 1973. Filmed copies of the records were made in June 1974. The Egyptians later received a second copy of the films in March and May 1975. In May 1974, Jordan made a similar request and received the films the following year. One reason why the Jordanians needed the material was that they had lost some of the original mandatory registers in their possession when Israel invaded and occupied the West Bank in June 1967. They also were trying to save wear and tear on the remaining registers. The Palestine Liberation Organization (PLO) also requested copies of the films in November 1982. Duplication finally was completed in May 1984 and the copies were handed over the PLO. They were stored at the PLO Economics Department in Damascus. On a related note, the UN's Committee on the Exercise of the Inalienable Rights of the Palestinian People also requested "an inventory of Arab property in Israel and the territories occupied by Israel" in 1976. The UNCCP agreed, and provided copies of the same information it provided to the Arabs.[92]

By the early 1980s, a number of parties across the globe had access to some of the voluminous records produced by the UNCCP Technical Office and the mandatory documents upon which they were based. Would this lead to action on the property issue? The answer to this had been presaged by the momentous events of June 1967.

## CHAPTER SEVEN

# REFUGEE PROPERTY QUESTION AFTER 1967

By late 1966 the UNCCP had closed its Technical Office, become moribund, and effectively continued to exist merely on paper. There was little likelihood of progress on the property compensation issue, as the regional climate did not at all lend itself to a breakthrough. It had been nearly twenty years since the refugee exodus, ten years since the Suez War had altered the Arab-Israeli Conflict, and no significant progress had been made on the question. The only real success over the years had been the UNCCP-brokered return of blocked bank accounts and safe deposit boxes. The parties to the conflict themselves were in no mood for movement on the refugee issue. Israel and Egypt were locked in an arms race, water issues complicated the Arab-Israeli conflict, and the rising tide of Palestinian nationalism symbolized by the establishment of the Palestine Liberation Organization in 1964 decried any attempt to negotiate with Israel or "sell" the refugees' land via compensation.

Within this unhopeful atmosphere, diplomats made a few inquiries anyway about Israeli willingness to compensate. UNRWA's Deputy Commissioner John Reddaway developed an idea in early 1967 for unilateral, unconditional Israel compensation. The U.S. embassy in Tel Aviv approached Israeli Foreign Ministry officials Yosef Teko'a and Mordekhai Gazit in January 1967 about this idea. The Israelis showed no real enthusiasm. State Department official L. L. Kinsolving also asked Dov Yinon of the Israeli embassy in Washington in February what thoughts Israel had about compensation. Yinon noted that the State Department had rejected most recent Israeli proposals because the proposals did not include repatriation, and the Americans felt the Arabs would surely have objected to it for that reason. Yinon's personal belief, he said, was that Israel should have pursued a quiet policy of making individual compensation payments after 1948-which Israel apparently was doing in the mid-1960s.[1]

Israel also developed an interesting policy in the 1960s that seemed to challenge its own insistence that it permanently had confiscated the refugees' abandoned land and incorporated it inalienably into the Israel Lands Administration (ILA) created in 1960. This policy involved trading some of the 1948 refugee property with Palestinian citizens who had stayed behind and become Israeli citizens. The ILA began trading absentee land lying within residential zones in inhabited Palestinian villages for rural land that legally was owned by the villagers. In this way the villagers could obtain much-desired real estate on which to build homes in their crowded communities since Israeli zoning laws forbade them from being constructed on their rural lands. In return the ILA obtained land to develop outside the built-up areas of Palestinian villages. But the exchange rate was very much to the ILA's advantage. Between 1965-80, the trade rate was 1:5.3. For every dunum that the ILA offered up, it received 5.3 dunums in return. Still, in "returning" formerly abandoned land to Arab usage after several decades this policy seemed to undermine Israel's insistence of the inviolability of its confiscation of refugee land.[2]

## 1967 War

Yet, overall, the refugee property question had slipped into tertiary status by the late spring of 1967. Indeed the military dimension of the Arab-Israeli conflict was heating up again. Four months after the American diplomats questioned their Israeli counterparts about compensation and heard their desultory response, war broke out again in the Middle East. The June 1967 war lasted only six days but permanently altered the Arab-Israeli conflict and with it the refugee property question. Israel's massive defeat of the combined armies of Egypt, Syria, and Jordan led to its conquest of the West Bank (including East Jerusalem) and Gaza, the remaining 23 percent of Palestine that had remained in Arab hands during the 1948 war. Beyond that, it occupied the Egyptian territory of the Sinai Peninsula and Syria's Golan Heights.

The overall effects of the 1967 war in changing the dimensions of the Arab-Israeli conflict are beyond the scope of this study. Suffice to say that the conflict, which already had shifted from a Jewish-Palestinian civil war toward an intra-state conflict by virtue of the 1948 and 1956 wars, became even more focused on Israel's relations with Arab states, rather than with the Palestinians. The increased involvement of the United States and the USSR in the conflict by virtue of their massive arms sales to the region only deepened the international focus on preventing further wars between Israel and the front-line Arab states. With passage of UN Security Council Resolution 242 of November 1967, diplomatic efforts to resolve the conflict largely focused on the "land for peace" formula instead of resolving lingering issues from 1948. Under this formula, Israel would withdraw from territories it conquered in 1967 in return for peace. The property question was subsumed within a general statement within Resolution 242 calling for resolution of the "refugee problem." Beyond this, global attention began focusing on a different aspect of the Zionist-Arab battle for control of land in Palestine. Israel quickly began laying hold of land in the West Bank and erecting both military and civilian settlements on it. Israeli land confiscation policies after 1967 posed a more immediate challenge to peacemakers and the Palestinian inhabitants of the Occupied Territories, and further helped push the question of 1948 refugee property off the diplomatic radar screens.

The war transformed the parties' attitudes toward the conflict and the refugees. The June War had demonstrated conclusively the Israeli military superiority presaged by the 1956 Suez War. For Israel, resolution of the conflict thereafter was clearly something that would be arranged on its terms by negotiations with its main enemies—the Arab states, not the Palestinians. Israeli cockiness later was shattered by the October 1973 war. However, armed with nuclear weapons since the 1960s, Israel decisively had asserted its military superiority over the Arabs. It now was becoming less and less subject to pressure from the United States or the world community to grant concessions to the Arabs, such as compensating the refugees for their abandoned property. An end to the conflict would involve trading recently occupied land for peace.

An interesting side aspect of Israeli policy toward 1948 refugee land that arose after its victory in 1967 was the issues raised by its occupation of the West Bank and Gaza. In the first place, Israel was now in a position to regain control over Jewish property in the newly occupied territories that had been sequestered by Jordanian and Egyptian authorities from 1948–67. The Order Concerning Jews' Property (the Gaza Strip and North Sinai) was passed in 1967, and a Commission of Jews' Property was established. In 1970, the Legal and Administrative Matters (Regulation) Law [Consolidated Version] generally allowed private Jews to seek the return of land sequestered by the Jordanians and Egyptians from the Israel Ministry of Justice's General Custodian (Heb.: ha-Apotropos ha-Kelali), which had taken possession of it upon the Israeli occupation in 1967. Jewish land that had been used by the Jordanians and Egyptians for public purposes, however, was not returned; the owners were paid compensation by the Israeli government instead. Other Jewish-owned areas were expropriated for construction of Jewish housing and urban renewal projects. Another dimension of this policy concerned Palestinians in East Jerusalem. When Israel extended its law to the area, it offered Israeli identity cards to Palestinians living there. Because Israel had allowed Jewish residents to regain lost property, a law was enacted allowing the Palestinian residents of East Jerusalem to seek compensation for any abandoned refugee property they had owned in Israeli West Jerusalem. The could not petition for restitution of the property, however.[3]

Israel also took its only serious action on compensation after the war in the early 1970s, but the effect was minimal and restricted to those Palestinians living in Israel. The Knesset passed the Absentees' Property (Compensation) Law of 5733/1973 on July 1, 1973 offering compensation for confiscated absentee property to those Palestinians who were residents of Israel (including East Jerusalem) as of July 1, 1973 or thereafter. The law required them to make claims within three years of that date or the onset of their date of residency. The law later was amended in 1976, 1982, and 1986. The 1986 version allowed claims to be filed up to fifteen years from the date of effect or two years from the date of residency.[4] The Ministry of Finance and the Justice Ministry were charged with executing the law. A commissioner was appointed to oversee this process. In April 1986, the Minister of Finance appointed the Custodian of Absentee Property to serve as the Commissioner of the Absentees' Property (Compensation) Law as well.

Considering Israel's overall dislike of the UNCCP and its methodology, it is interesting to note that the 1973 compensation law adopted the UNCCP Technical Office's approach to establishing a baseline figure for compensation. The law also noted that it would use mandatory rural land taxation categories for determining rural land values and mandatory "net annual value" (NAV) figures drawn from urban taxation records for reckoning the value of property in towns and cities. In the case of urban property, the law added that between 30 and 60 percent of the NAV would be added for urban property to help rectify the fact that the NAV was always a much lower figure than the actual market value of urban property. Since mandatory tax records were based on the value of the Palestinian pound, which was equal to the pound sterling, the resultant figures would be multiplied by 175 to obtain the corresponding figure in Israeli currency in 1973. Obviously, this did not affect the vast majority of Palestinian refugees living in exile. However, Israel also offered compensation to some Palestinians *outside* Israel as well. The Special Committee for the Return of Absentee Property, chaired by the prime minister's advisor on Arab affairs, approved 170 applications from such Palestinians between 1975-80 alone. Compensation was paid based on 1973 values plus an additional amount for inflation and four percent interest. It is not clear to the author how these claims were presented or how payment was effected.[5]

For its part, the United States also changed its attitudes toward the Arab-Israeli conflict and thus the property question after 1967. Beginning with the

Democratic administration of Lyndon B. Johnson but especially during the Republican administration of Richard M. Nixon, America drew increasingly closer to Israel. It provided Israel with more weapons (including top-of-the-line military aircraft) and aid. Nixon's preoccupation with containing the USSR was a product both of his world view and that of his National Security Advisor (and later, Secretary of State) Henry Kissinger. Nixon saw American interests at stake in almost every regional conflict around the globe in the early 1970s. Supporting Israel as a way of deterring Soviet influence in the Arab world was thus critical. When it came to peace-making, Nixon proved serious about the subject, but like Israel he viewed it as a matter for Israel and the Arab states to resolve—the Palestinians were not a factor.

The UN's role in solving the Arab-Israeli dilemma also was transformed by the events of June 1967. With the UNCCP moribund, the UN effectively relinquished its peacemaking role in the conflict to the United States after 1967. With the exception of the UN's inconclusive Jarring Mission of 1967–73, the real driving force behind diplomatic solutions to the Arab-Israeli conflict after 1967 would be the Americans. It was largely the failure of the UNCCP to effect a solution to the specifics of the refugee property problem that sealed the entire world body's fate in this regard. Yet this was not entirely its fault. As detailed in this study, the UNCCP was crippled in its efforts by a variety of factors, among them that the United States drew red lines around certain issues relating to the refugee question that largely coincided with Israeli positions. As the dominant force in the UNCCP, the Americans strove to maintain the inviolability of these red lines, were unwilling to pressure the Israelis, and did not possess sufficient standing with the Arabs to bring them on board U.S. positions. The result was that the UN's official organ for resolving the conflict, the UNCCP, was dead by 1966 as were future efforts on behalf of conciliation generally and refugee property specifically.

Finally, the Arab world was transformed by the 1967 war in ways that diminished its zeal to press for Palestinian refugee property rights. Egyptian President Jamal 'Abd al-Nasir was discredited by the war although he remained in power. Their armies in ruin and defiant in their defeat, the Arabs were in no mood to discuss much of anything with Israel let alone 1948 refugee property. Although UNRWA Deputy Commissioner Reddaway told the American ambassador in Tel Aviv in January 1968 that his recent talks with Israeli official Michael Comay revealed that Israel might be willing to pay compensation without prejudice to the right of return as part of a peace settlement,[6] the Arab states had decided on the "three nos" at the Khartoum summit of August 1967: no negotiations with Israel, no recognition of Israel, and no peace with Israel. No peace settlement developed, and the property question returned to the shadows.

The man who succeeded 'Abd al-Nasir upon his death in 1970, Anwar al-Sadat, became convinced that despite the "three nos" Egypt needed to withdraw from armed involvement in the Arab-Israel conflict. Even the Egyptian-Syrian assault on Israeli positions in the occupied Sinai and Golan Heights in October 1973 represented less of an all-out war on Israel than an attempt to break the diplomatic deadlock. Sadat continued his efforts to secure a diplomatic Egyptian exit from the conflict after the 1973 war. The Arab world's most powerful country had set itself on a course to transform the Arab-Israeli conflict once again.

One corner of the Arab world *did* actively pursue military confrontation with Israel after 1967, although ironically this also worked to the detriment of movement on the property question. The failure of either Arab military might or international diplomatic efforts to deal with the Palestinians' plight led to the rise of a host of political-guerrilla organizations like Fateh and the Popular Front for the Liberation of Palestine. These groups succeeded in taking over the Palestine Liberation Organization (PLO) in February 1968. With Fateh's Yasir 'Arafat as its new chair, the PLO became a major Arab player in the Arab-Israeli conflict while it served to change the focus of the Arab-Israeli conflict yet once again with tremendous consequences for the refugee property issue. This did *not* lead to the Palestinians championing the cause of compensating their own refugees. The Palestinian armed movement that engaged the Israelis from the late 1960s through the 1990s fought for a series of strategic goals vis-à-vis Israel, none of which included compensating the refugees for the abandoned property. Most PLO fighters believed that the refugees' salvation would come through a popular war of liberation aimed at defeating Israel and winning back their land. In the heady days of revolutionary optimism these fighters viewed compensation as treason, as the sale of the lost homeland to Israeli usurpers. Even when the PLO began replacing its exclusive commitment to armed struggle by pursuing diplomacy in the 1970s and especially after its defeat in Lebanon in 1982, the focus of its political efforts centered around creating an independent Palestinian state in the West Bank and Gaza, not the 1948 refugee issue.

The attitudes of Israel, the United States, the Arabs, and the Palestinians thus all were radically altered by the events of June 1967. The common result was increasingly less interest in the matter of the refugees' property. Whether through armed struggle or diplomacy, regional and international priorities toward the Arab-Israeli conflict had shifted. Little serious diplomatic attention thereafter would be given to the property question for the coming two decades.

## Declining Interest in the Property Question

By and large then the question of Palestinian refugee property faded into relative obscurity during the 1970s and 1980s. The longer the refugees lived in exile and the more the conflict drew attention away from them, the less the world thought about their property rights. This is not to suggest that the issue was forgotten altogether. Although they could not defeat Israel militarily on the battlefield, the Arab world continued to wage its diplomatic struggle in the halls of the UN. This effort served to keep the refugee property issue alive inasmuch as it became one of several political weapons in the hands of the Arabs.

The Arabs revived their earlier attempts to prompt the General Assembly into establishing a formal mechanism to protect the refugees' property rights. Instead of pushing for creation of a property custodian, they decided to seek the creation of a fund into which Israel would pay the income it generated from the refugee property. This effort finally succeeded in 1981 when the General Assembly passed Resolution 36/146 C on December 16 of that year. The resolution read in part:

> *Considering* that the Palestinian Arab refugees are entitled to their property in conformity with the principles of justice and equity, *Recalling*, in particular, its resolution 394 (V) of 14 December 1950, in which it directed the United Nations Conciliation Commission for Palestine . . . to prescribe measures for the protection of the rights, property and interests of the Palestinian Arab refugees . . . *Requests* the Secretary-General to take all appropriate steps, in consultation with the United Nations Conciliation Commission for Palestine, for the protection and administration of Arab property, assets and property rights in Israel, and to establish a fund for the receipt of income derived therefrom, on behalf of their rightful owners.

Despite passage of General Assembly Resolution 36/146 C, nothing happened to threaten U.S.-Israeli interests and the two remained concerned with other aspects of the conflict. In fact, the General Assembly reenacted the same property fund resolution for a number of years thereafter but nothing ever came of it. Nearly seventeen years later, the Arab League still was using the property question as part of its strategy in the UN. Arab League foreign ministers issued a declaration on September 16, 1998 calling on the UN to send a fact-finding mission to Israel to inspect the refugee land and to appoint a custodian to safeguard it. However, this was also a public relations exercise. The lack of action on the question and the Arabs' own nonchalance about such inaction merely underscored that for most of the Arab world the Palestinian refugee property issue merely had become a stick with which the Arabs sought to beat Israel at the UN.

## New Estimates of Refugee Property

On another less public front certain quarters demonstrated continued interest in the property question after the mid-1960s. Several serious new attempts to quantify the refugees' losses emerged starting in 1966. The studies are valuable because they offered some of the first detailed, public, nongovernmental studies of the value of refugee property and in so doing usually provided alternative methodologies to those used by the UNCCP. The first was conducted by the economist Yusif Sayigh. He was born in Syria in 1916, but grew up in Palestine after his family moved to Tiberias. During the mandate he was an official in the Bayt al-Mal, the fund of the Arab Higher Committee, as well as the head of the Palestinian branch of the pan-Syrian party of Antun Sa'ada, the Syrian Social Nationalist Party (also called the Parti Populaire Syrien). He was imprisoned by the Israelis during the 1948 war and exiled the following year. He was a good friend of Sami Hadawi, and requested and later received some documents from Hadawi relating to Palestinian land. Sayigh later went on to teach, advise governments, and serve the Palestinian nationalist cause, sitting on the PLO Executive Committee from 1968-74 and chairing its Palestinian National Fund from 1971-74.

Sayigh's study of the refugees' losses was part of his wider study of the Israeli economy that was published by the Arab League's Institute for Higher Arab Studies in 1966. His macro-level research produced a figure of £P7.567 billion in total personal losses suffered by the Palestinians. Table 7.1 reveals Sayigh's estimate of the scope and value of refugee land. Sayigh also developed figures for structures, which are shown in table 7.2. Finally, the figures he produced for abandoned capital and moveable property are shown in table 7.3.

Sayigh's study is significant for several reasons. First of all, it was the best assessment of refugee losses to have emerged in the Arab world since 1948.

TABLE 7.1 Scope and Value of Refugee Land According to Yusif Sayigh, 1966

| *Type* | *Scope (Dunums)* | *Value (£P)* |
|---|---|---|
| Citrus | 137,000 | 79,200,000 |
| Other orchards | 384,000 | 115,200,000 |
| Irrigated | 41,000 | 4,100,000 |
| Cereal | 4,400,000 | 176,000,000 |
| Potentially arable | 1,600,000 | 16,000,000 |
| Built-up | | |
| rural | 20,000 | 1,200,000 |
| urban | 29,250 | 11,700,000 |
| TOTAL | 6,611,250 | 403,400,000 |

Source: Yusuf 'Abdullah Sayigh, *al-Iqtisad al-Isra'ili* [The Israeli Economy] (Cairo: League of Arab States, Institute for Higher Arab Studies, 1966), p. 109

TABLE 7.2 Scope and Value of Refugee Buildings According to Yusif Sayigh, 1966

| *Type* | *Number* | *Value (£P)* |
|---|---|---|
| Homes | | |
| rural | 90,000 | 22,500,000 |
| urban | 60,000 | 150,000,000 |
| Mosques and churches | 1,500 | 4,500,000 |
| Factory buildings | 1,500 | 7,500,000 |
| Smiths, tailors, mechanics | 5,000 | 5,000,000 |
| Offices | 5,000 | 15,000,000 |
| Stores | | |
| rural | 2,000 | 800,000 |
| urban | 3,000 | 7,500,000 |
| Hotels | 1,000 | 15,000,000 |
| Restaurants, clubs, coffee houses | 2,000 | 4,000,000 |
| Plantation buildings | 2,000 | 5,000,000 |
| TOTAL | 173,000 | 236,800,000 |

Source: Sayigh *al-Iqtisad al-Isra'ili*, pp. 107–108

TABLE 7.3 Value of Refugee Capital and Moveable Property According to Yusif Sayigh, 1966

| *Type* | *Value (£P)* |
|---|---|
| Furniture, personal goods | |
| rural | 12,500,000 |
| urban | 50,000,000 |
| Factory equipment | 15,000,000 |
| Capital goods in offices, hotels, restaurants, coffee shops | 3,000,000 |
| Inventories | 5,000,000 |
| Farm animals | 10,000,000 |
| Bank accounts and insurance policies | 2,000,000 |
| Commercial vehicles | 15,000,000 |
| TOTAL | 112,500,000 |

Source: Sayigh *al-Iqtisad al-Isra'ili*, pp. 108–110

Sayigh also considered the value of "potentially arable" land in his study, something the UNCCP did not address. He also went far beyond the UNCCP and others in addressing the value of public institutions like mosques and churches as well as commercial properties like tailor shops and so forth. Sayigh's figures for compensation thus go far beyond the value of privately owned land which had always remained the focus of the UNCCP's efforts from 1952-64. His figures also went considerably beyond those that other Arabs had developed in the 1950s, which typically reflected the losses from the perspective of wealthy refugees rather than the Palestinian community as a whole. Sayigh tried to develop an exhaustive estimate that incorporated the sum total of the Palestinian community's losses in 1948.

Sayigh's friend Sami Hadawi later produced another detailed estimate of the property. Hadawi lived an active life after his involvement with the UNCCP and the Arab Land Experts conferences. Among other things, he worked with his friend Izzat Tannous' Palestine Arab Refugee Office in New York, headed the Institute for Palestine Studies in Beirut from 1965-68, and worked in the Arab League's offices in New York and Dallas. But his was a life marked by frustration and tragedy. He had been shunned from the third Arab Land Expert's conference and witnessed the overall tenor of the Arab-Israeli conflict shift away from issues regarding the 1948 refugees after the tumultuous events of 1967. Beyond that, his beloved Lebanese wife since 1931, Nora Nasib Badr, died in the United States in August 1965. Hadawi buried her in her native Lebanon and eventually retired and settled in Canada. He remained an avid writer on issues relating to the refugees and a became vocal critic of the UNCCP Technical Program's assessment of the scope of their property losses.

Hadawi was particularly critical of the Technical Office's methodology. In a number of books he authored, he scored the UNCCP for focusing exclusively on land that it could prove had been privately owned by Arabs. Like Sayigh, he felt that this narrow focus ignored other land that was clearly used by Palestinians individually or collectively but lacked the type of formal documentation utilized by the UNCCP. Hadawi contended that the UNCCP should also have taken account of communally owned land, land in the Beersheba district, and other land that he argued was part of the Palestinians' rightful patrimony. For this reason, he argued that the Technical Office's statistics on the scope of the property released in 1964 were far too low. In 1983, Hadawi found his chance to use his considerable expertise on the refugee property question to make a formal revisionist study of the issue when Jordan's Crown Prince Hassan agreed to provide $150,000 for a 12-month study of the matter under Hadawi's direction. The Jordanian government then approached the UNCCP as an interested party host to large numbers of refugees and asked for permission to view its records. Having secured permission, the Jordanians turned the project over to Hadawi and two assistants he hired who traveled to New York to go through the UNCCP material beginning in September 1983. Their work was completed the following September, after which Hadawi worked with the economist Atif Kubursi in arriving at conclusions about the refugee land's value. The study was finally published in 1988.[7]

Hadawi and Kubursi's study asserted that Palestinians had owned a much larger amount of land than either the UNCCP's 1951 Global Estimate or 1964 Technical Program had arrived at. The difference was largely the result of Hadawi's calculations of what constituted Arab land in the Beersheba district. He eventually determined that 19,031,012 dunums had been owned by Arabs in what became Israel, including the Beersheba district and including land owned by Palestinians who remained in Israel. This figure is detailed in table 7.4. Kubursi estimated that the total value of refugee land, presumably excluding the land of those Palestinians who remained in Israel, at P£528.9 million as shown in table 7.5.

Hadawi had finally published his definitive work on the subject with which he had been so personally and professionally involved for most of his adult life. The book was his rebuttal to the now-dormant UNCCP. He always had carried a grudge against the UNCCP not only for having fired him but

TABLE 7.4 Scope of Arab Land in Israel According to Hadawi and Kubursi, 1988

| *Type* | *Amount (Dunums)* |
|---|---|
| 1. Outside Beersheba District | |
| Urban | 112,000 |
| Citrus and banana | 132,849 |
| Village built-up | 21,160 |
| Cultivable (tax categories 5–8) | 471,672 |
| Cultivable (tax categories 9–13) | 2,937,683 |
| Cultivable (tax categories 14–15) | 444,541 |
| Uncultivable | 2,377,946 |
| Roads, etc. | 83,161 |
| TOTAL | 6,581,012 |
| 2. Beersheba District | 12,450,000 |
| GRAND TOTAL | 19,031,012 |

Source: Sami Hadawi, *Palestinian Rights & Losses in 1948. A Comprehensive Study.* Part V: An Economic Assessment of Total Palestinian Losses written by Dr. Atef Kubursi (London: Saqi Books, 1988) p. 113

TABLE 7.5 Value of Refugee Land According to Hadawi and Kubursi, 1988

| *Type* | *Value (P£)* |
|---|---|
| Urban land | 130,300,000 |
| Rural land | 398,600,000 |
| TOTAL | 528,900,000 |

Source: Hadawi, *Palestinian Rights & Losses in 1948*, p. 187

for ignoring his pleas to approach the entire Technical Program differently while he was employed there. After publishing his book in 1988, Hadawi thereafter remained interested in refugee property and the Arab-Israeli conflict. Although he possessed a British passport and therefore could travel to Israel, he refused to return and look at what had become of his home or his beloved aviary in West Jerusalem after he fled in 1948. His efforts on behalf of the refugees were not entirely unnoticed either. At age 93 in November 1997, the PLO awarded him the Palestine Prize for Documentation "for his role in the advancement of documentation specific to Palestinian land and his participation in raising the level of national culture."[8]

More recently a detailed new economic assessment of the scope and value of abandoned rural refugee land was published by a non-Palestinian. The scholar Frank Lewis determined that 5,667,400 dunums of rural land in Israel had been owned by Arabs as of 1948. Of this, he estimated that 4.8 million dunums belonged to refugees.[9] His statistics are presented in table 7.6.

Again, he felt that 4,800,000 of the 5,667,400 dunums belonged to refugees (the rest belonging to Palestinians who stayed). Lewis's study is noteworthy because he chose a novel new approach to determining the value of rural refugee land. Instead of capitalizing tax assessments as the UNCCP had done, Lewis chose "agricultural output" as the standard for determining the value of the refugees' losses. He ultimately determined that the value of the rural abandoned land was between £P144.5–180.7 million in 1945 prices.[10] Because it was not used for agriculture, Lewis did not try to set a value on abandoned urban land. Beyond that, Lewis also valued all Arab farm implements in Israel (both for refugees and those who remained) at £P3.3 million, livestock at £P10.2 million, and buildings at £P29.7 million. Of the resulting total of £P34.2 million, he estimated that £P24.3 million represented the losses sustained by the refugees. Lewis thus concluded that the total value of refugees' rural land, buildings, farm implements, and livestock amounted to between £P168.8 -205 million in 1945 prices. In 1993 U.S. dollars this totaled between $2.2-2.6 billion. With interest compounded at 3 percent per annum

TABLE 7.6 Scope of Arab-Owned Land in Israel in 1948 According to Frank Lewis, 1996

| | *Amount of Land In Tax Categories (Dunums)* | | | |
|---|---|---|---|---|
| *District* | *1–3* | *5–8* | *9–15* | *Total* |
| Galilee | 9,700 | 215,600 | 958,200 | 1,183,500 |
| Gaza | 22,000 | 57,200 | 2,530,500 | 2,609,700 |
| Haifa | 4,000 | 30,200 | 325,700 | 356,300 |
| Jerusalem | 0 | 43,800 | 390,600 | 434,400 |
| Lydda | 89,400 | 69,900 | 443,800 | 603,100 |
| Samaria | 14,400 | 38,000 | 428,100 | 480,500 |
| TOTAL | 135,900 | 454,700 | 5,076,800 | 5,667,400 |

Source: Frank D. Lewis, "Agricultural Property and the 1948 Palestinian Refugees: Assessing the Loss." *Explorations in Economic History* 33 (1996): 173

from 1948-93, the total compensation amount would reach between $8.1–9.9 billion in 1993 dollars.[11]

## Refugee Property and Diplomatic Sites in Jerusalem

The refugee property question also resurfaced in the 1980s and became embroiled in a diplomatic issue unrelated to compensation. For years pro-Israeli legislators in the U.S. Senate had tried to force the executive branch to move the American embassy in Israel from Tel Aviv to Jerusalem as a show of solidarity with the Jewish state. Like most countries, the United States had long located its embassy in Tel Aviv out of deference to the undetermined legal status of Jerusalem. The United States did maintain consulates in both East and West Jerusalem. After the Senate passed the so-called Helms Amendment of July 26, 1988, Public Law 100-459 set the stage for serious attempts by the administration of Presidents Ronald Reagan and George H.W. Bush to investigate the possibilities of moving the embassy to West Jerusalem. The Israelis were happy to oblige, anxious as they were to have the most powerful country on earth interested in moving its embassy to the disputed city that they claimed as their capital. The Americans located a site, but before signing the lease they carried out a "title search" on the property to make sure that the Israeli government had the legal right to lease the land. Satisfied, they signed a 99-year lease on January 18, 1989 by which they would lease 32.250 dunums of land just south of the Old City on the road to Bethlehem for the symbolic amount of $1 per year.[12]

The Americans wanted to avoid disputes over title because they had faced just such a problem in 1949: What to do when the land on which an American diplomatic facility is located is claimed both by the Israeli government and Palestinian refugees? The first American consulate in Jerusalem was located on Mamilla Road in West Jerusalem. Until the city was divided in 1948, it was the only American consulate in the city. The Americans later established another one on Nablus Road in Jordanian-controlled East Jerusalem. The original consulate leased the land on Mamilla Road from Darwish Da'udi, a member of the Dajani family of Jerusalem. In December 1946, two years before the onset of the massive refugee exodus, Da'udi left Palestine for Alexandria, Egypt and the Americans sent him the money at his new home. The consulate survived the 1948 fighting but the result was that the Americans did not pay rent to anyone for several months. In early 1949, Da'udi wrote to the Americans from Egypt seeking payment of all back rent, but in March

1949, the consulate received another letter from an Israeli lawyer representing the Israeli Custodian of Absentee Property requesting that the back rent be paid to the Custodian as the new guardian of the "abandoned" property.

Confused American diplomats wrote to Washington seeking advice. The Department of State eventually determined that the Israeli authorities were "within [their] legal rights" according to the Abandoned Property Ordinance to seek payment, but requested the diplomats in Jerusalem to ask the Custodian to make an exception in this instance so that Da'udi could be paid $600 in back rent for the 1947-48 year. The department's logic was that since rent was technically due in advance, Da'udi should have been paid before the war and before the Custodian was even in existence. Payments for the period after 1948 were another matter. Eventually, however, it was decided to pay all the back rent to the Custodian, who received £I108 for the period July 1, 1947–June 30, 1948, £I150- for July 1, 1948-June 30, 1949 as well as £I47.500 for July 1, 1949-October 24, 1949. The Americans also expressed an interest in buying the building, but the Custodian was not allowed to sell property under his control until after 1950.[13]

Thereafter American diplomats continued to monitor to question of other foreign diplomatic sites located on refugee property in Jerusalem over the years and what payment arrangements the governments in question carried out. In August 1962, the consulate general submitted a report on the subject to the Department of State in Washington. American officials in Jerusalem reported that at least three such sites were located on the land of refugees and that each government followed a different policy regarding whom to pay rent. The first was that of the Belgian consul's residence. In this case, the Belgian government paid rent on the property directly to the refugee, Constantine Salama, who was living in Lebanon. He was paid each month by Belgian diplomats who traveled outside Israel to transfer the funds. Apparently this policy annoyed the Israeli government, which once dispatched the police to threaten the Belgian consul with eviction for failure to pay rent to the Custodian of Absentee Property.[14] The second diplomatic site was the Venezuelan embassy. The Palestinian-owned building it occupied had formerly housed the Polish consulate. When the Poles left the building, the Custodian took it over as abandoned property and then rented it to the Venezuelans who sent payments to the Custodian. The final example involved the Italian consulate. In this case, the Italians avoided the diplomatic problem of whom to pay altogether by simply paying no one after 1948.[15]

Despite the Americans' confidence that they were not getting into the same trouble with the new Jerusalem embassy site, questions about the lease almost immediately were raised by Arab-American activists in the United States. In addition to objecting to the wider diplomatic implications of moving the American embassy to Jerusalem, these persons contended that the embassy site *did* consist at least in part of land that Israel confiscated from Palestinian refugees. In May 1989, the Attiyeh Foundation wrote to Representative Lee Hamilton, the chair of the Subcommittee on Europe and the Middle East of the U.S. House of Representatives, noting these points and moreover stating that part of the land of the proposed embassy site consisted of refugee waqf. The Department of State twice responded to Hamilton's inquiries that summer and fall, stating that it was aware of the claims of waqf but had conducted a title search that had revealed nothing. The department also claimed to know nothing of other claims to the land.

Unsatisfied, a group of Palestinian-Americans working with the Institute for Palestine Studies (IPS) decided to conduct a full investigation of the matter utilizing UNCCP archival material it obtained from the UN archives through the good offices of the PLO mission to the UN (see below), along with other archival and private family records. The Palestinian historian Walid Khalidi, head of IPS and the American Committee on Jerusalem that had been formed around the issue, publicly announced the results of the study on February 18, 2000. He noted that 71 percent of the proposed embassy site was refugee land that had belonged to 15 Muslim and 4 Christian families at the time of the 1948 war. Of their descendants, 88 heirs were U.S. citizens, 43 held Canadian or European citizenship, in addition to hundreds of others. The Department of State, unimpressed with the findings, tried to deflect the matter by claiming in late December 1999 that the United States had not yet "entered into" the lease and stating that the massive documentation produced by the group would be "kept on file."[16]

The episode would not be the last time that Israeli authorities attempted to lure embassies to the disputed city. The Israeli press reported in May 1998 that the government intended to set aside land in the 'Ayn Karm region of West Jerusalem for future embassy sites-a move that triggered more than 30,000 refugees from 'Ayn Karm to sign a protest petition directed to UN Secretary-General Kofi Annan.[17]

## Refugee Property and the Peace Process: Israel and Egypt, Jordan, Syria, and Lebanon

The late 1970s witnessed the beginning of peace talks and eventually even peace treaties between Israel and some of its Arab adversaries, marking yet another shift in the Arab-Israeli conflict that would affect the question of Palestinian refugee property. The Egyptian-Israel peace talks under U.S. auspices at Camp David, Maryland, in September 1978 led to the signing of a full fledged Egyptian-Israeli peace treaty on March 26, 1979, another fact that once again changed the nature of the conflict. Not only did the treaty remove the Arab world's largest and militarily strongest state from active confrontation with Israel, but also it seemed to validate the land for peace formula as the most appropriate way to resolve the conflict. The peace process also helped return the question of refugee property to greater public prominence, although ironically this has not yet led to resolution of the refugees' claims.

The peace treaty between Egypt and Israel opened the door for Egyptian and Israeli citizens to press for property claims in one another's countries since they were no longer at war. Article 8 of the peace treaty established a mutual claims commission by which the two sides could explore these topics after decades of inaction when they were at war and had no bilateral diplomatic relations. This is no doubt what earlier had prompted Clara Sursuq to write from Egypt to the UN in May 1950 inquiring about the fate of the property owned by George Lutf Allah Sursuq in northern Palestine.[18] Once peace had been concluded with Israel in 1979, Egyptian citizens who had abandoned property in Palestine in 1948 could seek legal redress. Egyptian Jews who were now Israeli citizens could also seek compensation for their own lost property. The author is unaware of any serious Egyptian Arab claims for compensation in this regard. As for Jewish claims, the leading Egyptian political figure Osama el-Baz claimed at a August 9, 2000 press conference that no Egyptian Jews ever sought to reclaim lost land. Dismissing the question as a "non-issue," el-Baz asserted that "not a single claim was presented. And we would welcome any of these people because we still have strong ties with them."[19]

However, Israelis of Egyptian extraction *did* look into the matter. Some hired Israeli lawyers to resolve their property claims after 1979, according to Moshe Sasson, Israel's first ambassador to Egypt. Sasson stated that some of these Israeli lawyers actually nominated local Egyptian lawyers to work on these cases for them.[20] In addition to those in Israel, Jews of other nationalities also sought to reclaim confiscated property in both Egyptian and foreign courts, in some instances even before the Israeli-Egyptian peace treaty. A Canadian Jew, Albert Metzger, brought suit in Egypt before the treaty to regain his property that had been seized after his expulsion in 1956. This property included the Cecil Hotel in Alexandria. In 1978, an Egyptian court ruled that his family was entitled to the land and the Court of Cassation upheld the decision in April 2000 following an appeal. More recently another Canadian

Jew, Raphael Bigio, obtained a decree from the Egyptian Ministry of Finance to have land confiscated from his family in the Heliopolis section of Cairo returned to him. The family were immigrants to Egypt from the Jewish community of Aleppo, Syria, in the early years of the twentieth century, and had leased their land to the Coca-Cola Company beginning in the 1930s. The Egyptian government expropriated the land in 1962, and the Bigio family fled Egypt in 1965. Coca-Cola then continued to lease the land from the Egyptian government until 1994, when it bought a substantial interest in the land. The Egyptian Ministry of Finance agreed to return the land to Bigio in 1980, but nothing ever happened. After the sale to Coca-Cola in 1994, Bigio and several other family members brought suit against the company in the U.S. Second District Court of New York in April 1997 to reclaim the land. Bigio brought the suit under the Alien Tort Claims Law, a U.S. law that allows foreign nationals to bring suit in American courts for violations of international law or for damages they incurred when such violations occur.[21] Although the court threw out the case, the dismissal was overturned on appeal by the U.S. Second Circuit Court of Appeals in December 2000 and the case was still alive at time of writing.[22]

Despite these efforts by individual Jews such as these, the Israeli government itself never has made any public efforts on behalf of Jewish property in Egypt after 1979. Given Israel's repeated public concern over the fate of lost Jewish property in the Arab world since the early 1950s, this might seem perplexing on the surface. With the Egyptian-Israeli peace treaty opening the door for the settlement of claims, one might presume that the Israeli government would have moved toward resolution of some of these claims with alacrity. However, as noted in chapter 3, the Israeli government's attitudes toward Jewish property essentially were based on its desire to leverage such claims against Palestinian refugee claims. The Israeli government therefore decided to defer presentation of formal government-to-government compensation claims with the Egyptians because it did not wish to use up this political capital until such future time that Palestinian claims might be discussed. It also has been suggested that Israel feared that making use of a mutual claims committee because that might open the door for Egypt to claim compensation for the oil that Israel pumped out of the Sinai oilfields it occupied from 1967–1975.[23] Another reason is that the Israeli government did not want to be seen as responsible for paying out claims to its own Egyptian Jewish immigrants.

This reticence was not lost on some Mizrahi Jews who had an interest in this subject. One such senior Mizrahi politician was Knesset member Shlomo

Hillel. Born in Baghdad in 1923, Hillel immigrated to Palestine in 1934. He played a role in Operation 'Ezra and Nehemya and served on Israel's Commission for the Registration of the Claims of Iraqi Immigrants in 1956. He later became a government minister, chair of the World Zionist Organization's Foundation Fund [Heb.: Keren ha-Yesod], and speaker of the Knesset. Hillel asked Prime Minister Menachem Begin on the Knesset floor in 1979 whether the Israeli-Egyptian treaty would lead to discussions over lost Jewish property in the Arab world. Begin told him that the treaty had created a claims committee, and "[w]hen the day comes, we will submit our claim for the return of illegally taken property."[24]

Nor was Israeli governmental reticence lost on Shlomo Cohen-Sidon of the Association of Egyptian Immigrants in Israel, the man who had sued the Israeli government in connection with Egyptian Jewish property claims in 1960. He was also quick to seize upon the peace treaty to remind his government of Egyptian Jewish property. In February 1980, Cohen-Sidon wrote to Begin insisting that it was the Israeli government that was now responsible for paying compensation to its Egyptian immigrants in light of the peace treaty and the claims committee it created. Deputy Director of the Ministry of Foreign Affairs Elyakim Rubinstein responded to Cohen-Sidon that it would be possible for Israel to raise these claims with the Egyptian government once the claims committee was formed but did not accede to Cohen-Sidon's argument that the Israeli government was responsible for paying out compensation in the meantime. To date the Israelis never have activated the mutual claims commission for this purpose.[25]

A revealing footnote to this story involves Elyakim Rubinstein's involvement in Israeli-Palestinian peace negotiations twenty years later. During the Camp David II summit of July 2000 (discussed more fully below), Rubinstein was one of Israel's lead negotiators. At the summit he openly confirmed that the reason that the Israeli government had deferred pressing for Jewish property claims against Egypt after 1979 was in order to keep such political capital intact until such time as Israel could bring it up in connection with Palestinian claims. When Palestinian negotiators asked their Israeli counterparts at Camp David II why Israel had not broached the question of Jewish property in Egypt much earlier with the government of Egypt and was bringing it up now with the Palestinians, Rubinstein responded, "We decided to keep this subject for the talks on the Palestinian refugees."[26]

Interestingly, on at least one occasion Jews outside the Israeli government have brought up the issue of Jewish property in Egypt, but not in connection with either the Israeli-Egyptian peace treaty or Israeli-Palestinian negotiations.

In this instance, the call was made to link the fate of Jewish property in Egypt with *American* aid to Egypt. In August 2000, World Jewish Congress (WJC) Executive Director Elan Steinberg suggested linking the compensation of Egyptian Jews with U.S. foreign aid assistance to Egypt.[27] It is unclear whether or how the savings to the U.S. treasury would be used to compensate either Jews from Egypt or the Israeli government.

Diplomatic efforts aimed at a peaceful resolution to the Arab-Israeli conflict continued throughout the 1980s, but led to no major breakthroughs until the early 1990s. The U.S.-led coalition's military victory over Iraq in the 1991 Gulf War paved the way for a new Middle East and new diplomatic efforts. The October 1991 Madrid peace conference convened by the United States and the USSR directly led to a series of bilateral and multilateral Arab-Israeli negotiations. As a result, Israel signed its second peace treaty with an Arab state, Jordan, on October 26, 1994. The refugee property question resurfaced although this time both the Jordanian government and private Jordanian citizens raised it in a more forceful way than had the Egyptians.

The Jordanian government almost immediately decided to use the provisions of the peace treaty to seek compensation for Jordanian citizens who had owned land in pre-1948 Palestine. This meant not only those relatively few East Bank Transjordanians who had owned property in Palestine, such as the large landowner Shibli Ibrahim Bisharat, but also the thousands of property-owing Palestinians who now held Jordanian passports. The Jordanians' rationale was that now that Jordan and Israel were at peace, Jordanian citizens no longer should be considered enemies or absentees under Israel's laws. Because many 1948 Palestinian refugees now held Jordanian passports this idea alarmed the Israelis, who quickly passed a law to stymie such efforts. The Knesset ratified the peace treaty by enacting the Law of Implementation of the Peace Treaty, article 6.b of which stated that Jordanian citizens who had been declared absentees prior to the peace treaty would remain classified as such. The Jordanian government was outraged.

Jordan's first ambassador to Israel, Marwan Muasher, sent a formal protest over the law to the Israeli government in August 1995. He claimed that the Knesset legislation violated article 11.b. of the peace treaty calling for both parties to abolish discriminatory legislation, and cited article 25 calling for creation of a claims committee to investigate financial claims. Muasher never received a formal response from the Israelis but was told informally that Israel was going to defer dealing with this matter until talks with the Palestinians, as they had done in the Egyptian case. The ambassador countered that this was a bilateral Jordanian-Israeli matter that should not be linked to wider regional issues. Nevertheless, he still never received a formal reply to his letter. The Israelis would not even give him the name and telephone number of Yehezkel Shammash, the Custodian of Absentee Property who had assumed his duties earlier in 1995. When Israeli Foreign Minister Shimon Peres came to Jordan later that October, he requested of Crown Prince Hassan that Jordan desist in continuing to bring up the issue.[28] The Jordanian government did go on to form a six-member committee to investigate the question of 1948 property compensation. Headed by the Minister of Finance, the group included current and past officials from the Department of Lands and Survey, the Ministry of Justice, and the Ministry of Interior. However, the committee met only three times and never accomplished anything concrete. Since that time, the Jordanian government has not made any significant public efforts on behalf of property compensation.[29]

Despite its reticence to pursue the matter publicly with vigor, the Jordanian government decided to prepare for the eventuality of negotiations with Israel on the compensation question in a more quiet, technical manner. It decided in 1999 to create a computerized data base of Arab landowners in Palestine using the films Jordan purchased from the UNCCP in 1974. The Ministry of Finance's Department of Lands and Survey was approached by the Department of Palestinian Affairs within the Foreign Ministry about undertaking the project. The Prime Minister's office later provided the funds for the project (which totaled JD200,000), and the two departments came to an agreement in March 1999. Thirty-five employees were hired as part of the project that was undertaken by the Department of Lands and Survey's Documentation Department. Data were extracted not only from the films but from extant British and Ottoman registers in the land department's possession since 1948.

In July 2001, the land department publicly announced that the project had been completed and the computerized data base assembled. However, the department tried to dismiss speculation that the project was political in nature and insisted that had been purely a "technical" undertaking. This was belied, however, by the fact that it also was announced that the public would not be granted access to the information contained in the data base for the time being.[30] A public statement made by Jordanian Foreign Minister 'Abd al-Ilah al-Khatib a few days before the announcement of the project's completion also hinted at Jordan's ongoing political interest in the property question. Al-Khatib told a gathering of refugees in the Baq'a camp outside Amman that Jordan had not forgotten about pressing Israel to compensate refugees in Jordan. "Jordan will not make any concessions on its citizens' right of return or on their right for reparations."[31] Some have noted the political subtext of the Jordanian announcement that it possessed a property data base: by positioning itself as the protector of abandoned property the Jordanian government might be trying to woo property-owning Palestinians away from the PLO in hopes that the Jordanian government might be better situated to realize a settlement of their property claims than the PLO.

The Jordanian government was not alone in raising the issue of refugee property in the wake of Jordanian-Israeli peace. So too did private Jordanian citizens. In February 1997 the issue rose to the level of a public controversy in Jordan when the Israeli embassy in Amman issued an announcement confirming that the 1948 property held by persons with Jordanian passports still was considered absentee property in accordance with Knesset legislation. The announcement also noted that the Israeli government considered this as being consistent with the Jordanian-Israeli peace treaty. In response, a number of Jordanians of both Transjordanian and Palestinian background formed an organization in March 1997 that was aimed at pressuring the Jordanian government to take more forceful issue with Israel's position. Nothing public eventually came of this action.[32] In addition, some private citizens have hired Israeli lawyers to look into ways they can seek redress. In some instances, these lawyers have traveled to the Jordanian Department of Lands and Survey in Amman seeking information on behalf of their clients.[33]

For its part, the Israeli government never used the opportunity of peace with Jordan to seek compensation for Jewish-owned land in Jordan. The Israelis never publicly discussed the 6,000 dunums of land along the Jordan River owned by the Palestine Electric Corporation (PEC), title to which apparently was later transferred to the JNF. To the author's knowledge, no other Jewish property claims have been raised diplomatically either. The question of Jewish land in Jordan was broached publicly in Israel however. In May 1997, the JNF published a list of property it claimed to own in Arab countries that included 16,000 dunums northeast of Amman. Apparently no mention was made of the PEC land.[34] According to Marwan Muasher, Israeli reticence to bring up the question of Jewish land in Jordan may be because Israel fears such action would set a precedent for Jordanian citizens to press for compensation for lost land in Palestine. Like the case of Egypt, Israel apparently did want to spend its political capital prior to serious discussions with the Palestinians.

Refugee property questions also have arisen recently in connection with peace moves between Israel and other Arab states as well. Israeli-Lebanese talks went nowhere in the early 1990s, but Lebanon nonetheless starting preparing for the possibility of a future peace deal. Lebanese citizens had lost land in Palestine in 1948, including from the Sursuq and Jabara families. In February 2000, Prime Minister Salim al-Huss called on Lebanese citizens who had owned land in pre-1948 Palestine to provide documentation to the Lebanese Ministry of Foreign Affairs. Al-Huss earlier had stated that Lebanon was preparing a legal case to seek redress for direct and indirect losses sustained by Lebanese citizens as a result of the 1948 Arab-Israeli war. A Lebanese newspaper cited a figure of $US8 billion that Israel owed Lebanon for property left in 1948 Palestine alone. The Foreign Ministry then announced in March 2000 that any interested Lebanese citizen should contact the ministry's Center for Legal Research in Beirut or the Lebanese embassy in Washington. Although the embassy refused the author's request to reveal how much land, if any, was registered, the Arabic press reported on the case of one such Lebanese citizen, Faruq Hamada, who had provided the Foreign Ministry with 45 documents and tax receipts from 1936-38 indicating ownership of three dunums in two villages.[35]

This was not the first time that the Lebanese authorities had tried to seek compensation for losses their nationals had sustained in the 1948 war. In March 1958, Lebanon's delegate to the UN asked the UNCCP to take note of a claim that a Lebanese company was seeking from Israel. The firm of Sabbagh and Abi al-Lama' had purchased the moveable assets belonging to the British army base at Azzib (al-Zib) on April 29, 1948 as the British prepared to withdraw. The Israeli army took over the camp during the fighting, and the company was seeking £UK2 million in compensation for their newly purchased but now disappeared property. The Lebanese delegate submitted the claim to the UNCCP, which then asked the UN Secretariat's legal department to study the matter. In June 1958, the UN counsel offered the opinion that the seized Lebanese property did not constitute a case of refugee property, since the Lebanese firm could not be construed as being a refugee, nor was it a matter of "war damages." Rather, it constituted a case of Israeli control over "enemy property" given that Israel and Lebanon had been and still technically were at war. Since the UNCCP's mandate only obliged it to work toward compensation of the refugees and not toward resolving claims of war damages and sequestered enemy property, the legal advisor stated that the Lebanese claim rightfully belonged on the agenda of any future Israeli-Lebanese peace talks. Still, the UNCCP told the Lebanese delegate that it "took note" of the claim and filed the detailed list of the lost property among its records that eventually were housed in the UN Secretariat archives in New York.[36]

Israeli-Syrian diplomatic discussions after the Madrid peace conference of 1991 also raised the possibility of compensation efforts between the two sides, although they did not produce a peace treaty. Syrians had owned land in pre-1948 Palestine, including prominent figures from the al-Shamma' family and even Shukri al-Quwatli, three-time president of Syria who led the country during the 1948 war. It is unclear to the author whether or not Syria has ever sought compensation for such persons. When Israeli and Syrian negotiators met under American auspices at Shepherdstown, West Virginia, however, in early 2000, the subject of Jewish property in Syria *was* raised, and in a public manner. Once again, however, this was not the doing of the Israeli government but the JNF, which publicly brought up the question of its lost land in southern Syria on January 6, 2000. The following day the JNF notified Israeli negotiators at Shepherdstown about the presence of JNF land in Hawran and Golan in order that the government not forget about the issue.[37] Two days later, JNF officials met to discuss the fate of this and other land it claims in Arab countries.[38] According to Yosef Kalesh of the Organization of Syrian Immigrants in Israel, his group also intended to approach the government of Prime Minister Ehud Barak and request that compensation for Syrian Jewish property be raised at the Shepherdstown talks. Kalesh told the Reuters news service: "The state of Israel needs to be compensated by Syria and it must then compensate the Jews here . . . . They are demanding every last centimeter of their land back [in the Golan Heights] so why shouldn't we demand every last centimeter of our property, every last house?"[39] Kalesh claimed that his organization possessed property lists, but the group's head, former Israeli ambassador to Egypt Moshe Sasson, denied this.[40]

Finally, some private Israelis even suggested raising property claims against Arab states that were *not* involved in the peace process. In the wake of the 1991 Gulf War, Yoram Dinstein, president of Tel Aviv University, suggested that the property claims of Iraqi Jews be linked with Iraqi compensation to the UN. Dinstein noted that the claims of those Iraqi Jews who were now citizens of nations that had gone to war with Iraq as part of the US-led coalition be added to the compensation list that was being demanded of Iraq. The Israeli Ministry of Foreign Affairs and organizations of Jews from Arab states like WOJAC reportedly were hostile to the idea because it therefore would impinge upon the Israeli government's ability to use these claims as leverage in its future peace negotiations.[41]

## Refugee Property and the Israel-Palestinian Peace Process

Surely it was the peace process between Israel and the PLO that revived most directly the decades-old question of refugee property and that spawned the most activity in the mid to late-1990s. The dramatic diplomatic breakthrough achieved between Israel and the PLO when they signed the Declaration of Principles on September 13, 1993 shifted the Arab-Israeli conflict back to its origins: two conflicting nationalist visions competing for the same territory. Although the so-called Oslo process led to a series of agreements that created the PLO-run Palestinian Authority in parts of the West Bank and Gaza in 1994, Israeli and Palestinian negotiators agreed to defer discussing issues relating to the 1948 refugees until "final status" talks would commence after an interim period. The prospect for forthcoming compensation talks engendered a host of activities related to the refugee property question on the part of Palestinians, Israelis, and others.

PLO negotiators and private Palestinian groups began preparing for talks on refugee property by seeking to acquire complete records of such property. The valuable property abandoned in West Jerusalem attracted particular attention. The Palestinian Society for the Protection of Human Rights and the Environment (LAWE) began compiling a database of Arab land ownership in pre-1948 West Jerusalem in 1996. The Institute for Jerusalem Studies, affiliated with the Institute for Palestine Studies, also collected and published information on Palestinian property in West Jerusalem in 1999.[42] More recently, the BADIL Resource Center for Palestinian Residency and Refugee Rights dispatched a delegation of refugees to Bosnia-Herzegovina in 2002 to study, among other things, the process of refugee property restitution in the wake of the bloody war that wracked that country in the early 1990s. This process was being supervised by the Commission for Real Property Claims, a body established by the 1995 Dayton Peace Agreement that ended the Bosnian war.[43]

Not just Palestinian NGOs were involved in such preparatory efforts. So too was the PLO. Geographers at the Arab Studies Society working in Orient House, the PLO's unofficial headquarters in East Jerusalem, began another project in 1995 to gather photographs and documents attesting to Palestinian ownership of land in West Jerusalem prior to 1948. According to the Arab Study Society's Khalil Tufakji, Palestinians owned some 5,700 homes in the western part of the city in 1948. Tufakji's information has been reportedly been assembled into a computerized GIS (geographic information system) database that includes both owners' names and maps detailing individual parcels of land.[44] In June 1998, the PLO official in charge of Jerusalem affairs, Faisal Husseini, who also worked out of Orient House, traveled to Turkey. Among other things, he spoke with officials of the Turkish archives about the possibility of Palestinian researchers using the archives to find Ottoman-era data on Arab ownership of land in West Jerusalem.[45] In July 1999, PLO

Chairman Yasir 'Arafat asked Turkish President Süleiman Demirel as well for permission to examine the Turkish archives for information on Arab property in Palestine.[46] It also was reported in December 1999 that the Palestinian Authority stated that refugees could register information about their 1948 property at Palestinian embassies worldwide.[47]

Perhaps the most significant Palestinian project to quantify the refugee losses involved working to put the massive collection of UNCCP property data into a useable form as the Jordanians had done separately. As noted earlier, the PLO acquired filmed copies of the UNCCP records in 1983 and deposited them in its Economics Department in Damascus. Given growing Syrian hostility to the PLO in the 1980s and especially after the onset of the peace process with Israel, the PLO leadership outside Syria could not gain access to these. To counter this, the PLO would need to obtain a second copy of the records from the UNCCP. This occurred at the same time that Walid Khalidi of the Institute for Palestine Studies (IPS) sought copies of the records to help determine whether refugees had owned the site of the proposed U.S. embassy in Jerusalem. Since the UNCCP would provide the films to only a small number of interested parties, including the PLO, the Institute approached senior PLO leader Mahmud 'Abbas (Abu Mazin) for help. Khalidi proposed that the PLO request new copies of the records, which IPS would then scan onto CD-ROMs. IPS agreed to carry out and pay for the work, in return for which it would give one copy of the CD-ROMs to the PLO and keep another for its own use. The two sides agreed to a plan that called first for scanning the UNCCP films and paper records and then formulating the data into a computer program.[48]

On June 13, 1997, the UNCCP authorized the project. IPS commissioned a Canadian-based company, TransCad, Ltd., to do the actual scanning work. TransCad employees spent several months starting in August 1997 scanning 5,625 maps, approximately 210,000 double-sided owners index cards, and 1,641 35mm films of mandatory land registers in the UNCCP collection that were housed at the UN Secretariat archives in New York. This first part of the project also scanned the more than 500,000 R/P1 forms produced by the UNCCP's Technical Project in the 1950s and 1960s. The project grew and soon involved a variety of parties. The UN's Committee on the Exercise of the Inalienable Rights of the Palestinian People coordinated the communication between the UN and the PLO. The UN offices involved in the work included the Division for Palestinian Rights, the UN Secretariat archives, and the UNCCP-still technically in existence. The PLO worked on the project through the Permanent Observer of Palestine to the UN, Dr. Nasser al-Kidwa.

Once the CD-ROMs had been produced for the PLO, the UN and the PLO then continued the second phase of the project on their own without IPS. This involved using the CD-ROMs to create a sophisticated GIS computer data base linking the property records with maps. The UN paid the bulk of the funds for this stage of the project because it wanted to store the UNCCP data on a more secure, more modern medium than the aging microfilms and paper copies. The basis for involving UN funds in the matter was General Assembly Resolution 51/129 of December 13, 1996, which repeated earlier resolutions calling for the 1948 refugees to be entitled to the income from their property. Beyond this usual declaration, the Resolution also called for the "preservation and modernization" of the UNCCP's records relating to refugee property. The Committee on the Exercise of the Inalienable Rights of the Palestinian People used this resolution as the justification for contributing some $500,000 from its budget to the second stage of the project, which was approved in May 1998. The PLO provided an additional $250,000, and work was undertaken once again by TransCad. The project was essentially complete by May 2000, and the resulting computerized data base contained all of the property owners' names, location of properties, and property values contained in the UNCCP's R/P1 forms and index cards. Both the PLO Observer Mission and the UN Secretariat archives in New York ended up with copies of the data base. However, like the Jordanians, neither of these thus far have allowed unrestricted public access to the records.[49]

This massive and sophisticated computerization project revealed a number of flaws with the UNCCP Technical Program's methods and data. It was discovered that not all R/P1 forms contained full information, and that many of the R/P3 forms (containing information on land not owned by individual Arabs) were missing. The technicians also determined that despite the Technical Program's methodology to produce one R/P1 form for each parcel of Arab-owned land, the total number of unique R/P1 forms exceeded the total number of unique parcels of land. Thus, the computerization project found that the Technical Program staff had compiled a total of 523,750 R/P1 forms. Of these, only 423,750 represented unique forms while the rest were duplicates, etc. Even considering this, the number of R/P1 forms still did not match the number of unique parcels of land. The Technical Program staff created 423,750 unique R/P1 forms although there are actually 458,210 unique parcels represented in the UNCCP records.[50]

The project to computerize the UNCCP data is important on a number of levels. For the first time the Technical Program records have been put into a readily accessible if still not publicly available format. Second, the database can serve a number of important scholarly purposes for the study of land in Palestine generally and not just refugee land. Third, aggregate figures derived from the new database provide a more accurate accounting of the UNCCP's original 1964 figures on the scope and value of Arab-owned land in Israel. For example, the figure of 458,210 individual parcels is greater than the general figure of 453,000 publicly cited by the UNCCP when it announced completion of its project in 1964. The new computer program also determined that the actual surface area of these unique parcels was 4,851,613.978 dunums, including the land of Palestinians still in Israel—less than the figure of 5,258,091 dunums publicly announced in 1964. The project furthermore determined that the value of the land, taken from the owners index cards, totaled £P224,815,931—less than Frank Jarvis's unpublished figure of £P235,660,250. Finally, the new database was able to determine that the number of Arab landowners in the part of Palestine that became Israel, including those Palestinians who stayed behind, was less than 100,000.[51]

Remarkably, the PLO's database was not immediately put at the disposal of PLO officials responsible for preparing for the eventuality of compensation talks with Israel. According to several Palestinians familiar with the issue, institutional Palestinian rivalries seemed to be the reason. Although they did not have access to the property database at the PLO mission to the UN, PLO negotiators formally brought up the property issue during the Israeli-Palestinian final status talks that opened in September 1999. This was according to senior Palestinian negotiator Yasir 'Abd Rabbo.[52] The two sides technically had opened the final status talks several years earlier in May 1996 but no major movement occurred. In large part this was because of the worsening Israeli-Palestinian relations that had replaced the halcyon days of 1993–1994. The resumption of violence and the election of Likud leader Binyamin Netanyahu as prime minister of Israel in May 1996 caused the talks to falter. Netanyahu had campaigned openly against the Oslo Accords and sought to limit further Israeli concessions to the Palestinians. Thus real Israeli-Palestinian discussions on final status issues such as the refugee property did not begin until after the election of the Labor Party's Ehud Barak as prime minister in May 1999. Even then, no real breakthroughs occurred.

Private Palestinian groups continued to pursue private efforts to keep the property issue alive. The Council for Palestinian Restitution and Repatriation was formed in Washington in early 2000 with the scholar Maysam Faruqi as its chair. The group reportedly was considering using courts to seek redress for 1948 property claims.[53] However, the question of compensation remained a controversial one among Palestinians. Some Palestinians feared the PLO might settle for a lump sum payment from Israel, rendering it impossible for them to receive individual compensation. To refute this, Palestinian official Muhammad Zuhdi al-Nashashibi denied in September 2000 that the Palestinians were seeking a fixed amount as general compensation for all refugee property. He insisted that negotiations would deal with individual claims for the use of or damage to their land since 1948, and that in all cases compensation was not a substitution for the right of return.[54] Some Palestinians did not even settle for such reassurances and continued to reject the notion of compensation altogether. Shaykh Ikrima Sabri, the mufti of Jerusalem, announced in July 2000 that he had issued a fatwa (Islamic juridical ruling) barring Muslims from accepting compensation for their lost property. Sabri equated compensation with sale of the land, stating this was something forbidden to Muslims inasmuch as Palestine constituted holy territory.[55]

The relatively tepid public and private Palestinian approach to the property question might strike some as surprising. It is also surprising that groups or individual Palestinians have not yet resorted to American courts to seek damages resulting from Israel's long usage of their refugee property (although the Palestine Litigation Project, a group of American lawyers and activists, was reportedly looking at just such action in mid-2002).[56] Given the intimate connection of the United Kingdom and British companies with Palestine, some individual Palestinian refugees as well as corporate entities raised claims against British banks and insurance companies decades ago. In October 1950, the Arab Bank sued Barclays Bank in London over assets frozen in Israel. The case, Arab Bank, Ltd. v. Barclays Bank (Dominion, Colonial and Overseas), was decided in 1954 when the House of Lords ultimately ruled against the Arab Bank (see chapter 3). In November 1950, two refugees sought redress from British courts in the case of F. & K. Jabbour v. Custodian of Absentee Property of the State of Israel, although they too lost their case in 1954 (see chapter 4). The much more recent Bigio case (see above) filed in New York in 1997 by a Canadian Jewish family originally from Egypt seeking compensation for confiscated land clearly shows that American courts are also willing to entertain property cases based on the U.S. Alien Torts Claims Law. As documented in chapter 1, a number of Israeli companies and bodies made use of refugee land over the years and in theory could be the targets of legal action, as the Coca-Cola Company was in the Bigio case. Belgian legislation that allows foreign claimants to bring human rights cases before Belgian courts also may provide room for compensation cases, although apparently none have ever been filed.

The Arab world was not alone in preparing for the day when compensation talks might resume, nor was it alone in the lack of precision, duplication of efforts, and crippling rivalries that characterized its efforts. Despite Israel's seeming lack of interest in bringing up Jewish property claims in bilateral talks with its Egyptian and Jordanian peace partners after 1979 and 1994, respectively, both the Israeli government and private and semigovernmental Jewish organizations pointedly have raised the issue of compensation for Jewish property sequestered in Arab countries since the beginning of the peace process in the 1990s. They have also exerted efforts to prepare statistics on Jewish property losses, but characteristically these have not been carried out directly by the Israeli government. This effort predated the peace process. In November 1975, the Israeli Knesset's Foreign Relations and Security Committee issued a statement stating *inter alia* "The Arab countries must pay the Jews who left them proper compensation on stolen assets and property."[57] Although the Knesset adopted the statement, the Israeli government itself did nothing public on the matter.

The same month that the Knesset committee adopted its statement, however, the World Organization of Jews from Arab Countries (WOJAC) was established in Paris. WOJAC emerged out of a gathering of Mizrahi Jewish groups organized in Tel Aviv earlier that year by Knesset Vice Chair Mordekhai Ben Porat, the Iraqi-born Mossad agent who played a key role during Operation 'Ezra and Nehemya. Ben Porat became one of WOJAC's two chairs along with Sir Leon J. Tamman, another Iraqi Jewish emigrant who at one time presided over TA'ALI—The World Movement for a United Israel—and who was the primary financial backer of the group. WOJAC held conferences in Paris in 1975, London in 1982, Washington in 1987, and four others in Israel. Despite the Israeli government's desire for deniability, the organization was supported financially in its efforts on behalf of publicizing the fate of Jewish land in Arab countries by both the Israeli Ministry of Foreign Affairs and the Jewish Agency until they ended their support in July 1999. A foreign ministry official told Ben Porat in 1976 that "the connection between the organization and the Foreign Ministry will be secret, so it is desirable to keep correspondence to a minimum." [58]

WOJAC was thus not an official Israeli government body, and could keep the compensation issue alive while the Israelis kept their distance. This tactic had first been utilized in the mid-1950s. Beset by financial problems, criticism that it was inactive, and an eventual cutoff of official Israeli government funding, WOJAC ended up in dire straights by July1999 when it announced it was ceasing to function.[59] However, the organization apparently still exists, and by early 2001 WOJAC official Moshe Shalal floated an estimated value of expropriated Jewish private and communal property in the Arab world:

US$30 billion. WOJAC Chair 'Oved Ben Ozer also claimed that the organization had lawyers in New York and Tel Aviv working on Jewish property issues, and the group claimed to have a file of 10,000 private Jewish property claims in Arab countries.[60]

As property compensation proved controversial among Palestinians, so too did the Jewish property issue lead to friction among Jewish groups and between Mizrahi Jews and the Israeli government. Some figures associated with WOJAC adhered to the Israeli government line about using Mizrahi property claims to cancel out Palestinian claims. Ben Ozer stated in 1993, "...the State of Israel — as the defender of the life, rights, and interests of Jews throughout the world — has full moral right to be charged with responsibility for the property left by Jews in their countries of origin." [61] Others were not always willing to allow Israel to represent their property claims vis-à-vis Arab states someday. Some of these activists were resentful that Israel would leverage their claims for a mutual cancellation of claims between the Israeli government and Palestinians instead of seeking compensation for individual Jews. The result of such an arrangement would be that individual Mizrahi Jews, especially those living outside Israel, would receive no compensation at all. A WOJAC official in the United States, Professor Heskel Haddad, was among such Jews who publicly insisted that Israel should not be allowed to represent their property grievances vis-à-vis the Arab world. At WOJAC's 1993 conference in Tel Aviv, Haddad stated:

> As a person living in the Diaspora, I want to point out the dangers of raising the arguments and rights of Jews who do not live in Israel. This was brought to my attention by Shimon Peres and Yossi Beilin in private conversations, and also by Yossi Hadas and Moshe Raviv in very private conversations. They are scared that our persistence regarding the Diaspora issue could open a Pandora's Box that would allow all Palestinians living out of the country to make similar claims.[62]

Haddad also disagreed with Ben Ozer, later noting in 1999 that "[Israel] has no legal right to represent the Jews from Arab countries that live outside of Israel, and it has no legal right to link our claims to those of Palestinians." [63]

Other Jewish organizations remained willing to support the Israeli government's strategy of taking the lead on the compensation issue and acting on behalf of aggrieved Mizrahi property owners. One powerful such group was the World Jewish Congress (WJC). The WJC had considerable experience dealing with compensation for Jewish property losses in Holocaust-era Europe.

WOJAC complained that the WJC had ignored its requests for assistance on the compensation question.[64] In fact the WJC chose to initiate its own campaign on the issue without WOJAC and its problems and in open support of the Israeli government's position. In January 1999, Avraham Hirchson, the Likud parliamentarian who was chair of the Knesset's Committee on Jewish Property Restitution, approached the WJC with an idea to create a national center in Israel for registering lost Jewish property in the Arab world.[65] On June 21 of that year, the WJC formally announced the start of a campaign to identify such property. The WJC later published a general report on the Jewish property question in 2000 based upon extensive research by journalist Itamar Levin that made use of archived Israeli government records.[66] Levin's summary was a preview for a much more thorough discussion of the subject that he published in 2001.[67] Levin estimated that the value of Jewish property left behind in Arab countries to be $US6-10 billion and openly admitted his agenda for completing the book when he did:

> The timing of this book is no accident. At the time this is being written, in April 2001, there is a good probability that the Palestinian authority, as they resume within the framework of negotiations with Israel for a permanent settlement, will demand compensation for properties confiscated from Palestinian refugees. This book presents decision makers and public opinion shapers with information on Israel's counterdemands, as regards property belonging to Jews from the Arab states. As early as 1951, Israel stated that at such time when Palestinian claims were discussed, it would demand parallel talks regarding Jewish claims. This statement has never been retracted. This book is intended as a basis for discussion on the question of whether to maintain the aforementioned policy and, if so, which claims deserve to be put forth.[68]

In addition to its own work, the WJC also worked with the American Sephardi Federation (ASF) in forming an organization for the purpose of registering claims called the International Committee of Jews from Arab Lands. Amram Attias, a Mizrahi Jew originally from Morocco, served as its chair. Attias was open about the aims of the campaign: to support the Israeli government by collecting information on Jewish property claims in order to cancel out Palestinian claims during negotiations:

> We want Israel to demand our property back in the negotiations. We are not against the Palestinians, but we consider them part of the Arab nation as they do themselves. They were driven out or left-and so were we.

> For each house they demand, a house of ours should be demanded. For each mosque, a synagogue. For each cemetery, a cemetery.[69]

In fact, it seems that this committee was yet another example of the Israeli government arranging for a "public body" to be formed at its behest to do the work of the Jewish property question in order to maintain a degree of deniability and distance. It was claimed in Israeli press reports that the committee was formed by the WJC and ASF at the suggestion of the advisor to Likud Prime Minister Binyamin Netanyahu for diaspora affairs, Bobby Brown, who contacted the ASF's president, Leon Levy (of Turkish Jewish heritage) and asked for the federation's help in researching the issue of Jewish property in Arab countries. The Netanyahu government reportedly was concerned about reports that the PLO was collecting data on 1948 Palestinian refugee property for use in the so-called final status talks between Israel and the PLO.[70] It clearly wanted to benefit from any future linkage of Jewish and Palestinian property claims but did not want to do the work of collecting the data itself.

Why has the Israeli government proven so reticent in this matter? First, it fears that its official efforts on behalf of Jewish property in Arab countries might revive hopes among Mizrahi Jews in Israel that they eventually would receive compensation payments *from the Israeli government* after negotiations with the Arabs are completed. Having a "public" body outside the Israeli government do the work of collecting data, such as WOJAC or the International Committee of Jews from Arab Lands, could provide the Israeli government with the requisite degree of distance. Just such a strategy had been openly discussed within the Israeli government as far back as 1951.[71] However, there is another more pressing concern among Israeli decisionmakers that explains why the Israeli government itself did not want to push the Jewish compensation matter with the Palestinians: it fears that the amount claimed against Arab states by Jews is dwarfed by the size of Palestinian claims. Far from canceling each other out, Israel would still end up owing a vast amount to the Palestinians. Itamar Levin quoted a "deeply involved source" in his study as stating the following in December 1999:

> The [Israeli] Ministry of Foreign Affairs conducted a tiny sample study of Jewish claims, and it was very hard to arrive at an estimated valuation. But according to that sampling, the ratio of claims is 22:1 in the Palestinians' favor . . . there's no question that there is a problem, because they [Palestinians'] speak very rationally about a minimum of $13 billion in property, in 1948 terms.[72]

As a "public body" separate from the Israeli government, the International Committee of Jews from Arab Lands tried to collect statistical information on Jewish property losses on its own starting in 1999. It initially made no apparent attempt to acquire the partial data on this subject that the Israeli government and certain Jewish groups had collected in the 1950s and 1960s. The committee instead distributed more than 100,000 questionnaires to Jews around the world seeking quantifiable information about property losses. By early 2001, the committee had not organized the resultant data to the point where it could hazard any concrete estimates of the value of this Jewish property. While Israeli parliamentarian Hirchson had envisioned the data being stored in Israel, the ASF intended to archive the data in an international data bank at the ASF Sephardic Wing of the Center for Jewish History in New York.

Internecine Jewish friction over how the property question should be brought up and by whom continued. Some Jews remained annoyed at the reticence of the Israeli government to become more publicly involved in the issue. In November 2001, the Jewish Agency hosted a gathering at Tel Aviv's Diaspora Museum commemorating the publication of Levin's book. Even though the Israeli Ministry of Defense had published the book, several speakers decried the Israeli government's previous lack of interest in the subject. The Chairman of the Jewish Agency's Executive, Sallai Meridor, called upon the Israeli government to work with the JA in seeking compensation from the Arab world. Mordekhai Ben Porat claimed that "a succession of Israeli governments has paid so little attention to the legitimate rights of Jews who fled from Arab lands that [Labor Party Minister] Yossi Beilin, during his term as Justice Minister, closed down the department in the Justice Ministry dealing with Jewish property claims in Arab lands."[73]

The fine-line distinction between the Israeli government and the International Committee of Jews from Arab Lands grew narrower in the spring of 2002 when the contours of the committee's project changed. In March 2002, the Israeli government announced that the Ministry of Justice would begin to register Jewish immigrants from Arab countries and Iran as well as collect material on "damages to property and the persecution of Jews" in those countries. Cabinet Secretary Gideon Sa'ar stated that the list was being established for the purpose of establishing claims with Arab states and international organizations.[74] Two months later, in May 2002, Minister of Justice Meir Shitrit, himself a Mizrahi Jew born in Morocco, announced that the ministry and the International Committee of Jews from Arab Lands had decided to work together on the data bank project. The project, entitled the Jewish Refugees from Arab Lands Project, aimed to microfilm the Justice Ministry's files on

Jewish property claims in Arab countries and then scan them into a computerized data base that would incorporate other materials gathered by the committee and other organizations. Additionally, the project will include Jewish property losses after 1940, not just after 1948 as the Israeli government formerly had collected. It was estimated that the resulting computerized data base would cost more than $1 million and require six to eight months' work to complete.[75]

Several months later, two additional developments on this front took place. In late September 2002 several major Jewish organizations established yet another group to raise awareness of issues relating to Mizrahi Jewish emigrants from Arab countries. Justice for Jews in Arab Countries was formed as an initiative of the WJC and ASF, as well as the Conference of Presidents of Major American Jewish Organizations and the Center for Middle East Peace and Economic Cooperation. Among those chairing the new group were the Israeli Mizrahi politician Shlomo Hillel, Canadian parliamentarian Irwin Cotler, former American diplomat Richard Holbrooke, and British noble Lord George Wiedenfeld. While not claiming to have formed the group to press for compensation claims, its leaders were trying to gain international recognition of the Mizrahi emigrants as "refugees." Holbrooke, noteworthy for his role in the diplomatic solution to the war in Bosnia in the 1990s, claimed that the Mizrahim are entitled to justice under UN Security Council Resolution 242 of November 22, 1967. He claimed that that resolution, which calls for ". . . . a just settlement of the refugee problem," includes the Mizrahi emigrants despite a traditional U.S. governmental understanding to the contrary (see chap. 3). [76]

Finally, it is worth noting in connection with Israeli-Palestinian compensation claims that the Jewish National Fund and one of its subsidiaries, Hemanuta, owns land that now lies under the jurisdiction of the Palestinian Authority in the West Bank and Gaza. This land could feature in future compensation talks. The JNF sought compensation from the Israeli government for handing over some of its land to the Palestinian Authority during the peace process of the 1990s. Israel eventually might try to seek compensation from the Palestinians in return. This JNF land reportedly includes several thousand dunums in the Palestinian-controlled part of Gaza, as well as other land in the so-called Areas A and B in the Palestinian-administered parts of the West Bank. This is in addition to some 25,350 dunums owned by Hemanuta in the Palestinian areas of the West Bank.[77]

With both Palestinians and Israelis preparing information for property claims and counter claims, it was inevitable that the subjects finally should be officially broached during the Israeli-Palestinian final status talks that began after the election of the Labor Party's Ehud Barak as prime minister in May 1999. The topic arose at the talks held outside Washington from July 11-25, 2000 (the Camp David II summit). These talks brought together Barak, PLO Chairman Yasir 'Arafat, and U.S. President Bill Clinton. It was at that gathering that the Palestinians brought up the issue. They did not just speak generally but pointedly asked the Israelis for the funds from the refugees' accounts that the Custodian of Absentee Property supposedly had been keeping. This reflects the official PLO position that the refugees still maintain their legal title to the land and are entitled to restitution, not compensation, which would erase their ongoing property rights. When Palestinian negotiator Yasir 'Abd Rabbo made this demand, Israeli negotiator Elyakim Rubinstein responded with a startling admission: the Israelis could not pay anything out from these funds because they no longer existed. Rubinstein claimed that Israel had spent all of the money it had generated from the refugees' assets, money that the Custodian of Absentee Property was legally bound to safeguard all these years. He told 'Abd Rabbo, "these funds no longer exist. We have used them up. It is up to the international community to create funds for this."[78]

Was Rubinstein's claim true? Had the Israeli government spent all of the money from the refugees' accounts? If so, how much money had been spent? A remarkable 1990 Israeli government document sheds some important light on this question. While it does not reveal whether the government spent the money or how much that might have been, the document clearly states that the Custodian of Absentee Property's office was in no position by 1990 to state with any certainty how much it still controlled in moveable refugee assets. These were the only type of assets it continued to manage by the mid-1950s once the Custodian sold landed refugee property to the Development Authority in 1953. Nor could such information about refugee accounts be found in the records of the Israeli Ministry of Finance. The document is a report from the Israeli State Controller's office. From April-July 1990, the Controller's office carried out an investigation into the work of the Custodian's office, which had been transferred from the Ministry of Finance to the Israel Lands Administration (ILA) in 1962. The Controller's report scored the Custodian's procedures and claimed that such incompetence was costing the state millions of shekels in unaccounted absentee assets. The Custodian's office did not respond to the Controller's request for information about unclaimed refugee bank deposits, safe deposit boxes, and tangible moveable property such as artwork, jewelry, etc. that was still under the Custodian's supervision. Nor could the Custodian produce solid information about shares he controlled in companies that formerly had been owned by refugees. The Controller's report eventually noted:

> According to the [1950 Absentees' Property] Law, the Custodian must safeguard all "property held" as defined by the Law (Absentee property vested in him and actually held by him, including any property acquired in exchange for vested property-and including the funds received in exchange for vested property) himself, or by means of others approved by him. To this end, the Custodian is authorized to make all expenditures and investments necessary for their safeguarding, holding, repair, and development, and all other related purposes, either himself or by means of others approved by him in writing.
>
> This inquiry examined the procedures of the Custodian for supervising and monitoring the moveable property in his charge, particularly the rights of absentees in various corporations. According to an initial, partial estimate, based on an examination of documentation within the office of the Custodian, the rights to only five of the companies whose shares are vested in the Custodian are worth a total of tens of millions of New Israeli Shekels. . . . Based on documentation of the activities of the Custodian found at the [Israel Lands] Administration's head office in Jerusalem, it was not possible to determine the number and names of all the companies in which shares held by absentees were vested in the Custodian. It was also not possible to determine the financial value of these shares.[79]

One of the reasons the Controller cited for this incompetence was the poor shape of the Custodian's records and the lack of both space and proper staff assistance provided to him by the Israel Lands Administration. During the first several decades of its existence, the Custodian of Absentee Property's office maintained thousands of files detailing the property it had controlled. Even when the Custodian sold landed property to the Development Authority, he maintained records about this property. For example, when British journalist Robert Fisk interviewed the Custodian, whom he named as Ya'akov Manor, in December 1980, he found that Manor was still able to lay his hands quickly on detailed information about any specific refugee's land that the journalist asked about even though control of the land had passed to the Development Authority and Jewish National Fund decades earlier. Manor had: "in his possession copies of almost every British mandate land registration document, file after file of papers recording in detail the Arab and Jewish owners of property in pre-1948 Palestine."[80]

But these files later were dispersed, hindering the ability of the Custodian to ascertain details about the accounts relating both to moveable and immoveable refugee property. Citing again from the 1990 report:

> The [Israel Lands] Administration provided the office of the Custodian and the office for Implementing the Absentee Property (Compensation) Law [of 1973] with only one small room in the building of the Administration's head office in Jerusalem. The current Custodian (and Commissioner [of the Absentee Property (Compensation) Law]) received three standard metal office cabinets from his predecessor, which held, among other things, stock certificates and other securities, as well as cloth sacks filled with various articles of Absentee property. The transmission of all of this was undertaken without being accompanied by any information or the registration of the contents of the cabinets, and without providing the Custodian with the appropriate means of safeguarding this material. The Administration placed one secretary-typist, an Administration employee, at the disposal of the Custodian (and the Commissioner) for only one hour each day .... Against the Custodian's wishes, the former director of the Administration ordered the splitting and redistribution of the Custodian's approximate 15,000 operational files that had accumulated over the years, which include information and documentation that he needs in order to perform his job. This resulted in the majority of files being moved from the Administration's head office in Jerusalem to the archive of the Administration's district offices, while only a small number were left in the Administration's head office where the Custodian is based. All this was undertaken without appropriate procedures of classification and registration.[81]

Indeed, when the author wrote to Custodian of Absentee Property Yehezkel Shammash in 1999 seeking general statistics on immoveable refugee property from 1948–1955, Shammash seemed to confirm this lack of available information when he replied that he had no such data nor was he certain that such information ever had been compiled.[82]

In summary, the Controller blasted the state of the Custodian's office and its lack of knowledge about refugee assets under its control as follows:

> An examination of the Custodian of Absentee Property's administration of moveable property in his charge reveals that he is not fulfilling his legally prescribed obligation to safeguard this property. The examina-

> tion also reveals that the Custodian is not exercising his powers regarding the expenditures and investments necessary to safeguard, hold and develop this property: the Custodian possesses neither exact data nor comprehensive information regarding the scope of different types of absentee property, their location and value, the manner in which they have been administered or the manner in which funds derived from them or their sale were invested. He also has no information regarding his financial rights and obligations, and his overall array of accounts. It is perhaps most serious that the Custodian does not possess comprehensive information regarding the value of his rights in various corporations, or even the total value of absentee bank deposits and safes. These properties have been estimated to value tens of millions of New Israeli Shekels at the very least.[83]

It thus seems clear that by the early 1990s, the Custodian of Absentee Property and the Ministry of Finance were in no position even to hazard guesses about the accounts Israel supposedly had been maintaining on behalf of the refugees over the years. In this regard these two Israeli government agencies were not in compliance with the Absentees' Property Law of 1950 that required them to safeguard all funds realized from the use and/or disposal of refugee property.

This chaotic situation is what perhaps led Rubinstein to tell 'Abd Rabbo that the refugees' money had been spent inasmuch as the Israeli government clearly did not seem to know anything about the accounts. If Rubinstein's claim was true, then how much in accumulated refugee accounts had the Israeli government spent or lost track of over the years? How much in proceeds had the Israeli government realized from its acquisition of refugee property? This is a different matter than that of the reputed value of such property as determined, for example, by the UNCCP. The author never has seen official or unofficial cumulative figures detailing how much money, either gross receipts or net profits, the Israeli government realized from moveable and immoveable Palestinian refugee property. Chapter 1 provides some very incomplete data for certain types of disposals in certain years and which is detailed in table 7.7. This table details only the gross receipts of funds, and does not list expenditures that the Israeli authorities paid out for repair, maintenance, taxes, etc., relating to abandoned property over the years. It also includes payments made by one Israeli governmental agency to another and theoretical sale prices of land that may or may not actually have changed hands.

TBLE 7.7 Sample of Funds Realized by the Israeli Government from the Disposal of Moveable and Immoveable Refugee Property, 1948–1958

| *Type of Disposal* | *Date* | *Amount* |
|---|---|---|
| Sale of Moveable Property | June 24, 1948– March 31, 1950 | £I 3,806,035 |
| Lease of Urban Immoveable Property | 1948–53 | £I11,453,543 |
| Same | 1957–58 | £I 2,114,700 |
| Sale of Olives | 1948 | £I 250,000 |
| Lease of Orange Groves | 1950 | £I 500,000 |
| Lease of Stone Quarries | 1948–54 | £I 102,618 |
| Sale of Land by Custodian of Absentee Property to Development Authority | 1953 | £I 46,000,000 |
| Sale of Land by Government to Jewish National Fund | 1949 | £I 23,421,685 |
| Same | 1950 | £I66,000,000 |

(see chapter 1 for sources)

An interesting footnote to this issue once again involves Elyakim Rubinstein. Beginning in July 1998, a Palestinian NGO in Israel began demanding that the Custodian of Absentee Property compile and release information on the refugees' moveable property. The group, Adalah, was prompted to action by the revelations contained in the 1990 Controller's report. When the Custodian refused, Adalah wrote to Rubinstein-who was Israel's Attorney General-in January 1999 asking him to force the Custodian's compliance. After more than two years of back-and-forth correspondence, Rubinstein eventually refused. He claimed that such action would take too much time and resources to compile and might damage Israel's foreign relations.[84]

In light of their claim at Camp David II to have spent all the funds derived from Palestinian refugee property, Israeli negotiators switched gears during the talks and countered with a new proposal about linking Palestinian refugee compensation with compensation payments to Jews who lost property in the Arab world but without stating that it would deduct such amounts from what it would pay the Palestinians. The proposal called for convening an international forum to deal with property claims from both sides. Any eventual payments to claimants from either side would be made from a fund created by international donors. In this way, the Israeli government itself would not be responsible for reckoning the amount it owed the refugees. It would not be expected to pay any amounts to its own Mizrahi Jewish citizens who claimed compensation. Also, it would not pay the Palestinian refugees itself; the world community would. This would avoid the problem that the Ministry of Foreign Affairs had studied earlier: that Palestinian claims were likely to be 22 times greater than Jewish claims. The new proposal seemed to offer the Israeli government a painless way out of its dilemma. Israeli press reports indicated that this idea was part of an American plan at Camp David II that an "international organization will be established for compensation and rehabilitation of refugees in their current location; Israel will participate in its financing."[85]

The Palestinians reportedly rejected the idea angrily and cited the lack of connection between the Palestinian refugees' claims and those of Jews from other Arab lands.[86] Palestinian hostility to linking Palestinian refugee property claims with those of Jews from Arabs countries reflected a longstanding PLO position. The Palestinians had long argued that Israel must respect their restitution/compensation claims irrespective of any claims that Israel or individual Mizrahi Jews may have against Arab governments. The Palestinians stated as much at the November 1992 second plenary of the Refugee Working Group (RWG) in Ottawa. The RWG had been created as part of the multilateral peace talks in the wake of the October 1991 Madrid conference. At the RWG meeting in Ottawa, the Palestinians rejected the Israeli notion proposed at the gathering that a population exchange had occurred in 1948 by which Arabs who fled Palestine had been replaced by Jewish immigrants who left Arab countries. They stated that compensation for such Jews should be raised by Israel in bilateral negotiations with the respective Arab states, just as the Palestinians would someday raise the compensation question in their own bilateral talks with Israel.[87] Daoud Barakat, head of the PLO's Department of Refugee Affairs, later reiterated this stance in 1999 when he stated, "There is no linkage here [between Palestinian and Jewish property]. Israel has to negotiate directly with Lebanon, Morocco, Egypt. I don't represent those countries."[88] 'Abd Rabbo restated this at Camp David II, telling Rubinstein, "This problem has nothing to do with us. Bring it up with the Moroccan authorities, the Yemenis, and so on."[89]

In the end, the Camp David II talks ended in failure, also ending the first significant Israeli-Palestinian negotiations to broach the topic of refugee property in fifty years. Not only did the two sides fail to reach an accommodation on this and other issues but also the Palestinians came away the clear losers from a public relations perspective as well. Both the Israelis and the Americans accused 'Arafat of passing up a golden opportunity to accept Israeli compromises on several issues at Camp David II, although new compromises on the property question do not seem to have been part of the Barak's so-called "generous offer." Despite the Palestinians' claims that they rejected linking their property claims with those of Mizrahi Jews, the Americans soon spread the word that the Palestinians *had* in fact indicated an "interest" in the idea of somehow connecting their claims to those presented by Israel. Not only did an annoyed President Clinton publicly indicate his belief that it was Barak who had taken a greater risk for peace than 'Arafat, he also gave the Israelis some political capital by publicly claiming that *both* sides had discussed favorably the matter of compensation for Jewish property losses. In an interview with Israel Television in late July 2000, Clinton stated, "There is, I think, some interest... on both sides, in also having a fund which compensates the Israelis who were made refugees by the war which occurred after the birth of the State of Israel."[90]

In the wake of Camp David II and the public backing that Clinton gave to the new Israeli proposal for an internationally subscribed fund for paying out mutual compensation claims, at least some Jews and Jewish organizations that had supported the Israeli government in the property compensation matter in the past echoed the new Israeli position. At a public meeting in Tel Aviv in November 2001, Avraham Hirchson, Mordekhai Ben Porat, and others made a similar call for establishment of such a fund made up of Israel, Arab states, the United States, and the European Union for compensating Jewish and Palestinian property owners. In contrast to other Israeli calls, however, the men stated that compensation must be paid on an individual and not a collective basis and so the internecine Jewish debate over the modalities of compensation continued.[91] Other Mizrahi activists also continued to pursue strategies on the property question that directly flew in the face of Israeli governmental efforts. In June 2002, just one month after it agreed to work with the Israeli Ministry of Justice on computerizing data on Jewish property losses, the International Committee of Jews from Arab Lands announced that it intended to bring suit against the Arab League seeking restitution of lost Mizrahi property. The committee's chair, Amram Attias, developed the idea and secured approval for it from the meeting of the World Sephardi Federation in Jerusalem that had been convened to coincide with the gathering of the World Zionist Congress. Attias did not seek monetary compensation but rather restitution for 200,000 homes, 6,000 synagogues, as well as other buildings and assets. While admitting that he did not expect any real results, Attias again noted the committee's ultimate goal of using the suit to raise public awareness of the Jewish property issue and to provide a "counterbalance" to Palestinian claims.

Despite this, the Israeli government's attitude toward the suit was predictably cool. Minister of Justice Meir Shitrit responded that while "[e]very organization can act independently as it feels fit... the goal of the Ministry of Justice is to gather information regarding the loss of Jewish property in the Arab states" not for generalized public relations usage but rather for future negotiations with the Palestinians. Shitrit's spokesperson, Yonatan Beker, pointedly called the Jewish property issue a "diplomatic tool" for deflecting Palestinian claims and stated that it should not be raised before such talks. Others greeted the news with hesitation as well. The executive vice chair of the Conference of Presidents of Major American Jewish Organizations, Malcolm Hoenlein, noted that an improperly pursued legal case at that time could prove damaging. The conference itself has prepared legal briefs on the issue for future use in legal cases or in negotiations. Attias ended up saying that he had no specific timetable for filing the suit against the Arab League and that he would consider postponing it if the Israeli government objected.[92]

Three months after the failure of Camp David II, the al-Aqsa Intifada broke out among Palestinians in the West Bank, Gaza, and even initially among some Palestinian citizens of Israel. Despite the new round of intense Israeli-Palestinian violence, a new series of significant Israeli-Palestinian talks took place in Taba, Egypt, from January 21-27, 2001. Both sides followed up on their discussions at Camp David. The result was the most far reaching, detailed Israeli-Palestinian discussion to that point that dealt with questions relating to refugee property. The Palestinian delegation, headed by veteran PLO negotiator Ahmad Quray' (Abu 'Ala'), was guided by the PLO's official negotiating policy calling not just for compensation but restitution as well. This policy notes:

> Moreover, real property owned by the refugees at the time of their expulsion should be restored to its lawful Palestinian owners or their successors. International law regards private ownership as sacrosanct. Accordingly, the various discriminatory laws and administrative schemes, notably the Absentee Property Law, enacted by the Israeli authorities since 1948 to seize the property of the refugees and transfer it to the state of Israel, its agencies, or to the hands of Jewish individuals must be repealed and the seized property should be restored whether the refugee chooses to return or not.[93]

Guided by such thinking, the Palestinians presented a detailed proposal that outlined three overall policies toward refugee property: restitution of lost land for refugees who would be repatriated to Israel, compensation for those persons' lost moveable property, and compensation for both moveable and immoveable property for nonreturning refugees. On the first point, the Palestinian position paper was brief and noted only two points:

> 27. Real property owned by a returning [repatriated to Israel] refugee at the time of his or her displacement shall be restored to the refugee or his or her lawful successors.
> 28. In cases where, according to criteria determined by the [proposed] Repatriation Commission, it is impossible, impracticable or inequitable to restore the property to its refugee owner, the refugee shall [be] restituted in-kind with property within Israel, equal in size and/or value to the land and other property that they lost.[94]

Such persons would be compensated additionally for the loss of moveable property. It was clear, however, that the PLO negotiators contemplated that the bulk of the refugees would be resettled and not repatriated, so their position paper devoted more than thirty paragraphs to the modalities of compensating these persons. The essence of the Palestinian proposal was that all landowning refugees are entitled to individual compensation for their property (unless the particular land in question had been collectively owned prior to 1948, in which case compensation payments would go to the proposed Palestinian state); that all refugees, including those without property claims, will be compensated for pain and suffering; that Israel should provide the funds for compensation; that such funds should be paid into an international fund such as that discussed at Camp David II; and that compensation would be disbursed by a compensation commission that would enumerate refugee losses and oversee the actual process of compensation. The fund would be managed by, *inter alia*, the United States, the World Bank, the European Union, a future state of Palestine, and donor countries, and would be based at the World Bank. The commission would consist of the same plus donor countries and "representatives from the parties" (i.e., Israel and Palestine), and would determine the *current* value of moveable and immoveable property and would use records of the UNCCP and the Israeli Custodian of Absentee Property to determine *prima facie* evidence of ownership. The Palestinian document also proposed that once restitution and compensation had been accomplished in their entirety, that the parties would consider that the refugee problem has been fully resolved. Both sides would therefore end all claims related to that problem.

The Israeli delegation at Taba was headed by Foreign Minister Shlomo Ben 'Ami, a Mizrahi Jew from Morocco, and generally responded positively to these proposals. The Israelis offered a written response to the Palestinian paper that also affirmed their desire to create both an international fund and an international commission for handling compensation claims. Israel would pay into the fund, but only up to an amount previously agreed upon; the international community would provide the rest. Israeli negotiators also called for an end to mutual claims and the end of "refugee" status for Palestinians following conclusion of these and all other measures relating to the final resolution of the refugee problem. Perhaps most significantly, the Israeli team formally abandoned the decades-old principle of linkage between Palestinian refugee property and the property losses suffered by Jews from Arab countries. The Israeli response noted: "Although the issue of compensation to former Jewish refugees from Arab countries is not part of the bilateral Israeli-Palestinian agreement, in recognition of their suffering and losses, the parties pledge to cooperate in pursuing an equitable and just resolution to the issue."[95]

A representative from the European Union, Miguel Angel Moratinos, was present at Taba as an observer. Based on interviews he conducted with the parties after each negotiating session, Moratinos drew up a type of minutes of the proceedings, a document that was euphemistically called a "nonpaper" because of its unofficial status (although by the summer of 2001 both sides had approved the amended version of the nonpaper as being accurate). The Moratinos nonpaper was subsequently leaked and published by the Israeli newspaper *Ha'aretz* in February 2002, and provides a fascinating account of the Taba talks. Moratinos noted that the Israelis rejected the Palestinian demand for property restitution for returning refugees, just as the Palestinians maintained that the subject of Jewish property was "not a subject for a bilateral Palestinian-Israeli agreement."[96] Both sides agreed, however, to the creation of an international commission to oversee the modalities of compensation and an international fund for financing this. Moratinos reported that the two sides also agreed that Israel would pay an agreed-upon amount into the fund. Where they differed was in how the value of abandoned property would be calculated. The Israelis called for a "macroeconomic survey to evaluate the assets in order to reach a fair value," while the Palestinian insisted that such value should be based on the records of the UNCCP and the Custodian of Absentee Property, among others. The Palestinians also called for establishment of a multiplier to be used in reaching a final "fair value."[97]

Despite making arguably more progress on the refugee property issue than at any time before in history, the Taba talks ended shortly before the Israeli elections of February 2001. Given that Prime Minister Barak of the Labor party was sure to lose to Likud candidate Ariel Sharon, both sides knew that the Israelis' mandate to negotiate would soon disappear. Indeed, the Israeli electorate chose Sharon as the country's new prime minister. The election of a hardliner like Sharon, combined with the ongoing Israeli-Palestinian violence, led to the virtual breakdown of the Oslo framework for peace by the summer of 2002. Five decades after their flight, the refugees and their descendants still had neither returned to their land, received it back through restitution, nor been compensated for it.

# CONCLUSION

This work was in the process of completion in late 2002 during the vicious cycle of killing and counter killing that characterized Israeli-Palestinian relations since the al-Aqsa Intifada broke out in October 2000. That outbreak of violence came only three months after Israeli and Palestinian negotiators at the Camp David II summit starting making the first significant public talks in decades on the question of Palestinian refugee property. No breakthrough occurred at the summit, nor at Taba in 2001, and no public discussions on this or any of the so-called "final status" issues have taken place since then, at the time of writing.. Serious discussions of compensation/restitution once again found themselves held hostage to the overarching high politics of the Arab-Israeli conflict. Part of the reason why the Israeli-Palestinian conflict continues is precisely because movement toward resolving these final status issues has not occurred. In this lies the dilemma: the Palestinian refugee property issue has been adversely affected over the decades by the longevity of the Arab-Israeli conflict, but that longevity itself is partly the result of the lack of movement on this and other refugee grievances. The conflict has prevented concrete steps to deal with the refugees, and the absence of such steps has led to bitterness and more conflict. *Plus ça change, plus c'est la même chose.*

The significance of this study of Palestinian refugee property extends far beyond the property question itself. Indeed, the property issue lies fairly close to ground zero in the entire Israeli-Palestinian conflict. The course that it has taken and its overall lack of resolution can tell us much about the nature of Arab-Israeli relations in general. For more than half a century the Arab-Israeli conflict has shifted and changed, waxed and waned. What has remained a constant, however,—despite the high politics of diplomacy and nationalism,—is that on the human level the conflict has become a personal tragedy for those persons on all sides who have suffered, died, fled, and/or seen their property abandoned and confiscated.

This study also details how the crux of the Arab-Israeli struggle, after all this time, still boils down to one crucial touchstone event: regardless of the intentions of its founders, Israel was created in 1948 at the expense of the Palestinian Arabs who had lived there. The Palestinians' loss in 1948 extended far beyond mere military defeat and constituted a political, socioeconomic, and demographic disaster of the first order of magnitude. The two most open manifestations of this disaster were the obvious presence of 726,000 persons in exile from their homes and the vast quantity of property that they left behind. Despite the passage of five decades, the holding of conferences, and the signing of treaties, these two glaring features of the refugee flight remain unresolved in full view of the world. Until they can be resolved in a manner that the refugees themselves can support, there will be no end to the conflict.

Can the refugee property question be resolved? This study has traced the various efforts and energies expended on the question from 1948–2001. It has also dug up records from the archives and revealed several creative compensation plans that emerged in the 1950s and 1960s that might provide the bases for fresh new thinking on the question in the future. While it is not my intent to offer a plan or issue a prognosis, this study hopefully has shed light on the major sticking points and controversies surrounding the property question that might prove helpful to peacemakers in the future. In the final analysis, what are some of these controversies? On the broad level this study has focused on five issues: What constitutes abandoned property and how much is it worth? Can refugee property compensation or restitution be carried out independently of the question of repatriation vs. resettlement? Is compensation/restitution unavoidably linked with Israeli counter claims? Is, or perhaps more relevant to our discussion, "was," Israel in a position to pay compensation, and if not, who would? Why was the UN unable to effect compensation or restitution despite its efforts and its prestige?

Central to the first issue is that no two parties have been able to agree on what types of property should be counted as refugee—or "abandoned," "absentee," or any word; even the words contain political connotations. Thus, even something as basic as quantifying the refugees' losses has proven controversial. There has been considerable debate over the past decades over exactly how much land the refugees left behind. This has led to widely divergent estimates of the scope and value of the property. However, this is not so strange as it first may seem. Even though "land" is real in the sense that one can run one's fingers through the soil, "property" is a socioeconomic construct reflecting cultural conceptualizations. "Land" might seem obvious and tangible, but "property" is not. To a Westerner steeped in the Roman tradition of unqualified possession, a parcel of land is a "thing" to be owned exclusively. In contrast, for certain Native American peoples, for example, land is an integral part of nature, part of "everything." One could no more own land than one could own the air. The Palestinian refugee property question similarly has been affected by different and conflicting conceptualizations of just what kind of "property" was abandoned by the refugees in 1948. Should only private property be included, or communal or even "public" land as well? Just what one considers "property" leads one to define "abandoned property" and thus get to the heart of the matter: how much "property" did the Palestinian refugees leave behind and what is it worth?

Israeli government officials and scholars over the years usually have taken a narrower view of what constitutes abandoned Palestinian property than have Palestinians and some others. Israeli officials almost immediately stated that they were willing to compensate the refugees but only for immoveable property. They claimed that moveable property had been lost, although various Israeli governmental bodies did acquire such property and sell it. Although it pledged to keep accounts of the monies it realized from such sales and keep them in accounts for the individual refugees concerned, this study has shown, in fact, that the money was immediately spent and by the 1990s the Israeli government had lost track of it.

More important has been the question of Israeli estimates of the scope of abandoned immoveable property. Here the government quickly announced that it was willing to pay compensation only for land that had been regularly cultivated. It refused to compensate for "waste" lands and other nonarable land even though this study has shown that the Custodian of Absentee Property profited from such land, generating income from abandoned stone quarries and even selling cactus fruit harvested from marginal land. The Israeli government also refused to consider as abandoned vast tracts of land that officially or informally were understood as land for common usage. Israeli authorities took over large areas particularly of southern Palestine by declaring them "state lands" to which they were entitled as the successor state to the British mandate. They claimed that they owed no compensation for such areas. Thus for Israel, compensation was generally something it reserved for arable lands it considered to have been privately owned by individuals.

In contrast Arabs usually have adopted a much more inclusive and expansive definition of abandoned property that includes both individually owned land as well as collective or communal property. They have viewed the question of abandoned land not merely in terms of what individual Arabs lost but have also considered the total economic loss to Palestinian society as a whole. Palestinian land experts have pointed out that marginal lands on the outskirts of villages, while not privately owned or even registered, were nonetheless economically important parts of the village economy deserving of compensation. Villagers utilized such areas for gathering firewood, allowing their animals to graze, and so forth. Over the decades they also have insisted that Israel compensate the Palestinians for their respective share of state property formerly owned by the mandatory government.

Arab estimates of the value of urban land and buildings as well as citrus groves usually have been much higher than Israeli estimates. One of the reasons is that the refugees reckoned the value of urban land and buildings as they left them whereas Israel maintained that the war damaged many buildings before it acquired control over them. In this lies yet another conceptual difference in understanding. How can one establish the value of land and property? The Israelis claimed that land prices in Palestine were artificially high because of Jewish demand and British restrictions on Arab sales to Jews in certain areas. Palestinians have pointed out that "marginal" lands on the outskirts of cities were much more valuable than their appearance because of their potential developmental usage through urban sprawl. Israelis can say that the abandoned land would have been worth much less had Israel and Zionism never existed, while Palestinians can counter that in Israel's absence, they would still be living on their land. One also can argue whether compensation should reflect some abstract standard of the land's value or should be calculated on the basis of the financial benefits Israel reaped from it (in terms of things like the savings to the Zionist movement from not having to pay for the land, the revenues it generated from their subsequent sale, etc.). Beyond just the question of varying Palestinian and Israeli ideas about what constitutes abandoned land there is a huge conceptual and practical difference between the abstract value of the land and the value of the financial benefits reaped by Israel from it.

Beyond this, the controversies over how much land the refugees left behind leads to another question: Do the refugees still own it? Should they receive it back through restitution, or merely be compensated for it and thereby concede its loss? Israel considers that the refugees' legal title to the land lapsed the moment it was taken over by the Custodian of Absentee Property. Israeli authorities consider that after that point they were free to do what they pleased with the property, including reaping any benefits from Israeli developmental efforts over the years. True, they stated they owed compensation for the lands' value but only as of 1948. They categorically refused to consider that the refugees maintained any "ongoing title" to the land itself and thus had any grounds to demand income from it or restitution of it. The Arabs, however, have never accepted the legality of Israel's confiscation of the land. For them, the property is still legally owned by refugee Palestinians who should benefit from it. In this regard, they viewed the refugees rather like absentee landlords who deserve to be paid rent, especially considering the circumstances behind their exile. For this reason, the Arabs began pushing in the 1950s for the UN to establish a property custodian to whom Israel would pay the income it received from the refugees' land. This allowed the Arabs to demand payment from Israel but in a form of payment that avoided the question of "compensation." By seeking compensation, they might be conceding the legality of Israel's confiscation. Demanding income was a way to seek reparations and still claim ownership. Not only did the UN General Assembly eventually pass such a resolution, but also this demand remains central to Palestinian negotiating strategies today. The author is aware that Palestinians already have carried out detailed studies of how much money Israel has generated from certain urban refugee land in terms of rents, sales, etc., over the decades.

This study also has shown how the UN and the world have understood these controversies—particularly the United States, given its power and influence within the international community and especially within the UNCCP. The UN General Assembly's partition resolution of 1947 specifically called on authorities in the proposed Jewish and Arab states to compensate members of the other community for any land that they subsequently expropriated. It also called for both Jews and Arabs to benefit from public property left behind by the mandatory government in each state. In subsequent years the UNCCP in particular adopted various conceptualizations of what types of property should be included within a future compensation scheme. Given its power within the UN and the UNCCP in particular, America's attitude toward these questions was of paramount importance. To cite but one example, the United States backed Israel's claim that its confiscation of the refugees' land severed their legal title to it. However improper the move may have been, the United States considered that Israel's confiscation of the land was a *fait accompli*. In American eyes, Israel owed the refugees compensation but had become the legal owner of the land. This explains why the Americans insisted that a title search showed them that the land on which they proposed constructing an embassy in Jerusalem in the 1980s was properly registered to the Israeli government and no longer belonged to refugees. Interestingly, the U.S. congress seems to have adopted quite a different standard in 1994 when it enacted the Helms-Burton Act, which denied the legitimacy of Cuba's land nationalization policies after 1959.

This leads to the second issue this study has examined. Is the question of compensation and/or restitution inseparably linked with the controversy over repatriation versus resettlement? The historical record suggests that the answer is "yes." Is payment and acceptance of compensation tantamount to an admission by refugees that they are accepting a *fait accompli* and somehow forfeiting what they call their right of return to their land? Whether openly stated or not, all parties to the drama, including Israel, the Arabs, the UN, and the United States, seem to have agreed that compensation is indeed something that will occur in lieu of repatriation. Israel and the United States have operated since the beginning on the assumptions that (a) massive refugee repatriation is out of the question; (b) compensation will be the financial vehicle for effecting refugee resettlement in the Arab world; and (c) refugees' acceptance of compensation nullifies their right to repatriation.

Israel vehemently opposed mass repatriation from the beginning. The greatest number of refugees it has ever offered to repatriate is 100,000. Resettlement of the vast majority of the refugees was the only option the Israelis would (and still do) discuss. Compensation payments to the refugees were not just a question of morality but would serve the practical purpose of providing the capital to assist in the refugees' absorption into the surrounding Arab countries. This is one reason why Israel has opposed the concept of compensating individual landowners and preferred compensation *en masse*: it feared that in the case of individual compensation a large amount of the total package would go to wealthy refugees who had possessed large estates and who already had resettled, leaving the bulk of the poorer refugees with little or nothing in terms of compensation to finance their absorption into the Arab world. The United States agreed, and from the beginning drew a red line around the equation linking compensation with resettlement. The UN also made this connection, although the UNCCP at various times also believed that even repatriated refugees were entitled to compensation if Israel had destroyed or damaged their property "illegally" and not as a direct consequence of war.

For their part, the Palestinians and the wider Arab world also have resolutely understood compensation as a surrender of the right of return and have refused to discuss it separately from repatriation. Their own ideological stance was deepened by others' insistence that the refugees must choose between compensation and repatriation. The property question for the Arab world has been a derivative of the refugees' central demand over the decades: the right of return. The Palestinians believe that the right of return is sacrosanct and must be dealt with separately from the property question. Many continue to argue that the refugees are entitled to property restitution or reparations, not compensation. They seek a return of the property to its owners, or payment for decades of Israeli usufructure, regardless of whether the refugees return to their homes.

Popular attitudes among Palestinians reflect this ambivalence about compensation and the understanding that it represents a surrender of the right of return. A summer 1999 poll conducted by the Palestinian Authority among Palestinians in the West Bank and Gaza, both refugees and nonrefugees, asked questions related to the question of compensation versus repatriation. The results showed that only about half of the respondents believed that compensation would be forthcoming as part of a final Israeli-Palestinian peace deal. A plurality responded to the question "what do you think will be the negotiated solution for the refugee question?" by saying compensation (46.7 percent). Of the rest, 24.9 percent said repatriation to Israel, 13.2 percent said resettlement, 12.7 percent said remaining in the refugee camps, and 2.5 percent said "other." Pollsters also asked those respondents who were refugees what they themselves *personally supported* as the solution to the refugee problem; the poll showed that compensation was much less popular than the right of return: 24.1 percent of refugees supported the right to compensation compared to 72.5 percent who supported the right of return. When asked what they would do if compensation were agreed upon by the parties as the final solution to the refugee problem, the plurality stated that they would refuse it: 10.7 percent said they would accept compensation with conviction, 32.8 percent said they would accept without conviction, 51.4 percent said they would try to make the scheme fail, and the remaining 5.1 percent offered other answers.(1) Firm convictions are also revealed in a slogan painted in October 2000 on a wall in the Balata refugee camp in the West Bank. It simply read, "One Choice—to Return or to Die."(2)

This ambivalence toward the concept of compensation also explains the recent insistence by some Palestinian groups that the refugees obtain justice through property restitution, not compensation. Official PLO negotiating positions include both concepts. But private Palestinian NGOs have been more forceful in insisting upon restitution instead of compensation. This is seen particularly in the positions taken by the BADIL Resource Center for Palestinian Residency and Refugee Rights and the Council for Palestinian Restitution and Repatriation.

A third important issue this study has discussed is whether Palestinian refugee property claims are linked inextricably to counter claims raised by Israel. Once again, the answer provided by the historical record seems to be "yes." The Israelis long insisted that any compensation they paid to the refugees must be reduced by amounts reflecting everything from war damages suffered by Israel in 1948, to economic damages suffered as a result the blockade of the Suez

Canal to Israeli shipping, to Jewish property abandoned in Arab countries. The last of these has proven to be the longest-lasting demand. A good proportion of the Jews living in Arab countries who fled those countries under duress in 1948 immigrated to Israel. Israel has insisted that it should receive compensation for the property they left behind as compensation for the costs it assumed in settling these immigrants. Muddling the issue is that many of these costs were assumed not by Israel but by the Jewish Agency, and that not all Mizrahi emigrants settled in Israel or even asked that Israel represent their claims for them. Israeli demands to link the two questions clearly have been directed at reducing or even canceling out the final amount that Israel might be required to pay. Some Mizrahi Jews have resented seeing their claims to individual compensation being "hijacked" by the Israeli state, and have felt that their legitimate demands for personal compensation are being threatened by Israel's attempt to reduce its own collective financial burden vis-à-vis the Palestinians.

This demand has proven particularly nettlesome for the Arabs too. The Palestinians categorically have refused to link the two questions. They have stated that they are not responsible for the policies of individual Arab states toward their respective Jewish citizens and therefore their refugee claims accordingly must not be reduced. At the Camp David II summit in 2000, Israeli negotiators continued to connect the two issues but indirectly: they sought the formation of an international fund that would pay individual compensation to both Jews and Palestinians. At Taba in January 2001, they finally admitted, after decades of arguing to the contrary, that the Jewish property issue would not be part of a bilateral Israeli-Palestinian agreement. However, they did demand that the two sides work toward progress on the question, and so it has still proven impossible to extricate Palestinian refugee claims completely from Israel counter claims.

This study has followed the course of another aspect of the property question. Is Israel able to pay the large amount of money required by a compensation scheme? Early compensation schemes developed both by the UNCCP and the United States clearly assumed that Israel could not pay the full amount, given the poor state of its initial post-1948 economy. These plans assumed that the bulk of the costs would be shouldered internationally. American strategists openly admitted as early as 1949 that it would be cheaper for the United States to contribute large amounts of money to these efforts than to allow the refugee problem to fester and lead to regional instability. Israel's concern over how it would pay compensation was clearly a driving force behind its raising of counter claims. This issue quickly became mired in controversy, especially once Israel began receiving massive German reparations and it became clear that the Jewish state was no longer the cash-starved nation it was in 1949. Today, Israel's economy is significantly better off than in the 1950s yet it remains concerned about its ability to pay. This is especially true in light of an Israeli governmental study showing that the Palestinians' compensation claims outstrip Israeli counter claims by a ratio of 22:1. At the Camp David II summit, Israeli negotiators claimed to have spent the funds Israel had generated from refugee property, funds it supposedly was setting aside for the refugees. The question of how to finance compensation payments and who would do so continues to surface today both in formal and informal studies of the issue.

Finally, this study has looked at the failure of the global community, the UN, and the UNCCP in particular to make any significant progress on the refugee property issue over the years. This failure was clearly not for lack of trying. However, the context in which these efforts were made worked against their success almost from the beginning. The conclusions that can be drawn from this history are sobering. The refugee property issue has bedeviled international attempts at solution for more than half a century. This comes despite the various global power shifts and despite the significant changes in international attitudes toward war and peacemaking that have taken place since 1948. What does this say about the ability of the UN, the superpowers, as well as regional actors to make any real progress in reconciling adversaries around the world? Certainly the issue this book has studied demonstrates that despite resolutions, commissions, study missions, conferences and the like, the UN is unable to solve nettlesome problems in the absence of clear and strong backing from the world's great powers, particularly the United States. The UNCCP ultimately proved incapable of creating serious movement on the property question because the United States and its allies, France and Turkey, were unwilling to pressure the parties, especially Israel. There were reasons for this attitude, among them that the United States viewed the Arab-Israeli conflict as subordinate to its wider strategic concerns like the Cold War. It cultivated allies and sought to isolate enemies, which had repercussions on its policies toward pro-Western Israel.

Idealistic UNCCP personnel like Gordon Clapp, Sami Hadawi, John Berncastle, Joseph Johnson, and Frank Jarvis truly believed in their missions, their plans, and their data. They and others correctly understood that unless systemic changes were created in the Middle East that addressed the fundamental concerns of the refugees, of Israel, and of other regional actors, that peace efforts would founder. However, their efforts continually were undercut by apathy, by inflexibility, by American red lines drawn around certain issues, and by the failure of the global community to exert serious efforts toward dealing with the entire Arab-Israeli *gestalt* in which the property question was situated. The UNCCP and others chose instead to dismantle the core problems inherent in the Arab-Israeli conflict into bit-sized, manageable pieces. These pieces ultimately proved less than manageable after all, and these efforts ultimately failed. The lessons of this failure also shed light on the inability of the present Israeli-Palestinian peace process to forge a lasting solution to the bitter conflict between Arab and Jew in Palestine/Israel. This recent peace process also seeks to dismantle the *gestalt* into bit-sized pieces that can be resolved through small-scale technical ventures carried out in a step-by-step process. The Oslo process focused on these small issues and chose to leave the key final status issues until the end. As we saw with the refugee property issue, however, the core issues of the Arab-Israeli conflict are so interconnected that they defy such efforts at a "piece-meal peace." The failure of the Oslo process to date thus comes as no surprise.

The tortured history of the Palestinian refugee property issue demonstrates that healing the humanitarian legacies resulting from bitter ethnic conflicts only can be accomplished by vigorous and creative international peacemaking efforts that respect the deeper conceptual issues presented by such conflicts and seek to address them. No amount of development aid or other technical approaches can succeed. Needless to say, such a task is exceedingly difficult. Nevertheless, we must consider the human and material costs that have gone into failed ventures. Not shouldering this task will prove even more costly for future generations.

# APPENDIX ONE

# COMPARISON OF STUDIES ON THE SCOPE AND VALUE OF REFUGEE PROPERTY

Note: one dunum = 1,000 sq.m.
Note: in 1948, £P1 = £UK1 = $US4.03

## Section One: Official Studies

### 1. Israeli Estimates

Weitz-Danin-Lifshits Committee, 1948

*Scope of Abandoned Land*

| *Type* | *Amount (Dunums)* |
|---|---|
| Rural | |
| Orchards | 92,615 |
| Bananas | 513 |
| Irrigated land, olives, fruit, grapes | 164,832 |
| Cereal | 1,645,183 |
| Built-up area in villages | 10,844 |
| TOTAL | 1,913,987 |
| Urban | |
| Acre | 1,430 |
| Safad | 3,699 |
| Tiberias | 3,861 |
| Jaffa | 10,639 |
| Lydda | 21,570 |
| Ramla | 37,961 |
| Jerusalem | 8,698 |
| Haifa | 6,269 |
| TOTAL | 94,127 |
| GRAND TOTAL: | 2,008,114 |

Source: ISA (130) 2445/3, "Report on a Settlement of the Arab Refugee [Issue]" (November 25, 1948), appendix 9; CZA A246/57, "Comments on Value Assessments of Absentee Landed Property" (November 12, 1962)

*Value of Abandoned Land*

| *Type* | *Gross Value (£I)* | *Net Value (£I)* |
|---|---|---|
| 1) Rural | | |
| Rural land | 46,498,000 | — |
| Rural buildings | 2,829,000 | — |
| TOTAL RURAL | 49,877,000 | 42,000,000 |
| 2) Urban (land and buildings) | | |
| Acre | 1,430,000 | — |
| Safad | 950,000 | — |
| Tiberias | 1,125,000 | — |
| Jaffa | 15,900,000 | — |
| Lydda | 2,200,000 | — |
| Ramla | 4,300,000 | — |
| Jerusalem | 14,600,000 | — |
| Haifa | 12,000,000 | — |
| TOTAL URBAN | 52,505,000 (excluding Beersheba, Baysan, al-Majdal) | 39,500,000 |
| GRAND TOTAL | 102,382,000 | 81,500,000 |

Source: ISA (130) 2445/3, "Report on a Settlement of the Refugee [Issue]" (November 25, 1948), appendix 9

Minister of Agriculture, 1949

*Scope of Abandoned Land*

| *Type* | *Amount (Dunums)* |
|---|---|
| 1. Total | |
| Cultivable | 1,373,000 |
| Waste and barren | 2,720,000 |
| Northern Beersheba | 1,700,000 |
| Southern Beersheba | 10,800,000 |
| TOTAL | 16,593,000 |

(only 400,000 dunums were deemed available for leasing)

Source: Aharon Tsizling, "Ways of Settlement Development in the State of Israel," *Kama* (1951), p. 111, in Granott, Agrarian Reform, p. 89; Labor Party Archives, IV-235–1, file 2251A, in Golan "The Transfer to Jewish Control," p. 423

Custodian of Absentee Property, 1949–1954

*Scope and Value of Refugee Land*

| *Date* | *Amount (Dunums)* | *Value (£I)* |
|---|---|---|
| March 24, 1949 | 3,986,493 | N/A |
| March 31, 1950 | 3,299,447 | 13,100,691 |
| March 29, 1951 | 4,500,000 | N/A |
| February 22, 1953 | 4,063,669 | N/A |
| September 5, 1954 | 4,450,000 | N/A |

Source: ISA (43) 5440/1578, "Interim Report on Real Estate Held by Custodian" (24 March 1949); ISA (43) 5440/1582, "Report of Custodian of Absentees' Office" (31 March 1950); ISA (130) 2402/4, "State Controller Report on the Custodian of Absentees' Property" (29 March 1951); CZA A202/97, "Custodian of Absentees' Property Report" (22 February 1953); CZA KKL5/22273, "Report on the Land Administration System of the State" (5 September 1954)

Ministry of Foreign Affairs, 1953

*Scope of Abandoned Land*

| *Type* | *Amount (Dunums)* |
|---|---|
| Cultivable | 2,600,000 |
| Non-cultivable | 900,000 |
| Underdeveloped urban land | 100,000 |
| GRAND TOTAL | 3,600,000 |

Source: NARA RG 59, 884A.16/5–453, Tel Aviv to Department of State (4 May 1953)

Ministry of Justice, Land Assessment Division, 1962

*Value of Abandoned Land*

Over £P140,000,000

## 2. Arab Estimates

Arab Refugee Property Owners in Palestine, 1951

*Value of Refugee Property*

| *Type* | *Value (£UK)* |
|---|---|
| 1. Cities (Jerusalem, Jaffa, Haifa) | |
| Land | 100–500/sq.m. |
| Buildings | 10–25/sq.m./floor plus value of land |
| 2. Towns | |
| Land | 3–30/sq.m. |
| Buildings | 10–25/sq.m. plus value of land |
| 3. Villages | |
| Built-up land | 250–500/sq.m. |
| Buildings | 3–10/sq.m./floor plus value of land |
| 4. Agricultural land in the plains | |
| Fruit trees | 300–500/sq.m. |
| Other | 75–150/sq.m. |
| 5. Agricultural land in the hills | |
| Fruit trees | 50–100/sq.m. |
| Other | 25–50/sq.m. |

Source: UNSA DAG 13–3, UNCCP. Subgroup: Reference Library. Series: United Nations/Box 10/ORG; Document: ORG/37, "Letter Addressed to the Conciliation Commission by the Committee of Arab Refugee Property Owners in Palestine" (May 7, 1951)

Arab Higher Committee, 1955

*Value of Refugee Property*

| *Type* | *Value (P£)* |
|---|---|
| Citrus | 100,000 |
| Banana | 1,000,000 |
| Orchards | 275,000,000 |
| Cultivable and Pasture Land | 250,000,000 |
| Urban and Rural Built-up | 1,100,000,000 |
| TOTAL | 1,626,100,000 |

Source: Arab Higher Committee, "al-Laji'un al-Filastiniyyun: Dahaya al-Isti'mar wa'l-Sahyuniyya" [The Palestinian Refugees: Victims of Imperialism and Zionism] (Cairo: 1955), pp. 81–93 and Arab Higher Committee, "Statement" (Beirut: 1961), pp. 19–24, both in Yusif Sayigh, al-Iqtisad al-Isra'ili [The Israeli Economy] (Cairo: League of Arab States, Institute for Higher Arab Studies, 1966), pp. 112–113

Arab League, 1956

*Value of Refugee Property*

| *Item* | *Value (£UK)* |
|---|---|
| Citrus plantations, including buildings, machinery, etc. | 100,000,000 |
| Banana plantations | 1,000,000 |
| Olive groves, fruit plantations, other trees | 275,000,000 |
| Cereal lands, good quality | 30,000,000 |
| Cereal lands, medium quality; grazing lands | 220,000,000 |
| Urban lands, buildings; factories, machinery; livestock, | 100,000,000 |
| Movables of all types | 200,000,000 |
| Blocked securities and deposits in banks | 6,000,000 |
| Blocked insurance companies' funds | 1,000,000 |
| TOTAL | 1,933,000,000 |

Source: J. Khoury, *Arab Property and Blocked Accounts in Occupied Palestine* (Cairo: League of Arab States, General Secretary, Palestine Section), 1956), p. 20

## 3. UN Estimates

### UNRWA Sample Study, 1950

*Refugee Property Losses According to Sampling of Refugees in Jordan*

| *Type* | *Number* | *% of Families With Losses* | *Number of Families With Losses* |
|---|---|---|---|
| 1. Structures | | | |
| Houses | 47,500 | 34 | 49,500 |
| Independent structures | 331 | N/A | N/A |
| Shops | 4,150 | N/A. | N/A |

2. Land

| *Type* | *Amount (Dunums)* | *% of Families With Losses* | *No. of Families With Losses* | *Amount/Family With Losses (Dun.)* |
|---|---|---|---|---|
| Cultivated | 2,000,000 | N/A | N/A | 36.2 |
| Citrus | 138,000 | N/A | N/A | 2.7 |
| Other Trees | 315,000 | N/A | N/A | 5.1 |
| Built-up | 5,540 | N/A | N/A | 0.1 |
| Other | 1,050,000 | N/A | N/A | 18.9 |
| TOT. LAND | 3,508,540 | 66.0 | 55,400 | 63.0 |

Source: UNSA DAG 13–3, UNCCP; Subgroup: Office of the Principal Secretary. Series: Records Relating to Compensation/Box 18/1949–51/Working Papers; Document: W/60, "Sampling Survey of Abandoned Property Claimed by Arab Refugees" (April 12, 1951)

## UNCCP Global Estimate, 1951

### *Scope of Refugee Land*

| *Type of Land* | *Mandatory Tax Categories* | *Amount (Dunums)* |
|---|---|---|
| 1. Northern and Central Palestine | | |
| Citrus | 1–2 | 120,564 |
| Bananas | 3 | 620 |
| Village built-up areas | 4 | 14,602 |
| Irrigated, plantations, etc. | 5–8 | 303,750 |
| Cereal land | 9–13 | 2,113,183 |
| Cereal land | 14–15 | 201,495 |
| Uncultivable | — | 1,431,798 |
| TOTAL | | 4,186,012 |
| 2. Beersheba District | | |
| Cultivable | — | 1,834,849 |
| Uncultivable | — | 10,303,110 |
| TOTAL | | 12,137,959 |
| 3. Jerusalem | | 5,736 |
| TOTAL | | 5,736 |
| GRAND TOTAL | | 16,329,707 |

### Value of Refugee Land

| *Type of Land* | *Value (£P)* |
|---|---|
| Rural land | 69,525,144 |
| Urban land | 21,608,640 |
| Jerusalem land | 9,250,000 |
| TOTAL | 100,383,784 |

Source: "Valuation of Abandoned Arab Land in Israel," p. 2. This report is found in several locations. One is UNSA DAG 13–3, UNCCP. Subgroup: Refugee Office. Series: Land Specialist/Box 35/1951/Reports: J.M. Berncastle; Document: MCP/3/51/9, "Valuation of Abandoned Arab Land in Israel" (14 August 1951). It can also be located in the Central Zionist Archives: CZA Z6/1995.

UNCCP Technical Program, 1964 [compare with amended figures below]

*Scope of All Rural and Urban Arab Land in Israel*

| *Sub-District* | *Total Area (Dunums)* | *Covered by R/P1 Forms (Dunums)* |
|---|---|---|
| 1. Excluding Beersheba | | |
| Acre | 795,357 | 507,707 |
| Baysan | 366,095 | 147,167 |
| Nazareth | 490,942 | 248,345 |
| Safad | 696,859 | 347,710 |
| Tiberias | 439,031 | 194,439 |
| Haifa | 972,312 | 405,580 |
| Janin | 257,212 | 228,407 |
| Nablus | 23,414 | 23,414 |
| Tulkarm | 503,676 | 332,571 |
| Hebron | 1,162,336 | 1,144,808 |
| Jerusalem | 296,943 | 221,482 |
| Ramallah | 6,240 | 6,240 |
| Jaffa | 285,084 | 140,425 |
| Ramla | 763,481 | 569,813 |
| Gaza | 815,437 | 675,983 |
| TOTAL | 7,874,419 | 5,194,091 |
| 2. Beersheba* | 12,445,000 | 64,000 |
| GRAND TOTAL | 20,319,419 | 5,258,091 |
| FINAL GRAND TOTAL** | | 7,069,091 |

* R/P1 forms were not drawn up for an additional 1,811,000 dunums of cultivable land in the Beersheba sub-district that were assumed to be cultivated by bedouin Arabs
Source: UN Document A/AC.25/W.84, "Working Paper Prepared by the Commission's Land Expert on the Methods and Techniques of Identification and Valuation of Arab Refugee Immovable Property Holdings in Israel" (April 28, 1964)
** adding the 1,811,000 dunums of land in Beersheba assumed to be cultivated by bedouin Arabs but for which no R/P1 forms were drawn up

*Estimated Scope of Land Owned by* Arabs Still Living in Israel

| *Sub-District* | *Amount (Dunums)* |
|---|---|
| Acre | 318,714 |
| Baysan | 9,390 |
| Nazareth | 190,182 |
| Safad | 30,222 |
| Tiberias | 50,323 |
| Haifa | 170,238 |
| Janin | 86,554 |
| Nablus | 0 |
| Tulkarm | 140,231 |
| Hebron | 7,649 |
| Jerusalem | 3,186 |
| Ramallah | 0 |
| Jaffa | 40 |
| Ramla | 5,320 |
| Gaza | 0 |
| TOTAL | 1,012,059 |

Source: UNSA DAG 13–3, UNCCP. Subgroup: Principal Secretary. Series: Records Relating to the Technical Office/Box 16/1952–57/Land Identification Project/Jarvis Report; Document: A/AC.25/W.83, "Initial Report of the Commission's Land Expert on the Identification and Valuation of Arab Refugee Property Holdings in Israel" (15 September 1961)

*Scope of Rural and Urban* Refugee *Land in Israel*

| *All Arab Land in Israel (Dunums) (on R/P1 Forms)* | *Land Owned by Palestinians Still Living in Israel (Dunums)* | *Land Owned by Refugees (Dunums) (on R/P1 Forms)* |
|---|---|---|
| 5,258,091 | 1,012,059 | 4,246,032 |

*Value of* All *Rural Arab Land in Israel*

| *Sub-District* | *Value (£P)* |
|---|---|
| Acre | 15,051,225 |
| Baysan | 3,464,834 |
| Nazareth | 5,595,879 |
| Safad | 7,323,092 |
| Tiberias | 3,805,192 |
| Haifa | 11,757,629 |
| Janin | 4,357,696 |
| Nablus | 540,660 |
| Tulkarm | 11,987,299 |
| Hebron | 12,443,989 |
| Jerusalem | 10,598,408 |
| Ramallah | 135,150 |
| Jaffa | 23,560,057 |
| Ramla | 22,190,429 |
| Gaza | 19,579,534 |
| Beersheba | 15,000,000 |
| TOTAL | 167,395,073 |

Source: UNSA DAG 13–3, UNCCP. Subgroup: Principal Secretary. Series: Records Relating to the Technical Office/Box 16/1952–57/Land Identification Project/Jarvis Report; Document: A/AC.25/W.83 ADD 1, "Initial Report of the Commission's Land Expert on the Identification and Valuation of Arab Refugee Property Holdings in Israel" (September 10, 1962)

*Value of All Urban Arab Land in Israel*

| *Area* | *Vacant Lots (£P)* | *Buildings (£)* | *Total (£P)* |
|---|---|---|---|
| Acre | 423,542 | 919,385 | 1,342,927 |
| 'Afula | 984 | 0 | 984 |
| Bat Yam | 1,683 | 0 | 1,683 |
| Baysan | 53,691 | 457,186 | 510,877 |
| Haifa | 4,311,086 | 10,467,644 | 14,778,730 |
| Holon | 123,441 | 890 | 124,331 |
| Jaffa | 7,559, 740 | 14,094,203 | 21,653,943 |
| Jerusalem | 6,371,160 | 12,062,701 | 18,433,861 |
| Lydda | 438,690 | 1,403,399 | 1,842,089 |
| al-Majdal | 94,960 | 728,976 | 823,936 |
| Natanya | 36,497 | 0 | 36,497 |
| Nazareth | 219,907 | 1,412,635 | 1,632,542 |
| Ramat Gan | 71,447 | 0 | 71,447 |
| Safad | 157,354 | 840,675 | 998,029 |
| Shafa' 'Amr | 52,814 | 284,330 | 337,144 |
| Tel Aviv | 2,366,740 | 134,020 | 2,500,760 |
| Tiberias | 201,253 | 524,084 | 725,337 |
| Beersheba (estimate) | | | 600,000 |
| Ramla (estimate) | | | 1,850,000 |
| TOTAL | | | 68,265,177 |

Source: UNSA DAG 13–3, UNCCP. Subgroup: Principal Secretary. Series: Records Relating to the Technical Office/Box 16/1952–57/Land Identification Project/Jarvis Report; Document: A/AC.25/W.83 ADD 1, "Initial Report of the Commission's Land Expert on the Identification and Valuation of Arab Refugee Property Holdings in Israel" (10 September 1962)

*Value of Rural and Urban* Refugee *Land in Israel*

| *All Arab Land in in Israel (£P)* | *Land Owned by Palestinians Still Living in Israel (£P)* | *Land Owned by Refugees (£P)* |
|---|---|---|
| 235,660,250 | 31,000,000 | 204,660,190 |

Source: UNSA DAG 13–3, UNCCP. Subgroup: Principal Secretary. Series: Records Relating to the Technical Office/Box 16/1952–57/Land Identification Project/Jarvis Report; Document: A/AC.25/W.83 ADD 1, "Initial Report of the Commission's Land Expert on the Identification and Valuation of Arab Refugee Property Holdings in Israel" (September 10, 1962)

UNCCP Technical Program Figures as Amended by Computerization of the Data, 2000

*Scope of Land (Including Land of Palestinians Still in Israel) in Dunums*

4,851,613.978

Value of Land (including Land of Palestinians Still in Israel) in £P

224,815,931

## Section Two: Unofficial, Academic, Other Studies

Studies of Yosef Weitz, 1948 and 1950

*Scope of Abandoned Land Outside the Beersheba District*

| *Type, Location* | *Amount (Dunums)* |
|---|---|
| 1. Good land | |
| Coastal plains | 959,701 |
| Jezre'el Valley | 128,714 |
| Hula Valley | 51,847 |
| Baysan | 81,274 |
| Galilee hills | 348,458 |
| Samarian hills | 82,476 |
| Judean hills | 85,910 |
| Judean lowlands | 331,890 |
| 2. Poor land | 136,530 |
| 3. Matruka | 751,730 |
| 4. "Government" land | 486,750 |
| 5. Land held by Custodian of German Property (included because this land had Arab tenants who later became refugees) | 39,320 |
| 6. Urban | 100,000 |
| TOTAL | 3,584,600 |

* included: land lying outside Israel belonging to villages lying within Israel

* not included: Beersheba district, land in partially-abandoned villages

*Value of Abandoned Land Appropriate for Settlement, Including Beersheba*

| *Type* | *Amount (Dunums)* | *Value (£I)* |
|---|---|---|
| Rural | 2,070,270 | |
| Urban | | 99,730 |
| Good land in Beersheba district | 1,230,000 | |
| TOTAL | 3,400,000 | 65,000,000 |

Source: Yosef Weitz, "le-Hanhil Adama Hadasha" [Bequest of New Land], *Molad* 2, 12 (March 1949), p. 325; Weitz, *The Struggle for the Land*, p. 113–114

Study of Yusif Sayigh, 1966

*Scope and Value of Refugee Land*

| *Type* | *Scope (Dunums)* | *Value (£P)* |
|---|---|---|
| Citrus | 137,000 | 79,200,000 |
| Other orchards | 384,000 | 115,200,000 |
| Irrigated | 41,000 | 4,100,000 |
| Cereal | 4,400,000 | 176,000,000 |
| Potentially arable | 1,600,000 | 16,000,000 |
| Built-up | | |
| rural | 20,000 | 1,200,000 |
| urban | 29,250 | 11,700,000 |
| TOTAL | 6,611,250 | 403,400,000 |

Source: Yusuf 'Abdullah Sayigh, *al-Iqtisad al-Isra'ili* [The Israeli Economy] (Cairo: League of Arab States, Institute for Higher Arab Studies, 1966), p. 109.

*Scope and Value of Refugee Buildings*

| *Type* | *Number* | *Value (£P)* |
|---|---|---|
| Homes | | |
| rural | 90,000 | 22,500,000 |
| urban | 60,000 | 150,000,000 |
| Mosques and churches | 1,500 | 4,500,000 |
| Factory buildings | 1,500 | 7,500,000 |
| Smiths, tailors, mechanics | 5,000 | 5,000,000 |
| Offices | 5,000 | 15,000,000 |
| Stores | | |
| rural | 2,000 | 800,000 |
| urban | 3,000 | 7,500,000 |
| Hotels | 1,000 | 15,000,000 |
| Restaurants, clubs, coffee houses | 2,000 | 4,000,000 |
| Plantation buildings | 2,000 | 5,000,000 |
| TOTAL | 173,000 | 236,800,000 |

Source: Sayigh *al-Iqtisad al-Isra'ili*, pp. 107–108.

*Value of Refugee Capital and Movable Property*

| *Type* | *Value (£P)* |
|---|---|
| Furniture, personal goods | |
| rural | 12,500,000 |
| urban | 50,000,000 |
| Factory equipment | 15,000,000 |
| Capital goods in offices, hotels, restaurants, coffee shops | 3,000,000 |
| Inventories | 5,000,000 |
| Farm animals | 10,000,000 |
| Bank accounts and insurance policies | 2,000,000 |
| Commercial vehicles | 15,000,000 |
| TOTAL | 112,500,000 |

Source: Sayigh *al-Iqtisad al-Isra'ili*, pp. 108–110

## Study of Sami Hadawi and Atif Kubursi, 1988

*Scope of Arab Land in Israel*

| *Type* | *Amount (Dunums)* |
|---|---|
| 1. Outside Beersheba District | |
| Urban | 112,000 |
| Citrus and banana | 132,849 |
| Village built-up | 21,160 |
| Cultivable (tax categories 5–8) | 471,672 |
| Cultivable (tax categories 9–13) | 2,937,683 |
| Cultivable (tax categories 14–15) | 444,541 |
| Uncultivable | 2,377,946 |
| Roads, etc. | 83,161 |
| TOTAL | 6,581,012 |
| 2. Beersheba District | 12,450,000 |
| GRAND TOTAL | 19,031,012 |

Source: Sami Hadawi, *Palestinian Rights & Losses in 1948. A Comprehensive Study.* Part V: An Economic Assessment of Total Palestinian Losses written by Dr. Atef Kubursi (London: Saqi Books, 1988) p. 113

Value of Refugee Land

| *Type* | *Value (P£)* |
|---|---|
| Urban land | 130,300,000 |
| Rural land | 398,600,000 |
| TOTAL | 528,900,000 |

Source: Hadawi, *Palestinian Rights & Losses in 1948*, p. 187

Study of Frank Lewis, 1996

*Scope of Arab-Owned Land in Israel in 1948*

| *District* | *Amount of Land in Tax Categories 1–3 (in Dunums)* | *Amount of Land in Categories 5–8 (in Dunums)* | *Amount of Land in Tax Categories 9–15 (in Dunums)* | *Total (Dun.)* |
|---|---|---|---|---|
| Galilee | 9,700 | 215,600 | 958,200 | 1,183,500 |
| Gaza | 22,000 | 57,200 | 2,530,500 | 2,609,700 |
| Haifa | 4,000 | 30,200 | 325,700 | 356,300 |
| Jerusalem | 0 | 43,800 | 390,600 | 434,400 |
| Lydda | 89,400 | 69,900 | 443,800 | 603,100 |
| Samaria | 14,400 | 38,000 | 428,100 | 480,500 |
| TOTAL | 135,900 | 454,700 | 5,076,800 | 5,667,400 |
| OF THIS, LAND BELONGING TO REFUGEES | | | | 4,800,000 |

Source: Frank D. Lewis, "Agricultural Property and the 1948 Palestinian Refugees: Assessing the Loss." *Explorations in Economic History* 33 (1996): 173

Value of Rural Abandoned Arab Property in Israel

| *Item* | *Value (£P)* |
|---|---|
| Land | 144,500,000–180,700,000 |
| Farm implements * | 3,300,000 |
| Livestock * | 10,200,000 |
| Buildings * | 29,700,000 |

* Includes non-refugees

| TOTAL VALUE OF ABANDONED LAND, BUILDINGS, IMPLEMENTS, LIVESTOCK | 168,800,000–205,000,000 |
|---|---|

APPENDIX TWO

# CHRONOLOGY OF EVENTS RELATING TO REFUGEE PROPERTY

## 1947

| | |
|---|---|
| November 29 | UN General Assembly Resolution 181 (II) partitions Palestine |
| December | Palestinian refugee flight begins |

## 1948

| | |
|---|---|
| March | Hagana creates Commission for Arab Property in the Villages |
| April | Creation of Supervisor of Arab Property in the Northern District and the Committee for Abandoned Arab Property |
| May | Israel creates Supervisor of Abandoned Property in Jaffa and Arab Properties Department |
| May 14 | Israel declares independence; UN General Assembly Resolution 186 (S-II) establishes Mediator for Palestine |
| June 20 | Israel blocks refugee bank accounts |
| June 21 | Israel passes Abandoned Property Ordinance |
| June 24 | Israel passes Abandoned Areas Ordinance |
| July | Israel creates Ministerial Committee for Abandoned Property |
| July 15 | Israel creates Custodian of Abandoned Property |
| August–Nov. 25 | Weitz-Danin-Lifshits Committee |
| September 16 | UN Mediator for Palestine Count Folke Bernadotte issues report calling *inter alia* for property compensation for non-returning refugees |
| October 11 | Israel passes Emergency Regulations for the Cultivation of low Land and the Use of Unexploited Water Sources |
| December | Israel creates Custodian of Absentee Property |
| December 2 | Israel passes Emergency Regulations (Absentees' Property) |
| December 11 | UN General Assembly Resolution 194 (III) establishes UNCCP, calls for compensating refugees for their property losses |

## 1949

| | |
|---|---|
| January 6 | Israel passes Emergency Regulations (Cultivation of Waste Lands) (Extension of Validity) Ordinance |
| January 27 | Israeli government sells "first million" dunums of refugee land to the Jewish National Fund |
| March 21–April 5 | UNCCP holds meetings with Arabs in Beirut |
| April 27–Sept. 12 | UNCCP convenes Lausanne Conference |
| June 14–Sept. 7 | UNCCP Technical Committee studies refugee question |
| Aug. 23–Dec. 18 | United Nations Economic Survey Mission for the Middle East [the Clapp Mission] |
| Oct. 20–Mar. 17 | Lif Committee |

## 1950

| | |
|---|---|
| January 30–July 15 | UNCCP convenes Geneva Conference |
| February 15 | UNCCP's Mixed Committee of Experts on Blocked Accounts establishes procedure for release of refugee bank accounts |
| March 14 | Israel passes Absentees' Property Law |
| July 31 | Israel passes Development Authority (Transfer of Property) Law |
| October | UNCCP creates Committee on Experts on Compensation |
| October 4 | Israeli government sells "second million" dunums of refugee land to the Jewish National Fund |
| November 8 | Sami Hadawi proposes creation of a refugee property trustee in letter to UNCCP |
| December 2 | UN General Assembly Resolution 393 (V) calls for creation of "Reintegration Fund" |

## 1951

| | |
|---|---|
| January 25 | UNCCP creates Refugee Office |
| March 19 | Israeli For. Min. Moshe Sharett states Israel will link Palestinian compensation with Jewish land seized in Arab countries |
| April 23 | UNCCP Refugee Office begins work on Global Estimate |
| August 14 | Refugee Office's John Berncastle issues report containing the UNCCP Global Estimate |
| Sept. 13–Nov. 19 | UNCCP convenes Paris Conference |

## 1952

| | |
|---|---|
| January 26 | UN General Assembly 512 (VI) concedes UNCCP has failed to make progress, states primary responsibility lies with states themselves |
| September 5 | UNCCP Technical Office created; Technical Program begins |
| September 12 | Luxembourg Agreement obliges Federal Republic of Germany to pay Israel reparations for Nazi crimes |
| October 9 | Israel agrees to first release of blocked refugee bank accounts |

## 1953

| | |
|---|---|
| February 24 | Custodian of Absentee Property Signs Agreement to Sell Refugee Property to the Development Authority |
| June 21–Dec. | Horowitz Committee |
| September 29 | Custodian of Absentee Property Signs Second Agreement to Sell More Refugee Property to the Development Authority |

## 1954

| | |
|---|---|
| September 27 | Israel agrees to second release of blocked accounts |
| November 25 | Izzat Tannous proposes creation of refugee property custodian in speech to UN General Assembly's Ad Hoc Political Committee |

## 1955

Arab Higher Committee issues estimates on refugee property

## 1956

Arab League issues estimates on refugee property

## 1959

| | |
|---|---|
| November 11 | Israel agrees to third release of blocked accounts |

## 1960

| | |
|---|---|
| July 25 | Israel Lands Administration created |

## 1961

| | |
|---|---|
| Aug. 21–Nov. 24 | UNCCP's first Johnson Mission |

## 1962

| | |
|---|---|
| Mar. 2–Aug. 31 | UNCCP's second Johnson Mission |

## 1963

| | |
|---|---|
| Spring–Summer | UNCCP "Informal Talks" |

## 1964

| | |
|---|---|
| May 13 | UNCCP Technical Program published |
| June | Jordan creates committee to study Technical Program report |

## 1966

| | |
|---|---|
| | Yusif Sayigh publishes estimate of refugee property |
| March 23 | First Arab land experts conference begins in Amman |
| July 25 | Second Arab land experts conference begins in East Jerusalem |
| September 22 | UNCCP agrees in principle to provide copies of its documents to the Arabs |
| September 30 | UNCCP closes Technical Office |

## 1967

| | |
|---|---|
| February 20 | Third Arab land experts conference begins in Beirut |

## 1973

| | |
|---|---|
| July 1 | Israel passes Absentees' Property (Compensation) Law |
| September | Egypt requests a copy of UNCCP films on refugee property |

## 1974

| | |
|---|---|
| May | Jordan requests a copy of UNCCP films on refugee property |
| June | Egypt receives copy of UNCCP films |

## 1975

| | |
|---|---|
| | Jordan receives copy of UNCCP films |
| March, May | Egypt receives second copy of UNCCP films |

## 1979

| | |
|---|---|
| March 26 | Egyptian-Israeli peace treaty |

## 1981

| | |
|---|---|
| December 16 | UN General Assembly passes Resolution 36/146 C calling for refugee property fund |

## 1982

| | |
|---|---|
| November | PLO requests a copy of UNCCP films on refugee property |

## 1984

| | |
|---|---|
| | PLO receives copy of UNCCP films |

## 1988

| | |
|---|---|
| | Sami Hadawi and Atif Kubursi publish estimate of refugee property |

## 1991

| | |
|---|---|
| Oct. 30–Nov. 1 | Madrid Conference |

## 1993

| | |
|---|---|
| September 13 | Israeli-PLO Declaration of Principles |

## 1994

| | |
|---|---|
| May 4 | Gaza-Jericho Agreement leads to creation of the Palestinian Authority |
| October 26 | Jordanian-Israeli peace treaty |

## 1996

| | |
|---|---|
| | Frank Lewis publishes estimate of refugee property |
| December | UN General Assembly Resolution 51/129 calls for, *inter alia*, "preservation and modernization" of UNCCP property records |

## 1997

| | |
|---|---|
| June | UNCCP authorizes PLO to copy UNCCP films and records |

## 1998

| | |
|---|---|
| May | UNCCP approves joint UN-PLO project to transfer property records to a computerized data base |

## 1999

| | |
|---|---|
| March | Jordanian government agrees to create computerized data base out of its copy of UNCCP films and other records on Palestinian refugee property |

## 2000

| | |
|---|---|
| May | UN, PLO complete computerized refugee property database |
| July 11–25 | Camp David II conference |

## 2001

| | |
|---|---|
| January 21–27 | Taba talks |
| 25 July | Jordan announces completion of computerized refugee property database |

# NOTES

## Notes to Introduction

1. Michael R. Fischbach, "Land," in Philip Mattar, ed., *Encyclopedia of the Palestinians* (New York: Facts on File, Inc., 2000), p. 241.

## Notes to Chapter One

1. Arnon Golan, "The Transfer to Jewish Control of Abandoned Arab Lands during the War of Independence," in S. Ilan Troen and Noah Lucas, eds., *Israel. The First Decade of Independence*. SUNY Series in Israeli Studies. Russell Stone, ed. (Albany: State University of New York Press, 1995), p. 406.

2. United Nations Secretariat Archives [UNSA], Record Group DAG 13/3, United Nations Conciliation Commission for Palestine (UNCCP). Subgroup: Principal Secretary. Series: General Records/Box 18/Period 1948–51/Working Papers; Document: Clapp Memorandum W32 (January 19, 1950), p. 9.

3. A[vraham] Granott, *Agrarian Reform and the Record of Israel*, trans. E. M. Epstein (London: Eyre & Spottiswood, 1956), p. 93.

4. J. Henry Carpenter, "The Arabs Can't Go Back," *Christian Century* 68, 26 (June 27, 1951): 764.

5. Kenneth W. Bilby, *New Star in the Near East* (Garden City, N.Y.: Doubleday & Co., Inc., 1950), p. 244.

6. United States National Archives and Record Administration [NARA], Record Group RG 59, Lot File 441/Entry 1107B/Gardiner Files/Palestine Refugee Files 1947–49/Box 3, Conciliation Commission for Palestine No. 2; Document: "The Arab Refugee Problem" (March 16, 1949).

7. Sabri Jiryis, "The Legal Structure for the Expropriation and Absorption of Arab Lands in Israel," *Journal of Palestine Studies* 2,4 (Summer 1973): 84–85.

8. Uri Davis and Norton Mezvinsky, eds., *Documents from Israel 1967–1973. Readings for a Critique of Zionism* (London: Ithaca Press, 1975), pp. 43–54.

9. See Benny Morris, *The Birth of the Palestinian Refugee Problem, 1947–1949*. Cambridge Middle East Library (Cambridge: Cambridge University Press, 1987).

10. Ghazi Falah, "The 1948 Israeli-Palestinian War and its Aftermath: the Transformation and De-Signification of Palestine's Cultural Landscape," *Annals of the Association of American Geographers* 86, 2 (1996): 256–85.

11. Walid Khalidi, *All That Remains. The Palestinian Villages Occupied and Depopulated by Israel in 1948* (Washington: Institute for Palestine Studies, 1992).

12. Basheer K. Nijim, ed., with Bishara Muammar, *Toward the De-Arabization of Palestine/Israel 1945–1977*. Published under the Auspices of The Jerusalem Fund for Education and Community Development (Dubuque, Iowa: Kendall/Hunt Publishing Company, 1984).

13. For example, see Avi Shlaim, "The Debate About 1948"; Benny Morris, "The Causes and Character of the Arab Exodus from Palestine: the Israeli Defense Forces Intelligence Service Analysis of June 1948"; and Nur Masalha, "A Critique on Benny Morris"; all in Ilan Pappé, ed., *The Israel/Palestine Question*. Rewriting Histories Series. Jack R. Censer, Series Editor (London and New York: Routledge, 1999).

14. Central Zionist Archives [CZA]. A246/7, Yosef Weitz, Handwritten Diary, Entry for December 20, 1940, pp.1090–91, in Chaim Simons, *International Proposals to Transfer Arabs from Palestine 1895—1947. A Historical Survey* (Hoboken, N.J.: Ktav Publishing House, Inc., 1988), p. 83.

15. Yosef Weitz diaries Vol. III, p. 288 (entry for May 20, 1948), in Benny Morris, "Yosef Weitz and the Transfer Committees, 1948–49," *Middle Eastern Studies* 22,4 (October 1986): 523. For more information on Weitz, see also Nur Masalha, "The Historical Roots of the Palestinian Refugee Question" in Naseer Aruri, ed., *Palestinian Refugees. The Right of Return*. Pluto Middle East Series. Nur Masalha, general editor (London and Sterling, Virginia: Pluto Press, 2001).

16. Israel State Archives [ISA], *Documents on the Foreign Policy of Israel Vol. 1*, ed. by Yehoshua Freundlich (Jerusalem: Israel State Archives, 1981) p. 163. Shertok to Goldmann (June 15, 1948).

17. Yosef Weitz, *The Struggle for the Land* (Tel Aviv: Lion the Printer, 1950) p. 87.

18. James G. McDonald, *My Mission in Israel 1948–1951* (New York: Simon and Schuster, 1951), p. 176.

19. NARA RG 59; Document: 867N.48/8–1248, Damascus to Department of State (August 12, 1948).

20. Pablo de Azcárate, *Mission in Palestine* (Washington: The Middle East Institute, 1966), p. 74.

21. *The New York Times*, June 3, 1948.

22. Don Peretz, *Israel and the Palestine Arabs* (Washington: Middle East Institute, 1958), p. 176.

23. NARA RG 59; Document: 867N.4016/5/549, London to Dept. of State (May 10, 1949).

24. *Ha'aretz*, June 17–July 3, 1951.

25. S. G. Thicknesse, *Arab Refugees. A Survey of Resettlement Possibilities* (London and New York: Royal Institute of International Affairs, 1949), p. 27.

26. NARA RG 59, 867N.48/8–248, Tel Aviv to Dept. of State (August 2, 1948).

27. Bilby *New Star in the Near East,* p. 213.

28. Morris *Birth of the Palestinian Refugee Problem*, p. 52.

29. Tom Segev, *1949: The First Israelis*. Arlen Neal Weinstein, English language editor. An Owl Book (New York: Henry Holt and Co., 1998), pp. 75, 80.

30. Ibid., p. 79.

31. Ibid., p. 334, fn. 25.

32. Ernest Stock, *Chosen Instrument. The Jewish Agency in the First Decade of the State of Israel* (New York: Herzl Press and Jerusalem: Hassifriya Haziyonit, 1988), p. 85.

33. Ibid., p. 86.

34. Israel, *Israel Government Yearbook 5711/1950*, p. 234.

35. Zvi Zinger [Yaron], "State of Israel (1948–72)," in *Immigration and Settlement*. The Israel Pocket Library (Jerusalem: Keter Publishing House, Ltd., 1973), p. 57.

36. Stock *Chosen Instrument*, p. 86.

37. Segev *1949*, pp. 86–87.

38. Morris *Birth of the Palestinian Refugee Problem*, pp. 135–37; Golan "The Transfer to Jewish Control," pp. 410–11.

39. Geremy Forman, "Jewish National Land After 1948: The Evolution of 'Israel Lands' and the Establishment of the Israel Lands Administration" (Unpublished manuscript, Haifa University, 1999), p. 12.

40. Ibid., p. 13.

41. NARA RG 84, Tel Aviv Embassy/General Records 1948/124.1–891; Document: 850, "Recent Economic Developments in Israel" (December 10, 1948).

42. Golan "The Transfer to Jewish Control" pp. 407–8.

43. Ibid., pp. 415–16.

44. NARA RG 84, Haifa Consulate/General Records, 1948/300–804.9; Document: 711.3, Lippincott to Secretary of State (June 22, 1948).

45. Golan "The Transfer to Jewish Control," pp. 417–18.

46. Minutes of the People's Council and the Provisional Council of State (June 24, 1948), p. 25, in Jiryis "Legal Structure," p. 83.

47. First published in *'Iton Rishmi* [Official Gazette) No. 7 (June 30, 1948).

48. Ibid.

49. First published in *'Iton Rishmi* [Official Gazette) No. 27 (October 15, 1948).

50. Jiryis "Legal Structure," p. 97.

51. Segev *1949*, p. 80.

52. Joseph B. Schechtman, *The Arab Refugee Problem* (New York: Philosophical Library, 1952), p. 93.

53. *Divrei ha-Knesset II* [Knesset Proceedings II], pp. 911–12, in Schechtman *Arab Refugee Problem*, p. 113, fn. 11.

54. NARA RG 59, Lot Files 441/Entry 1107B/Gardiner Files/Palestine Refugee File 1947–49/Box 4; Refugees—Background; Document: Tentative Policy Paper, Palestine Refugees (March 15, 1949).

55. First published in *Sefer ha-Hukkim* [Book of Laws] No. 37 (March 20, 1950), p. 86.

56. *Documents on the Foreign Policy of Israel* Vol. 5, ed. by Yehoshua Freundlich (Jerusalem: Israel State Archives, 1988), pp. 463–64. Sharett to Kaplan (August 6, 1950).

57. United Kingdom, Public Records Office [PRO]. Document: FO 371/91744.

58. *Israel Government Yearbook Vol. 5721/1960–61*, p. 199; *Davar*, August 27–28, 1950.

59. *Israel Government Yearbook Vol. 5717/1956*, p. 225.

60. *Jerusalem Post*, January 18, 1953.

61. UNSA DAG 13–3, UNCCP. Subgroup: Records of the Land Specialist. Series: Records of the Land Specialist 1951–1952/Box 35/ Diary (J. H. Berncastle); Document: Berncastle diary entry (June 4, 1952).

62. *Jerusalem Post*, June 18, 1951.

63. ISA (130) 2402/4, State Controller's report on the Custodian of Absentee Property (March 29, 1951).

64. *Medinat Yisra'el, Mivaker ha-Medina—Doh Shnati 41 (le-shnat 1990 ve le-shnat ha-ksafim 1989)* [State of Israel, State Controller's Annual Report 41 (for 1990 and Budget Year 1989)], pp.326–32.

65. ISA (43) 5440/1582, report of Custodian of Absentee Property (March 31, 1950).

66. *Israel Government Yearbook Vol. 5712/1951–52*, p. 87.

67. *Davar*, May 15, 1951.

68. *Davar*, August 27–28, 1950.

69. *Israel Government Yearbook Vol. 5711/1950*, p. 135.

70. *Digest*, July 22, 1949 and August 11, 1950, in Schechtman, *Arab Refugee Problem*, p. 113, fn. 8.

71. *Ha'aretz*, June 17-July 3, 1951.

72. *Jerusalem Post*, April 19, 1951.

73. *Zionist Review*, June 24, 1949, in Thicknesse, *Arab Refugees*.

74. *Jerusalem Post*, January 18, 1953.

75. UNSA DAG 13–3, UNCCP. Subgroup: Records of the Land Specialist. Series: Records of the Land Specialist 1951–1952/Box 35/ Diary (J. H. Berncastle); Document: Berncastle Diary entry (June 5, 1952).

76. Granott, *Agrarian Reform*, p. 72.

77. *Israel Government Yearbook Vol. 5719/1958*, p. 235.
78. Ibid., p. 236.
79. *Business Digest* [Haifa], May 18, 1950.
80. *Ha'aretz*, June 25, 1951.
81. Ibid.
82. Ibid.; *Davar*, August 27–28, 1950.
83. *Business Digest* [Haifa], April 13, 1950.
84. Peretz, *Israel and the Palestine Arabs*, p. 143.
85. *Ha'aretz*, June 25, 1951.
86. CZA A202/97, Custodian of Absentee Property report of February 22, 1953.
87. *Ha'aretz*, June 17–July 3, 1951.
88. *Ha'aretz*, June 21, 1951.
89. *Ha'aretz*, June 17–July 3, 1951.
90. *Ha'aretz*, June 21, 1951; *Davar*, August 27–28, 1950.
91. *Jerusalem Post*, May 14, 1951.
92. J.D. Ophen, "The Citrus Industry in Israel," *Middle Eastern Affairs* 5, 2 (February 1954), p. 54.
93. *Palestine Post*, April 5, 1950.
94. Peretz, *Israel and the Palestine Arabs*, p. 143; Ophen, "The Citrus Industry in Israel," p. 51.
95. *Israel Government Yearbook Vol. 5713/1952*, p. 119.
96. *Jewish Agency Digest of Press and Events* 3, 42 (July 6, 1951).
97. CZA A202/97, Custodian of Absentee Property Report of February 22, 1953.
98. *Davar*, August 27–28, 1950.
99. Ibid.
100. *Israel Government Yearbook Vol. 5714/1953–54*, p. 142.
101. *Ha'aretz*, June 17–July 3, 1951.
102. *Jerusalem Post*, January 18, 1953.
103. *Davar*, August 27–28, 1950.
104. Sharett's diary, entry for November 11, 1953, p. 150, in Livia Rokach, *Israel's Sacred Terrorism. A Study Based on Moshe Sharett's Personal Diary and Other Documents*. Introduction by Noam Chomsky (Belmont, Mass.: Association of Arab-American University Graduates, Inc., 1980), pp. 47–48.
105. *Davar*, August 27–28, 1950.
106. Michael Dumper, *Islam and Israel: Muslim Religious Endowments and the Jewish State* (Washington: Institute for Palestine Studies, 1994), p. 32.
107. Segev, *1949*, p. 83.
108. NARA RG 59, 867N.48/2–2849, McDonald to Secretary of State (February 28, 1949).
109. ISA (130) 2445/3, "Report on a Settlement of the Arab Refugee [Issue]" (November 25, 1948), pp. 6–8.

110. Ibid.

111. Ibid., appendix 8.

112. Ibid.

113. Ibid.

114. Ibid.

115. Weitz, *Struggle for the Land*, p. 97.

116. ISA (130) 2445/3, "Report on a Settlement of the Arab Refugee [Issue]" (November 25, 1948), appendix 8.

117. Ibid.

118. *Documents on the Foreign Policy of Israel Vol.* 2, ed. by Yehoshua Freundlich (Jerusalem: Israel State Archives, 1981). pp. 458ff.; NARA RG 59, 867N.48/2–2849 (McDonald to Secretary of State (February 28, 1949); NARA RG59, Lot file 441/Entry 1107B/Gardiner Files/ Palestine Refugee files, 1947–49/Box 3/Conciliation Commission for Palestine #2.

119. *Jewish Herald* [Johannesburg], January 5, 1951; Schechtman, *The Arab Refugee Problem*, p. 108.

120. *Ha'aretz*, July 28, 1948; NARA RG 59, 867N.48/8–1648 (Haifa to Department of State (August 16, 1948).

121. *Herut*, November 30, 1950.

122. *Business Digest* [Haifa], May 18, 1951.

123. Forman, "Jewish National Land," p. 16.

124. *Israel Government Yearbook Vol. 5719/1958*, p. 236.

125. CZA KKL5/22273, "Report on the Land Administration System of the State" (September 5, 1954); Geremy Forman, "The Transformation of Eastern 'Emeq Yizre'el/Marj Ibn 'Amer and 'Emeq Beit-Shean/Ghor Baysan: Changes in Settlement, Population and Land Tenure due to the 1948 War and the Establishment of the State of Israel" (M.A. thesis, University of Haifa, 2000), p. 135.

126. CZA A246/275, agreement of September 29, 1953.

127. CZA A246/276, "Development Authority Budget 1954–55 (Organizational and Operational)."

128. CZA A246/275, agreement of September 29, 1953; ISA (130) 1829-hts/12, Dagon to Comay (October 18, 1959).

129. *Israel Government Yearbook Vol. 5714/1953–54*, p. 144.

130. CZA KKL5/22273, "Report on the Land Administration System of the State" (September 5, 1954), sec. 14.

131. Ibid. and Forman "Transformation of Eastern 'Emeq Yizre'el," pp. 135, 137.

132. NARA, RG 59, 884A.16/10–1453, Tel Aviv to Department of State (October 14, 1953).

133. *Israel Government Yearbook Vol. 5719/1958*, p. 236.

134. See Golan, "The Transfer to Jewish Control," pp. 417–19, 421–22.

135. Ibid., pp. 419, 421–22.

136. Ibid., p. 423.

137. JNF, *Jewish Villages in Israel* (Jerusalem: 1949), p. xxi, in Walter Lehn with Uri Davis, *The Jewish National Fund* (London and New York: Kegan Paul International, 1988), p. 347, fn. 285.

138. Lehn and Davis, *The Jewish National Fund*, p. 108.

139. Weitz, *Struggle for the Land*, p. 139.

140. Ibid., p. 98.

141. NARA RG 59, 867N.48/2–2549, Tel Aviv to Department of State (February 27, 1949); Document: attached November 1948 issue of *Karnenu*.

142. Jewish National Fund, *Report to the 23rd Congress*, in Lehn and Davis, *Jewish National Fund*, p. 131.

143. Weitz, *Struggle for the Land*, p. 90.

144. Morris, "Yosef Weitz and the Transfer Committees," pp. 542–43.

145. Ben Gurion's diaries, cited in Ibid., p. 543.

146. Musa Goldenberg, *ve ha-Keren Odena Kayemet* [And the Fund Still Stands] (Merhavya: Sifrayat Po'alim Ketavim, 1965), pp. 207–11, in Lehn and Davis, *Jewish National Fund*, p. 247.

147. Ibid., p. 248.

148. Ibid., p. 251.

149. Schechtman, *Arab Refugee Problem*, p. 62.

150. NARA, RG 59, Lot File 441/Entry 1107B/Gardiner files/Palestine Ref. Files 1947–49/Box 4, "Refugees—United States Policy"; Document: "Palestine Refugees. Background and Policy Considerations" (May 1949).

151. Zeev Sharef, *Three Days* (Garden City, N.Y.: Doubleday and Company, Inc., 1962), p. 165.

152. Golan "The Transfer to Jewish Control," pp. 429–31.

153. Granott, *Agrarian Reform in Israel*.

154. CZA KKL10, Vol. 20, pp. 6–7; minutes of JNF board meeting (January 4, 1949).

155. JNF, "Report to the 23rd Congress," in Lehn, *Jewish National Fund*, p. 347, fn. 284.

156. Granott, *Agrarian Reform*, pp. 107–11.

157. See Figure 19.1 in Golan, "The Transfer to Jewish Control," p. 432.

158. *Karnenu*, November 1948.

159. *The New York Times*, June 10, 1949.

160. Weitz, *Struggle for the Land* p. 146.

161. Granott, *Agrarian Reform*, p. 111.

162. CZA A202/97, Custodian's report of February 22, 1953.

163. Granott, *Agrarian Reform*, pp. 108, 111; Lehn and Davis, *Jewish National Fund*, p. 132; FO 371/82257, Tel Aviv to Foreign Office (November 14,

1950); *Yediot Aharonot*, August 31, 1999, in David Blougrund, *The Jewish National Fund*. Policy Studies No. 49 (Washington and Jerusalem: Institute for Advanced Strategic and Political Studies, 2001), p. 7.

164. *Jewish Agency's Digest of Press and Events* 3, 20 (February 2, 1951), pp. 786–87.

165. *The New York Times*, January 21, 1951.

166. Granott, *Agrarian Reform*, p. 112.

167. Ibid., pp. 81, 253.

168. Ibid., p. 253.

169. *Israel Government Yearbook Vol. 5719/1958*, p. 236.

170. Israel Defense Force operations/intelligence to Shiloah (June 16, 1948), in Benny Morris, *Israel's Border Wars, 1949–1956. Arab Infiltration, Israeli Retaliation, and the Countdown to the Suez War* (Oxford: Oxford University Press, 1993), p. 116.

171. Weitz to Shertok (May 27, 1948), in Ibid., p. 117.

172. Ibid., p. 116.

173. Morris, *Birth of the Palestinian Refugee Problem*, p. 138.

174. Ibid., p. 148.

175. Weitz, *Struggle for the Land*, p. 6.

176. Golan, "The Transfer to Jewish Control," pp. 410, 428.

177. Forman, "Jewish National Land," p. 15.

178. Segev, *1949*, p. 83.

179. Weitz, *Struggle for the Land*, p. 149.

180. Israel, Ministry of Finance, *Development of Agriculture in Israel* (1953?), p. 17.

181. Zinger, "State of Israel (1948–72)," p. 159.

182. *Jerusalem Post*, January 18, 1953.

183. Peretz, *Israel and the Palestine Arabs*, p. 143.

184. Joseph Schechtman, "Meeting the Arab Claims on Israel," *Jewish Herald* [Johannesburg], January 5, 1951.

185. For more on this general phenomenon as well as the specific case of 'Ayn Hawd, see Susan Slyomovics, *The Object of Memory. Arab and Jew Narrate the Palestinian Village* (Philadelphia: University of Pennsylvania Press, 1998).

186. David Pinsky's article in *Der Tog*, October 1, 1949, in William Zukerman, *Voices of Dissent: Jewish Problems, 1948–1961* (New York: Bookman Association, Inc., 1964), pp. 140–41.

187. Bilby, *New Star in the Near East*, p. 239.

188. Yosef Weitz, "The New Land Policy," *Karnenu*, November 1948.

189. Morris, *Israel's Border Wars*, p. 28.

190. *Divrei ha-Knesset* 7 (January 2, 1952), p. 656, in Ibid., p. 122.

191. Glubb, "Note on Refugee Vagrancy," PRO FO 371/104778, in Ibid., p. 37.

192. Granott, *Agrarian Reform*, pp. 123–34, 256.

193. CZA KKL5/22273, "Report on the Land Administration System of the State" (September 5, 1954).

194. Ibid., sec. 9.

195. *Israel Government Yearbook Vol. 5717/1956*, p. 224; *Vol. 5719/1958*, p. 235.

196. Ibid.

197. Ibid., *Vol. 5717/1956*, p. 224.

198. Ibid., *Vol. 5718/1957*, p. 235.

199. CZA KKl5/22273, "Report on the Land Administration System of the State" (September 5, 1954), sec. 9.

## Notes to Chapter Two

1. UN document S/1025 (September 16, 1948).

2. Tel Aviv Embassy/Central Records/1948: 124.1–891/800, Statement of the Fighters for the Freedom of Israel (September 24, 1948).

3. NARA RG 59, Lot file 53D468/Records of the Bureau of Near East, South Asian, and African Affairs/McGhee Files 1945–53/Box 18, Palestine/"Memo of Conversation," Bunche and Thomas F. Power, Jr. (June 20, 1949).

4. UNSA DAG 13–3, UNCCP. Subgroup: Principal Secretary. Series: Records Relating to Compensation/Box 18/1948–51/Background Information Relating to Compensation; Document: W/36, "Returning Refugees and the Question of Compensation" (February 7, 1950).

5. UNSA DAG 13–3, UNCCP. Subgroup: Reference Library. Series: United Nations/Box 10/NC-Series; Document: NC/18, "Hearings of Non-Governmental Organizations Held by the Conciliation Commission in Beirut on 24, 25, 26 and March 28 1949" (March 29, 1948).

6. UNSA DAG 13–3, UNCCP. Subgroup: Office of the Legal Advisor. Series: General Records/Box 29/1949–50/State/ of Israel: Absentees' Property Law; Document: COM.GEN/W.2, "Note on the Emergency Regulations on Property of Absentees ('Absentee Property Act')" (June 21, 1949).

7. Ibid.; *Documents on the Foreign Policy of Israel Vol. 4*, ed. by Yemina Rosenthal (Jerusalem: Israel State Archives, 1981), pp. 26–27. Etyan to Etheridge (May 6, 1949).

8. *Documents on the Foreign Policy of Israel Vol. 4*, p. 63.

9. *The New York Times*, March 19, 1949.

10. *Documents on the Foreign Policy of Israel Vol. 2*, p. 446, Meeting with Members of the Conciliation Commission (February 24, 1949).

11. Ibid., p. 512, Eytan to Sharett (March 18, 1949).

12. Ibid., pp. 585 ff., Ben Gurion and Sharett at the Ministry of Foreign Affairs (April 22, 1949).

13. UNSA DAG 13–3, UNCCP. Subgroup: Office of the Legal Advisor. Series: General Records/Box 29/1949–50/State of Israel: Absentees' Property Law.

Document: COM.GEN/W.2, "Note on the Emergency Regulations on Property of Absentees ('Absentee Property Act')" (June 21, 1949).

14. NARA RG 59, Lot File 53D468/Records of the Bureau of Near Eastern, South Asian, and African Affairs/McGhee Files 1945–53/Box 18; Document: "Palestine Refugee Problem: Financing Repatriation and Resettlement of Palestine Refugees" (May 4, 1949).

15. Ibid., Document: "Intelligence Memorandum No. 180" (May 31, 1949).

16. NARA RG 59, Lot file 53D468/Records of the Bureau of Near Eastern, South Asian, and African Affairs/McGhee Files 1949–53/Box 17; Document: "The Palestine Refugee Problem."

17. NARA RG 59, Lot file 441, entry 1107B/Gardner Files/Palestine Refugee Files, 1947–49/Box 3, Palestine Refugees—2 Corr.; Document: "Arab Refugees in Israel" (June 16, 1949).

18. Walter Eytan, *The First Ten Years. A Diplomatic History of Israel* (New York: Simon and Schuster, 1958), pp. 57–58. For more on the refugee delegations at Lausanne, see Avi Plascov, *The Palestinian Refugees in Jordan, 1948–1957* (London: Frank Cass, 1981), pp. 20–21.

19. UNSA DAG 13–3, UNCCP. Subgroup: Office of the Legal Advisor. Series: General Records/Box 29/1949–50/State of Israel: Absentees' Property Law. Document: COM.GEN/W.2, "Note on the Emergency Regulations on Property of Absentees ('Absentee Property Act')" (June 21, 1949).

20. NARA RG 59, 867N.48/2–2549, Tel Aviv to Department of State (February 27, 1949).

21. NARA RG 59, Lot file 441, entry 1107B/Gardiner files/Palestine Refugee Files 1947–49/Box 4, Refugees—United States Policy. Document: "Palestine Refugees" (January 14, 1949).

22. Weitz, *The Struggle for the Land*, pp. 102–4.

23. *Israel Government Yearbook Vol. 5711/1950*, p. 213.

24. Ibid., *Vol. 5712/1951–52*, p. 155.

25. Ibid., *Vol. 5711/1950*, p. 213.

26. ISA (130) 2401/22, "Claims for Jewish Property Frozen in Arab States" (October 6, 1952).

27. UNSA DAG 13–3, UNCCP. Subgroup: Office of the Principal Secretary. Series: Records Relating to Compensation/Box 18/1948–51/Working Papers. Document: W/50, "Compensation to Refugees and the Question of War Damages" (August 4, 1950).

28. UNSA DAG 13–3, UNCCP. Subgroup: Office of the Principal Secretary. Series: Records Relating to Compensation/Box 18/1948–51/Background Information Relating to Compensation; Document: "Initial Steps on the Question of Compensation."

29. Plascov, *Palestinian Refugees in Jordan*, p. 172, fn. 63.

29. UNSA DAG 13–3, UNCCP. Subgroup: Office of the Principal Secre-

tary. Series: Records Relating to Compensation/Box 18/1948–51/Working Papers; Document: W/25 "Note on Certain 'Conservatory Measures'" (September 8, 1949).

30. NARA RG 59, 884.411/4–2651, Cairo to Department of State (April 26, 1951).

31. NARA RG 59, Lot file 55D643/Office of Near Eastern Affairs/Subject File Relating to Economic Affairs, 1927–51/Box 3, Blocked Arab Accounts. Document: "Frozen Balances of Arab Refugees" (April 27, 1950).

32. UNSA DAG 13–3, UNCCP. Subgroup: Records of the Land Specialist. Series: Records of the Land Specialist 1951–1952/Box 35/ Diary (J. H. Berncastle). Document: Alami to UNCCP (May 14, 1952), in Berncastle diary entry (May 14, 1952).

33. ISA (130) 2401/22/1, Custodian to Minister of Foreign Affairs (October 10, 1952); ISA (130) 2463/8, Research Department to Bendor (May 15, 1952); ISA (130) 2401/27, "Claims for Jewish Property Frozen in Arab States" (October 6, 1952) and memorandum of November 5, 1952.

34. Avi Shlaim, *Collusion Across the Jordan. King Abdullah, the Zionist Movement, and the Partition of Palestine* (New York: Columbia University Press, 1988), pp. 493–94.

35. NARA RG 59, Lot file 441, entry 1107B/Gardiner Files/Box 3, Palestine Refugee Files 1947–49/UN Conciliation Commission for Palestine #1; Document: W/8, "Note on Palestine Assets" (April 2, 1949).

36. UN Document A/1367/Rev. 1, "Conciliation Commission for Palestine Progress Report December 11, 1949–October 23, 1950."

37. David P. Forsythe, *United Nations Peacekeeping. The Conciliation Commission for Palestine*. Published in cooperation with the Middle East Institute (Baltimore and London: The Johns Hopkins University Press, 1972), p. 53.

38. Ibid.

39. NARA RG 59, Lot file 57D298/Records of the Office of Near Eastern Affairs/Subject File 1941–54/Box 4, Letters to and From Gordon Clapp; Document: Clapp to McGhee (October 20, 1949).

40. Ibid.

41. NARA RG 59, Lot File 53D468/Records of the Bureau of Near Eastern, South Asian, and African Affairs/McGhee Files 45–53/Box 18, Palestine 1948—Memoranda; Document: "Memorandum of Conversation" (November 2, 1949).

42. UNSA DAG 13–3, UNCCP. Subgroup: Office of the Principal Secretary. Series: Records Relating to Compensation/Box 18/1949–51/Working Papers on Compensation; Document: W/32, "Letter and Memorandum dated November 22, 1949 Concerning Compensation, Received by the Chairman of the Conciliation Commission from Mr. Gordon R. Clapp, Chairman, United Nations Economic Survey Mission for the Middle East" (January 19, 1950).

43. Ibid.

44. NARA RG 59, Lot file 55D643/Office of Near Eastern Affairs/Subject

File Relating to Economic Affairs, 1927–51/Box 3, Blocked Arab Accounts; Document: "Frozen Balances of Arab Refugees" (April 27, 1950).

45. UNSA DAG 13–3, UNCCP. Subgroup: Office of the Principal Secretary. Series: Records Relating to Compensation/Box 18/1949–51/Working Papers on Compensation; Document: W/33, "The Question of Compensation for Palestine Refugees," p. 6.

46. UNSA DAG 13–3, UNCCP. Subgroup: Office of the Principal Secretary. Series: Records Relating to Compensation/Box 18/1949–51/Working Papers on Compensation; Document: A/AC.25/W.53 "Note on the Problem of Compensation" (September 13, 1950).

47. UNSA DAG 13–3, UNCCP. Subgroup: Office of the Principal Secretary. Series: Records Relating to Compensation/Box 18/1949–51/Working Papers on Compensation; Document: "On Compensation for the Property of Refugees Who Decide Not to Return to their Homes" (April 22, 1950).

48. *Documents on the Foreign Policy of Israel Vol. 5*, pp. 584–86. Shiloah to Eytan (October 12, 1950).

49. PRO FO371/82257, Registry No. EE18213/1.

50. UNSA DAG 13–3, UNCCP; Subgroup: Office of the Principal Secretary. Series: Records Relating to Compensation/Box 18/1950/Compensation; Document: "Letter dated July 9, 1950 addressed to the Chair of the Conciliation Commission by the Foreign Minister of Israel" (July 13, 1950).

51. *Documents on the Foreign Policy of Israel Vol. 5*, p. 502. Sharett to Eban (August 27, 1950).

52. Ibid., pp. 604–5. Eban to Sharett (October 25, 1950).

53. PRO FO371/82257, Washington to Foreign Office (November 11, 1950).

54. Schechtman, *The Arab Refugee Problem*, pp. 104–5.

55. *Documents on the Foreign Policy of Israel Vol. 6*, ed. by Yemina Rosenthal (Jerusalem: Israel State Archives), pp. 113–15. Rafael to Eban (February 18, 1951).

56. *Foreign Relations of the United States 1952–54, Vol. 9* (Washington: Department of State, 1981), p. 1069. Document 524, Department of State to Tel Aviv (November 25, 1952).

57. Azcárate, *Mission to Palestine*, pp. 168–69.

58. *Documents on the Foreign Policy of Israel Vol. 6*, pp. 69–71. Avner to Nissan (January 30, 1951).

59. PRO FO 371/91410, U.K delegation to the UN to foreign office (December 19, 1951).

60. PRO FO371/91410, "Visit of Mr. Barco" (March 22, 1951).

61. *Documents on the Foreign Policy of Israel Vol. 6*, pp. 364–66. Comay to Lourie (June 7, 1951).

62. PRO FO371/91410, Walker to Furlonge (June 29, 1951).

63. UNSA DAG-13–3, UNCCP. Subgroup: Office of the Principal Secretary. Series: Issues Relating to Compensation/Box 18/1948–51/Working Papers; Document: W/59, "Note Concerning the Evaluation of Refugee Property" (February 26, 1951).

64. PRO FO371/91410, "Note by Mr. Myers" (July 7, 1951).

65. PRO FO371/91410, Tel Aviv to Foreign Office (June 14, 1951).

66. NARA RG 59, 325.84/6–1560, USUN to Secretary of State (June 15, 1960).

67. From Berncastle's final report entitled "Valuation of Abandoned Arab Land in Israel," p. 2. Berncastle's report is found in several locations. One is UNSA DAG 13–3, UNCCP. Subgroup: Refugee Office. Series: Land Specialist/Box 35/1951/Reports: J.M. Berncastle; Document: MCP/3/51/9, "Valuation of Abandoned Arab Land in Israel" (August 14, 1951). It also can be located in the Central Zionist Archives: CZA Z6/1995.

68. Ibid., p. 3.

69. Ibid., p. 4.

70. Ibid., p. 5.

71. Ibid., p. 6.

72. UN Document W/63 of May 1, 1951.

73. "Valuation of Abandoned Arab Land in Israel," p. 5.

74. Ibid., p. 9.

75. Ibid.

76. Ibid.

77. Ibid., p. 110.

78. UN Document A/AC.25/W.81/Rev. 2, "Historical Survey of Efforts of the United Nations Conciliation Commission for Palestine to Secure the Implementation of Paragraph 11 of General Assembly Resolution 194 (III)" (October 2, 1961), secs. 94, 95.

79. ISA (130) 1780/hts/22, Weitz to Ministry of Foreign Affairs (August 5, 1951).

80. CZA A246/57, "Comments on Value Assessments of Absentee Landed Property" (November 12, 1962).

81. UNSA DAG 13–3, UNCCP. Subgroup: Refugee Office. Series: Records of the Land Specialist/Box 35/Refugee Office Final Report; Document: UNCCP Final Report—Refugee Office (1951); Chapter II—Recommendations.

82. PRO FO371/91410, Chadwick to Furlonge (July 24, 1951).

83. PRO FO 371/98518, Tel Aviv to Foreign Office (January 18, 1952).

84. *Divrei ha-Knesset* Vol. 4 (November 4, 1951).

85. UNSA DAG 13–3, UNCCP. Subgroup: Records of the Land Specialist. Series: Records of the Land Specialist 1951–1952/Box 35/ Diary (J. H. Berncastle). Document: Berncastle diary entry (August 27, 1952).

86. PRO FO371/91410, "Arab Refugees" (December 14, 1951).

87. NARA RG 59, 884A.16/8–453, Tel Aviv to Department of State (August 4, 1953).

88. *Documents on the Foreign Policy of Israel Vol. 6*, p. 648. Eytan to Israeli delegation (September 16, 1951), p. 648; ibid., pp. 632–35. "Guidelines for the Israeli Delegation to the Paris Conference" (September 12, 1951).

89. Ibid., p. 652. Eytan to Sharett (September 19, 1951).

90. Ibid., pp. 791–97. Fischer's Statement before the Palestine Conciliation Commission (November 14, 1951); pp. 788–91. Eban to Fischer (November 14, 1951).

91. PRO FO371/98518, UNCCP document Restricted A/AC.25/W.78, "Practical Suggestions for the Commission's Future Activities in Connection with Compensation" (April 24, 1952).

92. *Documents on the Foreign Policy of Israel Vol. 6*, pp. 855–57. Memorandum on Sharett's meeting with Blandford (December 7, 1951).

93. PRO FO371/98518, UNCCP document Restricted A/AC.25/W.78, "Practical Suggestions for the Commission's Future Activities in Connection with Compensation" (April 24, 1952).

94. UNSA DAG 13–3, UNCCP. Subgroup: Records of the Land Specialist. Series: Records of the Land Specialist 1951–1952/Box 35/ Diary (J. H. Berncastle); Document: Berncastle diary entry (May 22, 1952).

95. Ibid.

96. Biran was probably Avraham Biran, who would later go on to become a world famous archaeologist.

97. Ibid., Berncastle diary entry (June 19, 1952).

98. Ibid., Berncastle diary entries (May 24–27, 1952).

99. Ibid., Berncastle diary entry (June 2, 1952).

100. Ibid., Berncastle diary entry (June 30, 1952).

101. Ibid., Berncastle diary entry (July 17, 1952).

102. Ibid. Berncastle diary entry (June 30, 1952); UNSA DAG 13–3, UNCCP. Subgroup: Principal Secretary. Series: Records Relating to Compensation/Box 18/1949–62/Selected Documents and Working Papers; Document: A/AC.25/W.80, "The Compensation Question" (March 8, 1955), pp. 65–68.

103. UNSA DAG 13–3, UNCCP. Subgroup: Records of the Land Specialist. Series: Records of the Land Specialist 1951–1952/Box 35/ Diary (J. H. Berncastle); Document: Berncastle to S.B. Shields, in Berncastle diary entry (June 12, 1952).

104. Ibid., Berncastle to Moe Sherwood, in Berncastle diary entry (September 8, 1952).

105. NARA RG 84, United Nations/USUN Central Files—UN Letters/2450; Document: "Blocked Arab Accounts." See also UNSA DAG 13–3, UNCCP. Subgroup: Principal Secretary. Series: Records Relating to Compensation/Box 18/1949–62/Selected Documents and Working Papers; Document: A/AC.25/W.80, "The Compensation Question" (March 8, 1955), pp. 65–68.

106. UNSA DAG 13–3, UNCCP. Subgroup: Principal Secretary. Series: Records Relating to Compensation/Box 18/1949–62/Selected Documents and Working Papers; Document: A/AC.25/W.80, "The Compensation Question" (March 8, 1955), pp. 65–68.

107. NARA RG 84, United Nations/USUN Central Files—UN Letters/2450/"Blocked Arab Accounts"; Document: "The Individual Assessment of Abandoned Arab Immoveable Property in Israeli Held Territory" (August 7, 1952).

108. UNSA DAG 13–3, UNCCP. Subgroup: Records of the Land Specialist. Series: Records of the Land Specialist 1951–1952/Box 35/ Diary (J. H. Berncastle); Chai to Berncastle in Berncastle diary entry (August 1, 1952).

109. Ibid., Berncastle diary entry (June 10, 1952).

110. Ibid., Berncastle diary entry (August 27, 1952).

111. Ibid., Berncastle diary entries (June 4, 1952) and (September 4, 1952).

112. Ibid., Berncastle to Chai (September 25, 1952), in Berncastle diary entry (September 25, 1952).

113. Ibid., Berncastle diary entry (September 26, 1952).

114. Ibid., Berncastle diary entry (October 6, 1952).

## Notes to Chapter Three

1. See the draft treaty in Shlaim, *Collusion Across the Jordan*, pp. 636–37.

2. *Documents on the Foreign Policy of Israel Vol. 5*, pp. 586–88. "Meeting: T. Kollek—B. Berry" (October 11, 1950); PRO FO 371/91410, Tel Aviv to Bevin (February 9, 1951).

3. *Documents on the Foreign Policy of Israel Vol. 6*, pp. 151–56. "Report on the Visit of L. Jones in Israel" (March 11–14, 1951).

4. Shlaim, *Collusion Across the Jordan*, p. 551.

5. *Documents on the Foreign Policy of Israel Vol. 6*, pp. 147–48. Eban to Eytan (March 6, 1951); Shlaim, *Collusion Across the Jordan*, p. 587.

6. PRO FO 371/82257, Foreign Office to Cairo [no date].

7. *Documents on the Foreign Policy of Israel Vol. 6*, pp. 71–73. Sasson to Sharett (January 31, 1950).

8. Ibid.

9. *Foreign Relations of the United States 1951, Vol. 5*; pp. 735–37. Palmer to Secretary of State (June 28, 1951).

10. ISA (130) 2453/3, Sasson to Divon (May 15, 1951).

11. *Documents on the Foreign Policy of Israel Vol. 6*, p. 270. "Report on Negotiations with King Abdullah" (April 28, 1951).

12. UNSA DAG 13–3, UNCCP. Subgroup: Records of the Land Specialist. Series: Records of the Land Specialist 1951–1952/Box 35/ Diary (J. H. Berncastle). Document: Berncastle diary entry (May 26, 1952).

13. Ibid., Berncastle diary entry (August 4, 1952).

14. ISA (43) 5595/gimel/4716, "The Report of the Committee to Examine the Issue of Compensation for Absentee Property" (March 17, 1950).

15. Ibid., section 11.

16. Ibid., section 7.

17. Ibid., section 9.

18. Ibid.

19. Ibid., section 14.

20. Ibid., section 16.

21. Ibid.

22. Ibid., section 17.

23. Ibid., section 18.

24. Ibid., section 20.

25. Ibid., section 23.

26. Ibid., section 27.

27. PRO CO733/140, Government House to Secretary of State (April 1, 1927).

28. Tsvi Ilan, "Nisyonot le-Rekhishat Adama ve le-Hityashvut Yehudit be-'Ever ha-Yarden ha-Mizrahi, 1871–1947" [Attempts by Jews to Purchase Lands and Settle in Transjordan, 1871–1947], unpublished Ph.D. dissertation, Bar-Ilan University, 1981, p. 402.

29. Blougrund, *The Jewish National Fund*, p. 9.

30. Jordan, Ministry of Finance, Department of Lands and Surveys, files of the Diwan; File: 6/3/jim, "Aradi al-Sultan 'Abd al-Hamid" [Lands of Sultan 'Abd al-Hamid]; Document: G.F. Walpole's memorandum of October 20, 1936; Ibid., Land Settlement Files/Ghawr al-Rama Files; File: Jadwal al-Iddi'a'at [Schedule of Claims]; Ibid., Land Settlement Files/Ghawr Safi Files; File: Qadiyyat [Case] 365/10; Document: Taqrir 'Umumi [General Report] (April 11, 1952).

31. For further information on this subject, see Michael R. Fischbach *State, Society, and Land in Jordan* (Leiden, Köln, Boston: Brill, 2000), pp. 178–87.

32. Supplement 1, October 8, 1953, to Jordanian *al-Jarida al-Rasmiyya* [Official Gazette] 1158, September 16, 1953: 560.

33. Supplement 1, April 8, 1954, to Ibid. 1177, April 3, 1954: 299–300.

34. Supplement 1, December 23, 1952, to Ibid. 1129, December 16, 1952: 576.

35. UNSA DAG 13–3, UNCCP. Subgroup: Refugee Office. Series: Summaries of Meetings/Box 35/1951/Summary Record of Meetings; Document: "Andersen's Report on Visits" (June 27, 1951).

36. See the various documents in NARA RG 59, Lot file 57D298/Records of the Office of Near Eastern Affairs/Subject file 1941–54/Box 2/Palestine Electric Corporation, Limited.

37. Supplement 1, April 8, 1954, to Jordanian *al-Jarida al-Rasmiyya* 1177, April 3, 1954: 299–300.

38. Ibid. 1959, October 10, 1966: 2010.

39. Ibid. 1625, April 1, 1963: 307.

40. Ibid.1702, August 1, 1963: 1019.

41. Jordan, Ministry of Culture, National Library/Center for Documents and Documentation. Government Files/File 8/2/6, Qadaya al-Aradi [Land Cases]; Document: 8/2/6/145, Jawda Salim al-Bakri to Prime Minister (May 4, 1967).

42. NARA RG 59 325.84/2–761, Jerusalem to Department of State (February 7, 1961).

43. *al-Waqa'i' al-Filastiniyya* [Palestinian Official Gazette] 2 (June 21, 1948). This journal was originally published by the British mandatory government in Palestine and continued, under the same name, by Egyptian military authorities.

44. See Ilan, "Nisyonot le-Rekhishat Adama" for more details.

45. Jesaias Press, "Die jüdischen Kolonian Palästinas," *Zeitschrift des Deutschen Palästina-Vereins* [Journal of the German Palestine Society] 35 (1912): 180–81; Aruts Sheva News Service, January 9, 2000; Ya'akov Meron, "The Golan Heights 1918–1967," in Meir Shamgar, ed., *Military Government in the Territories Administered by Israel 1967–1980. The Legal Aspects*, Vol. 1 (Jerusalem: The Hebrew University of Jerusalem Faculty of Law, The Harry Sacher Institute for Legislative Research and Comparative Law, 1982) p. 102.

46. Meron, "The Golan Heights 1918–1967," pp. 101–2.

47. PRO FO371/62116, Damascus to Foreign Office (July 17, 1947).

48. PRO CO 733/492/1, Wolfson to Chief Secretary (September 12, 1946); ISA (80) 5711/gimel/23, Salomon to Meir (August 15, 1957).

49. ISA (80) 5711/gimel/23, Salomon to Eshkol (December 31, 1958).

50. Meron, "The Golan Heights 1918–1967," p. 103.

51. ISA (8) 5721/gimel/23, agreement of December 31, 1958.

52. JNF, "Report to the Thirteenth Congress," p. 68, in Lehn, *The Jewish National Fund*, p. 73.

53. Aruts Sheva News Service, January 9, 2000; Blougrund, *The Jewish National Fund*, p. 8.

54. *Davar*, October 17, 1949; *New York Times*, October 16, 1949.

55. PRO FO 371/82478, 78773, Baghdad to Foreign Office (March 7, 1950). For more information on smuggling via Iran, see NARA RG 59, 887.411/3–2751, "The Position of Jews in Iraq" (April 5, 1951).

56. Mordechai Ben-Porat, *To Baghdad and Back. The Miraculous 2,000 Year Homecoming of the Iraqi Jews*, trans. Marcia Grant and Kathy Akeriv (Jerusalem and New York: Gefen Publishing House, 1998), p. 274.

57. PRO FO 371/82478, 78773, Baghdad to Foreign Office (March 7, 1950).

58. Ibid.

59. Histadrut Archives 14/393, "Summary Report" (July 12, 1950), in Moshe Gat, *The Jewish Exodus from Iraq 1948–1951* (London and Portland: Frank Cass, 1997), pp. 94, 149.

60. *Jewish Chronicle*, June 23, 1950, in Joseph B. Schechtman, *On Wings of Eagles. The Plight, Exodus, and Homecoming of Oriental Jews* (New York and London: Thomas Yoseloff, 1961), pp. 105–6.

61. Maurice Roumani, *The Case of the Jews from Arab Countries: A Neglected Issue* (Tel Aviv: World Organization of Jews from Arab Countries, 1977), p. 4.

62. Schechtman, *The Arab Refugee Problem*, p. 111.

63. NARA RG 59, 887.411/3–2751, "The Position of the Jews of Iraq" (April 5, 1951).

64. Ben Porat, *To Baghdad and Back*, p. 278.

65. ISA (130) 1836/hts/3, "The Control & Administration of Assests [sic] of Jews who denounced their Iraqi Nationality & the Work of the Custodian General" (April 17, 1951).

66. Ibid.

67. ISA (130) 1791/1, Kollek to Ehrlich (February 1950).

68. ISA (130) 2387,4/1, Danin to Minister of Finance (June 20, 1950).

69. ISA (130) 2563/2, Middle Eastern Department to Minister of Foreign Affairs (August 14, 1951).

70. ISA (130) 2463/8, Research Department to Bendor (May 15, 1952).

71. PRO FO 371/115767, Munro to Foreign Office (April 13, 1955).

72. ISA (130) 1836/hts/3, "The Control & Administration of Assests [sic] of Jews who denounced their Iraqi Nationality & the Work of the Custodian General" (April 17, 1951).

73. For example, see ISA (130) 2463/8, Research Department to Bendor (May 15, 1952).

74. NARA RG59, SOC 14–1 IRAQ, letter to William F. Ryan (April 13, 1964).

75. These can be found attached to several State Department dispatches beginning in the fall of 1964 in NARA RG 59, SOCI 14 IRAQ.

76. ISA (130) 2563/4, cited in Itamar Levin, *Locked Doors: The Seizure of Jewish Property in Arab Countries*, trans. Rachel Neiman. Forward by Abraham Hirchson and Israel Singer (Westport, Conn. and London: Praeger Publishers, 2001).

77. NARA RG 59, 883.411/7–2550, Damascus to Department of State (July 25, 1950).

78. Roumani, *The Case of the Jews from Arab Countries*, p. 4.

79. NARA RG 59, 883.411/10–1552, Damascus to Department of State (October 15, 1952), and RG 59 883.411/6–2553, Damascus to Department of State (June 25, 1953).

80. Levin, *Locked Doors*, pp. 182–84.

81. NARA RG 59, 883.411/3–752, Damascus to Department of State (March 7, 1952).

82. NARA RG 59, 890D.52/2–149, Damascus to Department of State (February 1, 1949).

83. NARA RG 59, 890D.5211/11–1249, Sutton to Department of State (November 12, 1949); RG 59, 890D.5211/12–1649, Damascus to Department of State (December 16, 1949).

84. NARA RG 59, 883.411/11–2553, Damascus to Department of State (November 25, 1953).

85. *The New York Times*, October 3, 1952. For details about Jews in Lebanon, see Kirsten E. Schulze, *The Jews of Lebanon: Between Coexistence and Conflict* (Brighton and Portland, Oregon: Sussex Academic Press, 2001).

86. Gottlieb Schumacher, *Northern 'Ajlun, "Within the Decapolis"* (London: Alexander P. Watt, 1890), pp. 27, 81; Carl Steurnagel, "Der 'Adschlun," *Zeitschrift des Deutschen Palästina-Vereins* 48 (1925): 206).

87. See Adaia and Abraham Shumski, *A Bridge Across the Jordan. The Friendship Between a Jewish Carpenter and the King of Jordan* (New York: Arcade Publishing, 1997).

88. NARA RG 59, 867N.48/2–2649, Cairo to Department of State (February 26, 1949).

89. ISA (130) 1836/hts/5, "Egypt's Plotting Against Jewish Property" (June 25, 1951).

90. Ibid.

91. Michael M. Laskier, *The Jews of Egypt 1920–1970. In the Midst of Zionism, Anti-Semitism, and the Middle East Conflict* (New York and London: New York University Press, 1992), pp. 254–56.

92. NARA RG 59, 874.411/2–657, "The Situation of Jews in Egypt at the Beginning of 1957," attached to Talmidge to Dulles (February 6, 1957); RG 59, 874.411/12–356, Cairo to Secretary of State (December 3, 1956).

93. Laskier, *The Jews of Egypt 1920–1970*, p. 256.

94. Schechtman, *On Wings of Eagles*, pp. 203–5.

95. NARA RG 59, 874.411/1–1457, attachment to Klutznick to Dulles (January 14, 1957).

96. Roumani, *The Case of the Jews from Arab Countries*, p. 4.

97. Schechtman, *The Arab Refugee Problem*, p. 127.

98. CZA Z6/2441, letter from Jews of Libya Association (January 10, 1973).

99. *Israel Government Yearbook Vol. 5711/1950*, p. 134.

100. ISA (130) 2401/22, "Claims for Jewish Property Frozen in Arab States" (October 6, 1952), and memorandum of November 5, 1952).

101. ISA (130) 2401/22, "Claims for Jewish Property Frozen in Arab States" (October 6, 1952).

102. ISA (130) 2401/22/1, Director of UN Department of Ministry of Foreign Affairs to Washington (November 5, 1952).

103. ISA (130) 2401/22, memorandum of November 5, 1952; *Jerusalem Post* (October 9, 1952), in Schechtman, *On Wings of Eagles*, p. 123.

104. ISA (130) 2563/7, Foreign Currency Department to Ministry of Foreign Affairs (February 20, 1956).

105. *Divrei ha-Knesset* (26), p. 1050 (February 10, 1959); Itamar Levin, *Confiscated Wealth: The Fate of Jewish Property in Arab Lands*. Policy Forum No. 22 (Jerusalem: Institute of the World Jewish Congress, 2000), p. 19.

106. Levin, *Locked Doors*, pp. 137–38.

107. Yehouda Shenhav, "The Jews of Iraq, Zionist Ideology, and the Property of the Palestinian Refugees of 1948: An Anomaly of National Accounting," *International Journal of Middle East Studies* 31, 4 (November 1999): 612–13.

108. Levin, *Locked Doors*, p. 52.

109. Ibid., pp. 614–15; ISA (130) 2387/4/1, Department of International Institutions to Ministry of Foreign Affairs (November 17, 1949).

110. *Documents on the Foreign Policy of Israel Vol. 4*, p. 117, Kollek to Sharett (June 10, 1949).

111. Zalman Lif was also a proponent of this idea. Levin, *Locked Doors*, pp. 31–33.

112. ISA (130) 2387/4/1, Danin to Minister of Finance (June 20, 1950); ISA (130) 2402/16, Kaplan to Danin (July 7, 1950) in Nur Masalha, *Israeli Plans to Resettle the Palestinian Refugees 1948–1972*. Monograph Series No. 2 (Ramallah: Palestinian Diaspora and Refugee Centre (SHAML), 1996), p. 21; Gat, *The Jewish Exodus from Iraq*, pp. 147–48.

113. PRO FO 371/82619, Tel Aviv to Baghdad (October 10, 1950).

114. See, for instance, CZA C2/1658, Peiss to Easterman (May 31, 1950).

115. Ben Porat, *To Baghdad and Back*, p. 275.

116. Ibid., pp. 277–79.

117. ISA (130) 1791/1, "Jewish Iraqi Property—Registration of Claims (Proposal)" (March 30, 1951).

118. Gat, *The Jewish Exodus from Iraq*, pp. 146–47; Levin, *Locked Doors*, pp. 30–31.

119. ISA (130) 2401/22, "Claims for Jewish Property Frozen in Arab States" (October 6, 1952).

120. *Divrei ha-Knesset* 26, p. 1050 (February 10, 1959); Levin, *Locked Doors*, pp. 63–64.

121. ISA (130) 2402/5, memorandum of March 13, 1952, in Masalha, *Israeli Plans to Resettle the Palestinian Refugees*, p. 26; ISA (130) 2402/15, memo of March 24, 1950, in Ibid., p. 25; and Yosef Weitz's diary entry for May 13, 1954, in Ibid. p. 28.

122. Masalha, *Israeli Plans to Resettle the Palestinian Refugees*, pp. 34–35, 37.

123. ISA (130) 1852/hts/11, Landau to Ministry of Foreign Affairs (November 27, 1955); Ibid., Eshkol to Landau (November 1955); Ibid., Migdal to Middle East Affairs Advisor (no date).

124. NARA RG 59, 867N.48/3–2249, Jerusalem to Department of State (March 22, 1949).

125. CZA Z6/1972, Easterman to Goldmann (March 13, 1959); Schechtman, *On Wings of Eagles*, p. 204.

126. Joel Beinin, *The Dispersion of Egyptian Jewry. Culture, Politics, and the Formation of a Modern Diaspora* (Berkeley, Los Angeles, London: University of California Press, 1988), p. 210.

127. Levin, *Locked Doors*, pp. 53–54.

128. *Documents on the Foreign Policy of Israel Vol. 1*, Document 357, Sharett to Comay (July 22, 1948). See also Document 380 on pp. 412–13.

129. *Documents on the Foreign Policy of Israel Vol. 6*, pp. 81–82.

130. Ibid., pp. 196–97, Eytan to Palmer (March 29, 1951).

131. *Documents on the Foreign Policy of Israel Vol. 7*, p. 227, Eban to Sharett (May 15, 1952).

132. ISA (130) 2563/2, Middle Eastern Department to Minister of Foreign Affairs (August 14, 1951).

133. *Documents on the Foreign Policy of Israel Vol. 6*, pp. 275–76, "Aide Mémoire from Government of the United States to the Government of Israel."

134. NARA RG 59, 887.411/3–2751, Berry to McFall (April 5, 1951).

135. NARA RG 59, 887.411/3–2751, McFall to Celler (April 6, 1951).

136. NARA RG 59, 887.411/3–2751, "The Position of the Jews of Iraq" (April 5, 1951).

137. ISA 130 2563/61 (May 30, 1951), in Shenhav "The Jews of Iraq," p. 622; ISA (130) 2401/22, "Claims for Jewish Property Frozen in Arab States" (October 6, 1952).

138. NARA RG 59, 884.411/12–259, Tel Aviv to Secretary of State (December 2, 1959).

139. NARA RG 59, REF 2 PAL, Cairo to Secretary of State (August 10, 1963).

140. NARA, John F. Kennedy Presidential Library, National Security Council Files, Box 119. Documents: Tel Aviv to Secretary of State, April 3, 1963; Department of State to Amman, Cairo, Damascus and Tel Aviv, April 13, 1963. Both are cited in Mordechai Gazit, *President Kennedy's Policy Toward the Arab States and Israel*. The Shiloah Center for Middle Eastern and African Studies Studies Series. (Tel Aviv: The Shiloah Center for Middle Eastern and African Studies, Tel Aviv University, 1983), pp. 126, 133.

141. Avi Machlis, "Compensation for Jews Who Fled Arab Countries," *Jewish Telegraphic Agency*, in *Jewish News of Greater Phoenix* 52, 50 (August 25, 2000) (on-line document: www.jewishaz.com/jewishnews/000825/fled.shtml).

142. "Reparations, German," *Encylopedia Judaica* (Jerusalem: Keter Publishing House, Ltd., 1971).

143. *Documents on the Foreign Policy of Israel Vol. 7*, pp. 533-38, "Meeting: A. Eban, D. Acheson and H. Byroade (September 22, 1952).

144. *Foreign Relations of the United States 1952-54, Vol. 9*, pp. 256-62, Hoskins to Byroade (July 25, 1952).

145. CZA Z6/888, Goldmann to Eshkol (February 13, 1954).

146. Shenhav, "The Jews of Iraq," p. 621; Carpenter, "The Arabs Can't Go Back," p. 764.

147. *Documents on the Foreign Policy of Israel Vol. 6*, pp. 364-66, Comay to Lourie (June 7, 1951).

148. UNSA DAG 13-3, UNCCP. Subgroup: Records of the Land Specialist. Series: Records of the Land Specialist 1951-1952/Box 35/ Diary (J. H. Berncastle); Document: Berncastle diary entries (June 20, 1952) and (July 3, 1952).

149. Ibid., Berncastle to Ladas (July 7, 1952), in Berncastle diary entry (July 7, 1952).

150. Ibid., Berncastle to Chai (June 11, 1952), in Berncastle diary entry (June 11, 1952).

151. Ibid., Berncastle to Chai (September 11, 1952), in Berncastle diary entry (September 11, 1952).

152. Ibid., Berncastle to Chai (July 10, 1952), in Berncastle diary entry (July 10, 1952).

153. NARA RG 59, Lot file 57D298/Records of the Office of Near Eastern Affairs/Subject Files 1941-54/Box 3/Refugee Program-Gen. 1. Compensation.

154. *Foreign Relations of the United States 1952-54, Vol. 9*, p. 1149, Davis to Department of State (March 5, 1953).

155. ISA (130) 2401/22II, "Meeting of the Committee Investigating the Arab Refugees" (September 15, 1953).

156. Ibid., Committee's Report.

157. Ibid.

158. *Documents on the Foreign Policy of Israel Vol. 7*, pp. 211-12, Eban to United States Division (May 5, 1952); pp. 216-17, Eban to Sharett (May 8, 1952).

159. NARA RG 84, United Nations/USUN Central Files-UN Letters/2450, "Blocked Arab Accounts"; Documents: "Memorandum of Conversation" (May 6, 1952) attached to US memorandum to UNCCP Chairman (May 22, 1952) and "Aide Memoire by the Ambassador (undated, but June 1952).

160. Ibid., Chai to Palmer (July 10, 1952).

161. Ibid., Memorandum attached to Chai's letter to Barco (July 28, 1952).

162. UNSA DAG 13-3, UNCCP. Subgroup: Principal Secretary. Series: Records Relating to Compensation/Box 19/1952-55/Question of Compensation; Document: Ladas to Chai (May 12, 1955).

163. NARA RG 84, United Nations/USUN Central Files-UN Letters/2450,

"Blocked Arab Accounts;" Document: "Paraphrase of cable dated May 22, 1953 from Reedman, to Mr. Chai."

164. Ibid., "Interim Memorandum on Results of First Instalment [sic] of 'Blocked Accounts' Release Agreement" (September 18, 1953).

165. Ibid., Memorandum of Conversation (October 1, 1953) and "Interim Memorandum on Results of First Instalment [sic] of 'Blocked Accounts' Release Agreement" (September 18, 1953); NARA RG 59, Lot File 57D298/Records of the Office of Near Eastern Affairs/Subject File 1941-54/Box 3/Refugee Program-Gen. I. Compensation; Document: Dulles to USUN (April 3, 1953).

166. NARA RG 59, 334.411/4-2651, Cairo to Department of State (April 26, 1951); NARA RG 84, United Nations/USUN Central Files-UN Letters/2450, "Blocked Arab Accounts;" Document: "Report of the Commission's Liaison Representative on the Status of the Scheme for the Release of the 'Blocked Accounts' of Arab Refugees."

167. *Jerusalem Post*, November 12, 1950.

168. NARA RG 84, United Nations/USUN Central Files-UN Letters/2450, "Blocked Arab Accounts:" Document: "Interim Memorandum on Results of First Instalment [sic] of "Blocked Accounts" Release Agreement" (September 18, 1953), p. 12.

169. Ibid., Ladas to Chai (October 20, 1954).

170. Ibid., Ladas to Chai (August 11, 1954).

171. *Israel Government Yearbook Vol. 5716/1955*, p. 170.

172. RG 84, United Nations/USUN Central Files-UN Letters/2450, "Blocked Arab Accounts;" Document: Barclays Bank to Ladas (October 30, 1955).

173. *Israel Government Yearbook Vol. 5717/1956*, p. 225; UN Document A/3199, 15th Progress Report of UNCCP (October 4, 1956).

174. NARA RG 84, United Nations/USUN Central Files-UN Letters/2450, "Blocked Arab Accounts;" Document: Ladas to Bang-Jensen (October 6, 1955).

175. *Israel Government Yearbook Vol. 5718/1957*, p. 236.

176. *Palestine Post*, March 31, 1950.

177. NARA RG 84, United Nations/USUN Central Files-UN Letters/2450, "Blocked Arab Accounts;" Document: "Preliminary Memorandum on Releases to Absentees" (September 8, 1953).

178. *Israel Government Yearbook Vol. 5718/1957*, p. 236.

179. NARA RG 84, United Nations/USUN Central Files-UN Letters/2450, "Blocked Arab Accounts;" Document: Ladas to Bang-Jensen (June 24, 1955).

180. *Israel Government Yearbook Vol. 5718/1957*, p. 236; *Israel Government Yearbook Vol. 5719-1958*, p. 236; UN Document A/AC.25/W.81/Rev. 1, "Historical Survey of the Question of Compensation" (May 23, 1960), pp. 62-63; UN Document A/6451, 24th UNCCP Progress Report (September 30, 1966).

181. NARA RG 84, United Nations/USUN Central Files-UN Letters/2450,

"Blocked Arab Accounts;" Document: "Note for the Chairman" [undated, but February 1956].

182. Ibid.; Document: Ladas to Bang-Jensen (January 12, 1956).

183. Ibid.; Document: Ladas to Bang-Jensen (February 9, 1956).

184. Ibid.; Document: Berncastle to Chai (June 28, 1957).

185. NARA RG 59, 325.84/6-1360, Tel Aviv to Department of State (June 13, 1960).

186. UN Document A/6451, 24th UNCCP Progress Report (September 30, 1966).

187. NARA RG 59, POL 3 PAL/UN, USUN to Department of State (July 13, 1966) and (February 1, 1967).

188. Fischbach, "Land," in Mattar, ed., *Encyclopedia of the Palestinians*, p. 242.

189. Schechtman, *Arab Refugee Problem*, p. 62.

190. *Newsweek*, April 8, 1963.

191. NARA RG 59, REF PAL, New York to Secretary of State (July 3, 1963), Tel Aviv to Secretary of State (July 8, 1963), Nicosia to Department of State (July 11, 1963), Nicosia to Department of State (July 18, 1963); RG 59, REF ARAB, Tel Aviv to Secretary of State (August 30, 1963).

192. NARA RG 59, REF ARAB, Tel Aviv to Secretary of State (August 30, 1963); RG 59, REF PAL, Tel Aviv to Department of State (November 7, 1963).

193. NARA RG 59, REF 3 UNRWA, Department of State Circular 977 (November 29, 1963); RG 59, POL 3 PAL/UN, Amman to Department of State (February 25, 1965); RG 59, POL ARAB, "Memorandum of Conversation" (July 15, 1965).

## Notes to Chapter Four

1. Sami Hadawi, *The Story of My Life (Memories and Reflections)* (n.p., 1996), pp. 237, 248, 270–71, 274, 276, 291; Interview with Sami Hadawi (March 1996 and July 2001).

2. UNSA DAG 13–3, UNCCP. Subgroup: Refugee Office. Series: Records of the Land Specialist/Box 35/1951/Correspondence; Hadawi file. Document: Berncastle to Azcárate (May 11, 1951). Berncastle's 1951 report entitled "Valuation of Abandoned Arab Land in Israel" also mentions this.

3. *The New York Times*, August 18, 1950.

4. Bilby, *New Star in the Near East*, pp. 98–99.

5. UNSA DAG 13–3, UNCCP. Subgroup: Refugee Office. Series: Records of the Land Specialist/Box 35/1951/Reports of J.M. Berncastle; Document: CP/3/51(a), "Valuation of Abandoned Arab Land in Israel."

6. PRO FO 371/91744, Chancery to Foreign Office (June 11, 1951).

7. "Valuation of Abandoned Arab Land in Israel" (Berncastle report; see chapter 2, note 67), p. 8.

8. UNSA DAG 13–3, UNCCP. Subgroup: Records of the Land Specialist. Series: Records of the Land Specialist 1951–1952/Box 35/ Diary (J. H. Berncastle); Document: Berncastle diary entry (May 21, 1952).

9. Azcárate, *Mission in Palestine*, p. 169.

10. Forsythe, *United Nations Peacekeeping*, pp. 79–80.10.

11 UNSA DAG 13–3, UNCCP; Subgroup: Office of the Principal Secretary. Series: Records Relating to Compensation/Box 18/1949–51/Working Papers; Document: A/AC.25/W.52, "Operations of the Custodian of Absentees' Property and Estimation of the Compensation Due to Arab Refugees not Returning to their Homes" (September 7, 1950).

12. UNSA DAG 13–3, UNCCP. Subgroup: Office of the Principal Secretary. Series: Transcripts/Box 12/1951/Conversation with Antoine [sic] Atallah.

13. NARA RG 59, Lot File 57D298/Records of the Near Eastern Affairs/Subject files 1941–54/Box 3/Refugee Program—Gen. 1. Compensation; Document: "Alternative Methods of Compensating the Arab Refugees" (May 7, 1953).

14. NARA RG 59, 884A.16/8–453, Tel Aviv to Department of State (August 4, 1953).

15. NARA RG 59, Lot File 57D298/Records of the Office of Near Eastern Affairs/Subject Files 1949–54/Box 3/Refugee Problem—Gen. 1. Compensation; Document: "Palestine Refugees: Alternative Methods of Compensation of the Arab Refugees" (May 7, 1953).

16. Ibid.

17. NARA RG 59, 884A.16/8–453, Tel Aviv to Department of State (August 4, 1953).

18. Ibid.

19. Ibid.

20. UNSA DAG 13–3, UNCCP. Subgroup: Principal Secretary. Series: General Records/Box 3/1962/J.P. Gaillard; Document: UN Document A/2629.

21. UNSA DAG 13–3, UNCCP. Subgroup: Refugee Office. Series: Records of the Land Specialist/Box 35/1951/Refugee Office—Final Report.

22. NARA RG 84, United Nations/USUN Central Files—UN Letters/2450, "Blocked Arab Accounts;" Document: Ladas to Bang-Jensen (June 30, 1955).

23. *The New York Times*, November 27, 1954.

24. Sharett's diaries, cited in Rokach, *Israel's Sacred Terrorism*, p. 47.

25. *Foreign Relations of the United States 1955–57, Vol. 14*, p. 203. K518 Alpha-Memoranda; p. 280, London to Department of State (July 8, 1955); NARA RG 59, Decimal File 320.511/5–957; Yossi Melman and Dan Raviv, *Friends in Deed. Inside the U.S.-Israel Alliance* (New York: Hyperion, 1994), p. 76.

26. UNSA DAG 13–3, UNCCP. Subgroup: Principal Secretary. Series: Records Relating to the Technical Office/Box 16/1952–57/Land Identification Project/Status Reports 1953, 1956 & 1957; Document: "Report on the Situation" (July 29, 1954).

27. UNSA DAG 13–3, UNCCP. Subgroup: Principal Secretary. Series: Records Relating to Compensation/Box 18/1949–62/Selected Documents and Working Papers; Document: A/AC.25/W.80, "The Compensation Question" (March 8, 1955).

28. NARA RG 84, United Nations/USUN Central File—UN Letters/2450 "Blocked Arab Accounts;" Documents: Draft UNRWA memorandum (April 28, 1955), "Report to the Conciliation Commission on the Question of Compensation" (April 20, 1955), and Ladas to Barco (April 26, 1955) .

29. Ibid., Bang-Jensen to Ladas (February 7, 1956).

30. UN Document A/3199, par. 15.

31. Ibid., annex B.

32. Ibid.

33. NARA RG 59, 320.511/9–1156, American Consul General, Jerusalem to Department of State (September 11, 1956).

34. PRO CO 733/494/3, Appendix II to Memorandum of J.F. Spry (October 1, 1948); Ibid., Memorandum to Spry (October 13, 1948).

35. PRO CO 733/494/3, Appendix II to Memorandum of J.F. Spry (October 1, 1948).

36. UNSA DAG 13–3, UNCCP. Subgroup: Records of the Land Specialist. Series: Records of the Land Specialist 1951–1952/Box 35/ Diary (J. H. Berncastle); Document: Berncastle diary entry (June 7, 1952); interview with Kamil Nasrawi (October 1993); interview with Iliyya Ya'qub 'Atallah (November 1996).

37. PRO FO 371/91742, Brin to Hunter (May 17, 1951).

38. PRO FO 371/91744, Clark to Hunter (July 24, 1951).

39. PRO FO 371/98817, Berncastle to Evans (January 4, 1951); Ibid., Wardrop's memorandum of January 17, 1952; Ibid. Hunter to Brin (February 14, 1952); FO 371/198818.

40. PRO FO 371/98817, Wardrop's memorandum of January 17, 1952; Ibid., Hunter to Brin (February 14, 1952).

41. UNSA DAG 13–3, UNCCP. Subgroup: Records of the Land Specialist. Series: Records of the Land Specialist 1951–1952/Box 35/ Diary (J. H. Berncastle); Document: Berncastle diary entry (August 10, 1952); CZA KKL5/22273, "Report on the Land Administration System of the State" (September 5, 1954).

42. NARA RG 59, POL 3 PAL/UN, Secretary of State to USUN (March 3, 1966).

43. NARA RG 59, 320.51/7–257, Wilcox and Rountree to Secretary of State (July 2, 1957), in *Foreign Relations of the United States 1955–57, Vol. 17*, p. 663.

44. NARA RG 59, 320.51/3–156, USUN to Secretary of State (March 1, 1956).

45. UN Document A/AC.25/W.81/Rev. 1, "Historical Survey of the Question of Compensation" (May 23, 1960).

46. NARA RG 59, 320.51/7–257, Wilcox and Rountree to Secretary of State (July 2, 1957).

47. Ibid.

48. NARA RG 59, 884.411/11–2157, "Palestine Refugee Problem" (November 21, 1957), p. 3.

49. NARA RG 59, 884.411/9–1957, "Memorandum of Conversation" (September 19, 1957).

50. NARA RG 59, 884.411/12–1360, Department of State to USUN (December 13, 1960); RG 59, 884.411/12–1360, "Memorandum of Conversation" (December 13, 1960); RG 59, 325.84/2–861, USUN to Secretary of State (February 8, 1961).

51. NARA RG 59, 325.84/3–1661, USUN to Secretary of State (March 16, 1961).

52. NARA RG 59, 325.84/2–2461, "Title to Arab Property in Israel" (February 24, 1961).

53. NARA RG 59, 325.84/3–2161, Secretary of State to USUN (March 21, 1961).

54. NARA RG 59, 325.84/4–661, London to Secretary of State (April 6, 1961). The court case was Fouad Bishara Jabbour and Kamal Bishara Jabbour (Trading as Messers. F. & K. Jabbour) v. Custodian of Absentee Property for the State of Israel.

55. NARA RG 59, 325.84/9–1461, Rusk to USUN (September 14, 1961).

56. NARA RG 59, 325.84/3–2161, "Memorandum of Conversation" (March 21, 1961); RG 59, 325.84/4–461, "Memorandum of Conversation" (April 4, 1961); RG 59, REF ARAB/UN (1963), "Memorandum of Conversation" (July 30, 1963).

57. NARA RG 59, 325.84/3–2361, USUN to Secretary of State (March 23, 1961).

58. NARA RG 59, 325.84/3–1061, Tel Aviv to Secretary of State (March 11, 1961); RG 59, 325.84/11–306, "Memorandum of Conversation" (November 30, 1961).

59. NARA RG 59, POL 3 PAL/UN, USUN to Secretary of State (June 28, 1963).

60. Ibid., Beirut to Department of State (November 30, 1964).

61. Ibid., USUN to Department of State (November 20, 1964).

## Notes to Chapter Five

1. NARA RG 84, United Nations/USUN Central Files—UN Letters/2450, "Blocked Arab Accounts;" Document: Chai to Berncastle (September 9, 1952); UN Document A/AC.25/W.80, "The Compensation Question" (March 8, 1955), p. 42.

2. UNSA DAG 13–3, UNCCP. Subgroup: Records of the Land Specialist.

Series: Records of the Land Specialist 1951–1952/Box 35/ Diary (J. H. Berncastle); Document: Berncastle diary entry (October 2, 1952).

3. UNSA DAG 13–3, UNCCP. Subgroup: Refugee Office. Series: Records of the Land Specialist/Box 35/1951/Correspondence/Hadawi file; Document: Berncastle to Azcárate (May 11, 1951).

4. Government of Palestine, *Supplement to A Survey of Palestine* (Jerusalem: Government Printer, 1946. Reprint edition: Washington: Institute for Palestine Studies, 1991), p. 29.

5. NARA RG 84, United Nations/USUN Central Files—UN Letters/2450, "Blocked Arab Accounts;" Document: Chai to Berncastle (September 9, 1952); UN Document A/AC.25/W.80, "The Compensation Question" (March 8, 1955).

6. Ibid.

7. UNSA DAG 13–3, UNCCP. Subgroup: Principal Secretary. Series: Records Relating to Compensation/Box 18/1949–62/Selected Documents and Working Papers; Document: A/AC.25/W.80, "The Compensation Question" (March 8, 1955).

8. NARA RG 59, 320.51/1–1359, Comay to Rook (December 4, 1958).

9. NARA RG 84, United Nations/USUN Central Files—UN Letters/2450, "Blocked Arab Accounts;" Document: Berncastle to Bang-Jensen (February 23, 1954).

10. UN Document A/3199, 15th UNCCP report (October 4, 1956).

11. NARA RG 84, United Nations/USUN Central Files—UN Letters/2450, "Blocked Arab Accounts;" Document: "Report to Mr. Bang-Jensen, Acting Principal Secretary of the Commission, from J. Berncastle, Land Specialist" (November 1, 1957); UNSA DAG 13–3, UNCCP. Subgroup: Principal Secretary. Series: Records Relating to the Technical Office/Box 16/1952–57/Status Reports 1953, 1954, and 1957; Document: "Conciliation Commission for Palestine. Land Identification Office. Progress Statement as at August 31, 1957."

12. NARA RG 84, United Nations/USUN Central Files—UN Letters/2450, "Blocked Arab Accounts;" Documents: Hadawi to Custodian (October 20, 1954), Levin to Hadawi (November 3, 1954), Meyer to Hadawi (December 24, 1954), and Hadawi to Chai (February 8, 1955).

13. Ibid., Hadawi to Chai (February 8, 1955); NARA RG 59, 320.51/2–1255, USUN to Secretary of State (February 12, 1955); NARA RG 320.51/4–1455, USUN to Secretary of State (April 14, 1955).

14. UNSA DAG 13–3, UNCCP. Subgroup: Principal Secretary. Series: Records Relating to the Technical Office/Box 16/1952–57/Land Identification Project; Document: "Report by the Acting Principal-Secretary Regarding the Office for the Identification and Valuation of Arab Property" (April 28, 1955).

15. UN Document A/3199, 15th UNCCP progress report (October 4, 1956); UNSA DAG 13–3, UNCCP. Subgroup: Principal Secretary. Series: Records Relating to Compensation/Box 18/1949–62/Selected Documents and

Working Papers; Document: A/AC.25/W.80, "The Compensation Question" (March 8, 1955); NARA RG 59, 320.51/7–855, USUN to Secretary of State (July 8, 1955).

16. NARA RG 84, United Nations/USUN Central Files—UN Letters/2450, "Blocked Arab Accounts;" Document: Berncastle to Bang-Jensen (February 16, 1956).

17. Ibid., Berncastle to Bang-Jensen (March 1, 1956).

18. Ibid., Berncastle to Bang-Jensen (March 8, 1956).

19. NARA RG 59, 320.51/5–2859, USUN to Secretary of State (May 28, 1959).

20. NARA RG 84, United Nations/USUN Central Files—UN Letters/2450, "Blocked Arab Accounts;" Document: Chai to Barco (April 11, 1958).

21. UN Document A/AC.25/W.84, "Working Paper Prepared by the Commission's Land Expert on the Methods and Techniques of Identification and Valuation of Arab Refugee Immovable Property Holdings in Israel" (April 28, 1964).

22. NARA RG 84, United Nations/USUN Central Files—UN Letters/2450, "Blocked Arab Accounts;" Documents: Ladas to Bang-Jensen (July 28, 1955) and Bang-Jensen to Ladas (August 4, 1955).

23. NARA RG 59, 320.11/9–1156, "Memorandum of Conversation" (August 29, 1956).

24. NARA RG 59, 320.51/7–257 (Wilcox and Rountree to Secretary of State (July 2, 1957); RG 59, 320.51/6–1757, USUN to Secretary of State (June 17, 1957).

25. UNSA DAG 13–3, UNCCP. Subgroup: Principal Secretary. Series: Records Relating to the Technical Office/Box 16/1955–60/Mr. J.M. Berncastle; Document: "Property Ownership in an Arab Village" (March 11, 1957)

26. NARA RG 84, United Nations/USUN Central Files—UN Letters/2450, "Blocked Arab Accounts;" Document: Berncastle to Chai (April 19, 1955).

27. UN Document A/3199, 15th UNCCP progress report (October 4, 1956); UNCCP. Subgroup: Principal Secretary. Series: Records Relating to Compensation/Box 18/1949–62/Selected Documents and Working Papers; Document: A/AC.25/W.80, "The Compensation Question" (March 8, 1955).

28. NARA RG 59, 325.84/7–160, Berncastle to Chai (June 16, 1960).

29. NARA RG 59, POL 27–14 PAL/UN, USUN to Department of State (January 24, 1964); NARA RG 59, Decimal File 325.84/5–1960, USUN to Secretary of State (May 19, 1960); NARA RG 59, 325.84/5–1360, "Valuation of Arab Refugee Property in Israel: an Appreciation May 1960."

30. From the R/P1 forms relating to 'Ayn Hawd. The author kindly thanks the Institute for Palestine Studies for allowing him to examine its copy of the UNCCP data.

31. From the R/P1 forms relating to Khalisa.

32. UNSA DAG 13–3, UNCCP. Subgroup: Principal Secretary. Series: Records Relating to the Technical Office/Box 16/1952–57/Land Identification Project/Jarvis Report; Document: A/AC.25/W.83, "Initial Report of the Commission's Land Expert on the Identification and Valuation of Arab Refugee Property Holdings in Israel" (September 15, 1961) .

33. UNSA DAG 13–3, UNCCP. Subgroup: Principal Secretary. Series: Records Relating to Compensation/Box 20/1961–64/Background Papers; Document: "Discussion of the Valuable of Movable Property" (December 1961), App. I, II, III.

34. UNSA DAG 13–3, UNCCP. Subgroup: Principal Secretary. Series: Records Relating to Compensation/Box 18/1949–62/Selected Documents and Working Papers; Document: "[Draft] Working Paper on the Problems Presented by the Paragraphs on Compensation Contained in the Johnson Proposal" (September 19 1962).

35. NARA RG 59, POL 27–14 PAL/UN, USUN to Department of State (January 14, 1966).

36. NARA RG 59, 325.84/9–2561, Department of State to USUN (September 25, 1961); NARA RG 59, 325.84/9–2661, USUN to Secretary of State (September 26, 1961); NARA RG 59, 325.84/9–2661, Department of State to USUN (September 26, 1961); NARA RG 59, 325.84/10–461, USUN to Secretary of State (October 4, 1961); NARA RG 59, 325.84/10–1361, USUN to Secretary of State (October 13, 1961).

37. NARA RG 59, POL 3 PAL/UN, Department of State to USUN (January 10, 1964); NARA RG 59, POL 3 PAL/UN, USUN to Department of State (January 27, 1964); NARA RG 59, POL 3 PAL/UN, Department of State to USUN (March 7, 1964).

38. NARA RG 59, POL 3 PAL/UN, Department of State to USUN (January 10, 1964); NARA RG 59, POL 3 PAL/UN, Department of State to USUN (April 29, 1964); NARA RG 59, POL 3 PAL/UN, USUN to Secretary of State (January 27, 1966).

39. NARA RG 59, POL 3 PAL/UN, USUN to Department of State (May 5, 1964).

## Notes to Chapter Six

1. Gazit, *President Kennedy's Policy*, p. 8

2. NARA RG 59, 325.84/8–1761, "Memorandum of Conversation" (August 17, 1961); RG 59, 325.84/8–1961, Rusk to Cairo (August 19, 1961).

3. NARA RG 59, 325.84/9–2961, "Memorandum of Conversation" (September 29, 1961).

4. NARA RG 59, 884A.411/10–1161, USUN to Secretary of State (October 11, 1961).

5. NARA RG 59, 325.84/9–2961, "Memorandum of Conversation" (September 29, 1961).

6. NARA RG 59, POL 3 PAL/UN, Department of State to USUN (April 12, 1966).

7. NARA RG 59, 884.411/7–2762, "The Plan"; RG 59, 884.411/7–2762, "Financial Implications of 'The Johnson Plan'" (July 26, 1962); NARA RG 59, POL 3 PAL/UN, Department of State to USUN (April 12, 1966).

8. NARA RG 59, 884.411/7–2762, "The Plan."

9. Ibid., and NARA RG 59, 884.411/7–2762, Johnson's Memorandum (July 27, 1962).

10. NARA RG 59, 325.84/5–162, (May 1, 1962).

11. NARA RG 59, 325.84/9–1462, Kennedy to Husayn (September 14, 1962); NARA RG 59, 325.84/9–1662, Amman to Department of State (September 16, 1962); NARA RG 59, 325.84/9–1962, Amman to Department of State (September 19, 1962).

12. NARA RG 59, 884.411, Talbot to Secretary of State (September 20, 1962).

13. NARA RG 59, 325.84/9–1862, London to Secretary of State (September 18, 1962). See also RG 59, 325.84/9–2162 (September 21, 1962) regarding Meir's meeting with Johnson.

14. NARA RG 59, 325.84/11–2162 (November 21, 1962).

15. NARA RG 59, 325.84/4–662, "Memorandum of Conversation" (April 6, 1962); NARA RG 59, 884.411/7–2462, Crawford to Talbot (July 24, 1962).

16. NARA RG 59, 884.411/7–2762, "Issues for the U.S. Government on the Financial Implications of 'the Johnson Plan'" (July 27, 1962).

17. NARA RG 59, 325.84/1–2463, Tel Aviv to Secretary of State (January 24, 1963). The phrase "that is gone" also appears in NARA, John F. Kennedy Presidential Library, National Security Council Files, Boxes 117-118, "Memorandum of Conversation Between Kennedy and Meir," cited in Gazit, *President Kennedy's Policy*, p. 108.

18. NARA RG 59, 325.84/1–3163, USUN to Secretary of State (January 31, 1963).

19. NARA, John F. Kennedy Presidential Library, Presidential Office Files, Box 119A. Document: State Department Brief re Dr. Johnson's Meeting with Kennedy, February 5, 1963, cited in Gazit, *President Kennedy's Policy*, p. 124.

20. NARA RG 59, 325.84/1–2863, USUN to Secretary of State (January 28, 1963); NARA RG 59, 325.84/1–2863, USUN to Secretary of State (January 28, 1963); NARA RG 59, 325.84/1–3163, USUN to Secretary of State (January 31, 1963).

21. UNSA DAG 13–3, UNCCP. Subgroup: Principal Secretary. Series: Records Relating to Compensation/Box 18/1949–62/Selected Documents and Working Papers; Document: "Note for the Record" (March 14, 1962).

22. NARA RG 59, POL 27–14 PAL/UN, "United Nations Conciliation Commission for Palestine. Aide Memoire by Land Expert" (January 24, 1964), attached to USUN to Department of State (January 24, 1964); UNSA DAG 13–3, UNCCP. Subgroup: Principal Secretary. Series: Records Relating to Compensation/Box 18/1949–62/Selected Documents and Working Papers; Documents: "Working Paper, United Nations Repatriation/Compensation Agency, Questions Requiring Prior Decision" (June 5, 1962) and Jarvis to UNCCP (November 24, 1961).

23. UNSA DAG 13–3, UNCCP. Subgroup: Principal Secretary. Series: Records Relating to Compensation/Box 18/1949–62/Selected Documents and Working Papers; Documents: "The Arab Refugee Problem. A Reappraisal and a New Concept [draft]," "Working Paper, United Nations Repatriation/Compensation Agency, Questions Requiring Prior Discussion" (June 5, 1962), and Jarvis' memorandum to UNCCP (November 24, 1961).

24. Forsythe, *United Nations Peacekeeping*, p. 118.

25. NARA RG 59, POL 3 PAL/UN, Department of State to USUN (March 13, 1965).

26. NARA RG 59, POL PAL/UN, Department of State to USUN (April 12, 1966).

27. NARA RG 59, POL 3 PAL/UN, USUN to Department of State (April 1, 1964).

28. UNSA DAG 13–3, UNCCP. Subgroup: Office of the Legal Advisor. Series: General Records/Box 28/1948–50/Claims for Damage; Document: Dajani to Bernadotte (August 14, 1948).

29. Ibid., Document: Helou to Lie (July 15, 1948).

30. Ibid., Shabib family to Palestine Accounts Section (January 17, 1949).

31. Ibid., Halaby to Clapp Mission (September 24, 1949) and Halaby to Reedman (October 29, 1949).

32. Ibid., Sanders to Lie (November 2, 1948).

33. UNSA DAG 13–3, UNCCP. Subgroup: Principal Secretary. Series: Records Relating to Compensation/Box 21/1958–73/The Question of Arab Land Ownership; Document: Kawar to Hammarskjöld (July 1, 1959); DAG 13–3, UNCCP. Subgroup: Principal Secretary. Series: Records Relating to Compensation/Box 21/1957–63/Properties and Blocked Accounts; Document: Kawar to Gaillard (January 28, 1963).

34. UNSA DAG 13–3, UNCCP. Subgroup: Office of the Legal Advisor. Series: General Records/Box 28/1948–50/Claims for Damage; Document: al-Hindi to Clapp Mission (October 21, 1949).

35. UNSA DAG 13–3, UNCCP. Subgroup: Principal Secretary. Series: Records Relating to Compensation/Box 21/1958–73/The Question of Arab Land Ownership; Document: Gaillard to Isaac (September 13, 1961).

36. UNSA DAG 13–3, UNCCP. Subgroup: Principal Secretary. Series:

Records Relating to Compensation/Box 21/1957–63/Properties and Blocked Accounts; Document: Gaillard to Jarvis (April 8, 1963).

37. February 25, 1946 memorandum by Yusif Sayigh of the Arab Higher Committee, submitted to the Anglo-American Commission of Inquiry, cited in *Village Statistics 1945. A Classification of Land and Area Ownership in Palestine. With Explanatory Notes by Sami Hadawi* (Beirut: Palestine Liberation Organization, Research Center, 1970), p. 27.

38. NARA RG 59, POL 3 PAL/UN, Department of State to USUN (March 7, 1964).

39. UNSA DAG 13–3, UNCCP. Subgroup: Principal Secretary. Series: Records Relating to Compensation/Box 21/1958–71/Property and Compensation; Document: Jarvis to Husein Mayassi (July 29, 1964).

40. UNSA DAG 13–3, UNCCP. Subgroup: Principal Secretary. Series: Records Relating to Compensation/Box 21/1961–67/Technical Office; Document: Jarvis to Nasif (August 23, 1966).

41. UNSA DAG 13–3, UNCCP. Subgroup: Principal Secretary. Series: Records Relating to Compensation/Box 21/1958–73/The Question of Arab Land Ownership; Document: Reich to Hall (September 14, 1967).

42. UNSA DAG 13–3, UNCCP. Subgroup: Principal Secretary. Series: Records Relating to Compensation/Box 21/1961–67/Technical Office; Document: Hall to Murr (June 6, 1967).

43. UNSA DAG 13–3, UNCCP. Subgroup: Principal Secretary. Series: Records Relating to Compensation/Box 21/1958–73/The Question of Arab Land Ownership; Document: Jamal to UNDP (March 21, 1968).

44. NARA RG 59, POL 3 PAL/UN, USUN to Department of State (February 24, 1965).

45. Ibid., Department of State to USUN (March 7, 1964) and (March 2, 1965).

46. Ibid., Amman to Department of State (July 8, 1964) and Beirut to Department of State (July 17, 1964).

47. Ibid., Tel Aviv to Secretary of State (June 9, 1964).

48. NARA RG 59, 325.84/3–2161, USUN to Secretary of State (March 21, 1961).

49. CZA A246/57, "Comments on Value Assessments of Absentee Landed Property" (November 12, 1962).

50. NARA RG 59, POL 3 PAL/UN, USUN to Department of State (April 1, 1964) and Department of State to USUN (April 29, 1964).

51. UNSA DAG 13–3, UNCCP. Subgroup: Land Identification and Valuation Office. Series: Records of the Land Specialist/Box 38/1964–66/Israel; Jarvis to Comay (November 13, 1964).

52. Ibid., Comay to Jarvis (December 23, 1964).

53. *'Al ha-Mishmar*, June 26, 1964.

54. NARA RG 59, POL 3 PAL/UN, USUN to Secretary of State (January 28, 1966) and USUN to Department of State (September 18, 1966); NARA RG 59, REF 3 UNRWA, Tel Aviv to Secretary of State (November 12, 1964).

55. NARA RG 59, POL 3 PAL/UN, USUN to Secretary of State (January 28, 1966).

56. Ibid., Beirut to Department of State (July 17, 1964) and (September 15, 1964).

57. Ibid., USUN to Department of State (September 1, 1964).

58. Ibid., Amman to Department of State (July 8, 1964), (July 15, 1964), (September 2, 1964), (September 9, 1964), and (September 30, 1964).

59. NARA RG 59, REF 3 UNRWA, Beirut to Department of State (November 30, 1964).

60. Ibid.

61. NARA RG 59, POL 3 PAL/UN, Beirut to Secretary of State (March 14, 1963).

62. UN Document A/AC.25/W.85, "United Nations Conciliation Commission for Palestine, Observations and Comments of the Host Countries on the Working Paper prepared by the Technical Expert of the Conciliation Commission A/AC.25/W.84 dated April 28, 1964" (May 11, 1966).

63. UNSA DAG 13–3, UNCCP. Subgroup: Principal Secretary. Series: Records Relating to the Technical Office/Box 17/1966/Observations of the Host Governments; Document: "United Nations Conciliation Commission for Palestine, Comments of the Technical Representative on the Paper Entitled 'Observations and Comments of the Host Countries on the Working Paper prepared by the Technical Expert of the Conciliation Commission A/AC.25/W.84 dated April 28, 1964'" (September 30, 1966).

64. UN Document A/AC.25/W.86, "Note Dated May 23, 1966 Addressed to the Chairman of the Commission by the Representative of Israel" (May 26, 1966).

65. *The New York Times*, July 17, 1966; NARA RG 59, POL 3 PAL/UN, Amman to Secretary of State (March 29, 1966), Beirut to Secretary of State (March 30, 1966), Beirut to Secretary of State (April 6, 1966), Cairo to Secretary of State (July 12, 1966); RG 59, REF 3 UNRWA, Beirut to Department of State (February 27, 1967).

66. NARA RG 59, REF 3 UNRWA, Beirut to Department of State (February 27, 1967).

67. Ibid.

68. Ibid.

69. UN Document A/SPC/91 (November 13, 1963), appended to A/5545, 21st UNCCP Report (November 1, 1963).

70. NARA RG 59, POL 3 PAL/UN, Department of State to USUN (February 17, 1965), (March 2, 1965), and (March 13, 1965).

71. NARA RG 59, REF 3 UNRWA, Amman to Department of State (January 21, 1966); NARA RG 59, POL 3 PAL/UN, USUN to Secretary of State (February 1, 1966).

72. NARA RG 59, POL 3 PAL/UN, USUN to Department of State (October 8, 1964).

73. Ibid., USUN to Department of State (January 6, 1965), (February 24, 1965), and (February 25, 1965).

74. NARA RG 59, POL 3 PAL/UN, Department of State to USUN (March 13, 1965).

75. Ibid., USUN to Department of State (February 24, 1965), Department of State to USUN (March 13, 1965).

76. Ibid., USUN to Secretary of State (February 1, 1966).

77. Ibid., USUN to Department of State (March 21, 1966), (March 23, 1966); Department of State to USUN (March 31, 1966); London to Secretary of State (April 22, 1966).

78. Ibid., Jarvis to Baker (May 18, 1966) attached to USUN to Secretary of State (May 20, 1966); UNSA DAG 13–3, UNCCP. Subgroup: Principal Secretary. Series: Records Relating to Compensation/Box 21/1958–73/The Question of Arab Land Ownership; various documents.

79. NARA RG 59, POL 3 PAL/UN, USUN to Department of State (January 6, 1965), (February 4, 1966); UNSA DAG 13–3, UNCCP. Subgroup: Land Identification and Valuation Office. Series: Records of the Land Specialist/Box 38/1963/Duplication of Microfilm—Memo and Note for the Record; "Note for the Record" (January 8, 1963).

80. NARA RG 59, 325.84/5–1660, USUN to Department of State (May 16, 1960); NARA RG 59, 325.84/5/1960, (May 19, 1960); PRO FO 371/151260, Pooley's letter of February 26, 1960.

81. NARA RG 59, 325.84/9–1461, Rusk to USUN (September 14, 1961).

82. UNSA DAG 13–3, UNCCP. Subgroup: Principal Secretary. Series: General Records/Box 3/1961–1967/Drafts of Correspondence with Host Governments; Gaillaird to members of the commission.

83. NARA RG 59, 325.84/3–262, Department of State to USUN (March 2, 1962).

84. UNSA DAG 13–3, UNCCP. Subgroup: Principal Secretary. Series: General Records/Box 3/1962/J.P. Gaillard; "Note on Microfilm Request from Syria" (July 12, 1963).

85. NARA RG 59, POL 3 PAL/UN, USUN to Secretary of State (June 25, 1963), (October 16, 1963); UNSA DAG 13–3, UNCCP. Subgroup: Principal Secretary. Series: General Records/Box 3/1962/J.P. Gaillard; Jarvis to Gaillard (July 16, 1963); Tarazi to Asiroglu (June 17, 1963).

86. NARA RG 59, POL 3 PAL/UN, USUN to Secretary of State (April 1, 1964).

87. UNSA DAG 13–3, UNCCP. Subgroup: Land Identification and Valua-

tion Office. Series: Records of the Land Specialist/Box 38/1963/Duplication of Microfilm—Memo and Note for the Record; "The Problem of the Microfilm"; UNSA DAG 13–3, UNCCP. Subgroup: Principal Secretary. Series: General Records/Box 3/1962/J.P. Gaillard; July 10, 1963 note on the Arab requests for films.

88. NARA RG 59, POL 3 PAL/UN, USUN to Department of State (February 4, 1966); Department of State to USUN (March 3, 1966); USUN to Department of State (September 16, 1966), (September 18, 1966), (September 23, 1966), (September 26, 1966).

89. UNSA DAG 13–3, UNCCP. Subgroup: Principal Secretary. Series: General Records/Box 3/1961–1967/Drafts of Correspondence with Host Governments; Arabs to Epervrier (February 3, 1967).

90. NARA RG 59, POL 3 PAL, USUN to Department of State (April 26, 1967), Department of State to USUN (May 27, 1967).

91. NARA RG 59, REF 3 UNRWA, USUN to Secretary of State (November 7, 1972); UN Document A/31/254, 30th UNCCP report (October 4, 1976).

92. UN Documents A/31/254, 30th UNCCP Report (October 4, 1976); A/38/397, 37th UNCCP Report (September 13, 1983); A/39/455, 38th UNCCP Report (September 6, 1984).

## Notes to Chapter Seven

1. NARA RG 59, REF 3 UNRWA, Tel Aviv to Department of State (January 26, 1967); RG 59, REF 1 ARAB, "Memorandum of Conversation" (February 8, 1967).

2. Oren Yiftachel, "The Internal Frontier: Territorial Control and Ethnic Relations in Israel," in Oren Yiftachel and Avinoam Meir, eds., *Ethnic Frontiers and Peripheries. Landscapes of Development and Inequality in Israel.* Published in cooperation with the Negev Center for Regional Development, Ben-Gurion University of the Negev (Boulder, Colo.: Westview Press, 1998), p. 57.

3. Eyal Benvenisti and Eyal Zamir, "Private Claims to Property Rights in Future Israeli-Palestinian Settlement," *The American Journal of International Law* 89:295 (1995): 308–10, 313–14.

4. Ibid., p. 301.

5. *The Times* [London], December 24, 1980.

6. NARA RG 59, REF 3 UNRWA, Tel Aviv to Department of State (January 2, 1968).

7. Sami Hadawi, *Palestinian Rights & Losses in 1948. A Comprehensive Study*. Part V: An Economic Assessment of Total Palestinian Losses written by Dr. Atef [sic] Kubursi (London: Saqi Books, 1988); interview with Sami Hadawi (July 2001).

8. Interview with Sami Hadawi (July 2001).

9. Frank D. Lewis, "Agricultural Property and the 1948 Palestinian Refugees: Assessing the Loss." *Explorations in Economic History* 33 (1996): 173, 179.

10. Ibid., p. 183.

11. Ibid., pp. 184–86.

12. Walid Khalidi, "The Ownership of the U.S. Embassy Site in Jerusalem," *Journal of Palestine Studies* 29, 4 (Summer 2000): 80–101.

13. NARA RG 84, Jerusalem Consulate General 1948–53/Classified General Records 1948–53/124.1/Genio to Consul General (March 23, 1949); Consul General to Secretary of State (April 20, 1949); Burdett to Buell (April 21, 1949); Secretary of State to Consul General (May 12, 1949); Burdett to Buell (September 3, 1949).

14. The Belgians continued this arrangement with Salama at least until the 1990s. *The Jerusalem Report*, November 2, 1995.

15. NARA RG 59, 325.84 (1960–63), Jerusalem to Department of State (August 1, 1962).

16. Khalidi, "The Ownership of the U.S. Embassy Site in Jerusalem;" *Middle East Newsline Weekend Report* 2, 71 (February 20, 2000).

17. *Jordan Times* Internet Edition, May 25, 1998.

18. UNSA DAG 13-3. Subgroup: Office of the Legal Advisor. Series: General Records/Box 28/1948–1950; Claims for Damage Suffered in Palestine due to Israeli Take-over; letter of Clara Sursuq (May 3, 1950).

19. "Egypt's Diminishing Jewish Community Beleaguered from Within, Without," Religion News Service (on-line document: www.religionnews.com/arc00/f_1011.html); Reuters, August 11, 2000.

20. Interview with Moshe Sasson (December 2000).

21. Marilyn Henry, " 'The Real Thing' and the Right Thing," *Jerusalem Post* Internet Edition, May 24, 1999.

22. "Egypt's Diminishing Jewish Community Beleaguered from Within, Without," Religion News Service (on-line document: www.religionnews.com/arc00/f_1011.html); *Jerusalem Post* Internet Edition, May 24, 1999.

23. Levin, *Locked Doors*, p. 146.

24. Shenhav, "The Jews of Iraq," p. 623.

25. Levin, *Locked Doors*, p. 146.

26. *le Monde Diplomatique*, September 2000.

27. Reuters News Service, August 11, 2000.

28. Interview with Marwan Muasher (January 2001); *The Jerusalem Report*, November 2, 1995.

29. Interview with Kamil Nasrawi (January 2000); *The Star* [Amman] Internet Edition, March 6, 1997.

30. *Jordan Times* Internet Edition, July 26, 2001; *Afaq 'Iqariyya* [publication of the Jordanian Department of Lands and Survey] 5 (July 1999); interview with 'Abd al-Mun'im Samara al-Zu'bi (August 2001).

31. *Israel's Business Arena-Globes*, June 25, 2000.

32. *Jordan Times* Internet Edition, February 26, 1995, and March 5, 1997.

33. The author personally observed this in the summer of 1997 at the Jordanian Department of Lands and Surveys in Amman.

34. *al-Dustur* [Amman], May 22, 1997; *Jordan Times*, May 24, 1997; *Yediot Aharanot*, June 17, 1997.

35. Agence France-Presse News Service, February 23, 2000.

36. UNSA DAG 13-3, UNCCP. Subgroup: Principal Secretary. Series: Records Relating to Compensation/Box 3/1958–1973/The Question of Arab Land Ownership; NARA RG 59, Decimal File 320.51/1-2659, Stavropoulos to Chai (June 6, 1958).

37. *Jerusalem Post*, January 7, 2000.

38. Reuters News Service, January 7, 2000; Aruts Sheva News Service, January 9, 2000.

39. Reuters News Service, January 7, 2000.

40. Interview with Moshe Sasson (December 2000).

41. Yehuda Shenhav, "Kehilot ve Mahozot shel Zikaron Mizrahi" [Communities and Districts of Mizrahi Memory] (Unpublished manuscript, Van Leer Institute and Tel Aviv University, 2000), pp. 51-52.

42. Salim Tamari, ed., *Jerusalem 1948. The Arab Neighbourhoods and their Fate in the War* (Jerusalem: Institute for Jerusalem Studies and Badil Resource Center, 1999).

43. *al-Majdal* 14 (June 2002): 8.

44. *The Jerusalem Report* 2000 (on-line document: www.jrep.com/Info/10thAnniversary/2000/Article-10.html); *The Jerusalem Report* November 2, 1995; Ahmad Jadallah and Khalil Tufakji, "Documenting Arab Properties in Western Jerusalem," in Tamari, *Jerusalem 1948*, pp. 237–39.

45. *Jordan Times* Internet Edition, June 7, 1998; *The Jerusalem Post* Internet Edition, July 5, 1998.

46. *ha-Tsofe*, July 18, 1999.

47. *Middle East Newsline* 1, 484 (December 20, 1999).

48. The author was involved with this project as a consultant. Some of the information contained in this section comes from his involvement in that work.

49. Adnan Abdel Razeq [sic], "Refugee Property: UN Modernizes Land Records," Pt. II, *The Jerusalem Times Insight Report* Internet Edition, October 10, 2001 (on-line document: www.jerusalem-times.net/tjt/insight/main.htm); Adnan Abdelrazek, "Modernizing the Refugee Land Records: Advantages and Pitfalls," Salim Tamari and Elia Zureik, eds., *Reinterpreting the Historical Record. The Uses of Palestinian Refugee Archives for Social Science Research and Policy Analysis* (Jerusalem: Institute for Jerusalem Studies and Institute for Palestine Studies, 2001); interview with Adnan Abdelrazek (September 2001).

50. Information provided by the Permanent Observer Mission of Palestine to the UN; Interview with Adnan Abdelrazek (September 2001).

51. Ibid.

52. *The Washington Post*, January 11, 2000.

53. Associated Press News Service, March 3, 2000.

54. *al-Dustur* [Amman], September 20, 2000.

55. Agence France-Presse News Service, July 25, 2000.

56. See on-line document: http://www.palestinemonitor.org/Activism%20pal%20solidarity/bringing_legal_action_against_israel.htm.

57. Levin, *Locked Doors*, p. 212.

58. Yehouda Shenhav, "Ethnicity and National Memory: The World Organization of Jews from Arab Countries (WOJAC) in the Context of the Palestinian National Struggle," *British Journal of Middle Eastern Studies* 29, 1 (2002), p. 52.

59. For more information on WOJAC's problems, see Levin, *Locked Doors*, pp. 217–23.

60. *Middle East Peace Report*, January 8, 2001 (on-line document: www.peacenow.org/nia/peace/v2i28.html); *Jerusalem Post* International Edition, April 1, 2001.

61. Shenhav, "Ethnicity and National Memory," p. 42.

62. Shenhav, "Kehilot ve Mahozot shel Zikaron Mizrahi," p. 41; Peter Hirschberg, "Private Property Keep Out!," *The Jerusalem Report* (on-line document: www.jrep.com/Info/10thAnniversary/1999/Article-11.html).

63. Shenhav, "Ethnicity and National Memory," p. 43

64. *Israel's Business Arena-Globes*, January 2, 2001 (on-line document: http://groups.yahoo.com/group/Support_Israel/message/120).

65. Agence France-Presse News Service, January 13, 1999; *Jerusalem Post*, January 13, 1999.

66. Levin, *Confiscated Wealth*.

67. Levin, *Locked Doors*. This was the English-language translation of Levin's original Hebrew-language version, *Sheki'ah be-Mizrah: Hisul ha-Kehilot ha-Yehudiyot be-Medinot 'Arav ve Shod Rekhushan*, which was published by the Israeli Ministry of Defense with assistance from the Jewish Agency.

68. Ibid., pp. xv–xvi.

69. *Ha'aretz*, September 23, 1999.

70. *Ha'aretz* Internet Edition, September 23, 1999; Hirschberg, "Private Property Keep Out!"

71. See ISA (130) 1791/1, "Jewish Iraqi Property-Registration of Claims (Proposal)" (March 30, 1951) for details.

72. Levin, *Locked Doors*, p. 223.

73. *The Jerusalem Post*, November 20, 2001.

74. *The Jerusalem Post*, March 3, 2002.

75. Jewish Telegraph Agency, June 18, 2002; Jewishweek.com, May 17, 2002; *The Jerusalem Post* internet edition, May 11, 2002.

76. See the group's web site at: www.jewishrefugees.org/JusticeForJews.htm;

see also "Justice for Jews in Arab Countries," *Jewish Post* (on-line document: www.jewishpost.com/jp0901/jpn0901a.htm).

77. Blougrund, *The Jewish National Fund*, pp. 8, 10.

78. *le Monde Diplomatique*, September 2000. This statement was confirmed to the author by a Palestinian source with access to top PLO official Mahmud 'Abbas (Abu Mazin).

79. *Mivaker ha-Medina-Doh Shnati 41 (le-shnat 1990 ve le-shnat ha-ksafim 1989)* [State of Israel, State Controller's Annual Report 41 (for 1990 and Budget Year 1989)], pp. 326–32.

80. *The Times* [London], December 24, 1980. The account was part of a series on refugee property that Fisk published in *The Times* in December 1980. The pieces from the series are also found in Fisk's book *Pity the Nation. The Abduction of Lebanon* (New York: Atheneum, 1990).

81. *Mivaker ha-Medina-Doh Shnati 41 (le-shnat 1990 ve le-shnat ha-ksafim 1989)*, pp. 326–32.

82. In a September 7, 1999 letter to the author.

83. *Mivaker ha-Medina-Doh Shnati 41 (le-shnat 1990 ve le-shnat ha-ksafim 1989)*, pp. 326–32.

84. Adalah Press Report E/05/2001, January 31, 2002.

85. "Report on Israeli Settlement in the Occupied Territories" 10, 5 (September-October 2000): 2.

86. Akram Hanieh, "The Camp David Papers" *Journal of Palestine Studies* 30, 2 (Winter 2001): 82; *Ha'aretz* Internet Edition, January 3, 2000; *Jerusalem Post International Edition*, April 1, 2001.

87. Salim Tamari, *Palestinian Refuge Negotiations: From Madrid to Oslo II* (Washington: Institute for Palestine Studies, 1996), p. 6.

88. Hirschberg, "Private Property Keep Out!"

89. *le Monde Diplomatique*, September 2000.

90. *Jerusalem Post* International Edition, April 1, 2001.

91. Global Jewish Agenda [Jewish Agency], November 22, 2001.

92. Jewish Telegraphic Agency, June 18, 2002.

93. See the web site of the PLO Negotiations Affairs Department at: www.nad-plo.org/permanent/refugees.html.

94. Palestinian Proposal on Palestinian Refugees, cited in *Journal of Palestine Studies* 31, 2 (Winter 2002): 145–48.

95. Israeli proposal presented at Taba; ibid., p. 150.

96. The Moratinos Nonpaper on the Taba Negotiations, Summer 2001, cited in *Journal of Palestine Studies* 31,3 (Spring 2002): 87.

97. Ibid.

## Notes to Conclusion

1. The poll was conducted by the Palestinian Authority's Committee for Information Service during the summer of 1999. A total of 1,080 questionnaires were completed, 560 in the West Bank and 520 in Gaza. The percentage of the respondents who were refugees was 44.6 per cent in the West Bank and 89.9 per cent in Gaza. *al-Majdal* 3 (September 1999): 9.

2. Deborah Sontag, "The Palestinian Conversation," *The New York Times Magazine*, 3 (February 2002): 40.

# BIBLIOGRAPHY


## Archival and Governmental Sources

### Institute for Palestine Studies, Washington and Beirut

United Nations Conciliation Commission for Palestine records on Arab property in Israel

### Israel. Prime Minister's Office, Israel State Archives, Jerusalem

43 (Prime Minister's Office files)
80 (Ministry of Finance files)
130 (Foreign Ministry files)
74 (Ministry of Justice files)

### Jordan. Department of Lands and Survey, Amman

Land Settlement files
Records of the Diwan

### Jordan. Ministry of Finance, Amman

Various files

### Jordan Ministry of Culture, National Library/Center for Documents and Documentation, Amman

Files of the Prime Ministry

### United Kingdom. Public Records Office, London

CO 733 (Colonial Office—Palestine. Original Correspondence)
CO 831 (Colonial Office—Transjordan. Original Correspondence)
FO 371 (Foreign Office—Political Departments files)

## United Nations. Secretariat Archives, New York

### *DAG 13/3 (United Nations Conciliation Commission for Palestine)*

Principal Secretary, 1948
Office of the Legal Advisor, 1949-unknown
Refugee Office, 1951–1952
Land Identification and Valuation Office (Technical Office), 1952–1966
Liaison Office, 1953-(Unknown)
Reference Library

## United States. National Archives and Records Administration, College Park, Maryland

RG 59 (State Department Central Files; Office or Lot files)
RG 84 (Foreign Service Post files)

## World Zionist Organization. Central Zionist Archives, Jerusalem

Z6 (Nahum Goldmann Office Files)
C2 (Files of the World Jewish Congress, British Section)
KKL5 (Files of the Keren Kayemet le-Yisra'el [Jewish National Fund], Jerusalem Headquarters)
KKL10 (Keren Kayemet le-Yisra'el Board of Directors Meetings Minutes)
A246 (Yosef Weitz Papers)
A202 (Avraham Granott Papers)

## Published Government Sources

Great Britain. A *Survey of Palestine. Prepared in December 1945 and January 1946 for the Information of the Anglo-American; Committee of Inquiry*. Jerusalem?: Government Printer, 1946–47; Reprint edition: Washington: Institute for Palestine Studies, 1991.

Israel. *Israel Government Yearbook* (various years).

——. Israel State Archives. *Documents on the Foreign Policy of Israel*. Jerusalem: Israel State Archives, various dates.

——. Knesset. *Divrei ha-Knesset* [Knesset Proceedings].

——. Ministry of Finance. *Development of Agriculture in Israel.*

——. Prime Minister's Office. "Background Papers: The Refugee Issue."

Jordan. *al-Jarida al-Rasmiyya* [Official Gazette]

United Nations. United Nations Conciliation Commission for Palestine, annual reports.
United States. *Foreign Relations of the United States*. Washington: Department of State, various dates.

## Secondary Sources

### *Unpublished*

Forman, Geremy. "The Transformation of Eastern 'Emeq Yizre'el/Marj Ibn 'Amer and 'Emeq Beit-Shean/Ghor Baysan: Changes in Settlement, Population and Land Tenure due to the 1948 War and the Establishment of the State of Israel." Unpublished M.A. thesis, Haifa University, 2000.
——. "The 'Backyardization' of Ramat Yisaschar: Changes in Population, Land-Possession and Land Ownership in Ramat Yisaschar-Gush Nuris, 1948–1958. Unpublished manuscript, Haifa University, 1997.
——. "Jewish National Land After 1948: The Evolution of 'Israel Lands' and the Establishment of the Israel Lands Administration." Unpublished manuscript, Haifa University, 1999.
Goldberg, David H. "The United Nations Conciliation Commission: an Historical Analysis." Unpublished B.A. thesis, Rutgers College, 1980.
Horowitz, Avery Justin. "U.S. Policy Toward the Palestinian Refugees, 1948–1956." Unpublished M.A. thesis, the University of Virginia, 1994.
Ilan, Tsvi. "Nisyonot le-Rekhishat Adama ve le-Hityashvut Yehudit be-'Ever ha-Yarden ha-Mizrahi, 1871–1947" [Attempts by Jews to Purchase Lands and Settle in Transjordan, 1871–1947]. Unpublished Ph.D. dissertation, Bar-Ilan University, 1981.
Nakkara, Hanna Dib. Untitled, unpublished manuscript on Israeli measures toward Palestinian property.
Procopio, Ilda Frances. "A Study of the Problems of Repatriation, Compensation, and Reintegration of the Palestinian Refugees January 1948 to June 1969." Unpublished M.A. thesis, The George Washington University, 1970.
Sabet, Dan. "The Palestinian Refugees and Their Effect on U.S.-Israel Relations: 1948- 1952." Unpublished B.A. thesis, The Ohio State University, 1998.
Shenhav, Yehuda. "Kehilot ve Mahozot shel Zikaron Mizrahi" [Communities and Districts of Mizrahi Memory]. Unpublished manuscript, Van Leer Institute and Tel Aviv University, 2000.

### *Published*

Abdelrazek, Adnan. "Modernizing the Refugee Land Records: Advantages and Pitfalls." Tamari, Salim and Zureik, Elia. *Reinterpreting the Historical Record. The Uses of Palestinian Refugee Archives for Social Science Research and Policy*

*Analysis*. Jerusalem: Institute for Jerusalem Studies and Institute for Palestine Studies, 2001.

Abu-Sitta, Salman H. "Documenting Arab Property in West Jerusalem. B: Notes on UNCCP Records on land and Landowners." Tamari, Salim, ed. *Jerusalem 1948. The Arab Neighbourhoods and their Fate in the War*. Jerusalem: Institute for Jerusalem Studies, 1999.

——. *The End of the Palestinian-Israeli Conflict. From Refugees to Citizens at Home*. London: Palestine Land Society and Palestinian Return Centre, 2001.

Abu Shakrah, Jan. "Deconstructing the Link: Palestinian Refugees and Jewish Immigrants from Arab Countries. Aruri, Naseer Aruri, ed., *Palestinian Refugees. The Right of Return*. Pluto Middle East Series. Nur Masalha, general editor. London and Sterling, Virginia: Pluto Press, 2001.

Azcárate, Pablo de. *Mission in Palestine*. Washington: The Middle East Institute, 1966.

Beinin, Joel. *The Dispersion of Egyptian Jewry. Culture, Politics, and the Formation of a Modern Diaspora*. Berkeley, Los Angeles, London: University of California Press, 1988.

Ben-Porat, Mordechai. *To Baghdad and Back. The Miraculous 2,000 Year Homecoming of the Iraqi Jews*. Trans. Marcia Grant and Kathy Akeriv. Jerusalem and New York: Gefen Publishing House, 1998.

Benvenisti, Eyal and Zamir, Eyal. "Private Claims to Property Rights in Future Israeli-Palestinian Settlement." *The American Journal of International Law* 89:295 (1995): 295–340.

Bernadotte, Folke. *To Jerusalem*. Trans. by Joan Bulman. London: Hodder and Stoughton, 1951.

Bilby, Kenneth W. *New Star in the Near East*. Garden City, N.Y.: Doubleday & Co., Inc., 1950.

Bisharat, George E. "Land, Law, and Legitimacy in Israel and the Occupied Territories." *The American University Law Review* 43 (1994): 467–561.

Blougrund, David. *The Jewish National Fund*. Policy Studies No. 49. Washington and Jerusalem: Institute for Advanced Strategic and Political Studies, 2001.

Buehrig, Edward H. *The UN and the Palestinian Refugees. A Study in Nonterritorial Administration*. Bloomington, Indiana and London: Indiana University Press, 1971.

Cahana, Shamay. *Differing and Converging Views on Solving the Palestinian Refugees' Problems*. Davis Papers on Israel's Foreign Policy, No. 51. Jerusalem: The Leonard Davis Institute for International Relations, The Hebrew University of Jerusalem, 1996.

Caplan, Neil. *The Lausanne Conference, 1949. A Case Study in Middle East Peacemaking*. Tel Aviv: The Moshe Dayan Center for Middle Eastern and African Studies, Tel Aviv University, 1993.

Carpenter, J. Henry. "The Arabs Can't Go Back." *Christian Century* 68, 26 (27 June 1951): 763–76.

Carr, Donald. "The Other Refugees." *Middle East Focus* 6 (March 1984): 4–5, 24.

Cohen, Abner. *Arab Border-Villages in Israel. A Study of Continuity and Change I: Social Organization*. Manchester: Manchester University Press, 1965.

Cohen, Hayyim J. *The Jews of the Middle East 1860–1972*. New York and Toronto: John Wiley & Sons; Jerusalem: Israel Universities Press, 1972.

Dash, Jacob. "Planning and Development." *Immigration and Settlement*. The Israel Pocket Library. Jerusalem: Keter Publishing House, Ltd., 1973.

Davis, Uri and Mezvinsky, Norton, eds., *Documents from Israel 1967–1973. Readings for a Critique of Zionism*. London: Ithaca Press, 1975.

De Felice, Renzo. *Jews in an Arab Land. Libya, 1835–1970*, trans. Judith Roumani. Austin: University of Texas Press, 1985.

Dumper, Michael. *Islam and Israel: Muslim Religious Endowments and the Jewish State*. Washington: Institute for Palestine Studies, 1994.

*Encyclopaedia Judaica*. Jerusalem: Keter Publishing House, Ltd., 1971.

Epstein [Elat], Eliahu. "Notes from a Paper on the Present Conditions in the Hauran." *Journal of the Royal Central Asian Society* 23 (1936).

Eytan, Walter. *The First Ten Years. A Diplomatic History of Israel*. New York: Simon and Schuster, 1958.

Falah, Ghazi. "The 1948 Israeli-Palestinian War and its Aftermath: the Transformation and De-Signification of Palestine's Cultural Landscape." *Annals of the Association of American Geographers* 86, 2 (1996): 256–285.

Felner, Eitan. *A Policy of Discrimination: Land Expropriation, Planning and Building in East Jerusalem*. Jerusalem: B'Tselem—The Israeli Information Center for Human Rights in the Occupied Territories, 1997.

Fischbach, Michael R. *State, Society, and Land in Jordan*. Leiden, Boston, Köln: Brill, 2000.

——. "The United Nations and Palestinian Refugee Property Compensation." *Journal of Palestine Studies* 31, 2 (Winter 2002): 34–50.

——. "Les Nations unies et l'imdemnisation des réfugiés palestiniens." Sanbar, Elie and Mardam-Bey, Farouk, eds. *Les Doits au Retour. le problème des réfugiés palestiniens*. Paris: Sindbad/Actes Sud, 2001.

——. "UN Conciliation Commission for Palestine: Land Records." Tamari, Salim and Zureik, Elia, eds. *Reinterpreting the Historical Record. The Uses of Palestinian Refugee Archives for Social Science Research and Policy Analysis*. Jerusalem: Institute for Jerusalem Studies and Institute for Palestine Studies, 2001.

——. "Land." Philip Mattar, ed. *Encyclopedia of the Palestinians*. New York: Facts On File, Inc., 2000.

——. "Settling Historical Land Claims in the Wake of Arab-Israeli Peace." *Journal of Palestine Studies* 27, 1 (Autumn 1997): 38–50.

——. "The Implications of Jordanian Land Policy for the West Bank." *Middle East Journal* 43, 3 (Summer 1994): 492–509.

Fisk, Robert. *Pity the Nation. The Abduction of Lebanon*. New York: Atheneum, 1990.

Forsythe, David P. *United Nations Peacekeeping. The Conciliation Commission for Palestine*. Published in cooperation with the Middle East Institute. Baltimore and London: The Johns Hopkins University, 1972.

Gabbay, Rony E. A *Political Study of the Arab-Jewish Conflict. The Arab Refugee Problem (A Case Study)*. Geneva: Librairie E. Droz and Paris: Librairie Minard, 1959.

Gat, Moshe. *The Jewish Exodus from Iraq 1948–1951*. London and Portland: Frank Cass, 1997.

Gazit, Mordechai. *President Kennedy's Policy Toward the Arab States and Israel*. The Shiloah Center for Middle Eastern and African Studies Series. Tel Aviv: The Shiloah Center for Middle Eastern and African Studies, Tel Aviv University, 1983.

Golan, Arnon. "The Transfer to Jewish Control of Abandoned Arab Lands during the War of Independence." S. Ilan Troen and Lucas, Noah, eds. *Israel. The First Decade of Independence*. SUNY Series in Israeli Studies. Russell Stone, editor. Albany, N.Y.: State University of New York Press, 1995.

——. "The Transformation of Abandoned Arab Rural Areas." *Israel Studies* 2, 1 (Spring 1997): 94–110.

Granott, A. [Avraham Granovsky]. *Agrarian Reform and the Record of Israel*, trans. E.M. Epstein. London: Eyre & Spottiswood, 1956.

Habash, Dalia and Rempel, Terry. "Assessing Palestinian Property in the City." Tamari, Salim, ed. *Jerusalem 1948. The Arab Neighbourhoods and their Fate in the War*. Jerusalem: Institute for Jerusalem Studies and Badil Resource Center for Palestinian Residency and Refugee Rights, 1999.

Hadawi, Sami. *Palestinian Rights & Losses in 1948. A Comprehensive Study*. Part V: An Economic Assessment of Total Palestinian Losses written by Dr. Atef Kubursi. London: Saqi Books, 1988.

——. *The Story of My Life (Memories and Reflections)*. N.p.: 1996.

Hamzeh, Fuad S. *United Nations Conciliation Commission for Palestine 1949–1967*. Beirut: Institute for Palestine Studies, 1968.

——. *International Conciliation*. Amsterdam: Djambatan, n.d.

Hanieh, Akram. "The Camp David Papers." *Journal of Palestine Studies* 30, 2 (Winter 2001): 75–97.

Hillel, Shlomo. *Operation Babylon*, trans. Ina Friedman. New York: Doubleday, 1987.

Jadallah, Ahmad & Khalil Tufakji, "Documenting Arab Property in West Jerusalem. A: Problems of Documentation." Tamari, Salim, ed. *Jerusalem 1948. The Arab Neighbourhoods and their Fate in the War*. Jerusalem: Institute for Jerusalem Studies and Badil Resource Center for Palestinian Residency and Refugee Rights, 1999.

Jewish Agency. *Jewish Agency's Digest of Press and Events* 3, 20 (2 February 1951).

Jiryis, Sabri. "The Legal Structure for the Expropriation and Absorption of Arab Lands in Israel." *Journal of Palestine Studies* 2, 4 (Summer 1973): 82–104.

——. *The Arabs in Israel.* Trans. by Inea Bushnaq. Foreword by Noam Chomsky. New York and London: Monthly Review Press, 1976.

Kark, Ruth. "Planning, Housing, and Land Policy 1948–1952: The Formation of Concepts and Governmental Frameworks." Troen, S. Ilan and Lucas, Noah, eds. *Israel. The First Decade of Independence.* SUNY Series in Israeli Studies. Russell Stone, editor. Albany, N.Y.: State University of New York Press, 1995.

Karmi, Ghada. "The Question of Compensation and Reparations." Karmi, Ghada, and Cotran, Eugene, eds. *The Palestinian Exodus 1948–1998.* Reading, U.K.: Ithaca Press, 1999.

Kellerman, Aharon. *Society and Settlement. Jewish Land of Israel in the Twentieth Century.* SUNY Series in Israeli Studies. Albany, N.Y.: State University of New York Press, 1993.

Khalidi, Walid. "The Ownership of the U.S. Embassy Site in Jerusalem." *Journal of Palestine Studies* 29, 4 (Summer 2000): 80–101.

——, ed. *All That Remains. The Palestinian Villages Occupied and Depopulated by Israel in 1948.* Washington: Institute for Palestine Studies, 1992.

Khouri, Fred J. *The Arab-Israeli Dilemma,* third edition. Syracuse: Syracuse University Press, 1985.

Khoury, J. *Arab Property and Blocked Accounts in Occupied Palestine.* Cairo: League of Arab States, General Secretary, Palestine Section, 1956.

Kossaifi, George F. *The Palestinian Refugees and the Right of Return.* Information Paper No. 7. Washington: Center for Policy Analysis on Palestine, 1996.

Koussa, E.N. "Memorandum on Properties Belonging to Arabs Living in Israel." *Ner* 2 (13 July 1951): 22–24 and (31 August 1951): 28.

Kretzmer, David. *The Legal Status of the Arabs in Israel.* Boulder, San Francisco, Oxford: Westview Press, 1990.

Kubursi, Atif. *Palestinian Losses in 1948: The Quest for Precision.* Information Paper No. 6. Washington: Center for Policy Analysis on Palestine, 1996.

——. "Valuing Palestinian Losses in Today's Dollars." Naseer Aruri, ed., *Palestinian Refugees. The Right of Return.* Pluto Middle East Series. Nur Masalha, general editor. London and Sterling, Virginia: Pluto Press, 2001.

Laskier, Michael M. *The Jews of Egypt 1920–1970. In the Midst of Zionism, Anti-Semitism, and the Middle East Conflict.* New York and London: New York University Press, 1992.

League of Arab States, Secretariat General, Press & Information Department. *Report on Sale of Arab Refugee Property by Israeli Custodian. Submitted by the Palestine Arab Refugee Office to the Palestine Conciliation Commission.* Cairo?: N.d.

Lehn, Walter with Uri Davis. *The Jewish National Fund.* London and New York: Kegan Paul International, 1988.

Levin, Itamar. *Locked Doors: The Seizure of Jewish Property in Arab Countries,* trans. Rachel Neiman. Forward by Abraham Hirchson and Israel Singer. Westport, Conn. and London: Praeger Publishers, 2001.

——. *Confiscated Wealth: The Fate of Jewish Property in Arab Lands.* Policy Forum No. 22. Jerusalem: Institute of the World Jewish Congress, 2000.

Lewis, Frank D. "Agricultural Property and the 1948 Palestinian Refugees: Assessing the Loss." *Explorations in Economic History* 33 (1996): 169–194.

Lustick, Ian. *Arabs in the Jewish State. Israel's Control of a National Minority.* Modern Middle East Series, No. 6. Austin: The University of Texas Press, 1980.

McDonald, James G. *My Mission in Israel 1948–1951.* New York: Simon and Schuster, 1951.

Masalha, Nur. *Israeli Plans to Resettle the Palestinian Refugees 1948–1972.* Monograph Series No. 2. Ramallah: Palestinian Diaspora and Refugee Centre (SHAML), 1996.

——, trans. and ed. *The Palestinians in Israel: Is Israel the State of All its Citizens and "Absentees"?* Nazareth: Center for Social Research and London: Scholarship Fund for Publications on Israel, 1993.

——. "A Critique on Benny Morris." Pappé, Ilan, ed., *The Israel/Palestine Question.* Rewriting Histories Series. Jack R. Censer, Series Editor. London and New York: Routledge, 1999.

——. "The Historical Roots of the Palestinian Refugee Question." Aruri, Naseer, ed., *Palestinian Refugees. The Right of Return.* Pluto Middle East Series. Nur Masalha, general editor. London and Sterling, Virginia: Pluto Press, 2001.

Melman, Yossi, and Raviv, Dan. *Friends in Deed. Inside the U.S.-Israel Alliance.* New York: Hyperion, 1994.

Meron, Ya'akov. "The Golan Heights 1918–1967." Meir Shamgar, ed., *Military Government in the Territories Administered by Israel 1967–1980. The Legal Aspects,* Vol. 1. Jerusalem: The Hebrew University of Jerusalem Faculty of Law, The Harry Sacher Institute for Legislative Research and Comparative Law, 1982.

——. "Why Jews Fled the Arab Countries," *Middle East Quarterly* (September 1995).

Morris, Benny. *The Birth of the Palestinian Refugee Problem, 1947–1949.* Cambridge Middle East Library. Cambridge: Cambridge University Press, 1987.

——. *Israel's Border Wars, 1949–1956. Arab Infiltration, Israeli Retaliation, and the Countdown to the Suez War.* Oxford: Oxford University Press, 1993.

——. "Yosef Weitz and the Transfer Committees, 1948–49." *Middle Eastern Studies* 22, 4 (October 1986): 522–561.

——. "The Causes and Character of the Arab Exodus from Palestine: the Israeli

Defense Forces Intelligence Service Analysis of June 1948." Pappé, Ilan, ed., *The Israel/Palestine Question*. Rewriting Histories Series. Jack R. Censer, Series Editor. London and New York: Routledge, 1999.

Nakkara, Hanna Dib. "Israeli Land Seizure under Various Defense and Emergency Regulations." *Journal of Palestine Studies* 14, 2 (Winter 1985): 13–34.

Nijim, Basheer K., ed. with Muammar Bishara *Toward the De-Arabization of Palestine/Israel 1945–1977*. Published under the Auspices of The Jerusalem Fund for Education and Community Development. Dubuque, Iowa: Kendall/Hunt Publishing Company, 1984.

Ophen, J.D. "The Citrus Industry in Israel." *Middle Eastern Affairs* 5, 2 (February 1954): 51–58.

Palestine Arab Refugee Office. *Report on Sale of Arab Refugee Property by Israeli Custodian*. Cairo: League of Arab States, Secretariat General, Press and Information Department, n.d.

Pappé, Ilan. "Britain and the Palestinian Refugees, 1948–50." *Middle East Focus* 9 (Fall 1986): 19–25, 31.

Peretz, Don. *Israel and the Palestine Arabs*. Washington: The Middle East Institute, 1958.

——. "Problems of Arab Refugee Compensation." *The Middle East Journal* 8, 4 (Autumn 1954): 403–416.

——. *Palestinian Refugee Compensation*. Information Paper No. 3. Washington: The Center for Policy Analysis on Palestine, 1995.

Plascov, Avi. *The Palestinian Refugees in Jordan, 1948–195*. London: Frank Cass, 1981.

Press, Jesaias. "Die jüdischen Kolonian Palästinas." *Zeitschrift des Deutschen Palästina-Vereins* [Journal of the German Palestine Society] 35 (1912).

Prittie, Terence and Dineen, Bernard. *The Double Exodus. A Study of the Arab and Jewish Refugees in the Middle East*. N.p., n.d.

Rempel, Terry. "The Ottawa Process: Workshop on Compensation and Palestinian Refugees." *Journal of Palestine Studies* 29, 1 (Autumn 1999): 36–49.

——. "Dispossession and Restitution." Tamari, Salim, ed. *Jerusalem 1948. The Arab Neighbourhoods and their Fate in the War*. Jerusalem: Institute for Jerusalem Studies and Badil Resource Center for Palestinian Residency and Refugee Rights, 1999.

Rokach, Livia. *Israel's Sacred Terrorism. A Study Based on Moshe Sharett's Personal Diary and Other Documents*. Introduction by Noam Chomsky. Belmont, Mass.: Association of Arab-American University Graduates, Inc., 1980.

Roumani, Maurice. *The Case of the Jews from Arab Countries: A Neglected Issue*. Tel Aviv: World Organization of Jews from Arab Countries, 1977.

Sayegh, Fayez A. *The Palestine Refugees*. Preface by Virginia C. Gildersleeve. Foreword by William Ernest Hocking. Washington: AMARA Press, 1952.

——. *Arab Property in Israeli-Controlled Territories. Israeli Measures for the Dis-*

*posal of Arab Property*, 2nd edition. New York: The Arab Information Center, 1956.

Sayigh, Yusuf 'Abdullah. *al-Iqtisad al-Isra'ili* [The Israeli Economy]. Cairo: League of Arab States, Institute for Higher Arab Studies, 1966.

Schechtman, Joseph B. *The Arab Refugee Problem*. New York: Philosophical Library, 1952.

——. *On Wings of Eagles. The Plight, Exodus, and Homecoming of Oriental Jews*. New York and London: Thomas Yoseloff, 1961.

Scholz, Norbert. *U.S. Official Statements: the Palestinian Refugees*. Washington: Institute for Palestine Studies, 1994.

Schulze, Kirsten. *The Jews of Lebanon: Between Coexistence and Conflict*. Brighton and Portland: Sussex Academic Press, 2001.

Schumacher, Gottlieb. *Northern 'Ajlun, "Within the Decapolis"*. London: Alexander P. Watt, 1890.

Segev, Tom. *1949: The First Israelis*. Arlen Neal Weinstein, English language editor. An Owl Book. New York: Henry Holt and Co., 1998.

Sharef, Zeev. *Three Days*. Trans. by Julian Louis Meltzer. Garden City, N.Y.: Doubleday & Company, Inc., 1962.

Shenhav, Yehouda. "The Jews of Iraq, Zionist Ideology, and the Property of the Palestinian Refugees of 1948: An Anomaly of National Accounting." *International Journal of Middle East Studies* 31, 4 (November 1999): 605–630.

——. "Ethnicity and National Memory: The World Organization of Jews from Arab Countries (WOJAC) in the Context of the Palestinian National Struggle." *British Journal of Middle Eastern Studies* 29, 1 (2002): 27–56.

Shlaim, Avi. *Collusion Across the Jordan. King Abdullah, the Zionist Movement, and the Partition of Palestine*. New York: Columbia University Press, 1988.

——. "The Debate About 1948." Pappé, Ilan, ed., *The Israel/Palestine Question*. Rewriting Histories Series. Jack R. Censer, Series Editor. London and New York: Routledge, 1999.

Shumski, Adaia and Abraham. *A Bridge Across the Jordan. The Friendship Between a Jewish Carpenter and the King of Jordan*. New York: Arcade Publishing, 1997.

Simons, Chaim. *International Proposals to Transfer Arabs from Palestine 1895–1947. A Historical Survey*. Hoboken, N.J.: Ktav Publishing House, Inc., 1988.

Slyomovics, Susan, *The Object of Memory. Arab and Jew Narrate the Palestinian Village*. Philadelphia: University of Pennsylvania Press, 1998.

Steurnagel, Carl. "Der 'Adschlun," *Zeitschrift des Deutschen Palästina-Vereins* 48 (1925).

Stillman, Norman A. *The Jews of Arab Lands in Modern Times*. Philadelphia and New York: The Jewish Publication Society, 1991.

Stock, Ernest. *Chosen Instrument. The Jewish Agency in the First Decade of the*

*State of Israel*. New York: Herzl Press and Jerusalem: Hassifriya Haziyonit, 1988.

Tadmor, Yoav. "The Palestinian Refugees of 1948: The Right to Compensation and Return." *Temple International & Comparative Law Journal* 8 (1994): 403–434.

Tamari, Salim. *Palestinian Refugee Negotiations: From Madrid to Oslo II*. Final Status Issues Papers. Washington: Institute for Palestine Studies, 1996.

Thicknesse, S.G. *Arab Refugees. A Survey of Resettlement Possibilities*. London and New York: Royal Institute of International Affairs, 1949.

Troen, S. Ilan. "New Departures in Zionist Planning: The Development Town." Troen, S. Ilan and Lucas, Noah, eds. *Israel. The First Decade of Independence*. SUNY Series in Israeli Studies. Russell Stone, editor. Albany, N.Y.: State University of New York Press, 1995

Tsur, Jacob. "The Jewish National Fund." *Immigration and Settlement*. The Israel Pocket Library. Jerusalem: Keter Publishing House, Ltd., 1973.

*United Nations Resolutions on Palestine and the Arab-Israeli Conflict*, Vol. 1 (1947- 1974), edited by George J. Tomeh; Vol. 2 (1975–1981), edited by Regina Sharif; Vol. 3 (1982–1986), edited by Michael Simpson; Vol. 4 (1987–1991), edited by Jody A. Boudreault. Washington: Institute for Palestine Studies, 1975, 1988, 1993.

Vainstein, Jacob. "Immigration and Settlement, 1948–1951." Cohen, Israel, ed. *The Rebirth of Israel. A Memorial Tribute to Paul Goodman*. London: Edward Goldston & Son, Ltd., 1952.

*Village Statistics 1945. A Classification of Land and Area Ownership in Palestine*. Explanatory Notes by Sami Hadawi. Beirut: Palestine Liberation Organization Research Center, 1970.

Weitz, Yosef. "le-Hanhil Adama Hadasha" [Bequest of New Land]. *Molad* 2, 12 (March 1949): 323–331.

——. *The Struggle for the Land*. Tel Aviv: Lion the Printer, 1950.

——. *ha-Ma'avak 'al ha-Adama* [The Struggle for the Land]. Tel Aviv: Hutsat Seferim N. Tevurski, 1950.

——. "Land Ownership." *Immigration and Settlement*. The Israel Pocket Library. Jerusalem: Keter Publishing House, Ltd., 1973.

Weitz, Raanan. "Settlement." *Immigration and Settlement*. The Israel Pocket Library. Jerusalem: Keter Publishing House, Ltd., 1973.

Yiftachel, Oren. "The Internal Frontier: Territorial Control and Ethnic Relations in Israel." Yiftachel, Oren and Meir Avinoam, eds., *Ethnic Frontiers and Peripheries. Landscapes of Development and Inequality in Israel*. Pub-lished in cooperation with the Negev Center for Regional Development, Ben-Gurion University of the Negev. Boulder, Colo.: Westview Press, 1998.

Zinger, Zvi [Zvi Yaron]. "State of Israel (1948–72)." *Immigration and Settlement*. The Israel Pocket Library. Jerusalem: Keter Publishing House, Ltd., 1973.

Zukerman, William. *Voices of Dissent: Jewish Problems, 1948–1961*. New York: Bookman Associates, Inc., 1964.

Zureik, Elia. *Palestinian Refugees and the Peace Process*. A Final Status Paper. Washington: Institute for Palestine Studies, 1996.

## *Newspapers*

*'Al ha-Mishmar*
*ha-Boker*
*Business Digest* [Haifa]
*Davar*
*al-Dustur* [Amman]
*Ha'aretz*
*Herut*
*Israel's Business Arena—Globes*
*Jerusalem Post*
*The Jerusalem Report*
*The Jerusalem Times Insight Report*
*Jewish Herald* [Johannesburg]
*Jordan Times*
*Middle East Newsline*
*Middle East Peace Report*
*The New York Times*
*The Palestine Post*
*The Star* [Amman]
*The Times* [London]
*ha-Tsofe*
*The Washington Post*

# INDEX

GPSR Authorized Representative: Easy Access System Europe, Mustamäe tee 50, 10621 Tallinn, Estonia, gpsr.requests@easproject.com

www.ingramcontent.com/pod-product-compliance
Ingram Content Group UK Ltd.
Pitfield, Milton Keynes, MK11 3LW, UK
UKHW030638120325
456013UK00006B/51/J

* 9 7 8 0 2 3 1 1 2 9 7 8 7 *